Mies van der Rohe

Hugo Erfurth Mies van der Rohe   FH 2389

Mies van der Rohe

An Architect in His Time

Dietrich Neumann

Yale University Press
New Haven and London

To Vivian

Contents

Introduction

Portraits of an Architect

> On the top floor of a rather dowdy old house in Berlin there lives a man who, in spite of having built little, spoken less, and written not at all, has somehow come to be considered one of the greatest architects of his time. Such is the power of personality and an idea.
> —George Nelson

In the summer of 1934, the young American architect George Nelson came to see Mies van der Rohe in Berlin, as he was writing a series of essays about European architects for the magazine *Pencil Points.* Nelson was twenty-six years old, fresh out of architecture school and on a two-year fellowship at the American Academy in Rome. His portrayal of Mies is one of the most personal and insightful that we have—and one of the most irreverent. "He is brilliant, slow, affable and vain....Physically he is strongly and heavily built, but lazy. A fine draftsman, he prefers to have his drawings done for him." Nelson recognized Mies as a "sure, sensitive artist, and in his handling of space and feeling for material he has no superior." He reported on Mies's hope to receive an important commission from the Nazis, especially at that moment, "with Mendelsohn, the Tauts and Gropius out of the country." Nelson concluded, prophetically: "His career, more than that of any other living architect, has been one of great promise and little realization, and the story of it leaves one with the feeling that more must be forthcoming."[1]

More was, indeed, forthcoming. Not in Nazi Germany, where Mies would spend another three years idle and desperate for work, but rather in the United States, where he would move in 1938; after five difficult years there without seeing anything built, he would rise to become one of the most influential architects of the twentieth century.

But in 1934, Mies was forty-eight years old, roughly at the midpoint of his career and in a place of utter uncertainty. One year into the Nazi dictatorship, everything had changed—the public discourse had become one-sided and volatile, while anti-Semitism and intolerance of dissent grew quickly. No part of life in Germany had remained unaffected. The way architecture was discussed, taught, and made was profoundly transformed. After a string of hopes and disappointments, Mies found himself performing precarious balancing acts between moral principle and willingness to compromise. Nelson's article is a case in point. When Nelson, back in the United States, was readying his essay for publication and contacted Mies for photographs, Mies panicked, as he feared the Nazis would take exception to his exposure abroad. "I would like to desist at this time from any publication of my work in foreign journals. I wish to maintain this intention under all circumstances," Mies wrote back immediately.[2] Thankfully, Nelson did not listen, published the essay anyway, and illustrated it with images copied from existing publications.

While it is unlikely that Nelson's article contributed to Mies being increasingly sidelined in Germany, it fit well into his rising fame in the United States, which had begun with his central role in the 1932 *Modern Architecture: International Exhibition* at the Museum of Modern Art (MoMA), still touring at the time, and continued unabated afterward. Just before Nelson's visit, in April 1934, one of North America's oldest and largest newspapers, the *Brooklyn Daily Eagle,* had claimed Mies was "regarded by many people as the foremost living architect."[3]

Nelson had found Mies at first reserved and unwilling to engage ("Of all the possible architects Mies was the hardest to interview"), but a good meal and glass of wine turned him into a "charming and mellow conversationalist"—leaving Nelson "enormously impressed by the keenness and extraordinary personal force of the man." While Nelson was skeptical of Mies's early visionary projects such as the glass skyscrapers—"which proved nothing"— or the Concrete Office Building—which someone else (Erich Mendelsohn) had executed "to great effect"—he acknowledged Mies's knack for propaganda and salesmanship: "By means of the printing press Mies entered upon the road to fame." Ultimately, it was Mies's personality that made all the difference, as none of his success would have happened "had this man been a dour dyspeptic."[4]

In his short piece, Nelson found a balance of respect and distance, acknowledgment and skepticism. The portrait of Mies that follows here pursues similar goals.

Mies is rightly celebrated as one of the most influential designers of the twentieth century. After apprenticeships in Aachen and Berlin, his independent work had begun modestly with a series of unremarkable, if competent, houses in Berlin's suburbs, fitting squarely into the fashion of *Reformarchitektur*, which was inspired by the rural vernacular around 1800 and less ostentatious than the historicist neo-Gothic or neo-Renaissance palaces popular before. It also lacked any of the flourishes of art nouveau that Belgian, French, and Spanish architects would have routinely applied to their residential architecture at that time.

In 1922, after adding the vaguely aristocratic-sounding "van der Rohe" to his last name, Mies reinvented himself as one of the stars of the architectural avant-garde. While still building conventional villas, he exhibited and published five visionary projects of two sky-scrapers, an office building, and two country houses to great public acclaim. Despite having built comparatively little, he was entrusted with the leadership of the Werkbund exhibi-tion in Stuttgart of 1927 and its model housing estate. He succeeded in bringing sixteen international modern architects together and crowned the estate with an apartment block of his own design. Several modern country houses followed, and the German Pavilion at the World's Fair in Barcelona in 1929—the most critically acclaimed building of its time. A year later, Mies van der Rohe became director of the Bauhaus art school in Dessau. When the Nazis reached a majority in the Dessau city council, the school was terminated there in 1932, and, after moving it to Berlin as a smaller, private institution, Mies again faced aggres-sive scrutiny in 1933, when the Nazis took over the Reich's government and the school was temporarily closed by the secret police. Mies's appeals to reopen the Bauhaus emphasized its apolitical nature, but also its compatibility with the new ideology. Just as the Nazis sig-naled their willingness to let the school continue, Mies closed it due to a lack of funds. Mies had been careful not to alienate the authorities—not just for the school's sake, but also

Figure 0.1. Werner Rohde, Mies van der Rohe, 1934. Bauhaus-Archiv, Berlin.

because he hoped (in vain, as it turned out) that his competition design for a new central bank in Berlin would be chosen for execution.

Having accepted a position as head of the architecture department at what would become the Illinois Institute of Technology (IIT) in Chicago, Mies went on to have a stellar second half of his career, focused on developing the campus architecture for his school, prototypical solutions for residential and office high-rises, and two major museums. His attention to the formal beauty of structural details and his proclaimed essentialism hit a nerve of his time, and pithy aphorisms attributed to him, such as "Less is more" or "God is in the details," helped to create an image of him as a thoughtful and stoic philosopher-architect.

It speaks to a heightened sense of self-reflection that Mies had two photographic portraits taken in that moment of uncertainty, 1934. We have, thus, a good idea of what he looked like when Nelson interviewed him. The earlier one was taken by the twenty-eight-year-old photographer Werner Rohde (figure 0.1). A fellow Werkbund member, he had started out as a painter and graphic artist, but then discovered photography and was immediately successful. Mies is elegantly dressed with a tie and watch fob and glances sideways, seemingly lost in thought—uncertain about the future, perhaps. There is none of the young man's swagger he had displayed when posing in the door of the Riehl House, his first commission, in 1910, nor the officious gravitas in Willy Römer's portrait of him as Bauhaus director in 1931, where a well-stocked bookshelf and several photomurals in the background suggest the home of a cultivated lover of art (figures 0.2, 0.3). Apart from occasional snapshots of Mies with his students (see figure 5.33), there is also a wonderfully sympathetic photograph in profile that Josef Albers took when Mies came to the Bauhaus about 1930 (figure 0.4).

For Rohde's portrait of 1934, Mies is positioned in front of a much-enlarged photograph of his German Pavilion at the Barcelona World's Fair, taken by Sasha Stone in 1929, which had adorned his office since then (see figure 4.17). It was not one of the much-published street views of the pavilion, but a perspective in the back toward the small pool with a female figure by prominent sculptor Georg Kolbe. The statue, however, is not visible

Figure 0.2. Ludwig Mies in the doorway of the Riehl House, Potsdam-Babelsberg, Germany, ca. 1910. Museum of Modern Art, New York. The Mies van der Rohe Archive, gift of the architect.

Figure 0.3. Willy Römer, Mies van der Rohe, 1931. Bauhaus-Archiv, Berlin.

behind Mies—and thus the well-known building not easily identified, a shrewd move given the political climate. We only see the receding sequence of reflective chromium posts and window frames on the right. Thus, only the broader themes of his architecture—the modernity of its materials, the separation of wall and support, its spatial depth and mastery of reflections—are on display.

When Mies had another portrait taken in 1935, his lot had worsened, several commissions had eluded his grasp, and his financial situation was dire (figure 0.5). The photographer, Hildegard Heise, was dedicated to the principles of Neue Sachlichkeit (New Objectivity). As such, her portrait had a particular veracity to it, showing Mies in the state he must have been in at the time—tired and frustrated, in ill health.

Given how meticulous Mies was about controlling the photography of his buildings, he was in all likelihood similarly involved in photos of himself. Most of Mies's staged early portraits are similar—perhaps hiding more than they reveal. As if heeding Gustave Flaubert's famous advice for artists, "Be regular and orderly in your life like a bourgeois, so that you may be violent and original in your work," Mies's demonstrative, calm demeanor and proclivity for tailored suits and good cigars belied a radical, even ruthless, streak that eventually led to architectural solutions in their utmost, minimalist essence—more than once at the cost of functionality or common sense.[5] Behind his bourgeois, even grand-seigneurial façade, Mies was also astonishingly thin-skinned and sensitive to criticism, and often indecisive and plagued by chaotic work habits, with many projects delivered late and over budget—or not at all.

Strikingly different is another portrait of Mies from the fall of 1934. The creator was Hugo Erfurth, twelve years Mies's senior and one of the most celebrated portrait photographers of the Weimar Republic. In a number of essays, Erfurth had described his artistic approach as that of a "painter with a black and white palette."[6] Apart from his regular clients, high-ranking politicians, businessmen, and military personnel, he sought out intellectuals and artists, members of the Dresden Secession and the Bauhaus, sometimes exchanging photographs for artworks for his gallery.[7]

After the Nazis came to power, however, Erfurth wanted to signal a new start in line with the regime, and in the fall of 1934 he moved to Cologne to distance himself from the left-leaning artistic circles he had frequented in Dresden.[8] The location of his new studio could not have been more prominent: the Goldschmidt House, across from the cathedral next to the central station. A Cologne newspaper welcomed Erfurth in October 1934, emphasizing qualities of his work that echoed the propagandistic rhetoric of the new rulers such as "straightforwardness, honesty, clarity."[9] Erfurth himself pointed out that his photography was aligned with the new *Weltanschauung* (the new political and cultural climate), as his portraits showed "truthful and unadulterated Germans."[10] In this context Mies van der Rohe might have sought him out, on one of his trips to nearby Aachen to visit his brother Ewald, or perhaps Erfurth contacted him, believing that Mies was going to have an important future in Germany. The result was a simple headshot: Mies looked straight into the camera, weary but defiant and steady, with deep shadows under his eyes (figure 0.6). Unlike the recent photographs by Römer and Rohde, with their evocative backdrops, the white wall behind him suggests a tabula rasa, a new beginning. Mies, at least for a moment, seemed willing to look the part of the "truthful and unadulterated Germans" whom Erfurth sought to present. Erfurth carefully edited and printed one copy with oil pigment and signed it. As intended, the softened image appeared more painterly, the lightened shadows under Mies's eyes and retouched neckline making him appear younger and slimmer (see frontispiece).

The one portrait in Erfurth's oeuvre that bears the closest resemblance to that of Mies is his 1927 photograph of the painter Max Beckmann (figure 0.7). We do not know if Erfurth recognized the kinship of the two men and suggested a similar approach, or if Mies chose it on his own, perhaps wishing to emulate the admired artist. Erfurth usually encouraged his clients to strike their own pose.[11] Beckmann, one of Germany's most prominent painters, was more of a household name than Mies at that moment. Since 1929, Mies had been friends with Beckmann's most important patron and supporter, Lilly von Schnitzler, wife of Georg von Schnitzler, who had commissioned the Barcelona Pavilion. Beckmann

< Figure 0.4. Josef Albers, Mies van der Rohe, ca. 1930. Harvard Art Museums, Cambridge, Mass.

Figure 0.5. Hildegard Heise, Mies van der Rohe, 1935. Bauhaus-Archiv, Berlin.

was two years older than Mies, and their career trajectories had had some parallels.[12] Alfred Barr, director of the Museum of Modern Art, had featured eight Beckmann paintings in his 1931 show on German painting and sculpture, just as Mies would be a central figure in the *Modern Architecture: International Exhibition* at MoMA the following year. In April 1933, Beckmann lost his professorship in Frankfurt due to the Nazis' rise to power at exactly the moment when Mies's Berlin Bauhaus was closed and the faculty salaries terminated. Both Mies and Beckmann, nevertheless, remained hopeful for recognition by the new regime, while they cautiously guarded their public profiles.[13] Contemporaries described them in comparable terms, as heavyset, cigar-smoking, quiet, proud, and taciturn men, both proletarian and intellectual, their portraits or self-portraits often in suit and tie.[14] They were too reserved to develop a closer friendship, and seem to have recognized the missed opportunity later.[15]

Even in the 1950s there are still photographs of Mies that mimic exactly the ones by Rohde and others in the 1930s (figure 0.8). Hand in hand with the most heroicizing essay on Mies in the postwar era, *Life* magazine's profile of 1957, came Frank Scherschel's brilliant portrait of Mies utilizing the myths that had emerged around him—as a calm, taciturn, cigar-smoking philosopher (figure 0.9). It was such a strong image that Yousuf Karsh could not help following with another profile shot a few years later (figure 0.10). Arthur Siegel found a perfectly heroic approach in his portrait of Mies with the model of IIT's Crown Hall around 1955, while Irving Penn, as part of the extraordinary campaign to advertise the Seagram Building, showed Mies and Philip Johnson locked in a pensive impasse during the design process (figures 0.11, 0.12). And, finally, there is the decidedly unheroic photo by Slim Aarons, taken in 1960 on the roof of 247 East Chestnut Street (with Mies's 860/880 Lake Shore Drive in the background) from an elevated vantage point that made Mies, in suit and hat, look like a man whose time had passed (figure 0.13).

Figure 0.6. Hugo Erfurth, Ludwig Mies van der Rohe, 1934. Museum Ludwig, Rheinisches Bildarchiv, Cologne, Germany.

Figure 0.7. Hugo Erfurth, Max Beckmann, 1927. Museum Ludwig, Rheinisches Bildarchiv, Cologne, Germany.

Figure 0.8. Otto Bettmann, Mies van der Rohe, 1958. Library of Congress, Washington, D.C.

Figure 0.9. Frank Scherschel, Mies van der Rohe, 1957. The LIFE Picture Collection.

Figure 0.12. Irving Penn, Mies van der Rohe and Philip Cortelyou Johnson with a model of the Seagram Building, New York, ca. 1957. National Portrait Gallery, Washington, D.C.

There are very few sketched or painted portraits of Mies. Mies's collaborator Sergius Ruegenberg sketched Mies testing the light reflections of the Curvilinear Glass Skyscraper sometime after he had joined the office in 1925 (figure 0.14). Barbara Buenger has suggested that Max Beckmann's *Der Architekt* of 1944 was inspired by a photograph by Pius Pahl showing Mies teaching at the Bauhaus (figure 0.15; see figure 5.33).[16]

In 1961, Hugo Weber, a Swiss-born painter teaching at the Institute of Design at IIT in Chicago, a colleague of Mies and friend and confidant of Mies's client Edith Farnsworth, created a series of portraits of Mies on the occasion of his seventy-fifth birthday (figure 0.16). His quick, almost subconscious sketches emphasized Mies's enigmatic, inscrutable personality and inaccessibility. Mies purchased one of them in 1961.[17]

And indeed, Mies turns out to be an astonishingly difficult subject. There are no diaries, no travel sketches; he said and wrote little, much of it clichéd and commonplace. Personal observations by acquaintances varied greatly. His student Hans Thiemann wrote in 1935: "I believe [Mies] is the most universal artist alive today. His art is in a way the synthesis of all contemporary movements; it contains André Gide as much as Hindemith or Strawinsky, Picasso and God knows who else!"[18] And then there is a disillusioned Edith Farnsworth: "Perhaps, as a man, he is not the clairvoyant primitive that I thought he was, but simply a colder and more cruel individual than anybody I have ever known."[19]

"Politically, Mies was the Talleyrand of modern architecture," historian Richard Pommer sarcastically noted, referring to the famously opportunistic diplomat Charles Maurice de Talleyrand-Périgord, who was active under different masters before, during, and after the French Revolution.[20] And indeed, a series of projects by Mies seem to suggest his indifference to political persuasions, be they the Bismarck Memorial, the Monument to the November Revolution, the Barcelona Pavilion, or the design for the Brussels World's Fair pavilion for the Nazi regime. Mies's stand was hardly a profile in courage, but rather driven by opportunism and a desire to maintain the respect of his many left-leaning friends, while keeping his options open with conservative clients or the Nazi regime. In the United States, he was suspected both of being a Nazi spy and questioned by Joseph McCarthy's House Un-American Activities Committee about Communist leanings due to the Monument to the November Revolution.

As our subtitle indicates, this portrait foregrounds the contemporary context and presents Mies as seen through the eyes of his peers, of journalists, clients, and jurors. It also draws

Figure 0.13. Slim Aarons, Mies van der Rohe on the roof of 247 East Chestnut Street with 860/880 Lake Shore Drive in the background, Chicago, 1960.

Figure 0.14. Sergius Ruegenberg, Mies van der Rohe testing the model of the Curvilinear Glass Skyscraper in the sunlight (detail), after 1925. Pencil sketch on paper, 6 5/8 × 7 7/8 in. (16.8 × 20 cm). Berlinische Galerie, Berlin.

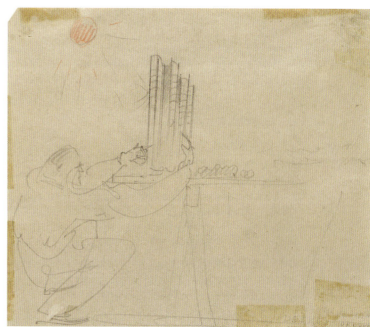

on much new research by myself and others in recent years. Some findings have been published as magazine articles or book chapters before, but many are introduced here for the first time. I am excited to be able to present newly identified buildings by Mies in Aachen, Wiesbaden, Stuttgart, and Indianapolis, previously unknown exhibition and furniture designs, and little-known patents for photographic wallpaper. These findings are noteworthy not in the way a newly discovered drawing by an adolescent Vincent van Gogh would create a sensation on the art market—independent of its quality—but because they complicate our understanding of a body of work that has often been presented as an unrelenting chain of masterpieces. In reality, there were just as many compromises, false starts, and missed opportunities—and they are usually just as interesting as the successes.

The fact that Mies would, occasionally, quote a line from Thomas Aquinas, or that one of his terse statements might echo the theologian Romano Guardini, whom he knew socially in Berlin, has tempted some critics to assign an unrealistic degree of philosophical proficiency to him. It is hard to know how much he truly understood of what he read and marked in the books he owned, and whether, consciously or not, it influenced his design decisions. Mies cared deeply about materials, structures, and their assemblage ("Architecture begins when you carefully put two bricks together," he told Christian Norberg-Schulz in 1958), and he had a keen eye for proportions and innovative spatial sequences.[21] He nonchalantly ignored blatant contradictions between his buildings and writings: for example, after having declared, in 1923, "Form is not the goal but the result of our work" and "Form as goal is formalism; and that we reject," he went on to become one of the most stubborn and glorious formalists of the twentieth century.[22]

Understanding the chronology of Mies's work is crucial; knowing which tasks were on the drafting tables and which collaborators were in the office helps us determine how individual projects came about. This allows us to see that Mies's visionary skyscraper designs coincided with utterly conventional residences designed for Berlin's suburbs (a fact noted with sarcasm by some of his contemporaries), or that his project for a war

Figure 0.15. Max Beckmann, *Der Architekt* (*Zwei Männer*) (The Architect [Two Men]), 1944. Oil on canvas, 23 5/8 × 15 3/4 in. (60 × 40 cm). Kurpfälzisches Museum, Heidelberg, Germany.

Figure 0.16. Hugo Weber, *Portrait Mies van der Rohe (6)*, 1961. Oil on canvas, 42 7/8 × 49 in. (109 × 124.5 cm). Private collection, Switzerland.

memorial in Berlin envisioned reusing material from the recently dismantled Barcelona Pavilion. Astonishing similarities between building tasks as different as the urban plan for the Stuttgart Weissenhof Estate and the Monument to the November Revolution, developed at the same time, reveal formal proclivities unencumbered by functional requirements or scale.

Where possible, I also have tried to show how other architects approached the same or similar building types or competition briefs. Sometimes, Mies turned out to be, indeed, ahead of his peers; in other cases, he nonchalantly adopted ideas from others—a fact that did not go unnoticed. Numerous less-celebrated architects and designers, such as Wilhelm Deffke, Hans Soeder, and Albert Kahn, are presented here as important sources of influence. And, of course, his relationship with Lilly Reich played a crucial role on his path to maturity.

In his later years, Mies's work became increasingly repetitive, posing an unusual problem for a biographer. For almost two decades, he responded with more or less the same laconic answers to commissions for office and apartment buildings and educational structures. At a time when Le Corbusier, Louis Kahn, and Gio Ponti were relentlessly inventing new forms for each project, responding to functional requirements, location, and lighting conditions, Mies essentially repeated approaches he had first developed around 1950 for high-rise apartment and office buildings. His longtime collaborator Joe Fujikawa recalled, "After 860 [Lake Shore Drive] [Mies] felt that he had solved the problem of the high-rise apartment house, because with all subsequent buildings, he really had just a casual passing interest in what was going on."[23] Mies stood his ground and declared in 1960: "I am, in fact, completely opposed to the idea that a specific building should have an individual character—rather a universal character which has been determined by the total problem which architecture must strive to solve....My idea, or better, direction, in which I go is towards a clear structure and construction—this applies not to any one problem but to all architectural problems which I approach."[24] Of course, reusing floor plans and details with only minimal adjustments many times over was also a pragmatic and lucrative business model—it saved time and allowed Mies to maintain a comparatively small office.

What Mies meant by "clear structure" was more often than not an appearance of clarity on the surface, paid for with compromises underneath—in other words, he would, usually, privilege aesthetics over functionality. And, he certainly stayed consistent in his priorities: condensation water collected inside his first American steel building at Lake Shore Drive in Chicago, just as it would materialize in veritable torrents at the Neue Nationalgalerie in Berlin twenty years later. Still, his great American discovery of structural detail as the locus for aesthetic intervention was a breakthrough of unprecedented gravity and consequence.

It is impossible to separate the work itself from the discourse surrounding it, as it was presented and received through magazine publications at first and, from 1947 on, through a long series of monographs. Much of the literature on Mies treated its subject with astonishing reverence, and one cannot help thinking of Werner Hegemann, the German critic and Mies's contemporary, who noted sarcastically in 1925 (vis-à-vis his colleagues' fawning over Frank Lloyd Wright and other architects): "The inability to differentiate between religion and architecture is quite common among architecture professors."[25] And, indeed, the critics' fiction of an unfailing, singular, visionary genius is first and foremost a religious concept—and has proven just as resilient. Mies himself was skillful at creating such an image from early on (a steady stream of admiring articles—often instigated behind the scenes by himself—appeared since 1922), which proved a perfect fit for the chaotic times in Weimar Germany and the hectic giddiness of America's postwar building boom, where Mies found enthusiastic supporters such as Philip Johnson at the Museum of Modern Art and Peter Blake at *Architectural Forum*, both superbly skilled at shaping public opinion. This, in turn would attract men such as Samuel Bronfman, client of the Seagram Building, for whom Mies was a perfect tool in his quest for polishing his own reputation.

In addition to the laudatory pieces, Mies also saw much reasonable critique by his contemporaries, who were by no means all ill-informed, narrow-minded, or even Nazis. Later biographers have widely omitted or flattened this discursive landscape. Ongoing digitization efforts, however, have greatly facilitated access to the reception of Mies's work in architecture magazines and newspapers and a wider range of contemporary debates, many of which are presented here for the first time. Mies's apartment block at the Weissenhof Estate in Stuttgart of 1927 may serve as an example: we can now square the succinct criticism of someone such as Marie-Elisabeth Lüders, parliamentarian and prominent women's rights activist, with the abundant praise by critic Max Osborn in the *Vossische Zeitung* (see Chapter 3).[26] What comes upon us over time is not always a "survival of the fittest," or the best and most accomplished, but rather also the result of selective archival access, of accident and bias and of successful propaganda efforts. A frustrated Edith Farnsworth noted how her visitors' expectations were colored by what they had read: "The big glossy reviews polished up their terms and phrases with such patience that the simpler minds that came to have a look expected to find the glass box light enough to stay afloat in air or water, moored to its columns and enclosing its mystic space. So 'culture spreads by proclamation' and one got the impression that if the house had had the form of a banana rampant instead of a rectangle couchant, the proclamation would have been just as imperative." Her quote—"culture spreads by proclamation"—came, apparently, from Mies himself.[27]

Following Pierre Bourdieu, who brilliantly linked our opinions about art and culture to our educational and economic standing, Catalan philosopher and professor of aesthetics Xavier Rubert de Ventós noted that sometimes people are "on cultural tiptoes" with Mies: "Trying to guess if it's good.…People don't know, because only if they are cultured they can say something about what it resembles, what it contrasts with, what it anticipates." Echoing Hannah Arendt's famous dictum, he concluded: "It's hard to see without these kinds of banisters."[28] Books such as this one, of course, are part of the discourse that provides such handrails. As the Afterword will show, the image of Mies has by no means been stable, but rather has continuously shifted. His legacy was most at peril in the 1970s and 1980s, when anguish over the negative impact his followers had on the built environment was a prominent reaction. By 2001, when the two largest exhibitions ever devoted to an architect were held in New York in his honor, a general sense of acceptance of his impact had set in.[29]

Rather than presenting Mies van der Rohe's designs as a series of undisputable masterpieces, I show them as responses to the contexts of their time—sometimes brazenly bold and sure-footed, sometimes tentative and compromised. Along the way, I hope to give a voice to architects and collaborators in Mies's orbit and, most importantly, to the critical reception accompanying his work. I consider contemporary politics, as well as technical and legal challenges, and I try to avoid automatic assumptions of agency, coherence, and linearity. As much as possible, I acknowledge the actual, sometimes inscrutable messiness of the creative process and the complexities of architectural production. What follows, then, is a gentle reevaluation of Mies. It aims for a more complicated, less heroic, and more humane picture, and ultimately for the *Sachlichkeit,* the "matter-of-fact-ness" that Mies and his colleagues evoked as a common goal.

One

Apprenticeships and Early Work

Aachen, Berlin, Wassenaar, 1905–22

> My father was a stone mason, and so it was natural that I would either continue his
> work or turn to building. I had no conventional architectural education. I worked
> under a few good architects; I read a few good books—and that's about it.
> —Mies van der Rohe

1886–1905   Youth in Aachen

Mies's typically laconic words about his upbringing suggest that there is, indeed, little in
his early years that helps us understand what put him on the path to becoming one of the
most influential architects of the twentieth century. Ludwig Maria Michael Mies was born
in Aachen, Germany, on March 27, 1886, the son of the stonemason Michael Mies and his
wife, Amalie, née Rohé, as the second youngest of five siblings. His birthplace still stands
(figure 1.1). Much of the family business was in gravestones, and his father's workshop was
located in close proximity to the city's western cemetery. Mies's parents would be buried
there in the late 1920s under an elegantly minimalist modern headstone designed in all likelihood by Mies himself.

After attending the Aachen cathedral school from 1896 to 1899 (age ten to thirteen), Mies
went to a vocational school (*Gewerbeschule*) for another two years (figure 1.2).[1] Mies
learned some French there, as well as mathematics, geometry, material science, wood-
working, drawing, and the sculpting of plaster ornaments. Mies pursued his education with dogged persistence. After graduating in 1901, he continued taking evening and
Sunday classes for craftsmen in the building trades such as construction, statics, mathematics, drafting, and life drawing. Simultaneously, at age fifteen, Mies started to work in
the building trade, at first as a mason's assistant, and then, from age sixteen on, for the
architect and plasterer Max Fischer, where he learned about drawing ornaments. In 1904,
Mies was hired by Albert Schneider, one of Aachen's preeminent architects, whose style
oscillated between historicism, Reformstil, and art nouveau. Mies was involved in at least
three projects there. The largest was the Tietz Department Store on the central square, in
a stripped-down neo-Renaissance style typical for this building type. Mies signed off on a
set of drawings when he picked them up at the city's building office. Construction lasted
from 1905 to 1910. Modernity arrived here via the enormous plate-glass windows on the
first floor, and the separation of the load-bearing steel structure and outside façade.[2] Mies
was also involved in the design of a townhouse for the affluent Levy family, and, more
importantly, a slim, mixed-use structure with a tavern and apartments above for a prominent Social Democrat and editor of a local newspaper, Joseph Oeben. A single stone arch
spanned the opening on the first floor, carrying the inscription "*Zur Neuen Welt*" (To the
New World). Apparently in a responsible role, Mies requested the city's inspection of the
finished building on May 6, 1905. From Schneider's early historicist sketch, the design
evolved into the protomodern, unornamented granite façade that was executed (figure 1.3).[3]

Mies moved to Berlin in the winter of 1905, following his childhood friend Gerhard
Severain, who had enrolled in the Berlin Kunstgewerbeschule (School of Arts and Crafts)
the previous year. Mies had accepted a position at the building department of Rixdorf, a
small, working-class town south of Berlin.[4] The department was headed by the charismatic
and talented architect Reinhold Kiehl, who had just designed a new city hall; construction
was about to begin (figure 1.4). Mies worked under project manager John Martens, who
had previously held a leading position in Bruno Möhring's office, where he was responsible for much of the German section at the 1904 World's Fair in St. Louis. Martens's reputation as generous and talented reached as far as Aachen, where Mies had heard about him.
At Martens's office, Mies met Max and Bruno Taut and Franz Hoffman, and remembered
designing wood paneling for the council chamber of the new city hall. Martens introduced

his assistants to the beauty of Gothic brick architecture, in particular that of the former Chorin monastery north of Berlin.[5]

Mies had to return to Aachen for his military draft in March 1907 and left the Rixdorf office. His time in the army was cut short by a lung infection, though, and he promptly returned to Berlin on June 1, 1907. His old job had been filled in the meantime, and so Mies joined Severain at the school of the Kunstgewerbemuseum (Museum of Applied Arts) in Berlin instead. Bruno Paul had just taken over as director of the school. Trained as a painter, Paul had become a prominent illustrator, caricaturist, and furniture and interior designer (notably for transatlantic cruise ships), who had transitioned from art nouveau to the recent, calm and unornamented, Reformstil. After playing a prominent role in the Munich Secession, Paul was tasked with reforming the school at the Kunstgewerbemuseum, and he supported training in crafts as the basis of artistic education. Architectural commissions had begun to come his way as well, and he was looking for students with architectural experience who would work in his office and pay a lower tuition rate at the school—an opportunity of crucial importance for the penniless Mies.

On October 6, 1907, Paul was back in Munich as one of twelve artists and industrialists who participated in the founding session of the German Werkbund—a group focused on making German design more competitive. (Mies would become the second director of the Werkbund almost twenty years later.) Paul was deeply immersed in furniture design at the time, his so-called *Typenmöbel* (type furniture) providing a pragmatic modernism for the middle class, with pieces that were mass-produced, simple, practical, and affordable— "one of the most significant, and frequently overlooked, directions in the history of progressive design in Central Europe."[6] His designs offered every type of furniture for a bourgeois home, could be easily combined, and came in a series of materials and finishes. The interiors of Mies's first houses looked similar to what Paul designed in those days, and

Figure 1.1. Steinkaulstrasse 29, Aachen, Germany, birthplace of Mies van der Rohe. Photograph by P. Brandi, 2007.

Figure 1.2. Gewerbeschule Martinstraße, Aachen, Germany, 1897. Stadtarchiv Aachen.

Figure 1.3. Albert Schneider with Ludwig Mies, Zur Neuen Welt, Aachen, Germany, 1905. Photograph by Daniel Lohmann.

Mies's own mass-produced furniture would become central to his success in later years. The notion of types—ideal, essential responses to a problem, universally applicable—was crucial for Mies's mature philosophy.

The founding of the Werkbund in 1907 was a culminating event in a development that had already driven the founding of the Kunstgewerbemuseum and its building by Martin Gropius (the great-uncle of Walter Gropius) in 1881 (figure 1.5). Modeled after Karl Friedrich Schinkel's Bauakademie (Building Academy) in Berlin, the square brick building, with its glass-covered courtyard, did not look like a conventional museum, such as the imposing temple of the recent Nationalgalerie (1875) by Friedrich August Stüler and Johann Heinrich Strack. This building's restrained brick façades were dominated by relentless sequences of large windows. The students entered through the main entrance, just like the visiting public. A lecture hall and the school's library were on the main floor, with classrooms, workshops, and studios on the second floor. The windows needed by the workshops and classrooms on the northern side became the defining factor in the spacing and size of the fenestration for the entire building, a fact that was stressed at the building's opening.[7] The building itself thus signaled the dominant importance of the school (rather than the museum) and of training in crafts and applied arts.

1907   Poster Competition, Hohenzollern Kunstgewerbehaus

Bruno Paul alerted his students to a poster competition for the prominent Hohenzollern Kunstgewerbehaus (Hohenzollern Arts and Craft House), for which he would be one of the jurors. Founded by Hermann Hirschwald in 1878, the Hohenzollern Kunstgewerbehaus was the premier store for interior decoration in Berlin and was approaching its thirtieth anniversary under new owners, the architects Ernst Friedmann and Hermann Weber. Its freshly renovated sales rooms were located at Leipziger Strasse 13 in Berlin, around the corner from the government district and a short walk from the busy commercial hubs of Potsdamer and Leipziger Platz. The store showed international design, from the Wiener Werkstätte to René Lalique. Henry van de Velde and Josef Hoffmann had created sections inside. Hermann Hirschwald had counted the crown prince of Prussia among his customers, who allowed him to use the family name, Hohenzollern, for his store.[8] "Nothing," modernist critic Max Osborn commented on the store's importance in 1915, "gives more profound expression of the soul of a people than the way it approaches issues of design." This store, he declared, was the leading force in forming a "culture of taste" in Berlin.[9]

Figure 1.4. Reinhold Kiehl, City Hall, Rixdorf (today Berlin Neukölln), Germany, 1908–14. Contemporary postcard. Private collection.

Figure 1.5. Martin Gropius and Heino Schmieden, Kunstgewerbemuseum, Berlin, 1881.

The poster competition had an enormous echo—265 entries. Apart from Bruno Paul, the most prominent member of the jury was Paul's friend Thomas Theodor Heine, another famous painter and illustrator. Graphic artist Charlotte Rollius won first prize, followed by painter and theater set designer César Klein and graphic designer Lucian Bernhard—all well-known artists. Given the large number of entries, the fact that Ludwig Mies and his friend Gerhard Severain received one of fourteen honorable mentions is certainly remarkable. Their design was purchased by the store and exhibited there in October 1907. All participants had to accommodate the same text and adhere to the same format. A comparison of the entry of Mies and Severain with the winners and other competitors is instructive (figure 1.6). Art historian Max Creutz noted that most entries displayed "a certain proclivity towards small scale ornaments in the Viennese sense, which might suffice when you look at a poster from closeup, but doesn't work for the distant view."[10] This could be read as an endorsement for Mies and Severain, who had refrained from decorating their entire poster via repeated patterns or decorative bands. Their small, central illustration introduced a bit of humor: in a "blue circle" (the code name of their entry) a heavy, seated bear (a reference to Berlin's heraldic animal) is clumsily contemplating a delicate piece of decorative art. Beyond that, there is the required text and little ornamentation. Much of the surface is left in an elegant charcoal black. The design provided a striking contrast to the work for sale at the Kunstgewerbehaus and the other entries.

1908–9   Riehl House

In early 1908, Alois Riehl, a prominent professor of philosophy, and his wife, Sophie, inquired at the Kunstgewerbeschule about a reliable young architect to design their

Figure 1.6. Poster for the Hohenzollern Kunstgewerbehaus. Competition entry by Ludwig Mies and Gerhard Severain, 1907. Private collection, Wiesbaden, Germany.

weekend retreat—in all likelihood not to discover future talent, but to avoid the costs and headaches that might come with the potentially large ego of a revered master. When they were introduced to the young Mies, however, he seemed too inexperienced. Mies recalled:

> I had a conversation with Mrs. Riehl and she asked: "What have you already built?" I said, "Nothing!" Whereupon she replied: "That won't do, we don't want to be guinea pigs." "Yes," I said. "I can build a house. I have never built one independently. But I have done it. Just think about it, if one would say to me 'Have you ever done this before?' until I am sixty or so." At that she laughed and said she would get me to meet her husband.... I said: "I work for Bruno Paul, and he wants me to build him a Tennis pavilion or a clubhouse. Why don't you ask him what he thinks of me!"[11]

When commissioned to design the clubhouse, Bruno Paul had indeed turned to Mies, who had more experience working in architecture firms. Mies, in turn, consulted with a friend from Joseph Maria Olbrich's office. Paul's pavilion at the Lawn-Tennis-Turnier-Club (today the Lawn Tennis Turnier Club Rot-Weiss) in Berlin Grunewald served as a small restaurant and bar, with an outside terrace overlooking a tennis court and the adjacent Hundekehl lake (figure 1.7). It was published in 1910, and certain motives echo those in Mies's Riehl and Perls houses, such as the flat, stucco pilasters and architraves, the pergola, and the row of tall windows with shutters.[12]

Once Mies had received the commission for the Riehl House, he left the Kunstgewerbeschule in the summer of 1908. The Riehls had suggested a *Bildungsreise*—an educational journey—to Italy for a few weeks, together with Adolf Propp, another student from the school, who was working with Mrs. Riehl on gardening projects.[13] The Riehls insisted that their first stop be a vast exhibition on arts and crafts in Munich, the *Kunstgewerbeausstellung*.[14] Several model houses by Richard Riemerschmid, whose work the Riehls admired, and a restaurant by Franz Zell seem to have impressed Mies (figure 1.8). Mies and Propp traveled on to Florence; Propp was more interested in museums, while Mies explored urban configurations. Apparently, they got as far as Naples, where Mies, as he recalled much later, realized how much he missed the overcast skies of Berlin.[15]

Right after his return from Italy, Mies entered the employment of the prominent architect Peter Behrens, whose office location was within walking distance from the Riehls' site, and began working on the house after hours. The Riehls were surely comforted by the fact that their young designer was embedded in an office where he could get help and advice from more experienced colleagues.

The philosopher Alois Riehl, mostly forgotten today, had enjoyed a stellar career with a sequence of professorships in Graz, Freiburg, Kiel, Halle, and finally Berlin. He was interested in the work of Immanuel Kant and in the immediacy of reception in the arts. His lectures were popular with the general public, and he certainly looked the part of the philosopher as well, with a full beard and a mane of long hair.[16] A visitor from Japan reported in the winter of 1907–8:

Figure 1.7. Bruno Paul with Ludwig Mies, Lawn-Tennis-Tournier-Club, Berlin Grunewald, 1909.

Figure 1.8. Franz Zell, watercolor rendering of temporary restaurant in the *Kunstgewerbeausstellung*, Munich, 1908. Contemporary postcard. Private collection.

The lectures on aesthetics were not about philosophical abstraction, but rather about something like the science of art, and as such they belonged to the newest style in this field....He often quoted the theories of the art historian [August] Schmarsow, sometimes he would talk about Michelangelo's sculptures at the Medici chapel or the beauty of music, for which he had a student play samples from Beethoven's 9th symphony on the piano, which made all of this accessible for a non-specialist like myself.[17]

Riehl was sixty-four at the time and about to retire. The planning of his weekend retreat was a deliberate and carefully published undertaking. The Riehls lived in a comfortable, large apartment house in Berlin's affluent Westend. In great contrast, the weekend house in Potsdam-Babelsberg was meant to look like a worker's cottage or a simple farmhouse. It was a calculated gesture of ostentatious humbleness on Riehl's part (he named it Klösterli, or little monastery), but of course, the sizable plot of land in an affluent neighborhood gave away the status of its owner. It was located on a northeastern slope between Bergstrasse, a quiet cul-de-sac, at the top, and Kaiserstrasse, a busier thoroughfare along the Griebnitzsee, at the bottom (today Spitzweggasse and Karl-Marx Strasse). The emperor (Kaiser) occasionally traveled along the lower street on his way between the nearby Babelsberg and Glienicke palaces (both important collaborations between Karl Friedrich Schinkel and landscape designer Peter Joseph Lenné). As Emperor Wilhelm II was little liked, even despised, by most German academics, Riehl's retreat to the furthest corner away from Kaiserstrassse could be read as avoiding any semblance of paying respect to the potentate, and the open loggia to the east would offer a splendid balcony to look down on the emperor on his way. In any event, there were more pressing and sensible reasons to place the house at the upper, southwestern corner of the lot: it was the quietest spot, secured for the main façade and the rose garden in front the best exposure to the sun, and offered the most enjoyable view toward the lake. With the main gate in the high garden wall placed at the far end, every visitor had to first walk through Sophie Riehl's carefully tended rose garden, then take a ninety-degree turn and approach the entrance on the central axis.

Naturally, in a collaboration between a sixty-four-year-old, image-conscious philosopher and a twenty-two-year-old novice architect, the ideas and wishes of the former will bear particular weight. In an entry in the Riehls' guest book, Mies acknowledged his role as that of a *Miterbauer*—a co-designer—of the Riehl House.[18] When Mies assembled material for his first monographic exhibition and its catalogue at MoMA, in 1947, he considered the Riehl House (as told by Philip Johnson) "too uncharacteristic to publish; but, according to a contemporary critic, 'the work is so faultless that no one would guess that it is the first independent work of a young architect.' Designed in the then-popular, traditional eighteenth-century style with steep roofs, gables, and dormer windows, it was distinguishable from its contemporaries only by fine proportions and careful execution."[19]

As someone who had devoted his life to studying the work of Kant, Riehl might have looked for inspiration in the lifestyle of the great philosopher, who had spent his last years in a house of his own in Königsberg, East Prussia (today Kaliningrad, Russia),

Figure 1.9. Unknown architect, Stukshof, near Langfuhr, East Prussia (now Wrzeszcz, Poland), ca. 1800.

Figure 1.10. Alfred Grenander, Villa Tångvallen, Falsterbo, Sweden, 1907.

where he lived simply and quietly, wrote, and occasionally gathered students and colleagues for lectures and discussions. Like Riehl's house, it was on a quiet street and adjacent to the parks of the royal palace. Kant's friend Johann Gottfried Hasse had published a description in 1804, the year Kant died: "When approaching the house, everything announced a philosopher. The house was a bit old, and on an accessible, but not much-frequented street, and its back bordered the gardens of the castle, hundreds of years old.... Entering the house, one encountered peaceful silence.... His room offered simplicity, and calm distance from the noise of the city and the world."[20] Hasse mentioned the white walls in the parlor and the study, the scarcity of furniture, and the resulting open space.

In their quest for potential models and stylistic inspiration, Mies and Riehl were helped by a general interest in Kant's time period. Paul Mebes's popular book *Um 1800* (Around 1800) appeared in 1908 and celebrated the stylistic simplicity of a century before, as "modern in the real sense of the word" and "refreshing after the undigested formal exuberance of the last decades."[21] The book offered potential models for the façade and volumes of the house—such as the "Stukshof" near Langfuhr, East Prussia (today Wrzeszcz, Poland), incidentally in the same region as Kant's hometown of Königsberg (figure 1.9).[22] Mies was probably also familiar with Alfred Grenander's Villa Tångvallen in Falsterbo, Sweden, finished in 1907, just when Mies was taking a class with Grenander at the Kunstgewerbeschule (figure 1.10).[23]

While the overall imagery and referential scope of the house might have strongly followed Alois and Sophie Riehl's preferences, Mies would have brought his skills to bear when it came to the internal organization and detailing of the Riehl House (figures 1.11, 1.12). The house was horizontally divided in three distinct zones—living rooms, main hall, and library on the first floor, family bedrooms upstairs, and a kitchen and maid's room in the basement.[24] The terrace on the sloped site necessitated a retaining wall, which Mies brilliantly combined with the eastern façade. This gave the kitchen and maid's room on the lower floor direct garden access and eastern sun exposure. Above, on the first floor, Mies placed an open loggia under a steep gable.

Figure 1.11. Ludwig Mies, Riehl House, Potsdam-Babelsberg, Germany, 1908–9. Northeastern side façade, view from garden below.

Figure 1.12. Ludwig Mies, Riehl House, Potsdam-Babelsberg, Germany, 1908–9. Main façade, view from rose garden.

Figure 1.13. Ludwig Mies, Riehl House, Potsdam-Babelsberg, Germany, 1908–9. Central hall, view northeast toward the pergola.

Figure 1.14. Ludwig Mies, Riehl House, Potsdam-Babelsberg, Germany, 1908–9. Central hall, view southwest.

From the entrance, a small vestibule leads straight into the large central space, which served as a dining room and could accommodate large gatherings. A traditional farmhouse would have been split in the middle by a long central hallway with a straight staircase up. Mies, instead, pushed his stair hall (three comfortable flights with low risers) out toward the back, freeing up a central space. That room was lit from two tall windows and a central double door on its northeastern side, darkened somewhat by the adjacent loggia. Two small rooms with a table or desk flanked the central hall on either side, and their windows provided additional light from the southeast in the morning and the northwest in the afternoon. They could be closed off by curtains. This spatial flexibility foreshadowed the arrangement at the Tugendhat House in 1930, where floor-to-ceiling curtains could separate room segments.

A gridded wood paneling unifies the central hall, providing a sense of coherence and enclosure.[25] The photographer who documented the house (probably under Mies's direction), moved the six chairs to the periphery to show off the generous space and the unusual six-legged table in its center (figures 1.13, 1.14). The Klösterli's seemingly bucolic simplicity went hand in hand with utmost modernity. The cellar contained a boiler for its central heating system, as well as a small generator. The focal point of the main hall is not an open fireplace, but a carefully designed radiator cover. The house was electrified (at a time when less than 3.5 percent of Berlin homes had electricity), and Mies boldly displayed naked light bulbs on the bedroom walls upstairs (figure 1.15).[26] The elegant and whimsical solution in the upstairs bathroom suggests that Mies might have based the size of the alcoves behind the semicircular mansard windows on a standard-size bathtub (figure 1.16).

Sophie Riehl, an avid gardener, embraced modernity in her field. She was one of the first clients of Karl Foerster, the garden designer and plant breeder, who had just established a nursery in Potsdam. He developed a philosophy of gardening as a reflection of nature's cycles and embraced and nurtured plants not usually found in gardens of Berlin's bourgeoisie, such as local ferns and grasses. When Foerster published his first book in 1911, *Winterharte Blütenstauden und Sträucher der Neuzeit* (Hardy Flowering Perennials and Shrubs of Modern Times), the Riehls' garden appeared in several (still rare) color images. A trellis on the southwestern wall was soon covered in ivy, and climbing plants were introduced on the southeastern corner as well. The geometric layout of the rose garden at the entrance level contrasted with a lawn and curved sloping paths at the lower level. A tea house was planned halfway down that path, but never executed.

Figure 1.15. Ludwig Mies, Riehl House, Potsdam-Babelsberg, Germany, 1908–9. Bedroom alcove upstairs.

Figure 1.16. Ludwig Mies, Riehl House, Potsdam-Babelsberg, Germany, 1908–9. Bathroom alcove upstairs.

In August 1909, the first guests were welcomed to the Riehl House.[27] Given the fact that its young designer was completely unknown, it received an astonishing amount of public recognition. In all likelihood, Alois Riehl was behind this, hiring the photographer (whom Mies could hardly have afforded) and contacting magazines. Through Peter Behrens, Riehl might have met the prominent critic Anton Jaumann, who had just published a lengthy, admiring piece on Behrens—surely required reading in the office. Jaumann had described Behrens as uncompromising, ruthless even, focused on the essential, reductivist result: "He does not want to be interesting....No part is redundant; all forms have a reason and a function."[28] Very similar terms would later be applied to Mies. In July 1910, Jaumann published an essay on the Riehl House, richly illustrated with twelve photographs, in which he managed to both acknowledge and critique Mies's work as he confessed his greater admiration for Behrens's generation. Mies's Klösterli, he wrote, was so "simply impeccable that one would never suspect it to be the first independent building by a young architect. To emphasize just a few things: How cleverly and almost naturally the connection of the small writing and chatting rooms to the dining room is solved, how simple is the means of bringing uniformity into the room by continuing the paneling across the doors. And Mies also succeeded brilliantly in making practical and artistic use of the mansard windows."[29]

Mies was "a model student," Jaumann explained, typical for a "new generation," more faultless and exemplary than its teachers, but also less exciting, "unaffected by the earlier, passionate and courageous urge forward." Instead, this generation behaved "as if they were the old ones...they detest all radicalism, aim for maturity, calmness, balance, moderation and a 'golden middle' between old and new...like a silent reproach" of their teachers. Jaumann preferred restless "daredevils" like Behrens, who didn't shy away from taking risks and making mistakes. They were more "fascinating and touchingly humane" and "may be of more use after all."[30] It would be difficult not to agree with Jaumann—the Riehl House was impeccably designed and executed, but contemporary houses by Behrens, be they Cuno and Schröder in Hagen or the astonishing Obenauer House in Saarbrücken of 1906–7 (back on the drawing boards in Behrens's office in 1910 for a new study and library), were more courageous and unusual (see figure 1.32).

In September 1910, critic Paul Klopfer praised the "classic simplicity" of the Riehl House in the journal *Moderne Bauformen,* and a month later Hermann Muthesius's popular 1907 book *Landhaus und Garten* (Country House and Garden) appeared in its second, much enlarged edition, which included a short description of the house with three outside photos and floor and site plans.[31] The overall costs were quoted as 50,000 Mark, "including the construction of terraces and interior" (a relatively high price given its small size).[32] The *Schweizer Bauzeitung* reviewed Muthesius's book in December 1910, showing the Riehl House as one of four examples.[33] The following year brought more international exposure when the *Studio Yearbook of Decorative Art* included two photographs of the Riehl House in an essay on "German Architecture and Decoration." The author, Werkbund member Ludwig Deubner, praised the handling of the sloping site with its southern terrace for the rose garden and access to the well-lit basement on the eastern side: "This shrewd solution gives to the house the appearance of being, as it were, a product of the soil—of having grown up out of the surrounding landscape; and this congruity between the building and its environment is again strengthened by the simple unpretending style, which is that of the old Brandenburgian rural architecture."[34] Riehl's students knew how much he proudly identified with the house. In her homage to his eightieth birthday in the *Vossische Zeitung,* philosopher Margarete Merleker made the house the centerpiece:

> The Klösterli in Babelsberg! It lies unrecognized behind its walls and hidden under its proliferous ivy. Only the initiated know of its beauty, know that the roses blossom here from May until Christmas, that this garden is known among the experts, that books on gardening contain its golden-yellow bushes and white benches. Almost a dream of the South, especially given the fact that paths among the roses are paved in the Roman tradition with irregular ashlar plates. But when we enter the house, this dream vanishes, as this is and wants to be a simple German country house. As a matter of course, the mind has penetrated and embraced location, nature, space, light and materials and brought them together into a whole. The result is a true home, symbol and representation of its owner, Alois Riehl.[35]

When Behrens was appointed artistic advisor for the Allgemeine Elektricitäts-Gesellschaft (AEG), he had rented the Erdmannshof, a house with a large garden in the Steinstücken area in southern Berlin, adjacent to Potsdam-Babelsberg. He had a simple, flat-roofed structure built as his "atelier" in the adjacent garden in 1908–9, and soon twelve draftsmen were busy there, later up to thirty (figure 1.17). Mies's friends from Aachen, Ferdinand Goebbels and Franz Dominick, were working there, as was Wilhelm Deffke, who would work with Mies in the early 1920s.

Mies rented a room in the immediate vicinity, at Villa Mehlhose in Teltower Strasse. When Mies had joined Behrens's office in September 1908, Behrens had just been commissioned to design his first major building for the AEG, a turbine factory, on a prominent street corner in Moabit, close to the city center. The design was submitted on December 17, 1908. The astonishingly short turnaround time was due to the fact that the structure itself was developed by the experienced engineer Karl Bernhard, while Behrens merely made a number of formal modifications. The building permit was issued on March 17, 1909, and construction began. The building was completed in October 1909 (figure 1.18).[36] This first major building for the AEG probably required "all hands on deck" in Behrens's small atelier, and Mies was presumably involved in some aspects of

Figure 1.17. Atelier Peter Behrens, Erdmannshof, Berlin Steinstücken, 1910, showing Wilhelm Deffke (far left), Walter Gropius (fifth from left), and Mies van der Rohe (eighth from left). Bröhan Design Foundation, Berlin.

Figure 1.18. Karl Bernhard and Peter Behrens, AEG Turbine Factory, Berlin, 1909.

it—however, it is unlikely that he had any influence on its design (as has occasionally been speculated).

Once construction of the AEG Turbine Factory was underway, Mies was engaged in other projects in the office. For example, he helped design and build a stage set for a performance of Otto Erich Hartleben's play *Diogenes* at a summer festival in Hagen in 1909. Mies stayed for almost another year in Behrens's office, increasingly busy with a string of factories at the AEG and several private homes. Walter Gropius resigned on March 5, 1910, apparently after Behrens blamed him for structural problems at the Schröder and Cuno houses in Hagen. His friend and close collaborator Adolf Meyer left with him. Gropius claimed that "Behrens underpaid everyone; one never seemed to feel human warmth in dealing with him. He was extremely egocentric and proud."[37] Mies left Behrens a few months later, at the end of June 1910, and returned home to Aachen.[38] The absence of another commission and the low salary at the office surely were important factors, as was the tension between Mies and Jean Krämer, Behrens's chief of staff.[39] Krämer was the same age as Mies, but had a proper architecture degree from Darmstadt and more experience.

1910 The Bismarck Memorial

Mies intended to start an independent practice from his parents' house in Aachen with his brother Ewald, who had taken over the family business but occasionally worked on architectural projects as well.[40] Their first (and only) joint project was a submission to the Bismarck Memorial competition.

One of most compelling examples of political architecture in late nineteenth-century Germany were so-called Bismarck Towers, of which about 240 were built all over Germany between 1869 and 1934. (A few even emerged in German colonies and in areas with large groups of German immigrants, such as Concepción, Chile; today, 173 still exist.) They speak to the quasi-religious cult around the powerful politician Otto von Bismarck, who had been the mastermind behind the German unification of 1871 and also introduced Germany's welfare state. After the inept Emperor Wilhelm II dismissed Bismarck in 1890, the building of Bismarck Towers and the celebration of his birthday became symbols of political resistance against the emperor. Bismarck died in 1898, and when what would have been his one hundredth birthday (in 1915) came into view, a national competition was held for a memorial overlooking the Rhine from the Elisenhöhe near Bingerbrück, 400 feet (120 meters) above the river. It surely must have been discussed among the young architects in Behrens's office, especially since Behrens had just designed an (unexecuted) Bismarck Memorial near Oldenburg, and had been asked to be on the jury, together with Theodor Fischer, Ludwig Hoffmann, Hermann Muthesius, and Fritz Schumacher.[41]

Each participant received a plan and five photographs of the site, which many would use in photo collages or as bases for the required perspective renderings. Entrants could also submit a model of the site, at 1:500 scale. The response was considerable. Between January 23 and 26, 1911, 379 entries were examined by the jury at the Düsseldorf Kunstpalast. Considered a matter of national importance, the results were widely discussed, as they touched on questions of politics and monumentality, abstraction and representation.[42] A number of types emerged. There were the familiar Bismarck Towers, large sculptures overlooking the Rhine (a portrait of Bismarck, sometimes in the harness of a medieval knight, or represented metaphorically as a lion or eagle), and round structures with cavernous interiors, inspired by the Mausoleum of Halicarnassus or the tomb of Theodoric in Ravenna.[43] There were medieval castles, a symbol of defense along the Rhine, or a ring of heavy piers referencing Stonehenge, and finally columnar structures surrounding a large, open space for gatherings and celebrations.

Surprisingly, the jury selected one of the most restrained and unmonumental proposals—of the Stonehenge variety—a simple ring of slender stone pillars connected by beams on top. In the center stood not a sculpture of Bismarck, but of Siegfried, the legendary medieval hero who had become a symbol of German nationalism. This being an anonymous competition, the designers were revealed after the winning entry had been picked. It turned out to be conservative architect German Bestelmeyer, a professor in Dresden (the sculptor was Hermann Hahn) (figure 1.19). The small scale, invisibility from afar, and lack of monumentality and deference to Bismarck failed to impress many members of the public, and in particular subscribers of the "Bismarck associations" in Germany. After much protest and critiques, the initial result was withdrawn and new deliberations were held in Wiesbaden on June 24, 1911, with a larger jury. Now, Wilhelm Kreis was given the first prize for a heavy mausoleum (figure 1.20). Discussions continued through the following year, followed by more meetings of committees, a brief reinstatement of Bestelmeyer's original winning design, and finally a confirmation of a reworked Kreis design on October 12, 1912.[44] The outbreak of World War I prevented the execution, but discussions continued through the 1920s, into the Nazi period.[45]

Forty-one designs had made it into the penultimate round, twenty-six of which were eliminated next, among them Ewald and Ludwig Mies's design, "due to the obvious transgression of the cost limitation. The indispensable substructure alone would lead to a substantial transgression of the financial estimate."[46]

The Mies brothers' proposal showed an open court flanked by two long, columnar halls with fifteen bays inside, and eighteen on the outside, wide enough to provide a stoa for contemplative strolls (figure 1.21). The colonnade anchored two tall pylons, flanking the semicircular exedra with an enormous Bismarck statue. One cannot help but see a similarity to

Figure 1.19. Bismarck Memorial at Elisenhöhe, Bingen, Germany. Competition entry by German Bestelmeyer, 1910. Perspective rendering.

Figure 1.20. Bismarck Memorial at Elisenhöhe, Bingen, Germany. Competition entry by Wilhelm Kreis, 1910. Rendering on photograph of the Bismarck Memorial. Contemporary postcard. Private collection.

Figure 1.21. Bismarck Memorial at Elisenhöhe, Bingen, Germany. Competition entry by Ludwig Mies and Ewald Mies, 1910. Perspective view of the courtyard by an unknown artist. Gouache on linen, 55 1/2 in. × 7 ft. 10 1/2 in. (140 × 240 cm). Museum of Modern Art, New York. The Mies van der Rohe Archive, gift of the architect.

Nationalgalerie, Berlin, 1965–68. The main
exhibition space upstairs after restoration,
2021. Photograph by Simon Menges.

the two pylons and colonnade at the Isis Temple of Philae in Egypt, much in the news at the time, due to its annual flooding from the British-built Aswan Dam of 1902, which was just being raised by 16 feet (five meters) (figure 1.22). To increase visibility, Ludwig and Ewald Mies pushed their memorial forward toward the river, necessitating a massive substructure. A similar boldness speaks from the proposal's representation: the official photograph was reprinted at a larger scale, with a photo of the model inserted and then two enlarged sections from the original photo added to accommodate the full length of the stoa and improve the overall proportion (figure 1.23).

The single image of the Mies brothers' design that appeared in the official publication was a photograph of an enormous gouache painting on a roughly 56-by-94-inch (141-by-240-centimeter) rectangle of heavy linen, which showed the central courtyard. Its painterly style is unique in Mies's oeuvre. In all likelihood it was commissioned in great haste from a local artist, who took pride in his work, as the word "*unfertig*" (unfinished) appears once in pencil inside the painting and once on a label tacked onto the wooden listel at the bottom. He seems to have used a discarded teaching tool typical in German classrooms at the time: images for biology, history, and geography lessons were printed on heavy linen, with wooden bars keeping it straight when on display and facilitating storage. A map of the German Reich (which Bismarck had created) would have made a particularly fitting substrate.[47] A large drawing of a side elevation (over three by seven feet, or one by two meters), on yellow tracing paper with a green wash was probably executed by Mies himself, as its style corresponds with similar drawings from Mies's hand at the time (figure 1.24).

The comparison between the Mies brothers' design and that of Walter Gropius and Adolf Meyer is informative. Gropius, Meyer, and Mies were still at Peter Behrens's office when the competition was announced, and might have discussed preliminary ideas. Just like Mies, Gropius and Meyer imagined a large courtyard, two tall pylons, and flanking, asymmetrical colonnades, one straight, one following the edge of the site in a meandering path (figure 1.25). Hans Poelzig and several others, such as Paul Bonatz, also designed a large gathering space, foregoing picturesque monumentality for communal functionality (figure 1.26).

1911   Meeting Ada Bruhn

Finally, in the summer of 1911, another commission beckoned in Berlin. Hugo Perls, a lawyer and an acquaintance of Alois Riehl, had begun collecting art after he had met his future wife, Käte. She was the daughter of wealthy Breslau industrialist Hugo Kolker and an avid art collector, just like her older sister Else, who was married to art historian Curt Glaser. Their remarkable collection included pieces by Max Beckmann, Ernst Ludwig Kirchner, Lovis Corinth, Henri Matisse, and Pablo Picasso. Mies would later be a frequent guest at Glaser's expansive apartment in Berlin. After Hugo and Käte Perls got married and commissioned Mies, they "went on their honeymoon, to Paris, to buy things for that house. There they met [art dealer Daniel-Henry] Kahnweiler and [artist Ambroise] Vollard and Picasso."[48]

Figure 1.25. Bismarck Memorial at Elisenhöhe, Bingen, Germany. Competition entry by Walter Gropius and Adolf Meyer, 1910. Photograph of rendering on gray illustration board, 5 7/8 × 8 3/4 in. (14.8 × 22.1 cm). Bauhaus-Archiv, Berlin.

Figure 1.26. Bismarck Memorial at Elisenhöhe, Bingen, Germany. Version A. Competition entry by Hans Poelzig, 1910. Perspective with landscape. Gouache and watercolor on photograph on illustration board, 18 × 23 1/2 in. (45.8 × 59.6 cm). Technische Universität Berlin, Architekturmuseum.

Mies returned from Aachen in the summer of 1911, resuming his job at Behrens's atelier and his regular visits at the Riehl House nearby.[49] In the meantime, Charles-Édouard Jeanneret (later Le Corbusier) had briefly worked for Behrens from November 1, 1910, to April 1, 1911.[50] While Mies remembered that he had met "a certain Jeanneret on the doorsteps of Behrens's office," this must have been during a visit to Berlin, as he only returned to work there after Jeanneret had left.[51] Like Gropius, Le Corbusier described Behrens as an aloof and demanding boss, with little personal warmth—a "monster," a "bear," "autocratic, tyrannical, and a brute who terrorized the office staff."[52]

An important aspect of Mies's return to Berlin had been the chance to see Ada Bruhn again, whom he had met at the Riehls' Klösterli in 1910 (figure 1.27). From a wealthy and cultured Berlin family, Ada had been the fiancée of popular art historian Heinrich Wölfflin, twenty years her senior, but their engagement was annulled when Wölfflin accepted a professorship in Munich. Mies and Ada got engaged at the Riehl House on January 6, 1912. Mies promised her a similar home: "When everything is settled I want to buy the land and then we will build a small house on the top of the mountain and a lot of sun will shine into our lives."[53]

Ada introduced Mies to a different world: she was a dance student at Heinrich Tessenow's new theater in Dresden Hellerau, where Mies encountered the essentialist vision of stage designer Adolphe Appia, music educator Émile Jaques-Dalcroze, and lighting designer Alexander Saltzman. Their large, universal space (a "cathedral of the future," as Appia later called it) fundamentally challenged traditional theater: thanks to a retractable orchestra pit, the stage and auditorium merged into a spiritual and sensory unit (figure 1.28).[54] Appia's stage design consisted of simple stairs and horizontal platforms, and ceiling and walls were lined with white cloth, behind which thousands of bulbs produced a diffuse, shadowless light, as if on a bright overcast day outside, "objective, neither cold, nor hot, but rather of a marvelously living consistency … with an imperceptible dynamism" (figure

Figure 1.27. Ada Bruhn, ca. 1912. Private collection.

Figure 1.28. Heinrich Tessenow, Hellerau Theater, Dresden, Germany, 1912.

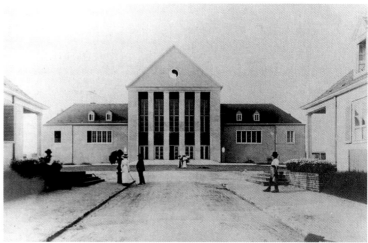

1.29).[55] While Mies wouldn't become an avant-gardist for another ten years, some of the revolutionary ideas he encountered here look like predecessors of his own later work. Ada introduced him to her roommates Marie Wiegmann (the future dancer Mary Wigman) and Erna Hofmann, the future wife of the famous psychiatrist Hans Prinzhorn, who became friends of Mies's.

One cannot but marvel at the poetic coincidences of these personal intersections. Ada Bruhn's previous engagement to art historian Heinrich Wölfflin had exposed her to his idea of the "affective experience" of a body moving in space to achieve an understanding of architecture, which helped pave the way for the notion of "flowing space" (introduced by Wölfflin's student Paul Frankl)—soon to be declared a trademark of Mies's architecture. The funds that had made Mies's early career possible came from Ada's father, Friedrich Wilhelm Bruhn, who had invented and produced a literal space-time machine— namely, the modern taximeter, which recorded distance traveled and time consumed in a taxicab.

To Ludwig Mies and Ada Bruhn's courtship, we owe some of the most authentic writing from Mies's hand. He wrote to her:

> A satisfying activity is the best thing we have. And when you do something with pleasure, it enriches. Every evening since Sunday I experience great joy with the little house. Really my dear, the hours in which you rise above yourself are of such deep bliss that you have to experience it yourself to know what it is like. Also, the struggle to form matter, while an image presents itself to the inner gaze is glorious, even if less great. Sacred are the hours when we listen to our innermost feelings, to bring them clearly formed to paper. The greatest and richest results I always achieve when I sit quietly in front of my work and dream. Creating forms is more technical work. Any person with taste and sensibility can do it. But one is really productive

Figure 1.29. Adolphe Appia, rhythmic drawing of set design project, 1909–10. Bibliothèque de l'Arsenal, Paris.

only when one stretches all one's fibers to the utmost and reaches beyond oneself. Maybe I should better say, when you have freed yourself from everything and connected to your deepest inner self. But perhaps what I'm saying is all nonsense. In such hours everything is blocked out and you only have to listen.

Mies went on to describe his new commission, the Perls House, in detail:

> Wait and see how different the Perls house will look from Klösterli, and artistically it will definitely stand high above it. But will it be as appealing and sweet? I don't know yet. It will look strange to some. But I am happy with it, and that is the most important thing. I have worked on it with the utmost concentration of my inner self, and returned again and again to refine it more. Now I am trying to turn the garden into a little paradise. I don't know if I will succeed. But the house is close to my heart.[56]

1911–12   Perls House

Mies worked on the Perls House after hours and was at pains to keep his moonlighting hidden from his employer, Peter Behrens. Ada was firmly instructed not to mention the house when she called for him at the atelier.[57] His friend Ferdinand Goebbels, who had originally come with him from Aachen and also worked for Behrens, partnered with Mies on the project. Mies also mentioned to Ada his work on a housing estate for federal employees and a display room at the Wertheim Department Store.[58]

The program, size, and rectangular footprint of the Perls House are, indeed, similar to the Riehl House, but the relationship between the two main façades is reversed (figure 1.30). At the Riehl House, one approached via a straight path through the garden, with the main entrance emphasized by a gable above, while the secondary, slimmer façade, with its three-bay loggia, overlooked the lake and street below. The second floor was integrated into the roof slope. At the Perls House, one enters on the short, northeastern side of the building, while the wide southeastern façade, with its three-bay open pergola, belongs to

Figure 1.30. Ludwig Mies, Perls House, Berlin, 1911–12.

Figure 1.31. Ludwig Mies, Perls House, Berlin, 1911–12. Addition for Eduard Fuchs in 1928. Three elevations. Pencil on tracing paper, 19 1/4 × 15 1/4 in. (48.9 × 38.8 cm). Museum of Modern Art, New York. The Mies van der Rohe Archive, gift of the architect.

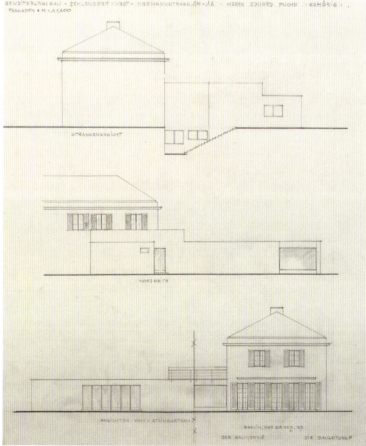

the dining room. A music room to the southwest has five large doors to the garden. While at the Riehl House, the site's slope had allowed for easy access to the basement, here, on a horizontal plot, Mies had a trench excavated to provide access and daylight to the basement kitchen and servants' rooms, and thus achieved a similar functional stratification. A section drawing of 1928 shows the basement access as well as the façade of a later addition, which Mies would execute for the house's new owner, art historian Eduard Fuchs, in 1928 (figure 1.31). While it has a flat roof and is more modern in appearance, it responds to its context by replicating the five French doors and shutters with a thin stucco line above Mies's original garden façade—a concession Mies had to make after an initially more restrained approach.

Apart from Behrens's contemporaneous Cuno and Schröder houses in Hagen, with their symmetrical façades and hip roofs, inspiration might have come from Karl Friedrich Schinkel's New Pavilion at the Charlottenburg Palace of 1824–25, with its thin stucco lines and a similar cornice below the onset of the roof (figures 1.32, 1.33). Mies knew that Perls was a great admirer of Schinkel.[59]

In 1912, Perls commissioned expressionist painter Max Pechstein to paint murals on canvas for the house's dining room (figure 1.34).[60] Pechstein created a panoramic paradise— a bucolic landscape filled with mostly female nudes—on three sides of the room. When they were published in June 1912, Perls was celebrated for his visionary patronage of monumental mural art.[61]

Facing financial difficulties during World War I (and disturbed by the stream of visitors the murals attracted), Hugo Perls sold the house to art historian Eduard Fuchs in exchange for five paintings by Max Liebermann. While he found the house "beautiful," he later recalled missing "cozy corners"—and probably wall space for his art, as indeed Mies had so many openings installed in the ground-floor rooms that there was little wall space left.[62]

The Liebermann paintings became the foundation of Hugo and Käte Perls's art gallery, which opened in 1921 on Berlin's elegant Bellevuestrasse. It existed until their departure

Figure 1.32. Peter Behrens, Cuno and Schröder houses, Hagen, Germany, 1909–10.

Figure 1.33. Karl Friedrich Schinkel, New Pavilion at the Charlottenburg Palace, Berlin, 1824–25.

Figure 1.34. Ludwig Mies, Perls House, Berlin, 1911–12. Dining room with murals by Max Pechstein, 1912.

from Berlin in 1931. They bought and sold art by cubists, impressionists, symbolists, and more, including the work of Edvard Munch, Picasso, Claude Monet, Vincent van Gogh, and Paul Cézanne. Munch painted a portrait of Perls and his wife in 1913.

1911–12 Working Again for Peter Behrens

One can only imagine the glee among Behrens's underpaid young apprentices and draftsmen, when among all the accolades about the AEG Turbine Factory, severe criticism could suddenly be heard from the most authoritative voice—the building's structural engineer, Karl Bernhard; this occurred just at the time when Mies was back in Behrens's office for the second time, in the fall of 1911.[63] Bernhard was nine years older than Behrens and had had proper training as an engineer and been responsible for a number of elegant bridges in Berlin. He was a lecturer at the Technische Universität Berlin and a prolific writer who argued for proper recognition of an engineer's aesthetic, since "architects were incapable of dealing with the demands of the structural tasks of large industrial buildings." "Beauty," he declared, "had to grow out of the 'thing itself,' checked by the knowledge of the engineer." The absence of this knowledge would lead to "half-baked results." One of those, in his opinion, was the main façade of the AEG Turbine Factory (see figure 1.18).[64]

No doubt, Bernhard was piqued by the fact that Behrens received all the credit for the building, after having only added a few formal flourishes to a structure that he, Bernhard, had designed. In a long essay, he listed the different contributions. Oskar Lasche, an AEG engineer, had developed the detailed program, and Bernhard had provided the accommodation of the two moving cranes, via the special foundation and support structure that their weight and lateral movement required. He was also proud of the interiors' excellent lighting, access to railroad tracks, and more. Bernhard chose the three-hinge arch system with a tension rod, the elevated base joints, and all technical details; as a result, "the building fulfills the tasks it was made for, with ease," he proudly stated.[65]

While the side façade, with its clear distinction of structural elements, was a "true and undeniable work of the art of iron architecture" (mostly designed by him, but he gave Behrens credit for the inclination of the windows between the piers), the main façade by Behrens, with its pedimented front, did not deserve such praise. Rather, "unfortunately, concrete has been used at the pedimented front on Huttenstrasse for large areas as a filling material, which creates an unjustifiable contrast.... The desired effect, namely, to make the

Figure 1.35. Peter Behrens with supervising site architect Ludwig Mies, German Embassy, St. Petersburg, Russia, 1911–12.

corners appear merely as a cladding, has not been achieved. While it consists of a thin skin of reinforced concrete on top of an iron construction, everyone considers the pediment a massive concrete structure: two corner pylons with a mighty pediment." Bernhard himself had even suggested the horizontal metal bands in the concrete in order to hint at the actually different material. The effect was different than intended: the metal bands read as joints between heavy concrete blocks. As a specialist in iron construction, Bernhard was particularly indignant that the AEG Turbine Factory had recently been praised for spearheading a new concrete style. Bernhard had made an important point—the main façade of the Turbine Factory displayed structural dishonesty, as its mighty reclining pylons on either side seemed to be carrying the enormous pediment above, while in reality, both pylons and pediment were thin sheet-metal constructions held by invisible cantilevers behind them. In sum, the much-discussed main front lacked "artistic truth," he concluded.[66] In response, Behrens declared that "structure does not yet mean culture," and that the "results of the engineer's work are by themselves not yet beautiful." He also pointed at the need for calm, monumental forms in the modern, fast-paced metropolis.[67] And, of course, Behrens had, rightly, decided that the creation of a powerful, memorable image was more important for AEG than the display of structural honesty.

This debate highlighted with great clarity a core conflict at the heart of modern architecture. Mies would take sides in the early 1920s, when he noted, "He who builds a factory as if it were a temple lies and disfigures the landscape" and declared, "Form is the result, and not the goal of our work"—but of course he would soon emerge as one of the most uncompromising formalists of the twentieth century.[68] When it was time for him to design an industrial building with a comparable brief, the Minerals and Metals Building on IIT's campus in Chicago in 1943, Mies must have surely remembered the Behrens-Bernard debate of 1911. The side elevation revealed its structural arrangement of steel and brick with brutal honesty (paid for, though, by a corrosive encounter with material physics, in the form of condensation water on the inside).

The main project on Mies's desk in Behrens's office at that time was the German Embassy building in St. Petersburg, executed in 1911–12 (figure 1.35). As construction manager, Mies was responsible for readying the project for execution. While a steel-frame building, it was clad in heavy ashlar, with a columnar façade on one side of its irregular plot, and notions of artistic or structural truths were hardly applicable. The site could not have been more prominent, right across from St. Isaac's Cathedral. Mies later recalled that he was astonished to see Behrens design the façade first, and then choose the material later. It ended up being the same red Finnish granite as in the cathedral, but rough, not polished. As a result, "of course, all the classical details vanished," Mies remembered with pride.[69]

1911–12 Kröller-Müller House

Mies's time in Behrens's office soon came to a sudden and dramatic end. Behrens had been asked by the mercurial art collector Helene Kröller-Müller to design a home and art gallery for her extensive collection on a piece of land ("Ellenwoude") in Wassenaar, in the Netherlands. Behrens had put Mies in charge of the project, as Mies's previous project of supervising the design and execution of the St. Petersburg Embassy had run its course. Helene Müller came from a wealthy German family. Her father, Wilhelm Müller, owned a company supplying transportation technology to the steel and mining industries and had urged her to marry Anton Kröller, his most capable employee, who came from a family of Dutch shipping and mining tycoons. Kröller soon led the Müller family business and moved the headquarters first to Rotterdam and then, in 1900, to The Hague. In the Dutch capital, the ambitious Kröller established important political connections. His profits grew exponentially during and after World War I through the sale and shipping of much-needed steel and iron.

Under the influence of her mentor, Hendricus Petrus ("Henk") Bremmer, Helene had begun collecting French and Dutch art, and in particular many works by Vincent van Gogh. Bremmer was a charismatic connoisseur, collector, and dealer who had an almost cultlike following among Dutch middle-class women who attended his lectures on aesthetics. When Helene died in 1939, she had assembled the largest private van Gogh

Figure 1.36. Peter Behrens, Wiegand House, Berlin, 1911–12.

Figure 1.37. Peter Behrens with Ludwig Mies, Kröller-Müller House project, Wassenaar, Netherlands, 1911–12. Main façade with greenhouse on the right and entrance pergola on the left.

Figure 1.38. Peter Behrens with Ludwig Mies, Kröller-Müller House project, Wassenaar, Netherlands, 1911–12. Open courtyard.

collection in the world: ninety-seven paintings and 185 drawings. Her purchases were also a smart business investment, in particular since Bremmer promoted the art he favored in a stream of publications, thus making it better known and more valuable.[70]

Behrens produced a design with Mies's help, and in March 1912 a 1:1 model on wheels was built in the park of Wassenaar, to be moved around the property, while Helene Kröller-Müller surveyed the sites on horseback. We do not know the extent of the individual contributions of Behrens and Mies, but the result was a stunningly modern design, its flat roof, dense rows of large, shutterless windows, and restrained massing a resolute step forward beyond Behrens's contemporaneous Wiegand House in Berlin (figure 1.36). There was a representative façade, a greenhouse and porte-cochere for the main entrance, but also several intimate courtyards (figures 1.37, 1.38). Mrs. Kröller-Müller did not enjoy her encounters with Behrens, but liked Mies and wanted him to take over the commission. She came from Essen, close to Mies's hometown of Aachen, and thus shared the same dialect and the Rhineland's friendly conviviality. Behrens, in contrast, a reserved northern German from Hamburg, was unable to bridge the gap of mentalities. At the end of April 1912, a meeting was scheduled between Helene Kröller-Müller, Behrens, and Mies in Berlin, and Sophie Riehl was invited to vouch for Mies. Behrens was asked to put Mies fully in charge of the design, but instead stormed out of the room and fired Mies shortly thereafter.[71]

Mies was promptly hired by Müller & Co. for a generous salary of 8,000 Reichsmark and sent to The Hague to work on the design for the Kröller-Müller House.[72] The company had just moved into a palatial seventeenth-century brick office building with tall windows, right in the heart of the city, where Helene also displayed her art collection. Mies was given a desk and got to work. He remembered: "About fifty van Goghs were hanging there. I became a van Gogh expert in spite of myself; there was no way of avoiding the pictures."[73] Mies stayed from April to September, interrupted by daily visits from Mrs. Kröller-Müller, who took him on sightseeing tours. She was seventeen years older than Mies and enjoyed his attention and companionship. He recalled, "I was driven around Holland for a couple of weeks, so that I got to know the country." Hendrik Petrus Berlage's Stock Exchange in Amsterdam "made a great impression" on him (figure 1.39). He recalled how impressed he was with "this careful construction, honest to the bone. That interested me the most. And the different spiritual attitude. You see, it had nothing at all to do with classicism, it had nothing at all historical, it was really a modern building. After Berlage, after I was in Holland, I fought a real inner battle with myself to get away from Schinkel's classicism."[74] Mies also

Figure 1.39. Hendrik Petrus Berlage, Stock Exchange, Amsterdam, 1898–1903. Gelatin silver print, 23 5/8 × 35 3/8 in. (60 × 90 cm). Photograph by Hans Spies. Nieuwe Instituut, Rotterdam, Netherlands.

recalled that it was in "1912 when I was working in The Hague, I first saw a drawing by Louis Sullivan of one of his buildings. It interested me."[75]

Helene Kröller-Müller's advisor, Henk Bremmer, had insisted that a more seasoned Dutch architect should also be consulted to build the Kröller-Müller House, and contacted Berlage. He was asked to collaborate with Mies (whom he had surely never heard of), but Berlage was not interested, and so they worked independently from each other and do not seem to have met.[76]

Mies faced a delicate problem regarding authorship. He had worked on the project as Behrens's employee, and Behrens's formal language was evident in its heavy ashlar, colonnaded courtyards, symmetrical and asymmetrical groupings, and a cornice below the roof's edge. Mies, however, might have been responsible for the flat roof, denser rows of windows, and an overall tighter disposition. Asked to develop the project further on his own, Mies stayed close to the formal language of the previous design, but rearranged the floor plan. The previous plan showed a compact sequence of grand spaces and interior courtyards, and solved the intermingling of spaces for visitors to the gallery and those for the family quite well. For Mies's design of the Kröller-Müller House, a number of model photographs, a perspective, and an elevation have survived, but the only floor plan we have is a sketch that Mies made twenty years later, in a conversation with students (figure 1.40). Howard Dearstyne preserved it and added a numbered key to its spaces and their intended uses.[77] In contrast to Behrens's compact scheme, Mies distributed the functions in a loose sequence around a central courtyard. The entrance is moved off to the side and marked by a porte cochere for vehicular access. To reach the large exhibition hall on the far end, one had to walk down a long, central corridor "for the display of porcelain" right behind the family sleeping

Figure 1.40. Ludwig Mies van der Rohe, Kröller-Müller House project, Wassenaar, Netherlands. Sketch plan of ground floor, ca. 1933. Pencil on tracing paper, 8 3/8 × 17 5/8 in. (21.3 × 44.7 cm). Museum of Modern Art, New York. The Mies van der Rohe Archive, gift of the architect.

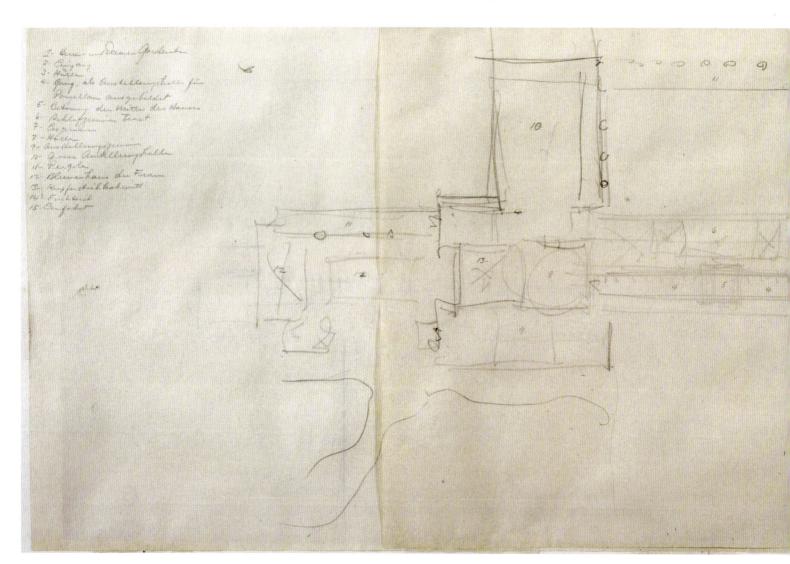

quarters and anchored by two "halls." While this arrangement seemed impractical and not fully worked out, Mies was clearly trying to get away from the typical symmetry and spatial sequence of upper-class homes and establish a memorable alternative, less focused on entertaining and more on presenting the clients' collections. Private and semipublic spaces for visitors are not separated. In an odd concession to conventional taste, a small protrusion in the middle of the long main façade is called "*Betonung der Mitte des Hauses*" (Emphasis of the middle of the house). This dynamic sketch certainly creates a stark contrast to the staid classicism of the model and perspectives of the design. If it correctly reflects Mies's approach of twenty years earlier, it points to the influence of Frank Lloyd Wright, whose "Wasmuth Portfolio" had appeared in 1911 and been discussed in Behrens's office. Designs such as Wright's Avery Coonley House of 1907 had a comparable centrifugal plan with long corridors and asymmetrically placed volumes.

On the reverse side of Mies's sketch of the Kröller-Müller plan, which required an extension onto a second, taped-on sheet of A4 writing paper, is another loose drawing by Mies, a floor plan of the Brick Country House of 1924 (figure 1.41; see figure 2.28). Clearly, Mies saw a connection between the two projects, and he would make sure that they were placed next to each other in the catalogue for the *Modern Architecture: International Exhibition* at MoMA in 1932. In 1927, he told Paul Westheim that one could easily "get rid of" the traditional, Schinkel-style façade at the Wassenaar project, "and then we would have a building just like we do it today. In other words, a building where the way of life is not determined by the arrangement of the house, but the house follows the process of dwelling." The house would change from a "stage set" to a "machine," where the lifestyle determined the "circulation from space to space, in order for domestic life to unfold as smoothly as possible."[78]

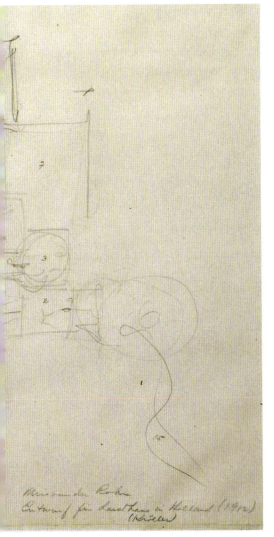

Figure 1.41. Ludwig Mies van der Rohe, floor plan sketch of the Brick Country House on the back of a sketch for the Kröller-Müller House, ca. 1933. Library of Congress, Washington, D.C.

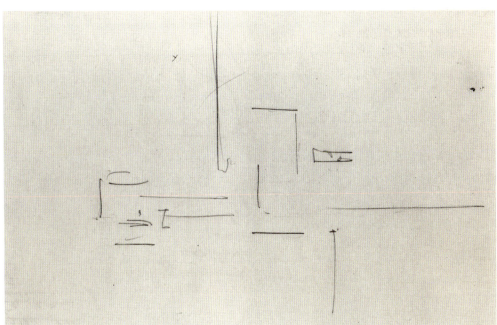

In September 1912 Mies presented the design in several drawings, a watercolor perspective, and a small plaster model (figures 1.42, 1.43). Just like Behrens's earlier design, a simplified façade was built on-site in 1:1 scale from wood and canvas—and, while Mrs. Müller apparently liked the design, her art advisor, Henk Bremmer, strongly favored Berlage, who had submitted his own design at the same time. Berlage's design had a symmetrical layout, hip roofs, and a clear distinction between private quarters and semipublic display areas. Nationalistic feelings ran high in the buildup to World War I, and Bremmer found the choice of a Dutch architect more appropriate.

Sensing the danger of losing this important commission, Mies sought support from the well-known art historian Julius Meier-Graefe. Meier-Graefe had helped to promote the art nouveau movement via his magazines *Pan* and *Dekorative Kunst* and established the Maison Moderne interior design store in Paris in 1897. By 1901, he had moved beyond the "Belgian line" and promoted reformed and restrained interiors in an influential essay on the "modern milieu," in which he had identified "the best of the modern principles" as applying as little art as possible.[79] Otherwise, his engagement with architecture had been minimal. The main reason why Mies solicited his opinion in Paris in the fall of 1912 might have been that this celebrated van Gogh expert was greatly admired and respected by Bremmer.[80] In his letter of support, Meier-Graefe congratulated Mies on avoiding a possible isolation of exhibition rooms from the residential area and mentioned the "agreeable asymmetry" of the architectural massing, in which "the gallery appears as a necessary part." He added, "Nothing is piecemeal, all parts hang together organically, evolve logically and the whole seems well suited for the flat land for which it is meant. Even the long corridor parallel to the living quarters, which could have appeared as a makeshift, is,

< Figure 1.42. Ludwig Mies, Kröller-Müller House project, Wassenaar, Netherlands. Plaster model, 1912. Klassik Stiftung Weimar.

Figure 1.43. Ludwig Mies, Kröller-Müller House project, Wassenaar, Netherlands. Perspective view from the garden, with pergola and large gallery in the foreground, 1912. Pastel and watercolor on print, 17 7/8 × 55 3/4 in. (45.4 × 141.5 cm). Collection Kröller-Müller Museum, Otterlo, Netherlands. Photograph by Rik Klein Gotink.

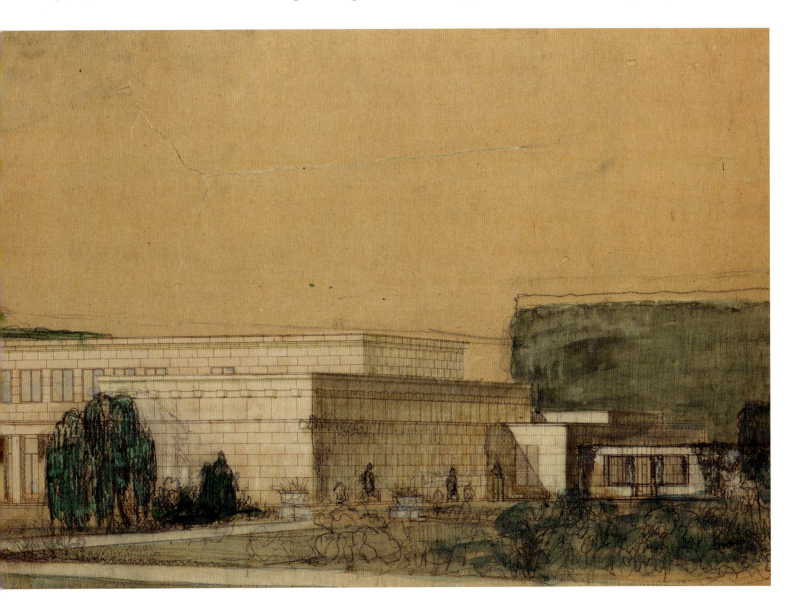

thanks to its depth, solved organically and seems felicitously organized." Meier-Graefe articulated a "minor objection," though—there were not enough spaces with side lighting, in addition to top-lit rooms, "since so many modern paintings look better with side lighting." But, Mies's simple façade appealed to him "through its impressive, never heavily monumental, appearance." He concluded that this project would give Mies "the opportunity of the artistic accomplishment of which you are capable."[81] While his trip to Paris did not have the intended outcome, it broadened Mies's purview of modern art, as Helene Kröller-Müller arranged for him to meet the art dealer and author Wilhelm Uhde, and the artists Wilhelm Lehmbruck and Amedeo Modigliani.[82]

When Meier-Graefe's letter arrived in The Hague on November 18, 1912, the decision to commission Berlage had already been made. More importantly, the overall circumstances had changed. News had arrived that a tram line would be built from The Hague to a planned development near her estate, and Helene Kröller-Müller feared for her solitude. The value of her land greatly increased, and so she decided to sell it and buy another, larger estate (75 acres, or 30 hectares) outside of Otterlo, called Hoge Veluwe.

How much had been at stake for Mies became obvious when Berlage was hired on a ten-year contract as company architect and executed several commissions, beginning with Holland House, the firm's London headquarters, with its relentless sequence of windows and strict vertical divisions (an important predecessor to Mies's later façade developments), the St. Hubertus Hunting Lodge in Hoge Veluwe, and a number of small farm buildings (figure 1.44). He never built the house museum, though.

In the mid-1920s, it became obvious that Anton Kröller had engaged in risky business practices. He lost his fortune and left many of his investors penniless. To protect their art collection, Anton and Helene created the Kröller-Müller Foundation in 1928, and ultimately donated the park and their entire collection of about twelve thousand objects to the state, stipulating that a large museum should be built. Berlage died in 1934, and Henry van de Velde ended up designing the Kröller-Müller Museum in the Hoge Veluwe park near Otterlo, which opened in 1938. Helene died the following year, her husband two years later.

1912–22 Conventional Houses

Having lost first his employment with Peter Behrens in the spring of 1912 and then the promising job of the Kröller-Müller House in the fall of that year, Mies luckily received another commission in October 1912—a house for the engineer Ernst Werner, right next to the Perls House in Berlin Zehlendorf. As with the Riehl House, models for similar structures with hipped mansard roofs and a central gable could easily be found in Paul Mebes's book *Um 1800* and in the contemporary work of Paul Schultze-Naumburg, Alfred Grenander, and others.[83] The conventional houses that followed over the next decade confirmed Anton Jaumann's dictum about the Riehl House: they were well executed, competent, but not exciting. Three of them were destroyed in the war or demolished afterward (the Warnholtz, Feldmann, and Kempner houses), making a full assessment difficult.

At the Werner House, Mies worked again with Ferdinand Goebbels, from their office in Mies's apartments in Steglitz (1912) and Lichterfelde (1913).[84] An interesting reversal had taken place here: the garden façade is the one that makes the grander statement, being more ostentatious and balanced with its central two-story projection and pediment, framed by a hipped gambrel roof, whose tiles cover the second floor. In contrast, the asymmetrical street façade spells out the adjustments made to accommodate the flow of life in and around the house (figures 1.45, 1.46). The visitor is led up three steps to a wide terrace in front of the entrance. The large dining room in the back seems to have pushed the kitchen toward the street, which now overlooks and shelters the entrance area. It is accessed from a service courtyard on the side. The interior spatial sequence is of particular clarity, as all representational rooms are interconnected while still being accessible from the central hall (figure 1.47). The dining room has a direct connection to an adjacent pergola, allowing sheltered access to the formal garden. A number of pieces of birch wood furniture in an elegant Empire style by Mies and Goebbels (probably a collaboration with a local cabinetmaker) have survived (figures 1.48, 1.49). Mies and Goebbels submitted a first plan in November

Figure 1.44. Hendrik Petrus Berlage, Holland House, London, 1916. Nieuwe Instituut, Rotterdam, Netherlands.

> Figure 1.45. Ludwig Mies and Ferdinand Goebbels, Werner House, Berlin, 1912. Garden façade. Photograph by Hassan Bagheri.

> Figure 1.46. Ludwig Mies and Ferdinand Goebbels, Werner House, Berlin, 1912. Perspective view from street. Pencil and watercolor on tracing paper, 10 3/4 × 21 3/4 in. (27 × 54.2 cm). Bauhaus-Archiv, Berlin.

Figure 1.47. Ludwig Mies and Ferdinand Goebbels, Werner House, Berlin, 1912. Central hall. Photograph by Hassan Bagheri.

Figure 1.48. Ludwig Mies and Ferdinand Goebbels, Werner House, Berlin, 1912. Dining room chair. Bauhaus-Archiv, Berlin.

Figure 1.49. Ludwig Mies and Ferdinand Goebbels, Werner House, Berlin, 1912. Sofa. Bauhaus-Archiv, Berlin.

Johann Julius Warnholtz, director of the Deutsch-Ostafrikanische Gesellschaft (German East African Society) and of the Deutsch-Ostafrikanische Bank (his signature adorned the German colony's Rupie notes), had commissioned a large house (no doubt financed by the fortune amassed in the colony) on a newly developed track of land at Heerstrasse in the northwest of Berlin. Emperor Wilhelm II, who had architectural ambitions, had personally authorized the development in a state forest and insisted on personally inspecting every design for the grand villas rising there. Mies, now without Goebbels, submitted his drawings in March 1914; the emperor approved, and topping out was celebrated seven months later. The formal language was similar to that at the Werner House, but the façades' roles had been reversed. The much larger street front, with its mansard roof and central gable above the entrance, was reminiscent of the Werner House's garden side, and sported heavy quoins at the corners and the main door (figure 1.50). The ground was lowered on the lateral sides, giving outside access to the utility rooms downstairs. The garden side lacked the composure of the front due to an abundance of windows of different shapes and sizes (figure 1.51). Nevertheless, the Warnholtz House was published years later (without naming

Figure 1.50. Ludwig Mies, Warnholtz House, Berlin, 1913–14. Street façade.

Figure 1.51. Ludwig Mies, Warnholtz House, Berlin, 1913–14. Garden façade from building file (detail). Pencil on paper, 16 1/4 × 19 3/8 in. (41.5 × 49.2 cm). Landesarchiv Berlin.

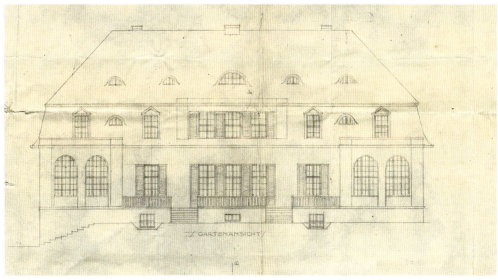

its architect) as a positive example of "quiet, self-assured obviousness" in a polemic against contemporary modernist mannerisms.[85]

When the house was nearing completion in October 1914, World War I broke out, and would rage on for the following four years. The fighting never reached Berlin or Mies's hometown of Aachen. Mies was initially not drafted, as he had been declared unfit for military service years earlier and could thus design and build another house, this time for the banker Franz Urbig, in Potsdam-Babelsberg, not far from the Riehl House. Mies worked with a new partner, Werner von Walthausen, whom he might have met through his wife, Ada. Walthausen had been project architect for Heinrich Tessenow in Dresden Hellerau when Ada was enrolled there as a dance student. Walthausen held degrees from Dresden's Technische Universität (Technical University) and Hochschule für Bildende Künste (Academy of Fine Arts) and had considerable work experience. He seems to have brought echoes of Tessenow's clarity and refinement to the design process and helped establish a new approach. Instead of a mansard roof and central pediment, a tall hip roof now centered a simplified, elegant street façade with its entrance between six shutterless, floor-to-ceiling windows on the first floor. The flat pilasters between them were intended to hold climbing plants. Windows are framed by travertine bands and on the first floor crowned by sculptural inserts (figure 1.52).

The terrace in the back expands east toward the river (above an extended basement) and south via a broad staircase, thus catching as much sun as possible, while offering views of the lake. The loggia on its northern end provides southern windows and an accessible flat roof (figure 1.53). The interior shows an elegant, restrained classicism with columns framing the main hallway and a monumental stair hall in the back. When the house was published with fifteen illustrations in the magazine *Innen-Dekoration* in 1920, the short commentary by Adolf Vogdt echoed Jaumann's judgment of the Riehl House in the same publication ten years earlier. He called the house "calm, well-balanced and firm…a good, normal achievement," but warned against underestimating the architect, "who seems to be driven by the times and by his temperament towards new, more courageous approaches."[86]

Mies was finally conscripted in 1917 to a railroad building contingent in Romania, where he did not see any military action. The war ended in November 1918, with Germany's defeat, millions of fallen or severely injured soldiers, and a global reorganization of the geopolitical landscape, as empires fell and new political systems were introduced. After a year of unrest, Germany abandoned the monarchy and adopted a democratic constitution in the small town of Weimar, where the politicians had retreated to escape the turmoil in the streets of Berlin. The Treaty of Versailles in June of 1919 ceded parts of Germany to neighboring Poland and France, and imposed steep annual reparation payments. Change came less suddenly in other spheres of life, as many artists and architects initially continued their work and ideas from before the war. Mies's postwar buildings, for example, continued his bourgeois style, and nothing indicated that he or his clients were affected by the dramatic turns in German history.

In early 1919, he received a letter from his old office pal Walter Gropius, who was positioning himself for the Bauhaus directorship, which was about to be decided. He was putting together a sales exhibition in a Berlin gallery on behalf of the newly founded Arbeitsrat für Kunst (Labor Council for Art), entitled *Ausstellung für unbekannte Architekten* (Exhibition for Unknown Architects). While Mies had initially signaled his interest in participating with his Kröller-Müller House design, he ultimately failed to submit it, possibly feeling that he was too established already to be seen as an "unknown architect." His instincts were proven correct: the exhibition ended up showing mostly unremarkable prewar work from architects who have remained little known to this day. The Luckhardt Brothers were the most prominent participants, but their spectacular glass cathedrals had not yet been designed.[87] There is no indication that Mies had any substantial interest in or contact with avant-garde artists before 1922.[88]

The year 1921 brought Mies three commissions at once, instead of the usual trickle of one job per year: the small Eichstaedt House and the larger Kempner and Feldmann houses. The main reason for these commissions was not necessarily Mies's growing popularity, but the economic climate. Delivering the first installment of the extraordinarily high reparation

Figure 1.52. Ludwig Mies and Werner von Walthausen, Urbig House, Potsdam-Babelsberg, Germany, 1915–17. View from street. Photograph by Hassan Bagheri.

Figure 1.53. Ludwig Mies and Werner von Walthausen, Urbig House, Potsdam-Babelsberg, Germany, 1915–17. Garden side, view from Lake Griebnitz. Photograph by Hassan Bagheri.

payments of the Versailles Treaty had increased Germany's inflation rate, while interest and construction costs had stayed low. This made loan payments easier and encouraged many who had purchased property to start building.

The bookseller Georg Eichstaedt commissioned a modest house in 1921 in Berlin's suburb Nikolassee, a cubic building with a shallow pyramidal roof above a stepped cornice and plastered outside walls. From a semicircular extension, three French doors open onto the adjacent southwestern terrace. Above is a balcony for a bedroom. The second of Mies's conventional postwar commissions came from Cuno Feldmann, chairman of the board of the Dr. Paul Meyer AG, a producer of electrical machine parts, closely connected with and later fully absorbed by AEG. Peter Behrens probably made the introductions, as he had accepted a professorship in Vienna and did not accept any more commissions in Berlin. The building followed the arrangement of the earlier Urbig House, with a central symmetrical entrance, a steep hip roof, and a servants' wing on the western side with a lower courtyard. An additional room on the eastern side undermined the strict symmetry, as did an adjacent tract with auxiliary rooms. The building was severely damaged during the war, greatly altered during its subsequent rebuilding, and finally demolished in 2000.

The most significant of Mies's commissions in the early 1920s came from the prominent lawyer and businessman Maximilian Kempner. Design began before August 1921, the date

Figure 1.54. Ludwig Mies van der Rohe, Kempner House, Berlin, 1921–23. Main elevation. Drawing by Carl Gottfried. Pencil on paper, 14 3/4 × 27 3/8 in. (37.4 × 69.5 cm). Landesarchiv Berlin.

Figure 1.55. Ludwig Mies van der Rohe, Kempner House, Berlin, 1921–23. Main façade.

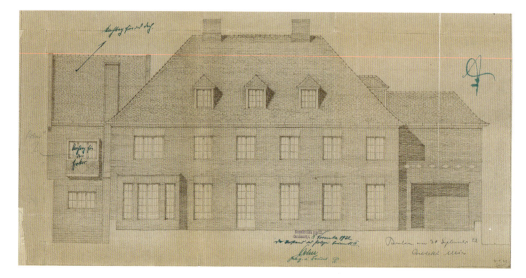

of the first building permit, but continued to evolve, necessitating a second permit a year later. Kempner enjoyed considerable clout with the city's building assessor, which proved a fitting corrective to Mies's sloppy design and submission habits.[89] While the façade followed the simplicity of the Urbig House, sheltered by a tall hip roof, the internal organization differed considerably, due to a central stair hall and two service wings in the back (figures 1.54–1.56). The house occupied the northeastern corner of a large (1.9 acres, or 0.8 hectare) property in Berlin with an existing garden and large trees. One approached the house through this garden, and entered from the side. The large living and dining rooms faced the garden beyond a broad veranda. The Kempner House was Mies's first design in exposed brick, and he applied flat brick rowlock arches above doors and windows and created detailed chimney patterns and simple ornamentation. The second permit application at the end of September 1922 shows the taller servants' wing in the back, with a Dutch stepped gable overlooking the service courtyard—one of Mies's most unexpected creations and a fitting complement to his Dutch-sounding new name (figure 1.57).

1921 A New Name and New Arrangements

The three building applications in the fall of 1921 reveal Mies's step-by-step adoption of the name Mies (initially spelled "Miës") van der Rohe, linking his surname to that of his mother, distracting from the negative associations of the word *"mies"* with "rotten" or

Figure 1.56. Ludwig Mies van der Rohe, Kempner House, Berlin, 1921–23. Main stair hall.

Figure 1.57. Ludwig Mies van der Rohe, Kempner House, Berlin, 1921–23. View toward the stepped gable of the servants' wing.

"dishonest."[90] The contrived "van der" had a Dutch ring to it, or to German ears a vaguely aristocratic association—a "pretentious fraud," as his daughter Dorothea later remarked.[91] Probably the new name was meant "to lend a visible sign of prestige" and enhance "his prospects of receiving commissions for conventional work from an upscale clientele."[92] Mies might have been inspired by the abovementioned art historian Julius Meier-Graefe, who had also combined his parents' last names, or by Dutch architect Theo van Doesburg, who had adopted the name of his stepfather (he was born Christian Emil Marie Küpper). Only two years later, the Dutch avant-garde of the De Stijl group had become a key source of influence, and Mies happily promoted its work in Germany. Critic Heinrich de Fries noted in confidence in 1925 that the name change indicated Mies's desire to be counted among Dutch architects.[93] With mock indignation, critic Werner Hegemann noted in 1927 that Mies van der Rohe was sometimes teased for having "awoken one morning as the Dutch nobleman van der Rohe.... Newly baptized," he had realized "that as a German Mies, one can build very decent houses with sloping roofs without attracting much attention, while with a Dutch name one only needs to design one very impractical, Dutch-style high-rise to gain both the enthusiasm of the young and the directorship at the 1927 Werkbund exhibition."[94]

Mies and Ada Bruhn had gotten married on April 10, 1913, and their three daughters were born in the following years—Dorothea in 1914, Marianne in 1915, and Waltraud in 1917. After first living in the southern suburb of Steglitz, in 1915 the family had moved into the apartment Am Karlsbad 24 in Berlin's Tiergarten central district (figure 1.58). Ada came from a family of wealth. Her dowry and eventual inheritance provided basic support over the coming years. Despite the introduction of women's suffrage in the Weimar Republic, the assets of a married woman were paid into her husband's bank account. Mies had full access to Ada's money, which allowed him to pursue his early career unburdened by financial worries. According to his daughter Dorothea, Mies "lived beyond his means all his life," and spent most of the available money on himself and his practice.[95] During World War I, when Mies served in Romania, Ada Bruhn and her daughters moved in with her parents, and she rented out the apartment.[96] The family was reunited at Am Karlsbad in 1919, but the familial bliss did not last long. With three new commissions coming in simultaneously, Mies claimed the apartment as office space, and Ada left with their three daughters and began a somewhat peripatetic life. Countless slips in the archive show how Mies would

Figure 1.58. Apartment house, Am Karlsbad 24, Berlin, 1858. Elevation.

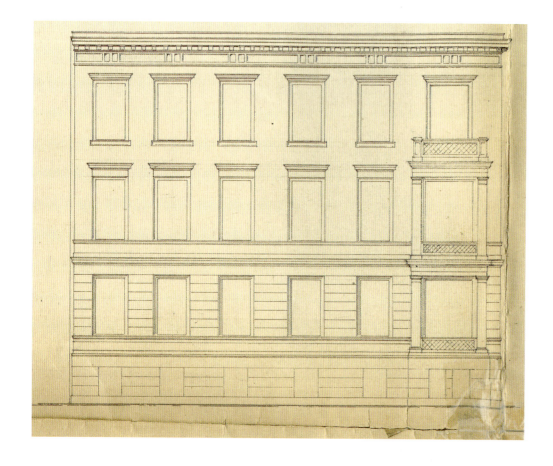

send supporting money from his account to his wife at different locations, often at spas in the Alps, where Mies would occasionally join them. At the eightieth birthday of Mies's first client, Alois Riehl, on April 27, 1924, Mies and Ada showed up as a family, with all three daughters signing the guest book.[97] Postcards from Ada show a continuously amicable relationship at least until 1925, when Mies began his relationship with Lilly Reich. Perhaps not coincidentally, a number of lucrative commissions emerged at that moment, and Mies became independent of his wife's money. After the Depression hit in 1929, and Mies's salary as Bauhaus director in Dessau was canceled two years later, both his and his wife's financial situation became quite dire. A long correspondence with the Salem boarding school where his daughter Dorothea was enrolled testifies to their lack of resources at that time.[98]

During World War II and after, Mies sent care packages from the United States via Lilly Reich to his wife, Ada. They never divorced. Ada died in Berlin in 1951, only sixty-six years old. Mies did not attend the funeral.

Two

Conventional Houses and Visionary Projects

Potsdam, Berlin, Wiesbaden, 1922–25

1922 Friedrichstrasse Skyscraper

Mies's entry into the circles of the avant-garde began with something that the eighteenth-century French philosopher Denis Diderot would have called an *"esprit de l'escalier"*—the common experience of finding the perfect comeback at a dinner conversation only after the party has ended, namely at the bottom of the stairs on the way out. Mies's famous and impactful design for a skyscraper at the Friedrichstrasse Railroad Station seems to have been such an afterthought (figure 2.1). It was, in all likelihood, never submitted to the 1921 competition for a high-rise in the center of Berlin (as he had claimed), but rather created after seeing the contest's results.[1] For a full five months, none of the many contemporary reviews showed or even mentioned Mies van der Rohe's spectacular design.

The design finally emerged in May 1922 in the avant-garde journal *Frühlicht* and in an article in the architecture weekly *Bauwelt*.[2] The *Bauwelt* author, Max Berg, municipal building director of the city of Breslau, had thought and published much about potential skyscrapers in his hometown, and was angered by the fact that the Berlin competition had been limited to members of the Bund Deutscher Architekten (BDA), the German independent architects' association, which had been founded two years earlier and did not admit architects who were state or city employees (such as himself).[3] The parochial interests of this organization, he declared, had prevented a broad participation in "one of the most important cultural questions of our time." As a result, "only a small number of useful attempts for further treatment of the high-rise question have emerged."[4] Mies's design, he claimed, was one of them—although he had certain reservations:

> The design…by Mies van der Rohe, Berlin, aims at utmost simplicity. But the floor plan does not respond to the varied and changeable needs of an office building. If the entire thing were just a warehouse, these spaces could be considered justified, especially since the outside walls, which consist entirely of glass, allow lighting for greater depth. The design presents a grand gesture, and can be considered an interesting and enriching attempt to master the formal problem of the skyscraper.[5]

Of the 144 entries, only forty are known through subsequent publications.[6] It is unlikely that Mies participated in the competition at all, as its limitation to members of the BDA excluded him, and he would have risked disqualification at the end, when the entries' authors were revealed. He also never seems to have produced the required model. But he wished that he had participated and upheld that fiction his entire life, recalling much later: "At that time a competition was exhibited in the old Berlin Rathaus. My design was placed somewhere in the darkest corner because they had probably taken it somehow as a joke."[7] Given the enormous impact that the design had on subsequent generations of architects, all of this matters little. Critics have seen it mostly as a formal statement, as "expressionistic,"[8] a demonstration of the "materialized demateriality or a dematerialized materiality"[9] of glass, and "as a manifesto [rather] than a practical piece of architecture."[10] And, indeed, the image of this sheer glass cliff rising from the dark melee of the busy streets of the metropolis has retained its evocative visual power to this day. Andreas Marx and Paul Weber have suggested that Mies took inspiration from the entry by Hans Soeder, who had designed a comparable six-armed star as a floor plan, and in one concept drawing reduced the façade to a simple grid of posts and beams (figure 2.2).[11] In great contrast, however, Mies seemed not to be interested in showing the structure, neither in elevation nor floor plan, as he focused on the glass's uninterrupted rise. All participants had to demonstrate the amount of usable floor space, an aspect of great importance to the businessmen of the Turmhaus AG (a skyscraper syndicate) who sat on the jury. In

Figure 2.1. Ludwig Mies van der Rohe, Friedrichstrasse Skyscraper project, Berlin, 1922. Perspective view from the north. Charcoal and pencil on tracing paper mounted on board, 68 1/4 × 48 in. (173.5 × 122 cm). Museum of Modern Art, New York. The Mies van der Rohe Archive, gift of the architect.

general, the competitors chose one of three ways to place their building on the triangular site: in a single slab on one side with lower perimeter buildings, in a triangular or round form with an internal courtyard, or as a star shape. Attempting to maximize office space, Mies chose the latter solution, and the three arms of his star nearly filled the site (figure 2.3). Between them were three small external light wells, providing daylight for stair-cases and sanitary rooms, as required by the Prussian building code.[12] Mies described his design process in 1924:

> The building site was triangular; I have attempted to make full use of it. The depth of the lot forced me to split up the fronts so that the inner core obtains light. Since I consider it senseless to drape the steel skeleton of the building with stone fronts, I have given the building a skin of glass. The objection has been raised that the glass wall does not adequately insulate against exterior temperatures. These fears are exaggerated. Buildings with large glass fronts already exist and it has not come to my attention that the large glass planes are considered disadvantageous. Furthermore, we have today Rude glass, a material that, on account of its vacuum layer, possesses considerable insulating capacity.[13]

As a result, the rooms were up to 49 feet (15 meters) deep, two times the legally permitted distance from a window.[14] Mies tried to compensate for this with tall ceiling heights (13 feet, or four meters) and his glass façade. By stacking twenty floors, he reached the maximum height of 262 feet (80 meters), a limit set by the soil conditions underneath. The result was a floor area of roughly 750,000 square feet (70,000 square meters), almost twice the amount offered by any of the winning entries. (W. G. Koch, who won third prize, offered the highest number with 400,000 square feet, or 37,000 square meters.) Mies and his small team produced a range of perspective views, some were inserted into photographs taken from two viewpoints up and down Friedrichstrasse.[15] The stunning, large charcoal perspective (about 69 by 48 inches, or 173 by 122 centimeters) on heavy brown paper had been published in Bruno Taut's magazine *Frühlicht* and montaged into a photographic street view in the magazine *Bauwelt* in 1922 (figure 2.4; see also figure 2.1). The

Figure 2.2. Schematic perspective of the sky-scraper at Friedrichstrasse Railroad Station. Competition entry by Hans Soeder, 1921. Bauhaus-Archiv, Berlin.

Figure 2.3. Ludwig Mies van der Rohe, Friedrichstrasse Skyscraper project, Berlin, 1922. Typical floor plan. Vandyke print with pencil, 23 1/2 × 25 1/4 in. (60 × 64 cm). Museum of Modern Art, New York. The Mies van der Rohe Archive, gift of the architect.

> Figure 2.4. Ludwig Mies van der Rohe, Friedrichstrasse Skyscraper project, Berlin, 1922. Drawing on photograph.

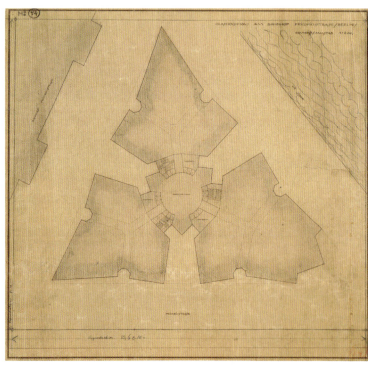

large size of the drawing lent its reproduction a degree of detail that was commensurate with the photograph that surrounded it, but it also, of course, was intended as a show-stopper at the *Grosse Berliner Kunstausstellung* (Great Berlin Art Exhibition) opening on May 19, 1922.

Since it was not clear if a skyscraper would actually be profitable, the cautious businessmen on the jury pushed the selection of lower buildings by the firm Brahm & Kasteleiner (first prize, fifteen floors) and the Luckhardt Brothers (second prize, fourteen floors) (figures 2.5, 2.6). Several architects, such as Hans Poelzig, ended up with twenty floors; Hugo Häring even showed twenty-one floors (figures 2.7, 2.8). Ultimately, nothing came of the competition, as the postwar economic crisis lingered

Figure 2.5. Perspective drawing of the skyscraper at Friedrichstrasse Railroad Station. Competition entry (and first-place winner) by Brahm & Kasteleiner, 1921.

Figure 2.6. Perspective drawing of the skyscraper at Friedrichstrasse Railroad Station. Competition entry (and second-place winner) by the Luckhardt Brothers, 1921.

Figure 2.7. Perspective of the skyscraper at Friedrichstrasse Railroad Station. Competition entry by Hans Poelzig, 1921. Drawing by Erich Zimmermann. Charcoal on transparent paper, 43 3/8 × 30 3/8 in. (110.1 × 77.2 cm). Technische Universität Berlin, Architekturmuseum.

Figure 2.8. Perspective drawing of the skyscraper at Friedrichstrasse Railroad Station. Competition entry by Hugo Häring, 1921. Pencil on transparent paper. Baukunstarchiv, Akademie der Künste.

for another two years. In all likelihood, the competition had mostly been intended to create publicity, boost confidence in the Turmhaus AG, and drum up financial support. But it was still one of the most visible and debated examples of what has been called the "German skyscraper craze," which produced literally hundreds of designs between the wars (see below).

Mies engaged in additional mythmaking about this project after he had moved to the United States. At his 1947 MoMA exhibition, he consistently dated it "1919"—in the wall labels, checklist, and catalogue. There is even a small, typewritten label in German ("Wettbewerb Hochhaus Friedrichstrasse Berlin 1919") on the back of the drawing. In all likelihood, the label was placed there when the rendering arrived in the United States in

1963, in order to back up Mies's claim.[16] The fictional date suggested an earlier turn to the avant-garde, placing its design in the context of visionary glass cathedrals by Bruno Taut, Hans Scharoun, and others. His early biographers, Philip Johnson, Arthur Drexler, Peter Blake, and A. James Speyer played along.[17] As soon as Mies died in 1969, Ludwig Glaeser corrected the date.[18]

1922   Curvilinear Glass Skyscraper

Mies's curvilinear alternative to his Friedrichstrasse Skyscraper was created at the same time and has the same glass sheathing, but is quite different otherwise (figure 2.9). Realizing that even a 13-foot- (four-meter-) high window could not sufficiently light a 49-foot- (15-meter-) deep room, Mies drastically reduced the footprint, and in turn the number of elevators from eighteen to nine, and emergency stairs from three to two. The height of the rooms remained at 13 feet (four meters). In both designs the staircases have twenty-six steps, with each riser a comfortable six inches (15 centimeters) in height. Unencumbered by competition requirements, Mies increased the building to thirty stories, resulting in a more soaring appearance. The outline seems to move arbitrarily within the borders of a trapezoidal plot of land (figure 2.10). At one point it follows the straight edge of the plot line, but soon falls back into its smoothly swinging rhythm. Mies explained:

> At first glance the contour of the ground plan appears arbitrary, but in reality, it is the result of many experiments on the glass model. The curves were determined by the need to illuminate the interior, the effect of the building mass in the urban context, and finally the play of the desired light reflection. Ground plan contours in which the curves were calculated from the point of view of light and shadow revealed themselves on the model, if glass was employed, as totally unsuitable. The only fixed points in the ground plan are the stairs and the elevator shafts.[19]

Critics have never been satisfied with Mies's laconic explanation for his Curvilinear Glass Skyscraper and have suggested formal crossovers with curvilinear designs by Hermann Finsterlin, Hans Arp, or Hugo Häring.[20] The detailed forms of the adjacent buildings in the model and the reference to the "the effect of the building mass in the urban context, and…the play of the desired light reflection" suggest a specific site and orientation. This was confirmed by Mies's collaborator Carl Gottfried in 1922, when he wrote: "The form of the building grew from the conditions of a given site," but he tantalizingly did not say more.[21] The roof of the Marine Panorama Building at Lehrter Bahnhof, visible in one model photo, suggests a location there; another possibility is at Alexanderplatz, where an appropriate plot had just been cleared in front of St. George's Church. Michele Caja has convincingly argued that a sketch by Mies shows the curvilinear skyscraper next to the Alexanderplatz traffic circle (see figure 3.48).[22] Bruno Möhring had recently suggested skyscrapers as urban markers at the five terminus railroad stations in Berlin.[23] Given Mies's explanation, the straight line in the composition suggests that that would be on the northern side, where no direct light hits the façade.

The representation of the project differed from that of the Friedrichstrasse Skyscraper. Mies produced an elevation, two floor plans, and a model, and had the model photographed from three different angles by Curt Rehbein (see figure 2.9). The prominent sculptor Oswald Herzog built surrounding historicist façades out of clay.[24] Neither the floor plan, nor the elevation, nor Mies's text reveal the intended method of construction, but circumstantial evidence and the voices of colleagues point to reinforced concrete, in particular the much discussed "mushroom column." Mart Stam analyzed the design in 1925 in his magazine *ABC*, devoted to concrete in architecture, and decided: "A circular plate, supported in its center, offers a maximum of floor area combined with a minimum of surface. Both, the stanchion as the vertical, the floor slab as the horizontal, produce an element that through addition creates a system."[25] Stam's explanatory illustration showed Mies's glass skyscraper together with a diagrammatic mushroom slab (figure 2.11). And Mies's model suggests, indeed, that the stanchions were placed in the center of circles of different sizes, whose arcs constitute the undulating borderline. Bruno Taut seemed to confirm Stam's interpretation when he claimed that Mies had been "the first one to use the mushroom construction architecturally."[26]

Figure 2.9. Ludwig Mies van der Rohe, Curvilinear Glass Skyscraper project, 1922. Model. Note the dome of the Marine Panorama Building (1892) at Lehrter Bahnhof in the background. Klassik Stiftung Weimar.

The reinforcement rods of a concrete column connected directly to those of the ceiling via the broadened head of the column rather than a ceiling beam, which led to "a better dissemination of air and light."[27] While the calculation, placement, and connection of the reinforcing rods was more complicated, the formwork became simpler. German building codes would include mushroom columns from 1925 on, and within a few years they were accepted as "the most proper area of the reinforced concrete construction,...rooms with mushroom slab ceilings are, if good proportions are applied, of such great beauty that eventually all embellishing additions can be shunned," Ludwig Hilberseimer wrote in 1928.[28] He was particularly intrigued by the Van Nelle Tobacco Factory, just nearing completion in Rotterdam (1926–30) (figures 2.12, 2.13). Mart Stam had worked with Johannes Andreas Brinkman and Leendert Cornelis van der Vlugt on the design, but the mushroom columns inside did not translate into a curvilinear outline (which would be impractical in other ways).[29] A second version of Mies's floor plan seems to suggest a different structural system, a grid of steel supports with a cantilevered outer edge (figure 2.14). However, the fifty-two anticipated columns would have affected the desired transparency.

Both of Mies's skyscrapers were sheathed in a homogeneous glass surface and lacked conventional features, such as a base, cornice, or ornaments, or even a visible main entrance. Their first publication in 1922 was accompanied by Mies's text:

> Only in the course of their construction do skyscrapers show their bold, structural character, and then the impression made by their soaring skeletal frames is overwhelming....When the facades are later covered with masonry this impression is destroyed and the constructive character obscured, along with the very principle fundamental to artistic creation....Above all we must try not to solve new problems with traditional forms; it is far better to derive new forms from the essence, the very nature of the new problem. The structural principle of these buildings becomes clear when one uses glass for the non-load-bearing walls.[30]

The text repeated rather commonplace positions. Appreciation for the aesthetic beauty of a steel skeleton underneath or scaffolding in front of the historicist façades of American skyscrapers had been voiced since the turn of the century and earlier.[31] From another

Figure 2.10. Ludwig Mies van der Rohe, Curvilinear Glass Skyscraper project, 1922. Typical floor plan. Vandyke print with watercolor, pencil, and wax pencil, 21 × 24 1/2 in. (53.1 × 62.2 cm). Museum of Modern Art, New York. The Mies van der Rohe Archive, gift of the architect.

Figure 2.11. Mart Stam, interpretation of the structural system of Mies van der Rohe's Curvilinear Glass Skyscraper. Published in *ABC-Beiträge zum Bauen* 3/4 (1925): 4.

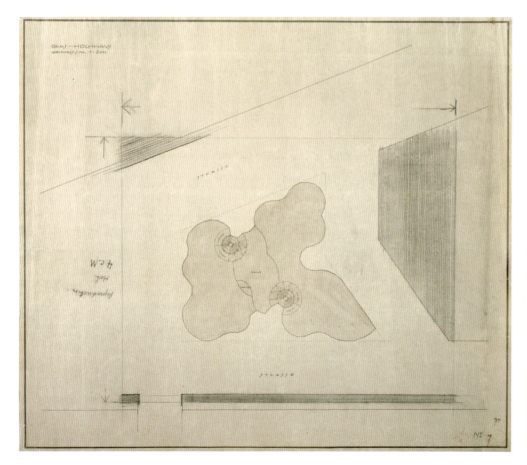

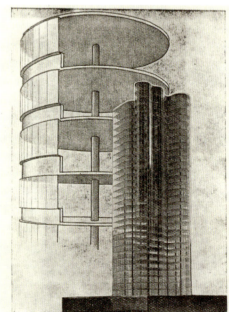

source, we know what Mies wanted the public to think about him and these projects. His draftsman, Carl Gottfried, published a very laudatory essay in the magazine *Qualität*, which was surely instigated by Mies—the first of many such instances of him creating positive publicity from behind the scenes.[32]

German architects, the piece claimed, were "clueless" when it came to designing a skyscraper—with one exception:

> The only significant design in Berlin's skyscraper competition at Friedrichsbahnhof, was that of Mies van der Rohe. The work of this architect shows new ways.... The building is a steel skeleton, its non-load-bearing outside walls are completely of glass.... Formed from a bold creative urge, this building, with its crystalline clarity and intense energy, is an expression of the defiant strength and greatness of our age.... These are the problems that Mies van der Rohe is working on in the spirit of our time. His designs for skyscrapers approach the problem from an entirely new angle. These are functional buildings, defined by their structure, created from purpose and material. Thanks to their artistic design they rise far above the concerns of the moment...they are impersonal, timeless, and therefore architecture in the highest sense.[33]

Figure 2.12. Leendert Cornelis van der Vlugt, Johannes Andreas Brinkman, and Mart Stam, Van Nelle Tobacco Factory, Rotterdam, Netherlands, 1926–30. Main façade. Het Nieuwe Instituut, Rotterdam.

Figure 2.13. Leendert Cornelis van der Vlugt, Johannes Andreas Brinkman, and Mart Stam, Van Nelle Tobacco Factory, Rotterdam, Netherlands, 1926–30. Interior. Het Nieuwe Instituut, Rotterdam.

Figure 2.14. Ludwig Mies van der Rohe, Curvilinear Glass Skyscraper project, 1922. Floor plan, alternative version with a steel frame. Pencil and charcoal on tracing paper, 30 1/2 × 37 3/4 in. (77.4 × 95.8 cm). Museum of Modern Art, New York. The Mies van der Rohe Archive, gift of the architect.

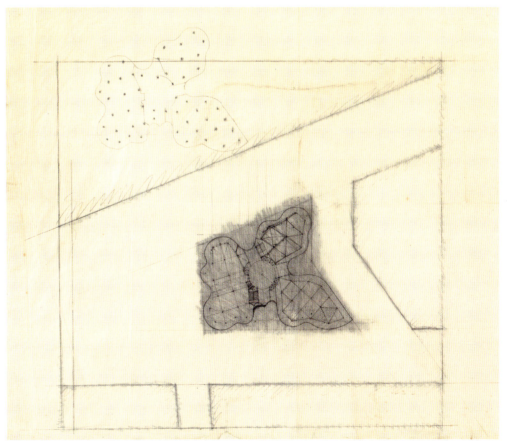

Mies ordered 150 offprints of the article to send out to friends and future clients. Both skyscraper projects were included in the *Grosse Berliner Kunstausstellung* from May 19 to September 17, 1922. This large annual exhibition, held since 1893, at the Landesausstellungsgebäude (State Exhibition Building) near Lehrter Bahnhof, was organized by three Berlin art and architecture organizations, the Verein Berliner Künstler (Association of Berlin Artists), the BDA, and the Novembergruppe. It provided Mies with a much larger audience than the brief showing of the results of the Friedrichstrasse competition would have done. While the majority of participants were painters and sculptors, architecture had been a big part of both the displays of the Novembergruppe and the BDA.[34] Mies had joined the Novembergruppe in the spring of 1922, probably in order to participate here, as the group had jurisdiction over its own segment of several rooms. Mies was not yet a member of the BDA.

The presentation of Mies's work at the exhibition was probably not as coherent as he had imagined. The model of the Curvilinear Glass Skyscraper shared a room with the work of several watercolor artists. In another small room, not adjacent, the large charcoal perspective of the Friedrichstrasse Skyscraper faced the similarly large drawing of Hans Poelzig's entry.[35] There were also several *Proun* drawings by El Lissitzky, and three of Oswald Herzog's dynamic, abstract sculptures. In yet another room, there was the Friedrichstrasse Skyscraper model by the Luckhardt Brothers, which had won second prize in the competition.

1920–29   *Hochhausfieber*

The so-called German skyscraper craze (*Hochhausfieber*) between 1920 and 1929 had triggered literally hundreds of projects for most German cities, which were widely published and enthusiastically discussed in the architectural periodicals of the day. The majority of these projects were developed by conservative architects who intended them as monuments to the German will to reemerge from the defeat of the war and the crushing burden of the reparation payments imposed by the Versailles Treaty. However, because there was neither an actual need for office space nor the money to build any high-rises, most designs remained on paper. Although most architects criticized the American historicism and argued for a genuine German version—less eclectic, less monumental, and more considerate of the urban environment—most proposals still emphasized central axiality and restrained neo-Gothic or neoclassical features (figures 2.15, 2.16). Prominent critic Adolf Behne wrote, "It is really not a building that represents anything special in particular. To make it into a symbol with seriousness, rigor and dignity has to be rejected. It is a building for offices and businesses, an accumulation of shops, cafés, restaurants, a movie theater and an arcade, elevators, staircases and storage rooms—therefore there is no reason for any pathos."[36] The complete absence of elements of conventional monumentality in Mies's two skyscraper projects reflected this attitude and took it a step further: the glass skin's reflection and transparency not only rejected monumentality and nationalistic connotations, but rendered the buildings immaterial and almost invisible.[37]

Mies's two skyscrapers had a remarkable echo abroad. In August 1923, the Danish architecture journal *Bygmesteren* became the first foreign publication to feature Mies's work, including images of the Friedrichstrasse Skyscraper, the Curvilinear Glass Skyscraper, and the Concrete Office Building. The author was the young Danish architect Knud Lonberg-Holm, who had visited Mies in the spring of 1923.[38] A month later, Berlin critic Walter Curt Behrendt published an essay, "Skyscrapers in Germany," in the *Journal of the American Institute of Architects,* in which he showed Mies's glass skyscrapers together with the contributions by Poelzig and Soeder at the Berlin competition. The majority of German architects were "in favor of introducing this building type, which appeals to them as a new and attractive problem of monumental architecture," he reported. He also mentioned the skyscraper competitions all over Germany, which were yielding "decisive contributions towards the solution of this architectural problem." While the German architects adopted the conventional steel cage, the "remarkable creative originality" of their plans and architectural treatment "surpassed the American models by experimenting in various and entirely new directions." To make this particular point, Behrendt showed Mies's projects.[39] Chicago architect George Croll Nimmons countered Behrendt's somewhat presumptuous conclusion with a number of caveats, such as the economic constraints of Mies's star-shaped plan, with the emergency stairs clustered in the center rather than spread out toward the edges, and a greater practicality of rectangular office spaces. But Nimmons diplomatically lauded Mies's "ideal" arrangement of the elevators at "the center of the circle" in his Friedrichstrasse design. The plan for the Curvilinear Glass Skyscraper fared less well; it was, Nimmons said, "so fantastic and impractical and so impossible to divide into any kind of usable or desirable offices or apartments that it is not likely that it would ever be executed."[40] Boston architect William Stanley Parker questioned Behrendt's conviction that skyscrapers were an "attractive problem of monumental architecture." Rather, he exclaimed, they were "a terrible necessity" and works "of sheer idiocy." He ended with a special *bon mot* regarding Mies's curvilinear skyscraper: "A picture of a Nude Building falling down stairs"—a reference to Marcel Duchamp's painting *Nude Descending a Staircase, No. 2*, which had created a scandal when shown at the Armory Show ten years earlier.[41] Nimmons is worth quoting for his thoughtful response to Mies's statement regarding the beauty of skyscrapers under construction and the need to express their

Figure 2.15. Emanuel Haimovici, Richard Tschammer, and Arno Caroli, Messeturm project, Leipzig, Germany, 1919.

Figure 2.16. Otto Kohtz, skyscraper project, Berlin, ca. 1922. Perspective drawing. Watercolor and ink on transparent paper, 13 7/8 × 18 1/8 in. (35.2 × 46 cm). Technische Universität Berlin, Architekturmuseum.

structure—it is oddly prescient, given Mies's frequent encounter with exactly this problem later. It is an "old ambition," Nimmons declared, and "volumes have been written about it," but it had remained unsolved:

> The principal difficulty appears to be that structural steel cannot be allowed to appear in the exterior design on account of corrosion and the danger of building collapse in case of fire; consequently, it must be covered by material that plays no part in holding up the main structure of the building. Furthermore, the strength of steel is so much greater than the materials which formerly supported buildings that all formerly accepted standards of proper sizes and proportions for the supports of buildings are upset. If the structure of skyscrapers was honestly and consistently expressed, the exterior design in the manner proposed by some of the advocates of this policy, would look like a huge birdcage, and there would not be enough surface left on the exterior to display any architecture whatever.[42]

Without a doubt, 1923 was the most dramatic year in Germany's interwar period. On January 11, French and Belgian troops had occupied the heavily industrialized Ruhr area, as Germany had defaulted on its reparation payments from the Versailles Treaty. Encouraged by the government, workers in the occupied area engaged in passive resistance and strikes. In scuffles with the occupying troops, 130 of them were killed. The government kept paying striking workers' salaries and soon needed to print more money. Inflation had already begun in the autumn of 1922 when the cost-of-living index saw a fifteen-fold increase and went on to reach unprecedented heights. On November 16, 1923, when one dollar was worth over 4.2 trillion Reichsmark, a new currency, the Rentenmark, was introduced (by cutting twelve zeros), and stabilization returned. The Dawes Plan restructured Germany's war reparations in 1924, which led to a withdrawal of the occupying troops by August 1925.

It is astonishing how many events of great consequence for Mies's career still happened during that year—be it the publication of the first two issues of the magazine *G: Material zur elementaren Gestaltung* in July and September 1923, the Bauhaus exhibition in August, the *Grosse Berliner Kunstausstellung* from May through September, or the De Stijl exhibition at Léonce Rosenberg's gallery in Paris from mid-October to mid-November 1923. Mies's first timidly modern house went up in Wiesbaden between April and November 1923.

1923   Ryder House

While Mies's public recognition as a member of the young avant-garde steadily increased, he was still involved in rather unassuming architectural efforts. In early March 1923, Mies had received a letter from his old friend Gerhard Severain from Aachen, with whom he had studied and lived after arriving in Berlin. Severain had moved to Wiesbaden in the meantime. He wrote: "I have been commissioned to build a small house. I ask you to help me with it."[43]

The timing seemed fortuitous, as Mies was just finishing up the large Kempner House project (it was inspected for occupancy on March 14, 1923) and had little income.[44] He busied himself with small projects designing stoves and furniture and tried to acquire new work.[45] We owe the detailed correspondence on planning and execution of the house to the fact that Mies lived far away from the construction site, and the political situation made travel difficult, as the city was occupied by French troops, as previously discussed.

The commission had come from an Englishwoman named Ada Ryder.[46] She lived in the same apartment building where Severain had his studio in the attic.[47] The building site was located in a prime residential area among the historicist villas along the street Schöne Aussicht, high above the city's park and casino.[48] Ryder had probably intended the building as an investment property. As a result of Germany's runaway inflation, foreign currencies had greatly increased in value, while at the same time unemployment and stagnating construction activity had led to a sharp drop in prices in the building industry. The house was meant to accommodate a family with two or three children and a maid. On the first floor there was to be a salon, a living room, a dining niche, from there a connection to the kitchen, and on the upper floor three bedrooms, a living room, a maid's room, and a bathroom. Severain asked Mies "whether one of these small house models that I saw at your place, with a flat roof, has been built.... Please send me, before we get to work, one of these models.... Or a drawing with a ground plan."[49] We know nothing about "these small house models... with a flat roof" in Mies's office, but they might have been similar to what Walter Gropius had developed in the run-up to the Bauhaus exhibition and shown there.

Mies explained to Severain in March 1923 (his figures reflecting the current hyperinflation): "The house with the rooms you mentioned would cost at least 50 million [Reichsmark]. The stones for this house would surely cost 8 million. None of the small houses has been built, but I would send you a drawing or a model immediately if I knew that the man would reflect on it even at this cost."[50] To ensure that his friend did not invest time in new design ideas (he was surely familiar with Mies's slow working habits), Severain asked if "perhaps the Riehl floor plan can be used as a basis?" Mies listened to his friend and quickly adopted the floor plan of the Riehl House, with its central hallway and adjacent alcoves. The second floor is fully built out under a flat roof. The kitchen at the back of the house would be reached via a separate entrance, three steps lower than the main floor, and thus with a higher ceiling. A hatch to the dining alcove would be accessible from the kitchen via this back-entrance area. On the upper floor, three bedrooms would face the street, while two rooms and a bathroom would face the garden side. On April 12, Severain reported that the client had approved the plans.[51] The fact that the building application for the simple, flat-roofed dwelling—probably the first in Wiesbaden—was accepted in May 1923, despite its marked contrast to the stately villas surrounding it, was probably due to the economic crisis, where any construction was welcome.[52] Work began immediately, and only a few weeks later, Severain proudly reported: "We are above ground with the construction and in 3 weeks we'll be all the way up."[53] Many letters document the desperate Severain asking Mies repeatedly for missing detail drawings in June and July 1923, while Mies was busy with the increased limelight in Berlin, due to the success of his drawings at the *Grosse Berliner Kunstausstellung* and his work on the new magazine *G* (see below). Mies had requested his fee payments, which Severain promptly paid in each case. Until July 14, he had transferred 3 million Reichsmark to Mies.[54] All the drawings and decisions about structural details were made by Mies and his collaborator Carl Gottfried, while Severain played the role of construction manager. Gottfried was an aide and accomplice in Mies's breakthrough to modernism, as his signature or handwriting can be found on the plans for the conventional Warnholtz, Feldmann, Kempner, and Mosler houses between 1914 and 1925, but also on the drawings for the two glass skyscraper designs of 1922 and the abovementioned exuberant article praising both.[55] Unfortunately, nothing else is known about him.

The introduction of the abovementioned Rentenmark in November 1923 not only ended inflation but also the disproportionate value of foreign money. In the fall of 1923, Severain reported that Ryder was broke, and the project was abandoned.[56] While Severain lost some

Figure 2.17. Ludwig Mies van der Rohe, with Gerhard Severain, Ryder House, Wiesbaden, Germany, 1923–27.

money, Mies had been paid in full, and advised Severain against taking legal action. His interest in a legal dispute and associated publicity was low, as he was just building a reputation as an avant-gardist in Berlin. A construction photo of the Ryder House from the winter of 1923 already reveals all the important features of the finished building: the flat roof, the stepped-back cornice, and the corner windows on the upper floor. Ada Ryder sold the unfinished house in 1927, and the new owner had the outside stuccoed and the sewer line connected and moved in in 1928 (figure 2.17). The house still stands, but a pitched roof was added in the 1980s.

After the somewhat accidental presentation of his glass skyscrapers at the *Grosse Berliner Kunstausstellung* in 1922, Mies made sure that things looked different in 1923, and joined the Novembergruppe's selection committee (he and Hans Luckhardt were responsible for curating the architecture section). Mies reserved a prime location for his own work in a large room next to the central hall. He showed the Concrete Office Building, the Concrete Country House (each in a model and a drawing), a drawing of an interior, and a drawing of a "residence in brick."[57] Rudolf Belling, Alfred Gellhorn, Max Taut, Hans Scharoun, and the Luckhardt Brothers provided comparative context in that room, as did Dutch architects and painters Mart Stam, Willem van Leusden, and Theo van Doesburg, the Norwegian Georg Jens Greve, and the Hungarian Vilmos Huszár. More Dutch architecture was shown in photographs.[58] Thankful for this prominent Dutch representation, van Doesburg invited Mies to join the De Stijl exhibition at Léonce Rosenberg's Paris gallery, L'Effort Moderne, in October 1923.[59] Mies sent illustrations of his glass skyscraper, the office building, and country house in reinforced concrete to van Doesburg, but was unable to travel to Paris himself.[60]

1923   The Concrete Office Building

The enormous charcoal perspective of the Concrete Office Building on heavy brown paper dominated room number twenty-six at the exhibition from May 19 to September 17, 1923 (figure 2.18). Its large size (about 55 by 114 inches, or 139 by 289 centimeters) made it visible from afar, and allowed it to compete with large paintings in the adjacent rooms. The Concrete Office Building would soon become one of Mies's best-known designs. Apart from being shown in the exhibition catalogue, it was also featured in the first issue of the new avant-garde magazine (more accurately, a single-page broadside) *G: Material zur elementaren Gestaltung*, edited by Hans Richter, Werner Graeff, and El Lissitzky, which appeared in July 1923 (more on this below).[61] In *G*, the perspective of the Concrete Office Building was paired with a short, emphatic text by Mies: "We reject all aesthetic speculation, all doctrine, all formalism. Architecture is the will of an epoch translated into space: lively, changing, new. Not yesterday, not tomorrow, only today can be given form. Only this kind of building will be creative. Create form out of the essence of the task using the methods of our time. This is our work." He claimed that this "house of work, of organization, of clarity, of economy" reflected the organization of the company and the austerity of the times: "maximum effect with minimal means."[62] Interestingly, he did not use the mushroom structure again, but imagined that the most economic approach would be a two-post frame where the columns spanned 26 feet (eight meters) and cantilevered 13 feet (four meters) on either side (resulting in a cross section of 52 feet, or 16 meters). The girders would be spaced at intervals of 16 feet (five meters). These numbers and the precision of the drawing allow us to read the structural rhythm of the side elevation on the right as 13, 26, 16, 16, 16, 16, 16, 26, and 13 feet (four, eight, five, five, five, five, five, eight, and four

Figure 2.18. Ludwig Mies van der Rohe, Concrete Office Building project, Berlin, 1923. Perspective view. Charcoal and crayon on paper, 4 ft. 6 1/2 in. × 9 ft. 5 3/4 in. (138.8 × 289 cm). Museum of Modern Art, New York. The Mies van der Rohe Archive, gift of the architect.

meters). The overall width of 161 feet (49 meters) suggests two 52-foot (16-meter) wings and a resulting 56-foot- (17-meter-) wide interior courtyard (figure 2.19).[63] Mies described reinforced concrete structures as "skeletons by nature. No gingerbread. No tank turrets…skin and bone construction."[64] Strictly speaking, a steel frame would have been a better fit for such a description, which suggested a clear distinction between the load-bearing structure and its envelope. But this was not a realistic proposition in Germany in 1923, as the country's heavy burden of reparations was largely being paid in a currency of steel and coal. In a reinforced concrete structure, the separation of "skin and bone" was not as obvious, as part of the load was taken on by the embedded steel reinforcement rods, and the concrete simultaneously served load-bearing and covering functions. Mies actually highlighted this latter quality when he described how the floor slabs would be turned up at their ends to form the building's outer skin.

Yet Mies made no mention at all of what is perhaps the most novel and mysterious quality of the design—namely, the incremental increase in the size of the floor plates. The progressive extension of each cantilever—barely visible from the vantage point of the perspective, but clearly indicated by the growing size of the corner windows—means, of course, that only one floor would have the 52-foot- (16-meter-) wide section Mies described (floors above would have been wider, those below narrower). Mies never talked about it, however, and critics have usually avoided addressing the issue, largely because this subtle, almost invisible gesture seems such an un-Miesian move in the context of his outspoken rationalism—one that comes dangerously close to the "aesthetic speculation" he so forcefully rejected.

There seem to be at least two rationales for the increasing floor size. The first is that Mies was trying to provide a clear drop from the edge of each floor in order to protect the concrete underneath from getting rain-soaked. The second is that he was giving visual expression to the reduction in weight toward the top. In any building where columns on each floor maintained the same diameter, they would be increasingly over-dimensioned for the load they have to carry, which decreases going up. Increased floor space was a way of compensating for this.[65] Such explanations, however, could be a case of what Mies would later call "a good reason" versus "the real reason"—which might simply be that the building looked taller this way, as the normal perspective foreshortening was undermined by the increased floor size.[66] An inspiration might have come from the Nijverheidsschool in Groningen, the Netherlands, of 1922, which showed similar ribbon windows, with each floor cantilevered slightly beyond the one underneath (figure 2.20). Hans Poelzig had designed a concrete office building in Breslau in 1912–13 that also had protruding floors

Figure 2.19. Ludwig Glaeser, reconstructed floor plan of Mies van der Rohe's Concrete Office Building, 1968.

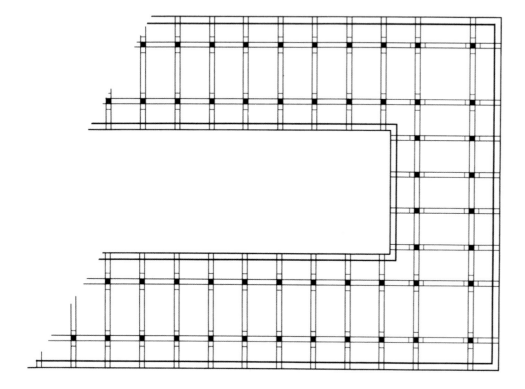

going up and successively slimmer piers. Mies painstakingly followed the city's height limitation of six floors, but provided eight usable stories by adding a basement level and a (probably top-lit) attic floor.

No indication was given as to a potential site for the Concrete Office Building, but one might recognize a certain resemblance between the silhouette of the building in the background of Mies's drawing and the neo-Renaissance Hotel Kaiserhof on Alexanderplatz—at the time there was much discussion about high-rises at Berlin's congested traffic hubs (see figure 2.18). Indeed, when a major competition was launched for the redesign of Alexanderplatz in 1928, Mies proposed a large, central traffic circle surrounded by a series of solitary blocks (see figure 3.47). The block next to the railway station, slightly more complex than the others, bears a striking resemblance to his office building design. The bird's-eye view suggests further parallels, revealing an oblong outline with an interior courtyard, thin ribbon windows, and the same number of stories, including a compressed top floor.

As usual, others were more precise and observant in their descriptions than Mies was himself. In an article on the potential of reinforced concrete, J. J. P. Oud seemed to refer to Mies's office building when he praised the "homogeneous combination of load-bearing and carried parts" of reinforced concrete. He stated: "The old post-and-lintel system only allowed us to build from bottom to top with an inward slant; we can now go beyond that and build from the bottom to the top slanting outward. With the latter, a possibility for a new architectonical plasticity has been created, which, in conjunction with the esthetic potential of iron and mirrored glass, can initiate the rise of an architecture of an optically immaterial, almost hovering character."[67]

Mies's friend Ludwig Hilberseimer described the office building in 1924 as follows:

> The dominant horizontal combined with the lack of piers on the façade completely changes the structural character of the building, and...creates an architecture of floating lightness. The layout and structure of this office building are of an uncommon clarity. It corresponds to its function perfectly. It is shaped out of the essence of the task, using the means of our time. The constructional function is conceived as architecture. The formal appearance stems from the structural idea. Construction and form have become one: clear, logical, simple, unambiguous, and regular.[68]

The large charcoal and crayon perspective that Mies showed at the *Grosse Berliner Kunstausstellung*, together with a small model, is the only surviving rendering of the project.[69]

Figure 2.20. Leendert Cornelis van der Vlugt and J. G. Wiebenga, Nijverheidsschool, Groningen, Netherlands, 1922.

An important potential collaborator on the Concrete Office Building project was Wilhelm Deffke, a graphic designer and talented draftsman, who had worked for Peter Behrens from February 1909 to April 1910 (helping to design the famous AEG logo), at the same time as Mies. While he had founded a graphic design agency in 1915, he also had architectural ambitions and between 1922 and 1924 worked with Mies in an occasional "cooperative for architectural projects."[70] According to Mies, they had worked together on a grain silo, probably Deffke's project in the Bulgarian port of Varna in 1922.[71] We have photographs of two charcoal drawings (the originals have been lost), whose rendering style is strikingly similar to that of Mies's Concrete Office Building (figure 2.21). The perspectival angle and the contrast between the rough charcoal and the precise contours of the ribbon windows suggest the same hand. The paper was evidently placed on a sheet of chipboard or plywood, whose rough-grained texture came through—an effective way of depicting the formwork of raw concrete. Looking more closely, we can see that both drawings have vertical lines suggesting 20-inch- (50-centimeter-) wide ribbons

Figure 2.21. Wilhelm Deffke with Ludwig Mies van der Rohe, Grain Silo, Varna, Bulgaria, 1922. North view. Photograph of a charcoal drawing, 5 1/4 × 15 1/4 in. (13.4 × 38.8 cm). Bröhan-Museum, Berlin.

Figure 2.22. Wilhelm Deffke, Reemtsma Office Building project, Erfurt, Germany, 1921. Pastel on paper, 5 1/8 × 9 1/2 in. (13 × 24.2 cm). Bröhan-Museum, Berlin.

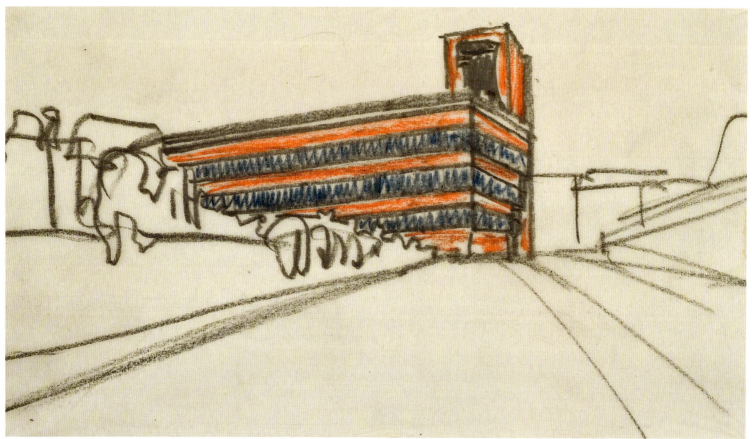

of veneer on a large plywood panel. Since Deffke worked in Mies's office at this time, it seems likely that both drawings were produced on the same board and possibly by the same hand, namely Deffke's.[72]

Deffke's 1921 project for an office building for the tobacco manufacturer Reemtsma in Erfurt suggests another connection (figure 2.22).[73] It had the same radical horizontality—bands of windows alternating with red spandrels, the color Deffke had selected for Reemtsma's corporate identity. Red would also be used, along with gray, for the spandrels in the model of Mies's office building. In one of Deffke's drawings, we find a remarkable detail: heavy crayon strokes in a far corner make clear that the building gets wider as it goes up, just as in Mies's Concrete Office Building. There is also a flat roof and the significantly lower top floor.[74] In other words, there is a high likelihood that Mies might have helped with Deffke's silo design, while Deffke, a talented draftsman, executed the large drawing for the Concrete Office Building and suggested ideas from his earlier Reemtsma design. A year later, Deffke accused Mies of "appropriating the ideas of others"—a hint that he might have had more to do with the Concrete Office Building (and perhaps other projects in Mies's office) than he received credit for.[75]

When the Concrete Office Building was on display in the annual *Grosse Berliner Kunstausstellung,* Mies managed to get it featured in the much-read weekend edition of a major national newspaper, the *Deutsche Allgemeine Zeitung (DAZ).* For the first time, one of his projects reached a mass audience, several hundred thousand readers, rather than the comparatively small readership of specialized architecture journals. *DAZ* typically reproduced only a handful of images, and so those that did appear tended to stand out. In those difficult postwar years, *DAZ* devoted much space to discussions of practical matters, such as the benefits of frugality and ingenious ways of doing more with less. Mies's project was not shown in the culture section, but on the first page of the *Kraft und Stoff* (Power and Materials) supplement, devoted to new advances in technology. Mies's starkly repetitive and brutally unadorned office building was presented as a functional and structural response to the austerity of the times. Mies had sent a photograph of his drawing and some technical notes by the due date, but struggled with the text and missed the deadline. The project appeared with a hastily written commentary from a staff writer, who missed its point.[76] Mies's own text (submitted after the Sunday supplements had already gone to press) shows his awareness of the importance of media:[77]

> It is no coincidence that important questions of architecture are being discussed in newspapers today. In focusing exclusively on aesthetics, the specialized art magazines—once the fulcrum of artistic life—have failed to take notice of the way modern architecture has evolved away from aestheticism and towards the organic, away from the formal and towards the constructive. Modern architecture has long since renounced the idea of playing a merely ornamental role in our lives. Creative architects want to have nothing, absolutely nothing to do with the aesthetic traditions of previous centuries. This area we gladly leave to the art historians.[78]

1923 The Concrete Country House

The second project Mies exhibited at the *Grosse Berliner Kunstausstellung* in the summer of 1923 was the Concrete Country House. Two model photographs and two perspectives (one executed in two different colored charcoal drawings) are the only surviving sources of visual information about this project (figures 2.23–2.25). They show a one- to two-story building with wings extending in four directions and surrounding, on three sides, a raised courtyard. The most striking features of the house are the long ribbon windows that are cut into its façades, not only beneath the cantilevered, projecting roof above the entrance and living areas, but also in the basement, where they wrap around the corner and thereby subvert the conventional expectations of structural support. Historians have attributed the influences for Mies's design to a number of different sources: to El Lissitzky's abstract "*Proun*" compositions,[79] to Wright's Willits House,[80] to the form of a swastika,[81] or to the spatial principles described in Oswald Spengler's contemporary bestseller, *Der Untergang des Abendlandes* (The Decline of the West).[82] Mies outlined his take on the material and his intentions in the September 1923 issue of *G* magazine, under the title "*Bauen*" (Building). He dismissed those who had used rounded corners to indicate concrete as a material as

Figure 2.23. Ludwig Mies van der Rohe, Concrete Country House project, 1923. Perspective view of garden façade. Drawing possibly by Wilhelm Deffke. Colored pastel and pencil on paper, 2 ft. 4 1/2 in. × 7 ft. 2 1/2 in. (72.3 × 219.3 cm). Museum of Modern Art, New York. The Mies van der Rohe Archive, gift of the architect.

Figure 2.24. Ludwig Mies van der Rohe, Concrete Country House project, 1923. Perspective view of garden façade. Drawing possibly by Wilhelm Deffke. Pastel on paper, 12 1/4 × 24 1/4 in. (31.1 × 61.6 cm). Museum of Modern Art, New York. The Mies van der Rohe Archive.

Figure 2.25. Ludwig Mies van der Rohe, Concrete Country House project, 1923. Plaster model.

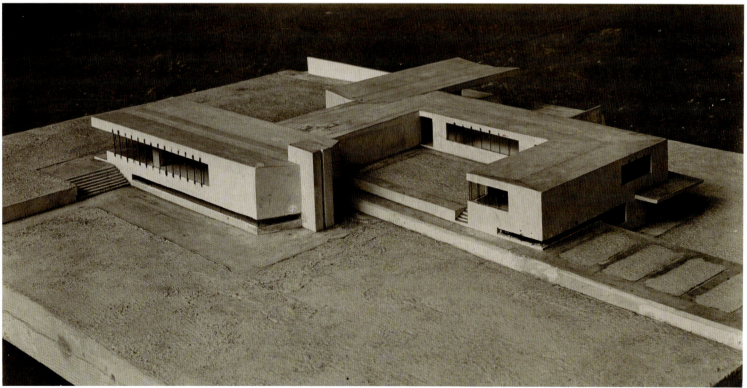

"entirely inconsequential," and claimed that the material had never been properly applied in residential buildings.[83] The often-cited disadvantage of poor insulation and sound conduct could be solved by using more insulation, rubber floors, sliding doors, and spaciousness, he suggested. What mattered most was "the opportunity to save a great amount of material" by concentrating "the bearing and supporting forces on only a few points in the structure." Thus, he proposed, "The main living area is supported by a four-post truss system. This structural system is enclosed in a thin skin of reinforced concrete, comprising both walls and roof. The roof slopes downward slightly from the exterior walls toward the center. The trough formed by the inclination of the two halves of the roof provides the simplest possible drainage for it. All sheet-metal work is thereby eliminated. I have cut openings in the walls wherever I required them for outside views and illumination of space."[84]

While far from being the breakthrough solution he suggested, this description still provides important clues to the building's structure. The carefully executed model confirms his interest in the placement of the troughs to ensure proper draining of the roof (see figure 2.25). Assuming that drain pipes would be placed next to support columns allows us to deduct their placement. The pastel perspective drawings and the model photographs help to position the two pairs of columns in the entrance and main living room area. The roof of each bedroom wing, with one central furrow, is supported by a single pair of columns. The transitional area between the entrance and the living room has a flat pitched roof, with its drainage furrows close to the outer walls, suggesting a space with load-bearing outer walls and no central column.[85] Mies had the perspective traced through and had two different versions drawn with colored charcoal—one in light gray, the natural color of concrete, the other in striking red. He commissioned a second, partial perspective that shows the house embedded in nature. These rarely published red versions suggest that Mies was interested in the current, but short-lived, practice of mixing colored pigment into cement (see figures 2.23, 2.24) and might have responded to the architect Bruno Taut's *"Aufruf zum Farbigen Bauen"* (Appeal for Colorful Architecture) of fall 1921, which Walter Gropius, Peter Behrens, and many others had signed. As city councilor for architecture and urban planning in Magdeburg, Taut realized about eighty colorful façade renovations in the city.[86]

In 1922, when Mies was experimenting with the potential of reinforced concrete, Emil von Mecenseffy's book *Die künstlerische Gestaltung der Eisenbetonbauten* (Artistic Design of Reinforced Concrete Buildings) appeared in a second edition.[87] The author emphasized the beauty of the sturdier dimensions of concrete, comparing them favorably to the lighter proportions of common ironwork. Cantilevered roofs above railroad platforms at Sonneberg and Langendreer (built in 1907 by the firm Dyckerhoff & Widmann) served as examples (figure 2.26). They are strikingly similar to the structure that appears in the model of Mies's Concrete Country House.

Mies's attempts to design as closely as possible to the structural conditions were hampered by his limited knowledge and lack of experience with reinforced concrete. Neither the 13-foot (four-meter) cantilever in the office building, the cluster of differently sized

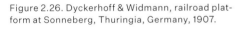

Figure 2.26. Dyckerhoff & Widmann, railroad platform at Sonneberg, Thuringia, Germany, 1907.

mushroom columns in the curvilinear skyscraper, nor the long ribbon windows here would have received approval from a civil engineer. They required complicated structural calculations and connections for the reinforcing rods and lacked accommodation for expansion and contraction.

1923   Bauhaus Exhibition

In June 1923, Walter Gropius wrote to Mies to say how impressed he had been by his projects at the *Grosse Berliner Kunstausstellung* (which was otherwise "a horrible chaos") and invited him to contribute to the *Internationale Architektur* section of the first major Bauhaus exhibition in Weimar, from August 15 to September 30, 1923. Gropius was particularly interested in the model of the Concrete Country House (which he mistook for a "flat office or factory building"), declaring it "new and lively." Mies accepted with alacrity and some caveats: "I can only place at your disposal a photograph of it and a charcoal drawing. The only models I could make available to you are the glass model of my tower and the wooden one of the large office building, and indeed I had thought of combining these two models, placing them next to each other so as to suggest a square. I tried it out, and the effect is wonderful; I believe that you too would understand then why the office building has only the horizontal articulation." Mies stressed that structural considerations held three of his recent visionary projects (the Curvilinear Glass Skyscraper, the Concrete Office Building, the Concrete Country House) together: "I would be delighted to be represented by the three projects, so that I could show how the same structural principle works out in three completely different assignments. Since I reject any and all formalism, and endeavor to develop the solution to an assignment out of its particular requirements, there will never be a formal relationship uniting the separate projects."[88]

A detail in the correspondence is telling: Mies offered a large drawing of the office building, "3.5m [11.4 feet] long and 1.5m [4.9 feet] high."[89] Since the well-known charcoal drawing (nine and a half feet, or 2.9 meters, long and four and a half feet, or 1.4 meters, high) was tied up in Berlin until September 17, Mies must have had another large

Figure 2.27. Bauhaus exhibition, *Internationale Architektur* section, Weimar, Germany, 1923. The models of Mies van der Rohe's Concrete Office Building and Curvilinear Glass Skyscraper are visible on the left. Bauhaus Museum Weimar.

drawing of the project, which he sent to Gropius.[90] It might not have ended up in the show, as Gropius indicated lack of space, and he had, in any event, found the project "too schematic."[91]

The model of the office building, however, shows up in an installation photograph from the Bauhaus exhibition, where it is paired with a model of the Curvilinear Glass Skyscraper in an urban constellation, just as stipulated by Mies (figure 2.27).[92] Across from it we see Gropius's own model for his *Chicago Tribune* competition entry and the accompanying perspective in a photograph. Less detailed than the model of the glass skyscraper or the Concrete Country House, the model of the Concrete Office Building presents a long, low structure with reflective ribbon windows and a much more pronounced upward increase in its floors than the more familiar perspective sketch. From the correspondence between Mies and Gropius, we know that the large drawing of the Friedrichstrasse Skyscraper was not exhibited. Gropius liked Mies's Concrete Country House so much that he included it in a report on modern architecture in Germany for Le Corbusier's magazine *L'Esprit nouveau,* where it appeared in 1924.[93]

Despite the unprecedented boldness of his visionary designs, Mies saw his own work as being more closely connected to the outstanding architects of the previous generation. After the Bauhaus exhibition in Weimar, when Gropius claimed to have received requests from "Berlin, Hamburg, Düsseldorf, Hannover" to take the show afterward, Mies developed other ideas.[94] He confessed in private how much he disapproved of the "wild constructivist formalism" and "artistic fog" at the Bauhaus exhibition; without telling Gropius, he set out to reframe and redesign the show (in close cooperation with Hugo Häring and Adolf Behne), retaining some of the material, notably his own, but flanking it with projects by Peter Behrens, Henry van de Velde, and H. P. Berlage (all of whom Mies contacted about this), along with Häring, Hans Scharoun, and others.[95] Potentially, Mies also wanted to include Frank Lloyd Wright, as he asked Berlage about material on Wright in December 1923.[96] When Gropius found out that his show was being usurped behind his back, he was livid, and in the end, nothing came of the scheme. Instead, the Bauhaus exhibition was shown in a reduced format (without any models) at the Provinzialmuseum in Hanover.[97] And Mies was commissioned by the painter and graphic artist Walter Dexel to curate his own show at the Jena Kunstverein (Art Association)—the second time Mies would act in this capacity (after his 1923 assembly of the Novembergruppe's architecture section at the *Grosse Berliner Kunstausstellung*). The exhibition, held in November 1924, featured the Concrete Office Building and other material from his Novembergruppe colleagues[98] under the title *Neue Deutsche Baukunst* (New German Architecture).[99] According to Dexel, it was an extraordinary success: "It truly responded to a desire of the public. The number of visitors was about five times as high as with our most popular special exhibitions of our most prominent painters."[100] The show traveled to the Gera Kunstverein and to Frankfurt's Städel museum afterward.

Mies was eager to play a leading role in avant-garde circles and so, together with Hugo Häring, he founded a small group of like-minded architects in order to regularly meet and discuss architecture in the winter of 1923–24. The Zehner-Ring (Ring of Ten) consisted of Mies, Otto Bartning, Peter Behrens, Hugo Häring, Erich Mendelsohn, Hans Poelzig, Walter Schilbach, Martin Wagner, and Bruno and Max Taut. When little beyond conversations emerged from these meetings, the group changed its name in 1926 to simply "Der Ring" and enlarged its membership.

1924 "Dualism"

Mies himself must have been aware that there was a gap between the boldness of his most recent designs and the conventionality of his buildings. But when he heard in January 1924 that Walter Curt Behrendt, who had presented his innovative skyscrapers to an American audience just months before, had accused him of "dualism" in a conversation with Hans Poelzig, he was deeply offended and took Behrendt to task by letter. Behrendt replied on January 30, 1924:

> Dear Mies, I understand that you feel hurt. It was my mistake that in a discussion with a third party, namely Poelzig, I cited your case as an example of a

possible dualism, before clarifying this issue, which still troubles me (I remind you of one of our last conversations at my place in the presence of Soeder), first in a personal discussion with you. The remark was made, as I said, in a heated discussion and taken out of context it seems more tragic than it was meant to be. There was no offensive or disparaging intention in it. This goes without saying in view of the respect I have for you and your work, and which I have always demonstrated to you and others. I sincerely regret that this incident has given you any doubt about my attitude towards your work. I hope, however, that the ill-feeling it has caused will soon be resolved to such an extent that nothing will stand in the way of a meeting and thus of an objective discussion of the question which concerns me.[101]

In any event, Mies's "dualism" continued for a while longer, as he was still dependent on the wishes of his clients, many of whom were uninterested in modern architecture. Mies surely must have been reminded of his exchange with Behrendt, when in July 1924 he submitted the building applications for the Mosler House (see below) and the conversion of the garage at the Urban House, and in October 1924 the application for a gymnasium at the Lyzeum Butte, and finally in September 1925 the application for the conversion of the Urban House itself. These projects—all traditional solutions—would last in part until 1926, while at the same time, with the Wolf House, his first completely modern building would be executed between 1925 and 1927 (see figures 3.12–3.15).

1924   Brick Country House

For the *Grosse Berliner Kunstausstellung*[102] in the summer of 1924 (May 31 to September 1), Mies again produced a modern design, presented in a floor plan and elevation, in which he had "abandoned the usual concept of closed rooms to produce a sequence of spatial effects instead of a series of individual rooms": a country house in Potsdam-Babelsberg, also known as the Brick Country House (figure 2.28).[103] The catalogue showed an additional sketch, a sweeping dynamic sequence of cubes in the style of Erich Mendelsohn.[104] The floor plan emphasizes the continuous spatial connection among several living rooms and auxiliary rooms (*Wohnräume* and *Wirtschaftsräume*) between two massive fireplaces. Faded pencil lines in the only existing photograph of Mies's drawings seem to suggest a second set of stairs going up to the bedrooms, which would mean that the visible full set of stairs indicates basement access. This makes considerably more sense for the internal organization, and for Mies it was customary to include a basement in his designs.

Clearly, his recent exposure to the ideas of Dutch architects bore fruit here. It is likely that Mies was aware of the drawings for Cornelis van Eesteren and van Doesburg's schematic artist's house, the Maison Particulière (Private House), which the two had drawn for an exhibition in Paris in October 1923, and which they had just published in *Bouwkundig Weekblad,* two weeks before Mies's design was due at the *Grosse Berliner Kunstausstellung* (figures 2.29, 2.30).[105] The Maison Particulière's cubically staggered ground plan, with its diagonally open spatial connections, is more likely a source of influence than van Doesburg's 1918 painting *Rhythm of a Russian Dance,* or Picasso's cubist drawing *Standing Female Nude* of 1910 that Alfred Barr assumed as a source in 1934 (figure 2.31). According to Barr: "In the history of art there are few more entertaining sequences than the influence by way of Holland of the painting of a Spaniard living in Paris upon the plans of a German architect in Berlin—and all within twelve years."[106] Mies rejected the idea years later, saying: "I think that was a mistake that the Museum of Modern Art made.... I never make a painting when I want to build a house. We like to draw our plans carefully and that is why they were taken as a kind of painting."[107] There are similar parallels to van Doesburg's follow-up design of a Maison d'Artiste which, together with the earlier design, was published in *L'Architecture vivante* in 1925—right next to Mies's Curvilinear Glass Skyscraper.[108]

The design of the Brick Country House gave Mies what was probably his greatest critical success to date, which may have encouraged him to continue working in this direction. Adolf Behne praised its "clarity and immediacy,"[109] and Walter Curt Behrendt (trying to make up for Mies's recent disgruntlement over his "dualism") emphasized how in this "stylized super-personal form...the traditional principle of order...that lines up the rooms on an axis…was abandoned in favor of the principle of function." He praised Mies's sense of proportion and his economic handling of the floor plan: "The sharp-edged, elegant building is most comparable to a machine product in its precise form."[110] For Hans Soeder, Mies's design was not only "the strongest and most future-oriented…project" of the exhibition, but "on a higher level the path of rational calculations was overcome, mathematics filled with music." Mies's design had left him speechless, Soeder confessed rather emotionally, and he was simply delighted "to see it, to be enchanted by it, to dream about it, and to admire the boldness of this spatial composition."[111] Mies's friend Hans Richter followed up a few months later, suggesting that the floor plan was "not a mathematical abstraction," but demonstrated habitation as a process that abandoned the "cozy corner" and separate rooms in favor of a "coherent living complex."[112] The illustration shown here, from the Kunsthalle Mannheim, is the only existing photograph of the project, as the original drawing has been lost (see figure 2.28). Its high resolution allows the reading of faded pencil lines, which usually do not appear in reproductions. Hassan Bagheri has carefully enhanced them, revealing a few previously unknown details, such as the lintels above the small windows in the auxiliary rooms on the right (rather than floor-to-ceiling openings), and the above-mentioned second staircase leading up.

Figure 2.28. Ludwig Mies van der Rohe, Brick Country House project, 1924. Perspective view and floor plan (lost). Gelatin silver print, 6 11/16 × 7 1/2 in. (17 × 19.1 cm). Kunsthalle Mannheim. (Note that the faded pencil lines in the original have been enhanced for better visibility by Hassan Bagheri.)

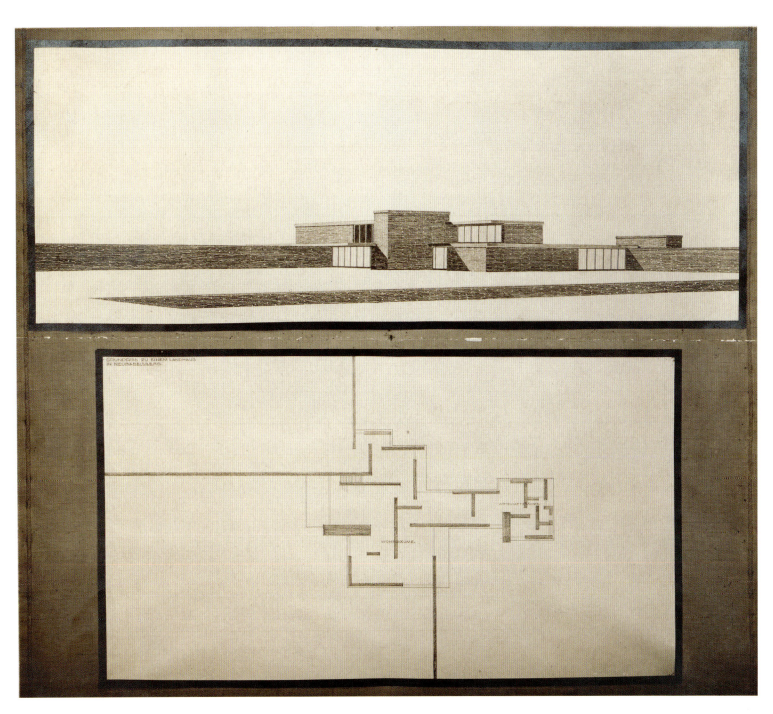

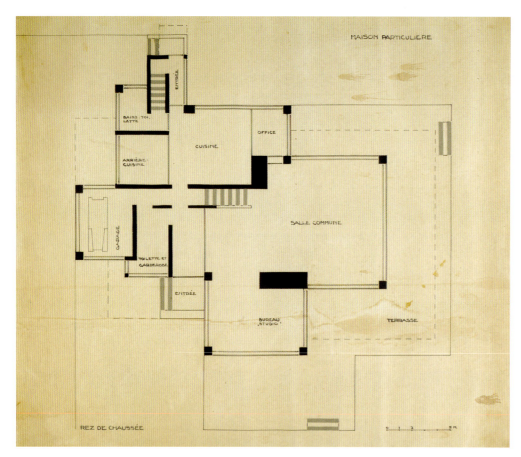

MAISON PARTICULIERE

REZ DE CHAUSSÉE

Figure 2.29. Theo van Doesburg and Cornelis
van Eesteren, Maison Particulière project, 1923.
Ground-floor plan. Ink and collage on paper, 32 7/8
× 31 1/2 in. (83.5 × 80 cm). Nieuwe Instituut
Rotterdam, Netherlands.

Figure 2.30. Theo van Doesburg and Cornelis
van Eesteren, Maison Particulière project, 1923.
Gouache and collage on paper, 22 1/8 × 22 1/8 in.
(56 × 56 cm). Nieuwe Instituut Rotterdam,
Netherlands.

Figure 2.31. Theo van Doesburg, *Rhythm of a
Russian Dance*, 1918. Oil on canvas, 53 1/2 × 24 1/4
in. (135.9 × 61.6 cm). Museum of Modern Art,
New York.

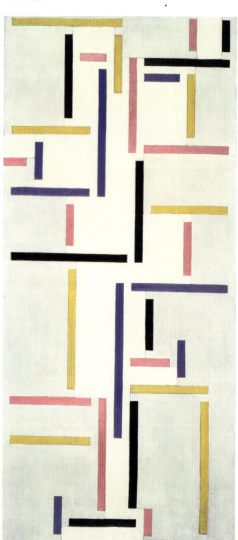

1924–26 Mosler House

Not far from the Riehl House, right on Lake Griebnitz in Potsdam-Babelsberg, Mies built the last of his conventional houses for Georg Mosler, a high-ranking manager at Dresdner Bank (figures 2.32, 2.33). The contact might have come about through Franz Urbig, whose house Mies had finished in 1917. Mies received the commission in early 1924, just when he was finalizing his plans for the Brick Country House for the *Grosse Berliner Kunstausstellung*. The application for a building permit was submitted in July 1924, some alterations followed in January and March 1925 (while Mies was working on the modern Dexel and Eliat house projects), and another application for a change to the basement was submitted during construction in January 1926. The house's façade was parallel to Kaiserstrasse—named for the fact that Emperor Wilhelm II occasionally traveled on it between his Babelsberg and Glienicke palaces. This location came with the disadvantage of its garden façade toward the lake facing northeast and thus getting little direct sunlight, except early in the morning. Mies repeated the type that he and Werner von Walthausen had introduced at the Urbig House—central axial symmetry, tall vertical windows on the first floor, smaller ones above, a steep hip roof with dormers. This symmetry was modified by the addition of the flat-roofed dining room on the northern side, with its own terrace toward the lake. Its windows faced southwest and northeast, which meant access to some evening sun in the summer. Upstairs were the family's bedrooms, while the kitchen and servants' rooms were downstairs.[113]

Mies created a disproportionately wide and deep garden porticus, with a wide terrace overlooking the lake from the suite of bedrooms upstairs. While this meant that the first-floor rooms underneath (library, music room, and study) would be quite dark throughout the day (when they were little used), the bedrooms above had superior lake views and morning sun. Mies's symmetrical floor plan led a visitor via the two-winged staircase

Figure 2.32. Ludwig Mies van der Rohe, Mosler House, Potsdam, Germany, 1924–26. Main façade, facing west. Photograph by Hassan Bagheri.

toward the entrance and into the hall, and straight ahead into the library, flanked by a music room to the left and the study or smoking room on the right. There were rococo-inspired wrought-iron balcony railings, which Sergius Ruegenberg, who joined the office in 1925, designed, as well as heavy marble rails for the main staircase and much wood paneling inside (figure 2.34).[114] Modern sensibilities were palpable in the absence of shutters (rolling blinds were installed instead, just as at the synchronous Wolf House) or ornamentation, and the presence of flat Flemish bricks, interrupted by the light gray of the travertine window framings.

1923–25 Publicity

While the Concrete Office Building had appeared in the first issue of *G: Material zur elementaren Gestaltung* (G: Material for Elemental Form-creation) in July 1923, the Concrete Country House was shown on the cover of *G*'s second edition, dated "September 1923" (its

Figure 2.33. Ludwig Mies van der Rohe, Mosler House, Potsdam, Germany, 1924–26. Garden façade toward Griebnitzsee. Photograph by Carsten Krohn.

Figure 2.34. Ludwig Mies van der Rohe, Mosler House, Potsdam, Germany, 1924–26. Main stair hall. Photograph by Carsten Krohn.

subscription price of 3.50 Marks, however, suggests that it actually appeared after the currency reform of November 15, 1923). Mies offered to fund the journal's third issue, which appeared in June 1924, and joined Werner Graeff and Hans Richter on the editorial board. As a result, this issue was decidedly different; at sixty-three pages, it was more voluminous than its two predecessors, which had been single-sheet, folded broadsides of 17 7/8 by 11 1/2 inches (45.5 by 29.2 centimeters). It was now smaller in format (9 7/8 by 6 3/4 inches, or 25 by 17 centimeters), and it was printed on high-quality paper. The word *"Material"* in the title was replaced with *"Zeitschrift"* (Journal). Mies designed an elegant cover on heavier stock, which featured an elevation of his Curvilinear Glass Skyscraper and the letter *G* in red, tilted to the side (figure 2.35). Mies insisted on a single new typeface throughout (there had been multiple typefaces on each page before)—a uniform sans serif, clearly constructed and unornamented, not imitating handwriting or classical lettering. No Berlin printer had enough of these letters available for an entire issue, and Mies ended up purchasing a complete set of lead types.[115] Not everyone was happy with the more luxurious appearance: "How odd of *G* to be inspired by De Stijl and end up as *Vanity Fair*," noted van Doesburg. El Lissitzky, who designed the first two issues, called it "a rather snobbish studio affair."[116] While *G* "only had a handful of paying subscribers," its editors nevertheless "sent as many as a thousand copies to artists, critics, art libraries, collectors, manufacturers," Graeff reported.[117] Mies's short stint as designer and publisher of a journal was not driven by altruism. Apart from the Curvilinear Glass Skyscraper on the cover, his Friedrichstrasse Skyscraper design was shown inside, and there was his essay on "Industrielles Bauen" (Industrial Building), as well as an essay by Hans Prinzhorn, "Gestaltung und Gesundheit" (Form-Creation and Health), written in the form of a letter to Mies. Finally, a long essay by Mies's friend Ludwig Hilberseimer, called "Konstruktion und Form" (Construction and Form), dealt mostly with Mies's Concrete Office Building and compared it favorably to recent buildings by Poelzig and Mendelsohn: "Mies van der Rohe was the first to recognize the latest design possibilities of the new structural ideas, and, in his design for an office building, he found the architectural solution for them....Construction and form have become one: clear, logical, simple, unambiguous and regular."[118]

In his own essay, Mies claimed—in his typically vague but emphatic style—that "industrialization of the building trade" was the "key problem of building in our time." He mentioned "companies using iron construction" as "the first to produce ready-to-assemble construction parts in their factories. Recently, the lumber industry has also sought to produce its construction parts by industrial means in order to turn building into a process of pure assembly." The examples he showed came from Breest & Co., a Berlin steel building company, and from the Deutsche Zollbau G.m.b.H. in Berlin Lichterfelde, which created large, curved wooden roof structures from grids of identical wooden studs—an early type of space frames. But, Mies claimed, "a new building material" was the first precondition for any industrialization of the building trade: "Our technology must and will succeed in inventing a new building material that can be produced technically and processed industrially; one that is solid, weather resistant, and sound- and heat-proof. It will have to be a light material, which not only permits industrial processes but demands them." As a result, the current building trade "will be destroyed," he claimed ominously. Possibly, Mies was thinking about Elektron (*"Elektronmetall"* in German), a much-discussed lightweight magnesium alloy, and recent German invention, used in the automobile and airplane industries.[119] Mies and Lilly Reich discussed that material when they met for the first time in Frankfurt in the early summer of 1925, and Reich followed up with additional information and a sample, which she had procured for Mies from the manufacturer.[120]

After the third issue of *G* appeared, Hans Richter published an extremely complimentary essay about Mies (perhaps in an attempt to secure his continued support for the magazine) in the journal *Qualität*, where Carl Gottfried's piece on Mies's skyscraper designs had appeared two years earlier. The journal was published by Ernst Hinkefuss, business partner of Wilhelm Deffke, who worked for Mies off and on in those years. While Richter's remarkable piece of laudatory prose (surely composed with Mies's input) might not have passed the editorial board of a mainstream journal, the personal connections between Mies, editor, and author allowed it to move forward, and thus it suggests some unfiltered insights into how Mies saw himself and his role at the time. Richter presented Mies as *the* prototypical *"Neue Baumeister"* (New Master Builder), the piece's title. The unsolved problems in the art of building, according to the text, stemmed from the absence of a clear order and

M. v. D. R.

its appropriate forms—in other words, from the lack of a building art that embraced ideals of both architects and engineers, and reached beyond them. The answer to this problem was Mies van der Rohe, "the first master builder who has succeeded in abolishing all preconceived notions of architecture and a bygone past before he even begins, who is so well-versed technically-practically and formally-historically and so deeply familiar with the building industry that he does not think about it any more than he thinks about his body. In him all forces are liberated and ready for the great task at hand: the task of building." While Mies was greatly respected, Richter explained, his many accomplishments had only been acknowledged individually, such as the facts that he had "invented a significant new type of ground plan, had recognized the fundamental potential of concrete, had created a simple and expandable system for office buildings with exemplary spatial and functional divisions, had clearly distinguished between the functions for new and old houses, had solved the problem of the continental skyscraper, etc." Mies van der Rohe's most important quality, however, had remained invisible, Richter explained—namely, that he represented a "new type of master builder," who not only builds buildings, but who "fights for a new philosophy of design." With Mies, "a tradition begins to reemerge that was once capable of building pyramids and that alone will be able to recognize and master the tasks of an internationally networked society. With him a new spirituality asserts itself, as well as a new type of man."[121]

Richter's emphasis on the title "master builder" in his essay coincided with a movement to start a professional organization for builders who were not members of the BDA (which gave preference to those with a degree from an architecture school). On October 18, 1925, at a meeting in Hanover, representatives from different vocational schools founded the Deutscher Bauschulbund (German Association of Schools for the Building Trade), which established "Baumeister" as a professional title. Mies apparently required collaborators and tradesmen, even his own chief of staff, Hermann John, to address him as "Herr Baumeister."[122]

Despite Richter's essay, the collaboration with Mies on the journal *G* did not continue, and it took two more years for the next issue to appear. Richter was its sole editor, and typefaces were as varied as they had been before.

Figure 2.35. Cover of *G: Material zur elementaren Gestaltung* 3 (1923). Design by Ludwig Mies van der Rohe.

Three

Housing and Urban Modernity

Berlin, Guben, Stuttgart, 1925–29

1925 The Dexel and Eliat Houses

On Thursday, January 9, 1925, Mies van der Rohe checked into Jena's best hotel, the Schwarzer Bär (Black Bear), for an important meeting with two prospective clients, Walter Dexel and his wife, Grete. The traditional hotel had existed since the fifteenth century and housed personalities such as the writer Johann Wolfgang Goethe and Chancellor Otto von Bismarck, for whose planned memorial Mies had submitted a design fifteen years earlier. Dexel had contacted Mies on January 3 and offered him his first opportunity to execute a truly modern house—a year after colleagues had chided him for his "dualism," the conceptual gap between his much-published visionary designs and his actual practice. Walter Dexel, a prominent abstract painter and designer, was the director of the Kunstverein (Art Association) in the city of Jena. As mentioned above, in November 1924, Mies had curated a successful exhibition there, on new German architecture.[1]

After the initial meeting with the Dexels, it became clear that there was enormous time pressure. Dexel's father-in-law, prominent Jena pedagogue Karl Brauckmann, was going to foot the bill, but he had set tight time limits on the design and submission of the building permit—the house had to be ready for occupancy, "for business reasons," on October 1, 1925. He wanted to inspect the "exterior design and floor plan" before leaving for Switzerland about a week later.[2] According to Dexel's son Bernhard, Mies "made some sketches on typewriter paper, at my parents' house on the occasion of his visit and 'on orders' from my mother."[3] The eight surviving sketches show that Mies was determined (and Dexel surely expected him) to move away from the imperious symmetrical façade and tall hip roof of the Mosler House, which was under construction at exactly the same time (figure 3.1). Four of them show evocative perspective views that suggest a centrifugal plan in the vein of his Brick Country House. The others drawings present conventional floor plans for two connected cubes of one and two stories. Dexel sent Mies a site plan shortly afterward, but Mies suddenly fell silent. A series of postcards and letters over the next few weeks reflects the Dexels' increasing desperation. "Perhaps the rule of not writing and not coming could be confirmed by an exception for once?" asked Walter Dexel. And his wife, Grete, described in another letter to Mies how she "trembled" when confessing to her strict father after his return that the design had still not materialized. Mies had promised a set of plans by January 24, but the day passed without any sign of life. Walter Dexel was "extraordinarily annoyed," especially since his "measure of patience is usually below rather than above the human average."[4] Nevertheless, the Dexels made one last attempt and went to Berlin to see Mies on January 29. He asked for another week. But this deadline also passed, as Mies had left to go skiing in Switzerland. In a sharp blow to Mies's ambitions, Dexel canceled the contract on March 3, 1925. Mies continued thinking about the project, and reported to his friend Adolf Behne on March 16 that he had finally "had the vision of the house," but the clients were no longer interested.[5]

Despite—possibly also because of—the repeated and increasingly desperate urging of the Dexels, Mies had gotten stuck after his initial sketches. He may have felt pressured not only by Dexel but also by the overall situation. After the spectacular success of his visionary designs, expectations were high for a first modern building from him. Jena was a city in the sights of modernism—Walter Gropius and his collaborator Adolf Meyer had fundamentally modernized the municipal theater there in 1921–22 and completed a modern, flat-roofed, cubic house for prominent physics professor Felix Auerbach in November 1924.[6] Mies thus faced a direct comparison. The fear of delivering a design that was not fully thought through may have led to a creative crisis.[7] "The project has to be good, otherwise I won't let it out of my hands," he had told the clients in January.[8] His collaborator Werner Graeff later recalled, "The Dexel case then somehow became a standing expression for anything that good old Mies had absolutely no desire to work on....We do not want to have another Dexel!"[9]

Immediately after withdrawing the commission from Mies, Walter Dexel approached Adolf Meyer, whom he knew as Gropius's capable collaborator on their Jena commissions. As expected, Meyer worked quickly. After receiving the commission in March, he submitted the building application in May. Mies's sketches, which had remained with the Dexels, served as inspiration. Echoes of the Auerbach House in Jena are also visible. The result was a dense, cubically staggered arrangement of living and outdoor spaces with a studio on the first floor and a workshop in the basement (figure 3.2). Without much hesitation, however, the city's building commission rejected Meyer's design because it would "appear as a foreign body in the landscape at this location."[10]

Dexel tried everything possible to change the committee's mind. He exhibited Meyer's drawings and a model in a reputable bookstore and asked the Werkbund for a positive opinion, which was published in the *Jenaer Volksblatt* on December 28, 1925. Peter Behrens, Hans Poelzig and, poignantly, also Ludwig Mies van der Rohe were the authors.

Figure 3.1. Ludwig Mies van der Rohe, Dexel House project, Jena, Germany, 1925. Sketch plan and perspective. Graphite on paper, 8 1/4 × 13 in. (20.9 × 33 cm). Canadian Centre for Architecture, Montreal.

Figure 3.2. Adolf Meyer, Dexel House project, Jena, Germany, 1925. Elevations. Ink and watercolor on paper, 7 1/2 × 25 3/16 in. (19 × 64 cm). Canadian Centre for Architecture, Montreal.

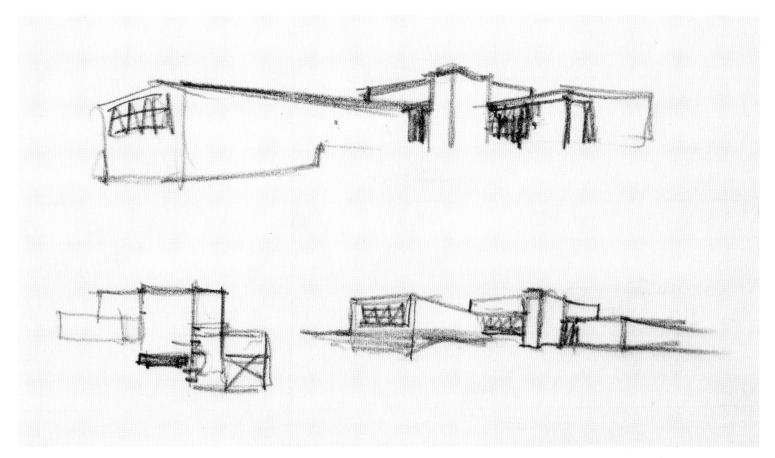

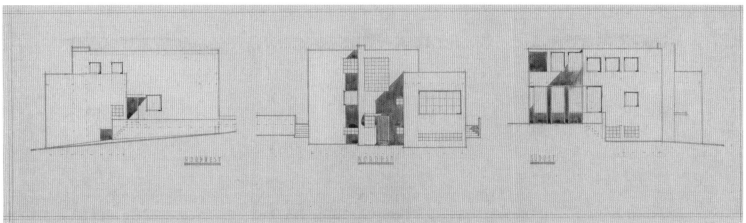

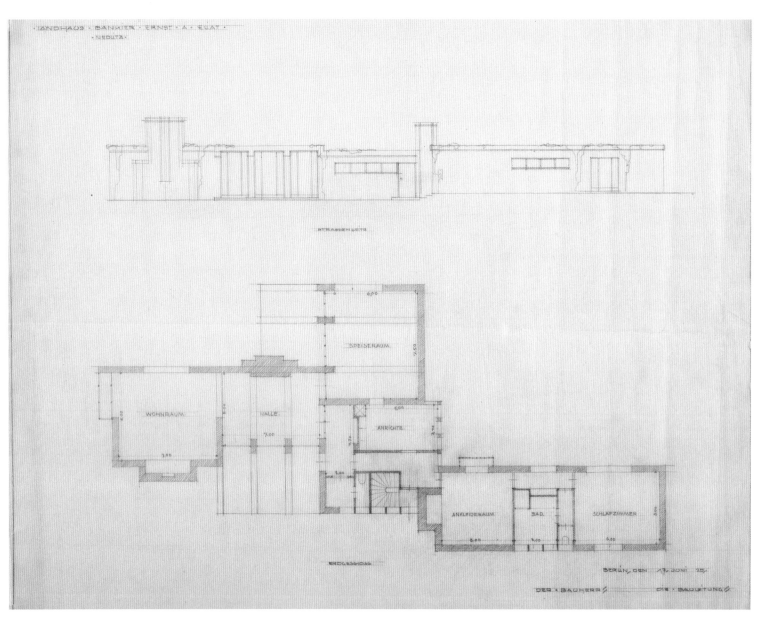

·LANDHAUS · BANKIER · ERNST · A · ELIAT·
·NEGUTA·

STRASSENSEITE

SPEISERAUM

WOHNRAUM   HALLE   ANRICHTE

ANKLEIDERAUM   BAD   SCHLAFZIMMER

ERDGESCHOSS

BERLIN, DEN 17. JUNI 25

DER · BAUHERR   DIE · BAULEITUNG

They praised "the arrangement of the individual rooms and especially the position in the terrain" and stated that they believed that "the simple cubic form of this building will fit well in the rolling hills in which it is skillfully embedded. We hope that this building will be realized soon." But to no avail, as the building administration stayed its course. Dexel consoled Meyer with a large exhibition at the Jena Kunstverein, in which the unbuilt house occupied a central place.[11] The review of Meyer's design on behalf of the Werkbund, which had been based on his own sketches for the Dexels, provided Mies with important insights for his Wolf House (see below) design which he developed simultaneously.

Another project is significant in this context. At the end of January 1925, at the time when Mies was supposed to start work on the Dexel House, he heard that the Berlin banker Ernst A. Eliat and his wife, the writer Helene Eliat, had hired the architect Werner March to design a house for them. Eliat had purchased a lakeside property in the Nedlitz district of Potsdam. March was a young, conservative architect who was just completing his first commissions for single-family houses—ornamentless, with steep roofs and careful spatial planning, as Werner Hegemann later remarked with admiration.[12] March would go on to build the Berlin Olympic Stadium, the Berlin Waldbühne, and the Yugoslav Embassy in the 1930s. March's design for Eliat has not survived and was not executed. Perhaps to make up for the loss of the Dexel contract, Mies approached Eliat with the offer to work out an alternative to March's design, and he was sent the site plan on March 17. Mies prepared a site plan, floor plans, elevations, and a watercolor perspective and submitted them in June, but the uncertainty about his future direction is still palpable. Mies adopted key elements from the Concrete Country House. Paired concrete supports with long cantilevers create deep canopies in front of an entrance hall and dining room (figure 3.3). What points ahead to the more sure-footed Wolf House design was the open, but not linear, connection among the living room, hall, and dining room, with higher ceilings than the adjacent utilitarian and circulation spaces. A full-size basement with a kitchen and staff rooms faces a lower service court. The watercolor perspective suggests a flat, horizontally protruding canopy without support beams, which would become a defining element at the Barcelona Pavilion (figure 3.4).[13]

1925–27 Afrikanische Strasse Housing Estate

At that time, Mies had just received a commission for a housing estate in Berlin with eighty-eight one-, two-, and three-room apartments. The client was the housing cooperative Primus, and the socialist Bauhütte was the designated builder. The complex was built in 1926–27. Mies owed the commission to progressive planner Martin Wagner, a fellow member of the Zehner-Ring who was in charge of the trade union's large social housing cooperatives. He had helped introduce a new tax in 1924, the *Hauszinssteuer*, levied on all property owners who had profited from postwar hyperinflation that had greatly reduced their mortgage debts. This tax financed most of Weimar Germany's social housing projects after 1925, and Wagner wanted to signal this new start with a decidedly modern approach. He brought Bruno Taut and Mies on board for the first executed examples. While Taut had many years of experience with building housing estates, Mies did not. Taut's spectacular brick-clad Schillerpark Estate in Berlin was designed in 1924, under the influence of recent Dutch social housing projects, and opened in 1926. Wagner also wrote and promoted the new *Reformbauordnung* (Reform Building Regulations) for Berlin in December 1925, when Mies began working on his design. These reforms suggested less dense housing estates in the city's outskirts and discouraged the creation of backyards via additional wings. To be financed via the new tax, apartments had to be smaller than 1,400 square feet (130 square meters). Only two- or three-story buildings were permitted. Wagner became city councilor for architecture and planning the next year and defined key housing policy and urban planning guidelines until the Nazis rose to power in 1933. All in all, he commissioned more than 140,000 apartments. Taut's "Onkel Tom's Hütte" in Zehlendorf and Hufeisensiedlung in Britz became two of the most iconic modern housing estates (each with over one thousand apartments) of their time. Mies, however, only designed the project at Afrikanische Strasse.

The Afrikanisches Viertel (African Quarter) in Berlin had been developed at the turn of the century, but not immediately built. The street names indicate the colonial ambitions of the late German empire: Zambesi-, Duala-, Uganda-, and Tangastrasse. In an unusual

Figure 3.3. Ludwig Mies van der Rohe, Eliat House project, Potsdam, Germany, 1925. Ground-floor plan and street elevation. Pencil on tracing paper, 17 1/4 × 21 in. (44.1 × 53.5 cm). Museum of Modern Art, New York. The Mies van der Rohe Archive, gift of the architect.

Figure 3.4. Ludwig Mies van der Rohe, Eliat House project, Potsdam, Germany, 1925. Perspective with watercolor wash, dimensions unknown.

constellation, the apartment blocks facing Afrikanische Strasse closed off the northeastern end of elongated plots parceled out for small, semidetached houses with gardens. Following Wagner's new guidelines, in his design Mies accommodated eighty-eight apartments in two- and three-story duplex units. The taller main wings consist of three such units, and connect at right angles to separate two-story secondary wings (figure 3.5).

Whereas in Taut's Schillerpark rows stood separately, opening the inner courtyard at the corners, Mies clearly wanted the inner space enclosed on three sides. A conventional perimeter block would have come with the dark *Berliner Zimmer* (Berlin Rooms) at the inner corner. By simply abutting the three-story main wings perpendicularly onto the two-story side wings (merely connecting them visually with hinge-like balconies), Mies avoided the dark inner corner, but also gave up precious real estate at the open corners. The project shows Mies torn between formal and functional considerations. He pragmatically introduced a sloped roof behind the straight edge of the façade, which meant that the attic on the top floor was significantly higher on the street side, and landed right above the small windows on the courtyard side (figure 3.6). For the main wing, Mies had designed spacious eat-in kitchens, whose loggias face the noon and afternoon sun and the quiet courtyard in the back. This ideal of having both sun and calm would have been reachable for half of the side wings as well (those facing southeast), but Mies decided otherwise. He wanted the photogenic deep and dark loggias visible across from each other on the side streets (figure 3.7). To achieve this symmetry, the street façades had to accommodate entrances and stairways, and as a result bathrooms and pantries ended up behind the loggia, depriving the kitchen-dining room of much light. Arthur Köster photographed the buildings around 1927, documenting the newly planted cypress trees and also severe water damage around the roof edge

Figure 3.5. Ludwig Mies van der Rohe, Afrikanische Strasse Housing Estate, Berlin, 1925–27. View to the northwest on Afrikanische Strasse immediately upon completion. Photograph by Arthur Koester.

Figure 3.6. Ludwig Mies van der Rohe, Afrikanische Strasse Housing Estate, Berlin, 1925–27. View to the southeast into the courtyard from Duala Strasse. Photograph by Hassan Bagheri.

Figure 3.7. Ludwig Mies van der Rohe, Afrikanische Strasse Housing Estate, Berlin, 1925–27. View to the northeast on Duala Strasse. Photograph by Hassan Bagheri.

(figure 3.8). However, Köster never recorded the less elegantly composed courtyard façades (no doubt on Mies's instructions).

1925 The Traffic Tower

When Mies had fled to Zuoz in Switzerland to escape Walter Dexel's constant demands, he was not entirely idle. On February 25, 1925, his office manager, Hermann John, reminded him by telegram of another project that awaited his attention—namely, the drawings for a traffic tower, as they were needed to construct a model.[14] It was the most metropolitan of projects—an elevated observation cabin for a traffic policeman at one of Berlin's busiest intersections, at Leipziger Strasse and Friedrichstrasse. Mies collaborated with Paul Mahlberg and Heinrich Kosina, two Berlin architects specializing in transportation architecture, currently at work on the future central airport in Tempelhof.[15] Half a year earlier, Berlin's (and Europe's) first *Verkehrsturm* had been established at the center of Potsdamer Platz on December 19, 1924—an instant symbol of Berlin's much desired status as a "world city" (figure 3.9).[16] Its architect was Jean Krämer, Mies's old adversary in Behrens's office; Mies's traffic tower was not just a response to the one on Potsdamer Platz, but also one-upmanship toward his former colleague.[17]

Traffic towers in New York (installed two years earlier at seven intersections on Fifth Avenue) had been the world's first. They were 24 feet (7.3 meters) tall and built of steel and cast bronze. Four slanted corner piers carried the glass-enclosed observation deck, a clock underneath, and the cornice above with red, yellow, and green lights. Despite their acanthus leaves, laurel garlands, and wingspread eagles, the traffic towers were seen as the epitome of modernity, thanks to the cool, incorruptible precision of their mechanism, impervious to discussions or requests for special treatment that traffic policemen routinely encountered. The discipline of New York's drivers and pedestrians immediately increased, noted the *New York Times*.[18] Krämer adopted the New York model for Berlin but removed the eagles and garlands, straightened the posts, and made the overall form a pentagon, reflecting the five incoming streets at Potsdamer Platz.

In great contrast, the tower design by Mies, Mahlberg, and Kosina broke free from the static New York model and its Berlin successor and suggested a dynamic approach, with the observation deck leaning into the intersection without blocking traffic.[19] From the protruding perch 18 feet (5.5 meters) aboveground, the traffic warden could survey all four streets and operate the signal lights on posts on the sidewalks. The single leg tower was to be built from cast iron and rest on a foundation grid that distributed the load (figure 3.10).[20]

Figure 3.8. Ludwig Mies van der Rohe, Afrikanische Strasse Housing Estate, Berlin, 1925–27. Façade of a two-story wing on Ugandastrasse immediately upon completion, with moisture penetration at the roof's edge. Photograph by Arthur Koester.

Figure 3.9. Jean Krämer, traffic tower in Potsdamer Platz, Berlin, 1924. Photograph by Georg Pahl. Bundesarchiv Bildarchiv.

Figure 3.10. Ludwig Mies van der Rohe, Paul Mahlberg, and Heinrich Kosina, traffic tower at the intersection of Leipziger Strasse and Friedrichstrasse project, Berlin, 1925.

Inside was a veritable control center, with small lights indicating the connection to the lamp-posts, a multiple lamp display indicating traffic flow nearby, a precise stopwatch, and direct phone lines to the police, traffic control, fire department, and so on. There was a megaphone to interact with the traffic warden in the street and an alarm bell to alert him.[21] Ultimately, the question of the foundation became an insurmountable obstacle, as a subway tunnel was right underneath.[22] The tower's location in Friedrichstrasse happened to be directly in front of the Adam Department Store, for which Mies would propose an extension three years later. The model of the tower and Mies's photomontage were presented to the press on June 3, 1925, at the elegant Hotel Kaiserhof.[23] Mies sent his friend Ludwig Hilberseimer to attend. The echo was considerable, all major papers reported.[24] This traffic tower was "not, like the tower at Potsdamer Platz, formed after American models, but a completely original idea," noted one.[25] "It only stands on one leg," observed another.[26] Mies clearly felt a sense of ownership regarding the tower. When Stuttgart architect Heinz Rasch claimed in a critical article that the street was too narrow for it, Mies paid him a visit to discuss it. A friendship resulted.[27]

1925   Magdeburg, Frankfurt, Lilly Reich

Mies and Lilly Reich had met for the first time when Mies became a member of the Werkbund in 1924.[28] Born in Berlin in 1885, Reich had studied under Josef Hoffmann in Vienna from 1908 to 1911 and had been invited to join the Werkbund in 1912. In 1920, she became the first woman on its executive board (figure 3.11). Also in 1920, she was in charge of the first Werkbund exhibition in the United States. At Berlin's fashion week event that year, she organized the Werkbund sections on craft and design. In 1924, she accepted a position at the Frankfurt Messeamt (Trade Fair Office) and opened a fashion design studio and tailor shop there.[29]

Apparently on Reich's urging, Mies was invited to apply for the Frankfurt planning director position in spring 1925, and Mies traveled three times to Frankfurt, in February, March, and June of that year.[30] In March, he seems to have seen Reich's apartment in Frankfurt, which a visitor described as follows: "I came for the first time in my life…into a modern apartment.…But what I saw there: light wood, very smooth, clear lines, everything designed simply, no frills or ornaments on the furniture…and at the same time it looked precious. I was completely thrilled and delighted."[31] Immediately after his return to Berlin in March 1925, Mies remodeled his own apartment at Am Karlsbad. Several invoices document the installation of wall coverings, silk curtains, and new lampshades. Clearly, Mies had been greatly impressed. Lilly Reich, in the meantime, traveled to the meeting of the Werkbund's executive board (where her voice was greatly respected) in Bremen on March 30, 1925. After the meeting, chairman Peter Bruckmann announced the planned Werkbund exhibition *Die Wohnung* (The Dwelling) in Stuttgart for 1927. Despite having built relatively little, Mies was appointed an advisor along with Hans Poelzig and Walter Curt Behrendt. He became director of the exhibition the next year.[32]

Figure 3.11. G. Engelhardt, portrait of Lilly Reich, ca. 1914. Gelatin silver print on Baryta paper, 6 1/2 × 4 3/8 in. (16.6 × 11 cm). Bauhaus-Archiv Berlin.

While Mies and Lilly Reich were still using the formal *"Sie"* when corresponding about a new lightweight metal with architectural potential (*Elektronmetall*) in the summer of 1925, by the fall they had switched to an informal "Du" and seem to have entered into a romantic relationship. They sent each other presents for Christmas 1925 (a handbag for Lilly Reich, a yellow silk dinner jacket for Mies).[33]

Mies was increasingly being considered for important posts. While the Frankfurt position went to Ernst May in the summer of 1925, Adolf Rading had asked Mies at the same time if he might be interested in a professorship at the Breslauer Akademie, where Hans Scharoun was also being considered. Mies turned down the offer with uncharacteristic speed on July 4, 1925, and supported the candidacy of Scharoun, who accepted the position.[34] But in the fall of 1925, Mies was in talks with representatives of the city of Magdeburg for the position of building deputy (succeeding Bruno Taut). His former collaborator Wilhelm Deffke, who had become the foremost modernist in Madgeburg, tried to sabotage the appointment by claiming Mies habitually appropriated the work of others.[35]

It seems natural to see a causal relationship between Mies's breakthrough to modernism and his next projects, in particular the Wolf House in Guben (today, Gubin, Poland) and the beginning of his partnership with Lilly Reich in the same year. Reich was strong-willed and assertive and may have given Mies the support with which he finally overcame the "dualism" that his critics had noted.

1925–27 Wolf House

The industrialist Ernst Wolf had approached Mies regarding a house in Guben, only a few weeks after Walter Dexel, on January 27, 1925. Two days later, they met at Berlin's Hotel Prinz Friedrich Karl, and Mies accepted the commission and visited the site, high above the river Neisse with a view toward the nearby town center. Wolf was a more patient client than Walter Dexel's father-in-law.[36] A second site visit to Guben took place on April 13, 1925, and Mies then developed the design over several months. Located east of Berlin, the smaller and little-known Guben—an industrial town with a population of fifteen thousand at the time (Jena had fifty-two thousand)—may have seemed more congenial to Mies for an experiment in modern architecture than the Jena limelight that came with the abandoned Dexel commission. On October 19, 1925, a first set of plans was ready and signed by Hermann John and the clients. As mentioned above, Mies was reviewing Adolf Meyer's design for Walter Dexel in Jena while he worked on a similar task in Guben. There are certain parallels in the distribution of rooms, the treatment of the terraces, and the single-pane windows. Mies's design, however, stood out for its unique handling of the spatial sequence inside.

The radical shift in Mies's approach becomes most obvious when comparing the Wolf House with the contemporary Kempner (1921–23) and Mosler (1924–26) houses (see figures 1.55, 2.32). The former had inspired Mr. and Mrs. Wolf to contact Mies, while the latter was still under construction. Both housed the usual enfilade of study, library, music room, and dining room typical for a bourgeois villa behind the conventional, symmetrical façade

Figure 3.12. Ludwig Mies van der Rohe, Wolf House, Guben, Germany, 1925–27. Floor plan. The walls outlining the sequence of representational rooms have been slightly darkened for better readability. Museum of Modern Art, New York. The Mies van der Rohe Archive, gift of the architect.

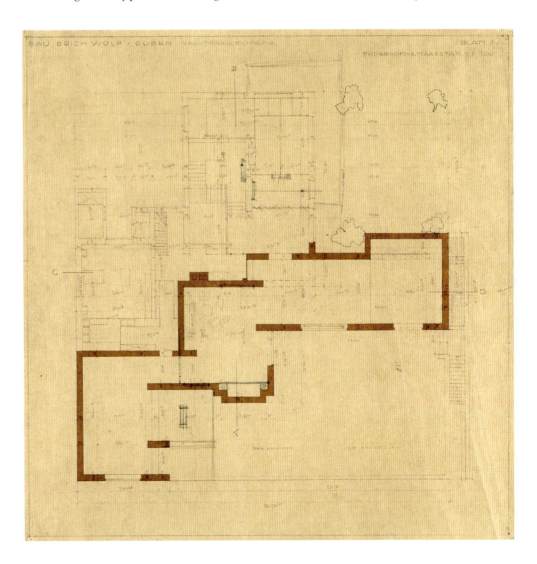

crowned by a hipped roof with dormers that Werner von Walthausen and Mies had first developed for the Urbig House.

It was this linear and horizontal sequence that Mies thoroughly rearranged in the Wolf House (figure 3.12). Instead of lining up the rooms according to an overarching formal-symmetrical concept, as he had done previously, here they were ostentatiously grouped according to their functions. To be sure, the cubically staggered arrangement is also a formal gesture, but the elimination of symmetrical relationships allowed for greater freedom in the placement of the rooms. These interconnected rooms fill the one-story wing toward the garden, staggered diagonally with projecting walls controlling the visual connections. The view from these four rooms faced southwest across the paved terrace, with its lowered planting bed, to the Neisse Valley below and to the city; above them was a spacious roof terrace. The living room however, turned perpendicularly, faced southeast, and thus had a straight view of the Gothic city church (the thirteenth-century Stadt- und Hauptkirche, with its sixteenth-century spire). The seating area in front of the living room was protected from sun and rain by a cantilevered concrete roof (figures 3.13, 3.14).

The adjacent two-story block contained an entrance hall and family rooms, a three-story block kitchen, and servants' quarters. The stair tower of the servants' wing projects boldly from the adjacent block, and a small storeroom next to the kitchen—an obvious afterthought that shows up only in a late-adapted plan—is simply added as a separate cube. Mies distinguished the different areas by their room heights: the representative wing had a ceiling height of 10 feet (3.1 meters); the adjacent entrance area had the same height; and the bedrooms above had a ceiling height of nine feet (2.8 meters). In the wing for the kitchen and staff there were three different ceiling heights, namely nine feet (2.7 meters) on the first floor, eight and a half feet (2.6 meters) on the second, and just over eight feet (2.5 meters) on the top floor. This made the horizontal connection between the family wing and the staff wing on the second floor complicated, as it required additional steps. The house has many different window sizes and proportions, from two floor-to-ceiling openings in the living room to a band of windows underneath the kitchen ceiling, but presents them with utmost confidence—a huge step beyond the hapless multitude of windows in the garden façade of his Warnholtz House ten years earlier (see figure 1.51).

Mies presented the materials and structure in a similarly programmatic manner: bright white mortar emphasized the load-bearing bricks, two heavy concrete beams of different thicknesses supported the canopy facing the garden, and a thinner cantilevered balcony slab enclosed the front corner and protected the entrance area.[37] The windows in many different formats were not divided as usual, but had large, vertical glass panes.[38] The clarity of

Figure 3.13. Ludwig Mies van der Rohe, Wolf House, Guben, Germany, 1925–27. Interior view of the living room with furniture by Mies and Lilly Reich, ca. 1927. Private collection.

the building's division into its three functional areas is unparalleled in the work of Mies. Never before or since would his work be so free of formal considerations. Only a year earlier he had declared that "form is not the goal, but the result of our work," and here he seemed to want to demonstrate this approach.

One would love to know how Mies was able to persuade his clients, who had obviously envisioned a cozy, upper-middle-class residence with a hipped roof in the style of the Kempner House (see figures 1.54–1.57), to agree to a utilitarian building of such radicalism. The street view of the Wolf House broke with all the traditions of a bourgeois home (figure 3.15). The main entrance was barely visible, the window formats varied, and an inexplicably high, bare brick wall on the upper floor at the street front looked rather forbidding. The service yard can be seen in the background, where two small additions of varying sizes create visual clutter and suggest late additions. Later photos show the stark brick wall toward the street first covered in ivy and then obscured from view by a large copper beech.

In 1927, Mies and Lilly Reich had asked Richard Lisker to design carpets for the Wolf House. Lisker was a former colleague of Reich's in Frankfurt, head of the textile department of the city's art school (he would become director of the famous Städelschule in 1934 and was dismissed by the Nazis in 1940). A letter from Reich to Lisker with floor plans and instructions gives a rare glimpse of design details for the interior, its coziness a striking contrast to the outside:

> For the dining room we are anticipating polished dark walnut furniture and chairs, potentially with black horsehair covers. Mies would like to have an all red carpet

Figure 3.15. Ludwig Mies van der Rohe, Wolf House, Guben, Germany, 1925–27. Street façade. Photograph by Arthur Koester. Klassik Stiftung Weimar.

here, different hues, which intersect in the form of large areas, thus no lines or ornaments but a unified grand form. For the living room corner, we are so far planning a big built-in sofabench, outfitted with large pillows, color as of yet undetermined, but the wood again walnut....The den is paneled entirely in walnut, will get big leather club chairs and a sofa. Here, Mies would like a dark cigar brown, so probably best the dark brown nature colored wool, potentially combined with a lighter natural color and some indigo or a beautiful green. Again, only large intersecting forms and shapes. Yesterday we matched some wool samples with the wood and we realized that only very pure, natural colors work, everything else appears dyed or dirty.[39]

The house was photographed by Arthur Koester in time for the Werkbund exhibition in Stuttgart in 1927, but before the interior and landscaping was finished. It was rarely published in the following years (and never with its revolutionary floor plan), as it was overshadowed by the coverage of the Weissenhof exhibition and then Mies's Barcelona Pavilion. The house was damaged in World War II and demolished afterward.

Where did the new formal language, which Mies applied with such certainty, come from? When he was designing the Eliat House in the summer of 1925, there was still palpable indecision about his new direction. Apart from the abovementioned engagement with Adolf Meyer's design for Walter Dexel, an important new influence came again from the Netherlands. While Mies had developed friendly relations with Theo van Doesburg, J. J. P. Oud, and other De Stijl members in the context of the 1923 *Grosse Berliner Kunstausstellung* (Great Berlin Art Exhibition) in Berlin, he was also open to the cubic brick modernism of Willem Marinus Dudok and others.

Dutch architecture had recently been featured in a number of essays in architectural magazines and in Heinrich de Fries's book *Moderne Villen und Landhäuser* (Modern Villas and Country Houses), which appeared in 1924 as one of Wasmuth Verlag's first major publications after the war and economic crisis.[40] De Fries celebrated new beginnings after the "monstrous cultural catastrophe" of World War I. Now began the age of "the third dimension, of spatial and spiritual depth," and of a new "autonomy of space in the floor plan," he declared.[41] The volume opened programmatically with Dudok's Sevensteyn House in The Hague (1920–22; figure 3.16). The influence of this building on Mies's Wolf House in Guben can hardly be overestimated. Flat roofs are used as terraces, corners are articulated by recesses, and cantilevered concrete slabs serve as canopies. The

Figure 3.16. Willem Marinus Dudok, Sevensteyn House, The Hague, Netherlands, 1920–22.

large windows have brick lintels and no shutters. Immediately afterward, Dudok designed the Bavinckschool in Hilversum (1921–22), showing a similarly clear, cubically staggered approach (figure 3.17). The formal vocabulary that had been invented here would be enormously influential for several years. The particularly forceful reception of Frank Lloyd Wright in the Netherlands played a role in this work, as did the expressive brick architecture of the Amsterdam School.

Another impressive example of Dutch brick cubism is Johannes Bernardus (Han) van Loghem's Stadswoonhuis 't Fort in Haarlem of 1924, published the same year (figure 3.18).[42] Here, too, the asymmetrical cubic arrangement, the careful brick details, and the chimneys as vertical anchors are striking.

Mies was by no means the only German architect succumbing to the Dutch influence. The Wolf House belongs to a group of private houses built in 1926–27, mostly in northern and western Germany, that arranged carefully detailed bricks or clinker cubes in asymmetrical staggerings using a similar formal language. A few examples may suffice: Hamburg architects Carl Gustav Bensel and Johann Kamps built a villa for Iserlohn merchant Otto Heutelbeck from 1924 to 1926. The client was active in the textile and fashion industry, just like Ernst Wolf. Its flat-roofed cubes are staggered from the one-story domestic wing to three stories on the valley side. Martin Elsaesser built his own residence in 1925–26 in the Frankfurt district of Ginnheim. It consists of two cubic blocks and has two roof terraces and careful brick detailing. Thilo Schoder, finally, built the Meyer House in Gera in 1926–27. An influence of the Wolf House on these designs can be ruled out, since it had not yet been published at the time of their creation.

Stuttgart architects Heinz and Bodo Rasch's small house for their uncle Ernst Rasch in Bad Oeynhausen may have been at least partially influenced by the Wolf House (figure 3.19). They were commissioned in the spring of 1926, and plans were submitted in June and approved in December 1926. On July 22, 1927, Ernst Rasch and his wife, Frieda, moved in.[43] Heinz Rasch had seen Mies's design for the Wolf House in 1926: "His house in Guben was almost finished, and he chose wallpaper, and I was allowed to choose a very bright tartan-like pattern for the walls and ceiling of the children's room. He invited me to a trip to Guben, I refused for some reason. The fact that I thought of a possibility shortly afterwards was of little use. Mies did not repeat a request again."[44]

Mies included the Rasch Brothers' building in the *Plan- und Modell-Ausstellung Neuer Baukunst* (Plan and Model Exhibition of New Architecture) at the Stuttgart Werkbund

Figure 3.17. Willem Marinus Dudok, Bavinckschool, Hilversum, Netherlands, 1921–22. Gelatin silver print, 14 1/8 × 18 7/8 in. (36 × 48 cm).

Figure 3.18. Johannes Bernardus (Han) van Loghem, Stadswoonhuis 't Fort, Haarlem, Netherlands, 1924. Gelatin silver print, 9 ft. 6 1/8 in. × 18 7/8 in. (36 × 48 cm). Het Nieuwe Instituut, Rotterdam.

Figure 3.19. Heinz Rasch and Bodo Rasch, Ernst Rasch House, Bad Oeynhausen, Germany, 1926–27.

exhibition, next to his Wolf House, his designs for country houses in reinforced concrete and brick, and Richard Döcker's Sebald House in Stuttgart.

One of Mies van der Rohe's most important, and still underrated, contemporaries was the Hamburg architect Karl Schneider. He had worked for Gropius and Behrens before setting up his own studio, and his Hamburg Kunstverein building of 1929–30 was represented in the *Modern Architecture: International Exhibition* at the Museum of Modern Art in 1932. His Müller-Drenkberg House in Hamburg Ohlstedt from 1928–29 is an asymmetrical, cubic brick building like the Wolf House, but with wide balconies on three sides (figure 3.20). Deprived of his teaching position by the Nazis, he ended up in Chicago in 1938, just like Mies. In great contrast, however, he was not able to gain a foothold as an architect, and worked as a designer for the department store giant Sears, Roebuck & Co. until his early death in 1945. It is not known whether Mies and Schneider ever had contact in Chicago.[45]

By 1925, critics had noted an emerging design pattern and vocabulary. Alfred Gellhorn, somewhat ironically, described the process:

> The house is divided up into always flat cubes of different height. The windows will ideally consist of wide bands of glass and are carried around the corner, canopies, walls, balconies are executed as plates. The surfaces are not divided through a horizontal or even vertical system, but treated asymmetrically through other means, such as its distribution of windows, or a plate-like cornice. You emphasize construction in your execution. But since a simple construction does not stand out, you try to find a difficult, albeit expensive execution. No ornaments.[46]

But still: the comparative examples above make clear that Mies did more than follow a recipe. His precise handling of masses, his emphasis on bricks as a module, the open spatial

Figure 3.20. Karl Schneider, Müller-Drenkberg House, Hamburg Ohlstedt, Germany, 1928–29.

connections inside, and the Wolf House's complex tripartite division show his extraordinary talent and are superior to the designs of many of his peers. Mies's work here was not necessarily singular or unique, but stood out as a *primus inter pares.*

1926 Monument to the November Revolution

Contemporary with the Wolf House, Mies designed a monument to Rosa Luxemburg and Karl Liebknecht, the founders of Germany's Communist Party, who had been murdered in 1919 by right-wing militias. The monument was placed in front of their graves and that of thirty-six other fallen revolutionaries at the Friedrichsfelde cemetery in Berlin. The commission had been arranged for Mies by the art historian and Marxist Eduard Fuchs. Fuchs had moved into Mies's Perls House, but, avid collector that he was, he soon ran out of space and contacted Mies in 1925 to discuss an addition, which was executed in 1928 (see figures 1.30, 1.31). At that occasion they discussed the planned monument. Mies recalled much later that Fuchs had shown him the model of an existing, neoclassical proposal with Doric columns and framed portraits. Mies laughed that this would be a "fine monument for a banker," and promptly was commissioned to design something more appropriate.[47]

Historical evidence suggests—somewhat differently—that the idea of a wall of "red sandstone or porphyry" had already been advanced by Fuchs (emulating the wall at Moscow's Kremlin where heroes of the Russian Revolution were buried) before he spoke with Mies. He planned to donate a cast of Auguste Rodin's sculpture *La Défense,* to be placed next to it. Names of fallen comrades would be listed on both sides. Communist politician Wilhelm Pieck presented this idea on July 12, 1925, at the tenth annual meeting of Germany's Communist Party.[48]

Thus, Mies's design of variously cantilevered, seemingly overlapping cubes might have originated from such an imagined wall of sandstone or porphyry blocks (as the clay model seems to suggest), and was only switched to brick when the fundraising did not progress as anticipated (figures 3.21, 3.22). The monument was 49 feet (15 meters) wide, 18 feet (5.5 meters) high, and approximately 13 feet (four meters) deep. At the bottom right, a protruding block provided a platform for speakers, and there was a flagpole and a five-sided, Soviet star with a hammer and sickle in front. The concluding quote from Rosa Luxemburg's last essay in the Communist newspaper *Die Rote Fahne*—"*Ich war, ich bin, ich werde sein*" (I was, I am, I will be), quoting nineteenth-century revolutionary Ferdinand Freiligrath—was meant to be attached in large letters to the front, but was not

Figure 3.21. Ludwig Mies van der Rohe, Monument to the November Revolution, Berlin Lichtenberg, 1926. Photomontage with clay model by Oswald Herzog. Gelatin silver print, 6 1/4 × 9 in. (16 × 23 cm). Photograph by Curt Rehbein.

executed. Regarding the formal approach, Mies (or at least photographer Arthur Koester, in his choice of angle) might have taken inspiration from Richard Herre's poster for the 1924 Werkbund exhibition in Stuttgart (figure 3.23).

For the monument, Mies used clinker bricks (similar to the ones at the Wolf House)—that is, bricks fired for a long time at high temperatures, a process that melts some clay components and thus hardens and darkens the brick. Clinker was used only sporadically before World War I, but came into fashion with the expressionism of the 1920s.[49] The brick courses do not follow the strict order of a particular bond, but rather mix headers and runners somewhat arbitrarily, with occasional full rows of headers. This might hint at the fact that the Sozialistische Baubetriebe (Socialist Building Associations) that executed the structure employed nonskilled workers alongside trained masons. In all likelihood, the structure had a core of concrete with embedded steel reinforcements to hold the protruding parts and support the rowlock course at the bottom of each projecting unit (which clashed with the regular height of adjacent courses). Bricks probably also served as formwork, and the liquid concrete would be cast into a shell of bricks.

Construction of the monument was completed by June 1926, and the official inauguration, which Mies attended, took place on July 11, 1926. A reviewer for *Die Rote Fahne* was impressed with its immense monumentality, but reported some initial hesitancy toward it:

> Colossal blocks are piled up in an irregular way. The monument is executed in dark hard-fired bricks, whose joints are painted black, giving it a gloomy, but ultimately all the more powerful appearance.... The first impression of the monument is surprising. It stands almost too massive in front of the 43 graves in front. But once that first impression is overcome, one realizes that this form is truly the correct expression for such a monument to the revolution. As critical as it was seen at first by the participants [at the opening] because of its unusual form, there was unanimous enthusiasm for this tremendous work in the end.[50]

1927   Stuttgart Weissenhof Exhibition

In 1924, the German Werkbund began planning for another major exhibition with a focus on architecture, after the inaugural exhibition in Cologne ten years earlier had been cut short by the onset of World War I. The Cologne exhibition had consisted entirely of temporary model buildings (of different types) and had only German participants (such as Walter Gropius, Bruno Taut, and Hermann Muthesius—the only exception being Henry van de Velde, who was, however, teaching in Weimar at the time). The new exhibition would complement its predecessor by being permanent, international, and tackling only one overarching topic, namely housing, in conjunction with an exploration of new building methods and materials and a survey of the building industry. In that latter respect, it continued the tradition of a *Bauausstellung* (building exhibition) or *Baumesse* (construction fair). The first of these exhibitions, the *Internationale Baufachausstellung* of 1913 in Leizpig, a "World's Fair for Building and Dwellings," was an important precedent, since its permanent, exemplary housing estate of forty-eight single-family and twenty-four apartment buildings formed the core of the city's garden suburb of Marienbrunn. Other cities had held similar, smaller building exhibitions, such as in Munich (1908) and Stuttgart (1908 and 1924). The success of these earlier initiatives convinced local industrialist and politician Peter Bruckmann, a cofounder of the Werkbund, and his friend Karl Lautenschlager, Stuttgart's mayor, of the advantages of another such enterprise. They suggested the development of a permanent housing estate, which would present models for modern living under the title *Die Wohnung* (The Dwelling). Bruckmann and Lautenschlager wrote:

> The drive toward efficiency in every aspect of our lives, has not ignored the question of housing, and the economic conditions of our time forbid extravagance and force us to achieve maximum results with minimum expenditure. This means using materials and technologies in the construction of apartments, and in the housing industry in general, that reduce costs as well as simplifying housekeeping and improving living conditions as a whole. Consistent encouragement of such efforts will also mean

< Figure 3.22. Ludwig Mies van der Rohe, *Monument to the November Revolution*, Berlin Lichtenberg, 1926. View from the front. Gelatin silver print, 10 × 8 in. (25.4 × 20.3 cm). Photograph by Arthur Koester.

Figure 3.23. Richard Herre, poster for the Werkbund exhibition *Die Form*, Stuttgart, Germany, 1924. Color lithograph on paper, 39 1/4 × 26 in. (99.8 × 66 cm). Staatsgalerie Stuttgart, Graphische Sammlung.

improvement in big-city housing, a better way of life in general, and accordingly a stronger national economy.[51]

Lautenschlager offered an attractive, city-owned site on the outskirts of Stuttgart, called Am Weissenhof, with a southeastern slope and views over the city, and funded the enterprise. The city expansion department conducted a feasibility study, which showed that twenty-nine single-family houses (in duplex and row formations) and a fourteen-unit apartment block could comfortably be accommodated, and the project received the blessings of Stuttgart's city council. It was an urban plan of great clarity, its eight duplex units accessible from opposite ends. As mentioned above, possibly thanks to Lilly Reich's prominent role on the Werkbund's executive board, Mies had been announced as artistic advisor, together with Hans Poelzig and Walter Curt Behrendt, editor of the Werkbund journal *Die Form*, after the board meeting on March 30, 1925. Mies later became the director and worked closely with Reich on all aspects.

Trouble emerged soon after Mies presented his alternative to the city's feasibility study. He submitted a sketch for its urban plan at a 1:200 scale in September 1925. Clearly, other projects on his desk at the time left their traces. Mies used the same corner abutment of rectangular blocks that he was developing simultaneously for his Berlin housing project at Afrikanische Strasse, and the model showed the irregular, staggered assembly of rectangular blocks that were the key element at the memorial for Rosa Luxemburg and Karl Liebknecht (figure 3.24). "The whole thing a sculpture!" Mies's collaborator Sergius Ruegenberg later recalled.[52] Most importantly, though, the arrangement of individual plots carefully followed and articulated the slope and its contour lines, creating a dense sequence of open terraces accessed by stairs and framed by staggered cubes, like so many Wolf Houses pushed together.

Mies wrote: "The layout is not at all meant to be final, because it will ultimately depend on the individual ground plans; but it does show what we are aiming for, and I believe it will be entirely adequate for negotiating purposes."[53] While the city expansion department

Figure 3.24. Ludwig Mies van der Rohe, first version of urban layout for the Weissenhof Estate, Stuttgart, Germany, 1925. Model.

was delighted with the increased density (and thus higher rental income) of Mies's plan and welcomed the general concept as a "pioneer architectural achievement," local architects were not impressed.[54] Not only were they unhappy that a little-known Berlin architect had received a plum commission on their own turf and paid for with their city's money, they also had doubts about the plan's feasibility.

For Paul Schmitthenner, the "formulaic" design resembled Italian hill villages, but did nothing to address "the rationalization of the housing question."[55] Paul Bonatz, an older colleague of Schmitthenner at the architecture school, nine years Mies's senior and vastly more experienced, wrote that the "assemblage of flat cubes" on a "succession of horizontal terraces" looked more "like a suburb of Jerusalem than dwellings in Stuttgart."[56] In sum:

> The whole thing is impractical, entirely based on decorative considerations, and in realistic terms impossible to execute. The utilities, retaining walls, terracing and so forth, would be roughly doubled, by comparison with building two simple rows of houses. Since I have a conviction that nothing but amateurism is shown by a man of whom I know nothing but a drawing of a skyscraper, and I have the impression that the plan is being handled in a completely impractical way, I, as an instructor at the Hochschule, regard it as my duty to protest and fight against it with all due force.[57]

A majority within the Stuttgart section of the Werkbund, however, was willing to let the Berlin leadership have its way, and Bonatz was sidelined. Other conservative architects, such as Schmitthenner, left the Stuttgart Werkbund in protest and were replaced by younger architects sympathetic to the modern movement. Richard Döcker was one of them. Eight years Mies's junior, he had been a student and associate of Bonatz, and had started his own very successful office, building a number of housing estates and a spectacular modernist hospital in Waiblingen. Weeks earlier, he had accepted an offer to join the organization Der Ring, which Mies had founded with Hugo Häring two years earlier (then called Zehner-Ring). Döcker, while not yet a Werkbund member, had published a long article about his own work and modern architectural conviction in *Die Form* in January 1926.[58] He must have assumed that Mies considered him an ally and would listen to his concerns. He confessed that, similar to his teacher Bonatz, he had been "startled" by Mies's proposal, since the siting of plots and houses was "so capricious that some rooms would never get either light or air." And he offered his help designing a new proposal that would be "realistic, practical, achievable, economic and organic."[59] Indignant, Mies rejected Döcker's offer and explained with considerable bluster that he had only shown the

> general forming principle, from which it would be possible to deduce the type and character of the development, but emphatically not such a thing as house sizes….Did you seriously suppose it possible that I would build rooms without light or ventilation, or that I would not give the buildings the right aspect to the sun?…At Weissenhof I consider it necessary to embark on a new approach, because I believe that the "New Home" will extend beyond four walls…I want to break new ground. This, for me, is the point, the only point, of our work. All the rest we could safely have left to Herr Bonatz and Herr Schmitthenner. These two have made it all too clear how they define a building problem. I would not waste an hour of my time on such work….Building to me is a thing of the mind: it is creative, not in details but in essentials.[60]

This rebuttal was the beginning of a long-lasting animosity between Mies and Döcker, which contributed greatly to the difficulties in planning and executing the exhibition. Bonatz and Döcker were, of course, correct in pointing out the complexities and impracticalities in Mies's first proposal, and after a number of iterations (without Döcker's input) over the following year, in the summer of 1926, Mies's plan ended up looking similar to the design that the city's planning office had put forward in the first place. Mies's evocative elevation drawing of July 1, 1926, still showed staggered references to the Wolf House, but also a large, central apartment block as the backbone of the entire arrangement (figure 3.25). Its dark color suggests that Mies thought of building it in brick. In any event, the planning had progressed sufficiently for a vote in the city council to move ahead on July 29, 1926.

Members of five parties of a broad political range were in favor. Only the Communists objected, saying:

> The building of villas is something that we may safely leave to private capital, or in other words to those who want to live in them. We cannot agree to experimental building within the framework of the public housing program, paid for by city funds.... We therefore propose...that the monies set aside for the Werkbund project be used in their entirety for the provision of 120 dwelling units at a cost of 10,000 marks each, and that these dwellings be placed on the housing market without delay. This would be an answer to the needs of the overwhelming majority of those in Stuttgart who are seeking homes. And above all we would be relieved of the odium of building villas for the affluent and banishing the underprivileged to a separate neighborhood.[61]

Döcker continued to needle Mies with condescending advice, stating the obvious when Mies had not provided detailed drawings for his apartment building by mid-December 1926: "For your designs, I would recommend drawing sections and basement and roof-level plans, as well as front and rear elevations corresponding to the lay of the land."[62] When Mies finally submitted the first set of drawings for his own building, it included twenty-four apartments instead of the fourteen the city expansion office had foreseen—thus offering the prospect of increased rental income (figure 3.26). In pursuit of additional savings, city officials asked Mies to reduce the length of his housing block, from about 276 to 236 feet (84 to 72 meters), while keeping the same number of units. Mies had to give up an intended store on the first floor and reduce the size of half the apartments.

For the Weissenhof Estate, Mies introduced a number of new elements that differed from his social housing project at Berlin's Afrikanische Strasse. There were generous roof gardens, flexible apartment layouts, and continuous, tall ribbon windows in slender steel frames (rather than the common wood frames of different sizes) (figures 3.27, 3.28). We are

Figure 3.25. Ludwig Mies van der Rohe, drawing of second version of urban layout for the Weissenhof Estate, Stuttgart, Germany, 1925. Site elevation study from east, 1926. Pencil on tracing paper, 16 1/2 × 45 1/4 in. (41.9 × 114.9 cm). Museum of Modern Art, New York. The Mies van der Rohe Archive, gift of the architect.

Figure 3.26. Ludwig Mies van der Rohe, apartment house, ground-floor plan. Weissenhof Estate, Stuttgart, Germany, 1926. Pencil on print, 11 1/2 × 35 3/4 in. (29.2 × 90.8 cm). Museum of Modern Art, New York. The Mies van der Rohe Archive, gift of the architect.

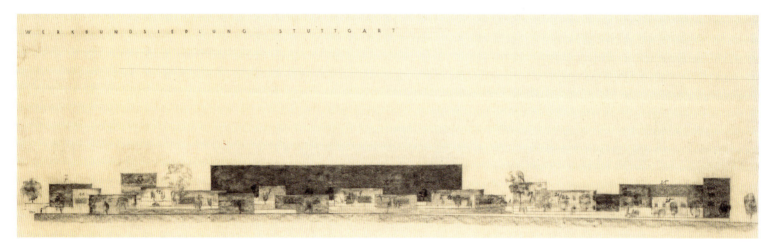

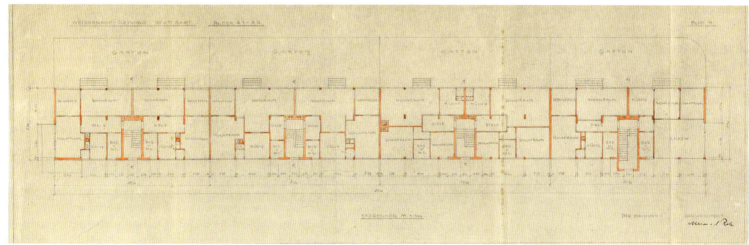

Figure 3.27. Ludwig Mies van der Rohe, apartment house, Weissenhof Estate, Stuttgart, Germany, 1926–27. Western façade with entrances and stair wells. Gelatin silver print, 6 5/8 × 8 7/8 in. (16.7 × 22.5 cm). Photograph by Dr. Otto Lossen & Co.

Figure 3.28. Ludwig Mies van der Rohe, apartment house, Weissenhof Estate, Stuttgart, Germany, 1926–27. Eastern façade with roof terraces. Gelatin silver print, 6 5/8 × 8 7/8 in. (16.7 × 22.5 cm). Photograph by Dr. Otto Lossen & Co.

reminded of the relentless ribbons of steel-frame windows in his Concrete Office Building project of 1923—one of many such transfers from utilitarian, commercial architecture into the domestic realm, increasingly typical for Mies at the time. He might have also been encouraged by Le Corbusier's design for his Double House at the Weissenhof Estate, which also featured roof gardens and continuous ribbon windows, albeit much slimmer (figure 3.29). Le Corbusier had submitted his designs on December 16, 1926—before Mies finished his own.

The most remarkable aspects of Mies's design for the Weissenhof Estate were the interior flexibility, as lightweight walls allowed for many different constellations, and its role as host to many designers. Mies himself designed three apartments, Lilly Reich one, and many of their acquaintances, such as Richard Lisker, Ferdinand Kramer, and Adolf Meyer from Frankfurt, and local designers such as Adolf Schneck, Camille Graeser, and the Rasch Brothers, presented interiors. The Swiss Werkbund presented six apartments.

Figure 3.29. Le Corbusier, Double House, Weissenhof Estate, Stuttgart, Germany, 1926–27.

Figure 3.30. Ludwig Mies van der Rohe and Le Corbusier at the Weissenhof exhibition, Stuttgart, Germany, 1927. Le Corbusier and Mies are second and third from the right.

Parallel to this process, after considerable wrangling, an international list of sixteen participating architects emerged, including Le Corbusier, J. J. P. Oud, Peter Behrens, Walter Gropius, Hans Scharoun, and Mart Stam (figure 3.30). The fact that only two Stuttgart architects (Richard Döcker and Adolf Schneck) were given commissions once again did not please the local group. But at least among the interior design firms, which helped to fit out individual apartments, the majority were from Stuttgart.

The exhibition, which opened on July 23, 1927, found a broad echo and greatly helped to spread the gospel of modern architecture (figure 3.31). The design rules that Mies had enforced, such as flat roofs, white stucco, and no roof overhangs, led to a uniform appearance that suggested an international modern movement of great coherence.

Architects and builders generally lacked experience dealing with flat roofs and walls unprotected from the rain due to the absence of roof overhangs. As a result, walls suffered from severe moisture penetration and subsequent discoloration and cracks in the stucco. The flat roofs had to be repaired several times in the following years. The slender steel-frame windows in Mies's block settled unevenly, leading to leaks and drafts. The west-facing bedrooms, exposed to the afternoon sun, heated up considerably, as they were unprotected by blinds or shutters. Mies's building was not finished when the exhibition opened, largely due to his tardiness in providing final plans. It was finally ready to receive visitors on September 6, 1927 (six weeks after the opening). The outside scaffolding had been removed for the opening celebrations, and thus Mies's block remained in its gray, unpainted stucco until the exhibition was over (see figures 3.27, 3.28).[63]

A number of unsightly failings such as cracks and moist walls were some of the reasons why photography (even sketching) by any visitors was strictly prohibited (figure 3.32). Only official photography by the studio of Dr. Otto Lossen & Co. (no doubt carefully vetted by Mies's office) was allowed over the course of the exhibition.[64]

Among the most prominent critics of the Weissenhof experiment was Hermann Muthesius, cofounder of the Werkbund and brilliant designer of comfortable homes in Berlin's suburbs. He noted sarcastically: "The daily use of the buildings will clarify for us, if, indeed the new generation, for which one apparently builds, will spend a significant amount of time on the roof, as in Arab countries, if they really want to freeze in front of large window panes in the winter, and if they want to expand their communal living in such a way that there is no enclosed room in the house, where one could concentrate, and if one really wants to give up all closets."[65] About Mies's housing block in particular, he wrote:

Figure 3.31. Weissenhof Estate, Stuttgart, Germany, 1925–27. The house by Hans Scharoun is in the foreground right, the two houses by Le Corbusier are on the left, and Mies van der Rohe's apartment house is central in the background. Gelatin silver print, 6 5/8 × 8 7/8 in. (16.7 × 22.5 cm). Photograph by Dr. Otto Lossen & Co, taken at the time of the opening.

It is the New Form that ordains the flat roof and causes acceptance of all the manifold still-to-be-foreseen disadvantages which that brings in its train. It is the New Form that leads us to the inordinate overlighting of rooms, because it dictates to its exponents that, at all costs, uninterrupted strips of window must run all around the house. It is the New Form that leaves the external walls defenseless against the weather by avoiding the roof overhangs which have hitherto been customary in our climate. All these things have absolutely nothing to do with rationalization, or with economy, or with structural necessity. These are purely formal issues. The ideal is the building of cubic masses.[66]

How much Mies anticipated such potential criticism became obvious when he wrote an open letter in January 1927 to the new editor of the Werkbund journal *Die Form*, Walter Riezler, asking him to change the journal's name—as he found it distracting. After all, he asked, "Is form really the goal? Isn't it in reality the result of a design process? Isn't that process the most important thing?" Riezler responded diplomatically that the name could not be changed, now that it was established, and that process and form would ideally be inseparable, while "formalism" (occasionally also visible in works of modern architecture, he pointed out) was to be avoided at all cost, just as much as formally unresolved solutions.[67]

Marie-Elisabeth Lüders, parliamentarian and prominent women's rights activist, noted Mies's ignorance of an apartment building's functionality. Lüders was truly an expert, having just founded the Reichsforschungsgesellschaft für Wirtschaftlichkeit im Bau- und Wohnungswesen (Reich Research Society for Economic Efficiency in Building and Housing), a government agency to explore affordable housing.[68] She noted, for example, that the large floor-to-ceiling windows at the stair landings blocked, when opened, the path of anyone going up or down. The sparse railings in front would not prevent children from climbing over or through them. Mies's uniformly high windows brought too much light for comfort into the living rooms, leading to overheating in the summer and freezing cold in the winter. They also, on occasion, heated up a pantry (spoiling any milk in the process) or blindingly lit up a bathroom. Stoves were too small and in a dark corner, windows could not be reached for cleaning, and there was no room for coats, shoes, or umbrellas near the entrance. Lüders concluded that public money should not go toward any housing project where women were not consulted.[69]

In great contrast, critic Max Osborn of the Berlin-based *Vossische Zeitung* found nothing but praise for Weissenhof, focusing, though, entirely on the outer appearance: "This

Figure 3.32. Ludwig Mies van der Rohe, apartment block, Weissenhof Estate, Stuttgart, Germany, 1925–27. Oblique view of the west (entrance) façade showing discoloration from humidity, 1932. Royal Institute of British Architects.

international group of buildings speaks the artistic language of our time as a whole and in all its details. There has never been anything like this. We have never been able to gain such a concrete idea of the possibilities of modern architectural expression."[70] The Werkbund exhibition did not achieve any of its alleged goals—namely, to demonstrate new ways of life, a new urban approach to housing, and new building techniques. But, as it was broadly and admiringly discussed, it ended up being one of the most successful advertising vehicles for the modern movement.

1927   Glasraum and Linoleumraum

Mies and Reich's Glasraum at the Stuttgart Werkbund exhibition in 1927 had been commissioned by the plate-glass industry to demonstrate the latest technological achievements and suggest new applications beyond display windows at department stores (figure 3.33). It presented a sequence of openly connected spaces between wall-high clear and translucent glass plates in different shades of gray that served as walls, windows, screens, and space dividers. The Glasraum stood inside a large exhibition hall and was evenly lit via suspended lamps above a ceiling of stretched white canvas, with a colorful linoleum floor underfoot. Sparsely furnished, the sequence of spaces had a vaguely domestic—but also rather unhomely— feeling. There was a suggestion of indoor and outdoor areas (indicated by the absence of a canvas ceiling): a small courtyard contained a sculpture by Wilhelm Lehmbruck, while the living room looked onto a second courtyard populated by a rather ominous lineup of rubber plants. The most striking elements were the lightness of construction, the reflections and different degrees of transparency, and the eerie evenness of the light, as if on a bright but overcast day. Siegfried Kracauer, the prominent cultural critic, observed astutely, if skeptically:

Figure 3.33. Ludwig Mies van der Rohe and Lilly Reich, Glasraum, Werkbund exhibition, Stuttgart, Germany, 1927.

In the exhibition halls we find a strange space, thought up by Mies van der Rohe and Lilly Reich. Its walls consist of opal and darkened plates of glass. A glass box, translucent, infiltrated by its adjacent spaces...any movement magically conjures up shadow plays on the wall, disembodied silhouettes, hovering in mid-air and getting mixed up with the reflections in the actual glass space. Conjuring up such an impalpable mirage, changing with the light reflections just like a kaleidoscope, demonstrates that the new domestic architecture is not yet the final word.[71]

Terms such as "mirage" and "kaleidoscope" equated the exhibit with a house of mirrors at an amusement park. Clearly, Kracauer disproved of such distracting optical effects in a future home.

In contrast, Mies's Dutch colleague Theo van Doesburg applauded what Mies and Reich had accomplished—an architecture of space and surface, and in his view the best example of interior architecture at the Werkbund exhibition, conquering "the material with all of its traits, such as weightiness, resistance, and transience." This, according to van Doesburg, had broader implications: "Weighing the energy and character of materials against each other and proportioning them well, most certainly belongs to the essence of the new architecture. Only thus can modern architecture realize what it has to offer in involuntary beauty...the new ideal of an empty space and a pure surface comes closer to realization." When he emphasized the importance of surface over structure van Doesburg unintentionally exposed the rift between Mies's theory and practice: "The development of the ultimate surface is essential, from the first stone to the last stroke of paint. Every architect having a visual sense for construction knows this, and with this glass display Mies van der Rohe proved to be on top of this new problem...only the surface is important. Man does not live within the construction or architectural skeleton, but

Figure 3.34. Ludwig Mies van der Rohe and Lilly Reich, Café Samt und Seide (Satin and Silk Cafe), *Die Mode der Dame* (Ladies' Fashion) trade show, Berlin, 1927.

touches architecture essentially through its ultimate surface…the new ideal of an empty space and a pure surface is coming closer to realization all the time."[72] Indeed, Mies had celebrated the surfaces of walls, windows, and ceilings while remaining unconcerned about expressing the structural means. The suspended canvas ceiling was weightless and transparent, creating entirely unrealistic lighting conditions. This formalism went so far that Alexander Dorner discovered "obvious similarities" between the Glasraum and the Raum der Abstrakten (Space for Abstract Artists) that El Lissitzky had recently installed at Dorner's Hanover museum.[73]

The Glasraum's floor consisted of different-colored linoleum and was accessible from the adjacent Linoleumraum, also designed by Mies and Reich, in which samples of colored linoleum were displayed on walls and floors. While linoleum, a product from the natural amber of trees, cork, and chalk, had been manufactured in Germany, in particular in Delmenhorst, since 1882, it had for the first decades generally been used in kitchens and bathrooms, then in the parlors of working-class homes, often with an ornamental, colorful pattern, as if to imitate an oriental rug on the parquet floor of a bourgeois living room. In recent years, the linoleum industry had consciously sought out modern architects and entered the discourse of modernity. Peter Behrens and Bruno Paul (both teachers and employers of Mies) had designed buildings and patterns for them, and members of the industry had helped to found the German Werkbund. Monochrome colors were introduced, and several linoleum companies joined forces in 1926 in the Delmenhorster Linoleum-Werke (DLW). The 1927 linoleum stand in Stuttgart, which showed the different monochrome colors on the floor and in samples, was followed by another, more elaborate stand in Leipzig (see below), which employed the large glass plates and cruciform columns that would become key elements of the Barcelona Pavilion and the Tugendhat House (see figures 3.51, 3.52).

1927   Café Samt und Seide

There was a similar emphasis on space and surface over structure in Lilly Reich and Mies van der Rohe's German silk section at the large trade fair, *Die Mode der Dame* (Ladies' Fashion), in the fall of that year (September 20 to October 9, then extended to October 30) (figure 3.34). There, the open spaces for a temporary café called "Samt und Seide" (Satin and Silk) were framed by silk curtains on horizontal metal rods suspended via cables from the ceiling. These curtains were of different colors, heights, and widths; two of them formed semicircular enclosures, while others presented the equivalent of a freestanding wall—disconnected, independent, surrounded by open space. Mies's newly designed chairs and tables populated the café.[74]

1927   Furniture Design

Mies seems to have habitually commissioned custom-made furniture for his early houses. Several of the pieces for the Werner House have survived (see figures 1.48, 1.49), and the interior photo of the Perls House shows a resemblance of the ornamental chair back rests with the window railings upstairs. In all likelihood, those pieces evolved in conversations with a cabinetmaker, rather than being properly and individually designed. Mies and Lilly Reich seem to have designed a first group of chairs with a table and a low bookshelf for the Wolf House (see figure 3.13), and Mies had a second set produced for his own apartment (figure 3.35). They were inspired by Bruno Paul's abovementioned *Typenmöbel*, simplified further and featuring a dark walnut veneer to cover any structural joints and unify the appearance of legs and tabletop.

In the run-up to the Weissenhof exhibition, Mies was exposed to new ideas. Dutch participant Mart Stam had experimented with chairs made out of commercial metal tubes, fortified inside with additional steel after their connections initially broke off, while Marcel Breuer was working on his own version of a tubular steel chair at the Bauhaus in Dessau. Mies, who had made essential reductivism one of his key working principles, found an immediate appeal in the idea of replacing the legs, seat support, and backrest with one continuous steel tube. Heinz Rasch and Bodo Rasch from Stuttgart, who had become friendly with Mies during that time, worked on wooden cantilevered chairs. When the show opened, the Rasch Brothers introduced their *Sitzfleischstuhl*, a cantilevered chair from

Figure 3.35. Ludwig Mies van der Rohe and Lily Reich, furniture for the Wolf House and his own apartment at Am Karlsbad 24, ca. 1926–27. Wood, veneer, leather. Photograph by Thomas Dix, 1998. Private collection.

Figure 3.36. Ludwig Mies van der Rohe, M10 and M20 chairs, 1927.

lacquered plywood, and Mies showed his MR 10 and MR 20 chairs, a great improvement over Stam's idea, by bending the steel tube in a large semicircle in front, which provided the desired elasticity (figure 3.36).[75] The semicircles came with the disadvantage of requiring more space than conventional chairs (inevitably colliding underneath a small table) and causing accidents when people's feet got caught in the protruding half circle as they got up.

Mies was the first one in the group who thought of patenting his cantilevered chair design—and thus before the colleagues from whose ideas he had profited. Mies included in his patent a paragraph that stated that his design was preferably from steel tubes, but added, "It is, indeed, possible to make it also out of suitably strong and resistible kind of wood."[76] Heinz Rasch recalled asking Mies for permission to produce his own cantilevered chair: "Well—I had hoped to get an authorization—I showed him photos of the models that had appeared in the meantime and the text of my trademark and promised him a share in it—but then I had a nasty surprise! With unusual vehemence, Mies said that the patent was his, so there was nothing for me to get out of it since he was the one who had all the rights!"[77]

1928   Adam Department Store

Several projects unfolded during the year 1928, while Mies and Lilly Reich began working on the Barcelona World's Fair, before and after they had been named lead architects in early June. The Adam family had owned a fabric and clothing business in Berlin since 1863. The founder's four sons ran the store since 1905, with Fritz Adam in charge of promotional activities, and his brother Georg managing the finances. Fritz had been instrumental in steering the firm toward fashion and sports clothing and equipment. Both brothers were in charge of an envisioned new building that would replace the neo-Renaissance structure at the intersection of Leipziger Strasse and Friedrichstrasse.[78] Changed building codes now allowed for the permission of additional floors on a case-by-case basis, and thus the opportunity for substantial real estate income at the city's most prominent location drove the project. Accordingly, the competition brief specified that only the lower floors would be used as a department store, while the floors above could be flexibly used as office spaces. Initially, only Peter Behrens, Heinrich Straumer, and Hans Poelzig were invited to submit proposals. All three were significantly older than Mies, ran big, well-established offices in the city, and had experience with large structures. Mies heard from Berlin building director Martin Wagner about the competition and asked Fritz Adam on April 2, 1928, to be considered as well.[79] Adam first turned him down, but then relented, perhaps pressured by Wagner and mindful of the fact that he would need Wagner's approval for building permits and height dispenses. The 1:100 drawings and 1:50 models were delivered by early July, and each contestant was awarded 2,000 Reichsmarks and reimbursed for the costs of the model.

In his design, Straumer (known among Berliners mostly for the Messeturm of 1926—the city's answer to the Eiffel Tower) stayed close to the existing cornice height by providing seven stories. Judging from his elegant brass model (its photo is all that remains), the prominent vertical piers are placed closely enough to lend an overall verticality to the façade and to allow single-pane windows between them. Poelzig also stuck to the existing cornice height, but set back two tiers of additional floors at the corner. The protruding verticals of his muscular structural system span wider than Straumer's and show abundant advertising on the heavy transoms above the ribbon windows. Behrens won the competition—he knew the Adam brothers personally and was most likely familiar with their ambitions.[80] He provided the greatest height (ten floors at the corner—in the eyes of Berliners, a veritable "skyscraper") and thus the most lucrative solution. Both versions of his design show a dense vertical grid covering the façades. With the competition results in hand, the Adams began to build their case for a building height dispensation, suggesting that Behrens's ten-story tower would be mirrored soon across the street at the Moka Efti and Equitable buildings and would perfectly correspond to Behrens's towers at Alexanderplatz—the outcome of the recent competition there (see below).[81]

Mies's elegant prototype for a future department store probably never stood a chance, but it provided a glimpse into his evolving thinking about commercial buildings since his Friedrichstrasse Skyscraper designs. Mies provided display windows on the first floor and an opal glass envelope on the remaining floors (figure 3.37). In one of his most evocative statements, Mies told Fritz Adam that he should aim for open space, flexibility, exemplary light conditions, and "lots of advertising." Making a building such an "economic tool," Mies explained, required courage from both architect and client:

> I therefore suggest to make the skin out of glass and stainless steel. The first floor will be transparent, all other floors translucent. Walls from such opal glass provide a wonderfully mild, but bright and even light. At night, the whole thing becomes a luminous body and you can apply as much advertising as you want. You can write "For your summer travels," or "winter sports" or "Four Days of Sales." Such writing on an evenly lit background will always have a magical effect. For the back of the display windows I would also like to suggest plate glass, in particular in a gray color, as indicated in the model. Your store has to reflect the character of your business and be a perfect match with sailboats and automobiles, or, in other words, with modern times and the people that represent them.[82]

Mies's design was a direct response to the famous glass front of Bernhard Sehring's Tietz Department Store (1899–1900), just down the block on Leipziger Strasse (figure 3.38). An important difference lay in the fact that Sehring's glass curtain wall faced north, while Mies's faced south and would have caused enormous heat increase inside.

None of the required technical drawings for the project have survived—only a photo of his model, one sketch, and a photomontage, which was important to Mies, as he requested it back from the family in order to publish it (figure 3.39).[83] It made it just in time to be included in Arthur Korn's book *Glas im Bau und als Gebrauchsgegenstand* (Glass in Construction and as a Commodity) that same year, and a bit later the conservative journal *Der Baumeister* celebrated it as an example of new façade treatments.[84] In early 1930, art historian Curt Gravekamp published a long, elegiac description of the project in *Das Kunstblatt*. Instead of treating the project as a missed opportunity, he suggested that it was about to "rise from the streets of asphalt at the center of the metropolis." While its walls consisted entirely of windows, Gravekamp mused, the glass here was neither wall nor window, but something completely different—this ancient material had found its ultimate destiny. While it had served in the choirs of Gothic cathedrals, it was also the most essential equivalent of modernity: "A modern commercial building with transparent glass walls is the contemporary form of spiritual realism, anchored in the social bedrock of our time."[85] Due to the onset of the Depression, the Adam family had not yet decided to move forward, and Mies—whose status as a leading modernist had been greatly enhanced by the success in Barcelona— might have hoped for another chance. Ultimately, the economic situation and then the

Figure 3.37. Ludwig Mies van der Rohe, Adam Department Store project, at the intersection of Leipziger Strasse and Friedrichstrasse, Berlin, 1928. Model. Private collection, London.

Figure 3.38. Bernhard Sehring, Tietz Department Store, Leipziger Strasse, Berlin, 1899–1900. Contemporary postcard.

> Figure 3.39. Ludwig Mies van der Rohe, Adam Department Store project at the intersection of Leipziger Strasse and Friedrichstrasse, Berlin, 1928. Photomontage, airbrushed gouache on gelatin silver print, 8 3/8 × 6 1/4 in. (20.3 × 15.2 cm). Private collection.

persecution of the Jewish population by the Nazis after 1933 prevented the execution of the project altogether.

1928 Stuttgart Bank and Office Building Competition

After submitting the Adam project, and awaiting the family's decision, Mies applied the exact same solution to another competition immediately afterward (figure 3.40). The city of Stuttgart was inviting architects to submit proposals for a large, mixed-use commercial building in a prominent location across from the railroad station. A bank and a department store were the intended clients, but some architects also demonstrated their designs' flexibility by suggesting restaurants, cafés, or apartments inside.

In his accompanying note, Mies could not help himself and put in a humorous sidesweep against Paul Bonatz, with whom he had had a rather public falling-out over the Weissenhof exhibition. In describing the advantages of the translucent, but not transparent, glass in his design across from Bonatz's railroad station, Mies pointed out that "a view of an unpleasant environment will be prevented" from inside. And he emphasized that his architecture of "quiet" and "lightness" was a counterweight to the heavily embossed station. Otherwise, just as in Berlin, Mies emphasized the suitability for advertising:

> The author...believes that advertising will become a factor more and more relevant in economy and that it will soon be the reason for changes in the arrangement of the facades of buildings. The author bases his arrangement of the building's exterior on this idea. He tries, as the model clearly shows, to keep the whole front empty for advertisements. Thus, he also tries to use the illumination of the interior for the effectiveness of the advertising. The building would glow at night. Any kind of advertisement could then be installed on these glowing glass walls.[86]

Figure 3.40. Stuttgart Bank and Office Building. Competition entry by Ludwig Mies van der Rohe, 1928. Photograph by Curt Rehbein, ca. 1928. Gelatin silver print of a photomontage, 5 1/8 × 8 1/8 in. (13 × 20.6 cm). Museum of Modern Art, New York. The Mies van der Rohe Archive, gift of the architect.

There had been eighty participants, and prizes were announced in early January. Mies won an honorable mention and 1,500 Reichsmark prize money; the jury called his glass façades "interesting but problematic," due to the insufficient illumination at the banking hall. Local critics noted the repetition of Mies's "favorite idea of a glass building" or scolded him for ignoring the historic context. Mies's design was published soon after by Wilhelm Lotz in *Die Form* and defended as a "simple and calm structure…individualistic and crystal clear."[87] *Das Kunstblatt* praised the "ingenious superiority" of Mies's design and chided the jury's lack of courage to admit to it.[88] Bonatz had the last laugh. While his design did not receive first prize, it ended up being the one executed.

1928–30   Esters and Lange Houses

Two neighboring houses in Krefeld for two silk manufacturers, who were friends and collaborators, are the most direct successors in Mies's oeuvre to the Wolf House in Guben (see figures 3.13–3.15).[89] The clinker-brick buildings show a related cubic order and formal language. They had a comparable, somewhat larger room program, and in each case, at the east end, a lower-lying service courtyard with a three-story building section for the kitchen and service staff.

Hermann Lange and Josef Esters had traveled to Guben at the end of August 1927 with Hermann John, Mies's office manager, and had inspected the Wolf House. "Both gentlemen were enthusiastic," John reported to Mies, "but cannot be dissuaded from the resolution that the individual rooms must be separated by doors."[90] Over the following months, Mies and John drew up the plans for the Esters House, very much in the spirit of the Wolf House. The plans were approved by the client on July 20, 1928, but not executed.

While Mies did not repeat the feature of three different ceiling heights, which had made the Guben project both spatially intriguing and complicated, he adopted and heightened other essential characteristics. The first Esters design was three stories tall at street level, and thanks to the sunken courtyard on the eastern side, reached four stories there (figure 3.41). Mies had a small model made. It was a remarkable design—a stern, rigidly vertical façade toward the street led first into a central, windowless hall, which gave access to the service wing and staircase up, but also to four different living rooms, a children's playroom, Mrs.

Figure 3.41. Ludwig Mies van der Rohe, Esters House, first project, Krefeld, Germany, 1928. Side elevations. Blueprint, 12 5/8 × 16 3/4 in. (32 × 42.5 cm). Der Oberbürgermeister, Stadtarchiv Krefeld.

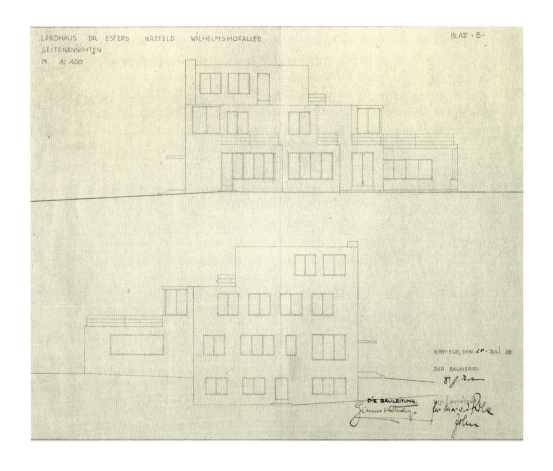

Esters's study, and the dining room. Only the latter two were interconnected with a large sliding door. The three westernmost rooms had both southern and western windows. The dining room connected to a southwest-facing terrace, protected eastward by a wall with a large window. The second floor contained the family's bedrooms, all with access to southern terraces, four bathrooms, and a guestroom. The third floor had three rooms for servants, another guestroom, and two rooms for storage and the drying of laundry. Additional servants' rooms faced the lower courtyard. In a departure from Mies's more conventional homes and the recent Wolf House, servants and family shared the same central staircase. The main entrances for both servants and inhabitants were of the same size and located next to each other on the street side, but they were marked by a subtle difference: only the main entrance had a protective roof above. The third floor, set back on the garden side, would have been part of a cascading southern front with a sequence of set-back terraces. In addition, the rooms on each floor receded in depth toward the west in order to provide maximum access to afternoon sun. Mies was familiar with the weather in Krefeld, just an hour north of his birthplace of Aachen, and its many overcast days. Harnessing the sunlight as much as possible was imperative. Never before or after did Mies tend so carefully to the impact of sunlight in one of his designs.

After Josef Esters had approved Mies's design in July 1928, Hermann Lange stepped in. Ten years older than Esters, he was the dominant figure in their friendship and had imagined two neighboring houses of equal and modest height and appearance. He objected to the three-story elevation. In haste, a new design was developed and applied to both projects, with only slight differences, and submitted for approval in October 1928. Both buildings ended up being merely two stories tall, wider in their layout, and with north-facing central halls for the display of art—although only Lange was a serious collector (figures 3.42, 3.43). The servants' rooms, formerly on the third floor with balcony access, were now much smaller, squeezed onto the second floor, where they shared circulation space with the family.

Ground was broken in October 1928, but debates about the design continued through the winter, while construction was on hold.[91] In January 1929, Lange suggested to build niches in the main hall for the presentation of sculptures. Mies managed to dissuade him from this idea, as he feared that the space would lose its calm disposition. Instead, he had four heavy travertine consoles cantilever out from the walls to carry three busts by Wilhelm Lehmbruck and a medieval figure. This was not an ideal solution either, as the

Figure 3.42. Ludwig Mies van der Rohe, Lange House, Krefeld, Germany, 1928–30. Street façade.

sculptures were too close to the wall, insufficiently lit, and presented precarious protrusions at eye level.

Hermann Lange was one of the most significant collectors of contemporary art in Germany, owning major pieces by Picasso, Georges Braque, Fernand Léger, and Wassily Kandinsky and by prominent German artists such as Paul Klee, Oskar Kokoschka, Emil Nolde, Lyonel Feininger, and many others.[92] A special storage room in the basement was dedicated to his collection, and a longitudinal opening in the floor above allowed easy transport into the gallery. Apparently, Lange enjoyed changing the display of his art often to surprise returning visitors. The need for frequent rotation was also caused by the fact that the central hall was not ideal for displaying art (figure 3.44). While its northern window provided even, indirect light, as the main circulation space it accessed five different doors and provided comparatively little wall space. An organ was built into the western wall and hidden behind a curtain. At night, the evenly spaced ceiling lights did nothing to highlight the art. A novelty was the hall's bookcase, recessed into and flush with the wall, thanks to a long steel girder hidden above it—an echo of the ribbon windows in the façade. The rooms on the garden side, with their large windows facing south and west, were too bright for precious paintings.

Hermann John's (and by extension Mies's) frustration with the design process was palpable when John expressed his hope "that we at least get *one* thing done in that house according to our vision."[93] It was probably around that time, in the winter of 1928–29, that Mies sketched out the garden view of the Esters House entirely dissolved in floor-to-ceiling windows. The building had already been reduced to its two floors and had become more horizontal in layout (figure 3.45). This was exactly the moment when Mies conceived the Barcelona Pavilion, the Tugendhat House, and the unbuilt Nolde House. "I wanted to

Figure 3.43. Ludwig Mies van der Rohe, Lange House, Krefeld, Germany, 1928–30. Garden façade with single-pane retractable windows on the first floor and open verandas on the eastern and western end.

Figure 3.44. Ludwig Mies van der Rohe, Lange House, Krefeld, Germany, 1928–30. Central hall with art collection.

Figure 3.45. Ludwig Mies van der Rohe, Esters House, Krefeld, Germany, 1928–30. Alternative garden façade. Pencil and pastel on paper, 14 1/4 × 23 3/4 in. (36.2 × 60.3 cm). Museum of Modern Art, New York. Mies van der Rohe Archive, gift of the architect.

make this house much more in glass, but the client did not like that. I had great trouble," Mies later recalled.[94]

Lange, at least, seems to have worked out a compromise with Mies and partially adopted the idea sketched out for the Esters House. There were six large, retractable windows on the first floor (figure 3.46). They did not reach quite from floor to ceiling, as heating units had to be accommodated in front of them. Windows of this size had previously only been used in commercial buildings and storefronts, such as Bohuslav Fuchs's Café Zéman in Brno (see figure 5.25), which Mies had probably seen on his first visit there. While a continuous open connection between rooms on the garden side was not realized, their external staggering with two-sided lighting to the south and west remained. The Lange House even carried the idea beyond the house itself by providing open, covered alcoves with a glazed window on the west and east flanks of the building. Especially the western terraces needed protection from the prevailing winds, while their windows still allowed access to the evening sun.

Each of the five bedrooms in the Lange House has its own interior bathroom, as in a modern hotel. The corridor in front of the single-span upper floor is lower, so that the bathrooms are lit and ventilated by skylights, while in the Esters House separate bathrooms are accessed across the corridor. A steel framework within the brick walls allowed greater freedom in load distribution. Compared to the Wolf House, some details were simplified: the dark clinker masonry, again used as a module, is now a simple block bond with alternating stretcher and header courses, instead of the Flemish bond used in the Wolf House. The mortar between the bricks is no longer strikingly white but dark gray, unifying the overall appearance. Each horizontal mortar joint has been scraped out diagonally so that a thin shadow line accentuates its darkness. The scroll layers that accentuated the roof edge have disappeared, and the balcony grilles have been greatly simplified. The

Figure 3.46. Ludwig Mies van der Rohe, Lange House, Krefeld, Germany, 1928–30. Interior view toward the garden with retractable window.

window frames are no longer made of white painted wood but out of much slimmer black metal profiles, making the transition from rough wall surface to glass reflection seem more abrupt. Hermann Lange died in 1942, and the family donated the house in 1955 to the city of Krefeld to be dedicated to the display of art. Josef Esters's house followed in 1966.

1928–29   Alexanderplatz Competition

In December 1928, Mies was invited by Berlin's urban planner, Martin Wagner, to submit a proposal for a redesign of Alexanderplatz, one of the busiest traffic nodes in the city. In a broadly eclectic mix of participants, Mies and the Luckhardt Brothers were most known for radical modern solutions, while Peter Behrens, the firm Mebes & Emmerich, Heinrich Müller-Erkelenz, and Johann Emil Schaudt had more experience and more moderate architectural tastes. Wagner had a clear vision for the "formal problem of a World City" and the resulting approach to a complicated intersection, such as Alexanderplatz. He took the unusual step of shepherding the participants toward his own vision by providing not only a plan of the anticipated solution, but also a detailed model (photographs by Arthur Koester were sent to the participants) (figure 3.47). A huge traffic circle would gather the incoming and outgoing traffic from five streets, and Wagner suggested a continuous façade above two of the incoming streets on its northeastern side (Neue Königstrasse and Landsberger Strasse).[95] The design was so complete and compelling that most participants were content with simply providing appropriate façades in their preferred patterns—except Mies, whose freestanding blocks eerily foreshadowed postwar reconstruction in German cities (and at Alexanderplatz).

Traffic circles were a fairly recent invention; while they consumed more space than traditional intersections, they promised continuous traffic flow and fewer accidents. Paris had introduced the first traffic circle at the Arc de Triomphe in 1906, followed by Washington, D.C.'s Thomas Circle in 1922. Both might have served as an inspiration. Wagner had taken on his role as *Stadtbaurat* (city councilor for architecture and urban planning) only two years before and had already made great strides with the planning of social housing projects. The planning of complicated intersections was new to him as well, and while he brilliantly imagined the continuity of street fronts, his envisioned traffic circle suffered from a fatal flaw. At five intersections, cars could join or leave the one-way, counterclockwise traffic flow. The two parallel tramlines in the center of two streets, however, were meant to continue straight through the heart of the circle, each crossing the vehicular traffic lanes twice perpendicularly. Thus, the circular flow would frequently be stopped to let trams pass.

The Luckhardts won the competition with a dynamic, fluid sequence of façades, bridging two streets and framing the traffic circle as suggested by Wagner. Curved edges and horizontal lines evoked continuous motion.[96] Peter Behrens had also designed

Figure 3.47. Model of Alexanderplatz, Berlin. Sample solution by Martin Wagner, 1928.

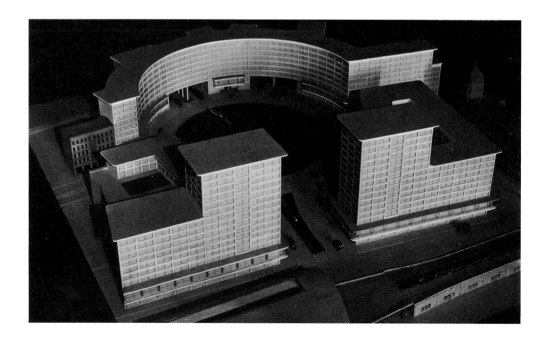

a monumental half circle on the square's northeastern side, flanked by two commercial wings on the southwestern side. Ultimately, it was Behrens who was invited by the investor to revise his proposal, and construction went ahead on Berolinahaus and Alexanderhaus, but not on the northeastern side of the circle. The world financial crisis put an end to the development.

Mies placed last. He had boldly ignored Wagner's limiting brief and vision. Working with urban planner Ludwig Hilberseimer, he arranged a set of eleven freestanding cubic volumes, instead of architecturally framing and containing the traffic circle. A central, sixteen-story tower was placed strategically on the western side of the new square and its huge traffic circle, thus effectively blocking the low western sun from the eyes of the drivers. While working on this proposal in early 1929, Mies was deeply immersed in his designs for the Barcelona Pavilion and the Tugendhat House. One cannot avoid seeing parallels between the commanding freestanding tower slab and the single onyx walls in Barcelona and Brno (figure 3.48, see also figures 4.15, 5.20). Mies went far beyond the scope Wagner had suggested and proposed a phalanx of six parallel apartment blocks along Alexanderstrasse (three are visible in the photomontage), lined up roughly in a north–south direction, thus providing all inhabitants with morning and evening sun. This meant, however—in a not exactly subtle political gesture—demolishing the city's huge police headquarters, an enormous brick building of 1890 called Die Rote Burg (The Red Castle) that was despised by many on the left.

The most interesting building in the aerial photomontage is shown directly adjacent to the railroad station. It has great similarity with Mies's 1923 Concrete Office Building, including a courtyard and the heavy concrete spandrels underneath the ribbon windows (see figure 2.18). It thus suggests a potential location for this design, and provided one example in Mies's taxonomy of façade solutions. The tall, sixteen-story tower slab was wrapped in the same glass curtain wall as his recent designs for the Adam Department Store or the Stuttgart Bank Building. For his office buildings, Mies showed both floor-to-ceiling glass walls and the concrete spandrels he had used in 1923. His apartment blocks received spandrels as well, and the vertical supports were moved to the surface of the façade in order to save space inside.

Most critics were not impressed with Mies's proposal, such as the Social Democratic *Vorwärts*, which noted Mies's "more expansive project with mighty cubic blocks, which, while providing a certain architectural greatness, still perpetuated the unfortunate disunity in the appearance of the square."[97] Critic Justus Bier declared Mies's approach fundamentally important but not applicable at Alexanderplatz, as private investors needed to see the project's profitability.[98] As was often the case, Mies's friend Ludwig Hilberseimer acted as a vocal supporter. Since seeing Le Corbusier's visionary plans for Paris in 1924, he had developed proposals for radically sequential housing and office blocks, which left their traces in Mies's design. Hilberseimer wrote in Martin Wagner's journal *Das Neue Berlin:* "Mies van der Rohe's project is the only one of the designs submitted that breaks through this rigid system (of frontages conforming to traffic flow) and attempts to organize the square independently of the traffic. The traffic lanes maintain their function, yet Mies has designed the square by grouping freestanding buildings according to architectural principles alone. By opening the streets wide, he achieves a new spaciousness which all the other projects lack."[99] He dismissed the façade architecture of the Luckhardts' winning entry and others who followed Wagner's ideas as a "stage set." Traffic should not be the driving force of architecture, he declared, in particular not the trams—the real traffic obstruction of Berlin.[100]

Wagner had been a supporter of Mies since their first collaboration, when Wagner's Bauhüttenbetriebe, a socialist building society, had executed his Afrikanische Strasse Housing Estate. Now, as the city's building deputy, he held considerable sway, and it is probably due to him that Mies was invited to both the Alexanderplatz competition, and that for a high-rise next to the Friedrichstrasse station shortly afterward, both administered by the Berliner Verkehrsgesellschaft (Berlin Transport Company).

1929 Friedrichstrasse Skyscraper Competition

January 1, 1929, marked a revolution in the management of Berlin's public transportation. Three large Berlin associations for urban buses, trams, and elevated trains were combined

Figure 3.48. Redesign of Alexanderplatz, Berlin.
Competition entry by Ludwig Mies van der Rohe,
1928. Photomontage.

in the Berliner Verkehrs AG, which introduced coordinated schedules and unified fares. It also invested in urban infrastructure and traffic planning. It had bought the triangular plot across from Friedrichstrasse Railroad Station, the site of the 1921 skyscraper competition, which inspired Mies's glass enclosed high-rise designs. While the previous competition had been open only to German architects in private practice who were members of the BDA (the German architects' association), this new competition was limited to just five architects: Mies van der Rohe, Erich Mendelsohn, Alfred Grenander, the firm of Mebes & Emmerich, and Heinrich Straumer. The competition was anonymous. Mendelsohn and Mebes & Emmerich shared the first prize. Both were remarkably mature renderings in high-rise design, anticipating stylistic tropes that would become prevalent in the immediate postwar period. Mebes & Emmerich placed two slabs shifted against each other with minimal overlap, accessible via a central stair and elevator core. A long, elegant passage led to a circular restaurant on the edge of the river. Mendelsohn suggested a single slab overlooking the river, accompanied by a six-story wing along the Friedrichstrasse.

Mies submitted two different designs under the code word "Red Circle." Critic Johannes Grobler found both versions "somewhat incomprehensible," as they "resolutely violated the holy spirit of the building code, which requests light and air for any space inhabited by humans."[101] Nevertheless, both are quite interesting. In one version, Mies provided a triangular space facing north toward the Weidendammer Bridge. This urban oasis was flanked by a concave, glass-covered front that was ten stories high. Behind it two parallel wings followed the initial curve as they fanned out over the wedge-like site. Interestingly, the distance between the supporting columns widens as the building's wings spread out. Equally fascinating is Mies's other version, where three curved wings seem to rotate around the central circulation core, providing access for stairs and bathrooms to somewhat narrow light shafts (figure 3.49). This version presents Mies's second façade solution, the sequence of horizontal transoms and ribbon windows he had developed for the Concrete Office Building in 1923 (figure 3.50).

1929 Leipzig Trade Fair Linoleum Stand

In great contrast to such grand urban schemes stands a little-known, but important, exhibition stand for the linoleum industry at a Leipzig trade fair from March 3 to 13, 1929, whose development coincided with or even preceded the crucial design phase of

Figure 3.49. Friedrichstrasse high-rise, Berlin. Competition entry by Ludwig Mies van der Rohe, 1929. Floor plan sketches. Library of Congress, Washington, D.C.

> Figure 3.50. Friedrichstrasse high-rise, Berlin. Competition entry by Ludwig Mies van der Rohe, 1929. Gelatin silver print with pencil drawing, 8 5/8 × 6 3/8 in. (21.9 × 16.2 cm). Museum of Modern Art, New York. The Mies van der Rohe Archive, gift of the architect.

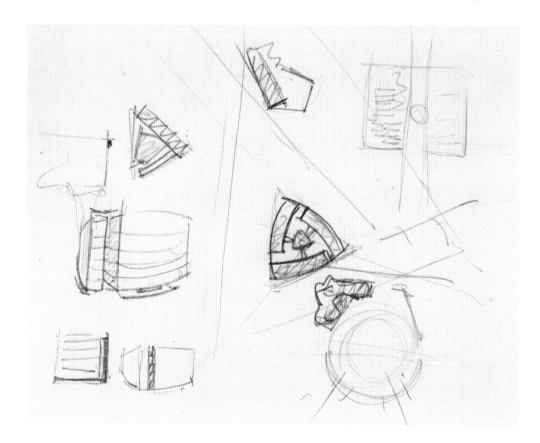

the Barcelona Pavilion. The Leipzig fair's section on building materials and machinery was housed in the sensationally modern steel and glass Exhibition Hall 19 (designed by Leipzig architect Walter Gruner, with Berlin structural engineers Breest & Co.). Upon entering, visitors would spot from afar the inscription "Deutsche Linoleum-Werke" on the high front of Mies's pavilion (figure 3.51).[102] Underneath the inscription were large display windows similar in size to those at the Barcelona Pavilion, two panes on the short side and four on the long side, facing the center of the hall. The open entrance was roughly as wide as two of the glass panes.[103] Different types of colored linoleum covered the floors and walls of the interior, accompanied by smaller displays in the center. Mies's MR 10 and MR 20 chairs were grouped in two seating areas (figure 3.52). Just as in Stuttgart, the lighting was provided by suspended lamps above a stretched white canvas ceiling. Most importantly, the stand contained the first examples of the cruciform, nickel-plated columns that would become a prominent element at the Barcelona Pavilion. Their placement was straightforward and logical—they carried the steel lintels above the display windows and the open entrance area, and their appearance was in line with the reflective surfaces of the nickel-plated window frames.

Four
Politics and Architecture

Barcelona, 1929

1929 Barcelona World's Fair

On June 11, 1929, Ludwig Mies van der Rohe and Lilly Reich left Barcelona by train from the vast iron vaults of the new Estació de França, never to return. Utterly exhausted and in desperate need of a vacation—Reich was running a high fever—they did not take the train straight back to Berlin, but rather headed west to the seaside resorts of Biarritz and San Sebastián for a two-week vacation. During this period of recuperation, they must have had rather mixed feelings about what they left behind in Barcelona. They had been in charge of twenty-five industrial sections with 268 different firms, in eight exhibition palaces, as well as a separate pavilion for Germany's electricity industry and, finally, the national pavilion. They clearly had no premonition that this unusual, temporary German Pavilion, created in utter haste and looking nothing like other national pavilions at world's fairs, would soon be hailed as one of the most important, most influential buildings of the twentieth century. Even before its realization, it proved to be the perfect foil for political and ideological projections, and it continued to elicit controversies long after it had been demolished at the end of the fair. The pavilion's clarity and pristine beauty stand in great contrast to the astonishing precariousness of its creation—it came from a country in considerable turmoil and was placed in another, similarly shaken by political upheaval. For Mies, this building (or rather the thirteen stark, black-and-white photographs that were soon all that was left of it) paved the way for his international prominence and subsequent career in the United States.[1]

Invitations to participate in the 1929 World's Fair had been sent out to European governments in February 1927, more than two years before the opening. It was an important prestige object for General Miguel Primo de Rivera, who had assumed power in Spain through a military coup in 1923. He was broadly disliked in Barcelona, as he had made a point of suppressing any signs of independent Catalan culture. The four columns in the center of the exhibition grounds had been taken down, as they were an important reference to the Senyera, the hallowed Catalan flag with its four stripes. (Mies was among several artists and architects at the fair who signed a letter of protest against the demolition.) In addition, Rivera's regime turned out to be militarily and economically inept. Protest demonstrations had flared up in the year leading up to the exhibition, and the universities had been closed.

Figure 4.1. Georg von Schnitzler, ca. 1920. Sanofi Hoechst Company Archive, Frankfurt-Friedrichsdorf.

In Germany a new, inexperienced government had just been sworn in, a coalition led by Social Democrats focused more on social programs than support for industry. Its reaction to the invitation was lukewarm and slow, but it finally consented in April 1928 and began the search for a general commissioner to oversee the details—someone with organizational skills and experience, diplomatic talent, connections to different industries, and enough wealth to do the job pro bono. Georg von Schnitzler, a forty-five-year-old Frankfurt industrialist and high-ranking manager at the chemical trust IG Farben, was asked and accepted in May (figure 4.1). His wife, Lilly, well acquainted with current trends in visual culture, knew Lilly Reich from her time in Frankfurt and urged her husband to appoint Mies and Reich as artistic directors (figure 4.2).

At that point, Mies had already been retained by the German silk industry for its section at the fair, thanks to his Krefeld clients, Josef Esters and Hermann Lange. Mies proposed an ambitious project in this context, namely, to appropriate a tower on the exhibition grounds for a nocturnal light installation, sponsored jointly by the silk, glass, and electrical industries.[2] The already planned tower at the Plaza de la Luz, between the textile and communication palaces, was to be covered entirely with "plate glass and multi-colored silk, to be changed frequently, all illuminated in a fantastic way. Apparently, it is something very original and surprising," the Spanish organizers reported. The Germans wanted "a strong representative statement" and promised to absorb the costs of those modifications or build their own tower if needed. Mies was poised to discuss the project on his first visit in June 1928.[3] The tower's clear or opal glass (similar to his recent projects in Berlin and Stuttgart), which would be silk-clad inside and backlit, would have produced richer luminosity and stronger colors than any floodlighting. We do not know why the project did not advance. The neoclassical tower in question was built as planned and floodlit each night (figure 4.3). Mies's white cube for the German electrical industry was placed next to it a few months later (see figure 4.25).

The German Sections

Von Schnitzler and Mies had reserved the right to veto any individual exhibit, and to determine the look of each industry's section—its overall design, lettering, and signage (designed by Gerhard Severain). This meant that every company had to forego its established corporate identity and instead adopt the uniform appearance that signaled the common quality standards of a product "Made in Germany." In creating this unifying visual language, Reich and Mies applied many of the solutions they had developed for the 1927 Werkbund exhibition in Stuttgart or the Café Samt und Seide in Berlin, such as white linoleum floors and backlit canvas ceilings, black letters and graphics on white backgrounds, and free-standing panels with large photographs. Glass and wall display cases, tables, panels, and structures for hanging fabrics were all designed by Lilly Reich.

Mies's MR 10 and MR 20 chairs provided a common signifier for the German section. The straight and semicircular forms of the nickel-plated steel tubes, with leather or cloth for the seat and backrest, seemed to confirm an image of a Germany associated with hygiene, lightness, sobriety, and elegance.[4] These pieces were much commented on and praised by visitors, whose delighted surprise led to designations such as "steel snakes" or "reptilian chairs."[5] At home, they were also occasionally mocked in caricatures in satirical magazines.[6]

Figure 4.2. Lilly von Schnitzler, ca. 1929. Published in *Diario oficial de la Exposición Internacional Barcelona 1929,* no. 12 (June 2, 1929): 2.

Figure 4.3. Tower at the Plaza de la Luz, Barcelona World's Fair, 1929. Contemporary postcard.

The Palace of Metallurgy, Electricity, and Motors, with its heavy concrete vaults and skylights, was located on the main axis of the exhibition grounds, the Avenida María Cristina, close to the German Pavilion. At one end of the building was the chemistry section, where, unsurprisingly, the products of von Schnitzler's company, IG Farben, featured prominently; it was ready to receive visitors on opening day (figure 4.4). Black-and-white photographs do not do justice to what must have amounted to veritable symphonies of color, as Reich had arranged the company's pigments, lacquers, and paints in chromatically sequenced geometric fields. The effect was heightened by the evenly distributed light from the suspended canvas ceiling above.

At the opposite end of the palace, the German machinery section could be found (figures 4.5, 4.6). Heavy machines sat like sculptures on an improbably white linoleum floor, as if to illustrate AEG director Paul Jordan's famous advice to Peter Behrens: "An engine should look like a birthday present."[7] To place the company names near their exhibits, a barely

Figure 4.4. Lilly Reich and Ludwig Mies van der Rohe, German section, IG Farben stands, Barcelona World's Fair, 1929.

Figure 4.5. Lilly Reich and Ludwig Mies van der Rohe, German section, Machinery Hall, Barcelona World's Fair, 1929.

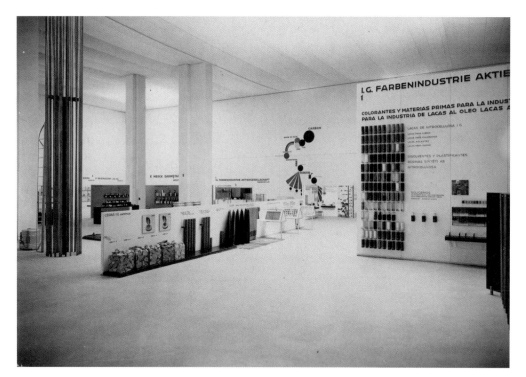

perceptible system of suspended wires created the illusion of letters floating in space. The German information section was also located in this northern section, upstairs on a balcony, to be reached via a narrow staircase on either end. It was made visible from below by a long row of monochrome photographs of German landscapes and tourist landmarks (among them, Trier's Roman city gate, Porta Nigra, and Neuschwanstein Castle). The space also featured MR chairs on a sisal carpet, an information desk, and two tables with German newspapers and information brochures (figure 4.7).

The same suspended lettering technique spelled out "Daimler Benz" or "Adam Opel" above the displayed cars, airplanes, and boats in the Palace of Communication and Transport across the street. Fittingly, this had a much lighter structure, with thin metal piers carrying several barrel-vaulted bays. Here, the German section was surrounded by enormous photographic murals up to 92 feet (28 meters) long showing all modes of transportation, by car, plane, train, suspended tram, zeppelin, and ocean liner.

Figure 4.6. Lilly Reich and Ludwig Mies van der Rohe, German section, Machinery Hall, Barcelona World's Fair, 1929. Note the German information section upstairs above the colonnade.

Figure 4.7. Lilly Reich and Ludwig Mies van der Rohe, German information section on the second floor of Machinery Hall, Barcelona World's Fair, 1929.

The Spanish organizers had urged all major participants to build a small "representative pavilion"—it did not need to be bigger than 3,200 to 7,500 square feet (300 to 700 square meters) or cost more than 70,000 Reichsmark—as national pavilions signaled a fair's international prestige and recognition. Georg von Schnitzler had only been given a small budget of 350,000 Reichsmark for Germany's participation in Barcelona and been told repeatedly by government officials that a separate pavilion was "out of the question"—it would cost too much, and there was not enough time left to design one. Von Schnitzler, however, brazenly ignored these directives, promised the Spanish organizers a German Pavilion, and commissioned Mies to design it.

In his later years, Mies van der Rohe would often claim that no one knew what a German Pavilion was supposed to look like and what role it should play: "When I got the job from the government, they told me 'we need a pavilion'—and I said: 'What do you mean by a pavilion?'—and they said 'We don't know—we have so much money for it—build it. But—please—not too much glass.'"[8] While this version made for a good story (and Mies's recollections may have been somewhat foggy decades later), it seems unlikely that he was unaware of the long-established building type of the exhibition pavilion and its important role in the architectural discourse of the day. Two of his teachers and employers, Bruno Paul and Peter Behrens, had contributed installations or entire buildings at the world's fairs in St. Louis 1904 and Brussels 1910. Country pavilions (or state houses) at world's fairs tended to be architecturally conservative, often resorting to a replica of a historic building at home. But their function was clear: they were to provide information about a country's attractions and accomplishments and space for festive gatherings and lectures.

In contrast, exhibition pavilions at industrial fairs (not burdened with the task of representing an entire nation) had increasingly become testing grounds for architectural innovation.[9] In September 1924, Wilhelm Deffke, the graphic designer and aspiring architect who worked with Mies in the early 1920s, had designed an exhibition stand for the cigarette manufacturer Tesma at the seventh Gross-Berliner Tabakmesse (Great Berlin Tobacco Trade Fair) in September 1924 (figure 4.8). The stand consisted of six full-height sheets of glass under a protruding roof plate, offset against each other in order to create exhibition spaces. It anticipated some central ideas for Mies's Glasraum of 1927 and the Barcelona Pavilion.[10] At the 1925 Exposition Internationale des Arts Décoratifs et Industriels

Figure 4.8. Tesma cigarette stand, at the seventh Gross-Berliner Tabakmesse, Berlin, 1924. Bröhan Design Foundation, Berlin.

Modernes (International Exhibition of Decorative and Industrial Arts) in Paris, Konstantin Melnikov and Le Corbusier had built evocative temporary pavilions. In 1928, Cologne had hosted Pressa, a large exhibition for the printing and publishing industries, with a series of decidedly avant-garde buildings, such as Erich Mendelsohn's superbly elegant structure for the Mosse publishing house (figure 4.9). Cologne architect Hans Schumacher built a large exhibition hall for the *Arbeiterpresse* (Workers' Press), whose main façade bears an uncanny resemblance to Le Corbusier's Villa Savoye, designed two years later. Wilhelm Riphahn's house for the *Kölnische Zeitung*, with its imposing symmetrical façade and luminous tower, became the best-known building of the fair. The Pressa exhibition was extensively discussed in the Werkbund journal *Die Form* in the summer and autumn of 1928, just when Mies was beginning to think about the design for the Barcelona Pavilion. Editor Walter Riezler argued that the exhibition's "elegant and intelligent" solutions could serve as models for permanent architecture and had to be taken seriously. Mies himself recognized the potential of exhibitions to address the "central problem of our time," namely, "the intensification of life," as they had the potential to "revolutionize the way we think."[11] Mies had not been involved at the Pressa, and it is plausible to read his Barcelona Pavilion as a contribution to the growing number of exhibition pavilions at trade fairs. Thus, rather than being a building without a model, its design grew out of a rich tapestry of peers and precedents. And, of course, Lilly Reich and Mies themselves had recently added to the range of stylistic, structural, and material innovations in that field with their Stuttgart Glassraum and the Café Samt und Seide in Berlin in 1927, and the linoleum stand in Leipzig in 1929 (see figures 3.33, 3.34, 3.51).

Design and Materiality

Mies had long been undecided about the design of the pavilion, and he delayed its presentation to the commissioner and a small committee until early February 1929. The site selection had happened late, when all spots in the international section up on Montjuïc Hill had already been assigned. France, equally late (and equally saved by an industrialist, André Citroën), was given the somewhat cramped inner corner of the two wings of the Palacio Alfonso XIII, facing the Plaza de Bellos Oficios. This plaza would fill up with a melee of commercial pavilions, food stands, and advertising kiosks; the small cube of the French Pavilion was never able to compete with the attention-seeking structures in front of it. The Germans were offered the equivalent on the other side, the inner corner of the Palacio Victoria Eugenia, but Mies asked instead for a large area at the western end of the adjacent

Figure 4.9. Erich Mendelsohn, Rudolf-Mosse exhibition stand, Pressa exhibition, Cologne, Germany, 1928. Bromide silver print, dimensions unknown. Photograph by Werner Mantz. Rheinisches Bildarchiv, Museum Ludwig, Cologne.

Plaza de Bellas Artes, not designated for any structure at that time. It was carefully landscaped with semicircular walls and hedges, and divided by a broad path and staircase in the center. This path was of strategic importance, as it would lead up to the Spanish Village, expected to be one of the biggest draws for the visitors (and an important propaganda tool, emphasizing Spanish cultural unity, rather than Catalan separatism). While this arrangement of copies of historic Spanish architecture was of great importance to the organizers, and became exactly the popular success they had hoped for, it probably had little significance for Mies—in fact, many in Germany expected it to be "unbearable kitsch" (figure 4.10).[12]

Probably thanks to Lilly von Schnitzler's close friendship with the Marqués de Foronda, the Barcelona businessman and director of the exhibition, Mies was given the go-ahead at his next visit on November 25, 1928—six months before the opening. Only then could he proceed with the design. A critic called Mies's insistence on this site "the architect's most important creative act."[13] In all likelihood, Mies had to make the concession to preserve access to the existing path in its center and the wide staircase behind. But if the organizers assumed that their largesse would inspire a cooperative attitude on Mies's part, they were mistaken. Mies seems to have been determined to render the path all but invisible. He clearly did not want his building to be experienced as a transitional space or, even worse, as some sort of entrance pavilion to the Spanish Village on the hill above.

Mies's collaborator Sergius Ruegenberg recalled later that the design unfolded with the help of a 1:50 scale model. On a base of white plasticine, 2 and 3/8-inch- (6 centimeter-) wide strips of glass and of cardboard covered with marbleized paper (representing the pavilion's height of almost ten feet, or three meters) were moved about to try out spatial sequences: "Once the room had been defined by the position of the walls, the ceiling was applied in the form of a piece of cardboard.... Mies made a couple of sketches, squatting in front of the model."[14] In one of those sketches a high enclosure on the left continues all the way toward the ascending stairs—blocking views not only onto the large pool and central open space, but also onto the path in the back (figure 4.11). In the final floor plan the pool is visible from the front, but the view to the path in the back is still blocked (figure 4.12).

The few comments that Mies himself offered on the design process came many years later, when the building had long been canonized as one of the masterpieces of modern architecture. In 1952, for example, he recalled the moment that led to the central onyx wall: "One evening, as I was working late on the building, I made a sketch of a freestanding

Figure 4.10. Spanish Village, Barcelona World's Fair, 1929. Contemporary postcard.

Figure 4.11. Ludwig Mies van der Rohe, German Pavilion, Barcelona World's Fair, 1929. Sketch of early version without columns and with a perimeter wall around the large pool. Pencil and colored pencil on tracing paper, 8 1/8 × 10 5/8 in. (20.6 × 27 cm). Preussischer Kulturbesitz, Kunstbibliothek, Berlin.

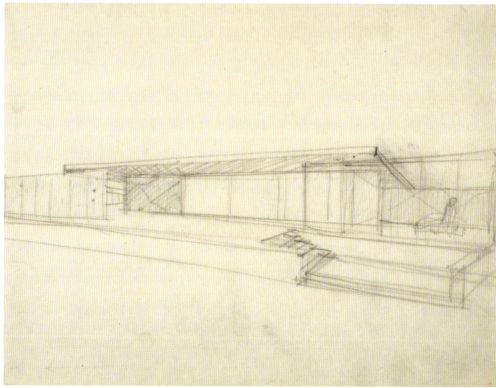

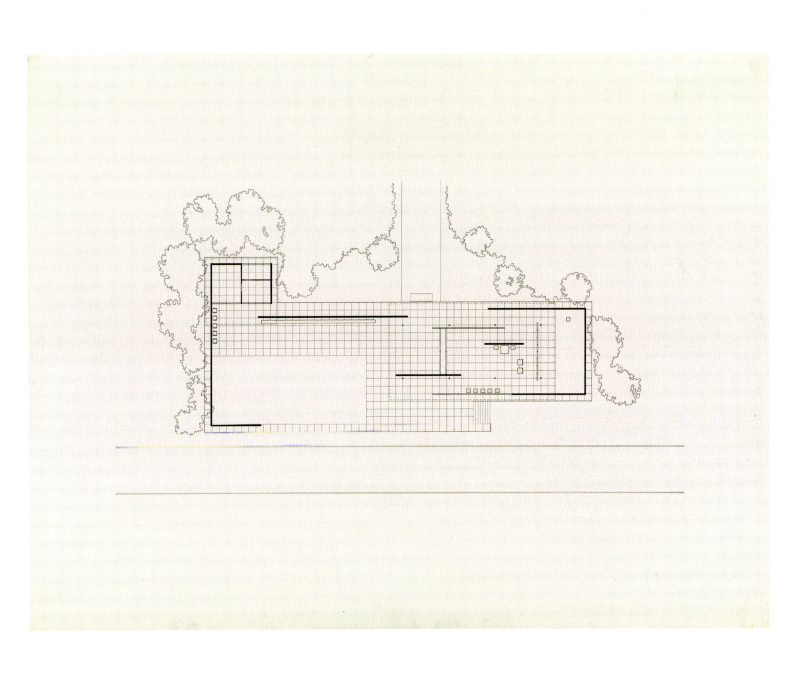

Figure 4.12. Ludwig Mies van der Rohe, German Pavilion, Barcelona World's Fair, 1929. Floor plan. Ink and pencil on paper, 22 1/2 × 38 1/2 in. (57.2 × 97.8 cm). Museum of Modern Art, New York. The Mies van der Rohe Archive, gift of the architect.

Figure 4.13. Ludwig Mies van der Rohe, German Pavilion, Barcelona World's Fair, 1929. View from the northeast, 1929. Photograph by Sasha Stone.

Figure 4.14. Ludwig Mies van der Rohe, German Pavilion, Barcelona World's Fair, 1929. View from the southeast, 1929. Photograph by Sasha Stone.

Figure 4.15. Ludwig Mies van der Rohe, German Pavilion, Barcelona World's Fair, 1929. Interior view, 1929. Photograph by Sasha Stone.

wall and I gave myself a shock. I knew it was a new principle."[15] Mies had actually made this discovery earlier—a solitary, freestanding wall already adorns the living room of his 1924 Brick Country House, a direct predecessor of the pavilion (see figure 2.28). Mies made that connection when he claimed a few years later that the pavilion would have been just as good a building in brick, but added: "I am quite sure it would have been not as successful as marble, but that has nothing to do with the idea."[16] In 1956, he recalled the onyx wall as a key generator for the building's scale:

> When I had the idea for this building I had to look around. There was not much time, very little time, in fact. It was deep in winter, and you cannot move marble in from the quarry in winter because it is still wet inside and it would easily freeze to pieces. So we had to find dry material. I looked around in huge marble depots, and in one I found an onyx block. This block had a certain size and, since I had only the possibility of taking this block, I made the pavilion twice that height.[17]

The freestanding onyx wall became the arresting center of an otherwise almost empty building on an oblong podium. Its expansive walls of travertine, marble, and glass formed a sequence of freely connected spaces, some underneath a thin, continuous roof slab, carried by eight cruciform, nickel-clad columns, while others were open to the sky—by turns luminous and dark, mysterious and inviting (figures 4.13–4.15). There were two shallow water basins: the larger one outside, flanked by a long wall and travertine bench, the smaller one in an interior court adorned with a female figure by the sculptor Georg Kolbe (figures 4.16, 4.17). The pavilion's center coalesced into an abstract intimation of domesticity, with a lush, black wall-to-wall carpet in front of the onyx slab, a wall-high red curtain, and a

Figure 4.16. Ludwig Mies van der Rohe, German Pavilion, Barcelona World's Fair, 1929. View of small courtyard and pool on the northern end with statue by Georg Kolbe, 1929. Photograph by Sasha Stone.

few pieces of strangely unsubstantial but heavy furniture (later called Barcelona chairs). This space provided the quiet center of the spatial sequence, midway between the entrance and the small reflecting pool. The two overlapping corridor spaces behind the onyx wall were much darker and suggested movement rather than stasis. For most visitors, the exit intuitively happened at the western back door, where they were released onto a small plaza behind the luminous wall, shielded from the view toward the exhibition grounds. Nothing remotely comparable had ever served as a national pavilion at an international exposition.

Mies was probably aware that his building was typologically closer to a temporary trade fair pavilion, where the language of modern architecture and spatial experiments were more common, than a traditional state's pavilion with certain programmatic expectations. In order to suggest the gravitas of a national pavilion, however, he decided to clad the entire 15,000-square-foot (1,400-square-meter) floor area in travertine, and all walls in travertine or polished marble. It was a gesture of such unapologetic, provocative extravagance that one cannot help but acknowledge his courage and recklessness in engaging in this extraordinary gamble. Such a display of profligacy could easily have backfired, appearing ostentatious at precisely the moment when the nations of Europe were willing to recover some common ground with Germany, eleven years after the world war it had helped to unleash. Financially and politically risky, it was also a risk aesthetically—a slap in the face to Mies's fellow modernists, who were committed not to pathos and luxury but to the ethics of Neues Bauen (New Building), which emphasized simplicity, structural honesty, affordability, and matter-of-factness. Mies did not explain away the obvious luxury with the building's important representational role, but rather claimed it as a way forward for the modern movement: "rich materials…marble in different colors, bronze, and glass

Figure 4.17. Ludwig Mies van der Rohe, German Pavilion, Barcelona World's Fair, 1929. View to the north along the western façade toward the statue by Georg Kolbe, 1929. Photograph by Sasha Stone.

are obligatory elements of the modern style," he told a Spanish newspaper—perhaps less guarded in his remarks than he would have been at home.[18] Mies might have sensed the need to make the modern movement, widely associated with progressive politics, acceptable to people like the von Schnitzlers. While his unique and temporary national pavilion at the Barcelona World's Fair turned out to be widely immune to criticism, disappointment with Mies became obvious when he applied a similar concept to the design of luxurious private homes at the *Deutsche Bauausstellung* (Building Exhibition) in Berlin and the Tugendhat House shortly afterward. Many on the left recognized a betrayal of the revolutionary goals of the modern movement; for a later critic, the Barcelona Pavilion meant "the ideological collapse of the modern project."[19]

In the following decades, countless critics would draw attention to the "flowing spaces" of the pavilion and the need to experience them while moving. Mies's comments at the time suggest the exact opposite. In a little-known essay published in 1930 (and probably written in 1929), he described how modern architecture sought rest and stasis to counterbalance the dynamism and impermanence of contemporary life:

> The Romans built for eternity: we build for a moment of rest. Our ancestors built firmly and enclosed, we prefer lightness and openness....We do not build for eternity, but for today and tomorrow; but we build for quietude. Repose and tranquility are what our houses are supposed to give us. The eye wants to rest, it wants to calm down, it wants to compose itself: hence the new lines, the emphasized line, hence the new steel furniture, the steel houses, hence the new architecture.[20]

In the completed pavilion such modern quietude came hand in hand with a surprising sensual richness. Brightness and temperature varied considerably between the blindingly white travertine of the outer terrace and the darker interior. The depth of the roof overhang would provide coolness and shade, and the resplendent play of light on the ceiling would echo the rippling of the water in the two pools, both open to the sky—one part of the outside terrace, the other part of the pavilion. The sounds of steps were muffled on the black carpet; the sharp echo from the marble walls diminished near the red curtain.

Some of the pavilion's aesthetic stemmed from recent technological developments, in particular in the design of storefronts and display windows. The three glass panes at the front of the building, almost 12 feet (3.7 meters) wide and 9.8 feet (3 meter) high, were so unusual in this setting that several visitors walked right into them, smacking their heads against the glass.[21] There were four kinds of glass: clear toward the plaza in front; green toward the small pool with Kolbe's statue; the darkest gray glass toward the back (once again, obscuring glimpses of the path toward the west); and a translucent and milky white opal glass for the luminous wall in the back. This rich palette was completed by three kinds of marble—onyx doré, Tinos, and verde antique—that gave the overall impression of a carefully calibrated composition.

And then there were the columns: never before had Mies used a series of freestanding, independent supports. There were, however, precedents among Mies's peers: Le Corbusier had used freestanding columns in his sketch for the Domino system in 1914 and then again at his double house at the Weissenhof Estate in Stuttgart in 1927 (with which Mies had been very impressed).[22] The Luckhardt Brothers' houses at the Rupenhorn in Berlin (1928) had also employed freestanding metal columns inside the main living room. Mies's assistant, Sergius Ruegenberg, even suggested that thin columns in African huts might have served as inspiration, just as the freestanding onyx wall might have been inspired in part by similarly freestanding walls for cult ceremonies in African architecture.[23]

Sketches and a floor plan of earlier versions of the pavilion without columns suggest that the supports may have been introduced as the design process unfolded in the winter of 1928 (see figures 4.11). Ruegenberg later gave credit to the engineer Ernst Walther, who "calculated the thinness and delicacy of the steel columns for the Barcelona Pavilion; Mies wanted them as thin as absolutely possible, he had actually only wanted a hovering plane as a roof. The columns could only be an intermediate element, almost invisible. That is why they were clad in reflective sheets of nickel."[24] The combination of four L-shaped, equilateral steel bands formed a strong column with the smallest possible footprint. It maximized strength while minimizing size and was by no means uncommon. The reflective surface of their nickel-covered casings further helped to dematerialize them, as their ninety-degree angle in the center prevented frontal reflections. The electroplating applied here, as well as in the window frames and the structural parts of the Barcelona chairs and ottomans, was a fairly recent innovation and was mostly used in cars, bicycles, and storefront display cases.

Other material finishes inside the pavilion included the translucent opal-glass screen that terminated the southern end of the main room. Made up of two almost 10-foot- (three-meter-) wide panes of light gray glass, the screen was reflective during the day, despite the elongated skylight above it. The three-foot- (one-meter-) deep space between the two panes housed sixteen suspended light bulbs, which were not fully functional until some months after the opening in mid-July. At night, this dull gray wall turned into a white luminous screen, providing the pavilion's only source of light. Offering respite from the symphony of colored illumination that spread across the exhibition grounds outside, the luminous wall integrated light into the pavilion's architecture of essential planes (figure 4.18). After two visitors had fallen into the small pool at night, the local supervisor asked to install additional lights, but Mies firmly rejected the idea.[25] Clearly, it was of crucial importance to limit the illumination to this one element, an integral part of the structure, keeping the space as uncluttered as possible.

Among the many astonishing qualities of the pavilion is that it was almost entirely prefabricated and shipped from Germany. ("Only the water seems to be Spanish," joked a German reporter.[26]) It had to be planned with great precision, and progress on the site

Figure 4.18. Ludwig Mies van der Rohe, German Pavilion, Barcelona World's Fair, 1929. View at night from the back. Photograph by Wilhelm Niemann.

was dependent on smooth transportation and working infrastructure. Instead of sourcing it from Barcelona, the stone was delivered from Köstner & Gottschalk, a marble supplier in Berlin, as Mies wanted to control its quality. Mies found the marble for the onyx wall in a depot in Hamburg, earmarked for vases on a cruise ship. He recalled: "They finally brought me a hammer and were very curious if I would really strike a corner off the block. I hit it very hard and off came a slice, the size of my hand, very thin, and I said go and quickly polish it, so I can see it. We then decided to use it, figured out the quantities, and then bought the material." It was cut into thin slices and sent to Barcelona. Apparently, Mies bought it on the spot using his own money—wondering on the train ride home what to do if the pavilion would not be built.[27]

The thin marble slabs would be attached to both sides of a steel framework, with shorter solid pieces at the end. This clever arrangement lowered the weight and amount of material needed, while still providing the appearance of solidity throughout. Inside the steel frame, flat, lozenge-shaped pipes drained water from the roof. Mies carefully arranged for the veneer's grain to form symmetrical patterns. Two sequential cuts would be placed next to each other with their patterns mirrored, a so-called book match, while four sequential cuts provided a "quarter" or "diamond" match. Diamond and book matches are visible in the verde antique wall of the main façade and around the small pool in the back. The onyx wall in the center consisted of larger pieces, 93 by 59 by 12 inches (235 by 149 by 30 centimeters). Here, Mies resorted to a random match, due to the configuration of the block he had purchased.

It was no wonder that Köstner & Gottschalk's bill amounted to 187,580 Reichsmark—about 55 percent of the overall cost of the pavilion. The next largest expenditures were 80,000 Reichsmark for Siemens-Bauunion, which had supervised the entire construction; and 28,759 Reichsmark for Berliner Metallgewerbe, which manufactured the nickel-covered supports, window frames, and Barcelona chairs. The total cost of the glass amounted to 16,000 Reichsmark. At that time, single-family houses could be had for between 10,000 and 30,000 Reichsmark.[28]

Politics

When Georg von Schnitzler's anticipated budget had swelled fourfold to 1.35 million Reichsmark in October 1928, he confidently requested additional funds, but did not hear back for six months, while work progressed on the site. To von Schnitzler's great surprise, the Reichstag finance committee rejected his request on March 2, and merely added another 150,000 Reichsmark. In great frustration, von Schnitzler canceled the pavilion and several sections and announced his resignation.[29] The minister for economic affairs, Julius Curtius, finally talked him into staying. But work on the pavilion stopped, and continued only on a starkly reduced number of sections. Mies and Lilly Reich took time out in San Sebastián.

We can only speculate what had motivated von Schnitzler's extraordinary gamble. He had commissioned the pavilion despite clear government directives against it, and without any available funds. He might have imagined (correctly, it turned out) that a photogenic pavilion by an avant-garde architect would do more for Germany's reputation than just a series of industrial exhibits, and he surely felt pressure from the Spanish organizers. He trusted that he would secure the consent of politicians, who were keen not to be outdone by Germany's "arch-enemy" once it became known that France was building a national pavilion. What saved the pavilion, in the end, was an intervention from Spain's proto-fascist dictator, Primo de Rivera, who expressed his great displeasure at an abandoned German Pavilion. This prompted a scramble for additional funds in Berlin, and a loan arrived some sixteen days later. Additional days passed with the hiring of workers, renting machinery, and installing electricity. The hiatus meant that none of the official maps would show the pavilion's location, and most visitors missed the German information section, which had been hastily relocated to the second floor of the Machinery Hall.

The delay also meant that the construction of the entire pavilion, from the foundations to its completion, had to be accomplished in a mere seven to eight weeks. By April 14, 1929, the foundations and the subfloor were nearing completion. The steel frame carrying the roof on its eight columns followed. There were night and evening shifts, agonizing delays in the delivery of materials, a shortage of workers, disagreements about the use of funds, and angry altercations between members of Mies's team. Partly due to this accelerated schedule, but mostly because of the brazen extravagance of cladding the entire structure in travertine and polished marble, it was by far the costliest pavilion at the exposition.

When it opened on May 27, 1929 (one week after the expo's official inauguration), a number of details remained unfinished, and some compromises were obvious. Painted stucco stood in for polished stone in the back, and the small structure on the southeastern end was not yet accessible, its front covered with sheets of drywall. The wall-high, dark-red velvet curtain, a key piece of the interior concept, had not been delivered in time, and the luminous glass wall, the only source of light at night, did not work. Most importantly, the inscription "Alemania"—the single word needed to identify the national pavilion's role and purpose— was missing from the façade. In all likelihood it had been held back—in an extraordinary gesture of defiance—by a disgruntled von Schnitzler. Money had run out again, and von Schnitzler had to request additional, personal loans, offering the pavilion itself as collateral. He ended up entirely pre-financing it and was, together with the contractor, the pavilion's

Figure 4.19. Opening ceremonies at the German Pavilion at the Barcelona World's Fair, May 27, 1929. Georg von Schnitzler and Alfonso XIII, King of Spain, are in front of the pavilion; Mies van der Rohe is on the left.

Figure 4.20. Opening ceremonies at the German Pavilion at the Barcelona World's Fair, May 27, 1929. Mies van der Rohe is in conversation with Alfonso XIII, King of Spain.

"sole owner" at the time of the opening.[30] The absence of the inscription for the first few months explains the confusion of many visitors on the grounds, who could not identify the building's purpose. Some visitors mistook it for an exhibition pavilion of the marble industry, since the marble supplier, Köstner & Gottschalk from Berlin, had applied its name near the entrance. The official photos taken by Berlin photographer Sasha Stone in June, which were widely distributed, show the building without its inscription.

At the brief opening ceremony Alfonso XIII, King of Spain (who was not known for his cultural interests) joked that he had anxiously driven by the building site every day to check on its progress until it dawned on him "that the Germans had delayed the opening of the pavilion on purpose, in order to show off their uncanny technical and improvisational skills to a world audience" (figures 4.19, 4.20).[31] In his own speech at the opening, however, the German commissioner, Georg von Schnitzler, began to frame a narrative that would become the foundation for many future interpretations:

> In a country less favored by the sun than yours, where the winters are long and dark, and there are many rainy days, a new spirit of the age has emerged, which aims to collect and radiate as much light and clarity as the natural conditions permit. We reject anything that is labyrinthine, obscure, overwrought, and complicated, we want to act clearly, and we want to surround ourselves with things that are clear, straight, and pure. Utmost simplicity has to be accompanied by the deepest profundity. The hard times that we have gone through have led us to consider simplicity as essential and to reject anything that is unnecessary as superfluous....We do not want to summarize our program with a catchphrase, but please consider it the expression of our serious desire to be absolutely truthful, giving expression to the spirit of a new era, whose essence will be sincerity.[32]

Many later critics read these remarks as an equation of the pavilion's forms with the political and moral ambitions of the Weimar Republic, a reading that has lasted to this day. In his bestselling survey, *Modern Architecture since 1900*, William J. R. Curtis wrote that the pavilion "had the honorific, not to say ambassadorial function of representing the cultural values of a new Germany, eager to distance itself from its imperialist past. The Weimar Republic wished to project an image of openness, liberality, modernity, and internationalism."[33]

The assumption that the pavilion had been deliberately selected to represent the young Weimar Republic and its democracy and was an endorsement of modern architecture made a lot of sense in retrospect, given the Nazis' opposition to both, but the reality was more complicated. As mentioned above, the government of the Weimar Republic, a coalition led by the Social Democratic Party, had firmly rejected the idea of a pavilion and denied additional funds. This was a financial decision and not based on the pavilion's architecture, which none of the politicians had seen. Lilly and Georg von Schnitzler were culturally progressive (Lilly a longtime supporter and confidante of expressionist painter Max Beckmann) but politically conservative. With her close friend, Austrian writer and aristocrat Karl Anton Rohan (who joined the Nazi Party in 1933), she edited the literary and political magazine *Europäische Revue*. It was the voice of the Europäischer Kulturbund (European Cultural Association), a conservative, antidemocratic association promoting the vision of a pan-European intellectual elite—of successful writers, artists, businessmen, and politicians—who would form a bulwark against Soviet Communism and American capitalism. The Kulturbund conference in October 1929 in Barcelona was titled "Le Problème sociale de la vulgarisation de la culture" (The Social Problem of the Vulgarization of Culture), and the delegates were treated to a tour of the pavilion on the first night. Lilly von Schnitzler's own 1929 article about the Barcelona Pavilion in the *Europäische Revue* conjured up some of the most lyrical descriptions celebrating Mies's achievement, describing it "as if from a fairytale, not from the *Arabian Nights*, but from an almost supernaturally inspired music of eternal space, not as a house, but as a drawing of lines in such a space by a hand that defines the human reach toward infinity." Mies had, she claimed, cast "our spiritual existence into form." She closed with a remark that can be read as a thinly veiled reference to the military dictatorship of Primo de Rivera, and her own willingness to tolerate a similar turn of events in Germany: "Spain seems to be Europe's last haven for conviction, attitude, character, metaphysics—the sole values through which Europe can recover and resist the impending Americanism....Spain's experiment in Barcelona, which is symptomatic for all of Spain to drive out the devil with the help of Lucifer, is for all of us a most enthralling adventure, whose result can become authoritative for us as well."[34] Max Beckmann placed the von Schnitzlers and Rohan at the center of a darkly prescient painting of a joyless Paris soiree in 1931, two years before the Nazis would take over power in Germany (figure 4.21).

In October 1929, immediately after the Kulturbund conference, a "German Week" was held at the World's Fair. Many details missing from the German Pavilion at the opening were now in place: the small office at the end was finished, the red curtain had been delivered, and the luminous wall, the only source of light at night, was functioning (see figure 4.18). Perhaps most importantly, the official word *"Alemania"* had finally been applied next to the access points in front and back (figure 4.22). Georg von Schnitzler had even requested an expert from Köstner & Gottschalk to come to Barcelona to re-polish the reflective stone surfaces.[35] A second opening celebration was held at the pavilion on October 19, and it turned out more festive than the first. The brand-new battleship *Königsberg* had traveled to Barcelona, and its military band played the Spanish "Marcha Real" and the German national anthem. Visitors from Germany had arrived, many expatriates attended, and Georg von Schnitzler gave another speech. Elated by the pavilion's positive reception in the press, he called it "a spiritual demonstration of our serious effort of collaboration in the world economy."[36]

The most significant event to take place at the pavilion happened a few days later at night, when, on October 23, 1929, the pavilion was to demonstrate its "essential purpose": instead of housing conventional gala dinners or lectures, for which it had not been laid out, it was to be presented as part and expression of a larger modern project, extending beyond architecture to art, dance, music, and technology.[37] Lilly von Schnitzler, the commissioner's wife, had discussed the details with Ludwig Mies van der Rohe and the Frankfurt publicist Heinrich Simon.[38] Their conversation about an exhibition of modern German graphic art at the pavilion suggests that the emptiness of the pavilion was not

Figure 4.21. Max Beckmann, *Gesellschaft Paris* (Paris Society), 1931. Oil on canvas, 43 × 69 1/8 in. (109.2 × 175.6 cm). Solomon R. Guggenheim Museum, New York. Prinz Karl von Rohan is shown in the center; left of him is Lilly von Schnitzler; Georg von Schnitzler is seated on the left.

necessarily programmatic, but a result of its chaotic genesis. They also discussed commissioning a documentary film about Germany to be shown at the pavilion or putting on a concert by the modern Amar-Hindemith Quartet or a dance performance by the Laban School.[39] Composer Paul Hindemith was part of the avant-garde circles that Mies frequented and had just written the music for and performed in Hans Richter's 1928 experimental film *Vormittagsspuk* (Ghosts before Breakfast). Rudolf Laban would have been an equally apt choice, as he was not only the prominent leader of the German *Ausdruckstanz* (expressionistic dance) movement, but also trained as an architect at the École des Beaux-Arts in Paris and deeply interested in human motion in response to built space.[40] Mies was a close friend of Laban's student, the famous dancer Mary Wigman. When both Laban and Wigman proved to be unavailable, two other modern dancers were hired for an evening performance at the pavilion: Ernst Matray and his wife, Katta Sterna, who had been a member of Max Reinhardt's ensemble, were among the most prominent progressive dancers in the Weimar Republic. Georg von Schnitzler, who paid their expenses and honoraria, invited Mies to attend: "I am giving a little party on Wednesday 23 October in the German Pavilion as part of German Week, where Mr. Matray and Mrs. Kattasterna [*sic*] will dance. It would be truly a great pity if you, the creator of this pavilion, were absent on this day, and I am asking you kindly to be there for at least a few days, and in particular on that Wednesday." Mies politely declined.[41]

The modern dance performance at the pavilion was the only nighttime activity ever scheduled there. Kolbe's statue was temporarily lit up for the occasion—a static echo perhaps of the dancers' movements. The day of the performance was carefully chosen to coincide with what the public would later remember as "the moment of greatest brilliance" of the German celebrations in Barcelona: the arrival of the famous, gigantic airship *Graf Zeppelin LZ 127* over the city, cruising above it for more than an hour in the afternoon.[42] It had completed a much-noted world tour earlier that year, and added a special trip to Seville and Barcelona. The hum of its motors overhead brought the citizens out onto their balconies or up onto their rooftops to wave at it with their handkerchiefs and take innumerable photographs. Unexpectedly, it reappeared at night and looped three times over the exhibition grounds. The powerful searchlights behind the National Palace were trained on it, incorporating it into the luminous spectacle. "Above the fires of the Exposition, the Zeppelin, touched by the beams of the searchlights, resembled an enormous fish swimming above in the bluish sea of the sky," wrote one journalist.[43] The guests attending the dance performance in the pavilion stepped outside to see the stunning play of lights overhead, reflected in the large pool. As the zeppelin finally turned back toward El Prat airfield and slowly vanished in the distance, it suddenly lit up again—picked out this time by the searchlights of the battleship *Königsberg* in the nearby port. It was a quintessentially modern moment.

It is significant that in front of the pavilion two different German flags were hoisted—the old flag of the Reich (black, white, and red) and the new one of the Weimar Republic

Figure 4.22. Concert at the German Pavilion during "German Week," October 23, 1929. Published in "Notas Gráficas," *La Vanguardia,* October 24, 1929, 3.

(black, red, and gold). While the new one had been made official by decree in 1919, many conservatives still felt a strong affiliation with the flag of the Reich, as did many Germans living abroad. A much-debated "flag controversy" had led to the downfall of Chancellor Hans Luther in 1926, after he had suggested hoisting both flags at consulates abroad, and it continued for a few more years. The merchant navy officially used the old flag for its better visibility.[44] (While the pavilion's inside color scheme of black carpet, red curtain, and golden onyx has occasionally been read as a reference to the Weimar flag, the white ceiling and floor together with the black carpet and red curtain also allow a reading of the Reich's colors.) The decision to fly both flags at the pavilion at certain times must have been made by Georg von Schnitzler, as it clearly violated government regulations, and it aptly signals the complexity of the pavilion's political affiliations.

Like many industrialists, von Schnitzler was close to the Deutsche Volkspartei (DVP, or German People's Party), which had opposed the new political system of the Weimar Republic, calling for the restoration of the monarchy (and had frequently expressed its preference for the old flag). In April 1933, merely three years after the pavilion had been dismantled, the Nazis came to power (von Schnitzler had donated to Hitler's election campaign on behalf of his employer, IG Farben). Five months in, he joined the "SA" (Sturmabteilung), a voluntary paramilitary organization, and the Nazi Party in 1937. He was convicted of war crimes at the Nuremberg trials in 1947 (figure 4.23).[45]

The Sculpture by Georg Kolbe

Similar to the arrangement at the Glasraum in Stuttgart, Mies imagined including sculpture in the pavilion. An early floor plan shows three pedestals for sculptures, and there are vaguely anthropomorphic forms in his sketches; but with the realization of the pavilion uncertain for several weeks in mid-March, the final decision was made rather late during a visit in Berlin in early April. Architect and critic Peter Blake, who knew Mies well, recalled that Mies would have preferred a figure by Wilhelm Lehmbruck, but when none was available, he "grabbed a taxi on one of his last days in Berlin before leaving for Barcelona, drove out to Kolbe's studio and borrowed the best substitute he could find."[46] That "best substitute" turned out to be the plaster cast of a female figure Kolbe jokingly called "Cecilie," as she was a replica of one of two bronze sculptures he had recently installed at the Ceciliengärten Housing Estate in Berlin. The sculpture was shipped immediately and arrived in time for the opening (see figure 4.16). It was painted to look like bronze. On the way back, it was damaged beyond recovery.

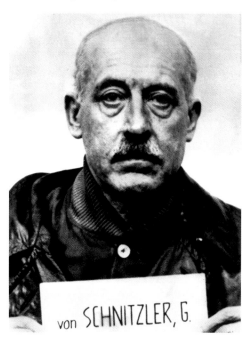

Figure 4.23. Georg von Schnitzler at the Nuremberg Trials, August 14, 1947. Von Schnitzler was sentenced to five years' imprisonment.

At the fair, most critics responded positively to the "extraordinarily beautiful" figure, assuming that it had been created for this specific location in the small pool at the back. Heinrich Simon, for instance, called her "Venus Anadyomene" (a Venus rising from the sea, reminiscent of the famous Titian painting of about 1520). Others referred to the figure as a *Badende* (bather), or noted that her raised hand shielded her "against the flood of light entering the open court."[47] Kolbe rarely burdened his figures with the bathos of metaphor. As a modernist, dedicated to Neue Sachlichkeit (New Objectivity), Kolbe explored the essence of human movements and described his sculptures as "Walking Woman," "Squatting Woman," "Standing Youth," and so on. It seems that the two statues in the Ceciliengärten were retroactively given the titles *Morning* and *Evening* by Kolbe's former collaborator, Margrit Schwartzkopff, and his granddaughter Maria von Tiesenhausen after World War II, when both women were busy establishing a Kolbe museum in his former home in West Berlin and eager to show Kolbe's contemporary relevance and gravitas.[48] Wolf Tegethoff, in 1981, introduced the title *Morning* for Kolbe's sculpture in the pavilion (after more than fifty years without a title), adopting the now common attribution in the Ceciliengärten. Since the large exhibition on Mies at MoMA in 2001, the title *Dawn*, or *Morning*, has found broad acceptance.[49] Given its placement, it is particularly convincing. The sculpture's position in the small reflecting pool in the northwestern corner secures her the first morning light, when the eastern sun makes her a luminous focal point for the entire structure.

In the weeks immediately after the opening of the 1929 fair, several writers used Kolbe's sculpture as a prompt to muse on the decoration of modern architecture. According to Swiss architect Hans Bernoulli, sculpture here adopted the "role hitherto played by leafy plants," and thus had to similarly "enrich and enliven" the "surrounding structure…and be understood as essential." American critic Helen Appleton Read agreed that "the vitality it imparts to the austerity of the scheme" presented "a brief for the use of sculpture in modern arrangements." Similarly, the architect Paul Bonatz saw at the pavilion "the most attractive example of a constellation of sculpture and architecture. It is inconceivable for a sculpture to have a better environment than the smooth walls, reflective marble surface, and the pool there."[50] Among the few hesitant voices was that of Walter Riezler, editor of the Werkbund journal *Die Form*, who found the "otherwise very beautiful figure" not "truly fitting: it still stemmed from the world of the old space." Unable to square the realism of the sculpture with his own association of "space–time," Riezler argued that Kolbe's sculpture instead represented stasis, and merely continued the spatial conditions of the Renaissance and baroque. Other sculptors—be they cubists, such as "[Alexander] Archipenko and his circle," or even naturalists, such as "Lehmbruck or [Ernst] Barlach"—were, in Riezler's view, closer to the new "sculptural attitude," reflecting "the new sense of statics in architecture; these figures don't stand solidly on the ground anymore, even where their motive has nothing to do with weightlessness, they seem to be levitating."[51]

Many years later, Reyner Banham would also note the striking difference in attitude between the sculpture and its abstract context—something he found so absurd as to be "faintly Dadaist." One would have expected, he explained, something entirely different among such "Mondrianesque abstract logical consistency."[52] Architectural historian Vincent Scully, at the same time, was unbothered by the sculpture's naturalism and found that it perfectly completed the pavilion—in fact, it created

> the constructivist environment around itself and, once seen, controlled the building completely. All the planes seemed to be deriving from it, positioned by it, even as its lifted arm could still be faintly perceived from the far end of the platform. Consequently, the union was optimistic and exact: mobility and enclosure were reconciled; the architecture of a precise but fluid environment was shown as created by the human act. The Barcelona Pavilion was thus the temple, perhaps appropriately temporary, of the International Style, and it embodied the ideal symbols of the European and American components which had gone into its creation.[53]

Scully's former colleague at Yale University, the architect Paul Rudolph, echoed these observations almost thirty years later when he visited the rebuilt pavilion. He found "the dialogue between the sculpture and the building…unlike any other dialogue between a work of art and a building that I know of." Kolbe's sculpture held the key to the pavilion's "profound mystery…the whole Barcelona Pavilion becomes most clear" from a place inaccessible to us—namely "the location of the sculpture": "If you stood where that sculpture stands…you would be seeing the layers of transparency and translucency, reflections of the unseen and seen and implied space presented in multiple ways.…You would have that multiple view of things all around you—the view the cubists always talked about."[54]

Reception

Mies himself seems to have been uncertain of the building's success. Contrary to his usual habit, he did not commission any professional photographs of it. At the end of June, weeks after Mies had left Spain, a prominent photographer, Sasha Stone, arrived at the behest of the German silk industry to document its exhibits. Stone also photographed the pavilion and sold his images to a news agency in Berlin. Rigorously composed around a horizontal symmetrical axis, the images lent the pavilion a stark gravitas, presenting it as a mysteriously beautiful, abstract composition of horizontal and vertical planes—its formal purity enhanced by the complete absence of visitors (see figures 4.13–4.17). Stone turned out to be, unwittingly, the most important accomplice on Mies's path to worldwide fame. His thirteen photographs were sent out from the news agency in Berlin and directly from Mies's office to countless architecture magazines, and became simply de rigueur for any books on architecture from then on. Restrictions on official photography during the fair meant that these images remained almost the only ones available of the pavilion after its demolition in

January 1930, and as such they illustrated and influenced many articles in newspapers and architectural journals over the following months.

What happened then is one of the most unusual success stories in the history of architecture: despite its short existence, and thanks to Stone's brilliant photographs, the building's reputation grew steadily over the following decades. Before long, it was considered a built manifesto for the modern movement, with its spatial and "spiritual" ambitions, and "one of the milestones of modern architecture." The pavilion itself was proclaimed "one of the great works of art of all time," "a virtual ur-hut" or "temple" of modernity, a true archetype akin to Donato Bramante's Tempietto in Rome, which holds a comparable emblematic position for the Renaissance.[55] Architects the world over would adopt the pavilion's formal and spatial vocabulary, making it a central strand of mid-century modern's DNA that is still vividly palpable today. Mies himself applied the pavilion's essential language only to two subsequent buildings—the Tugendhat House in Brno of 1930 and the House for a Childless Couple shown at the *Deutsche Bauausstellung* of 1931—but it reverberated, hauntingly, through his sketches and studio exercises all the way into the 1940s.

Political positions apparently did not color critics' judgments in those years. A German writer such as Guido Harbers, who had criticized Stuttgart's Weissenhof Estate of 1927 as "anemic" and "un-German," and who would eagerly join the National Socialist Party in 1933, was just as enthusiastic about the pavilion as Justus Bier, a progressive Jewish critic whom the National Socialists relieved of his post as curator of modern art in Hanover in 1936. Similarly, Spanish critic Francisco Marroquín, soon a fervent supporter of General Francisco Franco, loved the pavilion as much as Nicolau Rubió i Tudurí, a liberal critic and designer.[56]

Critical voices about the pavilion were rare at the time and far outnumbered by enthusiastic responses. A Stuttgart museum official found that the pavilion was merely an arrangement of "black or transparent glass panes," in fact, not "a building at all," and therefore "offensive" to the Spanish hosts. Several critics feared that the pavilion might only appeal to an intellectual elite and be "absolutely incomprehensible" to the less well-briefed, or similarly that a "shallow visitor" might wonder if he stood in front "of an unfinished building."[57] Such intellectual aloofness, a socialist critic noted, represented the "snobbish arrogance of the German on the intellectual world stage." Others were disappointed with the building's luxurious execution, "superbly cool, precious, well-proportioned," but ultimately "dead pomp."[58] A Berlin daily paper found the pavilion "an oddity…original, entertaining, perhaps even practical in the southern climate, but basically not German." While some critics had praised the boldness of a modern building "without a purpose," merely "dedicated to representation, to empty space, and thus to space itself," conservative magazines happily pounced at this contradiction with the movement's much-touted rationalism and functionalism: here, there was no "functional program…nor can it be used for anything—as the embodiment of an abstract architectural idea (how does the New Objectivity deal with that?!)."[59]

The Barcelona Chair

Mies and his team developed several pieces of furniture especially for the German Pavilion—a low, cross-legged ottoman and a small, square table and larger serving table, both with glass tops. Most important was the "Barcelona Chair"—meant ostensibly for the king and queen of Spain to sit on during the opening ceremony (figure 4.24). While the royal couple did not avail themselves of this opportunity, the chair would later become one of the most iconic pieces of furniture of the twentieth century. Here, after experimenting with hollow, tubular steel in previous years, Mies tried out flat-spring steel of a higher, flexible strength and a different carbon content, more commonly found in shock absorbers in trains and cars. As with his use of large display windows, opal glass, or nickel-plated columns, Mies had begun to transfer aesthetics or techniques from industrial or commercial applications into the home. His patent application for the Barcelona Chair and ottoman was submitted on May 1, 1929, just weeks before the pavilion's opening. The supporting text pointed out the crucial difference from a folding chair, which might look similar, but needed movable joints instead of a fixed connection at the center. Mies wanted to "exploit the spring of metal bands from a flexible material in order to arrive at an elastic seat and elastic back rest.… The arms of the cross of metal bands will be springy cantilevers and the result will be a soft, pliable seat, according to

the flexibility of the material."[60] The resulting chair was a hybrid—lacking armrests, it was not an armchair, but it provided the depth, comfort, and inclination of an easy chair.

The design of the Barcelona Chair was apparently a collaborative affair in Mies's office. Sergius Ruegenberg claimed in 1988 that he designed the chair after the cross-legged ottoman had been designed first: "Three days before my departure as supervisor of the building site in Barcelona, Mies asked me to design a chair. The steel stool had already been realized. One of my designs was taken by Kaiser to be produced." Willi Kaiser, also in Mies's office, later recalled that he too had worked on the chair with the same metal-worker who was responsible for the cruciform columns at the pavilion.[61] Ludwig Glaeser gave Lilly Reich credit for the design of the upholstery, choice of leather, and the details of its fastening.[62] Mies continued to work on the chair's central ideas in the following months and submitted a new patent application for a "seating furniture with a flexible frame" on November 18, 1930. It clarifies the intentions behind the chair and its unusual construction, highlighting the "leaf springs" and the flexibility of the frame for the way they "lessen the strain on the muscles."[63] Such a lessening was especially useful for elderly users or the more heavyset (such as Mies himself), in particular since there was no armrest to offer support.

Mies would use the same kind of springy metal bands for the easy chairs at the Tugendhat House in Brno, both for their supports and for a version with armrests, as well as for the Brno dining chairs. Countless drawings and a few more patents for further versions of chairs with curved metal bands followed in the next years, but none was put into production.

The Electric Utilities Pavilion

The second pavilion that Mies designed for the Barcelona fair—the Electric Utilities Pavilion, with an interior featuring large models, relief maps, photographs, and graphics—remains something of a mystery.[64] No drawings of it have survived, and only two photographs of the exterior exist (figure 4.25). The building is hardly mentioned in the voluminous correspondence. The decision to create a separate building only came late in December 1928 as the result of a complicated trading of space with the Spaniards, who needed more room in the exhibition hall for their own installation. The building went up in the Plaza de la Luz, a small space behind the Palace of Communications and Transport, but visible to anyone arriving from the city center by tram on the Gran Via. Above it rose the tower at the Plaza de la Luz, mentioned before as the proposed site for a German light installation by the silk, glass, and electrical industries. The pavilion was constructed as a white cube, about 50 feet (15 meters) high on a 66-by-66-foot (20-by-20-meter) footprint, and rose straight from the ground, without any base or plinth. Its façade was similarly unadorned and was interrupted only by the horizontal cutout of its entrance. Above this opening, black letters announced the Pabellón del Suministro de Electricidad en Alemania (German Electric Utilities Pavilion), while its sides showed four protruding pilasters supporting the roof's steel structure, with twelve square ventilation openings at the upper edge.

Design and construction unfolded at the same hectic pace as the official pavilion, with numerous night and weekend shifts. Late in the process, Mies developed an ambitious new tectonic concept that required a tripling of the planned foundations. He changed the building's structural system from a simple brick structure with a flat wooden roof to a steel exoskeleton with U-section beams, stuccoed brick infill, and a "most complicated" steel roof structure, which was installed the night before the opening, and sprang a leak as soon as the first drops of rain fell. Mies had initially estimated the costs at 40,000 to 50,000 Reichsmark, but final costs were around 140,000 Reichsmark.

Berlin architect Fritz Schüler, who worked for one of the electricity companies, was responsible for the interior design and supervised the pavilion's execution. The photographer Wilhelm Niemann (the owner of the Berliner Bild-Bericht agency) later claimed that he created the photographic murals inside and supervised the construction site from March 1929 onward.[65] The interior was illuminated with electric lights suspended above a canvas ceiling 33 feet (10 meters) from the floor. The central display (26 by 20 feet, or 8 by 6 meters)

Figure 4.25. Ludwig Mies van der Rohe, German Electric Utilities Pavilion, Barcelona World's Fair, 1929.

consisted of a contoured map of Germany, with small light bulbs indicating different types of energy production. Another model showed a section of Berlin's urban spaces as they were served by the famous Klingenberg power station. Two additional models contrasted conventional and renewable energies, with the coal-fired Golpa-Zschornewitz plant and the hydroelectric dam at Edertal, near Kassel. Three walls were covered by large photo murals on square plywood panels, whose central motifs linked them to the model in front.[66] One showed an assemblage of Berlin buildings in the style of Paul Citroën's famous *Metropolis* collages. On leaving, the visitor would face the entrance wall, viewing graphics and statistics about energy consumption by different user groups in Germany. The floor was covered in white linoleum, and a few MR chairs, stools, and a table are visible in one of the photographs (figure 4.26).

It is hard not to see this building as the deliberate opposite of the Barcelona Pavilion. There, Mies celebrated a complex spatial sequence, different qualities of natural light through the interplay of inner and outer spaces, and varied textures and colors of materials. The Electric Utilities Pavilion, on the other hand, was a building in black and white, with only one tall room, lit artificially from above, with a sequence of composite photo murals replacing any visible connection to the outside. It was Mies's second building in white stucco—which had become the lingua franca of the modern movement—and the first time that he used an exoskeleton, something that would reappear later in his work at IIT's Crown Hall or the Museum of Fine Arts in Houston. The only common elements of the two pavilions are their two rows of four columns on each side. Germany had the most advanced network of urban and rural electrification in Europe. For visitors from Spain, where cities were still widely lit by gaslight, Mies's mysterious white cube promised a veritable journey into the

Figure 4.26. Ludwig Mies van der Rohe and Fritz Schüler, German Electric Utilities Pavilion, Barcelona World's Fair, 1929. Interior with photo mural by Wilhelm Niemann.

future. Of course, the entire World's Fair—or rather, its European section in Barcelona—was a demonstration of the wonders of electricity, of sparkling colored floodlights and luminous fountains. The contrast to Mies's mysterious white Kaaba could hardly have been more didactic. The joyous display of electricity's magic met the cool and controlled mastery of its power.

Given the building's daring appearance, it is astonishing how little it was mentioned in the contemporary press, with the only recorded epithet being a Spanish critic's description of it as a "strange cubic pavilion" featuring an "excess of sobriety in the modern Teutonic style."[67]

The Building Type

What company did Mies find himself in? As to be expected, most national pavilions at the 1929 exposition followed long-established patterns and sought inspiration in celebrated historical monuments or vernacular architecture from home, while more adventurous and modern approaches were found among the commercial pavilions. All country pavilions (except those of France and Germany) were located in the international section on the hill, next to the National Palace and thus quite far away from the center of the exhibition. Belgium erected a large building in the style of a medieval town hall crowned by a tower, and Hungary was represented by a rather forbidding, vaguely pre-Columbian structure. The Danish, Norwegian, and Romanian constructions were reminiscent of each country's vernacular traditions, whereas France, Italy, Yugoslavia, and Sweden commissioned their architects to work in a contemporary idiom. As mentioned above, the French presence was bankrolled to a large extent by the industrialist André Citroën, who selected the little-known Beaux-Arts architect Georges Wybo, a designer of car showrooms and garages for his company. The small, cubic pavilion was placed diagonally in the inside corner of the two-winged Alfonso XIII exhibition hall. The mercurial Italian avant-gardist Piero Portaluppi reinterpreted a Palladian villa in an exuberant and fashionable Novecento style (figure 4.27). The most remarkable and determinedly modern pavilion after Mies's was the Yugoslav Pavilion by Zagreb modernist Dragiša Brašovan (figure 4.28). The small, two-story building had a planar façade with stark ribbon windows and a flat roof, but the little structure seemed to have undergone a process of violent folding, its walls zigzagging in and out in late-expressionist convulsions. German critic Walther Genzmer found that the unornamented Swedish Pavilion was the only other modern structure worth mentioning, besides Mies's pavilion (figure 4.29).[68]

Figure 4.27. Piero Portaluppi, Italian Pavilion, Barcelona World's Fair, 1929.

Figure 4.28. Dragiša Brašovan, Yugoslav Pavilion, Barcelona World's Fair, 1929.

In Barcelona, pavilions representing an industry or a company were also architecturally more adventurous, and many were modern in style, such as the pavilion of the Hispano-Suiza company by Eusebi Bona i Puig, the CSHE (Ebro Water Authority) Pavilion by Regino Borobio, and the Nestlé Kohler Pavilion right behind the German Pavilion (figure 4.30). In front of the southeastern corner of the German Pavilion, an elegant stand promoted the famous Swiss Maggi bouillon cubes, and until late at night the stand offered free samples of hot soup (figure 4.31).[69] Several visitors remarked how the restrained formal language of the German Pavilion, in particular, offered a welcome place of "sublime calm and uplifting silence," as a "refuge for anyone who feels burdened by the crazy commotion and loud noise of the buildings, towers and fountains."[70]

1986   Rebuilding the Pavilion

Known for more than half a century only through Stone's black-and-white photographs, the pavilion was rebuilt at its former location, just in time for the 1986 centenary of Mies's birth (figures 4.32–4.34). When Oriol Bohigas had first approached Mies with the idea of reconstructing the pavilion in 1957, the building's symbolic role as a representative of the democratic Weimar Republic had been firmly established. Bohigas belonged to a loose group of Catalan architects, Grup R (Grupo R, in Spanish), which between 1951 and 1961 moved the discourse beyond the regime's preferred monumentalism and neoclassicism, advocating instead a rediscovery of the ethics and aesthetics of prewar Spanish modernism. In rebuilding Mies's pavilion, they hoped not only to restore a significant part of the city's architectural past, but also to resist Francoist cultural politics. Nothing came of the proposal then, due to the loss of the original plans and the extraordinary costs associated with a recreation through Mies's office.

When, almost thirty years later, the project finally came to fruition (Bohigas had become city building deputy), the political context was entirely different. After Franco's death in 1975, Spain had returned to a democratically governed, constitutional monarchy and was busy catching up to its European neighbors. It had hosted the 1982 FIFA World Cup and was preparing to join the European Union in 1986. In the fall of 1986, Barcelona was selected to host the 1992 Olympics. Under its activist mayor, Pasqual Maragall i Mira (in office from 1982 to 1997), Barcelona lobbied successfully to place the work of Antonio Gaudí on the UNESCO World Heritage List. In this context, the rebuilt Barcelona Pavilion promised to boost cultural tourism, an important factor of economic growth. With its stone from Italy, Greece, and North Africa, and financial contributions from Germany, the EU, and Spain, one could hardly imagine a more potent symbol for the tides of its time than the new pavilion.

Given the almost complete absence of original construction documents, the new building is at best an approximation, and provoked a spirited debate about the value of reconstructions and the importance of authenticity. "How fundamentally does it differ from Disney?"

Figure 4.29. Pieter Clason, Swedish Pavilion, Barcelona World's Fair, 1929.

Figure 4.30. Unknown architect, Nestlé Kohler Pavilion, right behind Mies's German Pavilion, Barcelona World's Fair, 1929.

> Figure 4.31. Unknown architect, Maggi Pavilion, right in front of Mies's German Pavilion, Barcelona World's Fair, 1929.

Rem Koolhaas asked, while Alison and Peter Smithson wondered if, deprived of "its revolutionary intent," it would become "merely a tourist attraction."[71]

But even those uneasy with this "replica," "facsimile," or "parody" had to admit that the experience of the building in color and three dimensions offers rich new insights into its architectural concept. Its reincarnation also coincided with—and was probably helped by—wider changes in the discourse about historical architecture, notably, the rediscovery of a "Presence of the Past," as Paolo Portoghesi titled the first Venice Architecture Biennale in 1980, and the rise of a postmodern architecture. In this context, the very real, physical, presence of the reborn Barcelona Pavilion paradoxically helped to rekindle a renewed interest in the architecture of the modern movement, which postmodernism had ostensibly set out to replace. And while the pavilion certainly never regained the political connotations it carried in the 1920s or foreshadowed in the postwar period (when Mies's architecture and that of his peers returned to Europe, supposedly as an architecture of democracy and freedom), its careful execution, play with light and shade, and open spatial sequences have had a lasting impact on generation after generation of architects and critics. In the process, it has become the single most written about building of the modern movement.

163   Barcelona, 1929

Figure 4.32. Ludwig Mies van der Rohe, German
Pavilion, Barcelona World's Fair, 1929. Rebuilt at the
same location in 1984–86. View from the southeast.
Architects: Cristian Cirici, Fernando Ramos, and Ignasi
de Solà-Morales. Photograph by Hassan Bagheri.

Figure 4.33. Ludwig Mies van der Rohe, German Pavilion, Barcelona World's Fair, 1929. Rebuilt at the same location in 1984–86. Small pool with statue by Georg Kolbe. Architects: Cristian Cirici, Fernando Ramos, and Ignasi de Solà-Morales. Photograph by Hassan Bagheri.

Figure 4.34. Ludwig Mies van der Rohe, German Pavilion, Barcelona World's Fair, 1929. Rebuilt at the same location in 1984–86. View from the office at the southern end toward the main building with its luminous wall. Architects: Cristian Cirici, Fernando Ramos, and Ignasi de Solà-Morales. Photograph by Hassan Bagheri.

Five

Success and Changing Tides

Brno, Berlin, 1929–33

1930 Neue Wache Memorial Project

Thanks to the success of the German Pavilion at the 1929 World's Fair in Barcelona, Mies gained in national prominence. Three months after the pavilion had been dismantled, Mies was one of six architects invited to a limited government competition, which promised similar nationwide attention and required even more gravitas than representing the nation at a World's Fair. The government had decided to turn the interior of Karl Friedrich Schinkel's 1818 Neue Wache guardhouse on Unter den Linden Boulevard in the center of Berlin into a national memorial for the fallen soldiers of World War I.[1]

The trauma of the lost world war of 1914 to 1918, with a million Germans dead, countless maimed soldiers on the streets of Berlin, and the harsh conditions of the Versailles Treaty of 1919, weighed heavily on the collective psyche during the Weimar Republic. It had been a senseless war, triggered almost by accident, the result of incompetence, vanity, and pride, with no noble cause for which to fight or die. The rocky transition from monarchy to democracy that followed had led to pervasive political disunity and social tensions. Ten years after its beginning, the debate about how to commemorate the fallen had assumed particular intensity. Two projects that were discussed in 1924 demonstrate the breadth of the approaches. In August 1924, the foundation stone had been laid for a huge war memorial in Tannenberg, East Prussia (now Olsztynek, Poland), which commemorated the first major battle against the Russian army. The Germans had won this battle, but since they had lost the war, it was a meaningless triumph. The abstract, octagonal castle by the unknown Berlin architects Johannes Krüger and Walter Krüger was finished in 1927 (figure 5.1).

On the other end of the spectrum stood the proposal by art historian Frida Schottmüller, the first female curator at the Kaiser-Friedrich-Museum and a former student of Heinrich Wölfflin. In response to the Tannenberg Monument, she wrote:

> It is not necessary to honor the fallen of the war with a monument in the open, there is a building that is perfectly suitable for a memorial hall in terms of location, size and style, as if it had been conceived for this purpose.... The new guardhouse, which Schinkel built in 1816.... Today it stands empty and purposeless. It does not need to and should not be changed on the outside because of its beauty.... The interior, which apparently is architecturally insignificant, is to be adapted to the new purpose. Through the vestibule one should enter a square room, not too bright, with high windows or skylights. The walls are to be strictly and simply structured, perhaps with a bench-like plinth. In the center a simple sarcophagus, not too high: the grave not of the "unknown soldier," but instead of all the Germans whom the war took from us.[2]

When Emperor Wilhelm II had abdicated in 1918, the royal guard had been dissolved, and the building lost its functional purpose.[3] But it continued to be associated with the end of Napoleon's occupation and the long quest for German unification. Schinkel's first major commission had been a deliberately humble gesture—chosen over grander, triumphal manifestations (figure 5.2). A Doric temple front with allegorical depictions of war in its pediment was attached to a square building with corner pylons, reminiscent of a Roman castrum. The side walls consisted of exposed brick, and the building was surrounded by a grove of chestnut trees for quiet contemplation.

While the well-proportioned, Doric porticus made a confident contribution to Berlin's *Via Triumphalis,* Unter den Linden, between the Armory and Prinz Heinrich Palais, it had little to do with the rooms behind it, which were only accessible to the guards. Several utilitarian spaces on two floors (including a prison cell) surrounded a small atrium courtyard. The porticus thus did not signal a public entrance, as it normally would. Rather, Schinkel, who had begun his career painting theater decorations and panoramas, had created a veritable stage set here, merely a backdrop for the military ceremony in front. Guards would enter at the back of the building, change inside, and emerge in their colorful Prussian uniforms out front to perform their duties. This dissonance between form and function was already noted by contemporary critics.[4]

The Social Democratic prime minister of Prussia (Germany's largest state, to which Berlin belonged), Otto Braun, finally moved the idea of a new national memorial forward, and the competition was held in the spring of 1930. The invited architects included conservatives such as Hans Grube and Erich Blunck, and moderns of different persuasions such as Heinrich Tessenow, Peter Behrens, and Hans Poelzig. Mies van der Rohe was the youngest and most progressive participant. The government wanted a "simple" and "solemn" memorial "in organic relations with the exterior." The resulting space was meant to allow for the laying of wreaths and processions. The nature of the task and the seriousness of the time required "simple architectonic means." Schinkels's exterior was to remain untouched. Moving away from Schottmüller's vision, the brief suggested that an "atrium-like" approach with an open courtyard and a commemorative symbol at the center should be the basis of any solution.[5]

The selection committee featured a number of prominent names, such as critics Walter Curt Behrendt and Karl Scheffler, Reich art commissioner Edwin Redslob, Berlin urban planner Martin Wagner, and only one architect, the conservative Dresden professor Wilhelm Kreis. Out of nine jurors, five voted for Tessenow, three for Mies, and only one for Poelzig. At the end of July, the entries were exhibited in Berlin to great public interest, and Behrendt presented the results in the official *Zentralblatt der Bauverwaltung.*[6] As it turned out, those who had followed the brief and created an atrium (Grube, Blunck, Poelzig) had no chance at succeeding—their cramped designs showed that there simply was not enough space. Nevertheless, Poelzig, who had assembled eighteen columns around the central court, received the third-place prize; but he was understandably upset that the top prizes went to colleagues who had ignored the brief (figure 5.3).[7]

Tessenow won first prize, thanks to the simplicity of his approach, closest to Schottmüller's vision: under an open oculus sat a square block with a wreath; the walls were clad in the same ashlar as the front outside, and the side windows were blocked off (figure 5.4). According to the jury, "The silence of the room and the ultimate simplicity of its form give the memorial a solemnity full of consecration and compelling devotion. With the purest means of architectural design, the effect of the highest dignity and greatest monumentality is achieved here, as in Schinkel's building itself." The design was "timeless" and "ready for immediate execution."[8] The two organizing ministries were intent on demonstrating an efficient process: construction started right away, and the dedication followed a year later.

Figure 5.1. Johannes Krüger and Walter Krüger, Tannenberg Monument, Tannenberg, East Prussia (now Olsztynek, Poland), 1924–27.

Figure 5.2. Karl Friedrich Schinkel and Salomo Sachs, Neue Wache, Berlin, 1816–18.

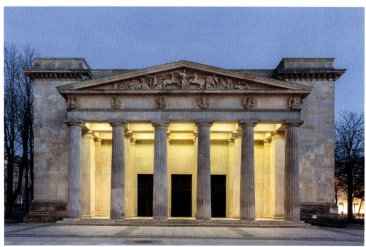

Mies placed second (figures 5.5, 5.6). While he also ignored the brief's quest for an atrium, not even providing lighting from above, he was more respectful of Schinkel's structure than anyone else. The two rows of windows (four and six respectively) on the side walls remained intact, and Mies gingerly inserted ten slender steel columns into the hollowed-out interior, about six and a half feet (two meters) clear of the walls. The columns carried five roof trusses for a lightly pitched roof, cantilevering out to the edge without putting weight on Schinkel's structure. They also carried horizontal supports for thin slabs of Tinos marble, making up the inner walls. The resulting space measured 46 by 46 by 30 feet (14 by 14 by 9 meters), with a ceiling of white stucco. Low travertine benches on either side invited contemplation; the five openings to the street were closed with gray transparent glass, admitting a dim light. Inside, they were flanked by six vertical candelabras for evening illumination. An indentation in the travertine floor held a low, square granite block with a relief of the Reich's eagle and the words *"Den Toten"* (To the Dead) on the side. A tall door on axis led to a shallow vestibule in the back (again, part of Schinkel's original design) and to the outside. Access was only provided from the chestnut grove in the back, thus forcing visitors away from the busy street, and maintaining Schinkel's handling of the porticus as merely a backdrop and an embellishment of the boulevard, instead of a public, triumphal entrance. The simple door in the back provided a more appropriate access to a space of mourning and reflection.

According to Behrendt, the jury appreciated the "noble pathos and strong symbolic power" of Mies's design, but found that the door in the back and the stone benches on two sides gave the square room "a pronounced longitudinal direction," depriving it of its peaceful atmosphere, almost suggesting "the character of a passageway."[9] The lighting was "unresolved," as it was impossible "to see into the darkened interior from the street," and the green marble all the way up to the ceiling led to "semi-darkness" and "a gloomy mood." The treatment and emphasis of the material gave the room "an exhibition-like and overly precious appearance, which contradicts its purpose and, moreover, is alien to the spirit of Schinkel's building, which is completely focused on its form."[10]

Reception

Not surprisingly, the competition found a broad echo in the press—the wide range of passionately held opinions apparently independent of political convictions. The Communist paper *Die Rote Fahne* dismissed the government's cheap gesture of "commemoration" at a time when hundreds of thousands of disabled, widows, and orphans were suffering from the effects of war and the Depression.[11] Modernist critic Adolf Behne rejected the location of Unter den Linden in the *Sozialistische Monatshefte* as too comfortable, driven

Figure 5.3. Hans Poelzig, design for a memorial for the fallen of World War I inside Karl Friedrich Schinkel's Neue Wache, Berlin, 1930. Interior perspective. Charcoal on transparent paper, 33 7/8 × 45 3/4 in. (86 × 116.1 cm). Technische Universität Berlin, Architekturmuseum.

Figure 5.4. Heinrich Tessenow, design for a memorial for the fallen of World War I inside Karl Friedrich Schinkel's Neue Wache, Berlin, 1930.

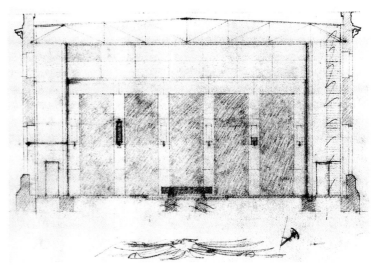

Figure 5.5. Ludwig Mies van der Rohe, design for
the Neue Wache Memorial project, Berlin, 1930.
Cross section.

Figure 5.6. Ludwig Mies van der Rohe, design for
the Neue Wache Memorial project, Berlin, 1930.
Black-and-white photograph of drawing by Sergius
Ruegenberg. Gelatin silver print on illustration
board, 4 3/8 × 5 5/8 in. (11 × 14.3 cm). Berlinische
Galerie, Berlin.

by concerns for appearances rather than true conviction. He arrogantly dismissed Frida Schottmüller's idea as "a housewife's proposal."[12]

Mies found praise on both sides of the aisle: the right-wing (soon to be Nazi) critic for a Munich daily, Kurt Karl Eberlein, found Mies's "dark marble chamber" the only acceptable solution.[13] The Social Democratic journal *Vorwärts* similarly found "Mies van der Rohe's design, undoubtedly, the solution to be considered here.…The sublime solemnity of the half-darkened room represents the strongest expression of the sentiment that we bear towards the victims of the war."[14] Similarly, Paul Westheim advocated for Mies in his monthly *Das Kunstblatt*. He found Tessenow's design "banal" in every respect, spiritually and formally, in great contrast to Mies's design: "a square space, the light subdued, marble walls, solemn and serious…simplicity, greatness, dignity and not least the spirit of Schinkel."[15]

Cultural critic Siegfried Kracauer agreed with Schottmüller on the need for an empty space, and found the language of modern architecture the only appropriate approach:

> It is simply the case that any positive statement seems impossible in our time.…The fact that modern churches look like grain silos or railroad stations is certainly no coincidence, just like the fact that strictly utilitarian buildings, which simply serve their purpose, seem most likely to have been designed for their own sake. They are the only true monuments of our time.…To be honest, a memorial for people killed in the world war must not be much more than an empty space.

However, he agreed with the jury and preferred Tessenow's "decent modesty," which abstained from both "dishonest sentimentality" and "booming objectivity without individual commitment." Mies van der Rohe, he declared, deserved credit for trying "to give full shape to the idea of the memorial…a container for memory, where it would find a proper place. With this intention, he designed a dark interior, lit only by the front windows. The walls of this mausoleum are made of dark marble, and in the middle of the darkness there is a tombstone with a bas-relief of an imperial eagle." Mies's design had not succeeded, however, he concluded (rather prophetically): "Against all expectations, it resembles certain comfortable vestibules, which are the pride of many a large company."[16]

Recycling the Barcelona Pavilion

Almost fifty surviving sketches show Mies's meandering, indecisive path toward a solution for the memorial. There are glass screens with visitors behind them, a phalanx of heavy piers, or different versions of a freestanding wall inscribed "Den Toten"—akin to the onyx wall at the Barcelona Pavilion and Tugendhat House (figure 5.7). This concept ultimately evolved into a low, square block of black granite, with the same inscription and the heraldic German eagle in flat relief on top, resulting in an open, uninterrupted space. Mies's code word for the competition was *"Raum"* (space), a noun that, due to the reception of the Barcelona Pavilion, many identified with Mies.[17] The presentation drawing was executed by Mies's assistant Sergius Ruegenberg, who had supervised the building of the Barcelona Pavilion.[18]

All materials and details mentioned here point to the Barcelona Pavilion: the slabs of thin Tinos marble on the walls, the square travertine floor plates, the stuccoed ceiling, and the low travertine benches. Even the gray glass in the façade to the street references the tinted glass at the pavilion. The German Pavilion had provided Mies with the most widespread praise of his career, and for many years he seems to have been unable to move beyond its formal vocabulary. The Neue Wache project was the first of these self-reflective designs.

Now let us consider the contemporary chronology. The Barcelona Pavilion was dismantled at the end of January 1930. After proposals to rebuild or sell it in Spain came to nothing, its marble and travertine slabs were shipped back to Hamburg to the ministries of finance and economic affairs, which had given a debt guarantee for this instance. Much of the exuberant cost overruns that Mies had produced in Barcelona had been covered by the German commissioner, Georg von Schnitzler, from both his private accounts and via loans he managed to secure. Mies had assured him that the building material for Barcelona would eventually be sold, and this income would offset the debt. How central that point was to the relationship between architect and client had become apparent when von Schnitzler invited Mies to return to Barcelona on October 23, 1929, for a celebratory event during "German Week": "It would be truly a great pity if you, the creator of this pavilion, were absent on this day, and I am asking you kindly to be there for at least a few days, and in particular on that Wednesday." Von Schnitzler slyly suggested that Mies should cover his own travel expenses, for which he would be reimbursed from the proceeds from the sale of the pavilion, which he had promised so often. Mies politely declined.[19]

The return shipment of the marble, travertine, and glass from Barcelona would have taken several weeks. It left Barcelona in March 1930 and would have arrived in Hamburg at precisely the moment when Mies was working on the Neue Wache design. It seems highly likely that Mies saw an opportunity here to reuse some of the pavilion's materials—in other words, to not just perpetuate its formal vocabulary but to use its *actual* parts. It would have proven his point to von Schnitzler by creating income to offset his debts, and also made Mies's current proposal more affordable. In Sergius Ruegenberg's central perspective for the Neue Wache project, the Tinos marble slabs and the travertine floor plates show the same size of those in Barcelona. The travertine benches could be assembled from the material for the long bench flanking the pool. The large panes of gray glass would have fit into the front openings. Each side of the cube inside the Neue Wache is 46 feet (14 meters) long and 30 feet (nine meters) high. Exactly 199 Tinos marble and 196 travertine slabs would have been needed. The Barcelona Pavilion had used roughly 600 travertine slabs, and around 133 Tinos marble slabs, although considerably more had been ordered by Mies's team. Those plates were now sitting in a Hamburg warehouse, waiting to be used.

We know from Ruegenberg's drawing what the interior view toward the north would have looked like, and the surviving cross section with a southern view allows for a similar reconstruction, which Hassan Bagheri has executed (figures 5.8, 5.9). The drawing makes clear that Schinkel's columns and lintels would have remained untouched, while two rows of Tinos verde marble slabs would have been placed above.

Figure 5.7. Ludwig Mies van der Rohe, design for the Neue Wache Memorial project, Berlin, 1930. Sketch, interior perspective view. Pencil on paper, 8 1/4 × 13 in. (21 × 33 cm). Museum of Modern Art, New York. The Mies van der Rohe Archive, gift of the architect.

Figure 5.8. Ludwig Mies van der Rohe, design for the Neue Wache Memorial project, Berlin, 1930. Rendering of Sergius Ruegenberg's interior perspective using the Tinos verde and travertine plates from the reconstructed Barcelona Pavilion. Photograph by Hassan Bagheri.

Figure 5.9. Ludwig Mies van der Rohe, design for the Neue Wache Memorial project, Berlin, 1930. Interior perspective looking south toward Unter den Linden Boulevard using the Tinos verde and travertine plates from the reconstructed Barcelona Pavilion. Photograph by Hassan Bagheri.

Since Mies knew several members of the jury, such as Walter Curt Behrendt, Martin Wagner, and Karl Scheffler, he might have found a way to hint at the availability of the Barcelona marble in a Hamburg warehouse, and the potential savings for the government that his scheme offered. One wonders if Behrendt surreptitiously referenced this connection when he found Mies's proposal "too precious" and "exhibition-like."

Mies's memorial in Schinkel's guardhouse occupies a rather unique position in his oeuvre. Apart from showing him pragmatically applying existing ideas and materials to new contexts, he also comes across as sensitive to the mood of the time and to the enormous task of responding to the national trauma of the catastrophic war and its aftermath. Perhaps most importantly, the Neue Wache project shows Mies in respectful conversation with a historic monument by the most significant German architect of the nineteenth century—it remained his only (and brilliant) example of adaptive reuse.

1931 *Deutsche Bauausstellung*

The *Deutsche Bauausstellung* at the Berlin fairgrounds from May 16 to August 3, 1931, the largest ever held in Germany, spread over 1.4 million square feet (130,000 square meters) and eight exhibition halls (figure 5.10). Much space was devoted to building products and machinery, a large section in hall one presented new approaches to urban planning the world over, and there was an outdoor display of buildings for rural areas. Mies and Lilly Reich were in charge of hall two and an exhibition called *Die Wohnung unserer Zeit* (The Dwelling of Our Time), which ended up being the most frequently discussed part of the show. The perimeter of the large hall showed examples of affordable housing on the first floor, such as Munich architect Robert Vorhoelzer's Boarding House, whose first-floor common room showed Mies's influence quite succinctly (figure 5.11).

Figure 5.10. View of the *Deutsche Bauausstellung*, Berlin, 1931. Mies van der Rohe's House for a Childless Couple is in the foreground, Lilly Reich's Single Story House is in the background. Gelatin silver print, 6 5/8 × 9 1/8 in. (16.8 × 23.2 cm). Museum of Modern Art, New York. The Mies van der Rohe Archive, gift of the architect.

Figure 5.11. Robert Vorhoelzer, Boarding House, *Deutsche Bauausstellung*, Berlin, 1931.

In the center, two houses by Mies and Lilly Reich took pride of place—connected by a wall, as if holding hands. Mies's own House for a Childless Couple was typologically close to the Barcelona Pavilion and adopted a similar design vocabulary (figure 5.12). The one-story structure contained a sequence of open spaces (vestibule, living room, dining room, and bedroom, as well as a small kitchen and room for a maid), protruding roof slabs, fifteen freestanding, round, chromium-covered steel columns, and a shallow water basin outside. The travertine and marble walls of Barcelona, however, were replaced here with white stucco and rosewood. Lilly Reich's adjacent "Single Story House," which had a similar

Figure 5.12. Ludwig Mies van der Rohe, House for a Childless Couple, *Deutsche Bauausstellung,* Berlin, 1931. Interior view of living room. Note the Barcelona chair in the foreground on the left and the Brno chair on the right. Gelatin silver print, 6 5/8 × 9 1/8 in. (16.8 × 23.2 cm). Museum of Modern Art, New York. The Mies van der Rohe Archive, gift of the architect.

program, was more compact, but came with a more generously sized kitchen and living space for a maid or cook.

Mies made a convincing effort to identify functional space, and the sequence of openly connected bedrooms for the two inhabitants, with a shared bathroom and dressing room between them, was superior to the arrangement at the Tugendhat House (figure 5.13; see figures 5.16–5.23). Similarly, the enclosed courtyard and pool outside the bedroom sequence shows a skillful handling of sight lines to preserve the privacy of the woman's section of the bedroom. The spatial generosity of the living quarters, however, stood in rather glaring contrast to the small kitchen and the adjacent maid's room, a tiny space made even more awkward by a freestanding column in its center. Another statue (again, a plaster cast) by Georg Kolbe was integrated into the spatial sequence, this time a "Tall Woman Walking."[20] Mies also designed a small apartment for a bachelor (figures 5.14, 5.15).

He declared, "The home of our time does not yet exist. But the changed needs of life demand its realization. The prerequisite for this realization is the clear elaboration of the real living needs. This will be the main task of the exhibition."[21] The contrast between Mies's and Reich's houses in the center and the examples of affordable workers' housing that stood alongside them did not escape the critics, who noted Mies's tone deafness in the face of the Depression and a real housing crisis for the working class.

In a scathing article, prominent critic Adolf Behne, who had often been supportive of Mies, found "stylistic dictatorship" and "aesthetic snobbism" in the exhibit. The apartments were not just "uninhabited," but lifeless and stuck in limiting formal fashions—"sterile, gray and glassy, as if a desert storm had swept through the house.…It has long been convincingly demonstrated that the more money you're able to spend on a dwelling, the more pleasant, spacious, and comfortable it will be." In reality, he continued, "the dwelling of our time— that is, the one needed with terrible urgency, is the dwelling for the people—the worker's dwelling."[22] Mies's house in particular, he pointed out, was clearly not meant for a worker, but rather for a person who did *not* have to work.

Another critic singled out Mies's house as a "show-off apartment of the future" that made a mockery of the needs of ordinary people.[23] The left-leaning weekly *Die Weltbühne* asked:

> Does Mies van der Rohe, whom up to now we had appreciated as an important architect, really believe that his one-story house…has created a building type for the future by avoiding the most burning questions of our time? Today we do not need an exhibition about dwellings for the man with too much money. The rich have always built homes adapted to their personal needs and taste. An exhibition funded

Figure 5.13. Ludwig Mies van der Rohe, House for a Childless Couple, *Deutsche Bauausstellung,* Berlin, 1931. Floor plan.

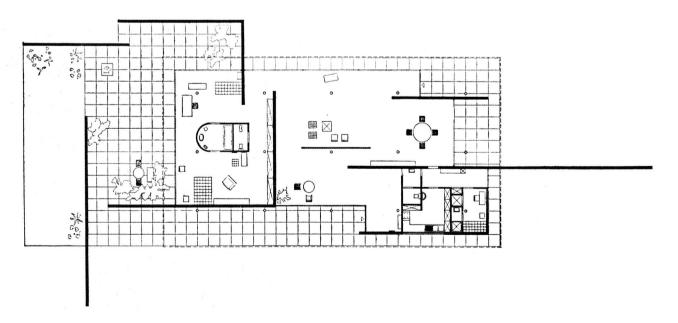

largely through public subsidies, however, should have more important problems to solve than luxurious housing for miniscule layers of our population.[24]

Czech architect Karel Teige observed that Mies's house was "a more or less irrational adaptation of his German Barcelona Pavilion," turned into a dwelling by simply adding "a toilet and a bathroom—and presto, the villa of the future has arrived! The whole concept is supremely impractical and governed by formal sculptural ambitions, which, in turn, are based on purely abstract notions of space composition—Raumkunst—executed with luxury materials.…This is theater and sculpture, not architecture—snobbish ostentation, but not a dwelling."[25] In contrast, while the Werkbund journal *Die Form* conceded that the encounter of the "working-class dwelling and a modern luxury object"[26] was, indeed, "a bit harsh," it found undeniable beauty in the house's "open spaces with their lively connection of interior and exterior," and Mies's "courage to think freely and unhampered about the future" while providing a purely spiritual direction for the dwelling and for the whole of modern architecture—in great contrast to the deplorable "violation of space" in the minimal dwellings and their lack of a discernible "desire for a new lifestyle."[27]

Philip Johnson, in the middle of preparations for his *Modern Architecture: International Exhibition* at MoMA, was clearly aware of the attacks on the building, and defended Mies in the *New York Times*. He acknowledged that the house "could have been built at a lesser cost and have been more economical of space and still have served equally well its function of living quarters for an unmarried couple." But then again, Mies had long passed beyond the purely utilitarian: "The Mies home is admittedly luxurious. For this reason, Mies is disliked by many architects and critics, especially the communists." After this adroit piece of political positioning, he went on to portray Mies as a stalwart defender of architectural beauty against "the exaggeration of functionalism into a theory of building where aesthetic considerations do not enter at all."[28] Johnson's friend Helen Appleton Read similarly dismissed those houses at the *Deutsche Bauausstellung* that were "too meagerly practical, too exclusively concerned with the problem of building inexpensive houses, to impress an American visitor with their importance." Instead, Read praised Mies's modernity, handling of space, and materials. We owe her the most precise eyewitness description of the house in that regard: "Varying shades of white are used in the woman's bedroom—a white, hand-tufted, rajah silk bedspread, a chair upholstered in white velours, a rug made of natural coloured grey-white wool, a marble shelf for flowers and books. Pale honey coloured wood…serves as one of the walls.…The curtains hang in straight, classic folds. Indigo-blue or black rajah silk are preferred. The man's room follows the same principle, but is done in indigo-blue with a rich wood for the cupboard wall." Ultimately, she found the building "curiously inspiring." After all, there "is an increasing need for a simplification of living, spiritually and practically. It is encouraging for those of us who have feared that this simplification necessarily entails drab standardization to have evidence to the contrary."[29]

Figure 5.14. Ludwig Mies van der Rohe, Apartment for a Bachelor, *Deutsche Bauausstellung*, Berlin, 1931. Floor plan.

Figure 5.15. Ludwig Mies van der Rohe, Apartment for a Bachelor, *Deutsche Bauausstellung*, Berlin, 1931. Interior view.

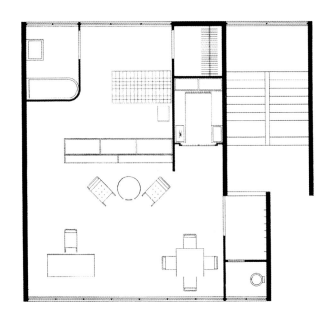

"Kann man im Haus Tugendhat wohnen?" (Can one live in the Tugendhat House?)—this provocative question in October 1931 signaled the continuation of the summer's debate about Mies's residential architecture at the Bauausstellung. Of course, Justus Bier's question was entirely rhetorical—after all, the Tugendhats apparently managed to live quite comfortably in their famous house. What Bier really meant was: *Should* one live in a house like that? Was it even morally justifiable? Evidently, in his eyes, it was not.[30] Before returning to this question, let us have a brief look at the genesis and context of the house.

The parents of both Grete and Fritz Tugendhat owned textile mills in Brno, Czechoslovakia (now Czechia)—called "Brünn" by the German-speaking population—and it was Grete's father, Walter Löw-Beer, who had given the plot of land at Schwarzfeldgasse 45 to the couple as a wedding present and then financed the house. It was situated close to his own house on the other end of a sloping large garden and enjoyed an enticing view over the city of Brno. The Tugendhats contacted Mies after seeing his Perls House in Berlin (1911–12) (then owned by the historian Eduard Fuchs), for which he had just built a modern gallery addition (see figures 1.30, 1.31); he suggested they also see the conservative Mosler House in Potsdam-Babelsberg and the Wolf House in Guben, on a comparable lot on a hillside overlooking the city. The Esters and Lange houses in Krefeld were under construction when Mies and the Tugendhats met.

Mies saw the site in September, and the essential elements were in place by the end of December 1928, when Mies presented his design to the clients. Construction of the

Figure 5.16. Ludwig Mies van der Rohe, Tugendhat House, Brno, Czechoslovakia (today, Brno, Czechia), 1928–31. Street façade, 1931. Photograph by Rudolf Sandalo.

Tugendhat House began in the summer of 1929, just after the German Pavilion had been opened on May 27, 1929.

While the size and program seem to align it with the two houses in Krefeld, spatially and structurally, the Tugendhat House appeared strikingly different (figures 5.16, 5.17). Instead of the mix of load-bearing brick façades and vertical and horizontal steel supports in Krefeld, the new design was based on a pure steel-frame construction, a precondition for the large expanses of glass on the lower floor. The structure and its masonry infill were covered in white stucco.

In response to its hillside location, the building's entrance from an unassuming, low elevation on street level leads into what is effectively the second floor of the building, containing a vestibule and the nanny's and family bedrooms, with direct access to a southwestern terrace overlooking the city. Visitors who entered the house would turn 180 degrees and descend on a semicircular staircase into the main living room (figure 5.18). This spectacular, light-filled space of 2,400 square feet (223 square meters) is, of course, the decisive and most conspicuous part of the building.

What must have struck many contemporary visitors as shockingly new in a residential environment was the complete replacement of the two outside walls with glass, with just the edges of floor and ceiling framing the view over the garden below and the city in the distance (figure 5.19). Two of the four large glass panels on the southern side could be lowered into the ground. The vastness of the room was enhanced by its radical emptiness and an unusual brightness that resulted from the unhindered influx of light reflected upward from the white linoleum floor and down from the white ceiling (figure 5.20). While there

Figure 5.17. Ludwig Mies van der Rohe, Tugendhat House, Brno, Czechoslovakia (today, Brno, Czechia), 1928–31. Garden façade.

were some chairs, tables, and built-in bookshelves, no provisions were made for the display of personal belongings or for family activities. The sparse furniture arrangements nevertheless hint at the key functions of a bourgeois home: reception, dining and living areas, and a library and workplace for the head of the household (figures 5.21–5.23). The space is divided by a solid Moroccan onyx wall parallel to the main front, and a semicircular Macassar ebony wood screen sheltering the dining area. The onyx wall is flanked by Wilhelm Lehmbruck's 1913 sculpture *Mädchentorso, sich umwendend* (Girl's Torso, Turning), and ten freestanding cruciform steel columns in a reflective chromium skin punctuate the space at regular intervals. Over the entire length of the eastern front a "winter garden" provides a green buffer zone, filtering the morning light and obstructing views from the adjacent sidewalk. At the western edge a door leads to a terrace and a wide staircase into the garden, for which Mies designed the landscaping.

Mies had been given the creative and financial freedom to create a classic Gesamtkunstwerk (a total work of art), in which everything from the building itself down to the furniture, curtains, and door handles was selected and designed by himself and Lilly Reich. Mies carefully chose the material for the solid, honey-colored onyx doré wall and made a special trip to Paris to find the right kind of Macassar wood. The radical innovation in the spatial-functional arrangements was equaled by the use of new materials and the application of recent technologies.

Behind the dinner alcove, a translucent wall of opal glass could be illuminated by fluorescent lights in the ceiling behind (which also furnished light to the adjacent food preparation area). The same opal glass was used in the entrance area, accompanying the hallway to the children's wing and tracing the descending, semicircular staircase. Then a recent invention,

Figure 5.20. Ludwig Mies van der Rohe, Tugendhat House, Brno, Czechoslovakia (today, Brno, Czechia), 1928–31. Living room. Photograph by Dietrich Neumann.

opal glass had quickly become a ubiquitous part of advertising displays in Berlin's streets and was widely discussed as a crucial element for a new luminous, ephemeral "architecture of the night." The *New York Times* believed that Berlin was the world leader in this application, naming it "the city of opal glass" in 1932.[31] Mies had used a similar wall of opal glass in Barcelona, and before at his recent designs in Berlin and Stuttgart, and the abovementioned glass exhibition room at the Stuttgart Werkbund exhibition in 1927 (see figure 3.33).

The Tugendhat House was fitted out with the latest technical amenities—apart from the abovementioned retractable windows, there was an early prototype of air-conditioning, a food elevator, and an electric alarm system. Numerous pieces of furniture were designed especially for the house, by both Mies and Reich—first and foremost the Brno Chair, which exploited the flexibility of flat steel bands similar to that of the contemporary Barcelona Chair, and several versions of a cantilevered chair, which improved upon Mies's 1927 version by removing the semicircular curve at its front in favor of almost vertical legs, and the separation of the seat support from the steel tubing. In addition, there were numerous simple shelves and tables with a Macassar veneer, as well as a sideboard that consisted of a horizontal frame with darkened glass on both sides and chromium columns that suggested the same separation of support and enclosure that characterized the Tugendhat House and the Barcelona Pavilion.

While the Tugendhat House has clear stylistic affinities to the Barcelona Pavilion and the house at the *Deutsche Bauausstellung*, it also presents a stylistic, structural, and organizational departure from Mies's previous buildings, and it seems worth speculating about potential reasons behind these changes. Brno had, for centuries, been part of the widely German-speaking Austro-Hungarian Empire. In 1918, a new Czechoslovak state had

Figure 5.21. Ludwig Mies van der Rohe, Tugendhat House, Brno, Czechoslovakia (today, Brno, Czechia), 1928–31. Dining alcove. Photograph by Dietrich Neumann.

Figure 5.22. Ludwig Mies van der Rohe, Tugendhat House, Brno, Czechoslovakia (today, Brno, Czechia), 1928–31. Library. Photograph by Dietrich Neumann.

Figure 5.23. Ludwig Mies van der Rohe, Tugendhat House, Brno, Czechoslovakia (today, Brno, Czechia), 1928–31. Floor plans.

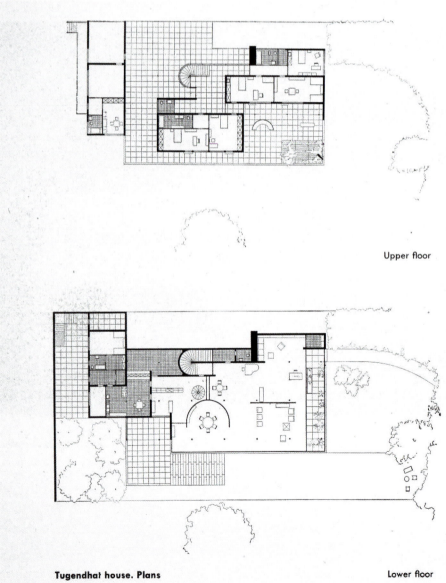

Upper floor

Tugendhat house. Plans

Lower floor

been proclaimed, uniting the Czechs and Slovaks into one country under a centralist, but modern, democratic constitution. As the inheritor of substantial industrial sites, Czechoslovakia (today, Czechia and Slovakia) was economically the most fortunate of the successor states of the empire. Brno, the country's second-largest city, was one of its centers of industrial production, which was dominated by metalworking and textile industries. In an astonishingly liberal political atmosphere, new Czechoslovak parties coexisted with parties such as the German Social Democrats and a party representing the interests of the German minority in Brno. More Czech-speaking schools than before catered to the Czech majority, but German schools continued to flourish. As German Jews, the parents of both Grete and Fritz had been active members of the Deutsches Haus (German House) in Brno, a cultural center advancing German language and culture.

Nevertheless, a certain amount of tension and competition among the different ethnic groups resulted from the recent political changes. In a conscious break with the forces of the past, many Czech intellectuals sought out new and different cultural alliances. After a visit to a lecture in Brno, Theo van Doesburg reported in an article in the Dutch magazine *Het Bouwbedrijf* in 1926 that the motto of many of Brno's modernist architects was "Free from Germany!" while they sought artistic affiliations with their Dutch and French colleagues, in particular with Le Corbusier.[32] They had wholeheartedly embraced the formal language of the International Style in publications and exhibitions and in a number of spectacular modern buildings, aptly symbolizing their decisive break with the past.

While Grete and Fritz Tugendhat's choice of Mies as their architect was certainly an affirmation of their cultural leanings toward Germany, both client and architect might have felt that a building of starkly exposed brick (as in his previous villas) would have provided a rather provocative—and presumably "Germanic"—contrast to the already existing modernistic formal coherence and the cultural identity for which it stood. Grete Tugendhat recalled the reasons for that decision differently forty years later, in 1969: "We particularly liked the most recent house we saw, that of a Mr. Wolf in Guben, a very generous brick building. Originally, our house also was meant to be out of brick, but it turned out that there were no beautiful klinker bricks to be had in Brno and also no masons who were capable of perfectly laying them."[33] In defense of Brno's modernists and the local bricklayers, it needs to be said that, while white stucco dominated in that period, someone like the brilliant local architect Arnošt Wiesner had done several decent brick buildings recently, and was, at that moment, finishing the city's crematorium, also in brick (figure 5.24). Similarly, Bohuslav

Figure 5.24. Arnošt Wiesner, Crematorium, Brno, Czechoslovakia (today, Brno, Czechia), 1926–29.

Fuchs, the city's most prominent modernist, had created Brno's city pavilion in brick at the local exhibition grounds in 1928.

Mies had been acutely aware that he was about to build in a city with a very active group of modern architects and probably the highest number of modern buildings anywhere in Europe. In the photo survey of contemporary architecture at the Stuttgart Werkbund exhibition in 1927, he had personally assembled the Czech section. Fuchs, Wiesner, and their pupils had designed so many modern buildings in Brno that all major building types were covered. During his 1928–29 visits, Mies could have stayed in Fuchs's 1928 Hotel Avion, had breakfast at Fuchs's 1926 Café Zeman, whose large floor-to-ceiling windows could open entirely, or even visited Fuchs at his own house (1928) on Hvezdarenska Street, whose interior arrangement was curiously similar to that of the Tugendhat House (figure 5.25). Literally down the street from there was Josef Kranz's Café Era (1927–29),

Figure 5.25. Bohuslav Fuchs, Café Zeman, Brno, Czechoslovakia (today, Brno, Czechia), 1926. Demolished in 1964, rebuilt in 1995 by Ateliér ERA.

Figure 5.26. Josef Kranz, Café Era, Brno, Czechoslovakia (today, Brno, Czechia), 1927–29.

where we might imagine Mies taking Philip Johnson after their visit to the building site in 1930, as Johnson included the building in the International Style exhibition in New York two years later (figure 5.26). The Tugendhats could send their children to the new German school building, also within walking distance from their house (Bohuslav Fuchs, 1929) or take them to the city's Zábrdovice public pool (Fuchs, 1929). At the edge of the city, an entire new estate called Nový Dům (New House) responded to the Weissenhof Estate in Stuttgart of the previous year with a more systematic and uniform approach, presenting individual, double, and triple houses in a mature modernist style. And Arnošt Wiesner had just recently created a spectacular series of modern houses, of which in particular a house for Eduard Münz (1924–26), the director of the Czech Union Bank, with its flat roof and broad staircase leading into the garden, might have inspired details of the Tugendhat House (figure 5.27). It was published in Germany just at the time when Mies began thinking about the Tugendhat House.[34] Despite a number of similarities between the Münz House and Mies's Tugendhat House (more obvious as seen through the eyes of the same photographer, Rudolf Sandalo), this comparison also shows the radical inventiveness of Mies's central idea—the large, fully glazed living room that bisects the house entirely and challenges structural expectations.

A large exhibition ground was being developed in Brno and inaugurated with the 1928 *Výstava Soudobé Kultury* (Exhibition of Contemporary Culture), which demonstrated Czechoslovakia's modern spirit and potential on its tenth anniversary. Grete Tugendhat's father, Alfred Löw-Beer, and Fritz Tugendhat's brother Emil both helped to finance the exhibition. There were several modern exhibition pavilions by Bohuslav Fuchs, a spectacular interior by Adolf Loos, and radical parabolic concrete structures by Josef Kalous.

Few contemporary modern architects escaped the spell of Le Corbusier—and Mies was no exception. Le Corbusier's seminal publication *Vers une architecture* (Toward an Architecture) had been translated into German in 1926 (under the title *Kommende Baukunst*) and, as Wassili Luckhardt remembered later, "expressed convincingly what we all felt."[35] Le Corbusier's Villa de Monzie (Stein) in Garches, France, with its separation of support columns from the walls, continuous band of large windows at the garden façade, and wide staircase leading to the garden, was frequently published. Its open plan, punctured by separate curvilinear elements, and the overall rather closed geometric form were all highly influential in Germany from 1927 onward, and their echo is certainly palpable in the Tugendhat design. Le Corbusier's double house at the Weissenhof settlement prominently displayed a row of free steel supports in its open first floor.

Back in Berlin, others equally fell under Corbusier's spell, such as Wassili Luckhardt and Hans Luckhardt, whose single-family residences in Berlin from 1929 to 1932 each contained a vast living room opening toward a terrace through six floor-to-ceiling windows, two of which could be opened entirely by being moved horizontally (figure 5.28).

Figure 5.27. Arnošt Wiesner, Münz House, Brno, Czechoslovakia (today, Brno, Czechia), 1924–26.

Figure 5.28. Hans Luckhardt, Wassili Luckhardt, and Alfons Anker, two houses on am Rupenhorn, Berlin, 1929–32.

Freestanding cylindrical steel columns inside were covered with chromium, and the main wall of the living room was polished onyx. A third, unexecuted building in this group would have been the most radical, containing a large living room with a greenhouse separated by a glass wall similar to the one Mies was about to use in Brno. Just literally a few meters down the street Am Rupenhorn, Erich Mendelsohn built his own house simultaneously with the Tugendhat House's construction. Mendelsohn had submitted the plans for his house in the summer of 1928, before Mies had been to Brno to inspect the site, and Mendelsohn's house was finished in March 1930, when the Tugendhat House was still under construction. Here, several large plate-glass windows in the enormous living room could be lowered into the floor and offered free access to the terrace, with its view over the Havel River. This living room was openly connected to a hall and a dining area. Polished wood and travertine contributed to the carefully calibrated color harmonies. The garden façade with its continuous band of glass windows has unmistakable similarities to that of the Tugendhat House.[36]

Reception

Mies's friends at the Werkbund journal *Die Form* got the critical reception of Tugendhat House off to a good start with a long, fawning essay, written by editor-in-chief Walter Riezler, and lavishly illustrated with fifteen photographs commissioned by Mies. Riezler called the central living room "an entirely new type of space," equivalent to modern music.[37] Surely no one could fail to notice—he prompted—"the impression of a particular, highly developed spirituality that reigns in these rooms, a spirituality of a new kind, however, which is tied in particular ways to the present and is entirely different, therefore, from the spirit one might encounter in spaces of earlier epochs....This is not a 'machine for living in' but a house of true 'luxury,' which means that it serves highly elevated needs and does not cater to some 'frugal,' somehow circumscribed lifestyle."[38]

Putting aside this dig at Le Corbusier's "machine for living in," Riezler's review, with its references to music and spirituality, and to an entirely new type of space, closely echoes the words that he and others used to describe the Barcelona Pavilion: "Everything static, everything sedate, recedes behind the dynamic of these spatial sections that glide into each other, whose rhythm finds its fulfilment only outside, when united with the all-encompassing space of nature. The space is, if you like, 'atonal' or 'polytonal' in the sense of modern music or painting, and thus the expression of a most general sense of the world, in which, just like in philosophy, an entirely new world view is apparent."[39]

What happened next, however, is significant. Whereas the Barcelona Pavilion, two years earlier, had been able to absorb any amount of this gushing hyperbole, the often rather harsh reception of Mies's building at the *Deutsche Bauaustellung* only months before had already shown a significant division among progressive architects and critics. *Die Form* had still stood firmly with Mies. Only a month or two later, it was the praise of the Tugendhat House in that same journal, as much as the house itself, that provoked one of the most engaged architectural debates of the time. Modern architecture's central claim—that new forms could be representatives and guarantors of social change—had quickly lost its legitimacy. Many protagonists of the "New Architecture" were also disturbed by the thought that architecture's beautiful new formal language could be so effortlessly coopted by a prototypical representative of the old system—a wealthy industrialist whose home housed more servants than family members. As a result, the modern movement had fallen from grace in the eyes of the political left.

The editors of *Die Form* now had to acknowledge the critical voices, and carried the abovementioned rebuttal to Riezler—"*Kann man im Haus Tugendhat wohnen?*" (Can one live in the Tugendhat House?)—written by the critic Justus Bier. This was the very same Bier who had so eloquently praised the Barcelona Pavilion in the same journal only two years before. Now, however, Bier found that the house suggested "ostentatious living."[40] He compared its main room to the sequence of representative rooms in a nineteenth-century house, but suspected that the inhabitants would be unable to exercise its different functions in the same way, and without disturbing each other. The pathos and spirituality of the space seemed unbearable to him.

If Bier's article already exposed significant rifts within the Werkbund, then the following month's issue of *Die Form* ramped up the argument, with the French Marxist Roger Ginsburger pointing out how little Mies had stuck to his famous dictum from 1923 that "Form is not the goal but the result of our work." Ginsburger claimed that it had been the Marxists who had consistently argued for a true functionalism with little concern for formal questions, so long as the necessities of a house were fulfilled properly and intelligently. He also suggested that such a display of luxury at a time of profound economic crisis, when millions were begging for food, was amoral and equivalent to theft.[41] Indeed, while a simple one-family home could be built for between 10,000 and 30,000 Reichsmark, Mies had spent 60,000 Reichsmark on the solid onyx wall in the living room alone.[42] The entire house probably cost close to 300,000 Reichsmark (which was still less than the Barcelona Pavilion). The footprint of the living room alone could have easily accommodated two or three workers cottages.[43]

Riezler was given the opportunity to comment on Bier's article, also in *Die Form*, in which he reiterated his earlier arguments, while Ludwig Hilberseimer was drafted in to reinforce the defense of the building.[44] Often giving a voice to his notoriously taciturn friend Mies, Hilberseimer emphasized in a short contribution the livability, even coziness, of the large Tugendhat room, the differentiation between functions in the upper and lower floors, the main room's "spatial-chromatic harmony," and the high quality of the building's technical execution.[45]

The conservative magazine *Der Baumeister* published a nuanced review, cautioning against the potentially oppressive nature of walls of precious materials, notably polished marble, in a living room, and about the fact that the open connection of all living areas requires absolute quietude: "Economy in a conventional sense is not a factor here."[46]

Czech architects, who had taken the social agenda of modernism very seriously, and were disappointed that this commission had gone to a German architect, either ignored the building or openly argued against it. For example, Jaromír Krejcar wrote that "while this looks from the outside like a functional and constructive building, a detailed inspection of the inside has convinced us that the format of a representational villa was really not abandoned. So, this is a design which belongs not to the future but to the past....This willingness to compromise is typical of Mies van der Rohe today and it might explain why the Brno industrialist, surrounded by several better local architects, gave the commission to someone from Berlin instead."[47] A year later, Krejcar called the building merely a "precious toy for the privileged," with no contribution to the real issues facing modern architecture.[48] His friend, leading Czech modernist Karel Teige, who worked on minimal housing solutions for the working class, agreed and called the Tugendhat House the "pinnacle of modernistic snobbism and the ostentation of a millionaire's lifestyle."[49]

The Wall Street crash in October 1929 had generally resulted in drastically reduced industrial production, soaring unemployment, and the steep deterioration of prices for labor and materials. The Brno textile industry was no exception, experiencing cutbacks in production and labor. While the Tugendhat House was being constructed, unemployment in the building trades climbed to 52.18 percent, and prices for materials and wages fell by at least 20 percent on the official index (a figure probably higher in reality). Some of the luxury in the Tugendhat House, we can thus speculate, was financed by savings brought about by the Depression.

Both Fritz and Grete Tugendhat defended the house and its designer against their critics in two separate letters in *Die Form*, though neither of them responded to the accusations of squandering enormous amounts of money at a time when many workers in their factories had just been laid off.[50] Grete Tugendhat acknowledged that a private home was, perhaps, not the best place for Mies's spatial ideas, but felt liberated by the expansiveness and ceremoniousness of the main room. Her husband endorsed the same view, describing the sense of beauty and truth he encountered there.

But how exactly this house and its famous central room functioned, and how the family lived in it every day, is something that has never been looked at in any detail.[51] We do not know whether the wealthy young couple found it difficult to forego the trappings that typically defined the homes of their peers—the inherited pieces of fine furniture, the portraits in the main living room, the displays of exotic travel souvenirs. Since Grete Tugendhat's parents, the Löw-Beers, lived further down the hill, on the same stretch of land, some family traditions might have continued there.[52] The life of a modern couple, as Mies suggested here, was supposedly unsentimental, free from the mementos of personal history and unburdened by the pressure to display tokens of a family's pedigree, wealth, and heritage.

In the large room, five different table and chair arrangements offered locations for simultaneous, different activities. It is no coincidence that one of the few social functions Grete Tugendhat would remember later happened to be a bridge tournament that her parents had organized. In the mid-1930s, Fritz Tugendhat took thirty-two photos of the house, which, probably mindful of the earlier criticism, present the building as a lived-in space. We see the children at play in the large room or on the terrace, involved in gardening activities or Christmas preparations. The recollections of the inhabitants shed some light on the living arrangements in the house: Mr. Tugendhat never used the desk that Mies had provided for him; Mrs. Tugendhat preferred her husband's bedroom for reading and working (her own bedroom lacked a desk) and looked forward to using her children's rooms once they left the house. The children had to eat dinner with the nanny upstairs in their own room, to which an elevator from the kitchen would bring the food. When there were houseguests, the nanny had to move in with the children, since no guest room had been provided. In addition, Mies's decision to place the bedrooms on the entrance level created an overlap between private and semipublic spaces that trapped parents and children in their bedrooms if they wanted to avoid meeting visitors in the entrance lobby. The conventional and time-tested arrangement at the Esters and Lange houses in Krefeld placed the main, semipublic spaces on the ground floor, close to the entrance. The more private quarters with parents' and children's bedrooms would be upstairs. At the Tugendhat House, Mies had to respond to the need for an entrance on the upper level. It would have been entirely possible to place the large living room on the upper floor and arrange for the living quarters underneath with direct access to the garden. It would have solved several issues with the current design. Three years later, when Mies designed a villa for Gerhard Severain's brother Alois in Wiesbaden, he successfully tried that solution.[53]

The entire arrangement of rooms on the upper floor seems strangely cumbersome—an enormous amount of circulation space serving five altogether uninspired rooms (see figure 5.23). The dense and economic clarity that characterized the arrangements of bedrooms, bathrooms, and adjacent terraces upstairs at the Lange and Esters houses is entirely absent. The less deft and surefooted handling of the complex room arrangements at the Tugendhat House might lie in the fact that the project architect was the young Friedrich Hirz, who had just joined Mies's office (after briefly working for Gropius) and was only twenty-one years old at the time. He was responsible for much of the detailed planning and supervision of the building site. According to Grete Tugendhat, the constellation of the upstairs rooms was redesigned after a conversation between clients and architects on December 31, 1928, when the Tugendhats requested that the freestanding columns be integrated into the walls.[54]

The Tugendhats had a married chauffer, two maids, a cook, and a nanny. All of them had comparatively small rooms. While the ratio between serving and served spaces in the Esters and Lange houses is about 0.5:1, in the Tugendhat House it is almost 1:1. The kitchen, food preparation, and pantry areas on the lower floor seem particularly large. Never much of a family man, Mies generally lacked interest in spaces of domestic function and, instead, designed noncommittal spaces, large enough to allow almost any pursuit (it is no coincidence that the main room functioned well later as a pediatric gymnasium).

The fact that a number of different functions had to coexist in the main living room had been one of the key criticisms of the main space, and the provision of curtains as space dividers was often mentioned in defense. But in the original photographs, they are rarely shown in this function. As light enters the space only from the southern and eastern sides (there greatly diminished by the greenhouse), the library area in the back, which is shielded from the southern façade by the onyx wall, is, even on bright days, rather dark (see figure 5.22). The placement of artificial lights in the main room is similarly puzzling. In order to keep the appearance of the room as empty and uncluttered as possible, only occasional ceiling lights by the Danish firm of Poul Henningsen (PH1) were provided, roughly aligned to a grid that did not correspond to the seating arrangement, except in the case of the dining alcove—resulting in highly awkward lighting conditions at night. The only contemporary image of the interior with all curtains drawn at night confirms this impression (see figure 8.22). Philip Johnson would note in 1977: "One thing he [Mies] was absolutely no good at was lighting. He just wouldn't focus on it—look at those fixtures in the Tugendhat House...the Tugendhat House was the worst of all."[55]

It is the great irony of the Tugendhat House, that, while it became one of Mies's most widely known and influential buildings, thanks to the dissemination of its striking photographs, it was also one his less successful responses to the requirements of a functioning home. Mies had not been able to fully meet the challenges that the house's sloping site had posed both for the interior organization and for the low street façade, which became the least convincing view of the building (see figure 5.16).

When the German philosopher and historian Walter Benjamin published his essay *"Erfahrung und Armut"* (Experience and Poverty) in a short-lived, German-language journal in Prague in October 1933, he might have thought of the striking images of the Tugendhat House. Benjamin knew about Mies, and had perhaps even met him through Hans Richter's magazine *G*, where both had been published, or at the house of art collector Eduard Fuchs, whom Benjamin had described in one of his pieces and who lived in Mies's Perls House. Without mentioning the Tugendhat House, Benjamin described the new steel and glass architecture as the enemy of secrets and possessions, as "prophet of a new poverty." After overcoming the crowded interiors of the nineteenth century, modern architects, he wrote, "have created rooms in which it is hard to leave traces," for "men who have adopted the cause of the absolutely new and have founded it on insight and renunciation." Wearily, Benjamin noted that the absence of experience and traces of human heritage in these contemporary buildings readied modern man for the dark times to come: "The economic crisis is at the door, and behind it is the shadow of the approaching war."[56]

Given the fact that the year 1931 had brought the most intense public critique of his work, in response to both the building at the *Deutsche Bauausstellung* and the Tugendhat House, it must have seemed a great relief and honor for Mies to be elected into the Preussische Akademie der Künste (Prussian Academy of Arts) on November 9, 1931, together with the architects Paul Mebes, Erich Mendelsohn, Bruno Taut, and Martin Wagner, among others.

1930 Four Apartments

In 1930, while finishing the Tugendhat House and working on the competition for the Neue Wache Memorial in Berlin, Mies and Lilly Reich designed the interiors of several apartments, among them two each in Berlin and one in New York. Franz Schulze would later call these commissions "bread-and-butter" jobs; these projects were a good measure of the applicability of Mies's vocabulary in environments that had not been created for them, and they stand out for their clarity and single-minded vision.[57]

Stefanie Hess's apartment was on the light-flooded fourth floor of a turn-of-the-century apartment building in the short Duisburger Strasse parallel to Kurfürstendamm in Berlin's wealthy Westend; it is clearly the most elaborate and successful of Mies's three interior projects. Surviving photographs show the main living room with a suspended heating unit on the wall, a generous built-in wardrobe, and Mies's chairs in front of a translucent curtain on the street side (figures 5.29, 5.30). There is also a custom-designed sideboard on the wall, a unique piece that did not show up anywhere else. Perhaps equally remarkable is a small study, containing a curious, built-in glass enclosed space for a rubber plant, comparable to the arrangement at the Glasraum in Stuttgart. Hess hired the photographer Marta Huth (wife of Berlin art historian Hans Huth) to document her apartment.

Mildred Crous, one of the daughters of Mies's current client Hermann Lange in Krefeld, and her husband, Carl Wilhelm Crous, commissioned another interior from Mies and Lilly Reich. It had Chinese mats on the floor, the influx of light was softened by transparent curtains, and it was apparently rather sparsely furnished with pieces by Mies and Reich.[58]

Philip Johnson's apartment in the brand-new, Emery Roth–designed Southgate apartment complex at 424 East Fifty-Second Street in New York consisted of three rooms; Mies and Reich provided drawings for the arrangement of furniture and curtains, but did not propose any architectural interventions (figure 5.31). Two years later, Johnson, together with his sister Theodate, moved to another apartment at 216 East Forty-Ninth Street in New York's Turtle Bay neighborhood (figure 5.32).[59] This was a duplex with a double-height living room and an upstairs gallery—a very Corbusian arrangement, reminiscent of his apartments at the Immeuble Villas. Johnson brought the furniture and curtains that Mies and Reich had specified for the previous apartment and tried to apply what he had learned from them.[60] He took out several separating walls in the three-room apartment, put in pale beige linoleum floors, finished the walls in white plaster, and introduced a "procession of curtains" of five different finishes (tan, blue, gray, black, and transparent fishnet). He had the result published in a lavish spread in *House & Garden,* where he was presented as a "young interior architect" (several years before he went to architecture school) with a fully formed theory of his own: "The effects achieved in the interiors he designs result from ingenious use of architectural principles rather than application of ornament. Theoretically, he sees a house or an apartment not as a collection of small or large boxes set within outer box-like walls, but as a series of interrelated planes to be arranged for maximum beauty and utility."[61] Johnson's other principles in the creation of space were, according to the magazine, the design and functional arrangement of the furniture and the "quality of lightness, both in weight and in color." The magazine, no doubt echoing Johnson's own claims, celebrated the theatricality of the space: "Drama enters with the curtains. Hung from wall to wall and from floor to ceiling, without lambrequins or swags, and with slender steel rails their unobtrusive support, they are not sides of a room-box but intersecting planes cut, although not stopped, by the equally limitless planes of

Figure 5.29. Ludwig Mies van der Rohe and Lilly Reich, Stefanie Hess Apartment, Berlin Wilmersdorf, 1930. View toward the entrance with built-in cabinets. Photograph by Marta Huth.

wall and floor. This sense of flow and continuity is of first importance in creating the illusion of space. It is the basic principle of what Mr. Johnson calls 'designing in planes.'"[62]

When Jan Ruhtenberg sent Mies a copy of the magazine, Mies was furious. He found that Johnson had copied his ideas without properly crediting him (except for "the pieces about the fireplace"), and in particular had produced some dining room chairs (Brno chairs with a flat bar frame) on his own, which, while based on Mies's design, were executed clumsily with rows of clavos (upholstery nails) in the back. Mies noted angrily that "the new architecture is considered increasingly simply a fashion in Amerika. This is very dangerous." Johnson sheepishly accused the magazine of not having printed what he had told them, and assured Mies that he was "not at all interested in modes or fashions in various kinds of modern." To redeem himself, he let it slip that, after all, he, Johnson, was the reason that Mies had become well-known in the United States, and "all modern architects hold you and your work…in great honor."[63]

1930–33 Teaching at the Bauhaus

Gropius had already proposed Mies for the directorship at the Bauhaus in 1928, but Mies, in the midst of preparations for the Barcelona World's Fair, had declined, and the Swiss architect Hannes Meyer had gotten the job. He only lasted two years, as his radical political and pedagogical approach led to opposition and disappointments among the faculty and concerns among the increasingly conservative city officials. László Moholy-Nagy, Marcel Breuer, and Herbert Bayer all resigned soon after Meyer came on board, and Oskar Schlemmer followed in 1929. But even those prominent teachers who stayed, in particular Wassily Kandinsky, Paul Klee, and Josef Albers, feared that their own work

Figure 5.30. Ludwig Mies van der Rohe and Lilly Reich, Stefanie Hess Apartment, Berlin Wilmersdorf, 1930. View toward the windows with Barcelona chairs and coffee table. Photograph by Marta Huth.

Figure 5.31. Emery Roth, Southgate Apartments, 424 East Fifty-Second Street, New York, 1932. Philip Johnson's apartment with furniture by Ludwig Mies van der Rohe and Lilly Reich, New York, 1930.

Figure 5.32. Architect unknown, 216 East Forty-Ninth Street, New York, 1910. Philip Johnson's apartment with furniture by Ludwig Mies van der Rohe and Lilly Reich, 1932.

and impact as painters would be increasingly sidelined. Mies was seen as apolitical and as someone capable of returning a sense of order and calm to the institution that had recently been troubled with much political activism and, apparently, libertine behavior among students. The fact that Meyer himself had engaged in a romantic relationship with one of his students, Lotte Beese, who bore his child, did not help—nor the fact that he forced her to leave the school early without her diploma, in order to avoid more publicity. When Meyer was asked by the mayor of Dessau, Fritz Hesse, to leave in 1930, he did not go quietly, but rather engaged in a protracted press campaign against the mayor and the circumstances of his dismissal.[64] He was able to achieve a favorable settlement with the city in the end.[65]

Mies assumed his post at the Bauhaus on August 1, 1930, and decided to pursue an uncompromising course toward depoliticizing the school (figure 5.33). When a group of left-wing students occupied the cafeteria to protest the dismissal of Meyer, Mies called in the Dessau police to evict them. A Bauhaus custodian named Fehn even recalled later that Mies had instructed him to "take a cudgel to disperse the students if necessary."[66] Mies decided to close the school two weeks early and to resume the next semester accordingly on October 21, 1930. Five foreign Communist students were asked to leave within twenty-four hours. Before the remaining 170 students could reenroll, they had to promise in writing to abstain from political activity (apparently even those determined to continue their activism still signed).

Figure 5.33. Pius Pahl, Ludwig Mies van der Rohe (third from left) teaching at the Bauhaus, 1931. Gelatin silver print, 3 1/4 × 4 5/8 in. (8.4 × 11.7 cm). Bauhaus-Archiv, Berlin.

During the break, Mies, in careful coordination with the mayor's office, the state education department, and the support group Freunde des Bauhauses (Friends of the Bauhaus), managed to calm the waves, and on September 9, 1930, the faculty published a unanimous,

supportive resolution. While acknowledging the best intentions of the previous Bauhaus director, Hannes Meyer, it stated: "The masters recognize that the development of the conditions at the Bauhaus made a change of leadership necessary. . . . They unanimously express their confidence in the new leader of the Bauhaus, Mies van der Rohe."[67] Mies reduced the school's departments to five: Architecture, Finishing and Completion (run by Lilly Reich), Weaving, Photography, and Fine Arts. Architectural training became central and shifted its focus from social issues to aesthetics.

When, shortly afterward, in late September, Ernst May left his position as building counselor in Frankfurt and moved to Moscow, several newspapers noted that Mies was considered for his job (in which he had shown interest in 1925), together with Martin Wagner and Richard Döcker from Stuttgart.[68] It is doubtful that Mies would have relocated at a time when his office was busy with the *Deutsche Bauausstellung* of 1931, several invited competitions, and the execution of the Tugendhat House. Possibly Mies had instigated these news items in order to inspire a renewed expression of confidence from the Dessau authorities, which they promptly gave.[69]

At a meeting with the Freunde des Bauhauses on November 25, 1930, Mies presented some of his plans to increase revenue and the school's reputation. He promised to bring in famous colleagues as visiting professors, and proposed to open a sister institute and exchange program in the United States.[70] He could present immediate results, as he had met Richard Neutra at a lecture in Berlin on October 13 and convinced him to give a talk on American modern architecture at the Bauhaus on November 5 and stay for a month to work with students on a competition entry for the Charkow Theater.[71] While nothing came of the imagined American Bauhaus (until former Bauhaus teacher László Moholy-Nagy established a short-lived Bauhaus in Chicago in 1937), contacts remained, thanks to Philip Johnson, who came to visit regularly from 1930 onward. As mentioned above, he commissioned Mies to design his New York apartment in 1930, and invited him to participate in the Museum of Modern Art's *Modern Architecture: International Exhibition*, which opened to many, if mostly skeptical, responses in February 1932. The chapter on Mies in the catalogue was the only one written by Johnson, while the others (on Frank Lloyd Wright, Gropius, Le Corbusier, J. J. P. Oud, Raymond Hood, Howe & Lescaze, Richard Neutra, and the Bowman Brothers) were written by Henry-Russell Hitchcock. Johnson had initially hoped that Mies would "plan the installation of the exhibition," such as "designing bases for the models, tables for the literature, chairs, photograph racks, and partition screens of glass and metal," in order to "show to some extent in actual objects what has been achieved in modern architecture."[72] While this particular collaboration failed to pan out, Mies's work was very much a centerpiece

Figure 5.34. Heinrich Siegfried Bormann, House Ceph, court house interior designed for Ludwig Mies van der Rohe's studio class, 1933. Watercolor and pencil on heavy paper stock, 16 × 22 7/8 in. (40.8 × 58 cm). Bauhaus-Archiv, Berlin.

of the exhibition, and photos of the Tugendhat House adorned the covers of both accompanying publications. Johnson summarized his high opinion of Mies: "As an artist of the plan, as a decorator in the best sense, as a creator of space, he has no equal."[73]

The New York exhibition was barely noticed in Germany, and Mies's increased international standing did not help him at the Bauhaus, where his troubles were by no means over. Not all Communist students had left, and they continued their activities (the group called itself Kostufra—for Die Kommunistische Studentenfraktion, meaning the Communist Student Fraction), attacking Mies quite regularly in their pamphlet called *Bauhaus,* just like the official school publication. They opposed the design of "churches and villas" for the ruling class, but also exploitative "rental prisons and minimum dwellings." Instead, architecture had to support the class struggle and should follow cooperative housing models in the Soviet Union. When Hannes Meyer returned from Moscow in 1931 to give a lecture in Leipzig, several Bauhaus students traveled to hear him. Mies was not happy—and refused to reimburse their travel expenses.[74] The *Arbeiter Illustrierte Zeitung,* the most widely read Communist pictorial newspaper in Germany (with a circulation of 350,000), declared in January 1931 that the Bauhaus was "on its way to Fascism."[75] As if to prove the journal wrong, in the winter of 1931, Mies's friend and colleague Ludwig Hilberseimer worked with seven Communist students on an urban plan for a communal workers' housing project outside of Dessau, called Fichtenbreite, for twenty thousand inhabitants.[76]

Despite the sustained criticism in response to both the Tugendhat House and the house at the *Deutsche Bauausstellung* in 1931, Mies remained confident that his new visual and spatial vocabulary deserved further exploration. He asked his students to design single-family homes of different sizes, but usually on a single floor and an ample lot, surrounded by a high wall. Mies did not discourage his students from copying his vocabulary, and thus emerged countless clones of his recent interiors, with open spatial connections, floor-to-ceiling glass walls, cruciform columns, and Barcelona or Brno chairs (figure 5.34). A certain stagnation in the architectural training at the Bauhaus was the result.[77] American student William Turk Priestley fondly remembered, however, how Mies challenged some established practices. Instead of developing a building via plans and elevations, Mies encouraged the recording of spatial experiences: "Step out of the automobile and draw me a freehand sketch of what you see. Go in the front door and draw me a freehand sketch of what you see. Turn right and take ten steps and draw what you see. Turn left."[78] Only after Priestley had produced many such freehand sketches was he allowed to work from plans and then models.

Over the following years, up to and immediately after his departure for America in 1937, Mies himself made countless sketches for flat-roofed houses with courtyards that rehearsed variations on the grammar of Barcelona. The German Pavilion had long been demolished, but ghostlike images of it (or rather of Stone's photographs of it) remained persistent in Mies's imagination for the next decade.

Despite the publicity that Mies's Barcelona Pavilion and Tugendhat House had enjoyed, new commissions were not forthcoming, surely due, in part, to the severe impact the Great Depression had on the German economy. Several projects had clients but did not come to fruition, such as the 1932 Gericke House on a sloping site on Lake Wannsee on the southwestern edge of Berlin. Herbert Gericke, the director of the German Academy in Rome, Villa Massimo, had asked several architects to produce designs, and Mies responded with an expansive and elegant arrangement of space over two floors, with an entirely glass-enclosed living room on the lower level.

1930   Golf Club

At the same time, Mies applied his newly found vocabulary to the design of a golf club in Krefeld, submitting a set of thirty drawings to a limited competition at the end of September 1930. Among the initiators of the project was Hermann Lange, Mies's client for a large house in Krefeld. In an overall pinwheel shape, Mies assembled changing rooms, administration offices, and a large space for entertaining adjacent to an open courtyard and terrace. He used cruciform, chrome-covered steel columns, a grid of travertine floor plates, and a boldly cantilevered flat roof. As if to demonstrate the validity of the original system, he imagined a wide roof above the parking area that rested on a single, central row of seven columns. In a temporary installation in 2013, the project was created as a 1:1 model in a field outside of Krefeld, which emphasized its temporary and model character by referencing, but not imitating, the intended materials, except the chromium-covered columns (figure 5.35). Walls and ceiling were made out of plywood, sometimes painted white, sometimes not, and there were window frames but no glass and occasional white curtains. It perfectly managed to represent the spatial sequences inside and demonstrated the building's closeness to the formal language of the Barcelona Pavilion and the house for the *Deutsche Bauausstellung,* which Mies was working on at the same time.[79]

1930 CIAM III Congress, Brussels

At the end of November 1930, Mies traveled to Brussels to participate in the Congrès Internationaux d'Architecture Moderne (CIAM) conference. Perhaps most importantly, it was an occasion to meet fellow modern architects, as it was particularly well attended. A group photo shows Mies right in the center of his forty-seven colleagues, among them Le Corbusier, Pierre Chareau, Richard Neutra, Henry van de Velde, Sigfried Giedion, Marcel Breuer, and his German colleagues Hugo Häring and Walter Gropius (figure 5.36).[80] The timing was particularly fortuitous—Mies had had international success with the Weissenhof Estate and the Barcelona Pavilion, and the critical fallout from the Tugendhat House and the house at the *Deutsche Bauausstellung,* which focused on Mies as a designer of luxury houses, was still to come. It would have provided an awkward contrast to the topic of the conference, namely the minimum dwelling and high-rise apartment blocks.[81] Mies already had enough troubles with left-leaning students at the Bauhaus, as he confided in Fred Forbát, a Hungarian architect and former Bauhaus teacher, with whom he traveled on the train to Brussels.[82]

Figure 5.35. Ludwig Mies van der Rohe, Golf Club project, Krefeld, Germany, 1930. Temporary 1:1 model at the envisioned site. Architects: Robbrecht en Daem architecten, Ghent.

1932 Dessau Trinkhalle

The Trinkhalle project in Dessau, never mentioned by Mies, but documented sufficiently in the Bauhaus archive, is both his smallest building and, in interesting ways, his most contextual. It also offers a pure example of his essentialist approach to design. Walter Gropius had worked with Carl Fieger and Ernst Neufert when designing the houses for the Bauhaus masters in 1926 and his own, larger, director's house—all within walking distance from the Bauhaus proper at the city's western edge. Gropius's sumptuous villa was the only one among the new houses that was surrounded by a long, six-and-a-half-foot- (two-meter-) tall wall. The local population disliked it (dubbing it *Klagemauer*," German for "Wailing Wall"), as it blocked the view toward the pine forest into which the masters' houses had been placed. Gropius deprived himself of a view east toward the "seven columns"—a folly in an eighteenth-century landscape garden across the street.

Mies's intervention at that spot, in the garden of the director's house, which he now inhabited—at least for a few days every week—was a so-called *Trinkhalle*. This type of a small sales kiosk had long been popular in German cities. Martin Gropius, the grand uncle of Walter Gropius, had designed one of the finest and most influential examples, for the sale of mineral water, in 1859.[83] Alfred Grenander created a freestanding type in 1909 that became ubiquitous in Berlin. At the Bauhaus, Herbert Bayer had designed a sales kiosk in 1924 as an example for applied advertising (figure 5.37).

To this day, many Trinkhallen or kiosks offer refreshments, cigarettes, magazines, and a few basic food items outside of normal business hours in German cities. Customers do not enter the "hall," but rather make their purchases from the outside, at a window under a protective roof. There is usually a small ledge where food and drinks can be consumed.

Figure 5.36. CIAM conference, Brussels, November 1930. Mies van der Rohe is at the center, in the second row, wearing a coat. Immediately in front of him, turned sideways, is Henry van de Velde. Le Corbusier is the fourth from the right in the front row.

Mies's Trinkhalle was not a freestanding structure. Instead, he simply cut a window and access door into Gropius's long wall, placed a single room with a foyer and toilet behind it, and put a flat concrete roof above, which simply extended above the wall and sales window. The window's two panes slide sideways into the adjacent walls, thus not impeding on the counter space. His talented student and later collaborator Eduard Ludwig drew up the plans, supervised construction, and took photographs upon its completion (figure 5.38).[84]

The Trinkhalle survived Dessau's heavy bombardment during World War II and still functioned for a number of years afterward. It was demolished in the early 1970s and rebuilt in a slightly simplified form in 2016, and is usually open for business on weekends in the summer months.

1932–33   Lemke House

The last house that Mies built in Berlin was a small courtyard house in the Hohenschönhausen section for Karl Lemke, the owner of a graphics and printing studio. Karl and Martha Lemke had asked Mies for a "small and modest home," and Mies delivered for roughly 16,000 Reichsmark (compared to 300,000 for the Tugendhat House). In 1930, the couple had bought a piece of land directly fronting a small lake. Mies received the commission in February 1932 and began to design a series of variations, some of them with two floors. Limited funds finally forced the comparatively small version, which received the building permit in July 1932. In March 1933, Mr. and Mrs. Lemke moved in. Mies connected a generous living/dining room and a large bedroom (both facing south, toward the lake) via a wide corridor in an L-configuration, attaching the garage on one side, and a kitchen and maid's room on the other (figure 5.39). The result was a simple, flat-roofed brick box. The bricks were laid in an elegant English bond with beaded joints; the steel-framed windows from the living room and corridor to the garden were wall high and included a section that could swing open (figures 5.40, 5.41). The garden design came from the office of Karl Foerster, a prominent landscape designer in Potsdam who had worked with Mies several times before.

Figure 5.37. Herbert Bayer, design for a newspaper kiosk, 1924. Tempera and cut-and-pasted print elements on paper, 25 3/8 × 13 5/8 in. (64.5 × 34.5 cm).

Figure 5.38. Ludwig Mies van der Rohe and Eduard Ludwig, Trinkhalle, Dessau, Germany, 1932.

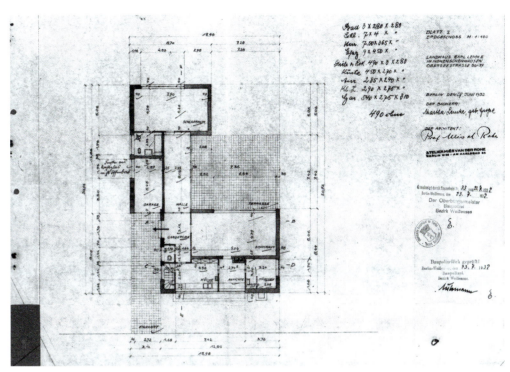

Figure 5.39. Ludwig Mies van der Rohe, Lemke House, Berlin, 1932–33. Floor plan.

Figure 5.40. Ludwig Mies van der Rohe, Lemke House, Berlin, 1932–33. View from the living room to the garden. Photograph by Hassan Bagheri.

The modesty and brilliant simplicity of the home would have been a perfect response to those critics, who had accused Mies of exclusively designing for wealthy clients. But it was only ready to be photographed after the Nazis had taken over power in Germany, and Mies never arranged to have it published.[85]

1933   The End of the Bauhaus

Nazis had already been voted into power in regional and city parliaments in 1932, such as in Anhalt in May and Thuringia in August. The city parliament of Dessau had twenty National Socialist members, who had since January loudly proclaimed their goal of demolishing the Bauhaus building. On August 22, 1932, their request to close the Bauhaus and to relieve all its teachers of their duties was voted upon and received a majority. Only the Communists were against, and the Social Democrats abstained, claiming that hardships during the Depression would have required a reorganization and different funding model for the school supported by all parties. That being impossible, the Social Democrats abstained from the vote.[86] Mies turned the Bauhaus into a private institution and the winter term was held in a former telephone factory in Berlin. One hundred fourteen students attended classes taught by Kandinsky, Albers, Hilberseimer, Reich, Peterhans, and Mies himself.

In the German Reich, the Nazi takeover happened in three dramatic steps in early 1933: President Paul von Hindenburg had made Hitler chancellor and head of a right-wing coalition on January 30. With his majority, Hitler immediately dissolved the Reichstag. On February 27, 1933, an arsonist set fire to the Reichstag building—just under a mile (one and a half kilometers) from Mies's apartment, the sky-high flames clearly visible from his north-facing balcony. The next day, Hitler and Hindenburg signed the "Reichstag Fire Decree," which was cemented into law on March 23 as the "Enabling Act," nullifying many civil

Figure 5.41. Ludwig Mies van der Rohe, Lemke House, Berlin, 1932–33. House seen from the lakefront. Photograph by Hassan Bagheri.

liberties. Amid all that, on February 10, 1933, the government had announced the competition for a Reichsbank extension building in the heart of the city.[87]

Just as the summer semester was about to begin, the Berlin Bauhaus was closed by the police on April 11, in order to execute a search warrant for Communist propaganda material among the unopened library boxes that had arrived from Dessau. Students on site without their passports were brought to a police station for questioning.

Mies asked Alfred Rosenberg, head of the Kampfbund für Deutsche Kultur (Militant League for German Culture), for an appointment, which was immediately granted for the following day, April 12 (ominously, rather late—at 11 p.m.).[88] Three days later, Mies jotted down what he recalled of the conversation with Rosenberg, a trained architect himself. Mies stressed the importance of working on design questions posed by industrial and technical progress. When Rosenberg asked if technical universities were not already doing this, Mies answered that universities offered too many different disciplines and had too many students, about one hundred to one hundred and fifty per professor. He, in contrast, had only thirty students and thus could work with each one. He asked Rosenberg to ensure that they were left alone and the Bauhaus could reopen. Rosenberg promised to look into it. Mies remembered:

> We also spoke about modern building. Rosenberg mentioned the urbanistically unsatisfying modern city expansions, mentioned "concrete boxes" and said that they find it important to use local materials and that they believed, following Goethe, that one should conduct experiments but not build them. I mentioned the technical materials, which industry provides today, such as steel and glass, and that these materials are superior to many others, and that the key task is to create perfect building designs with these materials. Rosenberg: why should one apply such alien material, and why don't we use the materials that belong to a particular region. Mies: I don't believe that we can avoid partaking in technical and industrial progress, just like agrarian science can't do that either. And, after all, steel is being found in Westphalia. Cultural Bolshevism is less of a threat to me than Americanism, and I see our main task to spiritually master the world of technology. Rosenberg: Then we agree that the art of building begins beyond the area of functions and rationality. Mies: Yes, indeed. But that is an approach which not all modern architects agree on, and for which I have been attacked most fiercely at many occasions. But I am of the opinion that the questions, which are presented by technical and industrial progress, are not to be avoided, but have to be conquered.[89]

Mies immediately started a campaign to reopen the school, but was, in all likelihood, mindful of the need for a low profile while the Reichstag competition, to which he had been invited (see below) was being decided. A group of Bauhaus students, probably mobilized by Mies, followed up with an open letter to Rosenberg, perhaps making the points that Mies had not stressed enough during their conversation. The students emphasized that, while, indeed, under Hannes Meyer, there was strong sympathy at the Bauhaus for the Communist Party, "Mies van der Rohe…tried to depoliticize the school." By removing about one-fifth of the student population, namely the Marxists, Mies succeeded in slowly establishing a new direction: "This fact has been overlooked outside of the Bauhaus, because it was not a sudden change, but rather a slow, but steady evolution." The students argued that "this de-politicization of the Bauhaus already created the basis for a positive collaboration towards the new Germany."[90] They pledged their allegiance to the new regime and asked for the reopening of the school. In additional conversations with Winfried Wendland at the ministry of culture in Berlin, Mies agreed to a number of conditions in order for the school to reopen, in particular sacrificing the positions of his friends Ludwig Hilberseimer and Wassily Kandinsky, whom the Nazis found particularly objectionable, and not employing any Jewish faculty members. By the time Mies received the green light to reopen the school, however, the financial situation had become untenable, as there were very few students left, no income from tuition, and no funds to pay the faculty. Mies closed the school.[91]

As the negotiations with Rosenberg and Wendland unfolded, Mies must have been reminded of a similar episode, literally just weeks before, when the Preussische Akademie der Künste was pressured to dismiss two of its members, Käthe Kollwitz and Heinrich Mann, for their progressive political engagement. The president of the academy, composer and conductor Max von Schillings, agreed to this on February 15 without consulting with Kollwitz or Mann. At a special meeting of the academy, many supported von Schillings; others, among them Mies's friend Martin Wagner, resigned in protest. On March 14, 1933, escalating pressure, academy president von Schillings asked all members for a declaration of support of the regime. Another wave of resignations followed by writers such as Thomas Mann and Alfred Döblin and the prominent painter Max Liebermann (the academy's previous president). Those who had ignored von Schillings's plea (Mies among them) received a follow-up note from him on May 15, 1933, asking them to resign. The architect Paul Mebes and the expressionist painters Otto Dix and Karl Schmidt-Rottluff followed his suggestion; the painter Ernst Ludwig Kirchner, the architect Erich Mendelsohn, and Mies van der Rohe did not. Mies told von Schillings on May 18: "I cannot convince myself to accept the suggestion in your letter of May 15, in particular, since in times like these such a step might be cause for misinterpretations."[92] Clearly, Mies did not want to be seen as resigning in protest, as that would have signaled opposition to the regime. He explained that any decision about his membership should be made officially by the ministry of culture and the entire academy. For Mendelsohn, who was Jewish, his refusal bought him merely a few months of time. Since April 7, 1933, the Gesetz zur Wiederherstellung des Berufsbeamtentums (Law for the Restoration of the Professional Civil Service) had paved the way for the removal of all Jewish citizens from state positions, and Mendelsohn was officially excluded from the academy on December 11, 1933 (recognition of his service at the front in World War I had provided a short reprieve). Von Schillings suspected that Mies might be Jewish too and asked the interior ministry's department of race research to check on his Aryan credentials on July 1, 1933. Before receiving an answer, von Schillings died suddenly on July 24, 1933, but the misgivings about Mies van der Rohe's membership in the academy continued behind the scenes and would lead to his final exclusion four years later, in the summer of 1937 (see below).[93]

1933 Reichsbank Competition

Chronology is of importance here. Mies had been invited as one of thirty prominent architects to participate in a competition for a new central bank building in Berlin, a 30-million-Mark project. Among the invited architects were Poelzig and Gropius. Each one received a generous 5,000 Mark honorarium. The Bauhaus closure by the police had happened on April 11, 1933—during the most intense work on the Reichsbank competition, less than three weeks before its May 1 deadline. Mies's subsequent efforts to reopen the school thus unfolded while he was waiting for the result, which was announced on September 21. Similarly, his refusal to resign from the academy in mid-May 1933 fell into that same time period when he was hoping for the commission. He clearly was not going to ruffle any feathers.

Figure 5.42. Extension of the Reichsbank. Competition entry by Ludwig Mies van der Rohe, 1933. Main façade to Kurstrasse.

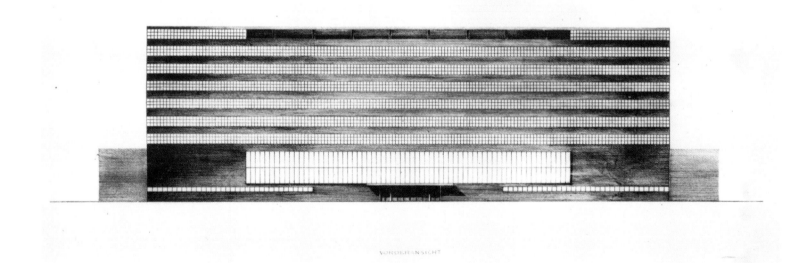

Most participants used the planned square in the north for a dramatic main entrance. Mies's design is fascinating and troubling in several respects. He had designed, but never built, office buildings before, beginning with his glass skyscrapers of 1922, the Concrete Office Building of 1923, and more recently his projects in Berlin and Stuttgart, but this was by far the largest building he had ever conceived. If its monumental façade and return to axial symmetry were meant to win favors with the new regime, or if it was simply the weight of the task that drove the formalism of this grand Beaux-Arts configuration, we do not know (figure 5.42). As one entered a low-ceilinged lobby in the center, two majestic staircases on either side led up into a 328-foot- (100-meter-) wide and 49-foot- (15-meter-) tall curved hall, lit by an enormous central, western-facing window. Three rectangular banking rooms were accessible from here, and slim office slabs rose above them (figure 5.43). The façades were meant to be clad in brick, alternating with ribbon windows flush to the façade. A curve in the southwestern corner of the plot had inspired the convex main façade in Mies's design, which faced the narrow Kurstrasse (figure 5.44). Most participants, such as Gropius, tried to lessen the impact of the substantial building, which was to house five thousand employees, by setting much of it back beyond a lower perimeter (figure 5.45). Not so Mies: his ten floors rise abruptly over the Kurstrasse.

Figure 5.43. Extension of the Reichsbank. Competition entry by Ludwig Mies van der Rohe, 1933. Floor plan.

Figure 5.44. Extension of the Reichsbank. Competition entry by Ludwig Mies van der Rohe, 1933. Urban context.

Figure 5.45. Extension of the Reichsbank. Competition entry by Walter Gropius, 1933. Perspective.

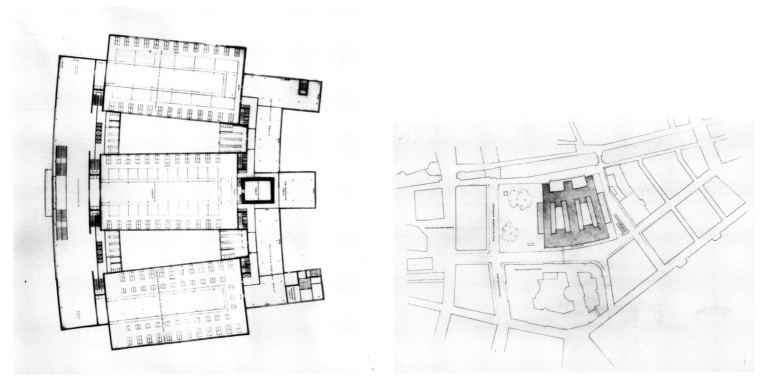

Figure 5.46. Extension of the Reichsbank.
Competition entry by Ludwig Mies van der Rohe,
1933. Perspective from the Kupfergraben (to
the northeast).

The jury was led by Martin Kiessling and included Peter Behrens, Paul Bonatz, Fritz Schumacher, and others. It decided to award shared first prizes to six architects, each one receiving 4,000 Reichsmark. Mies was by far the most progressive finalist, next to Fritz Becker, Kurt Frick, Mebes & Emmerich, Pfeifer & Grossmann, and Pinno & Grund.[94] While the jury had included Mies in this group (perhaps due to his former teacher Behrens), it was rather unkind in its judgment. It noted the missed opportunity of a northern entrance, critiqued the identical size of the three banking halls and the east–west orientation of the office slabs, which exposed their windows to either full southern sun or no sunlight at all (figure 5.46). The three wings facing the river violated current design guidelines. But still, even this critical jury had to note Mies's "impressive formal language." The shortcomings of Mies's design could have been easily fixed by turning the building ninety degrees to face the projected open space on its northern side.[95] The participation and prize money of 9,000 Reichsmark must have come as a welcome reprieve to Mies, who had lost his professor's salary and any support for the school. His income was reduced to proceeds from the licensing of his furniture, and some money left over from the sale of Bauhaus wallpaper patents. While Mies was spending time in Ticino, Switzerland, in September (see below), he still harbored hopes that his design might be selected for further development. When he returned to Berlin, he learned that Hitler had personally selected an earlier, conservative scheme by bank architect Heinrich Wolff.[96] The foundation stone was laid in 1934, and the building was finished in 1940. Wolff's design, however, hardly reflected Nazi architectural ideas, which at that moment were only just crystallizing. The design was typical of the conservative modernism at the time, as it was practiced by Pinno & Grund and many others. The unornamented façades with dense rows of windows and the large banking hall with skylights indicated the steel skeleton underneath (figure 5.47).

Figure 5.47. Heinrich Wolff, extension of the Reichsbank, Berlin, 1934–40. Photograph by Julie Woodhouse.

Six

On the Fence

Ticino, Berlin, Stuttgart, 1933–37

1933   Ticino

It is an image of sheer bliss. Mies is lying on an old stone bench in the midday sun, a wall of rough masonry behind him, a patch of unkempt grass in front (figure 6.1). His head rests on his folded jacket, protected from the heat by his hat. Mies is not sleeping, but rather puffing on a cigar and perhaps occasionally gazing out at the breathtaking panorama across Lake Lugano to the Collina d'Oro.

An opportunity for a stay in Switzerland's southern Ticino region had presented itself in September 1933 in the form of a vacant summer home to which his former student Paul Naeff had access. Mies decided to teach a course to ex-Bauhäuslers who would accompany him and Lilly Reich and receive design instruction. Each one paid a $200 fee. Apart from Naeff, two other Swiss students joined the group—Ettore Burzi, whose father, a landscape painter, lived in Lugano, and Frank Trudel from Zurich.[1] The Americans Howard Dearstyne and Jack Rogers came along as well, and one German student, Fritz Schreiber. There were boat tours on Lake Lugano, an excursion to Milan, where some of Mies's buildings were shown at the Triennale, and one day the group walked up to the isolated pilgrimage church of Santa Maria d'Iseo in Vernate (figure 6.2). Both Dearstyne and Schreiber took—almost identical—photos of Mies van der Rohe on the bench next to the church's door. Mies might have found this church particularly attractive—mentioned first in the fourteenth century, but with foundations going back to the ninth century on the former site of a Roman temple; several additions and restorations over time had resulted in a structure devoid of grand gestures. Its masonry, from local fieldstones, had lost its protective stucco, which made its timid moves toward baroque neoclassicism on the façade high above Mies's perch even more touching. According to Trudel, Mies loved the vernacular architecture in "the then still unspoiled villages in the Centovalli and Valle Maggia. There, Mies finally began to talk and called our attention to the often extraordinarily successful squares and the 'layered urbanism' which made the village into a whole. Probably, few architects were involved here, but that surely worked to the overall advantage of the whole ensemble."[2] Fritz Neumeyer has convincingly suggested that Mies was sensitized to the beauty of the unspoiled architecture in the Alpine foothills by Romano Guardini's *Briefe vom Comer See* (Letters from Lake Como) of 1927. Mies had met Guardini in Berlin, where the theologian taught at the university, and the rich pencil marks in Mies's copy of the book speak of a particularly intense encounter with this text.[3] Guardini described the vernacular simplicity of "very ordinary houses, built only for the use to which they would be put; no plasterwork, built only of stone, as it is quarried here, no mortar in between. But the way they juxtaposed the houses, the way they arranged the small square, unbelievable."[4]

Mies surely must have preferred this less popular area of Ticino to the more *en vogue* Ascona nearby. Its Monte Verità had been, at the turn of the century, the site of a "cooperative vegetarian colony" and later became a popular southern retreat for German artists, among them Mies's friend Mary Wigman, or Walter Gropius, who went there with several Bauhaus colleagues in 1930.

Mies knew that Hermann Hesse, perhaps the most prominent German writer of his time, had made a similar choice, settling a safe distance from the fashionable world of Ascona. Hesse had moved to a town called Montagnola, close to Lugano. He was at the height of his success: his novel *Steppenwolf* had appeared in 1927 and *Narziss und Goldmund* in 1930, and both were bestsellers. Hesse had contacted Mies van der Rohe in 1932 with a recommendation for his son to study at the Bauhaus in Dessau. Mies admitted Martin Hesse, who immersed himself in photography classes and later became his father's most important portraitist. Having witnessed Mies at work depoliticizing the school, Martin wrote to his father that he admired Mies as "a fantastic architect," but that he was "a reactionary man."[5] In 1927, Hermann Hesse and his wife, Ninon Dolbin, were photographed at the same pilgrimage church of Santa Maria d'Iseo in Vernate.

The serene image of Mies on his bench there in September 1933 betrayed the complicated reality in Berlin that he had left behind, and the uncertainty that awaited him upon his return. Ultimately, the decade that followed, from 1933 to 1943, was the least fruitful of Mies's career—marred by a long series of unexecuted projects under the Nazi dictatorship, inconsequential patent applications for furniture designs and wallpaper manufacturing, and finally his forced transplant to a foreign country whose language he did not speak, to an institution without a campus, dispersed over twenty-two locations in the vast, industrial city of Chicago. Creatively, Mies seemed trapped in a loop—unable, for those ten long years, to move beyond the vocabulary he had created for the Barcelona Pavilion in 1929. That short-lived building had triggered the most sustained amount of praise of his career, and this success might have made it hard to let go of its central elements. We find the same cruciform columns, freestanding central walls, and floor-to-ceiling windows under a flat roof in a number of unexecuted residential commissions and a golf club. In the United States, projects as different as the Resor House above a river in Wyoming, the private home for Joseph Cantor in Indianapolis, early ideas for the IIT campus, or a "Museum for a Small City" employed that same language. The students at IIT were exposed to the same courtyard house exercises that their Bauhaus peers had worked on before the institution was closed. Finally, in 1943, Mies's first building in the United States would go up on the IIT campus, and he began to develop a new architectural vocabulary of great stringency in response to the very different conditions of architectural production in his new homeland.

Mies also wrote one of his most insightful texts in 1933, for a prospectus for the plate-glass industry, which was never published. In it he speaks with rare clarity about his working method and essentialist ideas, as if he were taking stock at that moment of utter uncertainty. He talks about the "space toppling" power of steel, concrete, and plate glass, which, while then applied mostly in large utilitarian structures, would ultimately be applied in residential buildings: "Now it becomes clear again," he wrote, "what a wall is, what an opening, what is floor and what ceiling. Simplicity of construction, clarity of tectonic means, and purity of material reflect the luminosity of original beauty." In a first draft, he

Figure 6.1. Fritz Schreiber, Mies van der Rohe on a stone bench at Santa Maria d'Iseo in Vernate, Ticino, Switzerland, September 1933.

Figure 6.2. Santa Maria d'Iseo in Vernate, Ticino, Switzerland, 9th century–1677.

had also noted, "Only now can we articulate space, open it up and connect it to the landscape, thereby filling the spatial needs of modern man."[6]

1934   *Deutsches Volk—Deutsche Arbeit*

The year 1934 brought renewed hope for future employment or commissions. The Nazi mayor of Mannheim, Carl Renninger, contacted Mies in March 1934, potentially for a job as the city's building deputy, asking for samples of his work. Mies answered immediately, sending thirty-one photos and drawings of all of his major projects.[7]

Mies and Lilly Reich had been invited to work on a major Nazi propaganda show, *Deutsches Volk—Deutsche Arbeit* (German People—German Work), which celebrated the first anniversary of Hitler's rise to power and opened at the Berlin fairgrounds on April 21, 1934. The show was inspired by comparably staged exhibitions celebrating fascist achievements under Benito Mussolini in Italy. Here, swastikas were everywhere, on flags or stained-glass windows, or inside a giant cogwheel above a colonnade of four monumental hammers at the entrance to the pavilion of the *Deutsche Arbeitsfront* (German Workers' Front). The party's symbol had quickly become the ubiquitous sign of the German government, and the participation in such an event certainly signaled acquiescence with the new regime.

Apparently, Mies's office divided up the different tasks available to them: Mies passed on the opportunity to design a quasi-religious "Hall of Honor," dedicated to the history of the "German People," to his collaborators Sergius Ruegenberg and Ernst Walther. They created a simplified basilica, with an enormous stained-glass window by César Klein. Lilly Reich arranged a display of glass, ceramic, and porcelain on a mezzanine level in another hall. Reich and Mies together took on the mining section in the hall dedicated to energy and technology (figures 6.3, 6.4).[8] They employed a vocabulary similar to that of the industry sections at the Barcelona World's Fair. There were low walls, large photo panels, vitrines fully integrated into the wall, and a remarkable floodlighting system. Mies's childhood friend Gerhard Severain provided the modern sans-serif lettering for all inscriptions, just as he had in Barcelona. Other modern architects were represented at that exhibition as well. Walter Gropius and former Bauhaus master Joost Schmidt had taken on the nonferrous metals exhibit in the same hall, for which Schmidt designed a spectacular rotating metal tower.

1934   The Mountain House

After the intense work on the exhibition, and without any pressing obligations, Mies embarked on one of his habitual alpine vacations. After the previous summer's trip to Lugano, this year, he went to Sopra Bolzano in South Tyrol, Italy, an area suggested by his first client Alois Riehl, whose family came from there, and his wife, Ada Bruhn, who had

Figure 6.3. Ludwig Mies van der Rohe and Lilly Reich, *Deutsches Volk—Deutsche Arbeit* exhibition, Berlin, 1934. German mining section with freestanding walls of rock salt and granite.

Figure 6.4. Ludwig Mies van der Rohe and Lilly Reich, *Deutsches Volk—Deutsche Arbeit* exhibition, Berlin, 1934. German mining section with tar products in the center, and ore mining in the background.

Figure 6.5. Ludwig Mies van der Rohe, Mountain House sketch, 1934. No intended site known (possibly Merano, South Tyrol, Italy). Steel and glass structure on a hill site. Ink on paper, 4 1/2 × 8 in. (10.7 × 20.3 cm). Museum of Modern Art, New York. The Mies van der Rohe Archive, gift of the architect.

Figure 6.6. Ludwig Mies van der Rohe, Mountain House sketch, 1934. No intended site known (possibly Merano, South Tyrol, Italy). Stone structure with glass-enclosed central section. Graphite on paper, 9 × 11 3/4 in. (22.8 × 29.8 cm). Museum of Modern Art, New York. The Mies van der Rohe Archive, gift of the architect.

often spent summers nearby with their three daughters. Mies stayed at the opulent Hotel Friedl-Lang, with its celebrated postcard view onto the "Rosengarten," a dolomite mountain range, often glowing in warm pink on cloudless evenings. Ivan Bocchio has convincingly argued that Mies used his time in this idyllic location far from Berlin to think about an "alpine architecture"—not in the sense of the utopian, expressionist dreams of his colleague Bruno Taut sixteen years earlier, but simply a modern architecture that responded to the impressive landscape around him. While all of his projects to date had been resolutely metropolitan, or at the very least suburban, he now developed two versions of a mountain house (figures 6.5, 6.6).[9] Mies imagined this design to be located near a dolomite mountain pass that he could see from his hotel. Mies tested the range of his formal language: on one end an abstract, elevated glass box, filigrane and unobtrusive but in striking contrast to the rolling hills, rough peaks, and traditional architecture; or, on the other end, a modern vernacular with flat roofs but heavy, slanted walls made from local ashlar.

Mies's vacation was harshly interrupted when a telegram from his office alerted him to an invitation to a meeting about the small, limited competition for the German Pavilion at the World's Fair in Brussels. He was expected to appear at a government agency in Berlin on June 10, 1934, and then four days later in Brussels, in order to visit the site.[10] Mies rushed back home. At the two meetings he found himself in unusual company: among the six invited architects he was the only one with a former connection to the avant-garde. The others were Karl Wach, Emil Fahrenkamp, Ludwig Ruff, Eckart Muthesius, and Paul Schmitthenner, and all enjoyed success and recognition under the new regime. A photograph shows Mies, his collaborator Karl Otto, Fahrenkamp, and (probably) Muthesius in Brussels on June 14, 1934 (figure 6.7). If Mies was invited as a result of his previous design in Barcelona, or because he was considered a potential candidate for government commissions like the others, is not entirely clear. In any event, he was assigned the role of a spokesperson, in charge of the distribution of supportive material to the participants.[11]

The overall size of the project was 97,000 square feet (9,000 square meters), which included a central Hall of Honor, celebrating the motto "*Mens sana in corpore sano*" (A sound mind in a sound body), in anticipation of the Olympic Games in Berlin in 1936.[12] There was supposed to be a restaurant for 850 guests and a movie theater, in addition to sections about industry, manufacturing, and crafts. Mies's habit of working on projects to the very last minute probably meant that the bulk of the design happened between his return from South Tyrol and the deadline of July 2. He was in such a rush that he was unable to make copies of his drawings or take photographs of the model in the scale of 1:500, which the sculptor Oswald Herzog had produced.[13]

The general brief specified that the "totalitarian foundation of the Third Reich" and its "basic principles" should be represented[14] and that the pavilion in particular should "symbolize the attitude, fighting spirit and heroic determination of National Socialism."[15] Mies van der Rohe's text accompanying his design spoke a somewhat different language: not once did he mention "National Socialism," but rather he carefully educated the jury: "In recent years, Germany has developed a formal approach for its exhibitions, which increasingly moved away from ostentation and outward decoration to the essential." It had become evident over the years, in particular abroad, Mies explained, that such "clear and evocative language corresponds to the nature of German work."[16] The building should be nothing but a realistically organized and sensibly designed spatial framework. Mies emphasized, though, that the steel-frame building would consist entirely of "German Material" such as "clinker

Figure 6.7. Meeting in preparation for the 1935 World's Fair, Brussels, June 14, 1934, showing Mies van der Rohe (second from right), Emil Fahrenkamp (left of Mies), Karl Otto (second from left), Eckhardt Muthesius (first from left), and others. Gelatin silver print, 1934, reproduction, 1960s, 3 1/2 × 5 in. (9 × 12.6 cm). Bauhaus-Archive, Berlin.

bricks, travertine, limestone, glass, linoleum and precious woods from Germany."[17] (This presented a striking difference compared to the Barcelona Pavilion, where the marble and travertine had come from Italy, Greece, and Algeria.) Several consecutive drafts of Mies's text show him depoliticizing it. He had initially specified "*Schlesischen Marmor*" (marble from Silesia) for the two freestanding walls in the main hall, but then replaced that with "Danube Limestone." The former German province of Silesia (usurped by Prussia in the eighteenth century from Austria) had been divided up between Poland and Czechoslovakia with the Versailles Treaty. One of Adolf Hitler's belligerently proclaimed goals was to bring Silesia back. Suggesting Silesian marble thus seemed to support Hitler's position, and Mies moved away from that. Similarly, an early draft stated the installation of a "mighty bronze Reich's eagle" in front of one of the freestanding walls, while "a swastika is carved into the other wall"; both of these suggestions were not spelled out in the text's final version. An interior perspective with a large swastika on one wall, and the words "Deutsches Reich" on the other, has survived in the collection of Dirk Lohan.[18]

Critics have suggested that the design for the Brussels Pavilion was in some ways "the last version of the Barcelona Pavilion"[19]—and it was indeed a comparable project, albeit with larger dimensions, with a more specific program and a decidedly political charge.[20] Just like his cleaned-up text for Brussels, the design itself showed Mies on the fence, walking a fine line between appeasing the Nazi government and signaling, at least to those who knew him, his discontent.

Mies's sketches show the outside walls in brick (thus avoiding any outward semblance of profligacy) and a similar formal vocabulary: a grid of forty-nine cruciform columns, freestanding marble walls inside, expanses of tinted glass, shallow pools, enclosed areas open to the sky, and spatial variety (figure 6.8). It is highly instructive to trace the differences in

Figure 6.8. Ludwig Mies van der Rohe, design for the German Pavilion, competition entry, 1934, for the Brussels World's Fair (1935). Floor plan sketch (detail). Pencil on paper, 11 5/8 × 8 3/4 in. (29.5 × 22.2 cm). Museum of Modern Art, New York. The Mies van der Rohe Archive, gift of the architect.

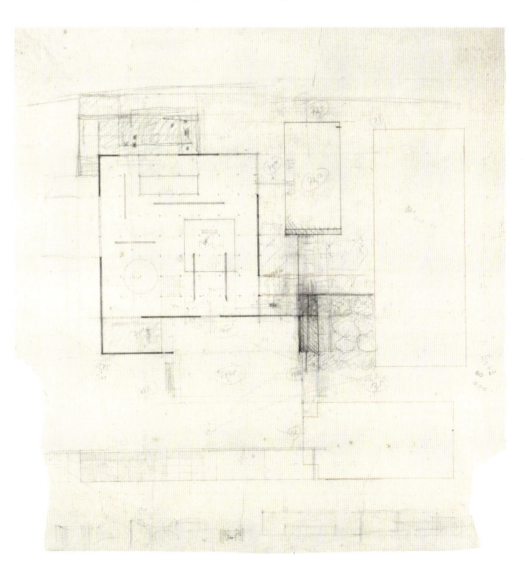

the treatment of several of the pavilion's elements. Mies might have been guided by a recent critique leveled at the Barcelona Pavilion by conservative historian Hermann Phleps, who had graphically analyzed all the "mistakes" Mies had made in Barcelona and suggested improvements. Columns and walls, he said, looked as if they could glide past and through each other, signaling instability. Therefore, the columns needed bases and capitals, and the glass walls plinths. The marble walls should be lower than the columns, to show their independence from the ceiling and non-load-bearing quality.[21]

Mies, indeed, gave the slim columns a type of capital—or rather, a deliberate absence of one—terminating their chromium or nickel cover just half a foot underneath the ceiling. The actual load-bearing cruciform steel inside was thus exposed, as it met a round metal plate above. Mies did not apply bases, though. As Phleps had recommended, the interior walls were now decisively lower than the ceiling and thus clearly non-load-bearing. Mies's sketch of the main façade suggests a slim opening between the outside wall and the ceiling plate to the same effect (figure 6.9). The interior arrangement appears to follow the stipulations of the brief (a hall and court of honor and exhibition spaces showing a "cross-section of German creative activity in the context of the Third Reich") (figure 6.10). Both the

Figure 6.9. Ludwig Mies van der Rohe, design for the German Pavilion, competition entry, 1934, Brussels World's Fair (1935). Elevation sketch. Pencil and colored pencil on tracing paper, 27 1/2 × 30 3/4 in. (69.9 × 78.1 cm). Museum of Modern Art, New York. The Mies van der Rohe Archive, gift of the architect.

Figure 6.10. Ludwig Mies van der Rohe, design for the German Pavilion, competition entry, 1934, Brussels World's Fair (1935). Interior perspective. Pencil on tracing paper, 10 1/2 × 17 1/4 in. (26.6 × 43.8 cm). Museum of Modern Art, New York. The Mies van der Rohe Archive, gift of the architect.

exterior sketch and the interior view show a strictly symmetrical arrangement. The entrance is in the center, flanked by two flagpoles; an eagle sculpture adorns the entrance, an embellishment that he had firmly rejected in Barcelona, while Mies's sketchy depiction of the swastika on two of the flags on the outside seems somewhat half-hearted.[22]

Perhaps most telling is a sheet with sketches by Mies, which again show the swastika flag as an incomplete scribble but also allows a reading of the main floor plan as a swastika. Clearly, Mies had his limits when compromising on design details, but seemed willing to accede to the political conditions in the hope of securing a commission (figure 6.11).

What exactly the submitted version looked like is hard to determine. The archive contains a series of drawings that appear more final in their execution and miss some of the above-mentioned elements (such as the separation of wall and ceiling) (figure 6.12). They also contain a new element in the background, a glass-clad structure, that seemingly took the glass curtain wall of the Dessau Bauhaus workshop wing to its extreme. Mies would revive that concept a few years later for an (unexecuted) field house at the IIT campus in Chicago in 1941, and a theater he designed before his 1947 MoMA exhibition.

According to the (not always reliable) recollections of Mies's assistant Sergius Ruegenberg, Hitler personally reviewed Mies's proposal for the Brussels Pavilion and found it wanting.[23] At the end of July, he selected the project by Ludwig Ruff as the winner of the limited competition.[24] Ruff was already at work on a huge amphitheater at Nuremberg's Nazi Party rally grounds and apparently had a chance of becoming Hitler's favorite architect

Figure 6.11. Ludwig Mies van der Rohe, design for the German Pavilion, competition entry, 1934, Brussels World's Fair (1935). Entrance and floor plan sketch. Pencil on tracing paper, 10 1/2 × 17 1/4 in. (26.6 × 43.8 cm). Museum of Modern Art, New York. The Mies van der Rohe Archive, gift of the architect.

Figure 6.12. Ludwig Mies van der Rohe, design for the German Pavilion, competition entry, 1934, Brussels World's Fair (1935). Elevation. Pencil on paper, 8 1/4 × 40 1/2 in. (21 × 102.9 cm). Museum of Modern Art, New York. The Mies van der Rohe Archive, gift of the architect.

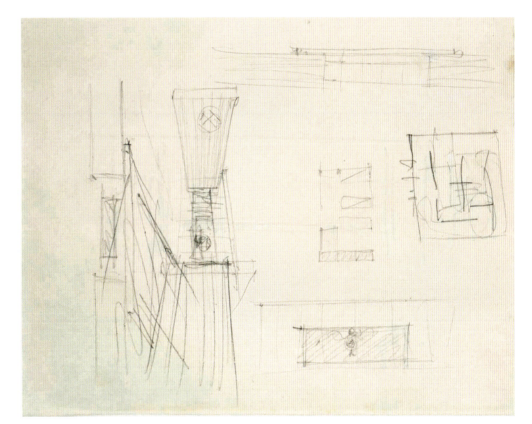

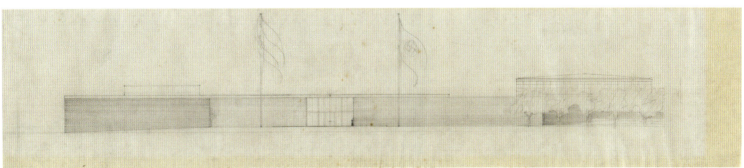

when Paul Troost died unexpectedly in January 1934. Ruff, however, also died suddenly in August 1934, and his son Franz continued the stadium's execution. Less experienced and less charismatic than his father, Franz Ruff did not ascend to similar prominence in the orbit of Hitler, who began working closely with Albert Speer the following year.

Throughout the fall, it still seemed likely that Mies and Lilly Reich would at least design the sections for the chemical and textile industries at the Brussels World's Fair, due to the influence of their former client Georg von Schnitzler of IG Farben, his assistant Erich von Kettler (who had managed the exhibition bureau in Barcelona), and Hermann Lange of the textile industry.[25]

1934 Public Pledge by the Creators of Culture

In mid-August, Mies was approached by the office of Hans-Friedrich Blunck, president of the Reichsschrifttumskammer (Reich's Literature Association), on behalf of propaganda minister Joseph Goebbels. Would Mies be willing to sign a public pledge of allegiance to Adolf Hitler?[26] An important plebiscite had been scheduled for the following week, on August 19, 1934, in order to consolidate Hitler's position by combining his role as chancellor with that of the president. The much-admired president Paul von Hindenburg had just died on August 2, 1934. The pledge was to be published shortly before the vote as a sign of widespread support. Therefore, time was of the essence, the sender politely emphasized, encouraging Mies to respond by telegram (reimbursement for expenses was included in the form of postage stamps). The text of the pledge, apparently written by Goebbels himself, read in part: "We believe in this leader who has fulfilled our burning desire for unity. We trust his work, which requires commitment beyond critical rationality, we place our hopes in this man, who is, beyond human and material things, faithful in God's providence.…The Führer has asked us to stand with him in trust and loyalty. None of us will be missing, when it comes to proclaim this."[27]

Hoping for his continued involvement at the Brussels World's Fair, and potentially other government work, Mies immediately telegraphed his consent. It is perhaps the most unforgivable of Mies's few political gestures, as many of his colleagues did not see a need to respond to Goebbels's overtures. Thirty-seven mostly conservative writers and artists signed—only four of them architects. One was the fervent Nazi Paul Schultze-Naumburg, who had been instrumental in closing the Bauhaus in Dessau under Mies's directorship the previous year. Another one was Emil Fahrenkamp, a moderately modern architect and co-competitor for the Brussels Pavilion. Georg Kolbe, the sculptor of the figure at the Barcelona Pavilion, also signed. The *"Aufruf der Kulturschaffenden"* (Appeal from the Creators of Culture) appeared in the Nazi paper *Völkischer Beobachter* and many other newspapers on August 18, 1934, and Hitler won the referendum with 89.9 percent of the vote (figure 6.13).

Mies's signature under this letter did not go unnoticed among progressives abroad. In November 1934, the Moscow exile magazine *Internationale Literatur* mentioned him in particular and called the appeal "a document of infamy, that deserves to be remembered for a long time."[28] The *Deutsche Freiheit,* a short-lived Social Democratic paper produced in Saarbrücken, a city just beyond Germany's western border at that time (integrated into the Reich after a plebiscite the following year), published the *"Aufruf der Kulturschaffenden"* under the headline *"Deutschlands Geistesgarde wählt Hitler"* (Germany's Intellectual Elite Votes for Hitler), and advised its readers at the end to "despise and forget" those who had signed the appeal.[29]

Internal correspondence reveals a deep division within the party about the *"Aufruf."* Chief Nazi ideologue Alfred Rosenberg, to whom Mies had turned for help when the Berlin Bauhaus was closed the previous year, chided Goebbels at the end of August for approaching people such as Ernst Barlach, Emil Nolde, and Ludwig Mies van der Rohe, whom "the Führer had personally clearly rejected. This rejection has been publicly and unequivocally declared several times and thus it remains regrettable that such personalities would be invited to sign." The issue still bothered him two months later. In another letter to Goebbels, he reiterated how "depressing it is to go begging for signatures among those whom we have been fighting vigorously for years." To demonstrate how fruitless such an

Figure 6.13. *"Aufruf der Kulturschaffenden," Völkischer Beobachter,* August 18, 1934.

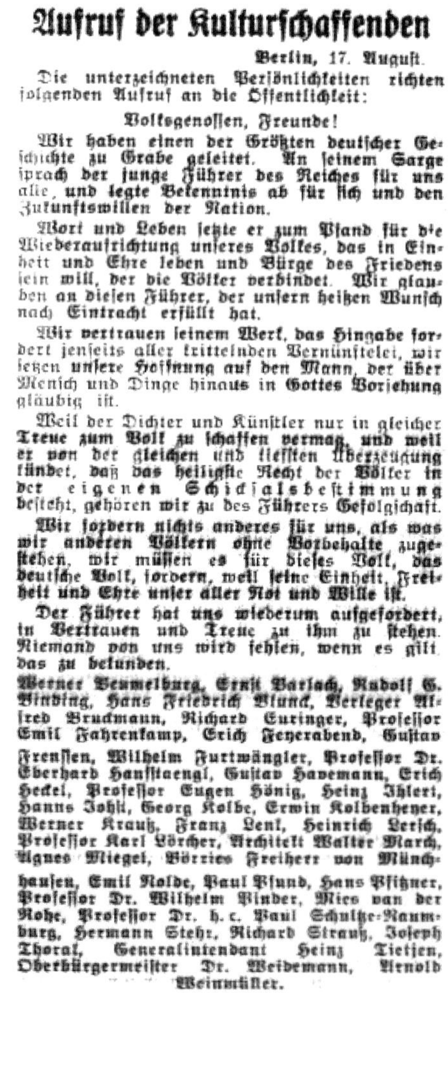

Aufruf der Kulturschaffenden

Berlin, 17. August.

Die unterzeichneten Persönlichkeiten richten folgenden Aufruf an die Öffentlichkeit:

Volksgenossen, Freunde!

Wir haben einen der Größten deutscher Geschichte zu Grabe geleitet. An seinem Sarge sprach der junge Führer des Reiches für uns alle, und legte Bekenntnis ab für sich und den Zukunftswillen der Nation.

Wort und Leben setzte er zum Pfand für die Wiederaufrichtung unseres Volkes, das in Einheit und Ehre leben und Bürge des Friedens sein will, der die Völker verbindet. Wir glauben an diesen Führer, der unsern heißen Wunsch nach Eintracht erfüllt hat.

Wir vertrauen seinem Werk, das Hingabe fordert jenseits aller krittelnden Vernünftelei, wir setzen unsere Hoffnung auf den Mann, der über Mensch und Dinge hinaus in Gottes Vorsehung gläubig ist.

Weil der Dichter und Künstler nur in gleicher Treue zum Volk zu schaffen vermag, und weil er von der gleichen und tiefsten Überzeugung kündet, daß das heiligste Recht der Völker in der eigenen Schicksalsbestimmung besteht, gehören wir zu des Führers Gefolgschaft.

Wir fordern nichts anderes für uns, als was wir anderen Völkern ohne Vorbehalte zugestehen, wir müssen es für dieses Volk, das deutsche Volk, fordern, weil seine Einheit, Freiheit und Ehre unser aller Not und Wille ist.

Der Führer hat uns wiederum aufgefordert, in Vertrauen und Treue zu ihm zu stehen. Niemand von uns wird fehlen, wenn es gilt das zu bekunden.

Werner Beumelburg, Ernst Barlach, Rudolf G. Binding, Hans Friedrich Blunck, Verleger Alfred Bruckmann, Richard Euringer, Professor Emil Fahrenkamp, Erich Feyerabend, Gustav Frenssen, Wilhelm Furtwängler, Professor Dr. Eberhard Hanfstaengl, Gustav Havemann, Erich Heckel, Professor Eugen Hönig, Heinz Ihlert, Hanns Johst, Georg Kolbe, Erwin Kolbenheyer, Werner Krauß, Franz Lenk, Heinrich Lersch, Professor Karl Lörcher, Architekt Walter March, Agnes Miegel, Börries Freiherr von Münchhausen, Emil Nolde, Paul Pfund, Hans Pfitzner, Professor Dr. Wilhelm Pinder, Mies van der Rohe, Professor Dr. h. c. Paul Schultze-Naumburg, Hermann Stehr, Richard Strauß, Joseph Thorak, Generalintendant Heinz Tietjen, Oberbürgermeister Dr. Weidemann, Arnold Weinmüller.

undertaking was, he mentioned Mies's duplicity: "Prof. Mies van der Rohe, the creator of a memorial for Liebknecht and Rosa Luxemburg, had finally agreed to sign, but he immediately apologized to his friends." Rosenberg had read this in the left-leaning Swiss newspaper *Basler Nationalzeitung*, which had written about Mies: "The former director of the Bauhaus signed with gnashing teeth but without objections and apologized to his friends the next day." The article pointed out that the sculptor Ernst Barlach persistently refused to sign, but finally gave in, after hearing that Mies, Nolde, Erich Heckel, and Kolbe had also signed.[30]

Mies was, nevertheless, willing to use his signature as convenient ammunition when, in January 1934, he was accused by the city of Dessau of unlawfully assuming patent rights that belonged to the city when the Bauhaus (under his directorship) was kicked out and moved to Berlin. Mies, at first, stood his ground in a follow-up letter, but after several more threatening notes from the Dessau city council, he finally gave in.[31] His lawyer wrote on September 18, 1934, that Mies was returning all rights to the city of Dessau, expecting that the case was now closed and any vilification of his client would cease: "Apart from the merely personal aspect, it makes no sense that the city magistrate of Dessau accuses Professor Mies van der Rohe of being a cultural Bolshevik, while the Reich's government commissions him to design buildings for the Brussels World's Fair and key figures of the Third Reich ask him to sign the *Aufruf der Kulturschaffenden*."[32]

This signature would haunt Mies again, eight years later, after he had immigrated to the United States. The Jewish German weekly *Aufbau*, published in New York since 1934, had become one of the leading anti-Nazi publications of the German press in exile. It counted many prominent German emigrants among its authors, such as Hannah Arendt, Albert Einstein, Thomas Mann, and Stefan Zweig. On February 22, 1946, six months after the end of the war, it published the *"Aufruf der Kulturschaffenden"* in its entirety, including its signatories, under the headline: "Ein Schmachdokument deutscher Künstler" (A Document of Shame for German Artists). Its preface was not without sarcasm: "In the current confusion both in Germany and in the cultural world beyond its borders, regarding the question of who should be accused—or not—of being a friend of the Nazis, this document might be of some help. Here we have a number of German intellectuals and artists, who happily confess their 'faith in Hitler.'"[33] Mies had just received his American citizenship and must have been panicked about his reputation. He was working on upcoming exhibitions at the Renaissance Society of Chicago and the Museum of Modern Art in New York for the following year, and his first high-rise building in Chicago was in the final planning stages. He needed quick damage control. A week later, a letter to the editor from prominent New York gallerist Karl Nierendorf appeared in the *Aufbau*. Mies knew Nierendorf and had probably asked him for help. Nierendorf claimed that "as far as he knew," the signatures of Ernst Barlach, Erich Heckel, Georg Kolbe, and Mies van der Rohe had been put wrongly under the *"Aufruf der Kulturschaffenden*," "without knowledge or authorization from these personalities." The headline read "Gefälschte Unterschriften" (Forged Signatures).[34] This seems to have put an end to it, for the time being. It was sheer luck on Mies's part that no one among the German-speaking readership of the *Aufbau* in New York or Chicago recognized his name and passed this information on to a major newspaper. It could have derailed his entire career.

The letter seems to have been forgotten after that, until, in 1963, it was reprinted in an East German publication, where Sibyl Moholy-Nagy found it and mentioned it publicly in the *Journal of the Society of Architectural Historians* in 1965. At that point, Mies had become untouchable. Major magazines were preparing for special editions celebrating his eightieth birthday in 1966, and Moholy-Nagy's letter to the editor had no measurable effect. In 1989, Elaine Hochman's *Architects of Fortune* appeared, which focused on Mies van der Rohe and the Third Reich and discussed the *"Aufruf"* again.[35]

1934   Severain House

Just when the appeal for Hitler's support appeared in the *Völkischer Beobachter* and many other newspapers, the last building that Mies designed in Germany before his emigration was finished. This previously unidentified house was designed for his friend Gerhard Severain's brother Alois, who owned a store for interior decoration and wallpapers in the center of Stuttgart. As with the Ryder House in Wiesbaden of 1923 (see Chapter 2), Severain had asked Mies to do the design work, while he signed the building application and helped with construction supervision on-site. Mies's collaborator at the time, Werner Graeff, remembered it being designed anonymously in Mies's office: "He had that friend from Aachen and he had a brother in Stuttgart with a house painting company.…And Mies kind of moonlighted for him.…We did it in the studio, but it didn't come under Mies's name.…That house in Stuttgart, for the brother of his friend…that looks like a poor man's version of Tugendhat."[36] The house does, indeed, have a significant similarity with the Tugendhat House in Brno, and it also avoids its often-critiqued ostentatiousness and functional shortcomings. Instead of white stucco, it is clad in brick, the vast window panes of the former are divided into smaller (and more affordable) units, and the street façade is more elegant (figures 6.14). Most importantly, Mies reversed the internal organization and thus improved it significantly: the wide-open living room (albeit much smaller than in Brno) with an adjacent greenhouse is on the upper floor, has a broad veranda, and is directly accessible from the entrance area (figures 6.15, 6.16). The freestanding wall in the living room is made of wood rather than onyx. Behind it is a work space and library, an arrangement similar to that at the Tugendhat House, but here receiving considerably more light (figures 6.17, 6.18). The private family rooms are underneath and enjoy direct access to the garden. The interior featured Mies van der Rohe furniture and some of the wallpaper that Alois Severain had designed. Mies was careful not to mention and publish this thoroughly modern house. He might not have wanted to undermine his friend's official authorship, and, as he was still hoping for government commissions, a flat-roofed modern house did not seem like a good calling card for himself. The Severain House in Stuttgart thus has been thoroughly forgotten but deserves to be recognized as a significant achievement.[37]

No other major commissions were realized in 1934 or in the remaining time while Mies was in Germany. His work for the Verseidag (United Silk Industry) in Krefeld, for which he had designed a factory in 1931 (only partially executed), dried up when the company's building department took over.[38] The core of the factory and office building in Krefeld still exist.

Mies's patent lawyer, Gottfried Bueren, whose firm, Bueren & Leineweber, had had the lucrative task of executing and defending Mies's furniture patents, mercifully gave Mies a job in the fall of 1934, which was, however, depressingly small—the conversion of a balcony into a glass-enclosed winter garden at his large villa in Nikolassee.[39] The project seems to

Figure 6.14. Ludwig Mies van der Rohe and Gerhard Severain, Alois Severain House, Stuttgart, Germany, 1934 (destroyed 1945). Street façade. Photograph by Adolf Lazi. Gelatin silver print, 6 3/8 × 8 7/8 in. (16.2 × 22.6 cm). Private collection, Wiesbaden.

Figure 6.15. Ludwig Mies van der Rohe and Gerhard Severain, Alois Severain House, Stuttgart, Germany, 1934 (destroyed 1945). Garden façade. Photograph by Adolf Lazi. Gelatin silver print, 6 3/8 × 8 7/8 in. (16.2 × 22.6 cm). Private collection, Wiesbaden.

Figure 6.16. Ludwig Mies van der Rohe and Gerhard Severain, Alois Severain House, Stuttgart, Germany, 1934 (destroyed 1945). Interior view of the living room looking toward the terrace. Note the greenhouse on the left. Photograph by Adolf Lazi. Gelatin silver print, 6 3/8 × 8 7/8 in. (16.2 × 22.6 cm). Private collection, Wiesbaden.

have been supervised by Herbert Hirche, who had studied under Mies at the Bauhaus and afterward occasionally worked in his office.

The striking difference in recognition abroad and at home became particularly apparent in October 1934, when Mies was invited to contribute several works to the centenary exhibition of the Royal Institute of British Architects in London (*International Architecture, 1924–1934*), an enormous show with about one thousand exhibits. Mies was careful about his selection and mindful of potential criticism at home. He included the Weissenhof Estate, the Lange House, and the Tugendhat House, but explicitly omitted his housing estate at Afrikanische Strasse (designed under socialist mayor Martin Wagner) as "not important enough," and he did not mention the Barcelona Pavilion, generally seen as a potent symbol for the Weimar Republic's young democracy, to the London organizers at all.[40]

While his Weissenhof Estate was on show in London, it was thoroughly discredited in Munich, where the Nazis had staged the *Deutsche Siedlungsausstellung* (German Settlement Exhibition) from June to October 1934, to mimic and outdo the Stuttgart Weissenhof exhibition with a "great manifesto of the new approach to building" and a sample estate on the outskirts.[41] Much larger than the Stuttgart estate, it contained 192 pitched-roof houses, mostly for single families, as well as duplexes and a few row houses, designed by sixteen different German architects, arranged as a garden city along curved streets and meant to be affordable to the middle class.[42]

Also, in October 1934, a new "architects' law" came into force. For the first time, it provided protection for the professional title, which led to consternation among many builders, who, often with similar or better educational experience, were excluded. The law specified that all architects "without exception" had to be members of the Reichskammer der bildenden Künste (Reich Chamber of Fine Arts) and were not allowed to practice if they were not. Previous members of the Bund Deutscher Architekten (BDA), which Mies had joined in 1924, were automatically integrated. Interestingly, as Anke Blümm has pointed out, all the German modernists were thus early members of this Nazi organization. Jewish members, however, were expelled shortly afterward.[43] The task of German architects, the charter spelled out, was a clear rebuttal to recent modernist and International Style efforts, namely to prevent the "further disfigurement of the German land through buildings which in no way respond to the needs of a German building spirit and sense of responsibility

Figure 6.17. Ludwig Mies van der Rohe and Gerhard Severain, Alois Severain House, Stuttgart, Germany, 1934 (destroyed 1945). View from the entrance area to the living room with a Makassar wood wall. Photograph by Adolf Lazi. Gelatin silver print, 6 3/8 × 8 7/8 in. (16.2 × 22.6 cm). Private collection, Wiesbaden.

towards the common goals."[44] Mies was a member of the chamber until he left for the United States.

In early December, Germany withdrew from the Brussels exhibition altogether due to a shortage of funds.[45] Mies and Lilly Reich had still hoped to be involved in some way. At the same time, local Nazi officials decided to destroy Mies's memorial to Karl Liebknecht and Rosa Luxemburg at the Friedrichsfelde cemetery, which had already been heavily damaged by members of the SA in February 1933. The demolition was executed shortly afterward, in January 1935.[46]

1935   Hubbe House

Sometime in 1935, Mies was contacted by Margarete Hubbe from Magdeburg, the widow of Gustav Hubbe, co-owner of the United Oil Company Hubbe & Farenholtz, who now led the company with Wilhelm Adolf Farenholtz. In 1925, Farenholtz had tried, with great personal engagement, to bring Mies to Magdeburg as the new head of the municipal planning and building office. Since Bruno Taut's tenure in this position in the early 1920s, the city had emerged as a center of modern architecture in Germany. Despite Mies's undeniable success in recent years, when, ten years later, Farenholtz needed a new office building for his company, he did not commission Mies but rather the equally prominent, but

Figure 6.18. Ludwig Mies van der Rohe and Gerhard Severain, Alois Severain House, Stuttgart, Germany, 1934 (destroyed 1945). Work area and library adjacent to the living room. Photograph by Adolf Lazi. Gelatin silver print, 8 7/8 × 6 3/8 in. (22.6 × 16.2 cm). Private collection, Wiesbaden.

conservative, architect Heinrich Tessenow, who designed a moderately modern building with a pitched roof. Farenholtz himself was a complex figure—greatly invested in the well-being of his workers, active in city politics, and a collector of contemporary, "degenerate" art by expressionist painters such as Emil Nolde, Erich Heckel, Lyonel Feininger, Karl Schmidt-Rottluff, and others. At the same time, he was also a fervent Nazi. Choosing Tessenow for his company headquarters was a politically prudent move, as Tessenow's craft-based vernacular was embraced by the new regime. Margarete Hubbe approaching Mies for ideas for a private home might have been a way to console him over the loss or impossibility of the larger commission for the company.

Hubbe owned a plot of land on the eastern side of the Werder Island in Magdeburg facing the older arm of the Elbe River. Mies developed several versions for the project. At first he produced a rather tight plan with a glass enclosed hall and a pergola on single supports all the way to a small belvedere at the waterfront and a semicircular terrace in front of the bedroom. A much larger and more generous design then provided one of the prototypes for Mies's courtyard house typology that he explored in countless versions throughout the 1930s. In this mature version, the broad, western entrance is protected by a flat roof on four cruciform columns, belonging to a central set of ten columns continued behind the wall that shielded the lobby. The path into the generous glass-enclosed living room behind it thus required a sequence of ninety-degree turns. Its centerpiece is a freestanding wall with a fireplace, perpendicular to the one closing off the entrance lobby. In front of it, the living room provides space for a grand piano and two seating arrangements, behind which is a dining table (figure 6.19). The wings on either side of the asymmetrically placed entrance contain bedrooms and bathrooms on the left and a service wing to the right with a wardrobe, guest bathroom, generous kitchen, and small living spaces for two maids.

Figure 6.19. Ludwig Mies van der Rohe, Hubbe House project, Magdeburg, Germany, 1935. Floor plan with furniture placement. Graphite on illustration board, 19 × 26 1/2 in. (48.3 × 67.3 cm). Museum of Modern Art, New York. The Mies van der Rohe Archive, gift of the architect.

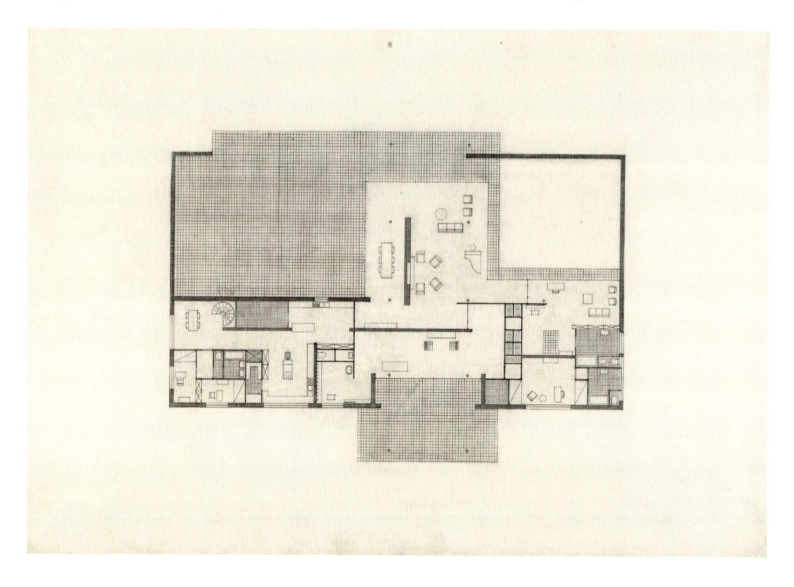

As grand as this plan is, Hubbe House is also an example of Mies's creative crisis. The design elements continue the spatial and formal language that had been fully formed in 1931 after the Barcelona Pavilion, the Tugendhat House, and the house at the *Deutsche Bauausstellung* in Berlin. His perspective sketches look like ghost images of Sasha Stone's photographs of the pavilion—the brilliant interpretation of the photographer had taken hold of Mies's imagination (figure 6.20). A large number of drawings in different collections (among them the MoMA, Library of Congress, the Art Institute of Chicago, the Getty, the Heinz Architectural Center, and the Canadian Centre for Architecture) have been assigned—somewhat unlikely—to this project, showing Mies endlessly varying the court house pattern and its intriguingly simple perspectives. Many of the sketches bear little resemblance to the one plan Mies published himself in the journal *Die Schildgenossen* in 1935, where he emphasized the plan's "beautiful alternation of quiet seclusion and open spaces…[for] social life and hospitality," adding:

> The house was to be built on the Elbe Island in Magdeburg, under old beautiful trees with a far-reaching view over the Elbe. It was an unusually beautiful site. Only the exposure presented problems. The beautiful view was to the east; to the south the view was dull, almost disturbing. This defect would have had to be corrected by the building plan. For that reason, I have enlarged the living quarters by a garden court surrounded by a wall and so locked out this view while allowing full sunshine. Toward the river, the house is entirely open and melts into the landscape.[47]

The magazine *Die Schildgenossen* was probably the only German publication in which Mies could still publish in 1935. Many other journals had either been discontinued under pressure from the Nazis (such as the Werkbund journal *Die Form*) or were tightly controlled. *Die Schildgenossen*, the small, intellectual journal of the Catholic youth organization Quickborn, was edited by two of Mies's acquaintances—its founder, Romano Guardini, priest and professor of theology in Berlin, and the architect and theologian Rudolf Schwarz. Mies knew Schwarz from the Werkbund board and greatly admired his starkly modern Fronleichnamskirche (Corpus Christi Church, 1928) in his hometown of Aachen. Schwarz's book *Wegweisung der Technik* (Technology's Directive) of 1928 had been centrally important to the evolution of Mies's design approach. Only months before, Schwarz had been relieved by the Nazis of his post as director of the Aachen Handwerks- und Kunstgewerbeschule (Trade- and Craftschool) which Mies himself had briefly attended two decades earlier. Guardini had been openly critical of the Nazis'

Figure 6.20. Ludwig Mies van der Rohe, Hubbe House project, Magdeburg, Germany, 1935. Perspective terrace. Pencil on illustration board, 19 × 26 1/2 in. (48.3 × 67.3 cm). Museum of Modern Art, New York. The Mies van der Rohe Archive, gift of the architect.

anti-Semitism. Just months before Mies's piece on "House H. in Magdeburg" appeared, an essay by Guardini emphasized the closeness of Christian and Jewish religions.[48] Thus, while Mies's short and descriptive sketches were clearly an outlier in this deeply intellectual and philosophical journal, they fit into its mold as one of the few spaces for critical resistance and discourse. Lilly Reich told the Dutch architect J. J. P. Oud: "Sadly, the Hubbe House was not built, for the lady client sold the property. Another small project for Krefeld has also had to be abandoned. All of this is not easy for us; I myself only have a few small jobs, but for M. it is especially difficult."[49]

1935 Ulrich Lange House

Another failed project, contemporaneous with the Hubbe House, was that for Ulrich Lange, the son of Mies's client Hermann Lange in Krefeld, who had gotten married in 1935. Here also, several versions have survived. One features a similar T-shaped plan, with a glazed-in living area, an enclosed court, and, through an opening in the surrounding wall, a distant view (figure 6.21). A second version has a straight brick wall with an oculus, similar to the recent Severain House, and a curvilinear wall in its center, two ample courtyards, one facing the kitchen and containing the garage, the other facing the living and bedrooms of the family. There are, as always with Mies in those years, extremely frugal rooms for household help, in this case two maids and two kitchen staff. Perhaps the most evocative part of the project is a series of perspectives that have been associated with it, not corresponding with either version, but giving special emphasis to the evocative power of the freestanding, central wall (figure 6.22). The project got as far as the application for a building permit. As Ludwig Glaeser tells it, when the Nazi head of the municipal building office in Krefeld required a street-facing berm to hide Mies's design, Mies refused to revise it accordingly and abandoned the commission.[50]

Figure 6.21. Ludwig Mies van der Rohe, Ulrich Lange House project, Krefeld, Germany, 1935. Plan and exterior elevation. Pencil and colored pencil on tracing paper, 15 × 21 1/4 in. (38.1 × 54 cm). Museum of Modern Art, New York. The Mies van der Rohe Archive, gift of the architect.

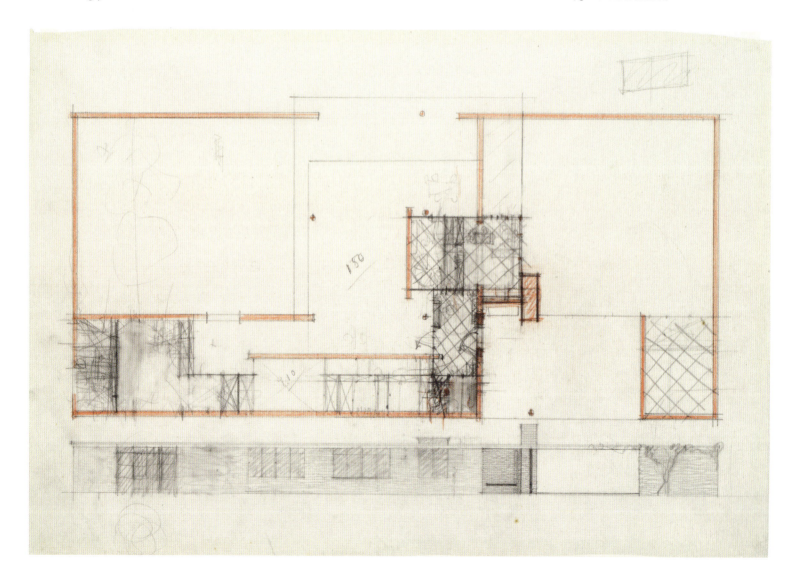

1935 Responding to Alvar Aalto's Furniture Patents

In 1927, Mies had patented his first cantilevered chair, and the patent for the Barcelona Chair followed two years later; these patents were the basis for lucrative licensing agreements with various furniture manufacturers. They provided an important part of his income in the late 1920s and during the 1930s.[51] In the mid-1930s, Mies spent a considerable amount of energy on more furniture patents, trying to revive his fortunes in this field and to stem the impact of the Finnish architect Alvar Aalto, whose furniture suddenly became popular and seemed to infringe on Mies's turf. Mies was unsuccessful on both counts. As a result, Mies's later furniture patents have been little noticed, but they are instructive, as they chronicle the evolution of ideas between the two architects. Mies and Aalto had met only once, briefly, at a meeting in Berlin of the directing council of CIAM, called CIRPAC, in June 1931.[52]

Mies had tried to protect broader ideas behind the Barcelona Chair in December 1929 in several countries; the patent was published in Switzerland on March 16, 1932, and in Germany on August 25, 1932. It described versions of chairs with flexible leaf springs in an astonishing array of rather baroque-looking versions and curved seats out of flexible sheet metal, plywood, leather straps, or woven fabric. Mies claimed that this chair would allow a "comfortable gliding into the seat" and supported a "facilitated rise" from it.[53]

The 1920s were a remarkable time for chair design. Countless architects discovered furniture design—and that of chairs, in particular—as an ideal area to try out and demonstrate fundamental principles. Stuttgart architect Adolf G. Schneck took stock of the recent developments in 1928 with an exhibition in Stuttgart and an accompanying book, titled *Der Stuhl* (The Chair) (figure 6.23).[54] Aalto had submitted several designs to the

Figure 6.22. Ludwig Mies van der Rohe, Ulrich Lange House project, Krefeld, Germany, 1935. Perspective sketch. Pencil and colored pencil on paper, 8 1/4 × 11 1/2 in. (20.9 × 29.2 cm). Museum of Modern Art, New York. The Mies van der Rohe Archive, gift of the architect.

exhibition, but they were not included in the catalogue. It is here that he might have encountered a new idea in chair design, which had nothing to do with comfort or fabrication, but rather addressed a quality that came to play when the chair was *not* in use, namely its stackability for quick, space-saving storage, which facilitated the modern idea of multipurpose spaces. Joseph Mathieu of Lyon had designed such a chair, patented it widely, and produced it in his hometown from 1922 on, through his Société industrielle des meubles multipl's (Production Company for Multiple Furniture).[55] The legs out of sheet metal had the cross section of an open quarter circle, tapering downward in such a way that the four legs of a second chair could be fitted into the one underneath. Mathieu's chair was the only stackable sample in Schneck's catalogue and the last, culminating image.[56] Other chair examples came from Charlotte Perriand, Marcel Breuer, and Mart Stam. Gerrit Rietveld was represented with both his famous Red and Blue Chair (in its early black version) and two versions of his recent Beugel (Bow) Chair of 1927, with a metal tube support and a continuous, curved seat from fiberboard (figure 6.24).[57] Both Mies's MR 10 and MR 20 chairs were included. Interestingly, the idea of stackability, conceptually close to Mies's preference for universal spaces, never seems to have impacted his chair designs. The catalogue, though, suggests possible cross-pollinations at the time.

Aalto might have discovered the notion of stackability here and the cantilevered metal tube chairs by Stam and Mies. He was surely also aware of Marcel Breuer's cantilevered chair, which, while not patented, would be mass-produced by Thonet a year later. Mies's patent for a "Seat with Springy Structure" was published in Switzerland in March 1932 and in Germany in August 1932. Aalto had never worked in curved steel, but now, in response to Rietveld and Mies, he patented a simple cantilevered chair (submitted in July 1932), which had two significant improvements over the status quo: the simple loop of a metal tube carried a continuous piece of bent plywood as both seat and backrest (figure 6.25).[58] Crucially, only the seat was supported by the metal tube. The plywood continued, unsupported, upward as a backrest, boldly demonstrating the strength and flexibility of the material. The second innovation addressed stackability via a subtle outward bend of the vertical supports to make room for a second chair, and more, to be pushed in from the front. The simplicity

Figure 6.23. Cover of Adolf G. Schneck, *Der Stuhl* (Stuttgart: Julius Hoffmann, 1928).

Figure 6.24. Gerrit Rietveld, Beugel Chair, 1927. Published in Adolf G. Schneck, *Der Stuhl* (Stuttgart: Julius Hoffmann, 1928), 56.

and brilliance of this design must have impressed Mies, even if it clearly challenged his own dominant position in the area of cantilevered metal tube chairs (figure 6.26).[59]

At the same time, Aalto worked out the technology of bending laminated wood and developed a wooden stackable armchair and stool. Their L-shaped legs were placed next to the seat rather than underneath it, which allowed a second, third, and more chairs to be placed on top, each chair protruding above the one underneath by the depth of a leg. The method of bending wood and Aalto's Paimio Chair were patented in England in February 1935, and in the United States in June 1936.[60] A separate patent covered Aalto's ingenious method of creating resilient curved laminated wood connections. Mies, in turn, also encroached on Aalto's turf by proposing cantilevered designs in materials other than metal, in particular bent wood and plywood.

Among Mies's many furniture sketches of the mid-1930s was a catalogue of the first Aalto exhibition in Zurich of 1933 under the title *Das Neue Holzmöbel: Aalto Wohnbedarf* (New Wood Furniture: Aalto Dwelling Supplies).[61] The twelve-page brochure, with its evocative cover by Herbert Bayer, presented a complete program of Aalto's ingenious work, starting with the stackable cantilevered metal tube chair, followed by several wooden cantilevered chairs and fauteuils, as well as elegant stackable wooden stools and tables (figure 6.27). Mies sent a copy of that brochure to his patent attorney Gottfried Bueren in July 1935, in order to find out what specific claims were made for three of Aalto's cantilevered wooden chairs.[62] Not satisfied, in 1937, Mies asked his collaborator Anton Lorenz to inquire further. Lorenz wrote to Aalto, reporting that he had been personally commissioned by Mies to "follow up on the sale of Aalto's springy cantilevered wooden chairs in certain European countries and in America."[63] Aalto was alarmed and contacted Mies directly in November 1937 to explain that his company, Artek, was mostly focused on Finland (which was clearly not the case) and that he hoped to have "an international impact intellectually speaking" and perhaps a future collaboration.[64] Mies was in Chicago at the time, and it is unclear if or when he received Aalto's letter. When Aalto came to Chicago in 1939 to see László Moholy-Nagy's New Bauhaus, he had lunch with John Wellborn Root, Jr., his wife, Moholy-Nagy, and others at the Tavern Club, but there is no evidence that he saw Mies as well.[65]

Perhaps the most direct response to Aalto's method of bending wood was a patent that Mies and Lilly Reich worked on for a number of years. A first version was submitted by Lilly Reich in 1935. Mies submitted it again in 1938, under his name (figure 6.28). It grew out of the realization that the stress exerted on the material of a cantilevered chair increases from the seat on down. Aalto increased the thickness of his bent, laminated plywood when the additional weight of the seat met it. Reich suggested a veritable taxonomy of responses,

Figure 6.25. Alvar Aalto, Chair 23, 1930. Tubular steel and bent plywood. Photograph by Maija Holma. Alvar Aalto Museum, Helsinki.

Figure 6.26. Ludwig Mies van der Rohe, chair with elastic structure, August 1932. Line drawing in patent application.

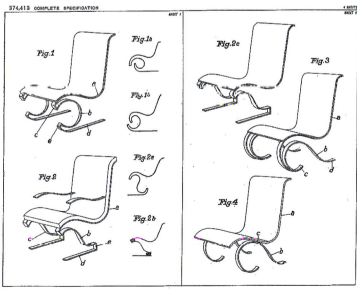

Figure 6.27. Studio Dorland, Berlin, and Herbert Bayer (attributed), brochure entitled *Das Neue Holzmöbel. Aalto Wohnbedarf,* for an exhibition of Alvar Aalto's furniture for the firm Wohnbedarf Zürich, 1932. Folded brochure with four loose pages, 5 7/8 × 8 1/4 in. (15 × 21 cm). Bauhaus-Archiv, Berlin.

Figure 6.28. Ludwig Mies van der Rohe, article of furniture, November 1938. Line drawing in patent application.

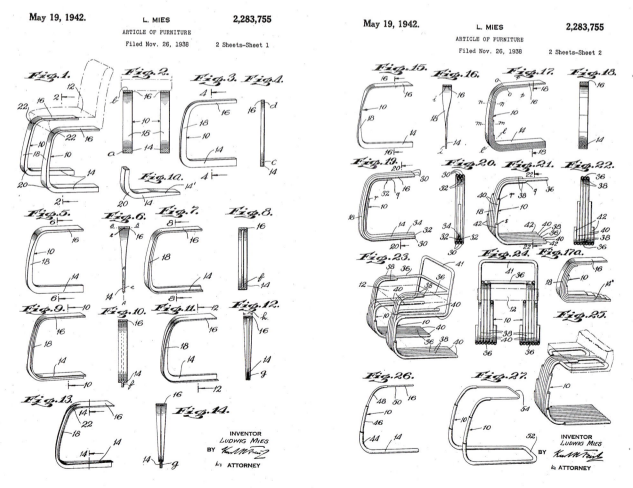

some of which are quite elegant. She was playing into contemporary sentiments when stressing that several solutions could be made from "relatively resistant German woods."[66]

The continuously curved sheet of plywood in Aalto's famous scroll chair for the Paimio Sanatorium (singled out on Herbert Bayer's cover) inspired Mies to work on an intriguing new chair patent, which he described initially as "Seat or Recliner out of Springy Sheet Metal."[67] These ideas found a first application in Mies's patent for a chair "especially for automobiles," which he filed on October 24, 1935 (figure 6.29). It consisted of a continuous piece of sheet metal, which worked somewhat like a spring, while an additional arc between seat and backrest maintained their angle to each other. Thus, the chair provided its own self-contained suspension system (in addition to that of the car), and ensured that the driver "always maintains the same distance to the steering wheel, which is of great benefit for the operational safety," as Mies pointed out.[68] But, while the patent office considered Mies's patent (it would be published in 1937), he and his patent attorney continued working toward a greater clarification of the central principle, namely a "Seat or Recliner out of Springy Sheet Metal," into the fall of 1936.[69] This version never made it into a patent application. If this radical chair had been realized as intended, it could have reinvigorated Mies's career as a furniture designer. He imagined it to be made from a continuous piece of springy, resilient material, "in particular stainless steel," or any other elastic material.[70] In response to Aalto's comparable cross section, Mies's design offered a substantial simplification, namely a reduction to one single material, providing support, seat, and backrest in one continuous piece. He mentioned the possibility of cutting out the armrest from the same piece of steel and of bending it in such a way that it rejoined at the curved front edge of the seat. While, in 1942, Frederick Kiesler designed chairs with similarly curvilinear sections out of oak and linoleum for Peggy Guggenheim's *Art of This Century* exhibition, it would take until 1986 that a chair out of continuously curved sheet metal would be introduced by the Israeli designer Ron Arad, his "Well-Tempered Chair."

One wonders if Mies's interest in seats for cars design was caused by Walter Gropius's great success in vehicle design in recent years. Between 1930 and 1933, Gropius had designed different versions for the bodies and seats of Adler limousines. Gropius's car designs received more press coverage than his architecture at that time.[71] In 1932, Mies had published an essay about "Expressways as an Artistic Problem," in which he suggested that their careful planning could "under certain circumstances...heighten the landscape." Advertising, he noted, should be carefully planned and "be subject to a central control."[72] The time of Mies's design for the elastic seat of 1935 coincided with the invitation to contribute to a limited competition for a prototypical gas station at the new Reichsautobahn, together with Otto Ernst Schweizer, Friedrich Tamms, Robert Vorhoelzer, Lois Welzenbacher, Otto Zollinger, and others. Mies developed a design, and the packing list of his Berlin office mentions the project, but it has not been found. Several sources suggest a collaboration with Werner March (mentioned above in connection with the Eliat House project), who executed a gas station near Hanover after the competition, but detailed proof has been elusive.[73]

1936 Disappointments and Hope

On the occasion of Mies's fiftieth birthday on March 27, 1936, his close collaborator Sergius Ruegenberg had published a short congratulatory piece in the architecture weekly *Bauwelt,* which tried rather hard to make Mies's work palpable to the Nazi regime and to position him for major commissions. While cautiously critiquing the country's recent return to neoclassicism, Ruegenberg pointed out that Mies was embracing that same style, having been inspired by Karl Friedrich Schinkel's Charlottenhof in Potsdam—not its "classical forms, profiles, capitals," but by its true essence, now realized with the means of his own time. This, he pointed out, laid the groundwork for the Barcelona Pavilion, "Mies's first work in this spirit"—designed in a "northern approach" under "the southern sun...driven by the desire to lend form to the German spirit. A strong sense of beauty does not need to overemphasize functionality. Careful execution goes hand in hand with progressive building methods."[74]

For the same occasion, a group of friends, colleagues, and former students got together to purchase a present. Lilly Reich suggested a painting by Max Beckmann, whom Mies greatly

Figure 6.29. Ludwig Mies van der Rohe, chair, in particular for motor vehicles, October 1935. Line drawing in patent application.

Zu der Patentschrift **652 791**
Kl. 63 c   Gr. 46

Bild 1.

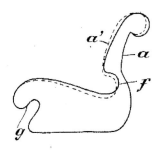

Bild 2.

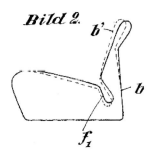

Bild 3.

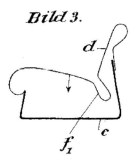

admired. Mies's assistant Herbert Hirche was sent to Beckmann's studio on an exploratory mission, but it was the painter himself who chose the canvas and gave a substantial discount. *Alfi mit Maske* (Alfi with Mask) shows a voluptuous, reclining woman whose face is partially obscured by a mask and headscarf (figure 6.30). It was a powerful meditation on the roles of a portrait, masking and revealing, returning the gaze, while protecting the subject's identity. Beckmann and his wife, Quappi, attended Mies's birthday party, where the painting was unveiled.[75] Mies wrote to Sergius Ruegenberg to thank him for his contribution to the purchase of the Beckmann painting: "I thought it was much too expensive. But it made me very happy. Not only to own it, but also to be able to examine such painting in regards to spaces we imagine." In all likelihood, Mies's reference here to space (less obvious in this particular painting than elsewhere in Beckmann's work) might have been inspired by the art historian Fritz Wichert, who had emphasized the centrality of space in Beckmann's art.[76]

A major topic of conversation at the party was a letter that Mies had just received from John Holabird in Chicago as chair of the search committee for a new director of the architecture school at the Armour Institute of Technology (which would later become the Illinois Institute of Technology). The school's president, Willard E. Hotchkiss, had been tasked by his board to enlarge and professionalize the school. Architecture classes had been part of the curriculum since the beginnings of the Armour Institute, together with classes in engineering, chemistry, and library science. Hotchkiss now wanted to introduce fifth-year master's courses in several areas. He asked if Mies "would, under any conditions, consider an appointment" as head of the architecture school. After thinking about the offer and discussing it with his friends, Mies signaled his interest, almost a month later, in a telegram on April 20, and a letter on May 4, under the condition that he would be free to completely reform the curriculum and to continue his own practice. Hotchkiss invited Mies

Figure 6.30. Max Beckmann, *Alfi mit Maske* (Alfi with Mask), 1934. Oil on canvas, 30 7/8 × 29 3/4 in. (78.4 × 75.5 cm). Solomon R. Guggenheim Museum, New York. Partial gift, Georgia van der Rohe, 1975.

to Chicago, so that he could get a personal impression of the school and deliver some lectures.[77] While Mies was thinking about this, two other, potentially better, offers arrived, and thus it took Mies three months to respond.

First, in June 1936, Alfred Barr of the Museum of Modern Art came to visit Mies in Berlin, as he had been authorized by MoMA's building committee to talk to Gropius, Mies, and Oud as potential partners of Philip L. Goodwin (who had already been selected as the local architect) in the design of a new building for the museum. Goodwin had studied architecture at Yale, Columbia, and the École des Beaux-Arts but had little building experience. He was a wealthy collector and a member of MoMA's board of trustees, where he was well-liked. The committee thought that he needed a partner to create the sensational International Style building it had in mind, and thus Barr was sent to Europe to talk to architects featured in MoMA's *Modern Architecture: International Exhibition* of 1932. Barr reported in June that only Mies, whom he clearly preferred, was both interested and available.[78] In the meantime, however, Abby Aldrich Rockefeller and her friends on the committee, who preferred working with an American architect, had changed their mind and hired the young, thirty-four-year-old Edward Durell Stone to partner with Goodwin on the design. Stone was by no means a bad choice. He had spent two years in Europe (1927–29) on a Rotch Travelling Fellowship and was intimately familiar with the work of European modernists.[79] Ironically, he might have been one of the very few American architects who saw Mies's Barcelona Pavilion with his own eyes. After his return from Europe, Stone had designed the spectacular Mandel House in Bedford Hills, New York (1933–35), followed by the Kowalski House in Mount Kisco, New York (1936). Both were generous and mature examples of the International Style, incorporating elements of Mies's Tugendhat House and Le Corbusier's Villa Stein (de Monzie) in Garches. They certainly qualified Stone as a capable and innovative architect.[80] As a bonus, since he was an American, there would be no language barrier, and he was an affable and convivial companion.

Barr heard about the board's decision while still traveling in Europe and had to tell Mies in July that the museum commission was not going to happen.[81] But they had also discussed the possibility of a position at Harvard, and Mies had signaled his interest in that as well. Harvard's dean of the Graduate School of Design, Joseph Hudnut, came to Berlin in August 1936, met with Mies, and was impressed. Famously, however, when Hudnut's follow-up letter mentioned that he was required to present two names to the president, and that Walter Gropius would also be put forward, Mies withdrew his agreement: "I am willing to accept an appointment, but not to make myself a candidate for a chair. If you stand by your intention to submit several names to the President of the University, kindly omit mine."[82] Gropius was promptly hired on February 1, 1937. After a three-month delay, Mies finally signaled to the Armour Institute of Technology that he was willing to consider its offer.

1937 Wallpaper Patents

On March 12, 1937, Mies submitted a patent application for a "Method for Printing Wallpaper."[83] It described "a process for printing rolls of wallpaper using photographic templates in halftones and full tones and in the commercially standard graphic printing processes (relief, planographic, intaglio) while maintaining the finest dotting as well as the customary print colors." Mies imagined printing from unusually large rolls with continuous patterns, in order to "produce an entire length of wallpaper in a single revolution." Each piece would have to be wall-high, to avoid cumbersome alignments and leftovers. (Ornamental patterns avoid this problem by repeating every few feet.) Of course, wall-high landscape imagery on wallpaper, produced in long, continuous pieces, was nothing new. From the late eighteenth century on, French companies such as Zuber and Dufour produced scenic wallpapers as woodblock prints—a very labor-intensive, expensive process. Of course, in Mies's case "no special wallpaper design" was necessary, since "it can faithfully reproduce photographic imagery." Mies had high hopes for the resulting spatial impressions: "This invention makes it possible to produce wallpaper having entirely new effects, in particular unprecedented effects of depths."[84] In order to achieve these effects, the print quality, detail, and color had to be as good as in book printing, and Mies and his collaborator, Walter Peterhans, addressed that challenge in separate patents regarding large screen printing (figure 6.31).[85]

The fact that Mies was seeking patents for photographic wallpaper production is historically interesting and somewhat contradictory. Two weeks after the Bauhaus had been closed by the Nazis (on April 11, 1933), Mies had sold all rights to the Bauhaus wallpapers to their manufacturer, Rasch, in Hanover on April 27, 1933. They had been the most commercially successful of all Bauhaus products, and Mies needed the money. The prize of 6,000 Reichmark allowed him to rent the telephone factory where the Berlin Bauhaus was located and pay salaries until July 1, 1933.[86] The Rasch company marketed "Bauhaus *Tapeten*" (Bauhaus wallpaper) successfully through the 1930s, apparently unencumbered by the association with the disgraced institution. In 1936, Mies contacted the company "to discuss a wallpaper problem," presumably his idea of photographic wallpapers.[87] Peterhans had studied mathematics, art history, philosophy, and photography and became a freelance photographer in 1927, participating in the exhibitions Pressa (Cologne, 1928) and *Film und Foto* (Stuttgart, 1929). In 1929, Hannes Meyer had invited him to establish the photography workshop at the Bauhaus, and he stayed on after Meyer departed. Peterhans's own photographs often show delicately illuminated still lifes from found materials such as feathers and blades of grass, fabric, glass, or metal fragments. Between 1935 and 1937, while teaching at the Reimann-Schule in Berlin, he published instruction manuals for photographic enlargement and development.[88] Peterhans's student at the Bauhaus, graphic designer Kurt Kranz, had patented a "Method for the Production of Images on a Grid" in 1933, an immediate predecessor to Peterhans's and Mies's patent.[89] Peterhans and Mies continued their work on the patent for screen printing on large surfaces, submitting a second application when they both were in the United States in 1940[90] and a third in 1946.[91]

The letters between Mies and patent attorneys Gottfried Bueren (Berlin) and Henry K. Feist (New York) testify to the exertion associated with the successful issuing of a patent.[92]

Figure 6.31. Ludwig Mies van der Rohe and Walter Peterhans, apparatus for the production of dot-composed negatives, June 1946. Line drawing in patent application.

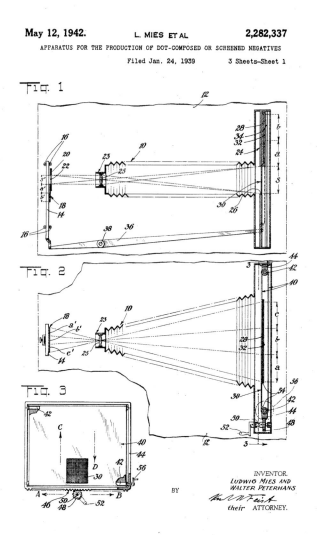

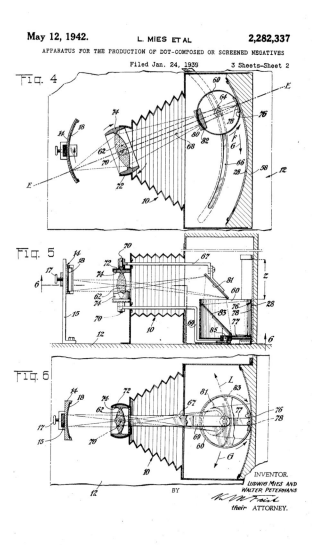

In the case of the screen-printing patent, approximately 260 documents have survived, and about sixty for the wallpaper patent.

The genesis of the wallpaper patent provides telling testimony of Mies's and Lilly Reich's evolving concept of the scheme.[93] Reich explained to the patent lawyer how the idea had come about: during a stroll in Berlin's Tiergarten, she and Mies had noticed the surface of a lake covered in fallen leaves, and thought of "using something like this for a wallpaper."[94] Based on this conversation, Bueren wrote a more comprehensive description of the patent in October 1939. He explained that it opened up "hitherto unknown possibilities for shaping space while at the same time offering a highly realistic reproduction of imagery," adding:

> It now becomes possible, for example, to place images of landscapes on a wall that visually dissolve its continuous surface, or to place perspectival images there, providing hitherto unknown effects of spatial depth. In this way, it becomes possible to endow smaller rooms with an impression of spaciousness, and vice versa. It also becomes possible, for example, to decorate a dark room say, one facing north with appropriately selected imagery in such a way that it is given a cheerful, sunny atmosphere. A warm room, for example, could be given a cooler feeling by means of wallpaper with arctic landscapes. With the faithful reproduction of seemingly warm textile materials, a room could very inexpensively be made cozy and warm.[95]

Mies and Reich had worked with large photographic reproductions at the Barcelona World's Fair or more recently at the Nazi propaganda show *Deutsche Volk—Deutsches Arbeit,* but these had been individual pieces, not mass-produced.[96] The "photomural" had already been considered a new modern art form, when Lincoln Kirstein staged the exhibition *Murals by American Painters and Photographers* at MoMA in May 1932 (right after its *Modern Architecture: International Exhibition*). In the catalogue, New York art dealer Julien Levy claimed an affinity between large-scale photographs and short-lived modern architecture: "The cost of execution for such murals would be minimum. When it is considered that the life of a modern building is usually something under seventy-five years, it is often desirable to secure the best possible decoration with the least expenditure."[97] The exhibition contained a dozen "photomurals," each seven feet (2.1 meters) high and 12 feet (3.7 meters) wide, by artists such as Berenice Abbott, Charles Sheeler, and Edward Steichen.[98] Around 1936–37, just as Mies was preparing his patents, several American architecture journals began publishing comprehensive reports and critical appraisals of the topic.[99] The arguments in these articles are similar to those in Mies's patent applications. In 1936, American photographer Drix Duryea observed that photographic wallpaper could make a dark room seem brighter or a confined space more open, as, for example, in the large-scale photographs of blossoming cherry trees in Huyler's restaurant in Chicago.[100] Under the title "Vanishing Walls," the magazine *Arts and Decoration* stated that photomurals would greatly improve contemporary homes, which had hardly any "architecture to speak of."[101]

Mies and Peterhans wanted to turn photomurals into an affordable mass product, while introducing color, depth, and detail, which would also allow the convincing reproduction of artworks. Was it a mere coincidence that Walter Benjamin's essay "Das Kunstwerk im Zeitalter seiner technischen Reproduzierbarkeit" (The Work of Art in the Age of Its Reproducibility) had just appeared in 1936 in *Zeitschrift für Sozialforschung*? If we look for potential evidence of photographic wallpaper in Mies's own designs, some drawings for the Ulrich Lange House in Krefeld of 1934 come to mind, which feature a strikingly colored, freestanding wall in the interior, perhaps a large reproduction of a work of art in lieu of a freestanding onyx wall (see figure 6.22). Perhaps Mies recalled Max Pechstein's wall-high murals in the Perls House of 1912 (see figure 1.34). It seems likely that his preoccupation with large photomurals (alongside other sources, such as current graphic conventions in advertising) helped to pave the way for the architectural collages, which became part of Mies's visual identity from the early 1940s on.

The notion that Mies van der Rohe imagined deploying illusionistic wallpaper with landscape photography or art reproductions, is, at first, somewhat disconcerting. Our image of him as a rigorous minimalist and structural purist has been too well established. Yet in each creative phase of his career, we find a pronounced sensibility for the potential of new materials and technologies and a delight in surprising contradictions—suggesting a more nuanced reading of Mies, and a less orthodox version of modernity.

1937   New Opportunities

Everything seemed to change in March 1937, when Mies received a letter from Vienna. It was sent by Clemens Holzmeister, president of the Akademie der bildenden Künste Wien (Vienna Academy of Fine Arts), offering Mies the professorship of Peter Behrens, who had accepted a position at the architecture school of the Preussische Akademie der Künste in Berlin. This was a prospect of great appeal. Mies would have been delighted to succeed his erstwhile teacher (and in a German-speaking country), and he responded enthusiastically.[102] Austria's political climate was only marginally different from that of Germany. The country's democratic government had also been disposed of early in 1933, and an "Austro Fascist" government had been introduced by Chancellor Engelbert

Figure 6.32. Ludwig Mies van der Rohe and Verseidag Building Department, Verseidag (United Silk Industry) Factory, Krefeld, Germany, 1930–31. Photograph by Hassan Bagheri.

Figure 6.33. Ludwig Mies van der Rohe, Verseidag (United Silk Industry) Office Building project, Krefeld, Germany, 1937. Model. Photograph by Hilde Löhr.

Dollfuss, modeled on Mussolini's regime further south. However, while in Germany areas of architecture and design were tightly controlled (as they were of great personal interest to Hitler), neither the Austrian chancellor, nor his Italian model, were overly concerned with stylistic expression. Thus, Mies could have expected to continue working as a modern architect, relatively unencumbered. Dollfuss was murdered in 1934 and replaced by Kurt Schuschnigg, who also did not exert drastic control over the field of design. In March 1938, however, Hitler annexed Austria, and Germany's system of government and different cultural conditions prevailed. Mies was never officially invited to join the Vienna academy as professor.

In the early summer of 1937, Mies received his last commission in Germany, from Hermann Lange for an office building for the Verseidag (United Silk Industry) in Krefeld. Mies had, in collaboration with the company's building department, designed a factory building there in 1930–31, which had set the visual framework for the continuing expansion by the company's building department. Mies had designed a shed-roofed hall and a two-story production facility with large ribbon windows (later topped up by two stories) (figure 6.32). The new office building followed a similar design approach. The bulk of it must have been designed between Mies's return from Paris after meeting clients Helen and Stanley Resor there on July 11, 1937, and his departure for the United States in August, as well as after his return in March 1938, before he left again that August. The project contains some remarkable details. A curved street along the site inspired a fan-shaped complex, reminiscent of the Reichstag design of 1933 (figure 6.33). There are three four-story office buildings in a U-configuration with an open central access spine and an elegantly glass-enclosed second floor above (figure 6.34).[103] This part in particular points ahead to the early designs for the IIT campus. The outbreak of World War II prevented the execution.

Lilly von Schnitzler, whose husband, Georg, had commissioned the Barcelona Pavilion, recalled how sometime in 1937, Mies asked her to use her political connections to help him find work. When, shortly afterward, she was seated at a dinner next to propaganda minister Joseph Goebbels, she asked him if he could do something for Mies. Goebbels answered: "Well, yes, he is our most outstanding architect, next to Troost." But, of course, he was unable to give him a commission: "Mrs. von Schnitzler…we are a totalitarian regime. We depend on the support of the masses. We dance, precariously, on a wave. If that wave ceases to carry us, we vanish overnight. I cannot do anything for Mies, as the masses behind me have entirely different ideas, and if I propose Mies, it won't be accepted."[104]

Figure 6.34. Ludwig Mies van der Rohe, Verseidag (United Silk Industry) Office Building project, Krefeld, Germany, 1937. Perspective courtyard. Photograph by Paul Schulz (dated on back July 28, 1938).

Seven

Difficult Beginnings
New York, Chicago, 1937–44

1937 Paris World's Fair

On Sunday, July 11, 1937, Mies met with two prominent American advertising executives, Helen and Stanley Resor, at the opulent Hotel Meurice in Paris, right across from the Tuileries Garden. At that location since 1835, the hotel's main entrance opened under the continuous arcades of Napoleon Bonaparte's most important urban intervention, the Rue de Rivoli. Behind its restrained limestone façades, the hotel proudly showed its Louis Seize interiors—a transitional style on its way from late baroque to neoclassicism and Empire, the French equivalent of the German Schinkel style, also known as *"Um 1800"* (Around 1800), as in the title of Paul Mebes's book, which had been important for Mies in his early career. This opulent environment provided the backdrop for an intense conversation about modern architecture. The Resors wanted Mies to build a summer house for them in the wild landscape of the Rocky Mountain foothills in Wyoming, across Mill Creek, a subsidiary of the nearby Snake River.[1]

Stanley Resor was president of J. Walter Thompson in New York, one of the world's leading ad agencies. His wife, Helen Landsdowne Resor, had worked for the agency as a copywriter, soon led major ad campaigns, and rose to become vice president. She was on the board of the Museum of Modern Art in New York and had witnessed the abovementioned discussions about an architect for the museum's new building. While the progressive wing of the trustees, led by Philip Johnson, Alfred Barr, and Helen Resor, had wanted Mies van der Rohe, a less adventurous group, led by Abby Aldrich Rockefeller, prevailed, and Philip L. Goodwin and Edward Durell Stone received the commission.

Helen and Stanley Resor had already started working with Goodwin on their ranch house but now decided to audition Mies for the job. They were vacationing in France in July, and the Paris World's Fair was on their itinerary. Johnson was also traveling in Europe; he had visited Mies earlier that summer and let the Resors know that Mies would also be in Paris, accompanying Lilly Reich as she was finalizing her presentation of German textiles at the International Hall. The meeting went well, as Helen Resor reported the next day to Barr: "I like him immensely. I have great respect for him and feel sure that after he sees the ranch, if he decides then to undertake the job, he will do a fine thing. He was allowed to take only $4 worth of marks out of Germany and had to ask for money when he arrived. Can you imagine how humiliating it must be?…He has talked very little of politics but I get the impression he is going to be very cautious even in America."[2] The Resors and Mies agreed that he would accompany them on their return to the United States in August to see the site.

It is a meaningful coincidence that on the day of Mies's meeting with the Resors in Paris, which paved the way for his move to the United States, the phone rang in vain in his apartment on Am Karlsbad in Berlin. A registered letter from the Preussische Akademie der Künste had remained unanswered, and academy secretary Alexander Amersdorffer was urgently trying to reach a number of members by phone. The unsuccessful phone call was followed by a telegram requesting a conversation, forwarded to Mies in Paris. Mies rushed back to Berlin and returned Amersdorffer's call on July 13. He was asked to resign from the academy, just as in 1933. This time, refusal was not an option. Mies asked for an hour to think it over and then agreed. His official letter followed on July 19, 1937. Remarkably, while several other resignation letters (by Ernst Barlach, Ernst Ludwig Kirchner, Rudolf Belling) dispensed with a complimentary phrase at the end, Mies ended with the obsequious *"Heil Hitler."*[3] Be that as it may, the exclusion from the academy was an unmistakable signal that his future in Germany did not hold much promise.

The preparation for the World's Fair had suffered from chaotic planning, strikes, and political unrest in Paris, and many palaces were far from finished when the fair officially opened on May 25, 1937. The German and Russian pavilions already confronted each other at the Pont d'Iéna on the main axis, and the Palais de Chaillot right behind them was ready for the opening gala. But the International Hall, where Lilly Reich's German textile division was to be shown, and many others were only nearing completion in mid-July. Some of Reich's drawings for her display stands date from July 13, 1937. They had evolved from a previous project, the *Reichsausstellung der deutschen Textil und Bekleidungswirtschaft* (Imperial Exposition of the German Textile and Garment Industry) in Berlin, for which Reich and Mies had initially been commissioned. After the announcement of Hitler's "Four-Year Plan" on October 28, 1936, the exhibition became an important propaganda tool, and Nazi architect Ernst Sagebiel took charge. The centerpiece of Mies and Reich's design had been a gray, curvilinear plate-glass wall, a vibrant successor to the heavy onyx walls in Barcelona and Brno. While Sagebiel, under the pressure of time, adopted some of their designs, he eliminated this striking element.[4] Reich adopted it for her participation at the Paris World's Fair.

Mies's sudden departure from Paris meant that he missed the installation of Picasso's painting *Guernica* in mid-July at José Luis Sert's Spanish Pavilion, which presented the plight of the Spanish Republic under attack by Franco's forces in the Spanish Civil War. Reich surely saw it and would not have missed the historic irony of the boastful tower of the German Pavilion dwarfing the nearby Spanish building, which showcased Picasso's remarkable painting of the bombing of a small Basque town by the Luftwaffe. The Nazis' onslaught on modern art happened at exactly that moment in Germany: on July 19, 1937, the notorious traveling exhibition *Entartete Kunst* (Degenerate Art) opened in Munich. It had been preceded by a nationwide campaign ridding all major museums of sculptures and paintings by expressionist and abstract artists. Five thousand pieces were confiscated, many by painters whom Mies knew well personally, such as Emil Nolde, Paul Klee, Max Pechstein, El Lissitzky, László Moholy-Nagy, and others. The opening of the exhibition on July 19 explained the urgency of Amersdorffer's telegrams and calls to several artists in the context of Mies's removal from the academy, such as Nolde and Pechstein. Their works were shown in the "Degenerate Art" exhibition—a fact not commensurate with their membership in the academy.

The architecture at the Paris World's Fair was more versatile and innovative than the often-published standoff between the classical German and Russian pavilions suggests (figure 7.1). Pierre Jeanneret and Le Corbusier's Temps Nouveaux Pavilion, a canvas structure with an exoskeleton, opened on July 17, and Mies would have witnessed its assembly.[5] Mies must surely have gone to the Finnish Pavilion by Alvar Aalto, whose recent furniture designs had been a source of concern for him. Jaromír Krejcar's Czech Pavilion, a steel structure clad in translucent glass, was exactly what Mies had unsuccessfully proposed for competitions in Stuttgart and Berlin in 1928 and 1929 (see figures 3.39, 3.40).

1937–38   New York

On August 20, 1937, Mies and the Resors left on the SS *Berengaria* from Cherbourg to New York.[6] They traveled onward by train via Chicago to Wyoming, where Mies stayed for several days in a log cabin on the site, apparently sharing it for some days with the prominent regionalist painter Grant Wood, a protégé of the Resors on vacation from his teaching job at the University of Iowa. Wood was probably able to muster a few words of German, since he had spent time studying art in Munich, while Helen and Stanley Resor might have had trouble communicating with their German visitor.

The Resors' ranch lies in the foothills of the magnificent mountain range of the Grand Tetons, which rise with stunning vehemence from the flat plane of the Snake River. When the Resors had bought the 400-acre (160-hectare) ranch in 1930, a neighbor from Connecticut had built them a simple log cabin. Helen Resor then hired Philip Goodwin, a fellow board member at MoMA, to build another log cabin as a guesthouse, where Mies and Wood stayed. Goodwin had already begun building the main house across the Snake River when Helen Resor changed her mind. A curved servants' wing with two ribbon windows had gone up on the eastern side, and two concrete piers had been placed in the river.

Figure 7.1. Paris World's Fair, 1937. Contemporary postcard.

Mies was back in Chicago on September 8 in order to meet with the Armour Institute of Technology advisory committee about his directorship of the architecture school. During a lunch at the Tavern Club with Bertrand Goldberg, William Priestley, Helmut Bartsch, and John Holabird, Sr., Mies mentioned that he had tried in vain to reach Frank Lloyd Wright and would like to meet him. Holabird promptly phoned Wright and arranged a visit for the next day; Goldberg and Priestley came along as translators.[7] The group stayed at Taliesin, Wright's estate in Spring Green, Wisconsin, from September 9 to September 13, and apparently got on splendidly (figure 7.2). Wright gave Mies a photograph of Taliesin and a woodblock print by Hiroshige. Wright accompanied the group back on their way to Chicago in order to give them a personal tour of the Johnson Wax Building in Racine, Wisconsin, still under construction; the Avery Coonley House in Riverside, Illinois; Unity Temple in Oak Park, outside of Chicago; and finally the Robie House on Chicago's South Side. On the next day, September 14, Mies had another meeting with the Armour Institute group. After that, Mies had no interest in staying in Chicago any longer and returned to New York by train.

Mies was not expected to design the Resor House while in the United States (as he had no working visa), but after his return to New York, he talked Stanley Resor into supporting him there, and extended his initial sixty-day visa for another two months, and then again until April 20, 1938.[8] Clearly, he was in no rush to get back to Berlin, where he had neither work nor money and the political clouds had darkened quickly.

Little is known about what else Mies did in those six months, what he thought of New York, where he went, or with whom he spent time. One wonders what he made of the 1899 University Club by McKim, Mead & White at Fifty-Fourth Street and Fifth Avenue, where Stanley Resor had put him up (figures 7.3, 7.4). In all likelihood, the building was larger and grander than anything he had stayed in before. Would he sit in the double-height library under H. Siddons Mowbray's ceiling paintings modeled after those in the Vatican apartments? Would he use its pool or billiard rooms? He mentioned in a later interview that he saw the Rockefeller Center from his breakfast table, and that it impressed him greatly with its sheer mass and thousands of windows. He sent a postcard of it to his former collaborator Eduard Ludwig.[9] One wonders if Mies took the elevator to the top of the Empire State Building nearby, or marveled at the illuminated American Radiator Building by Raymond Hood right behind the public library? Mies worked on the Resor project with Rodgers & Priestley, whose office was just up the street at 745 Fifth Avenue. They had picked up some German at the Bauhaus and thus could communicate with Mies. Mies also reconnected with another former student, Howard Dearstyne, who had come along on the trip to Ticino mentioned earlier, and after his return to the United States in 1934 worked for Wallace Harrison and J. A. Fouilhoux. On November 25, 1937, Walter Peterhans arrived for a visit. The Barrs, who spoke German, received a Christmas telegram from Mies.[10]

If Mies sought out other German-speaking modernists in New York, he might have reached out to William Lescaze, whose townhouse at nearby 211 East Forty-Eighth Street had been finished in 1934 and was generally considered the first modernist house in Manhattan. The Swiss-born Lescaze spoke German, and he and Mies could have commiserated about the fact that both had been briefly, but unsuccessfully, considered as architects for the Museum of Modern Art.

We know that Mies was in touch with several German art dealers whom he had known in Berlin and who had recently immigrated to New York.[11] J. B. Neumann had come in 1923, and Karl Nierendorf and Curt Valentin both arrived in 1937. Most often he visited the gallery of Nierendorf, a few doors down at 21 East Fifty-Seventh Street, only a short walk from the University Club (figure 7.5). Nierendorf held the exhibition *Three Masters of the Bauhaus* (Paul Klee, Lyonel Feininger, and Wassily Kandinsky) from December 1937 to January 1938, and Mies went on a veritable shopping spree at the end, purchasing five Klee paintings and watercolors—no doubt with the money that Stanley Resor had provided for him. Nierendorf and Mies even discussed becoming Klee's exclusive representatives in the United States. Mies bought more Klees when he was later back in the United States, and by 1940 possessed five oil paintings and ten watercolors.[12] Just a few blocks away was Alfred Stieglitz's gallery, An American Place, at Fifty-Third Street and Madison Avenue. We can only speculate if anyone thought of introducing the architect and the famous photographer to each other. While born in the United States, Stieglitz was from a German-speaking

Figure 7.2. Ludwig Mies van der Rohe (left) visiting Frank Lloyd Wright (second from left) at Taliesin in Spring Green, Wisconsin, September 9–13, 1937.

Figure 7.3. McKim, Mead, & White, University Club, 1 West Fifty-Fourth Street, New York, 1899. Exterior, ca. 1905. Photograph by Detroit Publishing Company.

family and had gone to high school in Karlsruhe and studied at a Berlin university. By 1938, however, Stieglitz's health was failing, and he suffered his first of a series of heart attacks. Dorothy Norman, Stieglitz's longtime lover, a photographer and social activist who enjoyed hosting dinner parties at her house (designed by Lescaze) with guests such as Ansel Adams, John Cage, and Lewis Mumford, also invited Mies one night, but exactly when remains unclear.[13]

While Mies was not a celebrity and not as well-known as Walter Gropius, most architects would have been familiar with his work, which continued to show up in magazines and exhibitions. Mies must have seen with mixed feelings how some of the vocabulary he had helped to create had already found ample distribution among architects and clients in the United States. In October 1937, for example, the floor plan of the Tugendhat House appeared in *Architectural Forum* as a "classic example" of the "flexible plan."[14] John Barney Rodgers and William Priestley might have shared with Mies architecture magazines eagerly promoting modern architecture, such as a recent issue of *Pencil Points* in July 1937 devoted to Richard Neutra's work in California.[15]

The office of Helen and Stanley Resor's J. Walter Thompson ad agency was about a fifteen-minute walk away from the University Club, on the eleventh floor of the Graybar Building at 420 Lexington Avenue, next to Grand Central Station. In all likelihood, meetings about the Resor House design were occasionally held there. Before the agency moved in, the Resors had commissioned Norman Bel Geddes in 1928 to design a two-story conference room and presentation hall. Mies thus saw a first-rate piece of American modernity there, which had been described as "machine-like in its efficiency, in its ability to help its occupants get through his day's work with a minimum of interference and distraction."[16] Mies would have also encountered the Resors' stylistic promiscuity, in the form of a somewhat surreal, quixotic intervention at their company headquarters. In 1938, just when Mies had delivered his design and was leaving for Germany, they dismantled a complete seventeenth-century living room from a Connecticut farmhouse they had purchased and reassembled it at their office. Lighting designer Richard Kelly, who ended up working with Philip Johnson and Mies van der Rohe years later, created the lighting for the "Colonial Dining Room" by backlighting scrims outside of the room's windows that did not have access to outside light.[17]

In any event, New York was a fascinating place in 1937. Emerging from the Great Depression, much cultural activity unfolded around the upcoming 1939 World's Fair and an American version of modernity in architecture, design, film, and music. Mies would have been invited to exhibition openings at MoMA, which had moved from the Heckscher Building on Fifth Avenue into temporary quarters on the concourse level of Rockefeller Center at 14 West Forty-Ninth Street. Mies's work was included in the summer exhibition

Figure 7.4. McKim, Mead, & White, University Club, 1 West Fifty-Fourth Street, New York, 1899. Main lounge on the first floor, 1939.

Figure 7.5. Karl Nierendorf in his gallery, 20 West Fifty-Third Street, New York, January 1937.

of the architecture gallery alongside Wright and Le Corbusier, and in an exhibition called *The Town of Tomorrow* in the fall, which pitched the fifteen model homes planned for the homonymous section at the 1939 World's Fair against photos of the Weissenhof Estate in Stuttgart of 1927—a contrast clearly intended to demonstrate the superiority of the latter. Among the—mostly conventional—houses for the World's Fair, two stood out as radically modern: the Plywood House and, in particular, the Pittsburgh House of Glass by Landefeld & Hatch, which applied Mies's and Le Corbusier's modern vocabulary quite convincingly, and was voted the most popular at the World's Fair two years later (figure 7.6).[18] Most obvious in its adoption of Miesian ideas was the "Masterpieces of Art" Pavilion by Wallace Harrison and Edward Durell Stone—an homage to the Barcelona Pavilion (figure 7.7).

A string of exhibitions in early 1938 celebrated modern architecture's recent progress in the United States. On January 25, 1938, a show about Frank Lloyd Wright's country house Fallingwater opened at the Museum of Modern Art, accompanied by a lavish catalogue and much fanfare in the press.[19] Mies might have found the encounter with Wright's masterpiece downright unavoidable, at exactly the moment when he was struggling with his own version of a house perched above a river. No doubt he felt that the two buildings would be compared one day. The Resor House's central wall of rough local stone, with its fireplaces that penetrate and anchor the building on the western side of the creek, might be read as a response to Wright. Publishing magnate Henry Luce, a board member at MoMA, made a concerted effort to present Wright as America's forceful architectural counterpart to Europe's modernists—prominently among them, of course, Mies van der Rohe.[20] Luce had commissioned Chicago photographer Bill Hedrich to record Fallingwater in November 1937. Hedrich's most iconic image repeated the viewpoint of Wright's famous drawing from the other side of the stream, looking up at the building (figure 7.8). In coordination with the opening of MoMA's show, Wright appeared on the cover of Luce's *Time* magazine (with the Fallingwater perspective as backdrop) as well as in Luce's other publications, *Life*, *Fortune*, and *Architectural Forum* (figure 7.9).[21] In an issue of *Architectural Forum* entirely dedicated to him, Wright dismissed MoMA's "International Style" show of 1932 as "more reflection of surface than substance."[22] The issue was advertised as "the most important architectural document ever published in America," presenting the "Modern Movement, from its inception to its present-day interpretation" as an American phenomenon.[23] It must have been of little solace to Mies that some of Wright's buildings, such as the Jacobs House or the House on the Mesa project, showed his own influence.[24] Thanks to Luce, Wright quickly became America's most popular architect.

Luce's demonstration of America's cultural superiority over Europe was part of a larger strategy. In tandem with the Wright show's opening and the accompanying press campaign, Luce released the semi-documentary film *Inside Nazi Germany* by Louis de Rochemont in his *March of Time* series. It was one of the first outspoken anti-Nazi films, fifteen minutes long and shown in movie theaters across the country before the main feature.[25] It

Figure 7.6. Landefeld & Hatch, Pittsburgh House of Glass, New York World's Fair, 1939. Photograph by Gottscho-Schleisner.

Figure 7.7. Wallace Harrison and Edward Durell Stone, "Masterpieces of Art" Pavilion, New York World's Fair, 1939. Charcoal drawing by Hugh Ferriss. Graphite on illustration board, 15 × 19 11/16 in. (38.1 × 50 cm). Cooper Hewitt, Smithsonian Design Museum, New York.

documented anti-Semitism in Nazi Germany and the country's rearmament under Hitler. It also warned that Nazis had begun to rally support in the United States through the German American Bund. One of the staged scenes in the films showed the upright citizens of Southbury, a small Connecticut town, as they prevent an American Nazi group from establishing a training center there. At the end, the voiceover warned ominously: "Expect any German anywhere to spread the Nazi creed." The *New York Times* just a few months earlier had offered a more generous take, entitled "America Imports Genius," which encouraged Americans to embrace intellectual refugees such as Albert Einstein, Walter Gropius, and László Moholy-Nagy.[26]

Other, equally pertinent shows at MoMA during Mies's stay at the University Club included *Machine Art* (March 7–31, 1938) and *Alvar Aalto: Architecture and Furniture* (March 15–April 18, 1938). The latter contained all the wooden cantilevered chairs that Mies had worried about since seeing them in Europe (minus the early steel tube chair), as well as Aalto's recent buildings such as the Paimio Sanatorium, the Viipuri Library, and the Finnish Pavilion at the Paris World's Fair.

1938 Armour Institute of Technology Architecture School Curriculum

While in New York, Mies started working on the curriculum for the Armour Institute of Technology. He was intent on clearly differentiating his approach from that of Walter Gropius, who had just presented ideas for the curriculum at Harvard. Gropius focused on a "language of vision" (picking up on ideas from László Moholy-Nagy and György Kepes), with its grammar and vocabulary, which would provide a universally understood framework for creative work based on "optical facts—such as proportion, optical illusions and colors."[27] These astonishingly formalist ideas stood in great contrast to where Mies was headed with the Armour Institute curriculum.

Working with Rodgers and Priestley, he got some help from an unlikely source. Charles W. Killam, a professor at Harvard's architecture school, had resigned in protest over Dean Joseph Hudnut's hiring of Gropius in January 1937. As a parting shot, he published an essay in the magazine *Pencil Points* about his teaching philosophy, clearly at odds with what Hudnut and Gropius were about to undertake. His spirited essay was "so crammed with common sense that we recommend it for reading by every serious practitioner," the

Figure 7.8. Frank Lloyd Wright, Fallingwater, Bear Run, Pennsylvania, 1937. Photograph by Hedrich-Blessing. Chicago History Museum.

Figure 7.9. Frank Lloyd Wright on the cover of *Time* magazine, January 17, 1938.

magazine opined.[28] For Mies, it provided welcome insights into what American architects, who were not in the thralls of the International Style, might be interested in.

Killham's point was clear: architects should stay away from current fashions and be trained to become solid practitioners, in order to gain a larger share of the building market: "It is not our first job to reform the universe; it is our first job to be competent architects." Killam made no secret of his disdain for the Bauhaus (without naming it) and for the "unreasonable ambition" of an "International Style." He stated that architects should not be "specialists in domestic work or low-cost housing. Not extreme modernists who can give their clients only bare boxes or glass hothouses....Not all-round geniuses who...also claim the ability to rearrange the regional and city plan, do the landscape work, and design the interior decorations and furnishings down to the chairs and dishes." Nor should they start by learning a trade: "The architect's work is so difficult that he has no time to waste in learning the qualities of materials by working with his own hands with any of them....The best way to learn to design in architecture is to design buildings themselves....It is a common habit of most students and of some practitioners to copy a design produced in Germany, Sweden, Holland, or England without having any idea whether the altogether different conditions in Maine, Florida, California, and Minnesota make its use economical or otherwise advisable for us. The student is not even sure that it was a reasonable design in the country of its birth. There may be incompetent architects in Europe. In this country, in normal times, we are not as poor as post-war Europe and we do not need to copy their starved architecture." Killam humorously identified "cantilever addicts" and noted that "columns set a few feet inside the exterior walls are in general more in the way than columns set in the wall itself....Students in a school of architecture should not be expected to create new types of architectural design or new types of structural design or new uses of materials, any more than engineering students should be expected to develop new types of bridges or tunnels, law students to establish new legal principles, or medical students to invent new techniques in surgery." Executing many simple design problems was the best approach: "The student should follow precedents which have proved their fitness in the past, modifying them as necessary to meet the needs of the present." Progress should come from "architects in practice, men who have had the background of a good training and the responsibility of actual building under the complicated conditions of our day and country."[29]

Mies, similarly, presented the Armour Institute curriculum as an alternative to Gropius's formal approach and closer to Killam's call for a sound education in the essence of architecture, its materials and structural and functional conditions, rather than in stylistic fashions. "Step I is an investigation into the nature of materials and their truthful expression," he wrote. Rodgers and Priestley carefully outlined a diagram that they had discussed with Mies. In a column on the left, under "General Theory," it listed mathematics, natural science, the nature of man, and culture as mandatory parts of the curriculum, and "Professional Training," which included drawing, as well as financing, structural design, and office practice. On the right were three general categories: "Means," which meant

Figure 7.10. Ludwig Mies van der Rohe with George Danforth and William Priestley, Resor House project, Jackson Hole, Wyoming, 1937–43. Floor plans. Delineator: John B. Rodgers. Pencil on tracing paper, 31 3/4 × 24 in. (80.6 × 61 cm). Museum of Modern Art, New York. The Mies van der Rohe Archive, gift of the architect.

Figure 7.11. Ludwig Mies van der Rohe with George Danforth and William Priestley, Resor House project, Jackson Hole, Wyoming, 1937–43. Elevation sketch, 1937–38. Pencil and colored pencil on tracing paper, 22 × 48 3/4 in. (55.9 × 123.8 cm). Museum of Modern Art, New York. The Mies van der Rohe Archive, gift of the architect.

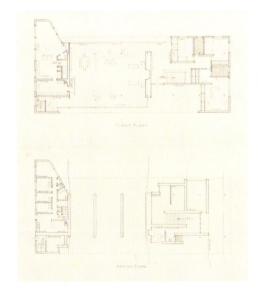

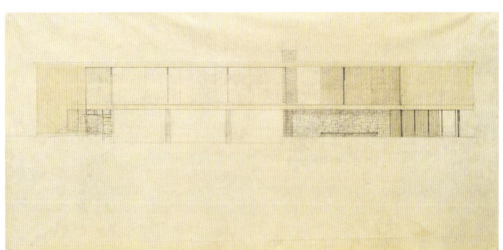

materials such as wood, brick, steel, and concrete; "Purposes," which listed building types; and finally "Planning and Creating," which seemed the least developed, as it mentioned "dependence on the epoch," "organic architecture," and architecture, painting, and sculpture as the "Creative Unity."[30]

1937–43   The Resor House

As mentioned above, some decisions had been made before Mies got involved with the Resor project, most importantly the idea of bridging Mill Creek. Philip Goodwin's unfinished servants' wing with wooden cladding and two ribbon windows had been built, as had two concrete piers in the creek.

Mies designed a huge open living room spanning the width of the creek, which ran roughly north–south (figures 7.10, 7.11). Thus, one side of the living room was facing south, the other north. Mies designed the same wall-high windows for both, specified as six sheets (96 by 180 inches, or 243 by 457 centimeters) of one-quarter-inch- (0.6-centimeter-) thick plate glass, with no provisions for shading. The driveway, garage, and main entrance were located on the western side. A generous staircase would have led upstairs into a small hall behind a rough stone wall, which contained the fireplace on the other side. This upstairs vestibule offered access to a porch facing north toward the magnificent Grand Teton Mountains and to the semiprivate area with the bedrooms of the Resors and their two children. From here, visitors would circumvent the masonry wall and enter the main living room, punctuated by four freestanding cruciform columns (figures 7.12, 7.13). All in all, fourteen columns were specified in Mies's plans, two invisibly embedded in the stone wall, two in the wall of the servants' wing. Six supported the roof above the bedroom area, two of them in the middle of a bedroom and one inside a closet. The central room cantilevered out on both sides beyond the concrete supports in the river. It was flanked by the service wing in the east, and the heavy ashlar wall with its fireplace in the west. Somewhat problematically, the kitchen, pantry, and servants' rooms were located on the eastern end, which meant provisions en route to the kitchen would have to be carried either across the living room or over a small wooden footbridge south of the house, which was also the only access route for the staff if they wanted to avoid crossing the living room. It was an impractical arrangement.

Early on, Mies decided to clad the entire building in vertical cypress boards (instead of the locally available pine), as he had "fallen in love" with its color and durability.[31] It would have to be transported up from Louisiana or Florida, its natural habitat. The large, single panes of glass that Mies had specified would have created structural and logistical problems. Wind velocity in the area exceeded the breaking strength of the quarter-inch glass, and the sheets he specified were too large to bring to the site, as the only street toward it led under a bridge too low for the required trucks.[32] The slender cruciform columns (here meant to be clad in bronze rather than nickel or chrome) would surely have to be

Figure 7.12. Ludwig Mies van der Rohe with George Danforth and William Priestley, Resor House project, Jackson Hole, Wyoming, 1937–43. Living room interior perspective with window blinds. Pencil on tracing paper, 8 1/2 × 11 in. (21.6 × 27.9 cm). Museum of Modern Art, New York. The Mies van der Rohe Archive, gift of the architect.

Figure 7.13. Ludwig Mies van der Rohe with George Danforth and William Priestley, Resor House project, Jackson Hole, Wyoming, 1937–43. Living room interior perspective. Pencil on paper, 17 1/4 × 23 3/4 in. (43.8 × 60.3 cm). Museum of Modern Art, New York. The Mies van der Rohe Archive, gift of the architect.

reevaluated once an engineer calculated the snow loads at the Grand Teton foothills (the area receives about 111 inches, or 282 centimeters, of snow annually, as opposed to 28 inches, or 71 centimeters, on average elsewhere in the United States).

By September 1937, a first study model had been made and presented to the Resors, and Mies had ordered samples of cypress veneer (figure 7.14). Rodgers and Priestley then produced a full set of drawings and construction documents while Mies stayed in New York. Some sketches demonstrate struggles to protect the interior from the impact of the summer sun; others document several variations of the eastern entrance area. Mies sketched a sculpture of a female figure, somewhat similar to Kolbe's statue in Barcelona, for a position next to the fireplace.

One of the most evocative drawings from Mies's hand shows his attempt at a dynamic sequence of masses and voids and material juxtapositions, as well as attempts at a curved central wall for the fireplace (figure 7.15). Mies's scribbles document his engagement with modern lighting and projection technology, and large-scale imagery in tune with his recent thoughts about photographic wallpaper: "Wall Decoration? Luminous murals? Space Illumination through projection of murals? Images as Space Decoration? Bright and subdued."[33]

Mies finally left New York on March 26, 1938, after delivering a huge package of about eight hundred drawings to the Resors' office. Stanley Resor did not waste any time. A telegram canceling the project reached Mies on April 5, 1938, while he was still on board the SS *Queen Mary* on his way back to Germany. But in his short note, Resor left open the possibility of another attempt at building the house, once Mies had returned to the United States and could work with an experienced local architect, "familiar with American conditions, prices, etc."[34]

Mies gave the project another try after his return, but the Resors finally abandoned it altogether in 1943, when a major storm washed away Goodwin's service wing and the supporting piers in the river. While this would have offered a clean slate for a new beginning, it also showed the precariousness of the site, and the Resors were busy with repairs at the existing structures on their land.

It was during this second iteration that Mies's collaborators George Danforth and William Priestley created a new type of architectural representation when they embedded photographs of the impressive landscape into simple interior perspectives (figure 7.16). In

Figure 7.14. Ludwig Mies van der Rohe with George Danforth and William Priestley, Resor House project, Jackson Hole, Wyoming, 1937–43. Study model, September 1937. Museum of Modern Art, New York. The Mies van der Rohe Archive, gift of the architect.

Figure 7.15. Ludwig Mies van der Rohe with George Danforth and William Priestley, Resor House project, Jackson Hole, Wyoming, 1937–43. Exterior perspective, sketches of fireplace, conceptual notes, ca. 1937–38. Pencil on note paper, 6 × 9 in. (15.2 × 22.9 cm). Museum of Modern Art, New York. The Mies van der Rohe Archive, gift of the architect.

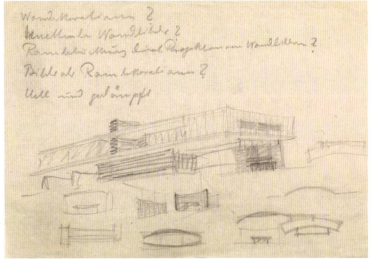

Germany, Mies had occasionally sketched onto site photographs to study and show a project's contextual impact—a common tool for architects. Now both process and perspective were reversed: instead of showing a building's impact on its context, now the (privileged) view from inside the structure was illustrated. For the Resor House, Danforth combined a large photo reproduction of an imagined view out, with a sparse line drawing of an interior column and window mullions, and a horizontal strip of wood veneer. In another rendering, a wall-high enlargement of Paul Klee's small lithograph *Colorful Meal* of 1939 (about ten by eight inches, or 26 by 20 centimeters), which the Resors had just purchased, completed the composition (figure 7.17). At first sight these collages seem perfectly "un-Miesian." After all, Mies had said, "I never make a painting when I want to build a house."[35] They compress "space into a strange, depthless void," and their role in the design process remained unspecific.[36] Such collages were produced for many of the later projects; sometimes (as in the early apartment buildings) they ended up in sales brochures to win over potential clients, sometimes to convince an existing client of a particular approach, and sometimes they were made for publication after the project was finished.

When Mies presented the Resor House at his 1947 exhibition at the Museum of Modern Art, it had undergone an astonishing metamorphosis (figure 7.18). A sleek, symmetrical model showed a horizontal box with cypress walls above a marble plinth. It retained the wall-high windows in the center but simplified the wood-clad parts on either end. One of the freestanding walls in the living room shows a wall-high enlargement of a Georges Braque painting. Most importantly, however, Mies coolly eliminated the entire ground floor. Now, the entrance area and private rooms on the western end had to share a much

Figure 7.16. Ludwig Mies van der Rohe with George Danforth and William Priestley, Resor House project, Jackson Hole, Wyoming, 1937–43. Interior perspective of living room (view through north glass wall toward Grand Teton Mountains). Pencil and photograph on illustration board, 30 × 40 in. (76.2 × 101.6 cm). Museum of Modern Art, New York. The Mies van der Rohe Archive, gift of the architect.

smaller space, while the access issues at the service wing on the eastern side remained. In what could be read as a deliberate snub, the Resors' living room is now so close to the water that the next river surge surely would have flooded or destroyed it. Mies also had the model photographed simply on a base without the river altogether. It had become a theoretical statement rather than a concrete proposal, and instead of floor plans only two collages were shown.

The Resor House project was tragic in its failure. A sympathetic and generous client offered Mies the project of a modern house in a region comparable to that of his recent mountain house studies. But Mies was unable to respond to the challenges presented by the site and its logistic constraints, trapped still in the formal language of the Barcelona Pavilion—and perhaps intimidated by the public success of Wright's Fallingwater.

1938   The Bauhaus Exhibition at the Museum of Modern Art

Sometime during Mies's time in New York, Walter Gropius and Herbert Bayer visited him to discuss the *Bauhaus: 1919–1928* exhibition at the Museum of Modern Art, which Alfred Barr had asked Gropius to organize for November 1938. After the meeting, Gropius was under the impression that Mies was on board, but he later heard from Barr that Mies had made derogatory remarks about the project. Gropius followed up with a letter at the end of June 1938, when Mies was briefly back in Germany, urging his participation. He assured him that he would present everything objectively, and that Josef Albers had already agreed to help with pulling material from the final years of the Bauhaus together.[37] Mies

Figure 7.17. Ludwig Mies van der Rohe with George Danforth and William Priestley, Resor House project, Jackson Hole, Wyoming, 1937–43. Graphite, collage of wood veneer, cut-and-pasted reproduction (Paul Klee's painting *Colorful Meal*), and photograph on illustration board, 30 × 40 in. (76.2 × 101.6 cm). Museum of Modern Art, New York. The Mies van der Rohe Archive, gift of the architect.

responded on August 2, claiming that he had stated earlier that he did not think it was a good idea, but denied having said anything negative about it to Barr. Bayer had called him in the meantime, he reported, and had "naively" dismissed his reasons as "exaggerated." Mies urged Gropius "to reconsider the plan for this exhibition with all of its consequences."[38] Gropius responded in September, after Mies had arrived in Chicago, disappointed over Mies's refusal and unable to grasp the reasons: "I suspect that your letter of August 2 can only mean that you wanted to have an alibi in the case of attacks by the Nazis. We have now decided to do the exhibition only about the time for which I was responsible."[39] Mies responded, saying, "Your assumption that I wanted to protect myself against possible aggression is not correct. This was not about me, but about the students, who could be exposed to potential animosities, and I did not want to be responsible for this."[40] When *Architectural Forum* had interviewed Mies upon his arrival in New York in November 1937, he insisted "that the Bauhaus was not closed on account of the German political revolution." The magazine quoted Mies (as translated by John Barney Rodgers) saying: "The Bauhaus in Berlin (following its removal from Dessau in 1932) was closed in 1933 because of purely financial grounds."[41] This was the only direct quote in the article, and clearly important to Mies. He was walking a fine line between trying hard not to alienate the German authorities while at least making his displeasure about the closing of the Dessau Bauhaus known.

Thus, contrary to the common assumption that Gropius had simply wanted to claim the Bauhaus entirely for himself, it was Mies who refused to participate, fearing reprisals from the Nazis (or at least diminished chances to build) when he returned to Germany. In the end, his contract at the Armour Institute was renewed, and this became a moot point. The Bauhaus exhibition at MoMA received mostly poor reviews, providing Mies with another reason for not wanting to be associated with it.[42] On January 19, Gropius sent Mies a copy of the catalogue, but Mies does not seem to have responded.[43] We can only speculate if Mies's fear of being exposed internationally in his first year abroad also helped Sigfried Giedion justify the fact that his magnum opus, *Space, Time and Architecture*, left Mies out almost entirely (figure 7.19). It was based on his Charles Eliot Norton lectures at Harvard in 1938–39, and developed in close cooperation with Gropius (the book appeared in 1941). Mies was not mentioned in the index, and only briefly in the text, with an image of the

Figure 7.18. Ludwig Mies van der Rohe with George Danforth and William Priestley, Resor House project, Jackson Hole, Wyoming, 1937–43. Architectural model for the 1947 MoMA exhibition *Mies van der Rohe*. Wood, plastic, paper, glass, copper, synthetic polymer paint, 5 3/4 × 48 3/8 × 28 1/8 in. (14.6 × 122.9 × 71.4 cm). Museum of Modern Art, New York. The Mies van der Rohe Archive, gift of the architect.

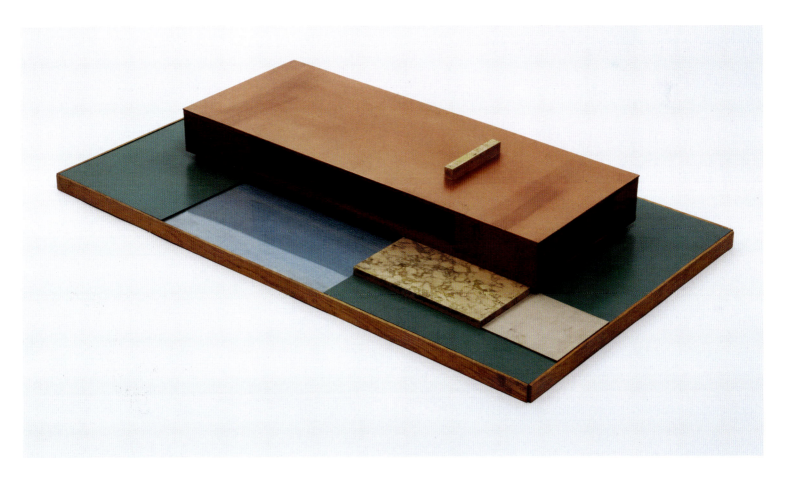

Curvilinear Glass Skyscraper described as a "modern excursion into the realm of fantasy" and "the dream of a European architect in the year 1921," which was, in any event, derivative of the "Reliance Building of some three decades earlier."[44] Giedion rectified the situation later, beginning with the 1954 edition.

1938 Beginnings in Chicago

After working for a few months on the Verseidag Office Building in Krefeld (see figures 6.32–6.34), Mies left again for the United States from Bremerhaven, on August 29, 1938. Both Walter Peterhans and Ludwig Hilberseimer, who would begin teaching at the Armour Institute of Technology as well that fall, had arrived separately before. After a month at the enormous Stevens Hotel on Chicago's Michigan Avenue, which had fallen on hard times, Mies moved across the street into the Blackstone Hotel, where he had stayed during his previous visit. Due to his two-year contract at the institute, he had to assume that he would potentially have to return to Germany in 1940. He did, however, apply for American citizenship on June 28, 1939 (a five-year process)—just in case. He ended up spending almost three years at the Blackstone, conveniently close to the Art Institute, where his architecture classes were held.[45] A year after his contract had been renewed, he moved into a generous 1916 apartment building in the style of an Italian palazzo at 200 East Pearson Street, designed by the same architect as the Blackstone Hotel, Robert Seeley DeGolyer (figure 7.20).

Chicago was a busy industrial city, blackened from soot, with steelyards, a commercial harbor, and the world's most extensive stockyards and slaughterhouses, whose stench often wafted across the future Illinois Institute of Technology campus. Upton Sinclair's dark novel *The Jungle* of 1906 had described the conditions there in excruciating detail. J. Ogden Armour, son of the institute's founder, Philip Danforth Armour, had been the inspiration for one of the plant owners in the novel, and the 1904 strike against Armour & Co. figures in the novel's plot. At the time of Mies's arrival, the city was still reeling from more recent labor unrest: the "Memorial Day Massacre" on May 30, 1937, which occurred at the Republic Steel plant, 15 miles (24 kilometers) south of the Armour Institute. To this day, it is considered one of the most important events in American labor history. While most large steel producers had agreed to unionization after a massive strike, Republic Steel and a few other smaller companies had resisted unionization. When a large crowd of steelworkers marched toward its gates to enforce a strike, a line of police officers shot into the crowd, killing ten workers and injuring 105.

Figure 7.19. Herbert Bayer, dust cover of Sigfried Giedion's *Space, Time and Architecture* (Cambridge, Mass.: Harvard University Press, 1941).

Figure 7.20. Robert Seeley DeGolyer, 200 East Pearson Street, Chicago, 1916. This was Ludwig Mies van der Rohe's residence from 1941 to 1968. Photograph by Hassan Bagheri.

The Great Depression had dealt a major blow to higher education, and many schools experienced serious financial problems as enrollment fell and endowments shrunk due to diminished philanthropy. The Armour Institute and another technical and home economics school, the Lewis Institute, decided to merge in October 1939 to form a more competitive unit. Henry Townley Heald, a thirty-five-year-old associate professor of engineering at the Armour Institute, had become president in 1938 and stayed on to head the new Armour Institute of Technology (soon to be renamed the Illinois Institute of Technology, or IIT). The charismatic and energetic Heald hired Mies to lead the architecture school and oversee the campus expansion. Of course, Heald knew that the campus expansion was a long-term project, and that Mies had no experience planning anything remotely comparable. But he needed to signal confidence and determination to his board for fundraising purposes. Hiring European architects to teach at American schools had become quite common; since 1903, Paul Cret from Paris had made the architecture school at the University of Pennsylvania one of the best in the country. The Massachusetts Institute of Technology (MIT) had hired Constant-Désiré Despradelle in 1893, and Princeton had hired Jean Labatut in 1928. When the cachet of the École des Beaux-Arts began to fade, American schools looked to European modernists for support. This is how Eliel Saarinen landed at Cranbrook in 1923, Jan Ruhtenberg at Columbia in 1934, and Gropius at Harvard in 1936. Modernist critics and curators also came, such as Justus Bier in 1937 (University of Louisville, Kentucky), Walter Curt Behrendt in 1934 (Dartmouth), and Alexander Dorner in 1938 (Rhode Island School of Design).

The spaces where Mies taught for the first eighteen years, on the top floor of the Art Institute, were not ideal: "The studios snake along under the skylights of the attic....In the summer, you roast," a former student had informed Mies in 1936 (figure 7.21).[46] Similarly, Mies's student Werner Buch recalled "these grotesque rooms, these halls up under the roof with iron supports, security windows, raw concrete floors and so forth. Here we had our workspaces, and here Mies presided."[47] The location in the center of town came with the advantage of being a short walk from the Blackstone and many restaurants nearby, where Mies took students and collaborators, such as "Harvey's" in the Straus Building across the street,[48] or the Berghoff at 17 West Adams Street.[49]

An intriguing opportunity for better studio spaces briefly presented itself after Mies's arrival. In 1938, Frances Glessner Lee had donated her parents' home, H. H. Richardson's John J. Glessner House of 1885–86, to the Armour Institute, and classes began to be conducted there immediately (figure 7.22). Mies expressed interest in it as a home for the architecture school when that possibility was mentioned to him during his visit in January 1938, and he requested the blueprints when he returned.[50] President Heald wrote to Lee on September 21, 1938:

> As you know, our School of Architecture is at the present time housed in the Art Institute, in quarters which are not entirely satisfactory. Professor van der Rohe has shown great interest in the Glessner House since he arrived in Chicago two weeks ago. He feels that the house is a "wonderful architectural document," and thinks it would be a fine place to house his School of Architecture....I still have definitely in mind the preference which you suggested for having the house used in connection with work in architecture, and, because of that fact, I thought you would be interested in van der Rohe's reaction to that possibility.[51]

Moving the Armour Institute's architecture school to 1800 Prairie Avenue would have put it in immediate vicinity to the Illinois Society of Architects at 1801 Prairie Avenue, and to the former home of local department store owner Marshall Field at 1905 Prairie Avenue, where the New Bauhaus under László Moholy-Nagy had just opened its doors on October 18, 1937. What a standoff that would have been: Mies and the Armour Institute architecture school in Richardson's masterpiece of 1887, and Moholy-Nagy with the New Bauhaus in a villa nearby of 1873–76 by Richard Morris Hunt.

Nothing came of those plans, not least because Glessner House was more than two miles (3.2 kilometers) away from the future campus, and its sequence of residential rooms was

Figure 7.21. Shepley, Rutan, & Coolidge, Art Institute of Chicago, 1893. Contemporary postcard.

Figure 7.22. H. H. Richardson, John J. Glessner House, 1800 South Prairie Avenue, Chicago, 1885–86.

not ideal for open studios. The New Bauhaus quickly ran into financial trouble and temporarily closed in October 1938.[52] In the spring of 1939 it opened again, as the Institute of Design. According to Katharine Kuh, Mies had objected to the term "Bauhaus," to which he, as its last director, claimed ownership. The Institute of Design offered a four-year course, training students "practically and theoretically as a designer of hand and machine-made products in wood, metal, glass, textiles, stage, display and for commercial arts, exposition architecture, typography, photography, modeling, and painting. An additional course of two years trains the student for architecture."[53] Just like at the Bauhaus, all students had to start with the preliminary course.

Recently, a number of excellent examples of modern architecture had sprung up in Chicago, which Mies must have heard about and seen. The architects William Keck and George Fred Keck (who taught temporarily at the New Bauhaus and Institute of Design) had designed a "House of Tomorrow" and Crystal House for the 1933–34 Century of Progress Exposition in Chicago to great acclaim (figure 7.23). (The latter even featured unauthorized replicas of Mies's furniture [figure 7.24]). Recently, they had built an apartment house for themselves and Louis Gottschalk, the chair of the history department at the University of Chicago in 1937, which was one of the city's earliest examples of the International Style. With a radicalism that must have appealed to Mies, the ground floor of the street façade consists of nothing but three garage doors, whose widths provide the scale for the three-partite façade above. Also in 1938, Alfred Alschuler, who had developed a preliminary plan for the expansion of the Armour Institute before Mies, had designed the Benson & Rixon Department Store at 230 South State Street (figure 7.25).[54] Possibly influenced by the work of Erich Mendelsohn, the curved façade of the six-story structure featured white bands of terra cotta and uninterrupted ribbons of glass blocks.

Mies might have initially preferred German-speaking acquaintances. Apart from Hilberseimer and Peterhans, who had come with him from Germany, there was, for instance, the architect Helmut Bartsch, like Mies a Rhinelander, from Düsseldorf, who had studied architecture in Berlin, received his diploma there in 1924, and come to Chicago in 1926 to join the office of Holabird & Root.[55] Bartsch often acted as translator at social occasions and would introduce Mies to his future companion, Lora Marx, on New Year's Eve in 1940.[56] Another acquaintance was Hans Huth, an art historian and curator at the Art Institute of Chicago from 1944 on, whose wife, Marta, a photographer, had documented modern interiors in Berlin, among them Mies's apartment for Stefanie Hess of 1930.[57]

It is hard to know how much Chicago architects knew about Mies when he arrived in 1938. His appearance was greeted with considerably less fanfare than that of Walter Gropius at Harvard a year earlier, who had been given a full-page portrait and several pages in the *Architectural Record* to explain his goals and vision, while Mies was merely greeted with a short interview in *Architectural Forum*.[58]

The *Chicago Tribune* had singled out Mies's work, though, when MoMA's traveling *Modern Architecture: International Exhibition* was hosted at the Sears, Roebuck & Co. department store in downtown Chicago in the summer of 1932. Mies had played an "important part…in the development of modern architecture," the newspaper declared, thanks to his many "successful buildings the world over," while the United States was "still fumbling" in this regard.[59] The same paper greeted Mies upon his arrival in September 1938 magnanimously as "an architect's architect. Big, quiet, methodical, publicity shy, he was a stone mason before he was director of the Dessau Bauhaus."[60] In the winter of 1938, Mies staged a small exhibition of his work at the Art Institute, which a reviewer found "clean cut, impressive and admirable."[61] But, she concluded, "A modern house is a rich man's house; the beauty and dignity of this type of building lies entirely with size, and quality of material. You cannot build an attractive modern house on a small scale; its greatest charm is the length of its lines."[62] The exhibition traveled on to the Albright Art Gallery in Buffalo, where it opened in September 1939, and to McCormick Hall at Princeton University in November.[63]

On October 18, 1938, Mies was officially welcomed in Chicago with a celebratory dinner at the Palmer House Hotel, hosted by the Armour Institute, the Chicago chapter of the American Institute of Architects, and the Illinois Society of Architects, with speeches

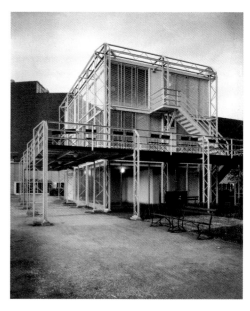

Figure 7.23. Keck & Keck, Crystal House, Century of Progress Exposition, Chicago, 1933–34. Exterior. Chicago History Museum.

Figure 7.24. Keck & Keck, Crystal House, Century of Progress Exposition, Chicago, 1933–34. Interior. Chicago History Museum.

Figure 7.25. Alfred Alschuler, Benson & Rixon Department Store, Chicago, 1938. Chicago History Museum.

given by Frank Lloyd Wright, Eliel Saarinen, William Emerson (dean of the school of architecture at MIT), and Rexford Newcomb, the dean of the College of Fine Arts at the University of Illinois.[64] Mrs. J. Ogden Armour, daughter-in-law of the institute's founder, announced a gift of $50,000 for the architecture school at that occasion.[65]

1939–58   Planning for Armour Institute of Technology/Illinois Institute of Technology

Philip Danforth Armour and his brothers had founded Armour & Co. in 1867 at Chicago's thriving Union Stock Yard and grown it into the city's largest meatpacking company. Armour's son J. Ogden Armour took over operations in 1901. Two major philanthropic undertakings were created, based on the progressive ethos of learning by doing—the Armour Mission (1886), a community learning center for children of all backgrounds, and the Armour Institute (1893), which taught engineering and library science to high-school graduates at nominal cost.

The Armour Institute had begun to systematically purchase adjacent lots for future expansion. Under President Heald, the land holdings of the Armour Institute of Technology and then Illinois Institute of Technology increased from nine to 85 acres (four to 34 hectares), assets grew from $2 million to $17 million, and student numbers from seven hundred to seven thousand.[66] By the late 1930s, it stretched between Thirty-First Street in the north, Thirty-Fourth Street in the south, State Street in the east, and the New York Central Railroad tracks in the west. The campus continued to grow and encompasses 120 acres (49 hectares) today.

The entire area of "Bronzeville," in which the Armour Institute was located and into which it expanded, was densely settled and one of the most vibrant African American neighborhoods in the United States. In the 1910s and 1920s, South State Street between Twenty-Sixth and Thirty-Ninth streets had been known as The Stroll for the crowds who would frequent its sidewalks, cafés, and jazz clubs. Among the many buildings demolished to make room for what would become IIT's expansion were Jesse Binga's Arcade and Bank at the corner of Thirty-Fifth and State streets—successful examples of Black entrepreneurship.

Lilly Reich came to visit Mies in Chicago from July through September 1939.[67] While her stay in Chicago included a trip with Mies to Pine Lake Lodge in Wisconsin, this was not a romantic getaway but rather a working vacation, where Ludwig Hilberseimer, George Danforth, and John Barney Rodgers joined them to work on campus plans for the future IIT. Danforth and Priestley fondly remembered Lilly Reich's presence at the school, her warmth and attention, and the fact that she spoke English.[68] The episode at Pine Lake Lodge in Wisconsin is also remembered for a neighbor reporting the German-speaking group to the FBI as potential spies.[69] But one might wonder if the experience of this log cabin had any impact on Mies's search for truthful display of structure and materials. After all, the logs are both structure and enclosure, load-bearing and insulating, looking the same inside and out. Mies would pursue such structural clarity for the rest of his life—coming up against the rather different thermic qualities of steel (a transmitter of temperature rather than an insulator) and code regulations for fire safety.

When Reich arrived back in Berlin in mid-September, the world had changed. Hitler had invaded Poland and World War II had begun. Mies's apartment and office at Am Karlsbad had been slated for demolition (to make room for Albert Speer's north–south axis), and Reich was in charge of clearing it out upon her return.

Mies's letters to Reich went up in flames during the war, but her letters to him allow us some glimpses into the late phase of their relationship. Reich consoled Mies from afar over his loneliness and health issues in Chicago, such as the flu, pain in his leg, and a toothache.[70] In May 1940, Mies learned that the Resor House was not going to be built, and he feared that his contract at IIT would not be renewed, due to the critical reception of his design for the school's future campus. Reich joked about his faulty German writing ("Due to his improved English?" she wondered) and teased him, "Why do you now always sign 'van der Rohe'?"[71] But she also noted the decreased frequency of his letters—"the gaps between them get longer and longer and it is not due to the mail"—and wistfully recalled their last half hour at the Art Institute of Chicago when "all the doors closed, probably forever."[72] She had become the administrator of Mies's business and private affairs, overseeing patent claims and a lawsuit over the cantilever chair,[73] and distributing funds and care packages, even to Mies's wife, Ada.[74]

While Mies sent her magazines such as *Architectural Record* and *Architectural Forum,* and an occasional issue of *Harper's Bazaar,* Reich pushed for intellectual conversations and recommended or sent books, such as Ernst Jünger's *Blätter und Steine* (Leaves and Stones) (which she found "superior, courageous, wise and youthful") and Wilhelm Pinder's *Das Problem der Generation in der Kunstgeschichte Europas* (The Problem of Generation in European Art History), and she challenged Mies on Rudolf Schwarz's *Wegweisung der Technik* (Technology's Directive), which she found "completely inaccessible," like "a foreign language…weighted down by symbols in an artificial interpretation after the fact."[75]

Reich's letters allow a glimpse into both of their initial thoughts about the campus:

> Your concerns about the project have surprised me, I would like to check on them with the help of the plans. But the different character of the solution with the plates and the glass buildings can lead to such thoughts. Especially if the bird's eye view makes the plates appear so rectilinear, rather than formally relaxed and easy. But essentially this is all going in the right direction. If you continue trying, I would go for the irregular approach and combine the school buildings with an interior courtyard, but probably the buildings not too big.[76]

Lilly Reich died in Berlin shortly after the war, on December 14, 1947. She had been in ill health and desperate for work. The intense collaboration with Mies on his projects from 1925 on had been of crucial importance for his success in Germany and helped pave the way for his career in the United States as well. Letters about the creative process, such as the one quoted above, are extremely rare, as much of their collaboration unfolded in conversations and via sketches on the drawing board, making it difficult to separate their voices in the resulting designs. And Mies certainly did not help. His rare comments on the design process would laconically describe it as a logical response to the conditions at hand. He never mentioned Lilly Reich's role in their partnership or her important input on individual designs.

The process of expanding the IIT campus was slow, and in all likelihood, Mies did not have many reasons to visit that part of town. In a conversation with his friend Katharine Kuh, he recalled many years later: "When I first arrived, I immediately went to the campus of the then Armour Institute (now the Institute of Technology). I felt I ought to turn around and go home."[77] It would take until 1956 before the architecture school could move into Mies's Crown Hall (two years before his retirement).

Mies's was not the original master plan: one had been fashioned in 1937 by the Chicago firm of Holabird & Root; another plan was developed by Chicago architect and Armour trustee Alfred Alschuler just before he passed away in 1940—while Mies had begun work on his own plan. Both the Holabird & Root and Alschuler plans showed the influence of Beaux-Arts principles in their central axis on Thirty-Third Street and symmetrical layout on either side. Both assumed preserving the Armour Institute's Main Building and Machinery Hall, and imagined solitaire buildings in a parklike setting, removed from the street's edge (figures 7.26, 7.27).

The first version of Mies's master plan (based on an earlier version by Alschuler and in collaboration with Holabird & Root) adopted many of these traits and showed a surprisingly symmetrical and uninspired arrangement of lecture halls and research and administrative buildings on either side of Thirty-Third Street, with the backbone of the urban arrangement between Thirty-First and Thirty-Fifth streets (figure 7.28). Flanking buildings on either end created entrance and exit gates and helped frame a vast open space in the middle, thanks to the elimination of two cross streets. (Reminders of this early planning phase are the symmetrical placements of Wishnick and Siegel halls, as well as the post-Miesian Hermann Hall and Galvin Library.) Throughout the planning process, Mies's sketches

Figure 7.26. Patton & Fisher, Armour Institute of Technology, Main Building, Chicago, 1891–93. Contemporary postcard.

Figure 7.27. Alfred Alschuler, Illinois Institute of Technology plan, Chicago, 1937–38. Illinois Institute of Technology Archive.

stubbornly refused to acknowledge the existence of any older campus buildings, such as the Main Building or Machinery Hall.

In great contrast to the existing architecture (and to what would be built later), most of Mies's envisioned buildings were partially lifted up from the ground by cruciform supports, creating a continuous landscape of complex vistas and pedestrian thoroughfares, which Mies would have greatly preferred and which was much discussed in his office (figures 7.29, 7.30). Mies "liked the idea because it did open up the view from the ground level through the campus. I think it was really pure economics that dictated that they not use the ground floor just for entrance and view because it would have meant adding another floor."[78]

President Heald supported Mies's ideas but would have to convince his board. In an attempt to win public support for the scheme, he published an essay in the *New York Times* reporting on Mies's concept, and hinting at a possible compromise:

> The "open plan," as applied to houses is described as conferring the feeling of living in space. As applied to buildings of a technological training center, that would be translated into a feeling of "working" in space, with the entire campus constituting one gigantic room. On the new campus this effect will be achieved by giving open first stories to six of the twelve buildings which will eventually make the architectural ensemble. By "open first stories" the architect refers to a type of construction which, while affording protection against the elements, employs transparent glass brick and similar materials in the walls to permit unimpeded view and the passage of light. In the plan it is the purpose to create a separate, utilitarian building to house each field of work.[79]

In the end, scarcity of resources accompanied the campus's extraordinary growth in those years and, tragically, led to the complete removal of this feature in favor of buildings that simply made full use of their ground floor. While the resulting architecture is less varied and evocative, perhaps it was this forced grounding of the buildings that helped Mies to finally overcome the creative loop in which he had found himself since the great success of the Barcelona Pavilion.

While the early drawings had still shown spindly cruciform columns holding the upper floors, now, Mies went the other way—instead of self-effacing, reflective supports, he now specified heavy, black, over-dimensioned columns, which framed and structured the beige brick façades. The load-bearing columns at the corners had to be encased in concrete for fire protection, and Mies developed an extraordinarily elegant corner solution.

Figure 7.28. Ludwig Mies van der Rohe, Illinois Institute of Technology plan, Chicago, 1939. Delineator: George Danforth. Pencil and conté crayon on illustration board, 39 15/16 × 51 in. (101.5 × 129.5 cm).

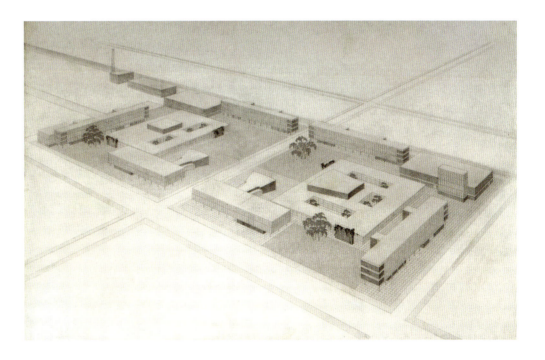

The concrete column would be encased in steel sheets, on which smaller vertical I-beams were attached in mirror symmetry to frame the brick walls. Mies's choice of buff-colored brick throughout stood in remarkable contrast to the older dark brick and brownstone buildings on the site, with the new structures emerging in their midst as superbly cool, clean, rational prophets of a new age. An IIT fundraising brochure of 1947 claimed that "While the immediate neighborhood presents blight in its worst aspects, costing the people of Chicago untold millions, the area has tremendous possibilities for improvement."[80] The mixture of new and old was repeatedly noted in the press. Mies developed a 24-foot (7.3-meter) module into which labs and classrooms of different sizes could comfortably fit, rendering it visible on the outside of most buildings in a steel or concrete framework.

Mies presented the IIT campus plan to the public in January 1942 at the Art Institute of Chicago.[81] His first design for an individual building on campus was probably the Field House for indoor sports and recreation, which the students and the athletic department started fundraising for in 1941.[82] It is likely that Mies provided a sketch for the building

Figure 7.29. Ludwig Mies van der Rohe, Illinois Institute of Technology campus, Chicago, 1939. Exterior perspective of classroom buildings along State Street. Delineator: George Danforth. Pencil on tracing paper, 19 × 26 1/4 in. (48.2 × 66.6 cm).

Figure 7.30. Ludwig Mies van der Rohe, Duncan School of Mechanical Engineering project, Illinois Institute of Technology campus, Chicago, ca. 1943. Delineator: George Danforth. Pencil and charcoal on transparent paper, graphite on illustration board, 30 × 40 in. (76.2 × 101.6 cm). Museum of Modern Art, New York. The Mies van der Rohe Archive, gift of the architect.

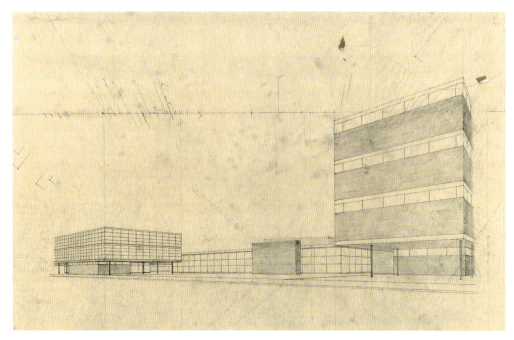

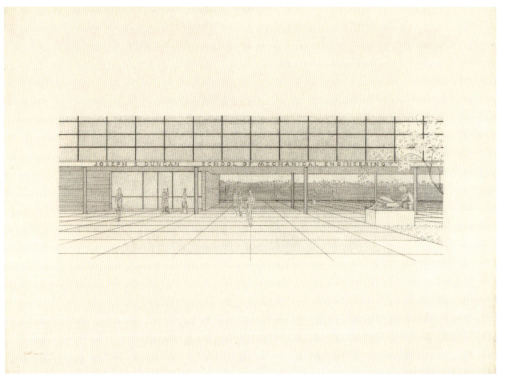

for that purpose, and it is clearly visible in many of the early drawings of 1940 next to the athletic fields on the northern edge of campus. There are several versions of it, but Mies published the one he was probably most fond of in the catalogue for his 1947 exhibition at MoMA (figure 7.31).[83] It was a spectacular vision—a transparent glass box on top of a recessed brick base, in which several indoor ball games could be played simultaneously. Mies used essentially the same design for the theater project he presented at the same occasion.

1942–43   Minerals and Metals Building

His first executed structure on campus, the Minerals and Metals Building, earmarked to support the war effort, consisted of a double-height main hall with a gantry and offices and workshops on two floors toward the street (figures 7.32–7.35). Mies described the design process with his habitual nonchalance and matter-of-factness, dismissing any thought of careful aesthetic considerations:

> People claim that I was influenced by Mondrian in the first building for the I.I.T. campus, the Metals Building. This one has a wall that they say looks like Mondrian. But I remember very well how it came about. Everything was donated for this whole building. The site—we had 64 feet [19.5 meters] from the railroad to the sidewalk; somebody gave them a travelling crane—it was 40 feet [12.2 meters] wide, so we needed 42 feet [12.8 meters] from center of column to center of column. The rest was laboratories, you know. Everything was there— we needed steel bracing in the wall, the brick wall. It was a question of the building code. You can only make an 8-inch [20-centimeter] wall so big, otherwise you have to reinforce it. So we did that. Then, when everything was finished, the people from the Minerals and Metals Research Building, the engineers, they came and said, "We need here a door." So I put in a door. And the result was the Mondrian![84]

Figure 7.31. Ludwig Mies van der Rohe, Field House, Illinois Institute of Technology campus, Chicago, ca. 1941. Pencil sketch, dimensions unknown. Museum of Modern Art, New York. The Mies van der Rohe Archive, gift of the architect.

The industrial architecture of Albert Kahn was of great importance here, which had been featured extensively in the August 1938 issue of *Architectural Forum*,[85] and published by Mies's Berlin visitor George Nelson as a separate book the following year.[86] Mies owned a copy and was "much interested" in it.[87] In particular, the plant for the Lady Esther

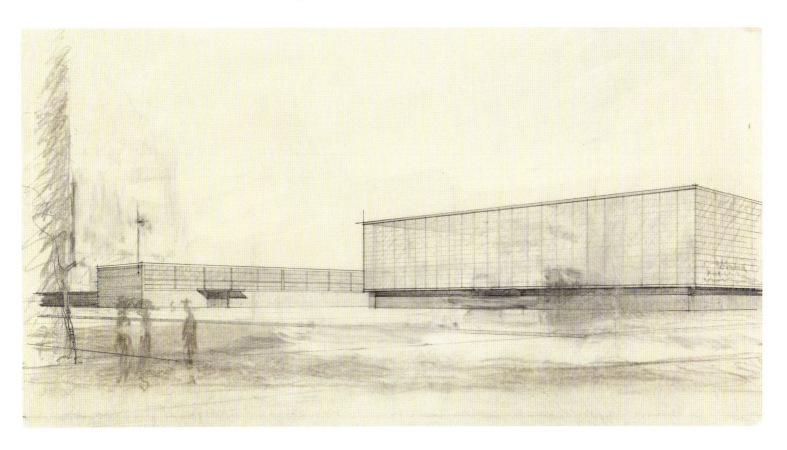

Figure 7.32. Ludwig Mies van der Rohe, Minerals and Metals Building, Illinois Institute of Technology campus, Chicago, 1943. Two exterior elevations, section and plan, structural details, perspectives, 1941. Pencil and yellow pencil on paper, 23 3/4 × 40 1/4 in. (60.3 × 102.2 cm). Museum of Modern Art, New York. The Mies van der Rohe Archive, gift of the architect.

Figure 7.33. Ludwig Mies van der Rohe, Minerals and Metals Building, Illinois Institute of Technology campus, Chicago, 1943. Exterior view. Photograph by Hedrich-Blessing. Chicago History Museum.

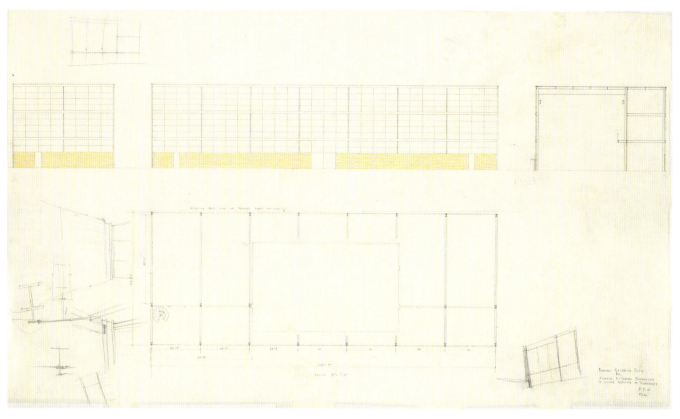

Figure 7.34. Ludwig Mies van der Rohe, Minerals and Metals Building, Illinois Institute of Technology campus, Chicago, 1943. Interior view from the second-floor gallery into the central space. The western façade toward the railroad tracks is on the left. Photograph by Hedrich-Blessing. Chicago History Museum.

Figure 7.35. Ludwig Mies van der Rohe, Minerals and Metals Building, Illinois Institute of Technology campus, Chicago, 1943. Interior view of the second-floor workshops behind the main, eastern façade. Photograph by Hedrich-Blessing. Chicago History Museum.

Cosmetics company in Clearing, Illinois, of 1938, or the Chrysler Tank Arsenal in Detroit, of 1940–41, bear a striking resemblance to Mies's design at the Minerals and Metals Building and other projects at the time (figures 7.36, 7.37). Mies hired the same architectural photographers, the company of Bill Hedrich and Henry Blessing in Chicago, and they endowed his building with the same perspectival drama. Carefully staged, several of them featured Mies and Hilberseimer in leading roles in their dark and beige trench coats at the doors; others were manipulated after the fact to look like scenes from a contemporary film noir—the asphalt blacked in front, the aggressive hood of a 1941 Hudson car dangerously close.

What greatly differed from Kahn was Mies's detailing. Kahn's glass façades were, in all likelihood, constructed from standard commercial panes, and the structural steel columns were placed right behind this skin, visible through the frosted glass, in the center of the panes. In Mies's case, the windows were custom made, with a flat, welded profile on the outside (figure 7.38). Aligned with the steel supports inside, each field of twenty-five

Figure 7.36. Albert Kahn, Lady Esther Cosmetics Factory, Clearing, Illinois, 1938. Photograph by Hedrich-Blessing. Chicago History Museum.

Figure 7.37. Albert Kahn, Chrysler Tank Arsenal, Detroit, 1940–41. Exterior view with a tank in the foreground, July 10, 1941. Photograph by Hedrich-Blessing. Chicago History Museum.

> Figure 7.38. Ludwig Mies van der Rohe, Minerals and Metals Building, Illinois Institute of Technology campus, Chicago, 1943. Exterior view. Photograph by Hedrich-Blessing. Chicago History Museum.

panes was carefully proportioned, as if Mies had relied on the regulating lines that Hendrik Petrus Berlage and Le Corbusier had used.[88] (Mies owned a copy of the German edition of *Vers une Architecture,* called *Kommende Baukunst.*) Each individual pane has the same proportions as the entire field of twenty-five. In other words, a diagonal drawn through the field cuts diagonally through five window panes. The main façade is strictly symmetrical—something that Mies had not done since his last conventional works in the early 1920s: there are seven bays, two entrance doors, and a central opening for deliveries. The elegantly proportioned eastern front façade differed from the western side toward the railroad line, which had smaller panes (seventy-two instead of the twenty-five in front) without proportional sophistication and marred by an additional layer of fire protection, as some of the passing trains transported combustible material (see figure 7.34).

When *Architectural Forum* published the building in November 1943, it became clear how much Mies had finally moved beyond the limited structural and aesthetic vocabulary of his German work. In detail drawings from the building's windowless, northern façade,

Figure 7.39. Ludwig Mies van der Rohe, Minerals and Metals Building, Illinois Institute of Technology campus, Chicago, 1943. Horizontal sections of structural details.

Figure 7.40. Holabird & Roche, Stevens Hotel, Chicago, 1927. Contemporary postcard.

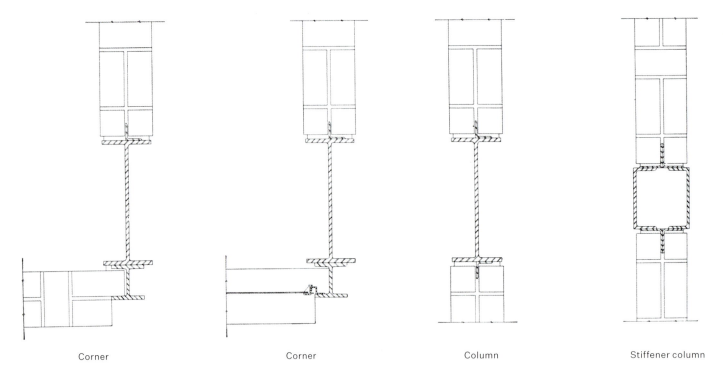

Corner   Corner   Column   Stiffener column

he showed embedded I-beams and their connection to the brick wall or glass (figure 7.39). *Architectural Forum* gushed: "The details of the construction of the research building were worked out with the utmost care to ensure that all of the different materials produced a thoroughly integrated structure. It was because of this care…that the exposed structure has a design interest rarely found in a building of this type."[89] While pleasing in their apparent purity, the details also signaled to anyone who had built with steel in Chicago that an I-beam exposed to an arctic winter outside and a blazing furnace within would produce torrents of condensation water inside—which is exactly what happened. The section of the brick base where the steel columns were embedded had to be replaced several times, as rust from the columns inside damaged the one layer of brick in front.

The building opened in January of 1943, a year after Mies's public presentation of his campus plan. It became obvious how academic an exercise this plan had been, as neither the building itself nor its location or size had been part of the plan or fit into its 24-foot (7.3-meter) module.[90] As mentioned above, a donated plot next to the railroad tracks and the size of an existing gantry established its perimeters. The fragility of Mies's planning efforts was proven again a few months later, when IIT president Heald decided to abandon the South Side campus altogether and instead purchase the three-thousand-room Stevens Hotel on Michigan Avenue to house the entire school (figure 7.40). His engineers had assured him that classrooms, lecture halls, labs, and offices could be created by removing partition walls; the grand ballroom would become the gymnasium, used for student dances, assembly meetings, and dinners; and the lobby would become the library reading room. At the end of September, Heald was outbid by the owner of the Blackstone Hotel, who paid the same price, $5.5 million, but in cash.[91]

1943 Museum for a Small City

Just weeks after the Minerals and Metals Building had opened, in early February 1943, Mies had been invited to participate in a special issue of the magazine *Architectural Forum*, which intended to showcase ideas for nonresidential buildings in the postwar American city.[92] Since the end of the war was nowhere in sight, the magazine called it "New Buildings for 194X." Charles Eames, Pietro Belluschi, William Lescaze, and Stonorov & Kahn were among twenty-three invited architects, charged with creating model solutions for different urban building types.

Support for the American entry into World War II had by no means been unanimous, and, in some areas, there was a broad effort toward changing public opinion. Henry Luce, the owner of *Architectural Forum* and *Fortune* magazine, had been a powerful advocate of the war effort and was now urging his advertisers and magazine editors to fall in line. There was hardly an ad in *Architectural Forum* that did not weave in the war effort and the expected building boom afterward ("Completed Piping Systems at Top Wartime Speed," "Add Aluminum in Color to Your Postwar Thinking," and so on.)[93] "New Buildings for 194X" belongs in this context. The editors of *Architectural Forum* and *Fortune* had begun a collaboration with city representatives and urban and financial planners in Syracuse, New York, to develop ideas for a "complete redevelopment of the city after the war."[94] The proposed urban layout was modeled on downtown Syracuse but took great liberties. Mies had at first been asked to design a church, but requested to do a museum, which was placed in the fictitious urban plan at an agora at the end of a tree-lined boulevard, next to Charles Eames's expansive city hall and across from a church by Lorimer Rich. Interestingly, Syracuse's urban density and historic streetscapes overall were kept mostly intact—in great contrast to the urban renewal projects that devastated urban centers in the 1960s—while some perimeter blocks opened up their center for parking. The results were published in May 1943.[95]

Most of the twenty-three participating architects had gone into great detail, presenting inside and outside perspectives, full sets of plans, detailed space calculations, and financial breakdowns. The hotel design by Louis Kahn and Oscar Stonorov was detailed down to the toothbrush holders behind the bathroom mirrors. In great contrast, Mies, despite having the Minerals and Metals Building behind him and the IIT plan in limbo, stood out for submitting the—by far—least substantial contribution, consisting of an elevation, a floor plan, two collages, and a short text.

Mies worked with his student George Danforth, who had developed a museum design for his final thesis with Walter Peterhans.[96] The end result was still dependent on the formal language of Mies's Barcelona Pavilion (figure 7.41; see figures 4.13–4.17). There was a grid of eight by fourteen columns à la Barcelona, carrying an enormous flat ceiling plate. An area of eight by eleven (equaling eighty-eight) columns was surrounded by glass, the roof stretched out over an adjacent open area of eight by four columns. The center of the main space received additional light from an open courtyard with plants. Other interruptions of its flowing space were a print department and a recessed area in the floor, "around the edge of which small groups could sit for informal discussions." The columnar grid was interrupted to preserve sight lines in the auditorium behind freestanding walls. Here, two overhead girders supported the ceiling from above—the first time this motive appeared in Mies's work. (It would be employed for a number of important projects in the following years, such as the Cantor Drive-In, the Mannheim Theater and, most importantly, Crown Hall.) There were six freestanding walls where "small pictures would be exhibited." Mies imagined mostly sculptures in this wide-open space, or paintings so large that they did not need a wall to support them. He explained: "A work such as Picasso's *Guernica* has been difficult to place in a typical museum gallery. Here it can be shown to its greatest advantage and become an element in space against a changing background."[97] One of Danforth's collages showed *Guernica* flanked by a pair of Aristide Maillol sculptures; photographs of leaves and the surface of water suggest views to the outside (figure 7.42).

The museum was placed upon a podium similar to the Barcelona Pavilion, accessible via several steps, and there was an outside reflecting pool. Many details remained unsolved. It is unclear where one would enter the building (presumably through the open area on the western side) or where ticket or information counters, coatrooms, or bathrooms would be located. Mies's text suggested that his museum was different from its metropolitan counterparts, a flexible "center for the enjoyment, not the interment of art." Sculptures would

Figure 7.41. Ludwig Mies van der Rohe, Museum for a Small City project, 1943. Pencil, ink, plastic film and airbrush on gelatin silver print, 8 × 10 in. (20.3 × 25.4 cm). Museum of Modern Art, New York. The Mies van der Rohe Archive, gift of the architect.

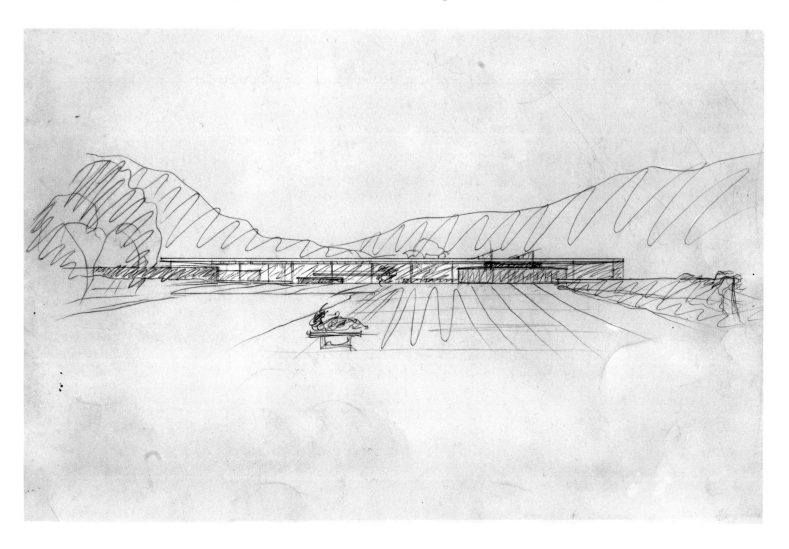

Figure 7.42. Ludwig Mies van der Rohe, Museum for a Small City project, 1943. Interior perspective. Note two sculptures by Aristide Maillol (*Action in Chains* [1905] and *Jeune fille couchée* [1912]) and a reproduction of Pablo Picasso's 1937 painting *Guernica*. Delineator: George Danforth. Graphite and cut-and-pasted reproductions on illustration board, 30 × 40 in. (76.1 × 101.5 cm). Museum of Modern Art, New York. The Mies van der Rohe Archive, gift of the architect.

be placed as in a garden, "defining rather than confining" them and removing a barrier between the art work and the community: "The building, conceived as one large area, allows every flexibility in use. The structural type permitting this is the steel frame. This construction permits the erection of a building with only three basic elements—a floor slab, columns and a roof plate. The floor and paved terraces would be of stone."[98]

1944 The Posada Exhibition

In contrast, Mies's actual museum work was rather modest. He had become friendly with the art historian and gallerist Katharine Kuh, who had studied with Alfred Barr at Vassar and then received a master's degree in art history from the University of Chicago in 1929. After her divorce from businessman George Kuh, she opened a gallery in Chicago in 1934, exhibiting European modernists such as Picasso, Wassily Kandinsky, Josef Albers, Fernand Léger, and Paul Klee, but also American photographers such as Ansel Adams. Apparently, they bonded when Mies visited several of her Klee exhibitions, and she became a sponsor for his citizenship application. When her gallery went out of business, Daniel Catton Rich hired her at the Art Institute of Chicago as curator for an educational "Gallery of Art Interpretation" on the first floor of the main building. She asked Mies to design the interior and develop the display. The opening exhibition in the spring of 1944 was titled *Who Is Posada?* and accompanied the Art Institute's *Art of José Guadalupe Posada* (April 13–May 14, 1944). The room Mies designed did not contain original

Figure 7.43. Ludwig Mies van der Rohe, exhibition design for *Who Is Posada?*, Art Institute of Chicago, 1944.

artworks but rather reproductions and explanatory panels, documents, and artifacts that traced sources of influence for the great Mexican graphic artist (figure 7.43). According to Kuh, Mies

> addressed himself to the design of that modest gallery with the same unfaltering standards that he brought to his most important architectural commissions. No detail was too negligible for his scrutiny. Each small problem he explored exhaustively, regardless of how long it took.... On three walls of the gallery he installed a group of horizontal wood panels that were to serve as backgrounds for changing exhibits. He gave the same dedicated attention to the quality, color, and grain of the wood as to the precise position and relationship of the panels.[99]

It is not hard to detect in the photos some typical Miesian elements, such as the elegant sans-serif lettering and the framing of the exhibits within a horizontal band of color or plywood. In the center of the space is a freestanding wall. Covered in dark-colored paper on one side, Mies showed the four plywood panels at the back and stabilized the wall via an adjacent vitrine. The veneer's wood grain is reminiscent of the marble pattern on the central walls in Barcelona and Brno or his Macassar wood panels elsewhere, and the carefully designed corners and base of the plywood vitrine give away Mies's hand. The installation remained in place for a number of follow-up exhibitions.[100]

Eight

Formation of a New Language

Chicago, 1943–56

1945–51 The Farnsworth House

One of the most fateful encounters of Mies's career happened one winter evening in 1945, in the old Irving Apartment Building at the corner of Oak and North State streets in Chicago—a short walk from Mies's home on East Pearson Street. He had been invited to dinner by the journalist, book dealer, and accomplished cook Georgia Lingafelt and her friend Ruth Lee. Also present was Dr. Edith Farnsworth, a doctor at Chicago's Passavant Memorial Hospital specializing in kidney diseases, who had just bought a piece of land on the Fox River in Plano, Illinois, an hour and a half west of downtown Chicago. She was forty-two at the time, seventeen years younger than Mies. Apparently, Mies had been mostly silent during the dinner—perhaps due to boredom, perhaps due to the fact that speaking English still caused him considerable effort, even seven years after his arrival in the United States. After dinner, when Lingafelt and Lee were out in the kitchen doing dishes, Farnsworth asked Mies, if "some young man" in his office could design "a small studio weekend-house" for her newly acquired property. As Farnsworth recalls in her memoir: "The response was the more dramatic for having been preceded by two hours of unbroken silence. 'I would love to build any kind of house for you.' The effect was tremendous, like a storm, a flood or other act of God."[1] This first conversation was followed by countless others and many visits to the site. A friendship evolved.

Mies had imagined glass-enclosed living rooms for quite some time, usually protruding from the core of the house and surrounded by glass on three sides, as at the Hubbe and Mountain House projects of 1932 and 1934, and his students' work also contained similar visions (see figures 5.34, 6.5, 6.19, 6.20). The support of the roof in such work was still derivative of the solution at Barcelona—slender, cruciform columns, standing freely in the room or close to the glass walls.

Mies's collaborator Edward Duckett developed elevation drawings for the Farnsworth House sometime in early 1946. He recalled that Mies "put a wash on two different sketches of the house with Edith Farnsworth standing right there watching. One scheme was on the ground and the other was with it raised up, the way it was eventually built."[2] Only the version hovering above ground has survived—it was clearly Mies's favorite and close to the final result (figure 8.1). Mies resisted suggestions to move the building out of the flood plane to a location higher up, as that would have eliminated the justification for the hovering cube. His impeccable sense of proportions (and not potential flood levels) dictated the distance of five feet (1.5 meters) from the ground. Mies's long-standing desire to reduce things to their absolute essence here led to a one-room weekend house defined entirely by its structural elements and the absence of conventional walls or windows—a simple rectilinear glass box, placed roughly east–west, 55 feet, 4 inches (16.9 meters) long and 28 feet, 8 inches (8.7 meters) wide, held aloft by eight heavy I-beams, with an open terrace on its southern side toward the river and a covered entrance area toward the low western sun (figure 8.2). The design was conceived in 1946, and additional work was done in the summer of 1947 for two upcoming exhibitions. Ground was broken in 1949, and it was finished in 1951.[3]

Noticing the abundance of mosquitoes close to the river, Mies planned for the open western end to be screened in, rendered it as such, and showed it in the model at the 1947 show at the MoMA. When the finished house was photographed in December of 1951, the screens had not yet been installed, enhancing its lightness and structural clarity.[4] Once they were in place, the building lost some of its visual appeal, and the house's next owner removed them again.

Figure 8.1. Ludwig Mies van der Rohe, Farnsworth House, Fox River, Plano, Illinois, 1945–51. North elevation; preliminary version, 1946. Pencil and watercolor on tracing paper, 13 × 25 in. (33 × 66.5 cm).

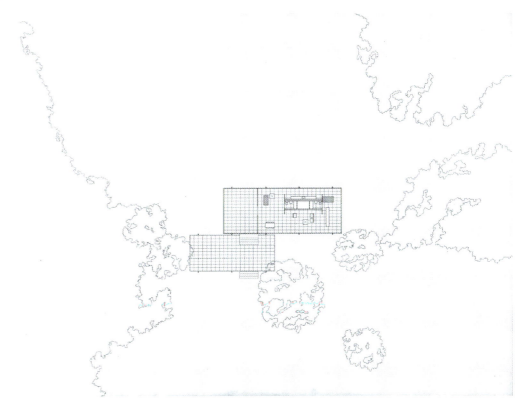

Figure 8.2. Ludwig Mies van der Rohe, Farnsworth House, Plano, Illinois, 1945–51. Plan; final version, ca. 1950. Ink on paper, 30 × 40 in. (76.2 × 101.6 cm). Museum of Modern Art, New York. The Mies van der Rohe Archive, gift of the architect.

According to Mies, at first, the building's construction was meant to be much simpler, "a steel construction, not welded, but bolted and as a more simple house—we were thinking even if we could do a lot of the work with the students on it....At this time, we were thinking about a concrete floor, and plywood for the core."[5]

In the end, the structure represented a decisive step toward a new direction for Mies. An exoskeleton of eight rolled, eight-inch (20-centimeter) flange steel beams, 22 feet (6.7 meters) apart, held both floor plate and ceiling, both 77 feet, 3 inches (23.5 meters) long and 28 feet, 8 inches (8.8 meters) wide. The self-effacing reflective slenderness of the supports in Barcelona had given way to assertive, heavy columns, proudly testifying to the rolling process in the foundry. *Architectural Forum* noted that their size was determined by formal rather than structural considerations, as they were strong enough "to support a much heavier structure, and some have misinterpreted their use as a functional impurity. They have not realized, perhaps, that there are demands of architectural expression quite as compelling as the demands of pure engineering, that the visual relationship of column thickness to depth of fascia and of column thickness to thickness of mullion can make or break a work of art as precise as this house."[6]

As there are no visible bolts, rivets, or welding seams, the glass house seemed "suspended...as if by magnetic force," *Architectural Forum* noted.[7] This magic trick was accomplished with so-called plug welds. All invisible steel connections (inside the terrace, floor, and roof structures) are bolted, but all visible connections on the outside are accomplished by a particular type of welding. While seams would ordinarily show up along the line where two metal parts had been merged under heat, plug welds made the connection invisible. Once the steel columns and floor and ceiling frames were fixed in place, welders would carefully target pre-drilled circular holes in the flanges of the I-beam and melt enough of the surface of the adjacent frame and the edge of the hole in the column to fuse them together with additional melted steel. This needed to be done with skill and care, as too much focused heat could burn through the frame, and too little could result in a weak connection (figure 8.3). As a result, these welds were hard to calculate, as their strength varied from case to case (and was, in any event, weaker than that of rivets or bolts). The "welding marks were ground flush after assembly. Mies did not like the texture of the structural steel next to the grinding marks and so the entire steel frame was sandblasted down to a smooth, matte silver."[8]

Mies applied the same method of sanding and polishing that he, a trained stonemason, would have used to reveal the essential quality of a piece of marble. He would have preferred to show the actual metal color, but stainless steel was not available and so he tried a coat of rustproofing zinc, but finally settled on four coats of white enamel paint (figure 8.4, 8.5).

These meticulous design decisions were lost on the average observer, but would excite visiting architects. Philip Johnson wrote to Mies: "The steel connections are so inevitable, so clean, so beautifully executed, that I believe no one will ever improve on them. Their problems are solved once and for all. Their execution is also a wonder to me. I am amazed that you found workmen to execute them so well. I cannot be specific, because each one is as good as the next. It exhausts me to even imagine what work you have been through" (figure 8.6).[9]

A profound artistic breakthrough had happened here—closely related to the façade solutions at Lake Shore Drive and the steel corners on IIT's campus, all happening at the same time. Mies never articulated it, as it stood in stark contrast to all of his proclamations. The approach developed here had nothing to do with "structural honesty"—in fact, it was its exact opposite, as Mies went to great length to conceal the structural conditions. Instead, a mundane steel connection had become the site for an aesthetic intervention, contrasting the industrial gravitas of a rolled I-beam—forged under enormous pressure in the foundry while moving back and forth, red hot, between ever tightening steel drums—with fine, meticulous craftsmanship on-site. The result was a unique formal solution, anticipating minimalist sculpture. To make all of this possible, equipment for gas welding, sandblasting, and appropriate energy sources had to be brought to the site,

Figure 8.3. Ludwig Mies van der Rohe, Farnsworth House, Plano, Illinois, 1945–51. Under construction, ca. 1949–50. Gelatin silver print, 8 3/8 × 10 1/2 in (21.2 × 26.7 cm). Canadian Centre for Architecture, Montreal.

Figure 8.4. Ludwig Mies van der Rohe, Farnsworth House, Plano, Illinois, 1945–51. Exterior view from the south. Photograph by Hassan Bagheri.

which was far from the center of Plano. New electric lines had to be connected and made invisible by being placed underground, just like the waterline and oil and septic tanks. Interestingly, while Mies had commissioned Hedrich-Blessing to photograph the construction of the Promontory Apartments and the details of Alumni Memorial Hall and other buildings on IIT's campus, there are very few photos of the Farnsworth House under construction, and they are all taken after the frame with its plug welds was already in place.

All this added to the enormous costs of the house, which, at $70,000 was almost ten times that of the median home price in the United States in 1950, and more than twice what Walter Gropius's own house in Lincoln, Massachusetts, had cost. (However, Philip Johnson's Glass House came in close, at $60,000.)

Even with all those additional expenses considered, one can't help but think that Mrs. Farnsworth was not given a fair deal by Mies and his team. The office claimed to have racked up an astonishing 5,884 billable hours for the design of the house—more than twice the number of hours billed for the Lake Shore Drive Apartments.[10] Mies's office organization and accounting were notoriously chaotic, and thus there was probably no way this could be verified. Compared to the amount of care devoted to the appearance of the columns, other areas at the house remained woefully unsolved. Since Thermopane glass did not come in the required sizes, the single-pane glass led, predictably, to streams of

Figure 8.5. Ludwig Mies van der Rohe, Farnsworth House, Plano, Illinois, 1945–51. Exterior view from the south. Photograph by Carol Highsmith.

condensation water inside in the winter. The fireplace had draft problems in the hermetically sealed house, working only when the front door was opened and let cold air in—somewhat undermining its purpose. The oil heating system produced a considerable amount of soot, and the flat roof leaked almost immediately. On the southern side, toward the river, the midday sun hit the large glass expanses without protection.

Thanks to the freestanding, tall central block with a fireplace, two bathrooms, and a kitchen, four distinct, but flexible, spaces emerged, becoming progressively less public—the entrance area, the main living area in front of the fireplace, the kitchen area behind it and at the end, facing east, the private sleeping quarters (figure 8.7). Both the kitchen section on the northern side and the fireplace directed the gaze and focus inward, rather than toward the surrounding landscape.

Philip Johnson, famously, had adopted the idea of a glass house after seeing Mies's model at the MoMA show, and built his own version within a year (figure 8.8). By May 1949, his new home was featured on New Canaan, Connecticut, modern house tours, and it was widely published in the fall of 1949.[11] While Johnson not only stole Mies's thunder by publishing his glass house before him, he also solved the spatial flow more elegantly, as his house was wider and shorter than Mies's design. The ceiling in Johnson's Glass House was considerably higher: 10 feet, 7 1/14 inches versus 9 feet, 2 3/8 inches (3.2 versus 2.8 meters). The row of kitchen appliances remained low, and the cylinder with the bathroom/

Figure 8.6. Ludwig Mies van der Rohe, Farnsworth House, Plano, Illinois, 1945–51. Detail of supporting I-beams. Photograph by Hassan Bagheri.

Figure 8.7. Ludwig Mies van der Rohe, Farnsworth House, Plano, Illinois, 1945–51. Interior view. Photograph by Hassan Bagheri.

fireplace combination obstructed the view less than the central, wall-high installation at the Farnsworth House. Richard Kelly's lighting installation made the building attractive and workable at night, while a separate, almost windowless brick box nearby served as the bedroom. In many ways, Johnson's was a better, more functional building. But it was no match for the visual radicalism of Mies's hovering box, whose stark white frame underlined the notion of detachment from ground and context.

Legal Troubles

A series of unfortunate events unfolded while the Farnsworth House was nearing completion. Edith Farnsworth had been remarkably patient and generous throughout, bankrolling Mies's experiments toward a new relationship between architecture, craft, and industry. The mood had finally soured when costs continued to spiral out of control and decisions were made without her consent, such as the selection of furniture. She eventually stopped payments and chose her own furniture by designers such as Florence Knoll, Harry Bertoia, Bruno Mathsson, Alvar Aalto, and others.[12]

At that time, in the spring of 1951, Philip Johnson noticed the financially unsustainable way in which Mies's Chicago office was run, and offered help in the form of his own business manager, Robert C. Wiley, for whom he was designing the magnificent Wiley House in New Canaan. Going over the books, Wiley noted $4,500 of outstanding construction costs at the Farnsworth House and approached Edith Farnsworth. Unhappy with some unsolved issues, Farnsworth offered $1,500 instead. Surely, they could have met somewhere in the middle.

Instead, Wiley contacted a major Chicago law firm, Sonnenschein, Nath & Rosenthal, and set up a meeting between senior partner David Levinson and Mies. Not surprisingly, Levinson recommended a lawsuit, and Mies decided to go ahead. "I think this was one of the most unfortunate things that could have happened," Myron Goldsmith noted later.[13] Mies came to greatly regret this decision, as he ended up deeply worried about the ensuing publicity and the possibility of losing his license during the four years that it took for the case to be solved in the courts. Guided by Levinson, Mies sued Farnsworth for an outstanding electrician's bill and his own fees (never before discussed), to the amount of roughly $33,000; Farnsworth countersued for $30,000—the difference between the $70,000 she had paid and Mies's initial estimate of $40,000. A complicated court system involving the expert opinion from a "special master" and a new judge appointed halfway through meant that the case lingered from 1951 until 1955, when a settlement was finally reached. Farnsworth paid $2,500 and ended up with the better deal. Her lawyer, one of her patients,

Figure 8.8. Philip Johnson, Glass House, New Canaan, Connecticut, 1948–49. Photograph by Carol E. Highsmith.

had worked pro bono, while Mies was stuck with the bill from Levinson. He did not receive the architect's fee he had demanded.

Edith Farnsworth continued to spend weekends at the house for the next twenty-one years, often making it available for visitors. She sold it in 1972 to British property magnate Lord Peter Palumbo for a reported $120,000 and retired to Italy, where she wrote her memoirs, translated Italian poetry, and died in 1977. A collector of modern art and architecture, Palumbo had commissioned Mies in July 1962 to design a nineteen-story office building in London, which he still hoped to execute after Mies's death (the necessary properties and titles at the site had not initially been available; see below). Palumbo added air-conditioning in 1972 and placed sculptures by Alexander Calder, Richard Serra, Henry Moore, and others on the grounds. The nearby Fox River flooded the house in 1954, 1996, 1997, 2008, and 2013. In 1996, the water inside the house was several feet high and destroyed most of the woodwork. Palumbo undertook a thorough restoration and opened the house to the public afterward. He sold it in 2003 to the National Trust for Historic Preservation for $7.5 million. While Edith Farnsworth did not quite double her investment, Palumbo multiplied his by a factor of over sixty-two. While these ratios would be lower when adjusted for inflation and factoring in the costs of restoration and repairs, they nevertheless reflect the different appreciation for Mies in the early 1970s and in 2003, in the wake of two monumental exhibitions at MoMA and the Whitney Museum of American Art in 2001 (see below).

Addressing the Court of Public Opinion

For four years, from 1951 to 1955, the unresolved case threatened to derail Mies's career and to inflict major financial losses on either party. Both tried their best to remain visible and vocal in the court of public opinion. Several fawning pieces about Mies appeared as soon as the lawsuit had been filed in the summer of 1951, just before depositions were taken, and then again in time for the final report of the appointed special master. In June 1951, for instance, the *Chicago Tribune* wrote of Mies's "devotion to simplicity" and described him as "a friend of steel." He was shown in deep contemplation looking at a model of the Farnsworth House, "now a family residence in Plano."[14]

In October 1951, the house was featured on the cover of *Architectural Forum*. Associate editor Peter Blake, another émigré friend and admirer of Mies, born in Berlin in 1920 as Peter Blach, wrote in the accompanying essay: "To some it may look like 'nothing much'—just a glass-sided box framed in heavy, white steel; but...the Farnsworth House near Chicago has no equal in perfection of workmanship, in precision of details, in pure simplicity of concept." Blake praised the "jewel-like perfection" of the house, comparable to the craftsmanship of the finest Japanese cabinetmakers. He slyly suggested that Edith Farnsworth simply might not have what it takes, as "such serenely beautiful spaces make heavy demands upon those who live in them"; he implied that they are not for everybody, but that "for those who are willing to enter Mies van der Rohe's world, there are [few] experiences as rich and rewarding." It is worth quoting the final paragraph of the essay:

> For while Mies subtracts and keeps on subtracting until all is skin and bones, the result is much like the reduction of a substance, in chemical analysis, to its crystalline parts. What remains after Mies' subtraction is a concentration of pure beauty, a distillation of pure spirit. Mies' buildings only seem to have a kind of nothingness at first glance; as time goes on, their subtle, indirect influence becomes increasingly apparent.... This subtle influence is likely to remain—the influence of a great artist, of a great work of art, of a great discipline, of a great belief that man in architecture should be free.[15]

When MoMA presented its exhibition *Built in USA: Post-War Architecture* from January 20 to March 15, 1953, Mies, naturally, played a major role, and the Farnsworth House was celebrated as showing most clearly "the relation between conspicuous space and the structure that generates it...indeed, a quantity of air caught between a floor and a roof."[16]

A year earlier, *House & Garden* magazine had already presented Mies's "Glass Shell That Floats in the Air" as an "American Idea in Houses," through the eyes of prominent photographer André Kertész. While Mies's supporters praised his work in the press, the other side was by no means idle. Elizabeth Gordon, successful editor of *House Beautiful* magazine, responded to the supposed American qualities of the Farnsworth House and the recent MoMA show with a lengthy text on "The Threat to the Next America" in the April 1953 issue of her magazine. It coincided perfectly with the report of the special master, issued on May 7, 1953. Gordon, who had interviewed Edith Farnsworth twice, started out with a photograph of the Tugendhat House, illustrating "The Cult of Austerity…the product of Mies van der Rohe's cold, barren design," and described Farnsworth as "a highly intelligent, now disillusioned woman, who spent more than $70,000 building a one-room house that is nothing but a glass cage on stilts."[17] It belonged to a movement, she declared, that promoted "the mystical idea that 'less is more'" and thus "unlivability, stripped-down emptiness, lack of storage space and therefore lack of possessions." Behind this, she claimed, was "a self-chosen elite who are trying to tell us what we should like and how we should live." And, she declared ominously, "accepting dictators in matters of taste" would lead to accepting "dictators in other departments of life." The fact that Mies was German certainly did not help. Executive editor Joseph Barry followed suit in the next issue with his "Report on the American Battle between Good and Bad Modern Houses," featuring the Farnsworth House as "a particularly fine example of a bad modern house." He quoted Edith Farnsworth, who felt unsafe and restless, and hemmed in by the design's stringency: "Mies talks about 'free space' but his space is very fixed. I can't even put a clothes hanger in my house without considering how it affects everything from the outside."[18]

Proof of Concept

While awaiting the result of the lawsuit, Mies tried applying the concept elsewhere, probably also in an attempt to show its validity. When approached by businessman Leon Caine, who wanted to build a home in Winnetka, Illinois, Mies scaled up the Farnsworth House for a family with three children and a maid. The result was a large, open glass volume with the same outside I-beams, four columns inside, and larger plates of glass. Its domestic landscape evolved from the earlier court house studies, providing an open, central area flanked by the children's and parents' bedroom wings. The house was meant to sit on a wide and deep podium over uneven terrain. It remained unexecuted.

Figure 8.9. Ludwig Mies van der Rohe, Core House project (also known as the "50 × 50 House"), 1952. Model. Photograph by Hedrich-Blessing. Chicago History Museum.

Aiming for a flexible type for mass production, Mies designed a house of a comparable size, known as the Core House (later often called the "50 × 50 House") but on a square plan of 50 by 50 feet (15.2 by 15.2 meters), yielding 2,500 square feet (232 square meters) (figure 8.9). The interior provided space for a couple with two children, two bathrooms, and a central fireplace. In his usual quest for thinking problems through to their absolute, radical end, Mies came up with the idea of having just one column in the center of each wall, thus bringing their number down to four (instead of eight at the Farnsworth House). The corners would be column-free, offering closer communion with nature. Of course, structurally, this was a terrible idea. Two 25-foot- (7.6-meter-) long cantilevers from a single point would have met under a ninety-degree angle at each corner. Any snow load, for example, would have pressed particularly hard onto those unsupported glass corners. Myron Goldsmith, a young architect and engineer in Mies's office, was tasked with working out the details. He had difficulties "calculating it out...trying all kinds of modifications to make it work." He drew several deflection diagrams to explain to Mies the effect of the center columns. At some point he sketched a diagonal grid instead, which would have been slightly advantageous, but he "didn't know if [Mies] would stand for it."[19] *Architectural Forum* barely concealed its skepticism: "Besides placing emphasis truly on the tensile qualities of steel, this approach removes the visual problem of the corner post—although at the same time it enlarges the structural problem of connections....The steel frame, for a house 50' × 50' [15.2 × 15.2 meters] would cost about 40% more than a steel frame with corner posts, but it looks as if might be well worth it."[20] About ninety sketches, thirty technical drawings, and photographs of a model exist in the archive.[21] An extensive article in the *Chicago Tribune* about the "Core House" emphasized its flexibility (it came in three versions of 40 by 40 feet, or 12.2 by 12.2 meters; 50 by 50 feet, or 15.2 by 15.2 meters; and 60 by 60 feet, or 18.3 by 18.3 meters) and multifunctionality: "Dinner in Yesterday's Bedroom: It's Possible in This Flexible Plan."[22]

Two commissions, which used elements of the Farnsworth House to demonstrate their validity for future mass production, were realized for clients in Mies's immediate orbit while the court case was pending. One was for Robert H. McCormick, one of the investors behind 860/880 Lake Shore Drive (built 1951–52); the other one was for Morris Greenwald, the brother of developer Herbert Greenwald.

As a prototype for mass production, the McCormick House in Elmhurst, Illinois, of 1952 had to forego expensively crafted details such as plug welds and the welding seams are visible at the edges of the steel posts (figure 8.10). The approach showed a similarity to the Lake Shore Drive Apartments, "with the difference that here he can leave out the columns entirely and let the mullions support the roof."[23] Rolled I-beams were applied to the façade in dense sequence, their structural role being quite different from the Farnsworth House. They did not touch the ground, but merely transferred the weight of the roof beams to the steel frame resting on the concrete foundation. Their dense sequence is less visually appealing than the light elegance at the Farnsworth House. Mies noticed that himself, and made the unlikely claim to a reporter that "the proper steel sections for vertical members were not available at the time of construction," and that, therefore, the sections in place were "one inch larger than was specified."[24]

The ceiling showed the I beams openly; the plywood partition walls were not load-bearing (figure 8.11). Similar houses, proposed for mass development by Robert McCormick and Herbert Greenwald, did not attract sufficient interest, and thus only two were ever built. One of the main reasons was the high cost, due to the price of steel and its abundant application in the house. The simple McCormick House, which combined two base units, had cost $45,000.

Morris Greenwald's house in Weston, Connecticut, was commissioned at the same time and based on the same concept, but only built in 1955.[25] The idea of prefabrication of housing was very much in the air and had experienced some substantial success in recent years. In Mies's orbit, Walter Gropius at Harvard, and Konrad Wachsmann, who had come to teach at IIT in 1949, had worked with great dedication on getting a prefabricated house off the ground. Their General Panel Corporation produced around five hundred houses altogether (instead of the anticipated ten thousand units annually), while the industry itself

was flourishing in the United States. There were seventy active firms, and about two hundred thousand units were manufactured during the war.[26]

One of Mies's students, Jacques Brownson, improved on Mies's concept for his own single-story glass and steel house, which he had built in Geneva, Illinois, between 1949 and 1952, working with Mies's structural engineers Frank Kornacker and Ernest Vlad. Apparently, Mies came to visit often during the court case against Edith Farnsworth, which unfolded at the courthouse nearby. The house has an exoskeleton (outside girders carry the roof) and a wider interior, and it sits firmly on the ground. While the living room in the front is fully glass enclosed and has a covered terrace, the back has brick infill walls for privacy and insulation.

1943–52   The Conchoidal Chair

The little chair that Mies had drawn into his elevation of the Farnsworth House merits some consideration (see figure 8.1). It was Mies's last attempt at designing a piece of furniture—another quest that lasted almost a decade, producing hundreds of drawings and ultimately (almost) no result. Mies responded to two current trends and events: the general conversation about plastics in furniture, and MoMA's 1940–41 competition Organic Design in Home Furnishings, followed by an exhibition of the same name in 1941, in which Eero Saarinen and Charles Eames presented several versions of a molded plywood chair on wooden or metal legs.[27] Encouraged by the formal freedom of the plywood designs in the *Organic Design* show, Mies recognized the potential of malleable plastic, culminating in a first patent application, together with Anton Lorenz, in 1943.

In October 1947, MoMA announced the International Competition for Low-Cost Furniture Design in collaboration with several prominent furniture producers (such as Knoll and Herman Miller).[28] Mies was asked to be on the jury, just as sketches of his own "Conchoidal Chair…to be manufactured in plastics" were shown in his own concurrent MoMA exhibition.[29] While this precluded him from participating, he was certainly mindful of his pending patent. With Lorenz he reconfigured their 1943 design, abandoned the initial patent, and resubmitted it in June 1948, clearly in an attempt to claim some turf in the expected surge of new, low-cost furniture pieces out of plastic. Mies now emphasized that the chair would be "of great strength and yet light in weight…readily manufactured

< Figure 8.10. Ludwig Mies van der Rohe, McCormick House, Elmhurst, Illinois, 1952. Exterior view.

< Figure 8.11. Ludwig Mies van der Rohe, McCormick House, Elmhurst, Illinois, 1952. Interior view.

Figure 8.12. Ludwig Mies van der Rohe, sketches of the Conchoidal Chair, ca. 1940. Pencil on cream light wove paper, 6 × 8 3/16 in. (15.2 cm × 20.8 cm).

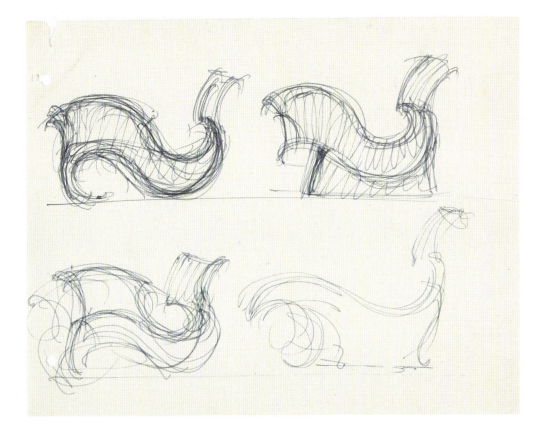

at low costs," and "shaped in accordance with the form of the body of an occupant." It was to be made from a "plastic material molded or pressed into shape." In Mies's early sketches, the chair, low slung and somewhat awkward, was made of one piece (figure 8.12). In the patent application of 1948, however, in an attempt to keep costs down and make production easier, there were two pieces—one that combined seat, armrest, and support underneath, and a second one with the backrest and the back supports.[30] The design emphasized qualities that could only be achieved with malleable plastic, but not plywood, namely varying thicknesses that responded to particular load conditions and provided weight reduction (figure 8.13). When the patent was finally granted, however, in 1952, its ideas were not innovative anymore.

The competition was an enormous success—receiving almost three thousand entries from thirty-one countries. Awards were announced in January 1949, and the museum exhibited the results from May 17 to July 16, 1950, entitled *Prize Designs for Modern Furniture,* and published a catalogue (figure 8.14). Charles and Ray Eames won second prize for a molded fiber glass chair, "close to the original concept" of their laminated plywood chair of 1940.[31] They also submitted a prototype of "La Chaise," an evocative piece in molded plastic on slender metal supports (figure 8.15).

Mies van der Rohe's role on the jury clearly had an impact on the competition's results. Several of his former students and devotees had participated as a group from the Armour Research Foundation (which had held onto the Armour name, while being part of IIT)— among them A. James Speyer, who had studied with Mies and was teaching at IIT, and Daniel Brenner, one of Mies's star students and professional partner of George Danforth. Speyer admired Mies's chair, as was obvious from his review of Mies's 1947 show at MoMA:

Figure 8.13. Ludwig Mies van der Rohe and Anton Lorenz, Conchoidal Chair, 1943. Line drawing in patent application.

Figure 8.14. Installation view of the exhibition *Prize Designs for Modern Furniture,* 1950, at the Museum of Modern Art. Museum of Modern Art, New York. Note the competition entry from the Armour Research Foundation on the left behind Charles and Ray Eames's "La Chaise."

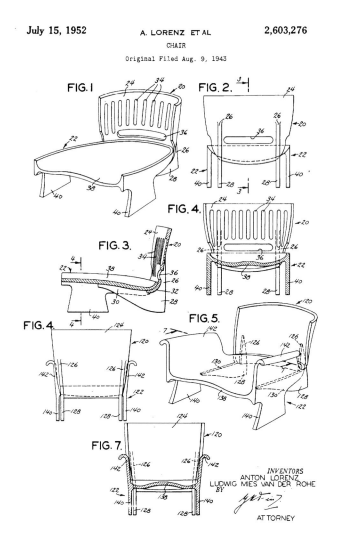

Among the most striking of Mies van der Rohe's latest developments is his design for a chair of sheet plastic. This has the same large scale and inference of comfort as the earlier metal examples. The art of his furniture derives from structure exactly as does that of his building. Difference in construction of the plastic and metal chairs reflects the difference in intrinsic qualities of the two materials.... The plastic chairs utilize continuous surfaces—the strong shell-like quality of the material. It is formed to the body for comfort, and constructed in a manner inspired by the formation of sea shells which the architect has been studying.[32]

Speyer's team produced a chair that was comparable to Mies's pending patent and similar to his drawings, "a large, comfortable one-piece chair in molded plastic designed to issue from its mold fully finished with integral coloring and perfect surface" (figure 8.16). According to the jury, which awarded it a $2,500 prize, the armchair "seemed somewhat overscaled for the average small home, a factor which in no way diminished its many other virtues."[33] In the exhibition, this one-piece chair was shown next to Charles Eames and Ray Eames's "La Chaise," which was never mass-produced during their lifetime, due to the complicated

Figure 8.15. Charles Eames and Ray Eames, full-scale model of the Chaise Longue ("La Chaise"), 1947–48. Hard rubber foam, plastic, wood, and metal, 32 1/2 × 59 × 34 1/4 in. (82.5 × 149.8 × 87 cm). Museum of Modern Art, New York.

Figure 8.16. Armour Research Institute chair design competition entry for the 1947 International Competition for Low-Cost Furniture Design at the Museum of Modern Art. Published in Edgar Kaufmann, Jr., ed., *Prize Designs for Modern Furniture* (New York: Museum of Modern Art, 1950), 45.

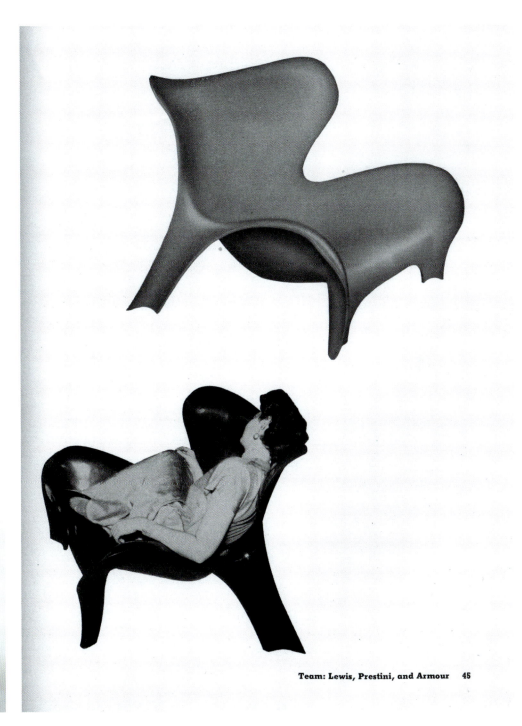

Team: Lewis, Prestini, and Armour 45

production process. Such complications were surely the reason why the Mies-inspired chair of the Armour Research Foundation did not have any future either. Werner Blaser dryly noted that "Mies' unmistakable influence shows in the many prizes awarded to the numerous designs proposing plastic shells."[34]

1945–46   Joseph Cantor's Drive-In Restaurant and House

In 1945, Mies had been approached by an entrepreneur from Indianapolis, Joseph Cantor, who was hoping to build a drive-in restaurant, a building type quickly gaining popularity. A recognizable image, visible from afar, would be important. It was an enticing proposition—while Mies was in Peter Behrens's office in Berlin in 1910, Behrens had described changing modes of perception from the motor car and their potential influence on architectural design: "When we race through the streets of our metropolis in a super-fast vehicle, we can no longer recognize the details of the buildings....Such a way of looking at the world, which has become a constant habit, needs an architecture with forms as coherent and calm as possible."[35] Mies had written an essay on the planning of highways in 1932, where he argued against a "rampant spread of advertising," which should be "clustered to indicate danger zones...restricted to the circumference of cities," and held in check by "central control" and design guidelines.[36]

Working with his assistant Myron Goldsmith, Mies came up with a simple glass box with a protruding roof on either side, presumably to protect parked cars. Two enormous steel girders would hold the ceiling and allow for a wide-open interior space without columns. Mies deployed these girders over the long side and greatly increased their size for dramatic effect. "Mies wanted a big statement, a visible statement," Goldsmith recalled.[37] One cannot help thinking of Hendrik Petrus Berlage's Amsterdam Stock Exchange (see figure 1.39), with its oversized girder above the main hall, mainly placed there for expressive purposes, and so heavy that its horizontal thrust cracked the side walls until it was tamed by tension rods. Mies's surviving floor plan does not indicate the functionality of a real drive-in where customers remain in their cars while ordering and eating. Waiters and waitresses (sometimes on roller skates) would come out to the vehicle to take orders and deliver meals on a tray to be attached to the inside of the door. Mies's interior had two sections, one with a long counter surrounding a square for the servers, a central kitchen, and tables and seats on the other sides. Bathrooms and storage were in the basement. Edward Duckett built a beautiful model, photographed by Hedrich-Blessing lit from underneath (figure 8.17).

Two sketches from Mies's hand, with and without the tall roof girder, show the luminosity inside the restaurant and large lettering ("Fairpost") outside—in one case as big

Figure 8.17. Ludwig Mies van der Rohe, Cantor Drive-In project, Indianapolis, 1946. Model. Photograph by Hedrich-Blessing. Chicago History Museum.

as the restaurant itself, spanning the adjacent parking lot (figure 8.18). Sadly, the project came to naught.

The home that Mies designed for Mr. Cantor, also unexecuted, was still very much in the vein of the Barcelona Pavilion, with an asymmetrical spatial expanse, barely visible columns, and a protruding roof (figure 8.19). Two additional commissions in Indianapolis would come from Cantor's friend Harry E. Berke, for an office building and an apartment tower; these, however, while also not built, were important steps in Mies's stylistic evolution (see figures 8.57, 8.58).

Cantor and Berke had been members of the Pi Lambda Phi fraternity at Indiana University in Bloomington, and the group commissioned Mies to design a new fraternity house in 1952.[38] Mies was quite invested, traveled to Bloomington, sent photos of the Farnsworth House and Lake Shore Drive, and, when money ran out, offered to work at cost.[39] The

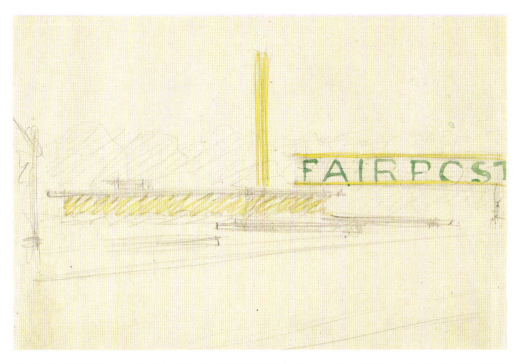

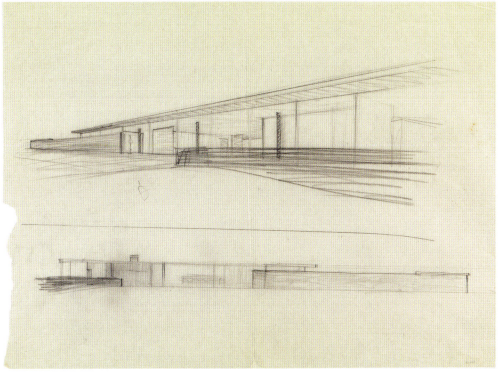

Figure 8.18. Ludwig Mies van der Rohe, Cantor Drive-In project, Indianapolis, 1946. Exterior perspective. Pencil and colored pencil on paper, 6 1/2 × 8 in. (16.5 × 20.3 cm). Museum of Modern Art, New York. The Mies van der Rohe Archive, gift of the architect.

Figure 8.19. Ludwig Mies van der Rohe, Cantor House project, Indianapolis, 1946–47. Exterior perspective and elevation sketch. Charcoal on tracing paper, 21 × 29 3/4 in. (53.3 × 75.6 cm). Museum of Modern Art, New York. The Mies van der Rohe Archive, gift of the architect.

project fizzled out in 1957, but was finally executed for the university's architecture school in 2020–21 (financed by Sidney Eskenazi, a later member of Pi Lambda Phi). The architect Thomas Phifer stayed as close to Mies's design as possible and thus added a spectacular, unique example to a taxonomy of Mies's building types. The Farnsworth vocabulary is fully evident, while the two-story elevation, receding lower first floor, and central opening provided ideas for the Bacardi Headquarters outside of Mexico City (see figures 9.41, 9.42).

1947   Two Exhibitions

While the Promontory Apartments in Chicago were readied for their groundbreaking on November 9, 1947 (see below), Mies finally received prominent recognition in the United States with two exhibitions and a first monograph. From May 16 to June 7, 1947, the Renaissance Society at the University of Chicago honored him with a show, in which a model of the Promontory Apartments was prominently displayed (figure 8.20). Curator Ulrich Middeldorf, like Mies a recent immigrant from Germany, and now chairman of the university's art department, was mindful of the local audience and the raw concrete of the Promontory Apartments about to go up, writing: "Mies van der Rohe's buildings are no dish for people spoilt by soft refinements or modern sensationalism."[40] He stated that they were "severe," even "rugged," but "extremely useable and livable for men of good and healthy tastes," and their architect was a man of "extreme seriousness, devotion to a task, an almost ascetic modesty, and an incorruptible honesty."[41] Despite its name, the society had, since 1915, shown contemporary art and architecture, such as recent exhibitions on László Moholy-Nagy, Richard Neutra, and Paul Klee. In the fall of 1947, Mies arranged and designed an exhibition about his old friend Theo van Doesburg, who had died in 1931 at the age of forty-one.[42] Van Doesburg's widow, Nelly, came to Chicago to help set it up, and Mies and Nelly were romantically involved for a few months.[43]

From September 16, 1947, to January 25, 1948, the Museum of Modern Art in New York held a larger Mies exhibition, receiving much attention. Mies worked closely with Philip Johnson on the display and the catalogue. Most of his pre-1938 work was still in Germany; original drawings thus only represented the later work. In contrast to Middeldorf, Johnson barely mentioned the Promontory Apartments (which were only shown in the catalogue) and emphasized Mies's "daring, clarity, refinement…technical soundness [and] finest possible craftsmanship."[44]

Figure 8.20. Installation view of the *Mies van der Rohe* exhibition at the Renaissance Society, Chicago, 1947. Photograph by Hedrich-Blessing. Chicago History Museum.

The most brilliant accomplishment on display was the arrangement of the show itself. The square room was punctured by four piers, against which Mies placed four wall-high (14-foot, or 4.3-meter) photomurals of an early project (figures 8.21–8.23). The visitor found himself face-to-face with the Monument to the November Revolution, inside the Barcelona Pavilion, or looking up at the two glass skyscraper designs. A 1934 sketch of a mountain house and an interior view of the Tugendhat House were shown in the same size on the perimeter walls. The interior view of the Tugendhat House was a particularly odd choice, as the curtains are fully drawn, rendering the striking glass walls invisible and exposing Mies's rather unsuccessful distribution of light sources. There was also a large reproduction of the Concrete Office Building drawing and additional photos from Barcelona and Brno, but no images of the Weissenhof Estate, Afrikanische Strasse Housing Estate, or the Wolf House in Guben (all shown in the catalogue, however).

Relatively little space was dedicated to the evolving plans of the IIT campus, of which the Minerals and Metals Building had been built and Alumni Memorial Hall was almost finished. There were models of the Cantor Drive-In restaurant in Indiana and the Farnsworth and Resor houses, the latter in an abstracted version, produced for the show. The two buildings became siblings, oblong boxes hovering above ground—one entirely open, with a dominant structure, the other closed, its structure a mystery. Barcelona and Brno chairs were assembled in three different configurations. Johnson's official press release did not shy away from grand claims: "This country may now be assisting at the birth of an architecture as expressive of the industrial age as Gothic was of its age of ecclesiasticism. A curious parallel between the now nameless master builders of the Middle Ages and one of the great architects of modern times is offered."[45]

The timing of the exhibition at MoMA was hardly ideal. The Promontory Apartments were just breaking ground, and several buildings on the IIT campus were under construction, months away from being photogenic enough for an exhibition. Thus, Mies quickly produced a number of visionary projects, such as the collage of a "Concert Hall," which George Danforth created with the help of an interior view of Albert Kahn's Glenn L. Martin Aircraft Plant. The caption read:

Figure 8.23. Installation view of the *Mies van der Rohe* exhibition at the Museum of Modern Art, New York, September 16, 1947–January 25, 1948. Note the 1:1 mockup of the corner of the planned Library and Administration Building at the Illinois Institute of Technology in the foreground. Photograph by Soichi Sunami. (Sunami retouched the lighting devices from the ceiling.) Museum of Modern Art, New York.

The entire hall is a design in free screens that seem to float in a huge cage of steel and glass. The blue is the sloping plane of the floor, the thin gray area above it marks the edge of the platform. The silver screen is the back wall of the auditorium. The yellow screen on the left and the black screen on the right form the sides of the hall, and the white area above is the acoustical ceiling. Of the steel and glass construction Mies says: "Factory construction—wide spans and bridge trusses—is the only true modern structural system. It is the duty of the architect to utilize this system in the practice of his art."[46]

In the catalogue, Philip Johnson called the Concert Hall Mies's "most astounding new creation," derived from the lecture hall at the Museum for a Small City: "There walls and ceilings are pulled apart and disposed within a trussed steel and glass cage. The concept of flowing horizontal space, first expressed in the brick country house of 1923 and carried on to its triumphant culmination in the Barcelona Pavilion, now expands: space eddies in all directions among interior planes of subaqueous weightlessness."[47]

Apparently, the project had begun with a design task for students around 1942, when Mies was working on the Metals and Minerals Building and was inspired by Albert Kahn's work. Mies had Kahn's image enlarged to three feet (one meter) wide and encouraged his student Paul Campagna to see "how you can hang paper—try to cut paper to make a room." Inspired by Campagna's collage, Mies and Danforth produced a larger version (five feet, or 1.5 meters, wide) for the MoMA exhibition.[48] That one Mies gave to his friend Mary Callery, who replaced the photograph of an Aristide Maillol figure in the foreground with that of an Egyptian scribe, and later donated it to the Museum of Modern Art (figure 8.24).[49]

The Kahn building that Mies and his student picked had the largest span ever constructed, at 300 feet (91 meters) long and 30 feet (9.1 meters) high. The Glenn L. Martin Assembly Building in Middle River, Maryland, produced bomber planes there, many of them used in the war against Germany. Neil Levine has pointed at the resulting political charge, but we do not know how consciously Mies responded to the building's function when he imagined a concert hall inside—if the old biblical admonition of "turning swords into plowshares" (Isaiah 2:3–4) ever crossed his mind.[50] After all, the photo of Kahn's building that Mies used was taken before the war in 1938; the MoMA show was after the war. In all likelihood, Mies was mostly interested in the uninterrupted, open space, succinctly different from the forest of columns in his Museum for a Small City.

Figure 8.24. Ludwig Mies van der Rohe, Concert Hall project, 1942–47. Collage over photograph, 29 1/2 × 62 in. (74.9 × 157.5 cm). Museum of Modern Art, New York. The Mies van der Rohe Archive, Gift of Mary Callery.

He paired the collage at MoMA with another one, a longitudinal, nine-foot- (2.7-meter-) long section of a "Theater" with a floating acoustic ceiling and raised auditorium, their curved sections reminiscent of his recent Conchoidal Chair (figure 8.25). They hovered inside a glass enclosed space like the Field House of 1941, his first unexecuted design for the IIT campus (see figure 7.31). This pristine glass box was divided into sixteen bays (at two panes each), with sixteen panes of glass stacked vertically in such a way that two panes horizontally had the same proportions as the entire building—a perfect application of the abovementioned "regulating lines" he applied at the Minerals and Metals Building. In great contrast to the Martin Assembly Building plant, this building had no structural elements, no roof trusses, and no girders to protect the tall glass walls from wind impact. The two illustrations next to each other represented the two poles between which Mies's work oscillated—the realism of necessary structure, and the idealism of essentialist form. A few steps from there at the exhibition, the model of the 1943 Cantor Drive-In suggested a solution: an exoskeleton could carry the roof load and stabilize the façade, and thus provide uninterrupted space inside. It would be applied at Crown Hall and the Museum of Fine Arts in Houston a few years later. The theater concepts presented here found an echo in Mies's unsuccessful competition entry for a city theater in Mannheim (1953), where two auditoria were freestanding inserts in a large, glass cube with an exoskeleton for its roof structure (figure 8.26). The influence of the Concert Hall collage could be found at the same time in Mies's project for a Chicago Convention Center, which he developed with three graduate students, Yujiro Miwa, Henry Kanazawa, and Pao-Chi Chang (figure 8.27). The two-way truss roof system,

Figure 8.25. Ludwig Mies van der Rohe, Theater project, 1947. Combined elevation and section. Graphite, ink, cut-and-pasted papers, and cut-and-pasted photoreproductions on illustration board, 48 × 96 in. (121.9 × 243.8 cm). Museum of Modern Art, New York. The Mies van der Rohe Archive, gift of the architect.

Figure 8.26. Ludwig Mies van der Rohe, Mannheim Theater competition project, 1953. Model. Photograph by Hedrich-Blessing. Chicago History Museum.

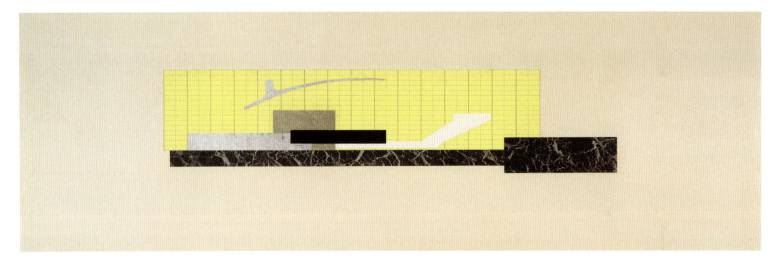

spanning an unprecedented 720 feet (219.5 meters), was supported on its perimeter by thin, cross-braced, and marble-clad outside walls, and underneath them twenty-four low piers—a daring arrangement given Chicago's occasional strong winds and heavy snow loads. A collage paired an interior model shot with *Life* magazine's photo of enthusiastic crowds at the 1952 Republican National Convention (figure 8.28). It is important in this context to recognize the presence at IIT of Konrad Wachsmann, the German-born pioneer of space-frame construction who taught from 1949 to 1964 at the Institute of Design (the successor to Moholy-Nagy's abovementioned New Bauhaus), which had been incorporated into IIT in 1949. His work and expertise had an important influence on Mies and his students designing wide-span structures. An appreciative piece on Mies by him appeared in 1952, when Mies was drumming up support in the press while the Farnsworth court case was lingering.[51]

The exuberant prose that Johnson had found for the Concert Hall at the 1947 exhibition was matched by his description of another unbuilt project, the Library and Administration Building for IIT, "possibly Mies's greatest single design" and "undoubtedly…one of the most impressive enclosed spaces in the history of modern architecture" (figures 8.29, 8.30).[52] In important aspects it was a predecessor of Crown Hall. Mies did not adhere to the general module for IIT of 24 by 24 by 12 feet (7.3 by 7.3 by 3.7 meters), but rather imagined each bay 64 feet (19.5 meters) wide and 30 feet (9.1 meters) high, for an overall length of 300 feet (91.4 meters) by 200 feet (61 meters). The offices would be enclosed by eight-foot- (2.4-meter-) high partitions, but enjoy the 30-foot- (9.1-meter-) high ceilings of the open space, except where a floating mezzanine in the center and the library stacks provided lower ceiling height. Similar to the Metals and Minerals Building, a largely single-story building did not require fire protection of its load-bearing structure, and a perspective and several detail drawings showed connections to adjacent brick or glass walls. It speaks to the importance assigned to this detail that it was featured as a three-dimensional centerpiece in the show as a 1:1 mockup of the corner connection (see figure 8.23). The mighty steel I-beam was a simulacrum of painted pinewood, produced by MoMA's installation department, but it was attached to real bricks, sourced to specifications from Mies's office (Johnson noted the poor craftsmanship of the brick layer).[53] It seems likely that no one among the visitors

Figure 8.27. Ludwig Mies van der Rohe, Yujiro Miwa, Henry Kanazawa, and Pao-Chi Chang, Chicago Convention Center project, 1953–54. Model. Photograph by Hedrich-Blessing. Chicago History Museum.

>> Figure 8.28. Ludwig Mies van der Rohe, Yujiro Miwa, Henry Kanazawa, and Pao-Chi Chang, Chicago Convention Center project, 1953–54. Interior perspective, preliminary version. Collage of cut-and-pasted reproductions, photograph, and paper on composition board, 33 × 48 in. (83.8 × 121.9 cm). Museum of Modern Art, New York. The Mies van der Rohe Archive, gift of the architect.

had ever seen a similar display in an art museum, nor tried to make sense of sixteen different detail drawings in the catalogue (figure 8.31).

The display at the 1947 MoMA exhibition was a watershed moment. Mies's early work loomed large in the black-and-white photos, arranged in the asymmetrical placement of freestanding walls, which Mies used here for the last time. The 1:1 corner model represented his carefully detailed structural solutions, which would dominate his American work. His interest in photomurals and their spatial impact bridged the two halves of his career. Several reviewers emphasized the unusual arrangement:

> First likely to impress visitors,…is the installation, supervised by the architect himself. Here spaciousness reflects the elements that more perhaps than any other single attribute characterizes the work of the distinguished modernist.…The exhibition…involves the customary use of plans, renderings, sketches, photographs and models. But these are presented with an almost breath-taking largeness of effect. Several of the photographs have been blown up to mural size. And excellent advantage has been taken of the museum's system of movable walls, which makes possible the creation of apparently enormous vistas.[54]

The young designer Charles Eames published a series of photographs (inexplicably taken from a shoe's vantage point) in the magazine *Arts and Architecture.* He wrote:

> The significant thing seems to be the way in which he has taken documents of his architecture and furniture and used them as elements in creating a space that says, "this is what it's all about." Certainly, it is the experience of walking through that space and seeing others move in it that is the high point of the exhibition.…In the sudden change of scale from a huge photo mural of a small pencil sketch, to quarter-inch-to-the-foot [roughly equivalent to a 1:50-scale] model, to man, to twice-life-size photograph, to actual pieces of furniture…one feels the…frame of reference from which the history of Mies van der Rohe's work can be examined.…The exhibition itself provides the smell and feel of what makes it, and Mies van der Rohe, great.[55]

Figure 8.29. Ludwig Mies van der Rohe, Library and Administration Building, Illinois Institute of Technology campus, Chicago, ca. 1944. Charcoal, graphite, and yellow pencil on tracing paper, 28 × 42 in. (72 × 106.7 cm). Art Institute of Chicago.

Figure 8.30. Ludwig Mies van der Rohe, Library and Administration Building, Illinois Institute of Technology campus, Chicago, ca. 1944. Perspective of the southeast corner. Delineator: Sing Mau Chau. Pencil on tracing paper, 44 × 34 in. (111.8 × 86.4 cm). Museum of Modern Art, New York. The Mies van der Rohe Archive, gift of the architect.

Figure 8.31. Ludwig Mies van der Rohe, Library and Administration Building, Illinois Institute of Technology campus, Chicago, ca. 1944. Horizontal section through steel column and brick connection at the corner. See the 1:1 model of this detail at the 1947 MoMA exhibition shown in Figure 8.23.

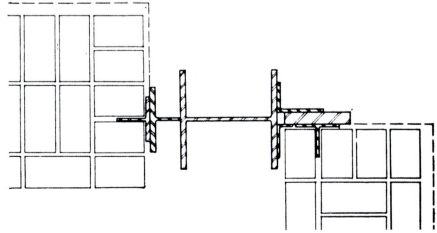

Reviewers of the accompanying book were less kind. Cambridge architect Robert Woods Kennedy noted that Johnson's text left "most of the questions one has about Mies still unanswered" as it was "almost purely a eulogy." His most pressing question referred to the structural detail of Mies's brick and steel corner for the IIT Library and Administration Building (see figures 8.23, 8.30, 8.31). Kennedy noted that the steel was "exposed both on the inside and the outside. There is much evidence to show, and it is generally believed, that this is very bad practice. One wonders whether or not condensation forms on the inside, whether convection heat losses are not far greater than necessary,...most of the detailing here displayed is based on practices studiously avoided by all architects, at considerable pains and expense."[56] Of course, Kennedy was absolutely correct. The corner shown at the exhibition would have produced much condensation water inside on a cold Chicago day, as the Minerals and Metals Building had already demonstrated. The detail could, however, claim to be "truthful"—it did show the essential construction itself, which could not be claimed for the solutions Mies settled on shortly afterward and applied continuously throughout the rest of his life.

A critic of the *New York Herald Tribune* noted a "sharp break in Mies's style" which he attributed to the "modern American building industry [being] radically different from the European building industry before the war....His architecture has calmly faced the reality of industrialized construction. It emerges naked as a factory....He is trying to show that honest building can still be beautiful building."[57]

When young art historian Joseph Rykwert reviewed Johnson's publication for the noble *Burlington Magazine,* he did not hold back. While he found the book disappointing, as it lacked any "attempt at a critical evaluation of van der Rohe's works, either in relation to one another or to the work of his contemporaries," what bothered him more was the quality of Mies's recent architecture itself. He felt that Mies's earlier work in Stuttgart, Barcelona, and Brno had lifted him to a level almost akin to that of Gropius or Le Corbusier, "but in 1945 many of his admirers were so disturbed by the publication of the scheme for the Metals and

Figure 8.32. Ludwig Mies van der Rohe, Alumni Memorial Hall, Illinois Institute of Technology campus, Chicago, 1948. Corner detail under construction. Photograph by Hedrich-Blessing. Chicago History Museum.

Minerals building of the Illinois Institute of Technology that alarm changed to despondency on the publication of the scheme for the whole Institute in 1947."[58] Rykwert chided the book for making "no attempt to account for the lapse which occurs when van der Rohe turns from his most experimental projects of the 'twenties to the flabby villas of the 'thirties; or for the violent change of attitude which produced the slick, lucid, sickening scheme for the Illinois Institute."[59] Rykwert was judging the campus designs from MoMA's publication, which still contained several images of Mies's original designs of partially elevated structures. What was currently under construction at IIT was unlikely to elicit a more positive response from him.

1947   Continuous Work at Illinois Institute of Technology

In the spring of 1947, Mies invited the firm of Hedrich-Blessing to photograph the construction phase of Alumni Memorial Hall at IIT (figure 8.32). It was highly unusual to invite a prominent, costly photo agency to document structural details on a building site, but it demonstrates the importance that Mies assigned to the construction process, and he might have envisioned the photographs as future teaching tools. Many were never published. Mies would continue the practice with most of his buildings in the following years. After he had to make his peace with the fact that his campus buildings were not going to be hovering aboveground on slender, cruciform stilts, to allow the free flow of space and pedestrian traffic across campus, he shifted his focus and energy to structural details. After his Minerals and Metals Building had been opened in 1943, finally Alumni Memorial Hall (originally called the Navy Building), as well as Wishnick and Perlstein halls, were under construction.

Being two- or three-story structures, their load-bearing steel frames had to be clad in concrete or other fire-retardant materials, which rendered them invisible. The corner detail Mies developed here was distinctly different from the one shown at his MoMA exhibition for the Library and Administration Building (see figures 8.23, 8.30), which had been based

Figure 8.33. Ludwig Mies van der Rohe, Alumni Memorial Hall, Illinois Institute of Technology campus, Chicago, 1948. Outside façade. Photograph by Hedrich-Blessing. Chicago History Museum.

Figure 8.34. Ludwig Mies van der Rohe, Alumni Memorial Hall, Illinois Institute of Technology campus, Chicago, 1948. Corner detail. Photograph by Hedrich-Blessing. Chicago History Museum.

on the assumption that the actual structure could remain visible, as much of the building consisted of a single, high-ceilinged, open floor. The new corner design was symmetrical on a diagonal axis at the corner. Different from the approach at the Farnsworth House, where load-bearing I-beams were placed on the outside, here non-load-bearing I-beams were welded to a steel plate covering the concrete column (with the actual load-bearing I-beam inside) and placed flush with the brick wall, providing stability and visual rhythm (figures 8.33, 8.34). Since steel contracts and expands, the joint between brick infill and I-beam deserved special attention. An indentation in the brick wall next to the steel flange created an elegant shadow line while providing an expansion joint. This seemingly elegant solution was paid for with decidedly unelegant details underneath: bricks had to be broken up and stuffed into the I-beam's hollow sides to create the recess. This was difficult and time-consuming to execute and undermined the brick's role as module (figure 8.35). The connections between the vertical and horizontal I-beams were welded and smoothed down for a continuous surface on the outside, while the actual load-bearing connections behind were bolted together. The vertical I-beams seem somehow to rest on a base of (softer) bricks, while in reality they sit halfway on an invisible concrete foundation, protruding just enough to be flush with the brick scrim that covers the concrete and then becomes a wall above.

Both here and at the Farnsworth House, Mies was navigating between a simple, Ruskinian idea of truthfulness, where a structure or material is simply visible in its purest form, and formal ideas about structural representation. This was the gap between "core form" and "art form," as German art historian Karl Bötticher had called it, or proof of Otto Wagner's assurance that "Every architectural form has arisen in construction and has successively become an art-form."[60] It also harked back to the discussion that Mies had witnessed as a young man in Peter Behrens's office in 1911, when the engineer Karl Bernhard publicly accused Behrens of dishonesty, as the main façade of the AEG Turbine Factory did not correspond to the structural realities behind it. Peter Blake addressed the issue:

> Anybody taking a walk on the Mies-designed campus of the Illinois Institute of Technology will find himself surrounded by two- and three-story-high buildings constructed of very simple-looking steel frames that are visible on every facade. If an engineer had designed those steel frames, the chances are that they would be quite complicated in their connections, that the steel sizes would vary depending upon the actual loads supported, and that the total effect would be clumsy and a little cheap. Inserted in I.I.T.'s neat steel frames the visitor will see precise panels of brickwork and tightfitting units of glass. Perhaps he will, at first, find the campus a little monotonous; but with time he may discover some very subtle variations in detail—and he may become conscious of an over-all concept of order that spells unity and design.[61]

1949–52   Illinois Institute of Technology Carr Memorial Chapel of St. Savior

When the commission for an interdenominational chapel on campus came along, Mies, who had been brought up Catholic, might have felt that his customary focus on the representation of structure would have to take a backseat to the building's purpose. An early sketch showed Mies still experimenting with a partial skylight and an exposed skeleton inside; the first developed perspective, which included a parish house nearby, showed a fully glazed western front and a closed eastern façade, and also exposed structural steel struts.

In the end, only the chapel itself, the Carr Memorial Chapel of St. Savior, was built, and a much calmer solution was found in the form of simple load-bearing brick walls with a roof of exposed steel beams (figure 8.36). It is 60 feet (18.3 meters) long, 37 feet (11.3 meters) wide, and 19 feet (5.8 meters) high. Three-fifths of the identical east and west façades are glazed, the only difference being that the western façade has translucent, not transparent, glass. Contrary to custom, the building is entered from the eastern side, and the altar—a solid block of Roman travertine on a black terrazzo podium—sits on the western end. A freestanding concrete block wall behind it is covered by a gray silk curtain with a slim stainless-steel cross suspended in front. The western orientation has the important advantage of western light streaming into the chapel on late afternoons, diffused by the translucent glass, and hidden from direct view by the protruding walls on either side, resulting

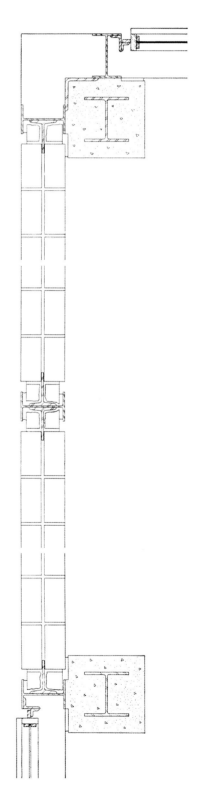

Figure 8.35. Ludwig Mies van der Rohe, Alumni Memorial Hall, Illinois Institute of Technology campus, Chicago, 1948. Corner and wall detail, horizontal section. Note the broken brick pieces inside the I-beam columns.

in a soft glow around the altar. On the occasion of the chapel's dedication on October 26, 1952, Mies told *Arts and Architecture* magazine:

> Architecture should be concerned with the epoch, not the day. The chapel will not grow old....It is of noble character, constructed of good materials, and has beautiful proportions....It is done as things should be done today, taking advantage of our technological means....Too often we think of architecture in terms of the spectacular. There is nothing spectacular about this chapel; it was not meant to be spectacular. It was meant to be simple; and, in fact, it is simple. But in its simplicity, it is not primitive but noble, and it its smallness it is great—in fact, monumental. I would not have built the chapel differently, if I had had a million dollars to do it.[62]

1946–49 Promontory Apartments

Two seismic shifts profoundly altered urban housing in postwar America: cars became affordable, and millions, especially families with children, left for the suburbs. The boom in high-rise apartments for the middle class and the wealthy in large cities had ended with the Depression, and urban apartment towers evolved into new types with smaller units and broader appeal. At the same time, high-rise housing for the poor became a main tool in federally funded urban renewal projects. In the short span of two years, Ludwig Mies van der Rohe made essential and lasting contributions to both.[63]

These contributions had begun in 1946 with the unlikely collaboration between the well-known, sixty-year-old architect—whose career, however, appeared to be floundering—and two inexperienced men in their thirties who were just starting out. Returning from the

Figure 8.36. Ludwig Mies van der Rohe, Robert F. Carr Memorial Chapel of St. Savior, Illinois Institute of Technology campus, Chicago, 1949–52. Main façade, facing east. Photograph by Hedrich-Blessing. Chicago History Museum.

war, Herbert Greenwald had decided to enter the real estate business instead of resuming his graduate studies in philosophy. He wanted to develop cheap apartment buildings for middle-class clients in formerly affluent neighborhoods and asked his friend and neighbor, architect Charles "Skip" Genther, to join him. Genther left his job with Holabird & Root and founded his own company, called PACE Associates (Planners, Architects and Consulting Engineers).

To impress financial backers and future owners, Greenwald needed an architect with an established reputation as an innovator. He was turned down by Frank Lloyd Wright, Eero Saarinen, and Walter Gropius, who, however, suggested Mies. As an IIT alumnus, Genther knew Mies and approached him. After eight years in the United States, Mies had only built three buildings on IIT's campus and—to his great disappointment—had just seen the commission for two dormitories go to Skidmore, Owings & Merrill.[64] Mies agreed to collaborate on Greenwald and Genther's project, whose outcome, however, must have looked rather uncertain. To add a third partner, Greenwald invited John Holsman, who had developed a financing model called Mutual Ownership Trust, in which prospective tenants purchased certificates for an apartment and then paid a monthly rent toward full purchase, while a board of trustees oversaw the building work and carried the financial risk. It took longer to secure the necessary construction loans, which he finally obtained from a Cincinnati life insurance company.[65]

Facing the lake, the Promontory is flanked by two apartment towers typical for the boom years of the 1920s: the sixteen-story Flamingo-on-the-Lake Apartments (1927, William Reichert), in the "Spanish style" with red brick, Portland stone trim, and dark roof tiles to the north, and the similarly elaborate nineteen-story Jackson Towers (1925, Walter W. Ahlschlager) to the south (figure 8.37).[66]

Amid the ostensible elegance of its neighbors, the Promontory arrived with the brashness of a self-assured newcomer. Its relentless grid of 160 identical units between nine exposed concrete piers made no concessions to architectural conventions—there was no discernible

Figure 8.37. Ludwig Mies van der Rohe, Promontory Apartments, Chicago, 1946–49. Main façade facing the lake. The Flamingo-on-the-Lake Apartments (William Reichert, 1927) are on the right. Photograph by Hassan Bagheri.

central axis nor any hint of the usual tripartite division of the façade.[67] Its aluminum ribbon windows spanned the full width of each bay and boldly faced the morning sun over the lake. Promontory Apartments was the first building by Mies van der Rohe in reinforced concrete and the first high-rise building in his career. It was also the first high-rise apartment building in Chicago since the war.

In great contrast, New York had recently seen a veritable flood of apartment towers for lower- and middle-income tenants, thanks to the collaboration of urban planner Robert Moses with investors such as the Metropolitan Life Insurance in so-called "slum clearance" projects. Many thousands of apartments were built throughout the 1940s in projects such as Parkchester (Bronx) in 1938–42, Riverton (Harlem) in 1943, and, most importantly, Stuyvesant Town and Peter Cooper Village in 1943–49, with eleven thousand apartments in thirty-five thirteen-story towers (figure 8.38).[68] They all followed the same design formula of sequential "cross plans" in which four short wings clustered around an elevator core, their steel frames clad with unadorned brick and rows of single windows.

The Promontory Apartments responded to the monotony of these New York projects with a structurally expressive design that referenced the visible frame and wide window openings of typical Chicago School office buildings. According to *Architectural Forum*, it was "a fresh victory for Chicago's way of 'building straight'" and, quoting Skip Genther, "A return to first principles in building."[69]

In an unpublished text of 1933, Mies had declared that the "architectural potential" of a "skeleton structure's clear constructive appearance" had emerged with "large utilitarian buildings," but would eventually be "fully realized in the area of residential architecture."[70] Adapting formal solutions or material applications from industry and commerce had long been one of Mies's key strategies. Whenever a utilitarian concept of this type was adopted, refinements were introduced. In the case of the Promontory Apartments, beige bricks were chosen instead of concrete blocks (and fitted precisely into the concrete frames), as well as wide aluminum windows with hinged lower sections. The use of air-entrained cement ensured a smoother surface and protection against temperature changes. Most importantly, though, Mies introduced setbacks for the concrete piers. The piers are deeper at the bottom, and then recede by about four inches (10 centimeters) above the sixth, eleventh, and sixteenth floors. In oblique sunlight, a staggered shadow line becomes visible (figure 8.39). The tapering thickness made structural sense, as the lower piers have to carry a greater

Figure 8.38. Richmond Shreve and Irwin Clavan, Stuyvesant Town, New York, 1943–49.

load (figure 8.40). Joe Fujikawa remembered: "If you look at Promontory, the columns step back. That was one of Mies's fundamental efforts in architecture, to express the structure of a building, and this did it very, very neatly. It's kind of Gothic in its character, the way it's stepped back; the buttresses reduce in size as it goes up."[71]

All the structural details were worked out by Georgia Louise Harris Brown from Topeka, Kansas. She had been among Mies's first students in Chicago, taking a summer course in 1939. Afterward, she enrolled at the architecture program at the University of Kansas in Lawrence. She returned to IIT as a visiting student for a year in 1942, again studying with Mies. After receiving a bachelor of architecture degree from Lawrence, she started working for Chicago architect Kenneth Roderick O'Neal, another former Mies student. Mies asked her to do the calculations for the Promontory Apartments—"her most exciting experience," as she later recalled.[72] She was then hired by Mies's structural engineer, Frank Kornacker, and ended up doing the statics for the Lake Shore Drive Apartments as well. In 1949, she was only the second female African American architect to get licensed in Chicago. Greenwald, Genther, and Mies worked with Kornacker "to use all possible economies, at the same time providing a building for apartments in the middle-income level,"[73] and at $8.65 per square foot (about $93.70 per square meter), the apartments cost "less than most of Chicago's slum clearance projects."[74]

The first floor contained a spacious, glass-enclosed lobby, recessed from the perimeter in order to create a protective colonnade (figure 8.41). Chicago's recently amended building code required for the first time a modest number of parking spots for apartment buildings— one space for every three apartments. The resulting forty spaces were placed in the back and accessed through open bays on either side of the building.[75]

The footprint's double-T design yielded the largest possible square footage. The layouts of the two- and three-bedroom apartments were more generous than those of their equivalents in New York's Stuyvesant Town. Only three apartments on each floor shared two elevators and two staircases (up to twelve apartments elsewhere), and each apartment had two entrances—the main access from the elevator lobby, and a service door to the kitchen from the emergency staircase (figure 8.42).[76] Circulation space was minimized thanks to an open connection from the foyer to the living/dining room. The comparatively low eight-foot (2.4-meter) ceilings were close to the permissible minimum of seven and a half feet (2.3 meters), considerably lower than in typical prewar apartments. Chicago's zoning code prescribed a height limit on the site (a "volume 3 district") of 198 feet (60.4 meters), into

< Figure 8.39. Ludwig Mies van der Rohe, Promontory Apartments, Chicago, 1946–49. Main façade facing the lake. Photograph by Hedrich-Blessing. Chicago History Museum.

Figure 8.40. Ludwig Mies van der Rohe, Promontory Apartments, Chicago, 1946–49. Façade cross section. Published in *Architectural Forum*, January 1950, 73.

Figure 8.41. Ludwig Mies van der Rohe, Promontory Apartments, Chicago, 1946–49. View of the entrance and ground floor. Photograph by Hassan Bagheri.

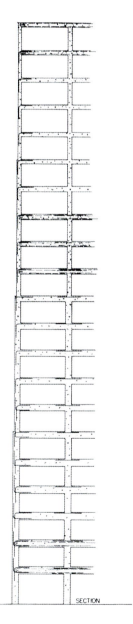

SECTION

which the Promontory Apartments managed to fit twenty-one floors, compared to nineteen floors in the Jackson Towers next door, which had the same overall height.

Mies hired Hedrich-Blessing again, who had already photographed his Minerals and Metals Building, and Bill Hedrich took on the assignment. His first job, on August 31, 1946, was to photograph the model for the Promontory's advertising brochure. According to Hedrich, it was typical for Mies to request changes to a model once he had seen the photographs of it, and then to request another round of photos: "Mies would study...the model, make another minor change and we'd shoot it all again. Oh, I can't remember how many times I photographed some of these models."[77] Worried about the unusually stark appearance of the first Promontory model, Mies had it reworked, giving it a larger base with landscaping and tall trees before being photographed again by Hedrich on September 24, 1946, from a higher vantage point, making the building less imposing. These photos then graced the front and back covers of the advertising brochure, which contained floor plans and penciled interiors with inserted photographs of views outside their wide ribbon windows. Mies and his team reversed a technique here that Mies helped pioneer in the early decades of the century, when he inserted drawings into photographs, for example, of his Friedrichstrasse Skyscraper design. The reverse technique—inserting photographs into larger drawings to suggest a view to the outside—was recently added to the office's

Figure 8.42. Ludwig Mies van der Rohe, Promontory Apartments, Chicago, 1946–49. Floor plan. Published in *Architectural Forum,* January 1950, 71.

Figure 8.43. Ludwig Mies van der Rohe, Promontory Apartments, Chicago, 1946–49. Photomontage in advertising brochure for the Promontory Apartment Building, Chicago, 1947. Lithograph, 9 × 12 in. (22.9 × 30.5 cm). Museum of Modern Art, New York. The Mies van der Rohe Archive, gift of the architect.

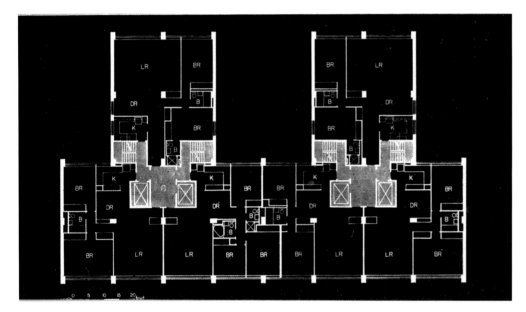

repertoire by George Danforth and William Priestley on the occasion of the Resor House project.[78] Independently, U.S. real estate advertising had begun to insert photos of landscape vistas into drawings of interiors to advertise homes with a view.[79] As Sandy Isenstadt succinctly put it, "Modernism itself [was] recast in the 1930s by its leading ideologues in terms of an individual's optical gratifications."[80]

These little-known montages show eastern views to the lake and the dome of the Museum of Science and Industry toward the south, probably taken from the neighboring apartment towers. The southern view, though, would in reality have been partially blocked by the Jackson Towers nearby. The most surprising aspect of these montages are the drawings of interiors, meant to appeal to the tastes of middle-class buyers and to soften the novelty of the enormous, curtainless windows. In one drawing, a rubber plant and modern sofa were joined by a neo-rococo footstool, picture frame, and coffee table, where three full martini glasses and a cocktail shaker seemed to suggest an impending visit by Mies himself (figure 8.43). The ensemble is placed on an ornamented area rug—one could hardly imagine a more un-Miesian arrangement.

Ground was broken on November 9, 1947, and when the concrete skeleton had been topped out at the end of September 1948, Mies asked Hedrich to photograph the empty, wide-open floor before partition walls came in, and to document the precise moment when the spandrels were inserted in the façade.[81] We see a mason filling in the frame with concrete blocks (figure 8.44). The Promontory Apartments were Mies's first reinforced concrete building, and they were, indeed, a "skin and bones" building, a term he had used in his famous text about the Concrete Office Building in 1923.

In the fall of 1949, the Promontory Apartments began to fill—the lake view apartments being snatched up first. Hedrich returned in January 1950 to photograph three apartments for publicity, after they had been furnished for the occasion (figure 8.45). Mies's own furniture was about to be produced exclusively by Mies's friend and former student Florence Knoll and her husband but was not yet available. Keenly aware of contemporary furniture design, Mies selected recent work by American designers (many pieces thus twenty years younger than Mies's Barcelona Chair, which would show up in time for the sales brochure and publicity shots at Lake Shore Drive). There are, for example, George Nakashima's Windsor chairs, produced by Knoll since 1946, as well as Charles Eames's wooden and metal DCM chairs, just introduced by Herman Miller.[82] Another room showed George Nelson daybeds with their characteristic "hairpin" or "V" legs—produced by Herman Miller since 1948.[83] Despite these interventions, the spaces continued to look uninviting, and many of these carefully staged interior photographs were never used. Hedrich

Figure 8.44. Ludwig Mies van der Rohe, Promontory Apartments, Chicago, 1946–49. Construction photograph before the spandrels under the windows were built. Photograph by Hedrich-Blessing. Chicago History Museum.

Figure 8.45. Ludwig Mies van der Rohe, Promontory Apartments, Chicago, 1946–49. Interior of a city-facing apartment. Photograph by Hedrich-Blessing. Chicago History Museum.

explained that in a "big, open room, there is a lot of ceiling and a lot of carpet showing, and it's very difficult to make them really exciting." Hedrich tried to find viewpoints where a "vase" or "column" in the foreground conveyed depth, and superimposed two images of different exposures in order to show both the inside and outside.[84] Mies had given Hedrich firm instructions: "Please do not use filters on my work....I want the sky to be white and I want to see reflections on the glass of my building. I want it to be in black and white."[85] Facing away from the window and with the help of additional light sources, Hedrich managed to give some interiors a more inviting look, showing the open spatial connection toward the kitchen and dining area, as well as a George Nelson–inspired storage wall with bookshelves and a built-in radio.

Concrete had been the only affordable option at the time, but Mies developed an alternative façade in steel, with two key elements of future approaches: he moved the columns inside and placed mullions "outside the building surface to form strong vertical accents" (figure 8.46).[86] He maintained the three-partite subdivision of each bay as well as equal width for each window. If the mullions already have the I-beam shape they got at Lake Shore Drive, it is impossible to tell.

1949 Algonquin I

Emboldened by the Promontory's apparent success, and before it was finished (in 1949), Herb Greenwald turned to his next project, the Algonquin Apartments, a few blocks further north, with the same group of collaborators. Two twenty-one-story high-rises with five-by-four and five-by-five bays were positioned on adjacent sites as solitaires, each accompanied by a parking lot and a generous garden. They used the Promontory's essential vocabulary of concrete piers and bays. Each one contained four apartments around a central core with elevators and staircases. The more expensive apartments in the five-by-five tower would have three bedrooms, their neighbors two. These unexecuted "twin

Fig. 8.46. Ludwig Mies van der Rohe, Promontory Apartments, Chicago, 1946–49. Alternative façade as steel curtain wall. Published in Philip Johnson, *Mies van der Rohe* (New York: Museum of Modern Art, 1947), 171.

Figure 8.47. Murgatroyd & Ogden, Tip Top Tap bar at the Allerton Hotel, Chicago, 1922. Contemporary postcard.

towers" occupy an important step in the evolution from the Promontory to the Lake Shore Drive Apartments.[87] Instead of windowless side façades, Mies now wanted windows all around, with continuous ribbons on two sides of a corner bedroom and floor-to-ceiling glass in the dining rooms and kitchens. He had never been closer to realizing a vision he had pursued since the early 1920s. This bold vision needed testing.

Mies and Genther had tested the view down from a corner room on the top floor without spandrels, to understand the visual impact of a floor-to-ceiling window.[88] Hedrich had been instructed to take a corresponding photo. And Mies happened to have a floor-to-ceiling window in his 1916 apartment at 200 East Pearson Street, but Clifford McElvain, manager of the mortgage division of Western & Southern Life Insurance in Cincinnati, who would be the main investor, needed convincing. He carried out his own experiment by taking his family to the famous Tip Top Tap bar at the top of the Allerton Hotel, which had floor-to-ceiling windows (figure 8.47). When his wife and daughter felt perfectly at ease next to the deep abyss outside, he approved the concept for the Algonquin (figure 8.48).[89]

Figure 8.48. Ludwig Mies van der Rohe, Algonquin I Apartments project, Chicago, 1949. Model. Photograph by Hedrich-Blessing. Chicago History Museum.

To drive the point home, the lakeshore views in the sales brochure seem taken from an unrealistic height—perhaps an airplane. The drawings now display resolutely modern furniture, by Charles and Ray Eames, Florence Knoll, and Alvar Aalto (figure 8.49).

1949–51 Algonquin II

If the Algonquin I project had been realized at that moment, it would have gone down in history as one of the more benevolent and sophisticated residential high-rises of its time. But a mortgage for the generous two-tower approach was hard to come by and, in the summer of 1948, Greenwald secured a piece of land in one of Chicago's wealthiest neighborhoods, right on Lake Shore Drive, and decided to apply his "twin towers" project there—catering to a different, more prosperous clientele.

With loans from the Federal Housing Association, the Algonquin project was turned into a pure moneymaker. Mies remained marginally involved, but, according to Skip Genther, he and John Holsman quickly redesigned the project, "at lunch on a paper napkin."[90] Instead of two towers surrounded by a large park, now six fourteen-story towers were crammed onto the same pieces of land, maximizing rentable space and income.[91] The formal language remained unchanged, including the setbacks in the outside concrete piers. The blocks had a simple rectangular form and contained apartments with two, three, and five rooms. However, the ground floor arcade (as at the Promontory) was given up, and Genther and Holsman played it safe and eliminated both the panoramic corner ribbon and floor-to-ceiling windows, fearing that their middle-class clientele might not warm up to them after all. The sales brochure was quickly adapted by filling in higher windowsills. The photographs of views outside were even more deceptive, as none of the apartments would have enjoyed lake views. The towers were ready for occupancy in 1951, and only exterior photographs were commissioned (figure 8.50).

Figure 8.49. Ludwig Mies van der Rohe, Algonquin I Apartments project, Chicago, 1949. Photomontage in advertising brochure for Algonquin Apartment Buildings, Chicago, 1949. Note furniture by Florence Knoll, Alvar Aalto, and Charles and Ray Eames. Lithograph, 9 × 12 in. (22.9 × 30.5 cm). Museum of Modern Art, New York. The Mies van der Rohe Archive, gift of the architect.

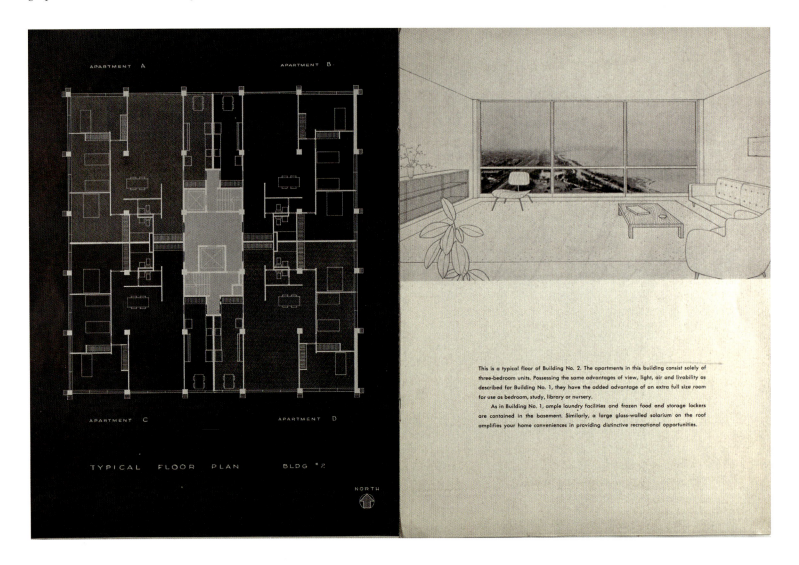

This is a typical floor of Building No. 2. The apartments in this building consist solely of three-bedroom units. Possessing the same advantages of view, light, air and livability as described for Building No. 1, they have the added advantage of an extra full size room for use as bedroom, study, library or nursery.

As in Building No. 1, ample laundry facilities and frozen food and storage lockers are contained in the basement. Similarly, a large glass-walled solarium on the roof amplifies your home conveniences in providing distinctive recreational opportunities.

Mies van der Rohe continued to use the Promontory's and Algonquin's formal language and structural approach when he was commissioned to design three dormitory buildings on the IIT campus in 1955, Bailey Hall, Carman Hall, and Cunningham Hall. Here, finally, panoramic corner windows were realized (figure 8.51).

The Type

Architectural Forum declared in 1949 that "through its architectural structure... Promontory's influence has already spread."[92] The Chicago Housing Authority (CHA) had finally agreed to permit high-rise apartment buildings for the urban poor.[93] One of the first to get a residential high-rise commission from the CHA was Skidmore, Owings & Merrill (SOM), who modeled its 1949 Ogden Courts "closely on Mies van der Rohe's Promontory Apartments."[94] It was the CHA's first project with a raw concrete skeleton, bay-wide ribbon windows, and comparable floor plans.[95] The price matched that of the Promontory at $8.65 per square foot (about $93.70 per square meter).[96] Chicago modernists Keck & Keck employed Mies's concrete frame, structural setback, and outside access corridors at the Prairie Avenue Courts of 1951–52.[97] SOM again followed the Promontory Apartments closely in their Harold Ickes Homes of 1955. So did Laurence Amstadter in 1957, in his designs for the Cabrini high-rise apartments at the Cabrini-Green Homes housing project (figure 8.52).[98] Often, the Promontory's unusual double-T layout was also adopted. From the front, it looked like a simple slab, and thus quite different from the "cross plans" common for high-rise housing in New York (as in Stuyvesant Town, see figure 8.38). Eventually, the simple rectilinear slab became the dominant mode

Figure 8.50. Ludwig Mies van der Rohe, Algonquin II Apartments, Chicago, 1949–51. Photograph by Hedrich-Blessing. Chicago History Museum.

Figure 8.51. Mies van der Rohe, Carman Hall, Illinois Institute of Technology campus, Chicago, 1955. Photograph by Hedrich-Blessing. Chicago History Museum.

and was considered "a major revolution in the housing field."[99] In 1960–62, Mies's collaborator Skip Genther built the William Green Homes—eight housing blocks of fifteen and sixteen stories with 1,096 units, using the Promontory vocabulary (figure 8.53). He applied the duplex layout with access from outside galleries—similar to those that had been on the drawing boards as an alternative for the Promontory Apartments.

Cabrini-Green became one of the most notorious housing projects in the country, plagued by overcrowding, poverty, drug abuse, gun violence, and gang activity. It finally had to be taken down—just like every single one of the abovementioned public housing projects.[100] Neither Genther nor Amstadter missed the irony of the lasting success of the Promontory Apartments and the complete failure of the same approach elsewhere. Genther recalled: "We thought we were giving people the same thing that people who lived along Lake Shore Drive had,…we gave them good views and livable space in a great location. We all had our hearts in it." Amstadter, architect of the Cabrini high-rises, agreed:

> The apartments at Cabrini are larger and almost nicer in some respects than the high-rises along Lake Shore Drive. If the decision were ever made to gentrify Cabrini and make it into middle-class condos, I think it would be extremely successful.…We thought we were playing God in those days.…We were moving people out of some of the worst housing imaginable and we were putting them into something truly decent. We thought we were doing a great thing, doing a lot of innovative design things, like putting open galleries on each floor so kids could play right in front of their apartments. We didn't foresee the kids throwing each other off them.[101]

1948, 1949   Rush Huron Co-Op and Berke Office Building

Mies and Greenwald were eager to apply their modern, essentialist approach to an office building as well. Pietro Belluschi's Equitable Building in Portland was celebrated in *Architectural Forum* in September 1948 as the first "long overdue crystal and metal tower" as it "catches the lightness of the multi-story cage" (figure 8.54). A concrete structure, clad in aluminum, with flush "sea-green" tinted windows of "sealed double glazing" filled most of the open space between floor and ceiling. These windows could not be opened, as there was air-conditioning throughout.[102]

Mies and Greenwald responded with their own project, the Rush Huron Co-Op Office Building in Chicago, which bore a certain resemblance to Belluschi's, and promised "the most functional and severely plain office building in the Midwest…with no ornamentation on the exterior walls. Interior walls will be of face brick. No plaster will be used. Partitions, placed where the tenant-owner wants them, will be of glass, aluminum, stainless steel, glass blocks, or other modern materials" (figure 8.55). Greenwald had purchased a piece of land at East Huron and North Rush streets on Chicago's North Side. He imagined applying the same cooperative ownership scheme and the same aesthetic as at the

Figure 8.52. A. Epstein & Sons (Laurence Amstadter), Cabrini Homes extension, Chicago, 1957. Photograph by Hedrich-Blessing. Chicago History Museum.

Figure 8.53. Skip Genther and PACE Associates, William Green Homes, 660 Division Street, Chicago, 1962. Photograph by Camilo José Vergara, 2004.

Promontory Apartments. It was to be a ten-story concrete structure on a three-by-five-bay footprint. Greenwald also promised a radiant heating system with pipes in the joists, artificial illumination from continuous cold cathode tubes, and natural light from "one of the largest window areas of any similar sized office structure in the city."[103] As promising as all of this sounded, it failed to capture the interest of enough investors and ultimately had to be abandoned. But it showed the fluid conceptual transition between apartment and office buildings.

Clearly, a revolution in office building design was underway. A groundbreaking ceremony for the much discussed, thirty-nine-story UN Headquarters Building in New York had been held in September 1948, and the building was fully finished in 1952.[104] A twenty-one-story headquarters for Lever House on Park Avenue in New York by SOM was announced in April 1950, promising a façade of "glass and stainless steel," and "designed to give the illusion of having no ground floor," due to its open space underneath the second floor and "glass enclosed lobby" (figure 8.56).[105] It opened officially on April 29, 1952.

Figure 8.54. Pietro Belluschi, Equitable Building, Portland, Oregon, 1948. Photograph by Ezra Stoller.

Figure 8.55. Ludwig Mies van der Rohe and PACE Associates, Rush Huron Co-Op Office Building project, Chicago, 1948. Photograph by Hedrich-Blessing. Chicago History Museum.

Figure 8.56. Skidmore, Owings & Merrill (Gordon Bunshaft and Natalie de Blois), Lever House, New York, 1951–52. Photograph by Ezra Stoller.

As mentioned above, Indianapolis businessman Joseph Cantor had introduced Mies to a friend, local developer Harry E. Berke. Berke loved modern architecture and remembered Mies's work from MoMA's *Modern Architecture: International Exhibition,* which had been shown at Indianapolis's Herron Art Institute in February 1933.[106] Berke commissioned Mies to design a four-story office block at Meridian and Michigan streets in Indianapolis in late 1949 (figure 8.57). Designed while Mies and his team worked on 860/880 Lake Shore Drive, this previously overlooked project is significant for the evolution of Mies's curtain wall. Similar principles were applied here—square columns behind the façade, with four floor-to-ceiling windows between them. The first floor, with large single panes, is partially recessed to create an arcade. Most importantly, the later much-discussed, nonstructural vertical element on the outside has been applied—a crucial step of great consequence beyond the stark structural display of the Promontory Apartment building. As the columns are embedded evenly in the façade, the regular distance between the vertical elements necessitated smaller windows on either side of the columns. From the model photos, it is hard to tell if the vertical elements have already taken on their future I-beam shape. Just as at the Rush Huron project, the building's function played no role in the structural and formal decisions, and the façade grid of a residential building was just as easily applied to an office building. Mies specified "stainless steel" for the outside—the material he wanted at Lake Shore Drive as well, since its honest materiality appealed to him.[107] He said: "It will startle those who are used only to buildings with masonry walls, as the entire outside walls, except where the stainless-steel framework will show, will be of plate glass, from ceiling to floor. Interior blinds will cut the glare from the sun, while the air conditioning will include summer cooling as well as winter heating."[108] Berke noted that a glass "curtain wall" would keep out weather, street noises, and dirt, while the steel framework would provide structural support: "The first floor would have 17,000 square feet [1,579 square meters] of floor space and the other three 19,000 square feet [1,765 square meters] a piece. One feature of the building would be that the windows are hinged, so all of them can be washed from the inside."[109]

When nothing came of this project, Berke commissioned a twelve-story apartment tower from Mies, similar to Lake Shore Drive, that was approved by the city of Indianapolis in June 1953 (figure 8.58). It was supposed to have fifty two- and three-bedroom units, with the second floor devoted to storage, laundry facilities, and offices, and there were to be parking spaces in the basement, a roof garden, as well as air-conditioning, operable

Figure 8.57. Ludwig Mies van der Rohe, Berke Office Building project at Meridian and Michigan streets, Indianapolis, 1949–50. Model. Photograph by Hedrich-Blessing. Chicago History Museum.

windows, and radiant floor heat.[110] The project failed as well, and Berke reported a $19,000 loss—it simply had been "too expensive, too elaborate…too stark for Hoosier tastes."[111]

1949–51 Lake Shore Drive Apartments

The Lake Shore Drive Apartments were developed by the same core team of Herbert Greenwald, Skip Genther with PACE Associates, and Mies as soon as the land in Chicago had been secured in 1948. Steel was now more readily available, and the steel industry was eager to enter the residential high-rise business.[112] Greenwald used a cooperative model similar to that in the Promontory Apartments and had no problems finding investors for the prominent lakeside location. The towers at 860/880 North Lake Shore Drive were based on a three-by-five grid and placed not along Lake Shore Drive, as previous apartment towers had been, but rather on the western edge of the site, away from the traffic, and tuned into the strictly east–west Chicago grid. One hundred parking spaces were provided in an underground garage. The glass-enclosed lobby was moved back from the periphery, providing a colonnade around the perimeter and emphasizing the load-bearing structure (figure 8.59). The promotional leaflets followed the format of their predecessors and now proudly included Mies's Barcelona chairs, ottoman, and table, as well as his MR 10 chairs, all finally available from Knoll. The exterior views embedded in the drawings were realistic views of the Chicago skyline and the lakefront.

Thanks to a more generous budget, lighting designer Richard Kelly was able to introduce new elements.[113] Strong projectors in the soffit created a "pool of light" on the granite floor

Figure 8.58. Ludwig Mies van der Rohe, Berke Apartment Building project, Indianapolis, 1953. Model. Photograph by Hedrich-Blessing. Chicago History Museum.

> Figure 8.59. Ludwig Mies van der Rohe, 860/880 Lake Shore Drive Apartments, Chicago, 1949–51. View looking south from Lake Shore Drive. Photograph by Hassan Bagheri.

along the building's perimeter. Kelly and Mies wrapped the auxiliary rooms next to the lobby in backlit translucent walls—a striking architectural element familiar from Mies's buildings in Barcelona and Brno. At night, the towers appear to be floating above a luminous cube (figure 8.60).

Mies could finally realize the floor-to-ceiling windows he had hoped for at the Algonquin project, and he applied the vertical element on the outside, which had first shown up on the alternative façade of the Promontory Apartments. It had evolved into a small, non-load-bearing I-beam attached to the window mullions, extending a regular vertical rhythm over the entire façade, while representing the load-bearing steel columns, embedded in concrete and hidden from view. Famously, a reporter asked Mies about the rationale behind them, in particular as they continue onto the cladding of the final column, where they do not seem as justified. The reporter relayed his conversation with Mies as follows:

> He says: "Now, first, I am going to tell you the real reason, and then I am going to tell you a good reason by itself. It was very important to preserve and extend the rhythm which the mullions set up on the rest of the building. We looked at it on the model without the steel section attached to the corner column and it did not look right. Now, the other reason is that this steel section was needed to stiffen the plate which covers the corner column so this plate would not ripple, and also, we needed it for strength when the sections were hoisted into place. Now, of course, that's a very good reason," he laughs, "but the other reason is the real reason."[114]

The steel-enclosed columns sit right in the façade and divide it up into readable bays of four windows each. To ensure the regular distance between the verticals, the windows adjacent to each column are slightly slimmer than the two in the center, leading to a subtle rhythm. As construction photos show, the spandrels and the vertical I-beams were welded together in two-story tall sections, alternatively with five or three mullions in the center (figure 8.61). The steel sheathing surrounding each corner column served as formwork for the concrete surrounding the steel post. The steel is painted with several layers of black enamel paint for weather resistance. A reporter recounted that Mies wanted "stainless steel, which he prefers to black-painted steel."[115] It would have revealed the material in its essence, rather than hiding it underneath a coat of paint. Noting that the same structural system was applied by Mies to a twenty-six-story tower and a simple four-story building, a reporter conveyed Mies's answer "that the proportions of

Figure 8.60. Ludwig Mies van der Rohe, 860/880 Lake Shore Drive Apartments, Chicago, 1949–51. View from Lake Shore Drive at dusk with Richard Kelly's lighting installation. Photograph by Hassan Bagheri.

Figure 8.61. Ludwig Mies van der Rohe, 860/880 Lake Shore Drive Apartments, Chicago, 1949–51. Under construction, 1950. Photograph by Hedrich-Blessing. Chicago History Museum.

structural members are not dictated only by the height of the structure. He accepts the strength of steel as a useful generality and lets his sense of proportion set the exact sizes—checked by engineers, of course."[116]

The ceiling height was raised to 10 feet (3 meters), versus eight feet (2.4 meters) in the Promontory Apartments. The *New York Times* noted that the building would have "more window space than any similar-sized structures in the country,"[117] and it was advertised as the "World's First Multiple Glass House."[118] Mies had finally been able to realize an essential manifestation of his design philosophy. All around, the windows reached from floor to ceiling; outside walls had been completely eliminated.

Regarding the interior's spatial layout, he still had to succumb to the developer's ideas: the large apartments he had originally laid out were scaled back in favor of smaller divisions (figure 8.62). *Architectural Forum* bemoaned the loss of these "breathtaking" plans with their open spatial flow. While the executed "closed bedrooms" were probably preferable to some, "the public corridor is increased, kitchens are smaller, passages have more kinks and corners."[119] Originally planned separate service entrances to each apartment also vanished. Bill Hedrich documented different phases of construction. The apartments were furnished in the fall of 1952. Skip Genther purchased one of the apartments, and Mies had it photographed by Hedrich in December 1952, after sparsely furnishing it (figure 8.63). The views came somewhat close to the vision spelled out in the

Figure 8.62. Ludwig Mies van der Rohe, 860/880 Lake Shore Drive Apartments, Chicago, 1949–51. Original floor plan. Note the load-bearing I-beams embedded in concrete and the small I-beams on the façade.

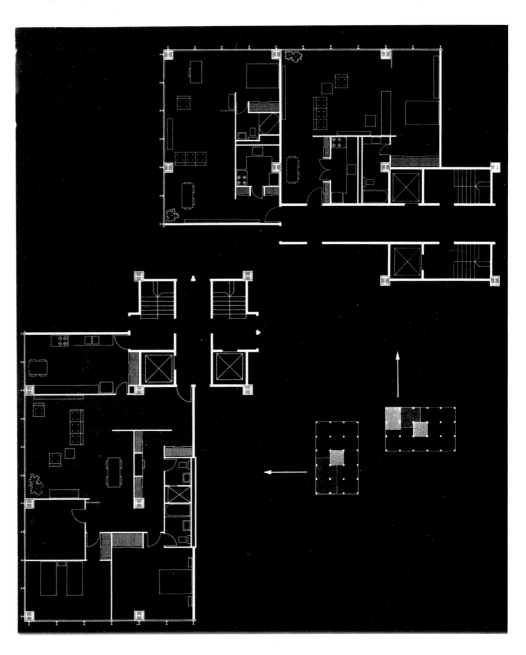

sales brochure, but had the same strangely tentative and unhomely quality of the interior shots at Promontory.

Not surprisingly, most magazines, upon receiving Hedrich's photographs, focused on the more photogenic exterior views. We do not know if a set was sent to *House Beautiful* magazine, but if so, the interior views certainly would have produced fodder for editor-in-chief Elizabeth Gordon, who was at that moment penning her famous "Threat to the Next America" article (with Mies in a starring role) to support Edith Farnsworth's pending court case. Her forceful campaign targeted European modernism in general, whose orthodoxy she equaled to a dictatorship, warning that its acceptance would lead to "dictators in other departments of life"—referencing recent history in Mies's homeland and the current fear of Communist infiltration. She wrote, "There is a well-established movement in modern architecture, decorating and furnishings which is promoting the mystical idea that 'less is more'…three or four pieces of furniture placed along arbitrary pre-ordained lines; room for only a few books and one painting at precise and permanent points." She considered the "glass-cube" to be "perhaps the most unlivable type of home for man since he descended from the tree and entered a cave."[120] While her article concentrated mostly on Mies's Farnsworth House, her observations there served as a general condemnation of the

Figure 8.63. Ludwig Mies van der Rohe, 860/880 Lake Shore Drive Apartments, Chicago, 1949–51. Skip Genther's apartment, 1952. Photograph by Hedrich-Blessing. Chicago History Museum.

International Style and the promotion of her own brand of a mellower modernism. Her annual series of so-called "Pace Setter" model homes showed colorful interiors with upholstered, brightly patterned furniture and luscious carpets.

As if to prove Gordon's point at the location of greatest impact, one of the inhabitants at 860/880 Lake Shore Drive hired interior designer James F. Eppenstein, a decorator of hotels, restaurants, and trains, who furnished the apartment with brightly colored curtains, upholstered furniture in the style of Gilbert Rohde, and his own designs. Photographed in May 1953 (just a month after Gordon's famous diatribe) by Hedrich-Blessing, it provides the impression of a dense, cozy, and modestly modern environment, suggesting a return to the interiority of a nineteenth-century bourgeois home. Most importantly, the views to the city or lake outside of the floor-to-ceiling windows—a major selling point for the projects, and central to Mies's vision—are blocked out by boldly patterned curtains.[121]

While the development of an identifiable and successful vision of an interior style remained somewhat elusive, Mies's concept of the fully glazed apartment tower prevailed. It was applied by him to a long series of apartment towers over the following years in Chicago, Newark, Detroit, Baltimore, and Montreal. His 860/880 Lake Shore Drive, however, remained a solitaire, a prototype, never surpassed in its elegance and structural immediacy, but also never repeated, as it required substantial modifications to be workable. Most frequently, the inhabitants had complained about the lack of air-conditioning (which the investors had eliminated) and overheating interiors on the eastern, southern, and western sides.[122] In the cold Chicago winters, condensation water appeared on window glass and structural elements; during rainstorms, water penetrated the insulation.

Peter Blake addressed the issue critically and perceptively:

> In Mies's arsenal of architectural solutions there is one large and, as yet, unclosed gap: to many critics it has seemed that Mies is being eloquent about the steel cage at the expense of making the space within that cage work properly in terms of mechanical equipment and indoor climate. Mies has tried to answer his critics by saying, brusquely, that "this is not my specialty"; yet, to most laymen, these problems are certainly part of the architect's responsibility....Unprotected glass walls may be exquisitely beautiful—but...exquisite beauty has a way of being elusive when the glass walls are backed up by improvised brown paper shades scotch-taped to the insides by sizzling and blinded humanity....Perhaps technology will again come to the rescue in the end—but that end is not yet in sight. For the present, at least, the architect must be the one to come to the rescue.[123]

1951 Arts Club of Chicago

When the Lake Shore Drive Apartments were nearing completion, Mies had finished several buildings on the IIT campus and had started working on Crown Hall. He had become a member of the Arts Club of Chicago, founded in 1916 in the wake of the impression the Armory Show had made at the Art Institute. It was housed at first in rented quarters in the Fine Arts Building on Michigan Avenue, then at the Art Institute, and finally in two different locations in the Wrigley Building. It was there that Mies attended an "All Percussion Concert" on March 1, 1942, presented by John Cage with eight musicians, who performed "their scores on kitchen utensils and wash tubs."[124] Cage was a visiting lecturer at László Moholy-Nagy's Institute of Design. We do not know what happened that night, or how much Mies and Cage conversed, but Mies's glass architecture would be mentioned frequently by Cage years later when researching the "Architecture of Silence."[125]

The Arts Club moved again in 1950 into an existing structure at 109 East Ontario Street, one block west of Michigan Avenue and four blocks north of the Chicago river. Mies was asked to design the interior, most notably the staircase to the exhibition spaces on the second floor (figure 8.64). This staircase, derivative of one Mies designed for the Verseidag in Krefeld just before he left Germany, was a most unusual intervention. In order to assure a comfortable rise, Mies divided the stair up into three flights with two landings. Rather than attaching it to the perimeter walls of the square lobby, as he had done at the Verseidag or, more recently, at Alumni Memorial Hall on the IIT campus, Mies placed the stairs

Figure 8.64. Ludwig Mies van der Rohe, Arts Club Chicago, 1951. Main entrance. Photograph by Hedrich-Blessing. Chicago History Museum.

Figure 8.65. Ludwig Mies van der Rohe, Arts Club Chicago, 1951. Interior upstairs. Photograph by Hedrich-Blessing. Chicago History Museum.

parallel to the outside wall in such a way that its side view with the landing, the elegant span, and the immaterial railing were visible from the outside, lending it a stronger visual presence than the simpler solution of attaching it to the perimeter. Mies's stair became the first work of art that any visitor would encounter. As Mies also insisted on placing the entrance door centrally in the enormous glass wall to the street, visitors had to be careful not to walk into the four-foot- (1.2-meter-) high landing right in front, or hitting their heads on the rising stair flank. Mies had the lobby clad in travertine and used wall-high curtains on both floors to shield from outside light and divide up space (figure 8.65). When the club had to move to another address a few blocks east on East Ontario Street, the staircase came along. Still claiming pride of place in John Vinci's new building of 1996, its positioning lost the original's stark immediacy.

1950–56   Crown Hall

Crown Hall was dedicated on April 30, 1956. After teaching for almost two decades in makeshift quarters at the Art Institute, Mies and his IIT faculty could finally access and command their own spaces, and in particular spaces that were generally considered a supreme expression of the gospel taught at the school—one of noble materials, structural expressiveness, and noncommittal, large spaces.[126] The building was dedicated to the memory of Sol Crown by his brothers Henry and Irving. They had founded and run the Material Service Corporation, dealing in construction and building materials and owning and operating factories, mines, and quarries around the world. When they sponsored Crown Hall, they owned the world's largest building (the Merchandise Mart in Chicago) and the world's tallest tower (the Empire State Building in New York).

Comparable to the story of Mies's involvement in urban renewal projects in Detroit and Newark (see below), IIT was built on the ruins of an African American neighborhood that fell victim to the campus's development. Over time, the new IIT buildings would slowly replace the existing structures in the area of Bronzeville, their light-beige bricks and black steel grid a stark contrast to the soot-stained brick and stone façades of the existing residential buildings.

The most striking examples for this displacement was the Mecca Flats apartment block at the corner of Thirty-Fourth and South Dearborn streets, a former hotel built for the 1893 World's Fair (figure 8.66). It had two spectacular glass-covered access courtyards (figure 8.67). After the fair it was converted to apartments, at first only accessible to white families, but later middle-class black families moved in. When IIT's presence grew in the area, the tenants engaged in a decades-long fight to save their building, which they finally lost

Figure 8.66. Willoughby J. Edbrooke and Franklin Pierce Burnham, Mecca Flats, Chicago, 1892. Outside view with Mies van der Rohe's Institute of Gas Technology Building (1947–50) in the foreground. Photograph by Wallace Kirkland. Chicago History Museum.

in 1952 (figure 8.68).[127] Upon Crown Hall's dedication, the press noted that on the school's "checkerboard campus…many of the squares are still occupied by derelict buildings awaiting eventual destruction."[128]

Many of the buildings on IIT's campus repeated the initial vocabulary—a 24-by-24-foot (7.3-by-7.3-meter) grid, concrete or steel frame, with beige brick or glass infill, two, three, or four stories, and a flat roof. The symmetrical corners of the steel frames showed the vertical I-beams welded onto the plates that covered the load-bearing post embedded in concrete (figure 8.69). Of the seventeen buildings that Mies realized during his tenure at IIT, between 1943 to 1958, Crown Hall is the most commanding, partly because it strayed from the straightjacket of this vocabulary (figures 8.70, 8.71). Mies recalled how, at first, the building was rejected by the buildings and grounds committee: "Then there came a new publicity manager. He wanted to have money for the building of the campus. You get money only for interesting things, not for stupid things. He knew that. He picked up the model and he got the money."[129] The generosity of the Crown family allowed for a formidable departure from precedent.

The footprint of Crown Hall measures 220 by 120 feet (67.1 by 36.6 meters), and its overall structure consists of only eight outside columns, carrying four solid web trusses above the roof. There are twenty-two-by-twelve bays, each 10 feet (three meters) wide. The interior is free of any structural elements. The smaller attached I-beams on the outside divide and strengthen the façade and connect the ceiling and floor plates with each other, but do not touch the ground. The connection is similar to that at the Farnsworth House, and flanges are welded invisibly onto the horizontal ceiling and floor plates. As everywhere around campus, the structural elements were painted black "using Superior Graphite 30, a standard product developed by the Detroit Graphite Company for painting bridges around the world."[130]

Figure 8.67. Willoughby J. Edbrooke and Franklin Pierce Burnham, Mecca Flats, Chicago, 1892. Interior courtyard. Photograph by Wallace Kirkland. Chicago History Museum.

Figure 8.68. Inhabitants of Mecca Flats protesting their eviction, 1950. Photograph by Charles Stewart, Jr. Chicago History Museum.

Figure 8.69. Ludwig Mies van der Rohe, Crown Hall, Illinois Institute of Technology campus, Chicago, 1950–56. Under construction, 1955. Photograph by Hedrich-Blessing. Chicago History Museum.

Figure 8.70. Ludwig Mies van der Rohe, Crown Hall, Illinois Institute of Technology campus, Chicago, 1950–56. Outside view of main entrance. Photograph by Hassan Bagheri.

Figure 8.71. Ludwig Mies van der Rohe, Crown Hall,
Illinois Institute of Technology campus, Chicago,
1950–56. Outside view from the southwest.
Photograph by Hassan Bagheri.

A floating set of stairs leads onto a landing and finally into the building. The eight-foot- (2.4-meter-) tall dividing walls out of white oak inside create three areas, two large studios on either side, and an exhibition or lecture hall in the center. To prevent distraction, the lower parts of the 10-foot- (three-meter-) wide glass panels on the perimeter are sandblasted, except at the six center bays on both sides. The first floor is elevated high enough aboveground to allow the basement to be lit from another band of frosted glass. The basement contains the library, bathrooms, and offices, and for a while housed Moholy-Nagy's Institute of Design (figure 8.72).

The reviewers agreed on the elegance of proportions and details, but also on a rather tenuous relationship between form and function: "As for the space itself: it is big. It is big and it is empty in a way which has nothing to do with furniture or inhabitants but derives from a sense of the vague, generalized purpose of the room. The evidence of intended occupancy and specific use is slight. One has the feeling that it is only incidentally a school of architecture and design," noted *Architectural Record* after the official opening.[131] Two years later, Peter Blake picked up the thread and explained how far removed Mies was from functionalism: "Functionalism rested…upon an exact organization of particulars.…If particular uses are going to change within the space we make, why then let's make a universal space that can take care of one and all possible uses! Said Mies: 'We do not let the functions dictate the plan. Instead let us make room enough for *any* function.' From this…Mies developed an entire vocabulary of universality; a vocabulary of universal details, of universal materials (brick, steel, glass), of universal proportions…for a universal architectural system of order that could provide answers to any problem. The particular solution, to Mies, was largely a thing of the past."[132] Of course, the lack of functional specificity, and thus fewer responses to program requirements, as well as the reuse of previously developed details, also meant a great simplification of the design process and allowed Mies to tackle a number of large projects with a comparatively small office.

When Mies visited the Architectural Association in London in May 1959, on the occasion of receiving the Royal Institute of British Architects' gold medal, he was asked about Crown Hall's open space and its potential impact on a student. He responded, "It is beautiful.… I like to work in this building. There is never any disturbance in the acoustics, only when the professor becomes emotional. He should not do that. Otherwise we have no disturbances. We work in groups together. I often did not see people."[133] On the same trip, Mies told British journalist Graeme Shankland, "I think the architects' building is the most complete and the most refined building and the most simple building. In the other buildings there is more a practical order on a more economical level and in the architects' building it is more spiritual order."[134]

Figure 8.72. Ludwig Mies van der Rohe, Crown Hall, Illinois Institute of Technology campus, Chicago, 1950–56. Interior downstairs. Photograph by Hassan Bagheri.

1954–58 Cullinan Wing at the Museum of Fine Arts, Houston

While Mies was working on Crown Hall for the IIT campus, the design of the Cullinan Wing at the Museum of Fine Arts, Houston, unfolded (figure 8.73). It is strangely under-represented in scholarship on Mies, perhaps due to the fact that it opened at the same time as the Seagram Building and was overshadowed by its reception in the press.[135] The Cullinan Wing was the northern extension of an earlier, neoclassical building of 1924 designed by William Ward Watkin, located on a triangular site with a central courtyard. Mies filled in the open center with his fan-shaped, 10,000-square-foot (929-square-meter) exhibition gallery and moved the main entrance from the south to the north. The curved façade there logically continued the arc suggested by the existing wings and offered a generous, three-bay glass façade on this northern side, which made the exhibitions held there perfectly visible at night. The lighting design picked up on Richard Kelly's contemporary work in the lobby of the Seagram Building, establishing invisible light sources around the edge of the suspended ceiling that would wash the three inside walls of the trapezoid exhibition space in bright light.

Figure 8.73. Ludwig Mies van der Rohe, Cullinan Wing, Museum of Fine Arts, Houston, 1954–58. Main entrance from the north. Photograph by Hedrich-Blessing. Chicago History Museum.

There were also office spaces and storage rooms underneath, and a front lawn for the display of sculpture. The support structure is the same as at IIT's Crown Hall. Four mighty girders carry the roof from above, thus eliminating the need for inside support. In contrast, however, here the structure was painted white, probably in response to the white marble cladding of the old building and mindful of the intense sunlight in Houston, which heats up black surfaces more than others. Critics pointed at the rarity of the curved element in Mies's work, naming the Reichsbank design and the Krefeld Verseidag Factory of 1932 and 1933 as predecessors.[136] Mies stated that he favored one large area for the museum, which would permit "complete flexibility.... The type of structure which permits this is the steel frame...with only three basic elements—a floor slab, columns, and a roof plate."[137] Clearly, what Mies described here was what he had in mind for the architecture studios in Crown Hall and the Bacardi Headquarters in Cuba at that time as well. And it foreshadowed his approach for the Neue Nationalgalerie in Berlin, a commission he received in 1961.

James Johnson Sweeney, the New York curator who had known and admired Mies since meeting him Berlin in 1933,[138] had left his position at Frank Lloyd Wright's controversial Guggenheim Museum to work in Mies's addition to the Museum of Fine Arts, Houston—"an exchange recognized in architectural circles as a voyage from the frying pan to the fire," as Ada Louise Huxtable put it in 1961, recognizing the difficulties that both museums presented to the curator.[139] Sweeney made Mies's large, open space workable for traditional exhibitions by hanging art on long wires from the ceiling. The idea of hanging painted panels in space had been pioneered in 1951 at the Colorado Springs Fine Arts Center by Mies's IIT colleague Hugo Weber, and might have been part of Mies's rationale in justifying his universal space at the Houston museum.[140] (When his Neue Nationalgalerie opened in Berlin in 1969 with an exhibition about Piet Mondrian, it adopted the same principle.) As soon as Sweeney had arrived in Houston, he began lobbying for the building's extension further north, which was finally executed (under Sweeney's successor, Philippe de Montebello), and opened after Mies's death in 1974 (figures 8.74, 8.75). The so-called Brown Pavilion used the same design language, also providing a curved glass façade and plate girders above the flat roof (this time painted black) and extended the pie-shaped earlier addition all the way to the street on the northern perimeter. Unfortunately, along the way, the new addition destroyed much of the convincing simplicity of the Cullinan Wing.

< Figure 8.74. Ludwig Mies van der Rohe, Brown Pavilion, Museum of Fine Arts, Houston, 1969–74. Interior at the intersection of the Cullinan and Brown pavilions. Photograph by Hassan Bagheri.

Figure 8.75. Ludwig Mies van der Rohe, Brown Pavilion, Museum of Fine Arts, Houston, 1969–74. Main entrance from the north. Photograph by Hedrich-Blessing. Chicago History Museum.

Nine

Universal Formulas

Chicago, Newark, Cincinnati, Detroit, New York, Baltimore,

Toronto, Montreal, Berlin, 1956–69

1955–57 Esplanade Apartments, 900/910 Lake Shore Drive

On March 14, 1955, at a luncheon at the Arts Club of Chicago, developer Herbert Greenwald, builder Samuel Katzin, and Ludwig Mies van der Rohe announced "one of the biggest private apartment building developments in Chicago's history."[1] It consisted of two projects, the two twenty-nine-story towers of the Esplanade Apartments at 900/910 Lake Shore Drive (next door to the earlier 860/880), and four towers (later reduced to two) at a site on Diversey Parkway and Commonwealth Avenue, three miles north, called the Commonwealth Promenade Apartments. Mies recalled the difficulties finding lenders for the project, and Greenwald's confidence in his "advanced" architectural ideas: "He turned down $12 million for the Commonwealth Promenade and 900 Esplanade apartments because one lender wanted a masonry spandrel and other modifications. Greenwald said no, the glass will go all the way to the ground. This takes courage."[2] According to *Architectural Forum,* both the Esplanade and the Commonwealth Promenade Apartments "would surely become two of the twentieth century's most famous apartment groups."[3]

The juxtaposition between the Esplanade Apartments at 900/910 and their already famous neighbors at 860/880 Lake Shore Drive makes their material, structural, and proportional differences particularly obvious. Mies had to mediate between the urgent need for structural and technical improvements and an established formal language that he considered essential. The result was, as the architect Minoru Yamasaki put it, "perhaps not quite so pleasing."[4]

The two towers of the Esplanade Apartments stand in a similar urban configuration to their neighbors on a deeper piece of land; one tower maintained the three-by-five proportion of its predecessors, the other one became a slab twice as long, made of three-by-ten bays (figure 9.1). The Esplanade Apartments offered 533 apartments and basement parking for four hundred cars underneath an accessible deck in the space between the two towers (figure 9.2). Mies reduced the ceiling height to eight and a half feet (2.6 meters), close to what he had used at the Promontory Apartments (the neighbor at 860/880 had boasted a generous 10 feet, or three meters). With a slimmer ceiling construction (the first flat slab concrete frame in Chicago), Mies could add three additional floors and thus increase revenue, while still ending up with a slightly lower building.

The most important change was its reinforced concrete structure, the tallest in Chicago at that time. The main reason for the switch to concrete was the unavailability of steel, due to the Korean War and dramatic developments in the steel industry, culminating in President Harry S. Truman's attempt at nationalizing all steel mills in April 1952 (struck down by the Supreme Court in June) and an accompanying two-month strike by the steel workers' union. It took until 1957 before steel construction could compete with concrete again in the building industry.[5]

Mies moved the piers inside, behind a glass curtain wall, which now had a uniform window size and a continuous rhythm, similar to his sketch of an alternative façade in steel for the Promontory in 1947. The façade still sported small I-beams on the outside, made from brown anodized aluminum and noticeably slimmer. Instead of being welded together like the steel I-beams at 860/880, these had regular gaps to account for the higher expansion coefficient. Importantly, but invisibly, they had lost their role as signifiers of the hidden, structural elements behind them. The load-bearing columns were solid reinforced concrete, instead of steel as before, and thus the aluminum attachments had become purely ornamental (figures 9.3, 9.4). There was a gap of eight inches

Figure 9.1. Ludwig Mies van der Rohe, 860/880 Lake Shore Drive, 1949–51, on the left and 900/910 Lake Shore Drive, Esplanade Apartments, Chicago, 1955–57, on the right. View from Lake Shore Drive. Photograph by Hassan Bagheri.

(20 centimeters) between the enclosure and the load-bearing frame, which allowed for rising ducts for the new air-conditioning units.

There is a disappointing fussiness at play in the freestanding piers on the first floor. They are clad in charcoal-colored aluminum and carry two vertical pilasters on each side, whose only purpose seems to be the resulting three-step corner profile. As a firm knock immediately demonstrates, they are thin and hollow—just like the I-beams, they are merely ornamental.

The glass is tinted to prevent overheating, and air-conditioning has been installed, leading to a ceiling grill on the first floor. Esplanade "boasted the city's first central air-conditioning for a residential tower; one of the first unitized, anodized aluminum curtain walls; and Chicago's first large-scale use of tinted, heat absorbing glass."[6] As we will see below, Esplanade also remained a solitaire, just like 860/880, but its structural solution became the direct predecessor to the Seagram Building, whose façade was designed immediately afterward, in August 1955.[7]

When ground was broken for both the Esplanade and Commonwealth buildings, *Architectural Forum* invited the architect Minoru Yamasaki, who had just completed

< Figure 9.2. Ludwig Mies van der Rohe, 900/910 Lake Shore Drive, Esplanade Apartments, Chicago, 1955–57. Under construction, 1956. Photograph by Hedrich-Blessing. Chicago History Museum.

Figure 9.3. Ludwig Mies van der Rohe, 900/910 Lake Shore Drive, Esplanade Apartments, Chicago, 1955–57. Corner view. Photograph by Hassan Bagheri.

Figure 9.4. Ludwig Mies van der Rohe, 900/910 Lake Shore Drive, Esplanade Apartments, Chicago, 1955–57. Horizontal section of corner detail with solid concrete pier and metal cladding.

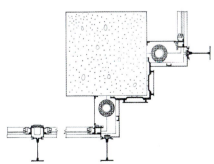

the Pruitt-Igoe housing project in St. Louis, to discuss new housing developments in Chicago, and in particular, "the Mies problem"—namely, the flood of less refined imitators. Yamasaki would become one of the least Miesian U.S. architects at mid-century, but he was gracious in his assessment: "Mies's buildings have integrity, ground space and great beauty. His contribution is tremendous. Questions such as the all-glass apartment house wall, with its inherent thermal and privacy weaknesses, must be judged in relation to the great beauty attained by the glass wall. Unfortunately, Mies is copied without understanding him or the details that make his buildings so successful." Questioned, however, about the similarity of Mies's apartment towers to glass office buildings, he said: "I agree apartments should look like apartments. If all the north side of Chicago begins to look like the downtown of Chicago, that is poor. Variation among the kinds of things that go on in buildings is what makes our cities interesting. And there is a need for richness, a psychological need for ornament which has been ignored too much. We are too prone to do things because they are 'functional.'" Yamasaki did not know yet that Mies was busy at exactly that moment transferring the details he had developed for an apartment building to the office building that would define the rest of his career and be imitated the world over, namely the Seagram Building in New York.

The article also noted that "many people are just not aware of what a good apartment—or house—is." After all, "for 15 years, through depression and war, housing construction was almost at a standstill." As a result, people "have been educated mostly from advertising." The article mentioned in particular the absence of balconies and interior kitchens without access to ventilation as common mistakes in modern apartment buildings (Mies was guilty on both counts).[8]

But still, Greenwald and Mies had managed to give their apartment towers an appeal that made clients flock to them despite these obvious shortcomings. Their calm clarity and promises of—by necessity—uncluttered interiors and unprecedented vistas seemed, at least to some, a perfect response to the problems and worries of the time.

1955–57 Commonwealth Promenade Apartments

The Commonwealth Promenade Apartments are a twin sibling to the Esplanade Apartments at 900/910 Lake Shore Drive in Chicago, but slightly larger, with 750 apartments and a 770-car parking garage (figures 9.5–9.7). The two projects were built at the same time, with Commonwealth about three miles (five kilometers) further north than Esplanade, also close to Chicago's lake shore. Originally, a complex of four towers was planned for Commonwealth, but only half of the project was executed, due to the untimely death of developer Herbert Greenwald in a plane crash in February 1959. The complex worked from a very similar set of blueprints and details as the Esplanade Apartments—the same concrete construction with an aluminum curtain wall. Most remarkable, however, is Mies's decision to now apply the natural color of the façade's material, aluminum—a silvery, light gray. While steel (unless it is an expensive stainless alloy) oxidizes and corrodes and thus requires a protective layer of paint, aluminum develops a thin, corrosion-resistant film of aluminum oxide of the same silvery color. This truthfulness in the material's appearance must have immediately appealed to Mies. The resulting difference between the Commonwealth Promenade and Esplanade apartments is astounding. At the latter, the tinted windows and the black anodized aluminum resulted in a homogenous, dark, and reflective surface. Here, the bright grid perfectly counterbalances the darkened windows in between. In all likelihood, the decision to dye the aluminum at the Esplanade Apartments black was made to create coherence with its neighbors at 860/880. Mies and his team stuck with aluminum for all their curtain walls in residential buildings going forward.

1958–60 Pavilion and Colonnade Apartments

As the Promontory Apartments in Chicago had, with their low cost and essentialist formal language, inspired several social housing high-rise projects in Chicago, Mies and his team now returned to affordable, middle-class housing themselves with two major urban renewal projects in Newark and Detroit. The structural execution and detailing are almost identical in both cities, while the size of the towers varied slightly. Most importantly, in order to save money, the team made an important breakthrough to greater material and

Figure 9.5. Ludwig Mies van der Rohe, Commonwealth Promenade Apartments, Chicago, 1955–57. Photograph by Hassan Bagheri.

Figure 9.6. Ludwig Mies van der Rohe,
Commonwealth Promenade Apartments, Chicago,
1955–57. Corner view with metal-clad column.
Photograph by Hassan Bagheri.

structural honesty. While the switch to a concrete skeleton had happened at the Esplanade and Commonwealth Promenade apartments already, it had not been visible from the outside, as the concrete piers were clad in anodized aluminum—which was structurally unnecessary. In Newark and Detroit, this cladding was eliminated, rendering the raw concrete visible and making the aluminum curtain wall a distinctly separate entity.

The project in Newark, known as Colonnade Park, was the last project on which Mies and Herbert Greenwald collaborated; the joyful groundbreaking ceremony with Mies, Herb Greenwald, and his wife, Lillian, happened just a year before Greenwald's fateful trip on February 3, 1959, from Chicago to New York, when his plane plunged into the East River as it approached LaGuardia Airport. Greenwald had been a seminal figure for Mies's American career, masterminding his early high-rise apartment projects and supporting Mies's structural and formal experiments. Mies considered him an ideal client: "He is very easy to work with. He has a sympathetic understanding of what we are trying to do. He could make a lot of money by building other buildings but he really is interested in good architecture. He is not afraid of our ideas. He wants to leave his stamp on the scene." And Mies continued: "I look forward to having lunch with him. He likes to talk about—and

Figure 9.7. Ludwig Mies van der Rohe, Commonwealth Promenade apartments, Chicago, 1955–57. Entrance vestibule. Photograph by Hassan Bagheri.

what is important he finds the time—to discuss—philosophy."[9] At Greenwald's memorial service on February 12, 1959, at Anshe Emet Synagogue in Chicago, Mies delivered a moving tribute:

> We will miss his brilliance, idealism, and his gallant spirit. He was so strongly a man of our age and yet he held to the best values of all the ages.... Herb needed no hope to begin, and no success to persevere. He accepted defeat with the same balance and good sense with which he welcomed success. In this, he was a real philosopher. I first knew him shortly after the end of the war—these were his early and most difficult years. Even then, I was astonished at the boldness of his thought and the fearlessness of his action. I saw him in many difficult and even hopeless situations, but to him the difficulty was a source of strength. Herb had an enormous capacity for learning and he learned quickly. He grew with each new piece of work to an amazing degree.[10]

The Newark project, the Commonwealth Promenade Apartments in Chicago, and Lafayette Park in Detroit were all underway at that point. The office had counted on Greenwald's patronage going forward, as Joe Fujikawa recalled:

> He said, "I'm going to build Mies buildings from New York to San Francisco."... We rented new office space on the fifth floor at 230 East Ohio Street—the whole fifth floor, all of 10,000 square feet [929 square meters].... and then the news came that Herb died in that plane crash, and we said, "Oh, my God, what are we going to do with all this space?" Those were frantic times, but Mies has always been lucky.[11]

After Greenwald's death, his real estate firm, Herbert Realty Co., was reorganized as Metropolitan Structures under the leadership of Bernard (Barney) Weissbourd, a character just as colorful and energetic as Greenwald. While Greenwald had studied to become a rabbi before being drawn to real estate, Weissbourd had studied chemistry, classics, and law at the University of Chicago. Under his leadership, Metropolitan Structures became the nation's largest commercial real estate firm. He continued to work with Mies, finishing the projects already underway, and overseeing One Charles Center and Highfield House in Baltimore, as well as 2400 North Lakeview in Chicago, and a development on Nuns' Island in Montreal.

The Newark project is located north of the downtown business district, next to Interstate 280 and east of Branch Brook Park, designed by Frederick Law Olmsted. Colonnade Park was one of the first urban renewal projects in the country, and the first in New Jersey (figure 9.8). It consisted of three twenty-two-story towers close to the city center, and opened in 1960, offering 1,240 apartment altogether on its 23.5-acre (9.5-hectare) site. The

Figure 9.8. Ludwig Mies van der Rohe, Pavilion and Colonnade Apartments, Newark, New Jersey, 1958–60. Model. The apartments bracket the Christopher Columbus Homes. Photograph by Hedrich-Blessing. Chicago History Museum.

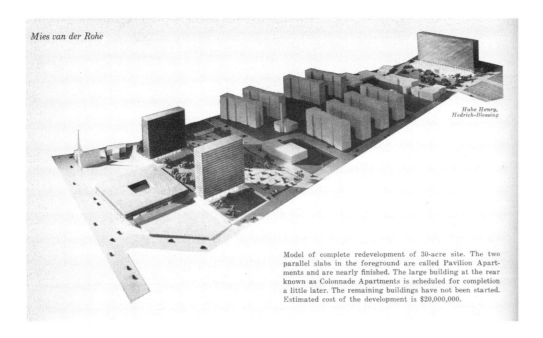

Mies van der Rohe

Hube Henry, Hedrich-Blessing

Model of complete redevelopment of 30-acre site. The two parallel slabs in the foreground are called Pavilion Apartments and are nearly finished. The large building at the rear known as Colonnade Apartments is scheduled for completion a little later. The remaining buildings have not been started. Estimated cost of the development is $20,000,000.

tower of the Colonnade Apartments on the western end measures 446 by 66 feet (136 by 20 meters) and houses 560 apartments. (It is Mies's most expansive structure.) Each of the two towers of the Pavilion Apartments, which face each other over a 500-foot (150-meter) distance, is 214 by 66 feet (65.2 by 20.1 meters), with 340 apartments each. The two eastern towers of the Pavilion Apartments are east–west oriented (its inhabitants having either purely north- or south-facing apartments), while the large tower of the Colonnade Apartments on the site's western edge is oriented north–south, and thus its inhabitants enjoy either morning or afternoon sun. Mies's formulaic approach to the design of his residential high-rise towers did not allow for design responses to the drastically different sun exposure in different apartments.

The towers applied the familiar pattern and details of the previous residential projects in Chicago, and thus made planning in Mies's office particularly efficient. As with its predecessors, the concrete structure is based on a square columnar grid, and the aluminum curtain wall sits in front (figure 9.9). The prefabricated vertical I-beam mullions provide the framework for the windows, but continue over the supporting piers, where they have no other function than to continue the rhythm, established by their "working" siblings. There is air-conditioning throughout. The glass-enclosed, double-height (16-foot, or 4.9-meter) lobby steps back one bay, about 20 feet (six meters) from the building's perimeter (figure 9.10). All three towers offer studios and two- and three-bedroom apartments. Kitchens, bathrooms, elevators, and staircases are clustered along the central spine, which provides access to all apartments. Inhabitants of the east-facing apartments of the Colonnade Tower can see the Manhattan skyline in the distance. As at the Detroit Lafayette Park

Figure 9.9. Ludwig Mies van der Rohe, Pavilion Apartments, Newark, New Jersey, 1955–58. View from the south across the Interstate 280. Photograph by Hassan Bagheri.

development, Mies's IIT colleague Alfred Caldwell designed the green spaces surrounding the towers.

The Colonnade and Pavilion Apartments were aimed at a middle-class clientele, trying to keep them in the city rather than losing them to the suburbs. In an interesting attempt at social engineering, Mies's towers bracketed (over a distance of half a mile, or 0.8 kilometer) a development of eight enormous social housing blocks for citizens with lower income, the Christopher Columbus Homes (figure 9.11). They had been commissioned by the Newark Housing Authority as one of several large-scale public housing complexes. Construction had begun in 1956, and the development consisted of eight thirteen-story-tall slabs with two hundred apartments each. It had promised to provide close proximity to schools, Broad Street Station, Branch Brook Park, and a newly constructed church. While the sequence of parallel housing blocks is reminiscent of one of Ludwig Hilberseimer's urban schemes, or Mies's own design for Berlin's Alexanderplatz in 1929, the architecture of the apartments followed a predictable public housing approach: bare brick façades and minimal

Figure 9.10. Ludwig Mies van der Rohe, Pavilion Apartments, Newark, New Jersey, 1955–58. Corner view with concrete pier. Photograph by Hassan Bagheri.

Figure 9.11. Newark Housing Authority, Christopher Columbus Homes, Newark, New Jersey, 1956. Note the two Pavilion Apartment towers by Ludwig Mies van der Rohe in the distance, 1994. Photograph by Camilo José Vergara.

finishes inside, accompanied by inadequate infrastructure and soon followed by deferred maintenance and an often volatile mix of inhabitants placed there by the Public Housing Authority as a result of urban renewal projects depriving them of their familiar neighborhoods. The buildings deteriorated quickly and became infamous for extreme poverty, violence, and crime. They were demolished in 1994 and replaced with two-story garden apartment buildings.

1956–63   Lafayette Park

Lafayette Park in Detroit was an immediate sibling to the Newark development, finished in phases shortly afterward with the same design vocabulary for its towers (figure 9.12). In great contrast, however, the space in between the three high-rises in Detroit was filled with low-rise apartments, also designed by Mies's office, and Lafayette Park became one of the most successful integrated urban renewal projects in the country. A 78-acre (31.6-hectare) site near the Detroit River and within walking distance from downtown was cleared; it included 4.8 acres (1.9 hectares) for shopping facilities and 18 acres (7.3 hectares) for a park and a new school. The initial proposal had included nine high-rise towers but was later scaled down to six and finally to three.

As with most urban renewal projects, Lafayette Park rose on a razed urban neighborhood. The area of Black Bottom had first been settled by Eastern European Jewish immigrants in the late nineteenth and early twentieth centuries. From the 1920s on, the Great Migration brought African Americans from the South to work in the auto industry. Segregation's restrictive covenants prevented them from living in most other parts of the city, and the wood-frame houses along Hastings Street were soon overcrowded. Condemnation of property had begun in 1946, and city funds for demolition increased after the National Housing Act of 1949 and the National Highway Act of 1956. Relocation assistance was minimal, and residents were usually only given a thirty-day notice. Many ended up in public housing projects, but not in their old neighborhood, Lafayette Park, which was newly designed for a middle-class clientele.

The twenty-story Pavilion Apartment block had gone up first (1955–59), an almost identical copy of the Pavilion Apartments in Newark (figure 9.13). There were only two marked differences: in Detroit the building was centrally heated and cooled, and therefore had no air intake grilles in the façades, while in Newark each unit had its own air conditioner. The other difference was Joe Fujikawa's work with a different window size, creating half-bay panels rather than the customary four smaller panels between the 21-foot- (6.4-meter-) wide bays. The result looks generous and well proportioned. The units are now framed vertically by pairs of flat U channels ("][") every 11.5 feet (3.5 meters), referencing and

Figure 9.12. Ludwig Mies van der Rohe, Lafayette Park, Detroit, 1956–63. The Pavilion Apartment towers are on the left, and Lafayette towers on the right. Photograph by Hassan Bagheri.

transcending the customary "I" mullions. For the two Lafayette Apartment towers in 1960, Fujikawa returned to the customary narrower sequence, making those two towers precise copies of the Pavilion Apartments in Newark (figure 9.14). Of course, economically, this was a shrewd move on Mies's part. Delivering the exact same project twice to different clients saved much time in the planning phase.

The most remarkable section of Lafayette Park, however, was not part of an evolving and repetitive typology, but a unique element in Mies's oeuvre—the one- and two-story townhouses and courtyard houses in a bucolic landscape accessed by cul-de-sacs and lowered parking areas, developed in collaboration with Ludwig Hilberseimer and Alfred Caldwell (figure 9.15).[12] The row houses offer a range of constellations—two-story walk-up flats, single-story row houses with enclosed gardens, and two-story townhouses (figures 9.16–9.18). The most ubiquitous is the elegant solution of the one-and-a-half-bay-wide first floor, whose second-floor bedrooms are two bays wide on one side, and one bay on the other. The structure combines a number of previous developments—the outside, load-bearing I-beam for every bay, with aluminum frames for the windows and their half-bay mullions. Mies could finally apply some of the strategies developed for the Farnsworth House on a multiple scale, as he had hoped in the early 1950s, when he was eager for vindication as the judgment in the very public court case against Edith Farnsworth was looming. The result here, begun just as the final verdict closed the case, is considerably more convincing than the

< Figure 9.13. Ludwig Mies van der Rohe, Lafayette Park, Detroit, 1956–63. Pavilion Apartment tower, 1956–59. Photograph by Hassan Bagheri.

Figure 9.14. Ludwig Mies van der Rohe, Lafayette Park, Detroit, 1956–63. Lafayette Apartment towers, 1960–63. Photograph by Hassan Bagheri.

Figure 9.15. Ludwig Mies van der Rohe, Pavilion
Apartments and Townhouses, Lafayette Park,
Detroit, 1956–59. Site plan by Ludwig Hilberseimer
and Alfred Caldwell, 1956. Ink on acetate, 25 × 31 in.
(63.5 × 78.7 cm). Museum of Modern Art, New York.
Mies van der Rohe Archive, gift of the architect.

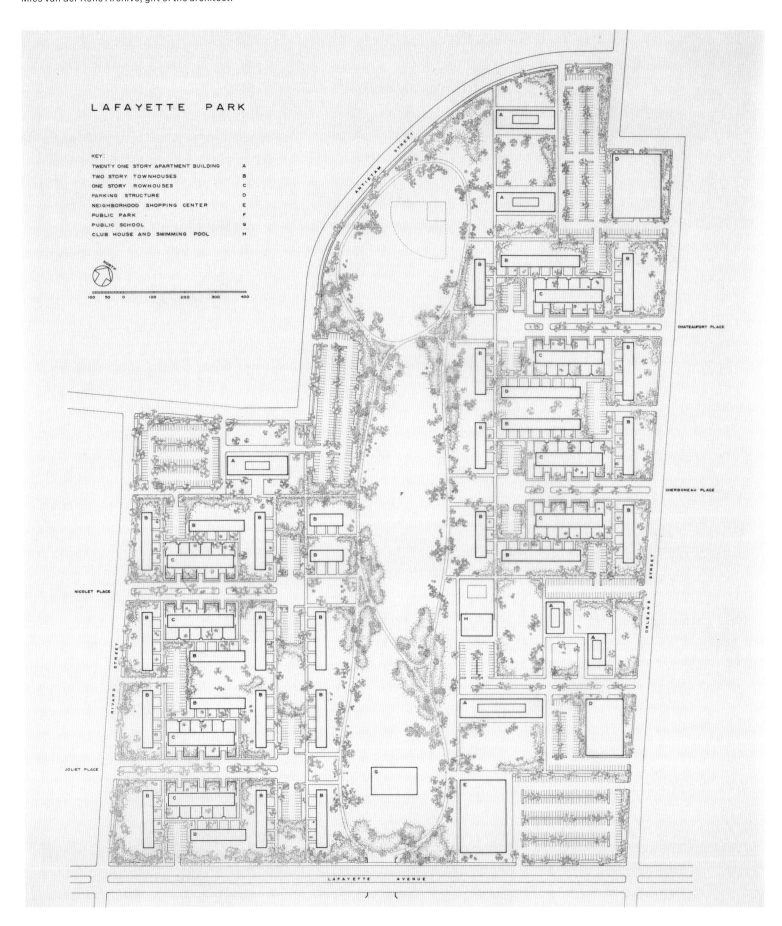

Figure 9.16. Ludwig Mies van der Rohe, Pavilion Townhouses, two-story version, Lafayette Park, Detroit, 1956–59. First-floor plan with different spatial configurations. Ink on acetate, 28 1/4 × 37 in. (71.8 × 94 cm). Museum of Modern Art, New York. Mies van der Rohe Archive, gift of the architect.

Figure 9.17. Ludwig Mies van der Rohe, Pavilion Townhouses, two-story version, Lafayette Park, Detroit, 1956–59. Photograph by Hassan Bagheri.

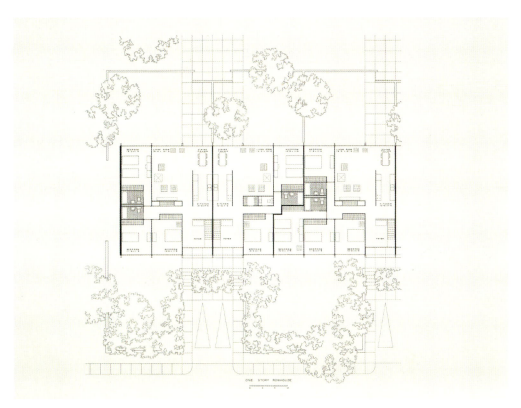

McCormick and Greenwald houses developed in that context. In fact, the first floor, with its glass façade on both sides, and the freestanding open kitchen line and bathroom unit dividing the space between living and dining room, is an elegant and economic solution.

Sadly, Mies and his team did not have another opportunity to build low-rise row houses, as the developers who targeted Mies in the late 1950s and 1960s worked with the large profit margins that luxury high-rise condominiums and clusters of office buildings delivered.

1962 2400 North Lakeview Apartments

While occasionally reviving the paradigm of the Promontory Apartments in Chicago for luxury condominiums in Baltimore (Highfield House, 1965) and Montreal (Nuns' Island Apartment Houses, 1969), Mies and his team mostly continued with the formal and structural vocabulary they had applied and developed since the Lake Shore Drive Apartments to a number of apartment buildings in the 1950s into the 1960s. The firm's last residential high-rise in Chicago, the 2400 North Lakeview Apartments (finished in 1962), again used a concrete frame with a light-colored aluminum curtain wall (figure 9.19). What changed here for the first time was the overall arrangement of six-by-four bays, with a denser columnar sequence on the shorter side, which allowed a different configuration inside. While the window size remained the same, the front façade had five windows per bay, while the

Figure 9.18. Ludwig Mies van der Rohe, Pavilion Townhouses, one-story version, Lafayette Park, Detroit, 1956–59. Photograph by Hassan Bagheri.

narrower side had three windows per bay, resulting in twenty versus eighteen windows on each side. The savings from sticking with the same window size overall and its established details outweighed the cost incurred by the additional steel. The difference is so slight that the building seems almost square as a result, and the façades look the same, except on the first floor.

1957 *Life* Magazine

At seventy years old, Mies found himself at the height of his career. Henry Luce's *Life* magazine published a carefully produced feature on him on March 18, 1957—almost thirty years after Luce's publishing empire had celebrated Wright's Fallingwater as *the* key piece of American modern architecture. Frank Scherschel, one of the magazine's star photographers, took hundreds of photographs of Mies at home and in his office, and of the construction of the thirty-eight-story Seagram Building on Park Avenue in New York.[13] The article in *Life* magazine, written by editor Richard Meryman, was a strategic piece in the

Figure 9.19. Ludwig Mies van der Rohe, 2400 North Lakeview Apartments, Chicago, 1963. Photograph by Hassan Bagheri.

unprecedented press campaign for the Seagram Building's opening (see below). It was titled "Emergence of a Master Architect" and lent Mies unambiguous American qualities of truthfulness, simplicity, and "sturdy nobility":

> Across the U.S. from New York to Texas, a stern but stunning new architecture has begun to tower on city horizons. Boldly rectangular, with skeletons of steel sheathed in glass, it is the inspiration and accomplishment of one of the great architects of the 20th century, Ludwig Mies van der Rohe....Today at 70, after living inconspicuously in the U.S. for 20 years, Mies is bursting into full, spectacular view. In Chicago he has built two tall apartment houses...whose steep piers, exposed at the base around a recessed lobby, give the building an effect of being on stilts. He is now finishing four more like them. In New York he is building a skyscraper. In Detroit his 76-acre [30.8-hectare] housing project is under way. In Houston ground is being broken for the wing of an art museum. This sudden surge of commissions is accepted by Mies as vindication of his lifelong principle that architecture must be true to its time. His own severely geometric, unembellished buildings have been designed to express in purest forms a technological concept of our technological age. They also, as may be seen on the following pages, express the simplicity and sturdy nobility of Mies himself.[14]

And, indeed, Mies's consistent portfolio of residential structures and university buildings had recently been broadened by more visible public commissions, such as the Seagram Building at Park Avenue and the Museum of Fine Arts in Houston. A year before, Crown Hall had opened to great fanfare on IIT's campus. Together with the Carr Memorial Chapel, it represented Mies's campus architecture in the *Life* magazine article, juxtaposed with the Lake Shore Drive Apartments and the almost finished Seagram Building. Additional photos showed Mies as a teacher, in conversation with the developer Herbert Greenwald or his client and collaborator Phyllis Lambert, and, finally, in solitude at home, reading "books about philosophy and science" in order "to find out what really is essential" in our time. The text tried, perhaps a little too hard, to drive the notion of the philosopher-architect home with a string of pithy aphorisms from Mies. After mentioning in passing his distinction of "skin and bones," "God is in the details," and "Less is more," Mies was quoted as saying, "We are not trying to please people. We are driving to the essence of things," or "We just solve problems." Similarly, "We do not build for fun. We build for a purpose." Careful pictorial editing matched the clouds from Mies's cigar in a full-page side portrait with those reflected in the glass façade of the Esplanade Apartments in Chicago. "For true greatness you have to go through the clouds," Mies supposedly said.[15] As shallow as some of these statements might seem, the article did much to turn Mies into the superstar of his profession, which secured him additional jobs, while the work at IIT, from which he would retire a year later, fizzled out at the same time.

A year after the article in *Life* magazine, Mies would be awarded the gold medal of the New York chapter of the American Institute of Architects; in 1959, the gold medal of the Royal Institute of British Architects, and then the Bundesverdienstkreuz (Federal Cross of Merit) of Germany, the country's highest civilian decoration; and in 1960, the gold medal of the American Institute of Architects.[16] The Presidential Medal of Freedom followed in 1963.

1956–58 The Seagram Building

The story of how a twenty-seven-year-old Canadian artist, Phyllis Lambert, living in Paris, rose up against her father, whose "fierce temper" had terrified her as a child, and interfered in his selection of an architect for the new company headquarters in New York is so well known that it long ago assumed the quality of an architectural myth, equal to, perhaps, the account of Frank Lloyd Wright sketching his famous perspective of Fallingwater between a phone call from the client, Edgar Kaufmann, Sr., and his arrival at Wright's home half an hour later.

One would ordinarily assume these stories to be too good to be true, having been embellished as they are told and retold over time. But the letter that Phyllis Lambert sent on June 28, 1954, to "Dearest Daddy"—eight densely typed pages, written over two long

Figure 9.20. Model of the Seagram Building (designed by Pereira & Luckman) for Seagram's annual national sales meeting, July 12, 1954, with Seagram president Victor A. Fischel. Canadian Centre for Architecture, Montreal.

Figure 9.21. Charles Luckman, interior of proposed Seagram Building, New York, 1954. Canadian Centre for Architecture, Montreal.

days, with all the writer's misspellings and handwritten additions—actually exists.[17] "NO NO NO NO NO," she cries out about the Pereira & Luckman design for the new company headquarters that her father had sent her (the same one that would appear in several newspapers a week later). "There is not ONE REDEEMING FEATURE . . . all vulgar surface with absolutely nothing behind it....It makes me too sick to go on." But then she explains to her father what he needs to do, tells him about Plato, Pythagoras, Vitruvius, and Alberti, about John Ruskin and Lewis Mumford, mentions Gropius, Mies, Le Corbusier, and William Lescaze, and summarizes beautifully the aspirations of modern architecture, pointing to Lever House and the United Nations as potential models: "You must put up a building which expresses the best of the society in which you live, and at the same time your hopes for the betterment of this society. You have a great responsibility and your building is not only for the people of your companies, it is much more for all people in New York and the rest of the world." In short, it is a wonderful letter that changed the course of twentieth-century architecture and should find its place in future anthologies.[18]

The famously bombastic model for Seagram's new headquarters by Pereira & Luckman that sparked Lambert's letter had been intended to uplift seven hundred sales representatives assembled in the ballroom of the Waldorf Astoria Hotel in New York for their annual meeting on July 12, 1954 (figure 9.20). The design had been requested only a few weeks earlier, and Pereira & Luckman had not been given an official commission. Charles Luckman later recalled that Samuel Bronfman wanted "old world charm in a modern setting," and even dreamed of placing an English castle atop the Park Avenue office building—which might explain the towerlike extrusions at the corners of Luckman's design. Given the appearance of Seagram's Montreal headquarters—a baronial granite castle of 1928, complete with crenellations and multiple turrets—this is entirely believable. In addition to the model, Luckman produced a series of drawings of club-like interiors with deep fauteuils and fireplaces (figure 9.21).

Following his presentation, Luckman received a "heartwarming" response from the audience, and Bronfman promised him the commission.[19] Phyllis Lambert, meanwhile, found an important ally in the pragmatic and farsighted Lou R. Crandall, president of the George A. Fuller Construction Company, the designated builder and a friend of her father. Crandall seems to have been one of the key players—"like an *eminence grise* or a deft puppeteer," as Lambert put it.[20] He convinced Bronfman that his daughter should select a new architect, and later he suggested the association of Philip Johnson with Mies, orchestrated the collaboration with the firm of Ely Jacques Kahn and Robert Allan Jacobs, and oversaw the financial aspects of the project. Most importantly, he had already been at work for two years on finding the best solution for the Park Avenue site.

In 1952, Crandall had commissioned the "Skytop" study from Kahn & Jacobs, who had plenty of experience building high-rises up and down Park Avenue (figure 9.22).[21] They produced a series of sketches to illustrate "various schemes showing allowable building size and comparable financial set up." It should be noted that most of them did not employ the setback scheme that the firm itself had frequently used, but that was considered outdated at that point. Among them was a scheme with great similarity to Lever House ("Scheme 3B"), and "Scheme 4A," a slab tower set back from Park Avenue with a plaza and fountain in front and "very close to Mies' solution" (figure 9.23).[22] Crandall had also assembled a list of competent potential architects, among them Voorhees & Walker, Foley & Smith, Eggers & Higgins, William Lescaze, and Pereira & Luckman. While Luckman's hasty design might not have been the last word (in particular since it came nowhere near any of Kahn & Jacobs's feasibility studies), and someone else on Crandall's list might have been given the commission eventually, the outcome probably would have been an acceptable but unremarkable (and certainly much cheaper) modern office building.

What Lambert's forceful intervention achieved was to move the discussion to a different realm, making architectural quality the most important asset of the building, and ultimately transforming architectural culture in New York. In fact, the choice of Mies—his design's extraordinary quality, its generous plaza, and the associated costs—became the central part of the public relations campaign that accompanied the construction and opening of the building. In the end, at a construction cost of $36 million (30 to

Figure 9.22. Jacques Kahn and Robert Allan Jacobs, 100 Park Avenue, New York, 1947–49. Photograph by the Wurts Brothers.

Figure 9.23. Jacques Kahn and Robert Allan Jacobs, massing study ("Skytop" study, "Scheme 4A") for the Seagram Building, New York, 1954. Canadian Centre for Architecture, Montreal.

40 percent above the average office building), the Seagram Building became the most expensive office tower ever built, "in Manhattan or anywhere else."[23] The capitalized building value from rental income (usually applied for tax purposes) was only $17 million, but, in a novel approach, the city decided to tax it at $21 million, applying something like a tax on "prestige." While this approach was unsuccessfully appealed, the architectural community protested it as a tax on architectural quality and the freedom of experimentation, one that would prevent the construction of good architecture in New York in the future (a suggestion that seemed to assume that additional costs automatically spell better architecture).[24] If this unusual approach to taxation did indeed, as Lambert suspected, result from puritanical prejudice against the Seagram Company's business practices during Prohibition, it certainly backfired.[25] The Seagram Building emerged in general opinion as a gleaming landmark of an altruistic, high-minded engagement with architectural culture, or, as Lambert put it, "what the company paid in real estate taxes it gained in reputation" (figures 9.24, 9.25).[26]

The lighting design, a crucial issue for the appearance and perception of the building and for the charm of the Four Seasons restaurant, lay mostly in the hands of Philip Johnson and lighting designer Richard Kelly (figure 9.26).[27] (Johnson liked to claim that Mies was

< Figure 9.24. Ludwig Mies van der Rohe, Seagram Building, New York, 1956–58. Outside view from the Lever House. Photograph by Hassan Bagheri.

Figure 9.25. Ludwig Mies van der Rohe, Seagram Building, New York, 1956–58. First-floor plan. Ink on illustration board, 27 1/2 × 20 in. (69.9 × 50.8 cm). Museum of Modern Art, New York. Mies van der Rohe Archive, gift of the architect.

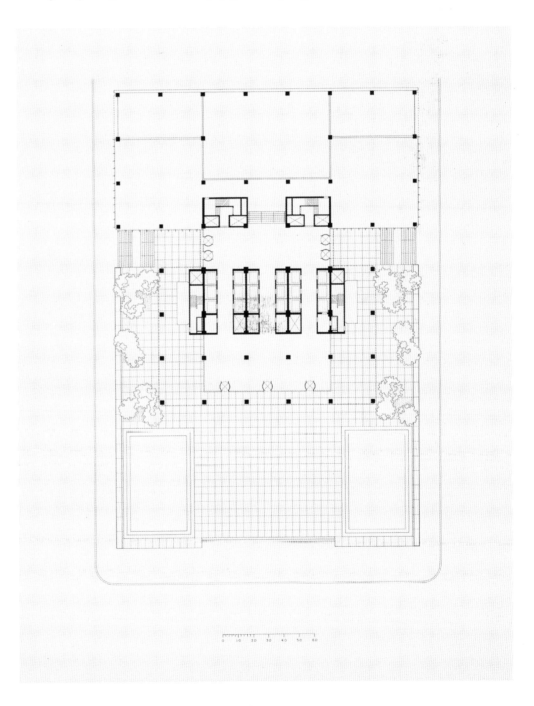

Figure 9.26. Ludwig Mies van der Rohe, Seagram Building, New York, 1956–58. Outside view with ceiling illumination. Photograph by Hassan Bagheri.

"lousy at lighting.")[28] Kelly was responsible for the perimeter lighting on every ceiling, with two dedicated circuits for day and night lighting, and for the recessed downlights and wall washers in the lobby. Kelly convincingly claimed that he talked Mies into covering the lobby's elevator shafts in rough white travertine rather than his customary polished green marble, in order for the grazing light from above to reflect out evenly from the rough surface of the stone, producing the intensely bright glow visible from Park Avenue.[29] Mies's team would apply the Tinos verde marble at later projects, such as the elevator shafts at One Charles Center in Baltimore or at the residential tower at 2400 North Lake View in Chicago (which proved Kelly's point). Recessed downlights were installed in the soffits around the perimeter of the building and along the front glass wall, in addition to two rows in the protruding canopy. The luminous footprint of the tower on the plaza floor helped maintain the transparency of the lobby's glass walls, readied the eye for the intense illumination of the core, and carried the suggestion of the building's interior glow onto the plaza—it became, according to *Architectural Forum,* "one of the best-illuminated buildings ever constructed."[30]

In the eyes of critic Lewis Mumford, this "regal mixture of black and gold that greets one from the lighted building at night" was not just "nighttime splendor," but "the highest aesthetic achievement of the building," even a "post-Whistler nocturne." Mumford hoped that this "integral illumination, divorced from advertising" might serve as an example of how to "enliven the townscape at night."[31]

The Seagram Building was designed and widely celebrated as a "bronze building," and the architects and engineers went to great lengths to work out the color and form of the bronze spandrels and extruded mullions, trying to anticipate the way they would change over time (figures 9.27, 9.28). It was the first skyscraper, as William Jordy once pointed out, that was "consciously designed to age . . . an architectural property as appropriate for Seagram's whisky as sheen for Lever's soap."[32]

As Kiel Moe has pointed out in a recent study, the "bronze" at the Seagram Building is not bronze in the technical sense (namely a copper alloy with 12 percent tin), but rather a material called Architectural Bronze, which is an alloy much closer to brass (a copper and zinc alloy), containing 56 percent copper, 41.5 percent zinc, and 2.5 percent lead. It is more malleable and has a lower melting point. Given Mies's deep interest in revealing the authentic color and structure of materials he worked with, here he could again employ a metal that revealed its genuine, essential hue. A coating of ferric nitrate and lemon oil was applied to Seagram's façade to achieve the desired patina. While inside the lobby the bronze surfaces have aged, as planned, to the rich golden brown of an "old penny" that Mies had cheerfully imagined, most of the building's outside surface has turned an uneven charcoal gray or black (close to the actual black he chose for the Lake Shore Drive Apartments or the IIT campus in Chicago), except in the areas that the cleaning crews would reach (figure 9.29). Understandably, the impact of New York's future air pollution was hard for the engineers of General Bronze to predict.[33]

Similar to the application at the Lake Shore Drive Apartments, small, vertical I-beams were part of the prefabricated façade sections, and continued across the entire façade (see figures 9.27, 9.28). Brass being softer than bronze or steel, the I-beams were not rolled, but extruded (in other words, forced through a die). Pretty much any cross section could be extruded. Gene Summers remembered: "So we tried shapes that were curved, shapes that were rectangular. And we tried in the drawing and then we tried in sketches, and then we would build it full size, a full-size model of it. But in the final analysis, the simple H-shape, like the steel wide-flange, was still the better aesthetic shape."[34] Philip Johnson agreed: "That H-column which makes that shadow, was an absolute revolution, because it gave you your third dimension…the application of a common, ordinary H-beam was a turning point…in façade design."[35] Two small lips on both ends of the flange in the I-beam's cross section demonstrate the process. They could only be achieved by extruding, not by rolling.

Mies would usually aim for the most authentic material appearance, and the stainless steel that he initially preferred was very expensive. The Inland Steel Company showed it off at its headquarters in Chicago by Skidmore, Owings & Merrill (SOM), which was finished at the same time as the Seagram Building (figure 9.30).[36] This was a remarkable counterpoint:

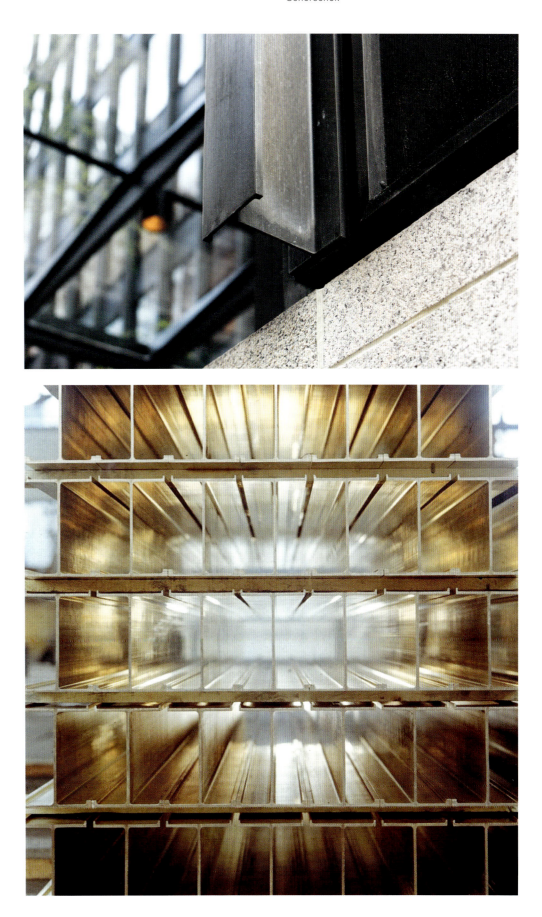

Figure 9.27. Ludwig Mies van der Rohe, Seagram Building, New York, 1956–58. Façade mullions. Photograph by Hassan Bagheri.

Figure 9.28. Extruded brass for the façade mullions of the Seagram Building. Photograph by Frank Scherschel.

its structural system was moved to the outside of the façade and, thanks to its shallower depth, it had column-free inside spaces. Stairs and elevator were placed in a separate tower. The façade also carries vertical, ornamental metal strips; in this case they were solid, rectangular in section, and featured a small indentation on the side.

The plaza in front of the Seagram Building was not entirely unprecedented—after all, the slim slab of the UN Building faced a plaza to the west, and Lever House had created an open space surrounded by an elevated second-floor structure across the street. Its main slab with its green-tinted glass and stainless-steel mullions sat perpendicular to Park Avenue. Kahn & Jacobs had included several comparable solutions in their "Skytop" study, though none quite as radical as Mies's proposal. Mies's careful attention to the plaza's proportion and appearance had much to do with the fact that the building appeared as a perfectly cubic solitaire, while in reality, the overall form was more complicated. There was a spine at the back, whose side walls were filled with dark Tinos verde marble (rather than glass), in order to hide the structural cross-bracing. Lower structures in the back of five and nine floors height created the "bustle." If one stands in the door of the Racquet and Tennis Club across the street, perfectly on axis, these protruding parts on either side are entirely invisible. Mies was unhappy that the new neighboring buildings north and south of the plaza did not go right up to Park Avenue, but included half-hearted plazas in front, and thus deprived the Seagram plaza of a strong definition.[37] What is usually overlooked is the fact that the building extends underneath the plaza all the way to Park Avenue, offering a spatially quite elaborate parking garage that Ezra Stoller found interesting enough to photograph (figure 9.31).

Architects and developers immediately recognized the advantages of the plaza in front, and the 1961 zoning ordinance explicitly encouraged it. Immediate successors in Manhattan included the Time-Life Building on the Avenue of the Americas and Fiftieth Street by Harrison & Abramovitz, the Equitable Life Assurance, Union Carbide Buildings, and the headquarters of Chase Manhattan in the Financial District by SOM. The *New York Times* reported, "The plazas have offset any loss of income by enhancing their buildings' appearance and the companies' prestige. The City Planning Commission, aware of the benefits of plazas to the city, is hoping that its proposed new Zoning Code will give builders an incentive to build more of them, despite the code's basic intention to reduce the bulk, if not the height of new structures."[38] The 1961 zoning ordinance included an incentive

Figure 9.29. Ludwig Mies van der Rohe, Seagram Building, New York, 1956–58. Side entrance. Note the bronze color in areas within reach of the maintenance crews. Photograph by Hassan Bagheri.

Figure 9.30. Skidmore, Owings & Merrill, Inland Steel Building, Chicago, 1958. Photograph by Hedrich-Blessing. Chicago History Museum.

mechanism that allowed developers to build 10 square feet (0.9 square meter) of bonus rentable or sellable floor area in return for one square foot (0.1 square meter) of plaza, and three square feet (0.3 square meter) of bonus floor area in return for one square foot of arcade.[39] Over the next forty years, more than five hundred such "Privately Owned Public Spaces" (POPS) have been built in Manhattan.

Reception

As always, Mies was of little help with the interpretation of the building. When asked, he resorted to his usual laconic reference to the conditions of production that led to the final result: "When we got the job, we tried to read the building code. That was impossible. Then we asked for the best office manager.... How do they want to work?

Figure 9.31. Ludwig Mies van der Rohe, Seagram Building, New York, 1956–58. Interior of three-story parking structure underneath the plaza. Photograph by Ezra Stoller.

How do they want to live in this place. And he gave us some sizes of offices....So we decided on a unit of four-feet-seven [1.4 meters]....Four-feet-seven and multiplication of that...gave us [the] skeleton structure....And then we made just a roster of [this] 27 feet [8.2-meter] bay and put it on this side. And, curiously enough, it worked....We had nothing to do with it."[40]

For Lewis Mumford, it was "the best skyscraper New York has seen since Hood's Daily News Building; in classic execution it towers above the doubled height of the Empire State building, while its nearest later rival, Lever House...looks curiously transitory and ephemeral when one turns from one to the other. Somber, unsmiling, yet not grim, 375 is a muted masterpiece—but a masterpiece." Mumford mentioned "a few urban drawbacks," such as "its municipally sanctioned congestion of occupancy, its lack of visual outlook for all but the occupants of outside offices, its wasteful disproportion of elevator shafts to usable floor space, and its inevitable over-mechanization make it not a desirable model for the city of the future."[41] William Jordy discussed the view from the offices to the outside, returning to the question that Mies had first addressed at 860/880 Lake Shore Drive: "There are those who have complained of giddiness at the openness of their aerie, even though the air-conditioning units provide a balustrade, partly physical, partly psychological, blocking contact with the window. The positive quality of the mullions affords further reassurance, while their columnar like division of the panorama imposes an order and foreground to the view which the fetish for 'picture window' denies." Probably without knowing about Mies's interest in panoramic wallpapers, Jordy still made the connection: "The city appears as an image of itself, somewhat as though it were a photographic mural pasted against the outside surface of the glass."[42]

Many critics agreed that the Seagram Building was just as finite a statement as the apartments at Lake Shore Drive had been. *Architectural Forum* reported: "In Mies's career, Seagram is something of a milestone: it is his first building in New York; it is the largest structure he has ever built anywhere; and it is, finally, the climax of Mies' 40-year search for a new kind of skyscraper—a slab that is, in effect, a sheer cliff of glass. The search began with a primitive but eloquent sketch, back in 1919; it is now concluded, and the evidence is a $43 million monument that will be recorded as one of the great events in twentieth-century architecture."[43] Of course, the Seagram Building was anything but a sheer cliff of glass and had little in common with Mies's Friedrichstrasse Skyscraper design (notably produced in 1922, not 1919), but its opaque, monolithic appearance, oblivious of its neighbors, suggested a calm, self-assured gravitas that had enormous appeal at that particular moment. While its formal language was pretty much identical to that of the Esplanade Apartments at 900/910 Lake Shore Drive in Chicago, the added ceiling height, urban placement, and strict axial symmetry made a significant difference and led to countless imitations worldwide.

Peter Blake saw beyond Seagram's uniqueness toward its potential ubiquity: "From this basic, classical notion of a universal plan and a universal space, Mies developed an entire vocabulary of universality; a vocabulary of universal details, of universal materials (brick, steel, glass), of universal proportions. The more unpredictable building technology and building needs became, the greater was the need, in Mies's eyes, for a universal architectural system of order that could provide answers to any problem. The particular solution, to Mies, was largely a thing of the past."[44] Of course, as a result, "Mies's school of simplification is...relatively easy to copy: any architect of discrimination who has absorbed the rigorous ground rules can produce a good 'Mies building' and, of course, many have," Blake continued. This meant that his staff at the office could continue working in the Miesian idiom.[45] This became more and more important, as Mies, now in his seventies, became increasingly immobile, due to crippling arthritis and later, cancer. In 1961 already, he had to miss the ceremony for his honorary doctorate degree at Columbia University due to ill health. He would be away from the office for months on end, but Gene Summers would drop by his apartment and keep him updated. Mies had become so famous that big jobs kept coming in. The fact that Mies was often not personally involved in design decisions did not mean that the quality of the work in the office suffered. And, besides, Mies had always relied heavily on collaborators, and his degree of involvement had varied greatly, probably similar to any principal's engagement with projects at a busy office. The variations that followed were all interesting in their own right, sometimes offering a better solution to problems that Seagram had not yet solved.

1962   One Charles Center

A twenty-three-story office building became the flagship building of a large (33-acre, or 13.4-hectare) urban renewal project, One Charles Center, in downtown Baltimore (figure 9.32). The project, advanced by the Greater Baltimore Committee around banker and developer James W. Rouse, was developed by urban planner David A. Wallace. It was widely praised for its unusual emphasis on the pedestrian experience, as a sequence of three public plazas above multilevel parking garages were connected by a network of pedestrian routes with bridges and staircases (responding to a 68-foot, or 20.7-meter, drop in topography). It also won praise for the incorporation of several existing buildings, rather than pursuing the customary "clean-slate" approach of such developments. While conceding that "Charles Center, like all urban redevelopment, will cause hardship and perplexing injustices to some people now on the site," urban theorist Jane Jacobs praised this "New Heart for Baltimore" for providing "precisely the things that belong in the heart of downtown—offices, entertainment facilities, a hotel, stores, a transportation terminal."[46] Ultimately, the ambitious expectations for revitalizing downtown did not come to fruition, as the stores at Charles Center continued to struggle, and the squares remained unpopulated. In great contrast, Rouse's

Figure 9.32. Ludwig Mies van der Rohe, One Charles Center, Baltimore, 1962. Photograph by Hassan Bagheri.

subsequent development of Harborplace, five blocks south, became a rousing success when it opened in 1980.

While belonging to the family of what Philip Johnson once called "Sons of Seagram," One Charles Center responded to the plan's ambitions and to the site with astonishing flexibility. The glass-enclosed lobby facing Charles Street was set back to the third bay. A vast terrace on that upper level extended far on the southern side above a row of shops and underground parking. The building's square piers on its western side, toward Center Park, extend to the lower level, thus anchoring the building in the square, while allowing the open terrace above the lower row of shops to continue.

Its T-shaped floor plan provides a cleaner overall outline than the Seagram Building's "bustle," but in other respects it echoed Seagram's details. Instead of panels and I-shaped mullions out of bronze, the material here is cheaper brown anodized aluminum. Since soft aluminum is extruded rather than rolled, just like bronze, the I-beams carry the same cross section as Seagram, sporting two lips at the end the flanges. The structure is reinforced concrete rather than the steel used at Seagram, and there are four equal window modules between each column.

There is no perimeter lighting in the ceilings, but rather the familiar downlighting to create a "pool of light" around the recessed, transparent lobby. The elevator banks are clad in green marble, rather than the light travertine that prevailed at Seagram, with the disadvantage of a darker appearance at night, and a more focused reflection of the

Figure 9.33. Ludwig Mies van der Rohe, One Charles Center, Baltimore, 1962. The landing of the outside staircase to the lower plaza (demolished). Photograph by Hedrich-Blessing. Chicago History Museum.

recessed ceiling lights. Sadly, alterations in 1990 included the removal of the floating stair leading down to the square on the building's west side, as well as the replacement of the travertine paving and marble cladding on the podium (figure 9.33).

1963–69   Toronto-Dominion Centre

To this day, the Toronto-Dominion Centre complex serves as the headquarters of the TD Bank (the result of a merger of the Bank of Toronto and Dominion Bank in 1963), with about twenty-one thousand people working in the complex. The project was initiated by the bank's president, Allen Lambert, whose brother Jean had been married to Phyllis Lambert. The couple had divorced at exactly the moment when Phyllis Lambert got involved in her father's search for an architect for the Seagram Building. After Gordon Bunshaft of SOM submitted an unconvincing proposal, Lambert, who had become a consultant to the project, insisted on inviting Mies van der Rohe, who worked with the Canadian architects John B. Parkin Associates and Bregman & Hamann. When the TD Bank Tower was finished, its 731 feet (222 meters) and fifty-four stories made it the tallest in Canada (figure 9.34). The Banking Pavilion and Royal Trust Tower (today TD North, forty-four stories) followed in 1968 and 1969. The one-story pavilion at the center, a fifteen-bay square, has a columnless interior underneath a welded steel grid ceiling.

Two towers (TD West and TD South) followed in 1974 and 1985, both in Mies's recognizable idiom, but not part of his initial plan, resulting in a cluster of five Miesian towers, with the low banking pavilion between them. They are accessed via two diagonally connected public plazas—which, thanks to the towers' east–west orientation, receive enough sunlight, making this the most convincing urban cluster in Mies's idiom. All five towers achieve the uninterrupted, simple geometric form that Mies had not been able to accomplish in New York or in Baltimore.

1959–73   Federal Center

As part of a federal program to enhance the government's administrative presence in the late 1950s, the General Services Administration instituted a major building campaign. Mies, whose firm collaborated with Schmidt, Garden & Erikson, as well as C. F. Murphy Associates, luckily got the commission for the Federal Center in Chicago at a moment when his office "had next to nothing"; he would build two high-rises, of thirty and forty-two floors, and a single-story, square post office building between them on the corner of South Dearborn and West Adams streets in the downtown Loop—coincidentally close to Mies's favorite restaurant, the Berghoff (figure 9.35).[47] The idiom is the same as at Seagram Building, but Mies and his team managed again to place all the auxiliary spaces, such as stairs, elevators, and lavatories, at the core of each tower, and thus avoided the spine and bustle there. The urban constellation with open space surrounding the post office is somewhat affected by the tall John C. Kluczynski Federal Building, which sits on the plaza's southern side and thus blocks sunlight during the entire day. Holabird & Roche's 1895 Marquette Building faces the plaza, while Burnham & Root's Monadnock is blocked off from it. According to Joe Fujikawa, Mies was mostly concerned with the proportions and arrangement of the plaza, rather than the historical context of the neighboring buildings.[48] Alexander Calder's red steel sculpture *Flamingo* was installed on the plaza in 1974.

1964–67   Westmount Square

The Westmount Square development in Montreal combines two apartment building (twenty-one floors each) with an office building (twenty-two floors) surrounding a low office building and a first-floor shopping center (figure 9.36). Due to a light slope on the site, access to the plaza and entrance level of all three buildings from busy Ste. Catherine Street has to proceed from a lower level without immediate access to the entrance area of the towers. The two-story office block in the center projects out into the streetscape to announce the project. The fact that both the office tower and the two residential towers use the exact same formal language that Mies had first developed for the Esplanade Apartments in Chicago in 1955, then applied at Seagram and elsewhere, brings us back to the beginning

Figure 9.34. Ludwig Mies van der Rohe, TD Bank
Tower, Toronto-Dominion Centre, Toronto, 1963–
69. Photograph by Hassan Bagheri.

Figure 9.35. Ludwig Mies van der Rohe, Federal Center, Chicago, 1959–73. Photograph by Hassan Bagheri.

of this evolution. It also demonstrates the independence of form from function in Mies's design thinking. While all residential towers after the Esplanade had used light-colored aluminum frames and either an aluminum-clad or exposed concrete structure, here Mies chose to create visual coherence along the lines of the Seagram Building, unifying both apartment and office blocks. The fact that Phyllis Lambert, who had been instrumental in getting Mies involved at the Seagram Building, acted as one of the sponsors of the project might have contributed to this decision. The functional mix of office and apartments has proven successful.

1968 Mansion House Square

When the eighteen-story tower for Mansion House Square in London was commissioned by British entrepreneur Rudolph Palumbo in 1968, to be occupied by Lloyd's Bank, it had already encountered protests from the Royal Fine Art Commission and the Greater London Council because of its height being close to that of St. Paul's.[49] Still, the application was approved under the condition that Palumbo acquire the entire site. The tower followed the visual language of the Seagram Building closely, but had unusually wide bays at the front (six windows per bay) and smaller ones at the side (four windows per bay), similar to the contemporary solution at 2400 North Lake View in Chicago (figure 9.37).

Fourteen years later, in 1982, Palumbo's son Peter, also a developer and admirer of Mies, who had recently purchased the Farnsworth House, revived the scheme after having patiently acquired all necessary property titles.[50] Sensing renewed headwinds, he presented

< Figure 9.36. Ludwig Mies van der Rohe, Westmount Square, Montreal, 1964–67. Photograph by Hassan Bagheri.

Figure 9.37. Ludwig Mies van der Rohe, Mansion House Square project, London, 1968. Photomontage with model, 1968. Royal Institute of British Architects, London.

the scheme to the public in an exhibition at the Royal Institute of British Architects, supported by the institute's president, Michael Manser. Richard Rogers, Norman Foster, and James Stirling jointly declared it "a great architectural addition to London; in fact, a masterpiece,"[51] and architectural historian John Summerson saw "a marvelously exciting architectural adventure."[52] A lively debate followed, touching on questions of urban design, Mies's architectural philosophy and its appropriateness for the present time, and the enduring value of the goals and philosophy of modern architecture.[53] Slowly the tides turned, as traditional urbanism and postmodern planning ideas gained ground, and the debate came to a head in 1984—just when the Barcelona Pavilion's new incarnation was beginning to rise. Hearings were held, editorials published, and countless letters reached the editors of London's papers. The Greater London Council, the Royal Fine Art Commission, the Victorian Society, and Save Britain's Heritage publicly declared their opposition. On May 30, 1984, on the occasion of the 150th anniversary of the Royal Institute of British Architects, Prince Charles called the building a "giant glass stump, better suited to downtown Chicago than the City of London." (In that same speech, he famously dismissed Peter Ahrends's winning design for an extension to the National Gallery as "a monstrous carbuncle on the face of a much-beloved and elegant friend.")[54] Other headlines were equally unflattering, such as "A Monument to the Dead"[55] or "Palumbo's Pile."[56] Architectural historian John Harris doubted that, due to the lateness of the design, Mies had anything to do with it at all,[57] and Henry-Russell Hitchcock conceded that Mies could have at best only been involved in "preliminary work" on the tower—a fact that had been contested by Mies's collaborators Peter Carter and William Holford when the building had first been discussed.[58] David Watkin considered the demolition of historic buildings for Mies's scheme a "disaster…unparalleled since the destruction of London by Hitler's bombs."[59] Philip Johnson found the design a "posthumous and unimportant piece of architecture…one of many sons of Seagram," while lacking Seagram's greatest asset: the square in front. Mies deserved "better monuments," he added.[60]

In May 1985, the venerable London *Times* took a stand in favor of Mies's scheme, lauding its magisterial architecture, the open space it offered, and the fact that it was ready for action, providing 178,000 square feet (16,500 square meters) of office space.[61] Only weeks later, the final, negative, decision was made by Prime Minister Margaret Thatcher, who had personally inspected the model,[62] in a written answer to a parliamentary question.[63] Peter Palumbo selected James Stirling as his new architect.[64] After long delays and protests regarding the demolition of John Belcher's 1870 Mappin & Webb Building on the site, Stirling's No. 1 Poultry was, posthumously, erected in 1997—at a time when a Miesian skyscraper already looked again more contemporary than the strained, multicolored confection the aging Stirling had cobbled together before his death.[65] After his painful defeat in 1985, Peter Palumbo consoled himself by purchasing Frank Lloyd Wright's Kentuck Knob (1956), a rural weekend house south of Pittsburgh, Pennsylvania, in 1986.

1960s Mid-Size Buildings

The unique fact that Mies's office had established a recognizable style, had worked out most of the details, and had no problems applying formally similar solutions to many different building tasks made it easy to accept commissions and execute them swiftly with a comparatively small staff. It was an economically shrewd philosophy, and there is probably no other American office whose style remained so consistently recognizable over fifteen years. As a result of the extraordinary press coverage that had come with the Seagram Building and other high-profile projects, new commissions kept coming in throughout the 1960s, as Mies himself was retiring more and more from the office.

The Federal Savings and Loan Association Building in downtown Des Moines, Iowa, for example, was designed in 1959 and opened in 1962 in an unusual square, three-by-three bay footprint (figure 9.38). Mies's team had initially experimented here with an exoskeleton of exposed roof girders, similar to the unexecuted design for the Cantor Drive-In in Indianapolis, but then decided on this conventional approach. Also, in Des Moines, Drake University commissioned Meredith Hall (1961–65), and so did Duquesne University in Pittsburgh, with its Mellon Hall (1968), and the University of Chicago, with its Crown Family School of Social Work, Policy and Practice (1965). Washington, D.C., commissioned the Martin Luther King Jr. Memorial Library (1969–72) (figure 9.39). Here, Mies's fame surely helped to overcome the hesitation of the Washington, D.C., planning commissions, as it permitted a building in the International Style in the city center, where neoclassicism was still very much de rigeur.

1957–68   Bacardi Headquarters, Museum Georg Schaefer I and II, Neue Nationalgalerie

Very few architects have the good fortune of ending their career with a building so astounding that it seems like a final word or gesture, a proud summary of an accomplished life. Both Frank Lloyd Wright and Mies van der Rohe were so lucky.

Ludwig Mies van der Rohe had been commissioned by the Bacardi distillery in 1956 to design its new headquarters in Santiago de Cuba on the southern coast of the Caribbean island. Bacardi president José M. Bosch had seen Crown Hall and wanted a glass-enclosed, open-plan office for his staff, with a sample bar and sales rooms in the basement. The decisive design sketches were made in April 1957 on letterhead from the Hotel Nacional de Cuba in Havana. The Hotel Nacional, by the way, had been designed by McKim, Mead & White, and opened in 1930 as the most luxurious hotel in Havana. Probably unbeknownst to Mies and his collaborator Gene Summers, it had been the site of two historically significant events: the 1933 coup by Cuban military officer Fulgencio Batista, paving the way to his presidency (1940–44) and military dictatorship (1952–59), which ended with the Cuban Revolution; and an infamous 1946 mob summit, when the hotel hosted mafia delegations from New York, New Jersey, Buffalo, Chicago, New Orleans, and Florida.

Figure 9.38. Ludwig Mies van der Rohe, Federal Savings and Loan Association Building, Des Moines, Iowa, 1959–62. Photograph by Hedrich-Blessing. Chicago History Museum.

As Mies and Summers sat under the protective canopy of the hotel's veranda gazing out over the ocean, envisioning the Bacardi Headquarters, they realized that a glass façade would have to be deeply shaded in this climate. As Summers remembered: "We were sitting under this overhang which was quite interesting, it was probably twenty feet [six meters] high, it had long sort of colonial like columns [with] probably twenty feet…between the column and the wall and we were sitting very comfortably on lounge chairs having a drink and I said to Mies, 'this is kind of what we need to shelter the glass and to offer shadow and to keep the sun out of the inside. At least in the summertime.'"[66] They designed a wide, cantilevered square roof (177 by 177 feet, or 54 by 54 meters), held aloft by just two tapered concrete supports on each side (figure 9.40). This was a return to ideas Mies had explored when he was trying to develop the Farnsworth House into a prototype for mass production. The "50 × 50 House" of 1952, which was supposed to only have one column on each side, for example, is a direct predecessor to this concept. For the Bacardi Headquarters, desks, office cabinets, and six-and-a-half-foot- (two-meter-) high room dividers were to accentuate the wide-open space into "executive space" and "office space," for a staff of seventy-five. A broad staircase led downstairs to the retail and tasting room, as well as storage space and the legal department. Twenty people were supposed to work on this windowless lower floor.

The roof structure was designed as a two-way grid of prestressed concrete beams, as steel was hard to come by in Cuba. There was a suspended ceiling underneath, and "above this ceiling five separate air-conditioning units will be set into the roof slab." When construction was about to begin, the design made it onto the cover of *Architectural Forum* in February 1959, where Peter Blake celebrated it as "Mies's one-office office building."[67]

Weeks before, Fidel Castro had come into power, marching into Havana on January 9, 1959. José M. Bosch was, at first, confident that he could stay and execute the structure for his growing company: "Now that we have democracy and justice in Cuba, we can have this building built," he declared.[68] He ended up fleeing the impending nationalization of his company in 1960 and moved its headquarters to Mexico City, where Mies and his team designed a new building for him, better suited to the climate and easier to execute. It

Figure 9.39. Ludwig Mies van der Rohe, Martin Luther King Jr. Memorial Library, Washington, D.C., 1969–72. Photograph by Hassan Bagheri.

was finished in 1961 and a sibling to the (then still unexecuted) fraternity building at the University of Indiana in Bloomington of 1952 (figures 9.41, 9.42).

Mies's original design for Bacardi ended up in a drawer of his Chicago office. A year later, Georg Schäfer, a German industrialist and collector of medieval art (and also the father-in-law of Mies's grandson Dirk Lohan), decided to build a museum for his collection in his hometown of Schweinfurt; he commissioned Mies's office in 1960. The resulting design (apparently done by Gene Summers without much involvement by Mies, who was ill and did not come to the office much) was approved by Schäfer—a glass box with brick walls for the hanging and positioning of his collections and a tall band of light above.

According to Franz Schulze and Edward Windhorst, the first Schweinfurt design (begun in February 1961) was ready in December 1961, and Summers went to Germany to show it to Schäfer, who then sent a telegram to Mies confirming that he liked and accepted the design. Sometime in January or February 1962, Mies returned to the office and decided to instead revive the Bacardi concept. It was redesigned in steel, and precise drawings, a model, and some collages were created. The windowless basement had a big lecture hall with 242 seats, bathrooms, storage rooms, and study rooms for scholars consulting the collection.[69]

All this was presented to Schäfer, who, however, preferred the early design, as he told Summers (but apparently not Mies himself). In the meantime, Mies had been contacted by West Berlin's senator for building, Rolf Schwedler, who congratulated him on his seventy-fifth birthday in March 1961 and held out the prospect of a commission for the Galerie des 20 Jahrhunderts (Gallery of the Twentieth Century). (In a case of Cold War brinkmanship, it was later called the Neue Nationalgalerie [New National Gallery], in contrast to the Alte [Old] Nationalgalerie in East Berlin, and thus claiming

Figure 9.40. Ludwig Mies van der Rohe, Bacardi Headquarters project, Santiago de Cuba, Cuba, 1959. Model. Photograph by Hedrich-Blessing. Chicago History Museum.

the "national" label for a building in the western sector.) Mies was officially commissioned in the summer of 1962. The director of Bacardi gave Mies permission to use his design, and Schäfer agreed that Berlin could have the later Schweinfurt design (which he had found impractical anyway). Why the first design for Schweinfurt was then never realized remains a mystery.

For the museum, the design of the glass-enclosed hall remained largely unchanged, the planned concrete structure was replaced by steel, and the whole thing was made slightly larger—the room height grew from 23 to 28 feet (7 to 8.4 meters).

While Mies was working on the designs for Cuba, an article in *Architectural Forum* of March 1958 must have caught his attention: it described the new Air Force Academy Cadet Dining Hall (today called Mitchell Hall) in Colorado Springs, designed by Gertrude Lempp Kerbis in the office of Skidmore, Owings & Merrill (figure 9.43). The Cadet Dining Hall was designed to feed three thousand Air Force cadets at the same time—within half an hour. The roof is a perfect square, its side length 308 feet (93.9 meters), and the free span between the columns is 266 feet (81 meters). There are no columns inside, and three of its four sides are fully glazed. Four (originally two) columns on each side stand close to the glass and wall enclosure, and the roof cantilevers out two bays beyond. Its enormous steel grid roof truss, weighing over 1,000 tons (about 2,400 tonnes), was assembled on the ground and then lifted into place, 24 feet (7.3 meters) above on its sixteen load-bearing columns, with the help of sixteen hydraulic presses. It was the first structure of this type and clearly a precise model for Mies's approach at the Neue Nationalgalerie in Berlin, several years later.[70] Kerbis had studied architecture at the University of Illinois, then under

Figure 9.43. Gertrude Lempp Kerbis (of Skidmore, Owings & Merrill), Cadet Dining Hall, Air Force Academy, Colorado Springs, 1958. Photograph by Hedrich-Blessing.

Gropius at Harvard, and returned to Chicago to study under Mies. While still a student, she married Walter Peterhans, one of Mies's closest collaborators. After graduating, she worked for SOM and became responsible for the Cadet Dining Hall.[71]

While about a third smaller (with a 216-foot, or 65-meter, side length versus 308 feet, or 93 meters), the Neue Nationalgalerie followed a comparable principle (figure 9.44). It relied on only two columns on each side, but placed them at the roof's edge, rather than in the plane of the glass wall, which would have been structurally easier. Each of the eighteen-by-eighteen square modules measures 12 by 12 feet (3.7 by 3.7 meters). There is a span between the outside columns of eight by 12 feet, equaling 96 square feet (2.4 by 3.7 meters, equaling 29.2 square meters), and cantilevers on each side of five by 12 feet, equaling 60 square feet (1.5 by 3.7 meters, equaling 18.3 square meters) on each side. The girders have stiffening steel sections (in Colorado they are an open square grid with diagonal braces) of different thicknesses and also different steel qualities. The stresses are higher in the center and above the supports, and therefore high-tensile steel is used in those areas. Mies was very concerned about the straight appearance of the horizontal ceiling grid, which "resulted in a considerable deviation from the mathematically pure plane. When all dead loads are finally applied the roof should have a camber of four inches [10.1 centimeters] in the center and two inches [five centimeters] in midspan, at the edges, and at the four corners."[72] In other words, the grid was ever so slightly curved upward in the center to give the appearance of complete horizontality (figure 9.45). Before being hoisted into place, the steel roof was assembled on the ground (or rather four feet, or 1.2 meters, above it, to give the welders easier access to each quadrant) from prefabricated sections—eight box girders (12 feet, or 3.7 meters, wide each), four edge girders, and one center girder. Each one was divided into three 72-foot- (22-meter-) long sections.

Figure 9.44. Ludwig Mies van der Rohe, Neue Nationalgalerie, Berlin, 1965–68. View from the northeast, 1968. Photograph by Balthazar Korab.

If the Bacardi hall would have been built, the use would have at some point been adapted to the building, and not vice versa. "Functions are not constant," Mies said when attending the groundbreaking ceremony in 1964 in Berlin.[73] What he had sketched with his assistant in Havana corresponded to what he had been working on for decades: a clear, column-free space that could be used in a variety of ways and at the same time bring out the essential elements of architecture—space, structure, material, light.

The carefully balanced relationship of the supports to the roof slab, for example, aimed for the greatest possible lightness: Mies pursued the ideal of pure architecture—a new, absolute clarity on the tabula rasa of the destroyed city, an architecture that also saw itself as a counter-design to the expressionism of Hans Scharoun's Berliner Philharmonie (Philharmonic) right next to it. Bruno Taut's post–World War I vision of a "city crown," a sophisticated new urban center with a light-flooded glass temple for a religion of pure architecture, served in different ways as an inspiration for both Scharoun's and Mies's designs for a future unified capital.

What perhaps even Mies did not fully anticipate was the additional function that would fall to his Neue Nationalgalerie in the years to come. Its elevated position offered a panoramic view, a belvedere comparable to Schinkel's *"Grosse Neugierde"* (Great Curiosity) in Klein-Glienicke Park. The visual contact with the surrounding city, reminding visitors of their role as citizens of a community, also exists in other museum buildings. In Schinkel's Altes Museum, the large open stairwell took on this task—as did the roof access that was initially possible. And at Leo von Klenze's Alte Pinakothek in Munich, it was the long walkway on the upper floor with a view of the city skyline—which fell victim to the war.

Figure 9.45. Ludwig Mies van der Rohe, Neue Nationalgalerie, Berlin, 1965–68. Entrance area, 1968. Photograph by Balthazar Korab.

From the Neue Nationalgalerie, this panoramic view fell on the badly damaged Matthäi-kirche, on Scharoun's Philharmonie, on endless fields of ruins, and a section of the wall at Potsdamer Platz. "Look at this city"—Berlin mayor Ernst Reuter's words from his famous 1948 speech may have rung in the ears of many at the time.[74] The counterpart to Mies's open space for the contemplation of art and the city is the *hortus conclusus*, the walled-in sculpture garden on the lower level in the back, which turns the gaze inward, providing the only source of natural light for the galleries of the permanent collection.

Mies had come to the museum's groundbreaking ceremony in September 1965, and he came again for the topping-out ceremony. By then, he was eighty-one years old and suffering from painful arthritis. The circle was complete—about 1,500 feet (500 meters) away, on the other side of the Landwehr Canal, had been his own apartment: Am Karlsbad 24. It had fallen victim to Albert Speer's capital planning already before the bombing. Mies had lived and worked there from 1915 until his emigration to America in 1938. His visionary designs for glass skyscrapers and a concrete office building had been created there, as had the drawings for the Barcelona Pavilion and the Tugendhat House in Brno—all of them ground-breaking events in twentieth-century architecture.

Joined by his old colleague Hans Scharoun, who had built the philharmonic hall nearby, Mies watched as the roof was slowly raised to the height of 27.5 feet (8.4 meters) by hydraulic presses on April 5, 1967. The process took ten hours. As soon as there was enough room, the architect limped slowly but purposefully on his crutches under the 1,200-ton (1,088-tonne) steel roof. He was full of confidence in the engineers' calculations. He ponderously took a turn and looked around—thrilled that his ideal building was becoming a reality on this very spot. "I had almost forgotten how wonderful it is to be an architect," he said.[75]

Reception

At the opening ceremony a year and a half later, on September 15, 1968, leaflets rained down on the dancing guests in the sculpture garden. From the terrace above, students protested against the "temple of glory" of the city's establishment, arguing that politics and private interests had joined forces to "assassinate the city" (figure 9.46). Inhumane social housing projects were just as much part of the city's corruption as the "reparation architecture" of the Neue Nationalgalerie, which was built without a competition and was a symbol of a "new heavy *Gründerzeit*."[76] The students juxtaposed photos of the Neue Nationalgalerie with Mies's monument to the November Revolution, stating: "Since today Berlin has the opportunity to inaugurate a late work by Mies van der Rohe, we see it as an obligation to the history of the city and the architect to rebuild this structure—one of the few he realized in Berlin."[77] As mentioned above, Mies's 1926 monument in Friedrichsfelde's central cemetery, honoring Rosa Luxemburg and Karl Liebknecht, had been destroyed by the Nazis eight years later. Now the students wanted it rebuilt on the banks of the Landwehr Canal, where the two politicians had been murdered in 1919. They presented their clay model first on the museum terrace and then at a symbolic groundbreaking ceremony at the anticipated site nearby. One thousand visitors signed the appeal; many of the young coauthors would later become prominent Berlin architects—Hinrich Baller, Jonas Geist, Josef Kleihues, Nikolaus Kuhnert, Goerd Peschken, and Jürgen Sawade.

There was hardly a newspaper or architectural magazine in Germany that did not report on the new building. From rapturous enthusiasm to detached analysis and amused rejection, all shades were represented, depending on how much weight a critic attached to the museum's functionality, the political climate, or the breathtaking construction. An overview would best begin with *Bauwelt*, whose editor-in-chief, Ulrich Conrads, had been campaigning for a building by Mies in his former hometown since 1961.[78] A year later, Mies received the commission for the Galerie des 20 Jahrhunderts. At the opening, Conrads proudly wrote: "Wish and request have become tangible reality. The work stands before us." He was impressed by Mies's "entirely confident, entirely certain, entirely undramatic space creation." He said that much reminded him of the Barcelona Pavilion (by now considered in absentia the best building of the twentieth century), but the architect had become someone else entirely since. Asymmetry had given way to the strictest symmetry—"Mies van der Rohe walking most decisively arm in arm with

Figure 9.46. Student protests at the opening of the Neue Nationalgalerie, Berlin, September 15, 1968. Note their model of Mies's Monument to the November Revolution.

Schinkel." Yet even Conrads found some things downright "impossible"—such as the gloomy automat café in the basement and the coat checks and ventilation shafts under the floating steel roof. The absolute primacy of the structural idea had led to "drawbacks" and "misunderstandings."[79]

Perhaps inspired by the demonstrations at the opening, some critics addressed the political unrest that shook Berlin and many other cities in the late 1960s. Discussions about the future of the museum as an institution were part of the cultural reorientation of the time—parallels to today's debates about decolonization are immediately striking. Camilla Blechen of the *Frankfurter Allgemeine Zeitung*, for example, recognized the "beginning of a change of conditions": the museum would no longer be "an object for a reverent attitude," but a place for "emotional charging and entertainment, a museum for everyone." And while the radical left "considered the 'museum an instrument of oppression,' sociologically, the institution is in top form."[80] Jürgen Beckelmann of the *Frankfurter Rundschau* similarly speculated that the "New National Gallery was not designed for the...elite clique of art lovers, but for everyone," especially those "who have never ventured into a museum before. The 'public atmosphere' of this 'train station of a building' will be instrumental in overcoming the false reverence for art. Critical debate can and should take place here. And for that reason alone, the museum, which at first glance seems 'quite impossible,' is an ideal museum."[81]

In the weekly *Die Zeit,* Gottfried Sello half-heartedly conceded that the building was "probably a masterpiece," but also "deeply depressing" as a missed opportunity. It marked "the magnificent endpoint of museum development, but not a new beginning." After all the discussions about un-museum-like museums, Berlin had received another temple of art "like we've had a hundred times, only just not quite as comfortable, not quite as perfected....Forty years ago, the new building would have been an avant-garde beacon. Today, just inaugurated, it is an anachronism."[82] Architectural historian Julius Posener agreed. Situating the building so close to the Berlin Wall amounted to a hollow political gesture, and as a building type, it was an anachronism. A museum building of a future socialist society would have to look different and not so "austere, monumental, significant."[83]

Mies responded to his critics in a conversation with (and prompted by) his daughter Dorothea. He said: "This is such a large hall in Berlin, which of course brings great difficulties for the exhibitions and the man who makes them. Of course, I am fully aware of that. But it has such great potential that I don't take those difficulties into account at all."[84]

The three major American architecture magazines reported extensively about the building. Mies's old friend and editor-in-chief of *Architectural Forum,* Peter Blake, a native Berliner, came to the opening. He sympathized with the protesting students: they "should have been admitted to the ceremony, instead of some of the elders," and in any event he was pleased "that even the most radical of the radical students in the world today consider Mies one of their own." He was less taken with the model-making skills of the young revolutionaries: "Mies would have scolded the person who made that model, by the way!"

The building itself, according to Blake, was "the most beautiful building ever created by Mies van der Rohe," and "made most of 20th-century architecture look nearly amateurish." While agreeing with other critics that the Mondrian exhibit in the Great Hall was not ideal (a giant Jackson Pollock would have been a better fit), he found the basement rooms spacious and well-lit (figure 9.47).[85] *Architectural Record,* the largest-circulation architectural magazine in the United States, shared Blake's enthusiasm, supported by Balthazar Korab's brilliant photographs. The building was a "consummate masterpiece," and "one of the finest buildings ever built."[86]

In great contrast, *Progressive Architecture* complained that Mies had avoided any political or social stance, creating merely the largest and most precious work of art for the museum's own collection, a monument to itself and its creator. It was only partially up to its task, the magazine declared, as displaying art behind walls of glass was not a good idea, the pedestal was too wide, and the surroundings too empty: "It's exquisite and uplifting to behold, but it bears little relation to the tumult of Berlin life, and perhaps even to the tumult of contemporary art."[87]

Luckily, most of the reviews appeared in the summer of 1968, before the cold Berlin winter brought along the predictable floods of condensation water on the inside of the large, single-pane glass plates. The architects had promised that the "hot air stream directed upward just inside the glass walls prevents accumulation of condensation," but this unproven technique did not deliver the anticipated results.[88] The museum management requested woolen blankets from army supplies to catch the water at the foot of the glass wall.[89]

It was no coincidence that the Museum of Modern Art in New York held an *Architecture of Museums* exhibition to coincide with the opening in Berlin, in which the Nationalgalerie took center stage with a model, a wall-sized photograph, and several smaller photographs (alongside buildings and projects by Le Corbusier, Frank Lloyd Wright, Philip Johnson, Marcel Breuer, and others). The curator, Ludwig Glaeser, was in the process of organizing the transfer of the Mies estate to New York (see below), and the appropriate appreciation was important to both the office and the museum, which had taken on the estate. In his introduction to the catalogue, Glaeser noticed that Mies, more consistently than anyone else, had applied his architectural concepts to exhibitions: "Paintings and sculptures are used as if they were walls and supports, defining the open space."[90]

Figure 9.47. Ludwig Mies van der Rohe, Neue Nationalgalerie, Berlin, 1965–68. Opening of the *Piet Mondrian* exhibition, 1968. Photograph by Balthazar Korab.

When the Neue Nationalgalerie reemerged in 2020 after a spirited five-year restoration by David Chipperfield, the mixed reception it had received sixty years ago had become irrelevant (figures 9.48–9.50). Its unique configuration was a simple fact that invited responses

Figure 9.48. Ludwig Mies van der Rohe, Neue Nationalgalerie, Berlin, 1965–68. Outside view after the restoration by David Chipperfield, 2021. Photograph by Simon Menges.

Figure 1.22. Temple of Philae in Egypt, 6th century BCE. Early 20th-century stereocard. Private collection.

Figure 1.23. Bismarck Memorial at Elisenhöhe, Bingen, Germany. Competition entry by Ludwig Mies and Ewald Mies, 1910. Model view inserted in a site photograph. Collage gelatin silver photograph, direct carbon photograph, ink on illustration board, 40 × 50 in. (76.5 × 102 cm). Museum of Modern Art, New York. The Mies van der Rohe Archive, gift of the architect.

Figure 1.24. Bismarck Memorial at Elisenhöhe, Bingen, Germany. Competition entry by Ludwig Mies and Ewald Mies, 1910. Longitudinal side elevation. Pencil and colored pastel on tracing paper, 39 3/4 × 7 ft. 9 1/2 in. (99.5 × 214 cm). Museum of Modern Art, New York. The Mies van der Rohe Archive, gift of the architect.

DEUTSCHLANDS DANK

Figure 9.50. Ludwig Mies van der Rohe, Neue Nationalgalerie, Berlin, 1965–68. Exhibition spaces downstairs after restoration and before art installation, 2021. Photograph by Simon Menges.

but not criticism. Building technology had progressed in the meantime to allow solutions closer to Mies's original vision, in particular in regards to the large single panes in the outside wall. Their higher insulation coefficient will reduce, but not entirely eliminate, the forming of condensation water in the winter—a reminder of Mies's nonchalant stance toward the precarious tension of form versus function.

Mies had not been present at the opening and died a year later, at eighty-three years old. At the time of his death, Mies had thirty people working in his office, three of whom he had recently made partners. Bruno Conterato, Joe Fujikawa, and Mies's grandson Dirk Lohan continued to work as the Office of Mies van der Rohe and, after 1976, as Fujikawa, Conterato, Lohan & Associates. Their initial focus was on buildings that had been commissioned when Mies was still alive, such as the office building at 111 East Wacker Drive, also known as One Illinois Center (1966–70), and the fifty-two-story IBM Center (1969–72) in Chicago (figure 9.51).

Figure 9.51. Ludwig Mies van der Rohe, IBM Center, Chicago, 1969–72. Photograph by Hassan Bagheri.

Afterword

Legacy

One early morning in the summer of 1962, a truck with East German security agents appeared unannounced in front of August Ludwig's carpentry shop in Mühlhausen, a picturesque town behind the Iron Curtain in Communist East Germany (figure 10.1). The commander asked to see crates that the family had stored in a back room. When Mr. Ludwig obliged, the crates were immediately confiscated, loaded onto the truck, and transported away—in a "military style" operation that left the family shaken.[1] After traveling 186 miles (300 kilometers) north, the truck unloaded its cargo at the Akademie der Künste (Academy of Arts) in East Berlin. The crates contained the entirety of Mies van der Rohe's and Lilly Reich's work from before 1937.[2] The raid in Mühlhausen was a key moment, the crucible in the unique process of establishing and defining Mies's legacy for posterity.

The archive's odyssey has all the trappings of a Cold War drama, deeply entwined as it was with the political tides of its time. When Mies immigrated to the United States in August 1938, he had left his Berlin office and apartment in the hands of Reich—initially thinking he would be gone for only two years.[3] Contrary to his expectations, his contract in Chicago was renewed in 1940.[4] In any event, by then, World War II had broken out, and a return or even a visit to Germany was out of the question. At the same time, Albert Speer's megalomaniac redesign of Hitler's Berlin as "Germania" had commenced with demolitions for an intended broad north–south axis. Mies's home since 1915, Am Karlsbad 24, in the elegant Tiergarten district, was one of the first casualties. Once the permit was issued on June 3, 1939, the inhabitants were notified and given a time frame to relocate.[5] Shortly after receiving this news, Lilly Reich left to visit Mies in Chicago from July through September 1939, and after her return she started to pack up the office.

This was the moment when Mies's drawings and paperwork and many of Reich's were put into crates for storage. The building was taken down in November 1940. Toward the end of the war, when bombardments were imminent, Reich entrusted the crates to their collaborator and former student Eduard Ludwig, who brought them to his parents' home in Mühlhausen, which was unlikely to be bombed. After the war, Communist East Germany was cumbersome to reach from the West, requiring costly visas and much advance planning. Ludwig kept Mies informed, writing a few weeks after Lilly Reich's death on December 14, 1947: "According to a list among Mrs. Reich's papers, there are many plans and original drawings of your early work in the boxes that are with my parents in Thuringia." He promised to look through them on his next visit, to "see what can be used to get better image reproductions."[6]

Three years later, Ludwig again updated Mies about his estate: "The boxes with your work are still in Mühlhausen/Thüringen in the Eastern Sector. They are safe there, and I can't risk transporting them through the Soviet Zone....It would be a pity if they got lost....Even sending the material in small individual packages to Berlin is impossible, since every package is being opened and censored."[7] By 1958, West German art historian Hans Maria Wingler had heard about the boxes. While writing a history of the Bauhaus, he contacted Ludwig and then went to Mühlhausen several times in 1959 to look through them.[8] Not wanting to alert the authorities, he did so clandestinely—officially, his mission was to study medieval architecture nearby. Ludwig explained: "If the location of these works is known, they will be immediately confiscated by the government of the Eastern Sector."[9]

The political climate between East and West Germany became more volatile, the Berlin Wall went up in August 1961, and the inner German border was fortified with minefields, dog runs, and motion-activated machine guns. Little could be hidden from East German intelligence, and Wingler's repeated visits might have caught the attention of the Stasi and triggered the abovementioned raid.

Apparently, no one in East Berlin quite knew what to do with the boxes, once they had arrived at the Akademie der Künste. But then luck intervened. Kurt Liebknecht, one of the most prominent architects in East Germany, director of the Institut für Theorie und Geschichte der Architektur (Institute for the Theory and History of Architecture) of the Bauakademie, and a high-ranking politician (a member of the party's powerful Zentralkommittee from 1954 to 1963), heard of the boxes at the academy and went to see them. Liebknecht was the nephew of the murdered Communist activist Karl Liebknecht and had worked for Mies in 1927, just after the latter had designed the Monument to the November Revolution. He remembered his time in Mies's office fondly and wrote to him in September 1962 to assure him that he supported efforts to get his material to him, but asked for permission to make some photocopies first, and also asked Mies for samples of his more recent work, to make it better known "in the countries of the socialist camp."[10] His elevated position in the party hierarchy gave him considerable clout. Any material pertaining to the Bauhaus and Mies's role as director was taken out and transferred to the Bauakademie. The East German government had begun to embrace the Bauhaus and saw itself as the legitimate custodian of its legacy. The rest of the boxes were released in the fall of 1963. We can imagine a film noir–style transfer of crates from one truck to another in the middle of the night at a heavily guarded Checkpoint Charlie. The man who had brought them to Mühlhausen, Eduard Ludwig, had died in a car crash in 1961, so they ended up in the care of Ludwig Glaeser, whom Eduard Ludwig had considered stepson and heir, as he had been close friends with his mother, Käthe Glaeser.

Figure 10.1. The building that was once August Ludwig's carpentry workshop, Mühlhausen, Germany, ca. 1900. Photograph by Dietrich Neumann, 2021.

Ludwig Glaeser had studied architecture at the Technische Universität Berlin. After he graduated, apparently Eduard Ludwig had instructed him not to pursue a career as an architect, as "he would never be another Mies."[11] Instead, Glaeser prepared for a career as a historian and curator and studied art history and anthropology at the Freie Universität in West Berlin, where he received his PhD. Meanwhile, Mies had made up his mind that his drawings should go to the Museum of Modern Art in New York, his office and personal papers to the Library of Congress, and his library to the University of Illinois at Chicago.[12] According to family lore, this decision (which meant that the material in the boxes was now official American property) had been related to the secretary of state in Washington, D.C., and as a result, the U.S. ambassador in Moscow spoke to government officials there. This apparently helped move things along in East Berlin.

Glaeser turned out to be a shrewd negotiator: once the boxes were in his hands, conversations with Mies's office and the Museum of Modern Art ensued. The result was an unusual quid pro quo: in exchange for releasing the material, Ludwig Glaeser was hired by the museum as an assistant to chief curator Arthur Drexler. He arrived in New York in 1963 (months before the boxes landed in Chicago). Glaeser first gathered experience with a number of small exhibitions before becoming associate curator of architecture in 1964, curator in 1968, and curator of the Mies van der Rohe Archive in 1972. He turned out to be excellent at this job, organizing a number of exhibitions and publications about Mies's work, which were measured and thoughtful in their analysis. He initiated an oral history project, interviewing many of Mies's surviving colleagues, clients, and collaborators, such as Werner Graeff, Herbert Hirche, John Barney Rodgers, and Lilly von Schnitzler.

The boxes themselves had first gone to Chicago, where they arrived in December 1963, and Mies apparently was in no hurry to look at them. The one box labeled "Lilly Reich," he never opened at all.[13] They were stored in the basement of Mies's office at 230 East Ohio Street in Chicago. Finally, Ed Duckett, supervisor of the model workshop, took charge and made them available to curious visitors, such as Arthur Drexler from the Museum of Modern Art.[14]

In 1965, Mies made an initial gift of eighty-six drawings to MoMA, which celebrated the event with the show *Mies van der Rohe: Architectural Drawings from the Collection* in

Figure 10.2. Installation view of *Mies van der Rohe: Architectural Drawings from the Collection*, Museum of Modern Art, New York, February 2–March 23, 1966.

February and March 1966 (figure 10.2). Most of the drawings were minor renderings of unexecuted courtyard houses, such as the Gericke and Hubbe houses, but the real show-stopper was the large charcoal perspective of the Friedrichstrasse Skyscraper of 1922 (see figure 2.1). Two years later, the Art Institute of Chicago followed suit with a large exhibition in which the Friedrichstrasse Skyscraper was joined by a drawing of the Concrete Office Building in the lobby of the museum (figure 10.3). That same year, MoMA placed the Neue Nationalgalerie in Berlin at the center of a show about new museum buildings.

The pieces that Mies gave the Museum of Modern Art outright were labeled "gift of the architect," while the rest became part of his bequest and would arrive after his death in 1969, when the Mies van der Rohe Archive was established (figure 10.4). Philip Johnson provided initial financial support for the archive to begin cataloging and conservation. Substantial annual contributions from Phyllis Lambert and the Friends of the Mies van der Rohe Archive, a group chaired by Myron Goldsmith, secured its continuation. It is worth pausing for a moment to recognize the important and unusual fact that Mies decided to preserve all traces of his work and practice from around 1922 onward—right after he changed his name, converted the family rooms at home into office space, and joined the avant-garde with several eye-catching, visionary projects. He also, simultaneously, began to engage in publicity on his own behalf, initiating articles, submitting images to publications and exhibitions. He seems to have suddenly understood both the importance of his work and the importance of shaping its public perception. There is an obvious correlation between the existence of a vast personal archive and an architect's legacy. Wright, Le Corbusier, Kahn, and Ponti all carefully documented their work. In Mies's case, it took many lucky breaks

Figure 10.3. Installation view of *Mies van der Rohe Retrospective,* Art Institute of Chicago, April 27–June 30, 1968.

for his material to survive, and there is a certain irony in the fact that a Communist functionary in East Germany, Kurt Liebknecht, and an architect and curator in the United States who had sympathized with the Third Reich, Philip Johnson, contributed substantially to his archive's existence. In retrospect, the raid in Mühlhausen probably helped to keep the material together and prevented its loss, damage, or dispersal on the art market.

Mies passed away on August 17, 1969, only days before the mammoth, two-thousand-piece *50 Years Bauhaus* exhibition opened at his Crown Hall at IIT. The opening reception on August 24 had been conceived as a tribute to (and with) Mies and turned into a memorial instead. The enormously influential show had been organized by the Federal Republic of Germany and traveled to Stuttgart, Amsterdam, London, and several North American cities. At IIT it was enhanced by examples from Mies's teaching and practice. One of its curators was Hans Maria Wingler, whose clandestine research in Mühlhausen had caused the abovementioned raid. His separate, massive book on the Bauhaus appeared in an English edition at the same time. Obituaries to Mies in newspapers around the world praised him as a "patient genius," his art "as immutable as life and death," raising "structural reality to beauty," thanks to his "uncompromising adherence to absolute standards of art and excellence."[15]

Once the Mies Archive had been established, the work to sort and document its fifteen thousand items began, and much was accomplished in time for what would have been Mies's one hundredth birthday in 1986. Wolf Tegethoff, a young German PhD student (and later director of the Zentralinstitut für Kunstgeschichte in Munich [Central Institute for Art History]), was the first to make extensive use of the holdings at MoMA for his PhD thesis on Mies's villas and country houses, which appeared as a book in 1981, accompanied by an exhibition in Krefeld, Germany, and in 1986 at MoMA.[16] Franz Schulze's biography, which appeared in 1986, also made extensive use of the newly available material.[17] Arthur Drexler, Schulze, and George Danforth edited a twenty-volume catalogue raisonné of Mies's architectural drawings from 1986 to 1992.[18] This monumental accomplishment in collaboration with the now defunct Garland publishing house made much never-before-seen material available to researchers around the world, and solidified the central position of MoMA's archive for any research on Mies. By today's standards, however, the reproductions in black and white do not have high enough resolution—often details and inscriptions are murky and indecipherable. Thankfully, MoMA has put almost two thousand works by Mies online. The accompanying office files at MoMA are tremendously helpful in establishing context for each project. Often, the letters from clients contained there are not exactly flattering. They address late or nonexistent delivery of plans, cost overruns, and structural damages.

Figure 10.4. The Mies van der Rohe Archive at the Museum of Modern Art, New York. Photograph by Dietrich Neumann, 2012.

While the project files and drawings were sent to the Museum of Modern Art, Mies's correspondence and personal papers were delivered to the Library of Congress in two installments, in 1971 and 1973. They consist of about twenty-two thousand items on 27 feet (8.2 meters) of linear shelf space. The smaller section from the years 1921–38 came in the boxes from Berlin; the larger, second part consists of the correspondence kept by his Chicago office staff. Perhaps due to the fact that Lilly Reich had to pack up the contents of Mies's office quickly and without him being present, nothing was sorted or edited. As a result, there are delightfully mundane notes and receipts that allow glimpses into Mies's private life in those years. There are money wires to his wife and daughters (as head of household, he was in charge of the finances, which stemmed mostly from his wife's inheritance), or transfers he called in from his office staff while on one of his frequent vacations. There is his selection of two handbags as Christmas presents for Reich in 1925 (from an assortment she had sent)—and his receipt of a yellow padded silk dinner jacket from Reich in return (see Chapter 3). A tailor's bill from July 1925 speaks to the need to have his suits widened.[19] More importantly though, many letters document the details of his organization of exhibitions and the sending and receipt of models and drawings, and there is much correspondence with colleagues and associations. These documents have often helped to establish precise chronologies of Mies's activities. The selection of documents became more professional in the 1940s, once his Chicago office staff dealt with it.

Every architect's archive will be dogged by questions of authorship, as building is naturally a collaborative process, and both working drawings and presentation drawings are often done by draftsmen in the office. Mies was proud of acquiring drawing skills in his youth, and later would fondly recall impressing his students with them.[20] As noted in the opening chapter, George Nelson observed that Mies preferred "to have his drawings done for him." And indeed, Mies's own quick design sketches ("Mies is a master of the scribble," William Jordy observed), with their identifiably loose style, bear no resemblance to the precise charcoal and crayon perspectives or watercolor renderings of his office's presentation drawings.[21] Even if a photograph of 1928 shows Mies with charcoal in hand, seemingly at work on a floor plan, any practitioner would notice the impossibility of sketching on a piece of paper on a table, one hand in a pocket, without steadying the rendering (figure 10.5). It speaks to the nature of the archive and its focus on Mies alone that the question of authorship has never been seriously examined. To his credit, Drexler briefly addressed it on the occasion of the Garland publication. He asked: "What constitutes a drawing by Mies van der Rohe?" And he concluded that only those loose sketches in pencil or ink, usually from a small notepad, are "indubitably by Mies and Mies alone." Everything else posed "considerable uncertainty."[22]

Figure 10.5. Ludwig Mies van der Rohe with a drawing of the Esters House in Krefeld, Germany, spring 1928. Acetate film negative, 3 1/2 × 4 3/4 in. (9 × 12 cm). Photograph by Preß-Photo, Berlin. Bauhaus-Archiv, Berlin.

Among his early drawings, we can recognize a strong similarity between the perspectives for the Werner House and Kröller-Müller House project (see figures 1.46, 1.42), as well as the lost perspective of the Eliat House (see figure 3.4). They all show quick, impatient scribbles and equally impatient washes of watercolor for vegetation, and seem to rely on the same sturdy yellow paper for background—those might be the only large-scale drawings from Mies's hand. As noted above, the drawings of the Concrete Country House and Concrete Office Building, and possibly even the Friedrichstrasse Skyscraper perspective, were, in all likelihood, executed by Wilhelm Deffke, and Carl Gottfried was responsible for other drawings for the Friedrichstrasse Skyscraper project. Later, Sergius Ruegenberg executed meticulous presentation drawings for the Barcelona Pavilion, the Neue Wache proposal, and the proposed pavilion at the Brussels World's Fair.

The arrival of the crates in the United States, the subsequent establishment of the Mies Archive at MoMA, and the publications it inspired were essential contributions to creating Mies's legacy. They demonstrated his gravitas, cultural value, and relevance at a moment when many critics were getting tired of him and his successors, and they shored up the importance and legitimacy of the Museum of Modern Art as well. In fact, the reviews of MoMA's first exhibition with Mies's freshly acquired drawings in 1966 reveal the growing irritation with the damage that Mies's followers had unleashed on American cities. Ada Louise Huxtable remarked: "The World has mislearned the lesson of Miesian architecture, and then lost the ground he had gained for modern architecture in the span of his own lifetime....In too many cases the Miesian principle has been ignored and the Miesian example simply 'knocked off' in the cheapest 7th Avenue terms."[23] According to Arthur Drexler, Mies was aware of the disenchantment with the work of his followers, wistfully telling him one day: "We get up in the morning...and we sit on the edge of the bed and we think 'What the hell went wrong?' We showed them what to do...why don't they do it?"[24]

In 1968, on the occasion of the large Mies retrospective at the Art Institute of Chicago, Huxtable noted that "an entire generation of architects has turned its back on Mies," due to a lack of understanding of his legacy.[25] This became quite obvious when the *Chicago Tribune* reported "A Mies van der Rohe Panning" right in his hometown. At a conference at DePaul University, Sibyl Moholy-Nagy, widow of László Moholy-Nagy and a formidable critic, had declared: "You could lay a Mies building on its side and chop off two stories for a museum, 20 for a business building and 40 for a federal building." The structure "could be placed on the lake shore, in the middle of a business district—anywhere at all—and it would be self-contained and innocent of any give and take with its surroundings....Such buildings don't serve the people in them but only the economic power structure....This submission to a narrow functionalism is destroying architecture."[26] Moholy-Nagy followed up with an essay entitled "Hitler's Revenge" a few months later.[27]

Robert Venturi had crystalized growing sentiments in his book *Complexity and Contradiction in Architecture* of 1966 when he inverted Mies's austere dictum "Less is more" to "Less is a bore."[28] Mies died in 1969 to much attention and accolades in the press worldwide, but the criticism grew more succinct after his passing. In 1973, critic Charles Jencks devoted an entire chapter of his *Modern Movements in Architecture* to "The Problem of Mies." He wrote that while the "Platonic world view" had worked at the ideal solution of the Barcelona Pavilion, elsewhere it had led "to an inarticulate architecture" marred by "damaging...technical and functional mistakes" and a lack of connection to site, climate, and place.[29] Four years later, in *The Language of Post-Modern Architecture,* Jencks took Mies to task for his simplistic, "univalent," "impoverished," "fetishized," and "confusing" architecture.[30] When Peter Carter's *Mies van der Rohe at Work* appeared in 1975, James Maude Richards, the British critic and editor of *Architectural Review,* was clearly bored: "Can there be a need for yet another book on Mies van der Rohe, who has been more exhaustively written about than any other of the hero figures of modern architecture?" he asked.[31]

And, indeed, there was a lull in the production of books on Mies in the late 1970s (when postmodernism provided a major distraction), and MoMA fed the general interest in an architecture before modernism with an exhibition about the École des Beaux-Arts in 1975.

But as soon as what would have been Mies's one hundredth birthday in 1986 came into view, it was "about to be celebrated in no uncertain fashion," as Huxtable put it.[32] Major exhibitions and accompanying publications saw the light of day—and a replica of the Barcelona Pavilion was unveiled at its original site. William Jordy claimed that "the extent of the Mies celebration in America is without precedent for any architect....All this enthusiasm is the more astonishing because only yesterday, it seems, Mies was the modernist of greatest stature at the bottom of the postmodernist barrel."[33] Jordy argued that while the 1986 exhibition at MoMA presented "the return of Mies into the spotlight," it "offered no substantial fresh insights into Mies's achievement—and seems, indeed, to have been intimidated by Mies's reputation," due to the fact that "Mies uniquely belongs to MoMA" (figure 10.6). Philip Johnson and Alfred Barr had fully supported him, and the archive had become "the most important source for scholarship on the architect anywhere in the world. So, the exhibition at MoMA is something of a family affair."[34]

Some reviewers, though, let their disenchantment with Mies shine through when discussing MoMA's centennial show and Franz Schulze's biography. Mark Girouard found Mies's legacy "disastrous, because of the appalling cumulative impact of the Mies-type buildings designed with none of his flair all over the world....He was a powerful character who could inspire great devotion, but his life was as reductivist as his architecture—occupied by drink, sex, cigars, St. Thomas Aquinas, his own buildings, and remarkably little else. It was not a basis from which to build humane buildings."[35] In the *Washington Post*, Paul Richard conceded that "no architect of our age has had an influence so broad,"

Figure 10.6. Installation view of *Mies van der Rohe Centennial Exhibition,* Museum of Modern Art, New York, February 10–April 15, 1986.

but then proceeded to list the flaws of his vision: "Nobody who loved him once, who felt he honored the truth, can see this retrospective without feeling to some small degree misled, abused, betrayed," because "his art, despite its pristine beauty, is in crucial ways dishonest." None of his buildings were mass-produced or prefabricated, Richard pointed out, but expensively custom-made and often finished by hand. The attached I-beams on his buildings were "glued on decorations," and Mies had no interest in his clients' programs. His often proclaimed "logic" stopped short of responding to heat exposure in glassed interiors, or applied the same design to the different climates in Cuba and Berlin. "Post-Modernism's silliness…may soon fall out of fashion," Richard concluded darkly, "but Mies' day is gone."[36]

Quipping that "Postmodernism could just as well be called Post-Miesianism," Robert Campbell of the *Boston Globe* found Mies "an instance of the disastrous confusion between art and architecture that has been (and continues to be) a persistent characteristic of the twentieth century. Mies's buildings can only be understood as visual artworks, as sculpture. Mies's buildings don't, for example, aggregate into good streets or good cities." Ultimately, "it simply isn't possible anymore…to take this rather grim designer quite so seriously as he invariably took himself."[37]

Even the Museum of Modern Art itself, Campbell noticed, was determined at that moment to avoid the impression "that it's trying to spark a Mies revival," as he discovered a rather "insouciant tone" and "iconoclastic sniping" in some of the exhibition labels. For example, Drexler and his team commented on Mies's Alexanderplatz proposal of 1928 as follows: "The street perspective suggests buildings now familiar to everyone, just as their grouping suggests the near-destruction of the normal city wrought by bombs, architects and planners.….It produced barrack-like blocks symptomatic of urban despair through renewal."[38]

Figure 10.7. Installation view of *Mies in Berlin*, Museum of Modern Art, New York, June 21–September 11, 2001.

Reviving Mies's reputation fifteen years later, the Museum of Modern Art and the Whitney Museum of American Art staged two joint exhibitions in New York in 2001. The ninety-five-year-old Philip Johnson was guest of honor at the opening. While MoMA documented the first half of Mies's career under the title *Mies in Berlin* (curated by Terence Riley and Barry Bergdoll), the Whitney focused on *Mies in America* (curated by Phyllis Lambert) (figure 10.7). Together, the two shows were probably the largest exhibition project ever dedicated to a single architect, closely rivaled by the famous Frank Lloyd Wright exhibition at Florence's Palazzo Strozzi in 1951.[39]

And yet the two simultaneous exhibitions in New York could not have been more different, with visitors to both institutions that summer encountering an unexpected reversal of roles. The show at the Whitney, known for its engagement with contemporary art, celebrated Mies as a no-nonsense high-modernist, and its installation, designed by Iñigo Manglano-Ovalle with wall-high photographs, film projections, and countless drawings was reminiscent, in its sparse linearity, of Mies's 1947 retrospective at the Museum of Modern Art. In contrast, MoMA made a decisive attempt to "postmodernize" Mies, thus capping thirty-five years of attempts to prove the continuing relevance of Mies in a hostile, anti-modern climate. Emphasizing qualities in his work that appealed to Robert Venturi's now well-worn gospel of complexities and contradictions, the exhibition focused on Mies's early work, and in particular on his lesser-known, conventional private residences in Berlin's suburbs. In a stark departure from convention (and somewhat ironically), the models of these early structures—such as the Riehl, Urbig, and Eichstaedt houses—were not the monochrome abstractions one would usually encounter on such occasions, but instead were manufactured by a model-maker for commercial real estate (Howard Architectural Models), with brightly colored bases, realistic finishes, and a high degree of quotidian detail.

Also counter to convention, at MoMA Mies's drawings were interspersed with large-scale photographs by the contemporary German artist Thomas Ruff, featuring studies of several early projects, some newly taken, others adapting archival material. The most strikingly successful was a view of the Barcelona Pavilion—its sky manipulated into the color of pink lemonade—that adorned the catalogue cover, announcing the exhibition's irreverent, postmodern approach (figure 10.8). The gamble paid off. The reviews were exceedingly positive, and the griping about Mies's responsibility for monotony in our urban environments seemed forgotten. Instead, Ada Louise Huxtable now celebrated Mies as "the inventor of cool" and "one of history's greatest architects." Even his buildings' functional failures, which had puzzled earlier generations of critics (including a younger Huxtable), were now considered a fair price to pay: "Aesthetically absolute, his buildings can be dauntingly resistant to those who have their own agendas, or to the compromises imposed by messy, ad hoc, reality.... Like all great works of architecture, Mies's buildings elevate human experience. He raised a structural and ideological revolution to the highest level of art."[40]

The many authors that followed generally accepted Huxtable's verdict, while looking anew at different aspects of his work. Jean-Louis Cohen's 2007 volume analyzed a number of projects in conjunction with carefully selected quotes to let Mies "speak for himself." A particularly insightful chapter presented new details about Mies's complicated relationship with the Nazis (or rather the Nazis' complicated relationship with him). In 2012, Franz Schulze coauthored with Edward Windhorst a new and revised edition of his 1985 monograph that included much new material, in particular juicy quotes gleaned from resurfaced court records of his case against Edith Farnsworth. In 2013, Phyllis Lambert published a magisterial and balanced account of the design, construction, and afterlife of the Seagram Building. Detlef Mertins's *Mies* appeared the next year as, according to its publisher, the "definitive study of Mies's life and work," a claim backed up by the tome's monumental scope: the 12-by-9-3/8-inch (30.5-by-20.8-centimeter) volume, with 542 pages and 600 illustrations, weighs six and a half pounds. It remains an extraordinary resource. Finished by several of Mertins's colleagues (Barry Bergdoll, Ed Dimendberg, Felicity D. Scott, and Keller Easterling) after his untimely death in 2011, it acknowledges "complexities and contradictions" in Mies's work, accessed via its cultural context in art and philosophy, and guided by the books in Mies's library. Carsten Krohn's *Mies van der Rohe: The Built Work* appeared in the same year, 2014, and brought together the author's extraordinary photographs and line drawings. A series of monographs on selected aspects of Mies's work or individual buildings has appeared since. In addition, recent years have seen renewed interest in the work of Lilly Reich, in particular by Spanish scholars Laura Lizondo-Sevilla and Laura Martínez de Guereñu.[41]

Thomas Ruff's abovementioned photograph on the cover of MoMA's 2001 exhibition catalogue shows the Barcelona Pavilion in a horizontal blur, as if the viewer (or the building) were moving at high speed. This absence of clarity and precision hinted at the uncertain historical role of the rebuilt pavilion and deliberately undermined qualities usually associated with Mies. In a broader sense, it serves as an apt reminder of the continuously shifting nature of our look at history.

With its emphasis on primary sources and much newly discovered material, this volume aims at a more complete and less monolithic picture of Mies's work. It acknowledges collaborations with others and allows for the fact that not all of Mies's buildings and designs were equally successful. In fact, the ongoing fascination with Mies's architecture reminds us how important it is to critically reassess, now and then, the criteria with which we measure a building's quality. As pointed out at the beginning, we cannot separate Mies's success from the discourse that surrounded and caused it, often carefully manipulated by Mies himself and those who supported him. Mies surely sensed and fed into a thirst for clarity and essentialism during the conflicted years of the Weimar Republic, and similarly during the giddy postwar abundance in the United States.

When ground was broken for the Lake Shore Drive Apartments in the fall of 1949, King Vidor's *The Fountainhead* was playing in Chicago's movie theaters. Based on Ayn Rand's successful novel, it tells the story of a heroic architect (Howard Roark, played by Gary Cooper) who refuses to compromise on his aesthetic vision, even if it means losing his most important commission. While Rand had been inspired by an encounter with Frank Lloyd Wright, set designer Edward Carrere's model of an unexecuted high-rise for the film's key scene is strikingly Miesian. The film enjoyed a respectable four-and-a-half month run in

Figure 10.8. Thomas Ruff, *d.p.b. 02*, 1999. Chromogenic print, 51 1/4 × 75 1/4 × 1 1/2 in. (130.2 × 191.1 × 3.8 cm).

Chicago, its popular success in great contrast to its unanimous panning by the critics. Frances Peck Grover of the *Chicago Tribune*, for instance, found the film "incredibly stupid," in particular its "idiotic conception of the importance of architecture."[42] There is a distinct possibility that Mies went to see the film, as it played at the State-Lake Theater, just a few blocks from the Art Institute. Mies might have found his own steadfast pursuit of his aesthetic vision and disregard for clients' requests or comfort encouraged by the film, and he might have picked up on Roark's penchant for pithy epithets. Roark said, "I don't build in order to have clients—I have clients in order to build," and "Buildings have integrity. Just like a man...and just as seldom." What set Mies apart from the clichéd image of the self-centered architect, however, was his insistence on the universal nature of his work. While contemporaries such as Wright, Le Corbusier, Kahn, and Ponti would, naturally, meet each project on its own terms and come up with one-of-a-kind solutions (showing off their creative prowess along the way), once Mies found a fitting response to a building type or structural problem, he would apply it again and again with little variation. This way, he took himself as creator out of the equation. "Who wants to know the names or cares about the accidental personalities of their architects?" he had asked in 1924—referring to antique temples and Gothic cathedrals—and concluded: "Architecture is the will of the age translated into space."[43]

Mies leaves us with several paradoxes—an architecture that became impersonal and formulaic, while by many accounts it was exactly his personality (perceived as forceful, reserved, philosophical) that won people over to his approach. His proclamations had little to do with the actual work. While he reliably met questions about a building's genesis with a laconic account of a simple, logical response to the conditions at hand, the reality was often exactly the opposite—the result of a painstaking search for a beautiful and photogenic simplicity that used function or structure merely as aesthetic inspiration, while adding complications and costs behind the scenes. Mies sensed that his buildings would be judged more by their appearance than their ability to fulfill their purpose well. In other words, Mies treated architecture as a largely autonomous art form, skirting the constraints that normally force architects' hands. While the "age," whose will Mies's architecture supposedly translated into space, was surely different from ours (we now rightly expect buildings to be responsible stewards of the environment and help engender social change), his emphasis on the epochal gravitas and relevance of architecture—from corner details to urban configurations—is surely one of his greatest legacies.[44]

Acknowledgments

One of the great delights in finishing a project that evolved over a number of years is thinking back on the many encounters and engaging conversations with colleagues, archivists, and librarians who helped along the way—many more individuals than I am able to mention by name below. I'll start with what the late Jean-Louis Cohen called the "Miesologues"—other Mies researchers who shared ideas, knowledge, and critiques; of course, Jean-Louis being one of them—who helped shape the book's contents and intellectual trajectory. Helmut Reuter's assistance and feedback—and, in particular, his trove of historic image files—were crucial for this book's genesis. I am grateful for conversations with Fritz Neumeyer, Aya Soika, and in particular the always generous Annette Droste in Berlin; with Phyllis Lambert in Montreal; and with Michelangelo Sabatino in Chicago. Conversations with Barry Bergdoll and Wolf Tegethoff over the years helped shape the trajectory of this project. Without Guy Nordenson I would not have understood the importance of the "plug weld" at the Farnsworth House. Tim More explained the legal intricacies of the court case regarding taxation of the Seagram Building. Adrian Täckman from Copenhagen, working on Knud Lonberg-Holm, was very generous with information, as was our Dutch friend and colleague Herman van Bergeijk in Rotterdam. Michele Caja in Milan, Lars Scharnholz in Cottbus, Cammie McAtee in Montreal, and Hans-Georg Lippert in Dresden also shared ideas and discoveries, and Carsten Krohn provided images and feedback. Barbara Buenger, an expert on Max Beckmann and his supporter, Lilly von Schnitzler, helped in countless ways. Tom Tisch suggested using the introductory quote. I have learned a lot from the incredibly resourceful and creative Mies scholars in Spain, in particular, Juanjo Lahuerta, and the younger generation including Valentín Trillo Martínez, Pablo Gallego Picard, Laura Martínez de Guereñu, and Laura Lizondo-Sevilla. There is a wider circle that includes Mies's family members and his collaborators or clients, whom I had the pleasure of getting to know over the course of my research, such as the abovementioned Phyllis Lambert; Mies's grandchildren Dirk Lohan in Chicago and Frank Herterich in Berlin; the grandson and great-grandchildren of Mies's friend and partner Gerhard Severain (Sever, Rea, and Reo Severain) in Wiesbaden; Christiane Lange in Krefeld; and Hans Flaskamp in Berlin; Countess Isabel Hoyos and Count Franz Seefried; Evelin and Armin Homburg in Raeren; Edward Glaeser in Cambridge; and the late Wilhelm Wolf in Montevideo. Also crucially helpful were Wita Noack, director of the Mies van der Rohe Haus in Berlin, and Reinhard Wegener at the Parzival School in Berlin (in Mies's Perls and Werner houses).

The search for new information in different archives with their particular atmospheres has always been for me the most exhilarating part of any scholarly work. The delightful encounters with archivists who understand the urgency and excitement of such quests is an added bonus. I am thinking of Paul Galloway and Pamela Popeson at MoMA, Andreas Matschenz at the Landesarchiv Berlin, Robert Dupuis at the Bezirksamt Neukölln, and Stephan Dinges at the Sanofi Hoechst Archive in Frankfurt.

I would also like to acknowledge the kindness of many strangers, whom I only met via email but who nevertheless went out of their way to quickly provide photographs, image rights, scanned documents, or pieces of information. I am thinking in particular of Kai-Annett Becker at the Bauhaus-Archive, Joyce Faust at Art Resource, Angela Hoover at the Chicago History Museum, Christoph Moss at the Stadtarchiv Krefeld, Christoph Kaufmann at the Stadtgeschichtliches Museum Leipzig, Sabrina Walz at the Rheinisches Bildarchiv in Cologne, Matthias Pühl and Andreas Nutz at the Vitra Design Museum in Weil am Rhein, François De Heyder at CIVA Fondation in Brussels, Christoph Brachmann at the University of North Carolina at Chapel Hill, and Simone Vermeer and Roel van As-Krijgsman at the Kröller-Müller Museum near Otterlo. Hermann Kühn, photographer and librarian at the Technical University Hamburg-Harburg was immensely helpful with detailed knowledge and a vast bibliography. Frank Herre, Anna Mas, Kiel Moe, as well as Julia Pechstein kindly provided information and image permissions as did photographers Thomas Ruff and Camilo José Vergara. Karen Bouchard, Arts & Humanities Librarian at Brown University, helped me out countless times with scans and quick information, when I was far from a library. I owe a special note of appreciation to Hassan Bagheri, who not only took almost all of the contemporary views of Mies's work in this volume but also created renderings of Mies's project for the Neue Wache in Berlin.

I am grateful for all of the help from my sister Elizabeth, who provided material from German archives, and for the unflagging support, patience, and joyful enthusiasm with which my wife, Vivian, accompanied this project during its long incubation. The book is dedicated to her. I fondly remember countless hours spent at the Fineprint café in Hong Kong over final reviews of the manuscript. The Wendy Strothman Award, several Humanities Research grants, and Research Funds from Brown University helped offset costs for research trips and copyrights. And finally, I would like to acknowledge the patience, kindness, and professionalism of the team at Yale University Press who saw this book through to completion—editorial director Katherine Boller as well as designer Luke Bulman, graduate fellow Julian Day, production manager Rachel Faulise, managing editor Alison Hagge, copy editor Laura Hensley, editorial assistant Elizabeth Searcy, indexer Krister Swartz, and proofreader Kati Woock.

Notes

Introduction

Epigraph: George Nelson, "Architects of Europe Today: 7—Van der Rohe, Germany," *Pencil Points* (September 1935): 453–60, quote at 453. Nelson's essays were reprinted with an introduction by Kurt W. Forster in *Building a New Europe: Portraits of Modern Architects, Essays by George Nelson, 1935–1936* (New Haven: Yale University Press, 2007).

1. Nelson, "Architects of Europe Today," 459–60. Nelson referred to Erich Mendelsohn, Bruno and Max Taut, and Walter Gropius, three prominent modernists who had recently left the country.
2. Mies van der Rohe to William Nelson, July 20, 1935, Library of Congress (hereafter LoC), MvdR, Container 1 ("N"). See also Cammie McAtee, "Alien #5044325: Mies's First Trip to America," in *Mies in America*, ed. Phyllis Lambert (New York: Harry N. Abrams, 2001), 132–91.
3. Helen Appleton Read, "Machine Age Ethics and Esthetics," *Brooklyn Daily Eagle,* April 1, 1934, "Sunday Review," 13, 14.
4. Nelson, "Architects of Europe Today," 453, 454.
5. Gustave Flaubert to Gertrude Tennant, December 25, 1876, in Gustave Flaubert, *Correspondance* (Paris: Louis Conard, 1910), 4:280.
6. Hugo Erfurth, "Zur Erkenntnis der Ähnlichkeit," *Photographische Kunst* 9 (1910/11): 311, quoted in Bodo von Dewitz, "Hugo Erfurth. Ein Photograph und die vielen 'Köpfe seiner Zeit,'" in *Hugo Erfurth 1874–1948. Photograph zwischen Tradition und Moderne*, ed. Bodo von Dewitz and Karin Schuller-Procopovici (Cologne: Wienand, 1992), 10–27, quote at 26nn40, 41. All translations, unless otherwise noted, are my own.
7. Erfurth took portraits of Erich Mendelsohn and Walter Gropius, and Bauhaus masters such as László Moholy-Nagy, Oskar Schlemmer, Paul Klee, and Wassily Kandinsky.
8. Von Dewitz and Schuller-Procopovici, *Hugo Erfurth,* 20.
9. Heinrich Schwarz, "Hugo Erfurth," *Kölner Stadtanzeiger,* October 14, 1934, quoted in von Dewitz and Schuller-Procopovici, *Hugo Erfurth,* 20, 27n71.
10. Hugo Erfurth in Wilhelm Schöppe, ed., *Meister der Kamera erzählen. Wie sie wurden und wie sie arbeiten* (Halle: William Knapp, 1935), 6–12, quoted in Claudia Gabriele Philipp, "Bildmässige Photographie. Zur künstlerischen Legitimation des Photographen," in von Dewitz and Schuller-Procopovici, *Hugo Erfurth,* 37–44, quote at 41, 44n39.
11. "Wie Dührkopp, Erfurth, Grainer, Smith, Taut Arbeiten?," *Photographische Kunst* 9 (1910/11): 2, quoted in von Dewitz and Schuller-Procopovici, *Hugo Erfurth,* 16, 26n39. Perhaps ultimately repulsed by Hugo Erfurth's growing affinity with the Nazis, neither Mies nor Beckmann ever used the photographs he took of them.
12. See also Lea Baerens, *Raum und Figur bei Beckmann und Mies van der Rohe* (Norderstedt: Books on Demand, 2020).
13. Similar to Mies trying to cancel the Nelson article, in January 1934 Beckmann told his gallerist to either cancel a planned exhibition or limit it to some "carefully selected" pieces to avoid "unnecessary attention," and he expressed his belief that things would get much better within a year. Olaf Peters, *Vom Schwarzen Seiltänzer. Max Beckmann zwischen Weimarer Republik und Exil* (Berlin: Reimer, 2005), 291.
14. See, for instance, Wilhelm Hausenstein's 1924 description of Beckmann, or Perry Rathbone's from the 1950s, in Sabine Rewald, *Max Beckmann in New York* (New York: Metropolitan Museum of Art, 2016), 16, 30.
15. In August 1939, Max Beckmann told New York art dealer Curt Valentin that he wanted to paint a portrait of Mies and asked for a photo (Beckmann was in Amsterdam at the time, Mies in Chicago). Mies's collaborator Gene Summers recalled many years later: "Mies always said he regretted the fact that Beckmann—if you recall Beckmann did a number of double portraits, it would be he and another person—Beckmann wanted to do one with Mies. Mies said, 'Doggone it, I never did that, I should have done that.'" Peters, *Vom Schwarzen Seiltänzer,* 310; Paulina A. Saliga, "Interview with Gene Summers," *Chicago Architects Oral History Project,* Ernest R. Graham Study Center for Architectural Drawings (Chicago: Art Institute of Chicago, 1993), 68.
16. Peters, *Vom Schwarzen Seiltänzer,* 310; Barbara Buenger, "Max Beckmann in Paris, Amsterdam, and the United States, 1937–50," in *Exile and Emigrés: The Flight of European Artists from Hitler,* ed. Stephanie Barron (Los Angeles: Los Angeles County Museum of Art, 1997), 58–67, reference at 58.
17. Vivian Endicott Barnett, "The Architect as Art Collector," in Lambert, *Mies in America,* 90–131, reference at 121.
18. Hans Thiemann to Paul Naeff, July 26, 1935, Bauhaus-Archiv Berlin. I thank Professor Magdalena Droste for this reference.
19. Quoted in Franz Schulze, *Mies van der Rohe: A Critical Biography* (Chicago: University of Chicago Press, 1985), 193, quoted from Edith Farnsworth's handwritten memoir in the Edith Farnsworth Papers (boxes 1 and 2) at the Newberry Library, Chicago, https://ia903004.us.archive.org/24/items/mms_farnsworth/mms_farnsworth.pdf.
20. Richard Pommer, "Mies van der Rohe and the Political Ideology of the Modern Movement in Architecture," in *Mies van der Rohe: Critical Essays,* ed. Franz Schulze (New York: Museum of Modern Art, 1989), 96–145, quote at 96.
21. Christian Norberg-Schulz, "A Talk with Mies van der Rohe," *Baukunst und Werkform* 11, no. 11 (1958): 615–18. See also Katharine Kuh, "Mies van der Rohe: Modern Classicist," *Saturday Review of Literature* 48 (January 23, 1965): 22–23, 61, quote at 23.
22. "Building," *G,* no. 2 (September 1923): 1, quoted in Fritz Neumeyer, *The Artless Word: Mies van der Rohe on the Building Art* (Cambridge, Mass.: MIT Press, 1991), 242.
23. Quoted in Phyllis Lambert, "Mies Immersion," in Lambert, *Mies in America,* 192–589, quote at 571.
24. Quoted in Phyllis Lambert, "Mies Immersion," in Lambert, *Mies in America,* 391.
25. Werner Hegemann, "Holland, Wright, Breslau," *Wasmuths Monatshefte für Baukunst* 9, no. 4 (1925): 165–67.
26. See Chapter 3. Marie-Elisabeth Lüders, "Baukörper ohne Wohnungen," *Die Form* 2, no. 10 (October 1927): 316–19; Max Osborn, "Die Wohnung der Zukunft," *Vossische Zeitung,* no. 402, morning edition, August 26, 1927, 1–2.
27. Quoted in Schulze, *Critical Biography,* 155; Farnsworth, "Memoirs," chap. 13.
28. *Mies en Scene: Barcelona in Two Acts,* directed by Xavi Campreciós and Pep Martín (Spain, 2018). Hannah Arendt had advocated a "thinking without banisters."
29. *Mies in Berlin,* Museum of Modern Art, New York, June 21–September 11, 2001; *Mies in America,* Whitney Museum of American Art, New York, June 21–September 23, 2001.

Chapter One. Apprenticeships and Early Work

Epigraph: Quoted in Katharine Kuh, "Mies van der Rohe: Modern Classicist," *Saturday Review of Literature* 48 (January 23, 1965): 22–23, 61, quote at 61.

1. Much new material about Mies's early years in Aachen is in Maike Scholz and Daniel Lohmann, "'Zur Neuen Welt'—Towards the New World: Ludwig Mies and His Architectural Youth in Aachen," in "The Heritage of Mies" special issue, *Docomomo* 56 (2017): 7–15.
2. Daniel Lohmann and Maike Scholz, "Warenhaus Leonhard Tietz," in *Mies im Westen,* ed. Norbert Hanenberg, Daniel Lohmann, Ursula Kleefisch-Jobst, and Peter Köddermann (Aachen: Geymüller, 2022), 103–9.
3. Daniel Lohmann and Maike Scholz, "Volkshaus 'Zur Neuen Welt' Für Joseph Oeben," in Hanenberg et al., *Mies im Westen,* 112–18.
4. Notorious for its taverns and amusement sites, Rixdorf changed its name to Neukölln in 1912 to signal a new beginning. It became part of Greater Berlin in 1920.
5. Robert Dupuis, "John Martens (1875–1936). Architekt, Bildhauer und Baukeramiker," in *Ein Schwede in Berlin. Der Architekt und Designer Alfred Grenander und die Berliner Architektur (1890–1914),* ed. Christoph Brachmann and Thomas Steigenberger (Korb: Didymos, 2010), 471–80.
6. W. Owen Harrod, "Bruno Paul's Typenmöbel, the German Werkbund, and Pragmatic Modernism, 1908–1918," *Studies in the Decorative Arts* 9, no. 2 (Spring/Summer 2002): 33–57. They were presented to the public in 1908 at Munich's Vereinigte Werkstätten für Kunst im Handwerk (United Workshops for Art in Handicraft)—an important predecessor to the Werkbund.
7. "Das Kunstgewerbe-Museum in Berlin," *Centralblatt der Bauverwaltung* 2, no. 40 (October 7, 1882): 363–64, floorplan at 365; *Centralblatt der Bauverwaltung* 2, no. 41 (October 14, 1882): 367–68, reference to window sizes at 368; *Centralblatt der Bauverwaltung* 2, no. 42 (October 21, 1882): 380–82.
8. Ludwig Pietsch, "Das Hohenzollern-Kunstgewerbehaus—Berlin," *Deutsche Kunst und Dekoration* 15 (1904/5): 169–76.

9. Max Osborn, "Das Hohenzollern-Kunstgewerbehaus in Berlin," *Innen-Dekoration* 26 (February 1915): 55–80.

10. Max Creutz, "Die Plakatausstellung im Hohenzollern-Kunstgewerbehaus," *Berliner Architekturwelt* (1908): 403–12. Creutz was editor-in-chief of the magazine *Berliner Architekturwelt* and would become director of the Kaiser-Wilhelm-Museum in Krefeld in 1922 and a key advisor for art collector Hermann Lange, one of Mies van der Rohe's most important clients.

11. Quoted in Fritz Neumeyer, ed., *Originalton: Ludwig Mies van der Rohe. Die Lohan Tapes von 1969* (Berlin: DOM, 2021), 64–65.

12. "Professor Bruno Paul-Berlin. Sportshaus des Berliner Lawn-Tennis-Clubs," *Deutsche Kunst und Dekoration* 25 (1909–10): 214–17.

13. Adolf Propp, an assistant to the painter and graphic artist Emil Orlik at the school, designed a bird bath for the garden of the Riehl House and helped Mrs. Riehl with a competition for bird bath designs. Neumeyer, *Originalton,* 16–17. Propp later became a graphic artist and book illustrator.

14. The exhibition was held from May until October at the Theresienwiese fairgrounds.

15. Neumeyer, *Originalton,* 68.

16. Riehl published eight of his lectures in 1903. Alois Riehl, *Zur Einführung in die Philosophie der Gegenwart* (Leipzig: Täubner, 1903).

17. Kuwaki Genyoku (1925), quoted in Niels Gülberg, "Alois Riehl und Japan," *Humanitas,* no. 41 (2003), 1–32, http://www.f.waseda.jp/guelberg/publikat/riehl.htm#4.

18. Mies signed the Riehls' guest book on October 25, 1909. See Fritz Neumeyer, "Mies's First Project: Revisiting the Atmosphere at Klösterli," in *Mies in Berlin,* ed. Terence Riley and Barry Bergdoll (New York: Museum of Modern Art, 2001), 314.

19. Philip Johnson, *Mies van der Rohe* (New York: Museum of Modern Art, 1947), 10.

20. Johann Gottfried Hasse, *Merkwürdige Äusserungen Kant's von einem seiner Tischgenossen* (Königsberg: Hering, 1804), 4–6.

21. Paul Mebes, *Um 1800. Architektur und Handwerk im letzten Jahrhundert ihrer traditionellen Entwicklung* (Munich: Bruckmann, 1908), 2; Paul Mebes, *Um 1800. Architektur und Handwerk im letzten Jahrhundert ihrer traditionellen Entwicklung,* ed. Walter Curt Behrendt (Munich: Bruckmann, 1918), 1–6.

22. Mebes, *Um 1800* (1908), 2:81.

23. Mies was enrolled in a class taught by Alfred Grenander at the Kunstgewerbeschule from June 1, 1907, on and then joined Bruno Paul's class in early October. On May 15, 1908, he took a leave of absence to work on the Riehl House; Universität der Künste, Berlin, Archiv, Best. 7, Nr. 241, 242, acceptance lists 1906/7 and 1907/8. Thomas Steigenberger, "Mies van der Rohe—ein Schüler Bruno Pauls," in *Mies van der Rohe. Frühe Bauten. Probleme der Erhaltung—Probleme der Bewertung,* ed. Johannes Cramer and Dorothée Sack (Petersberg: Imhof, 2004), 151–62, esp. 157f; Brachmann and Steigenberger, *Ein Schwede in Berlin,* 101–8.

24. The basement plan was never published, but could be reconstructed when the house was renovated in 1998. Jörg Limberg, "Haus Riehl, Neubabelsberg, Sanierung und denkmalpflegerische Begleitung," in Cramer and Sack, *Frühe Bauten,* 26–41; Heiko Folkerts, "Haus Riehl, Neubabelsberg, Sanierung," in Cramer and Sack, *Frühe Bauten,* 43–55.

25. Thomas Steigenberger has made a convincing connection to Bruno Paul's teachings. Thomas Steigenberger, "Mies van der Rohe—ein Schüler Bruno Pauls," in Cramer and Sack, *Frühe Bauten,* 151–62, esp. 156.

26. Gert Kähler, ed., *Geschichte des Wohnens. 1918–1945 Reform-Reaktion-Zerstörung* (Stuttgart: Deutsche Verlagsanstalt, 1996), 287.

27. Neumeyer, "Mies's First Project," 310.

28. Anton Jaumann, "Neues von Peter Behrens," *Deutsche Kunst und Dekoration* 23 (June 1909): 343–57, quote at 353.

29. Anton Jaumann, "Vom künstlerischen Nachwuchs," *Innen-Dekoration* 21 (July 1910): 265–73, quote at 272.

30. Jaumann, "Vom künstlerischen Nachwuchs," quotes at 266, 272.

31. Paul Klopfer, "Architekt Ludwig Mies. Villa des Herrn Geheimen Regierungsrats Prof. Dr. RIEHL in Neu-Babelsberg," *Moderne Bauformen: Monatshefte für Architektur und Raumkunst* 9 (September 1910): 42–48.

32. The most expensive example is Muthesius's Freudenberg House in Nikolassee of 1907–8 at 230,000 Mark; the cheapest is a small model summer home for 3,000 Mark by Oswald Milne. Hermann Muthesius, *Landhaus and Garten: Beispiele neuzeitlicher Landhäuser nebst Grundrissen, Innenräumen und Gärten,* 2nd ed. (Munich: Bruckmann, 1910), 28–30, 50, 51, 175.

33. "Landhaus und Garten," *Schweizerische Bauzeitung* 56 (December 17, 1910): 336, 337, 345, plates 69–72, Riehl House at 70.

34. Ludwig Deubner, "German Architecture and Decoration," in *Studio Yearbook of Decorative Art* (London: International Studio, 1911), 147–210, Riehl House at 150, 178.

35. Margarete Merleker, "Alois Riehl. Zum 80. Geburtstag am 27. April," *Vossische Zeitung,* April 26, 1924, morning edition, 2–3.

36. Tilman Buddensieg, *Industriekultur. Peter Behrens und die AEG. 1907–1914* (Berlin: Mann, 1979), D. 12.

37. Quoted in Stanford Anderson, "The Atelier of Peter Behrens, 1908–18," in *Jean Krämer Architect and the Atelier of Peter Behrens,* ed. Stanford

Anderson, Karen Grunow, and Carsten Krohn (Weimar: Weimarer Verlagsgesellschaft 2015), 24–67, quote at 55. This stands in contrast to a warm, personal note from Behrens to Gropius of 1916, in which he suggests traveling to Constantinople together and congratulates him on his recent marriage to Alma Mahler. Peter Behrens to Walter Gropius, September 28, 1916, Bauhaus-Archiv, Berlin.

38. A farewell visit with the Riehls is recorded in their guest book on June 8, 1910. "I hate leaving Klösterli but do so confidently, and sincere thanks once again for the possibility of its creation," Mies wrote. See Neumeyer, "Mies's First Project," 314.

39. Salomon van Deventer to Helene Kröller-Müller, August 29, 1911, cited in Franz Schulze and Edward Windhorst, *Mies van der Rohe: A Critical Biography,* new and rev. ed. (Chicago: University of Chicago, 2014), 39.

40. Daniel Lohmann and Maike Scholz, "Ewald Mies," in Hanenberg et al., *Mies im Westen,* 48–69. See in particular his Homburg House in Raeren.

41. "Bismarck-National-Denkmal," *Deutsche Bauzeitung,* 42/2, no. 93 (November 18, 1908): 640; Fritz Hoeber, *Peter Behrens* (Munich: Müller und Rentsch, 1913), 96.

42. Karin Wilhelm, "Der Wettbewerb zum Bismarck-National-Denkmal in Bingerbrück (1909–1912). Ein Beitrag zum Problem mit der Monumentalität," *Kritische Berichte* 2 (1987): 32–47.

43. As the tomb of Mausolus (377–353 BCE), it had provided the source for the term.

44. "Das Bismarck-National-Denkmal von Professor W. Kreis-Düsseldorf," *Bismarck-Bund* 10, no. 11 (November 1912): 141–48.

45. Ekkehardt Mai and Peter Springer, eds., *Das letzte Nationaldenkmal. Bismarck am Rhein: Ein Monument das nie gebaut wurde* (Cologne: Böhlau, 2013).

46. "Protokoll der Sitzungen des Preisgerichtes für das Bismarck-National-Denkmal auf der Elisenhöhe," *Bismarck-Bund* 9, no. 6 (May 1911): 82–86, quote at 84. See also "Das Bismarck-National-Denkmal," *Bismarck-Bund* 9, no. 2 (February 1911): 18–29.

47. The painting was purchased by the Museum of Modern Art from Ewald Mies's family in 2000.

48. Augusta von Oertzen, "Berliner Salons: Ein Haus der Kunst. Montagsempfang beim Direktor der Staatlichen Kunsbibliothek Professor Curt Glaser," *Weltspiegel. Berliner Tageblatt,* March 31, 1929; Klaus G. Perls, preface to *The Perls Collection in the Metropolitan Museum of Art,* by Kate Ezra (New York: Metropolitan Museum of Art, 1991), xiii–ix.

49. His name is recorded at a party there on October 15, 1911. See Neumeyer, "Mies's First Project," 314.

50. H. Allen Brooks, *Le Corbusier's Formative Years: Charles Edouard Jeanneret at La Chaux-de-Fonds* (Chicago: University of Chicago Press, 1997), 236.

51. Stanislaus von Moos, *Le Corbusier: Elements of a Synthesis* (Cambridge, Mass.: MIT Press, 1979), 12.

52. Brooks, *Le Corbusier's Formative Years,* 238.

53. Mies van der Rohe to Ada Bruhn, February 21, 1912, private collection (Frank Herterich, Berlin).

54. Tamara Levitz, "In the Footsteps of Eurydice: Gluck's *Orpheus and Eurydice* in Hellerau, 1913," *Echo: A Music-Centered Journal* 3, no. 2 (2001), http://www.echo.ucla.edu/article-in-the-footsteps-of-eurydice-glucks-orpheus-und-eurydice-in-hellerau-1913-by-tamara-levitz.

55. S. D. Gallwitz, review in an unnamed journal, translated into French and quoted in Adolphe Appia, *Oeuvres complètes,* vol. 3, ed. and trans. Marie L. Bablet-Hahn (Bonstetten: L'Âge d'Homme, 1988), 206.

56. Mies van der Rohe to Ada Bruhn, October 25, 1911, private collection (Frank Herterich, Berlin).

57. Mies van der Rohe to Ada Bruhn, September 28, 1911, private collection (Frank Herterich, Berlin).

58. Mies van der Rohe to Ada Bruhn, February 21, 1912, private collection (Frank Herterich, Berlin).

59. Hugo Perls, *Warum ist Kamilla schön? Von Kunst, Künstlern und Kunsthandel* (Munich: Paul List, 1962), 16.

60. Annika Weise, "Max Pechstein im Haus Perls," in *Mies—Episoden. Oder wie Martha Lemke einmal im weissen Kleid auf der Terrasse stand,* ed. Wita Noack (Berlin: Form + Zweck, 2021), 79–102.

61. H. Friedeberger, "Ausstellungen. Die XXV. Ausstellung der Berliner Sezession (Zeichnende Künste)," *Der Cicerone* 4, no. 23 (December 1912): 895–97, quote at 895. Donated to the Nationalgalerie, the Pechstein canvases were confiscated and vanished in the buildup to the "Degenerate Art" exhibition of 1937. Aya Soika, "Im Kreis von Freunden Max Pechstein und die Förderer seiner Kunst," in *Gemeinsames Ziel und eigene Wege. Die "Brücke" und ihr Nachwirken. Almanach der Brücke 1,* ed. Hermann Gerlinger and Katja Schneider (Munich: Hirmer, 2010), 78–89.

62. Perls, *Warum ist Kamilla schön?,* 16, 62, 64.

63. Alan Windsor, *Peter Behrens, Architect and Designer* (New York: Whitney Library of Design, 1981), 91–94.

64. Karl Bernhard, "Die neue Halle für die Turbinenfabrik der Allgemeinen Elektricitäts-Gesellschaft in Berlin," *Zeitschrift des Vereins deutscher Ingenieure* 55, no. 39 (September 30, 1911): 1625–31, 1673–82; a shortened version is repr. in Buddensieg, *Industriekultur,* 307–12.

65. Bernhard, "Die neue Halle," quote at 1681.
66. Bernhard, "Die neue Halle," quotes at 1629–30.
67. Peter Behrens, "Kunst und Technik" (lecture notes from 1911), in *Peter Behrens. Zeitloses und Zeitbewegtes. Aufsätze, Vorträge, Gespräche 1900–1938*, ed. Hartmut Frank and Karin Lelonek (Hamburg: Dölling und Galitz, 2015), 382–89, quotes at 383.
68. Mies van der Rohe 1928 notebook, quoted in Fritz Neumeyer, *The Artless Word: Mies van der Rohe on the Building Art* (Cambridge, Mass.: MIT Press, 1991), 71. "Building," *G*, no. 2 (September 1923): 1, quoted in Neumeyer, *The Artless Word*, 242. Mies van der Rohe, "Zum Neuen Jahrgang" (letters to Walter Riezler), *Die Form* 2, no. 1 (1927): 1; 2, no. 2 (1927): 59.
69. Ulrich Conrads and Horst Eifler, "Mies im Gespräch II" (recorded by RIAS Berlin, October 1964), published as a phonograph record as *Mies in Berlin* (Bauwelt Berlin, 1966), quote at 9:16 min., https://www.bauwelt.de/rubriken/videos/Mies-im-Gespraech-II-2123186.html.
70. At first there was a monthly portfolio with high-quality reproductions and accompanying essays, *Moderne Kunstwerken* (1903–10), and then a monthly journal, *Beeldende Kunst* (1914–38).
71. Mies van der Rohe to Ada Bruhn, April 26 and 29, 1912, private collection (Frank Herterich, Berlin).
72. Mies van der Rohe to Ada Bruhn, April 29, 1912, private collection (Frank Herterich, Berlin).
73. Conrads and Eifler, "Mies im Gespräch II," quote at 6:28 min.
74. Conrads and Eifler, "Mies im Gespräch II," quote at 8:12 min.
75. Kuh, "Modern Classicist," 22–23, 61, quote at 61.
76. Christopher Vernon, "Berlage in America: The Prairie School as 'The New American Architecture,'" in *The New Movement in the Netherlands 1924–1936*, ed. Jan Molema (Amsterdam: 010, 1996), 131–51; Hendrik Petrus Berlage, "Neuere Amerikanische Architektur," *Schweizerische Bauzeitung*, 60, nos. 11–13 (1912): 148–50, 165–67, 176.
77. 1. Men's and Ladies' cloak room, 2. Entrance, 3. Halls, 4. Corridor, executed as exhibition space for porcelain, 5. Emphasis of the middle of the house, 6. Sleeping room section, 7. Dining room, 8. Hall, 9. Exhibition room, 10. Great Exhibition Hall, 11. Pergola, 12. Lady's flower house, 13. Cabinet for Etching, 14. Fish pond, 15. Driveway. Dearstyne studied with Mies at the Bauhaus from 1928 until 1934. Sketches from classroom discussions might have been easier to come by when the Bauhaus had moved to Berlin, as teaching became more informal and the number of students had dwindled.
78. Paul Westheim, "Mies van der Rohe: Entwicklung eines Architekten," *Das Kunstblatt* 11, no. 2 (February 1927): 55–62, quotes at 56–58. Thirty-two years later, Mies similarly said: "Certainly I was influenced by Schinkel, but the plan is not in any way Schinkel's." Henry Thomas Cadbury-Brown, "Ludwig Mies van der Rohe in Conversation with H. T. Cadbury-Brown," *AA Files*, no. 66 (2013): 71.
79. Julius Meier-Graefe, "Ein modernes Milieu," *Dekorative Kunst* 8 (1901): 249–65.
80. Meier-Graefe had written the first monograph on the artist: Julius Meier-Graefe, *Vincent van Gogh* (Munich: Piper, 1910).
81. Julius Meier-Graefe to Mies van der Rohe, November 18, 1912, Museum of Modern Art, MvdR, Early Projects, Folder #1.
82. Marcia Winn, "Front Views and Profiles: This Changing World," *Chicago Daily Tribune*, January 28, 1942, 17.
83. Correspondence House Werner, 1912–1914, Archive Parzival School, Berlin, Quermatenweg 6.
84. Christiane Kruse, "Haus Werner—Ein ungeliebtes Frühwerk Mies van der Rohes," *Zeitschrift für Kunstgeschichte* 56, no. 4 (1993): 554–63.
85. Markus Jager, "Das Haus Warnholtz von Ludwig Mies van der Rohe (1914/15)," *Zeitschrift für Kunstgeschichte* 65, no. 1 (2002): 123–36; Edgar Wedepohl, "Form und Raum: Gespräch im Berliner Grunewald," *Wasmuths Monatshefte fiir Baukunst* 10 (1926): 393–95.
86. Adolf Vogdt, "Ein Landhaus in Neu-Babelsberg," *Innen-Dekoration* 31 (1920): 184–98; Clemens Klemmer, "Vom Neoklassizismus zur Moderne: Werner von Walthausen (1887–1958), ein Meister des Neuen Bauens—Partner von Mies van der Rohe," *Werk, Bauen + Wohnen* 78, no. 7/8 (1991): 78–82.
87. Andreas Marx and Paul Weber, "Ludwig Mies's unrealisierte Teilnahme an der 'Ausstellung für unbekannte Architekten' (1919). Materialien zur Entwicklungsgeschichte Mies van der Rohes," in *Berlin in Geschichte und Gegenwart. Jahrbuch des Landesarchivs Berlin 2009*, ed. Werner Breunig and Uwe Schaper (Berlin: Mann, 2010), 195–263.
88. Dietrich Neumann, "Mies—Dada—Montage: Notes on a Reception History," in *Mies van der Rohe: Montage, Collage*, ed. Andreas Beitin, Wolf Eiermann, and Brigitte Franzen (Aachen: Ludwig Forum, 2016), 65–69.
89. Andreas Marx and Paul Weber, "Konventioneller Kontext der Moderne. Mies van der Rohes Haus Kempner 1921–1923. Ausgangspunkt einer Neubewertung des Hochhauses Friedrichstrasse," in *Berlin in Geschichte und Gegenwart. Jahrbuch des Landesarchivs Berlin*, ed. Jürgen Wetzel (Berlin: Mann, 2003), 63–107.
90. Andreas Marx and Paul Weber, "From Ludwig Mies to Mies van der Rohe: The Apartment and Studio Am Karlsbad 24 (1915–39)," in *Mies and Modern Living: Interiors, Furniture, Photography*, ed. Helmut Reuter and Birgit Schulte (Ostfildern: Hatje Cantz, 2008), 36–37.
91. This did not prevent her from also claiming the name for herself. See Georgia van der Rohe, *La donna è mobile: Mein bedingungsloses Leben* (Berlin: Aufbau, 2001), 14.
92. Marx and Weber, "From Ludwig Mies to Mies van der Rohe," 36–37.
93. Richard Lisker to Mies van der Rohe, July 19, 1925, Library of Congress, MvdR, Private Correspondence, Folder L; Lisker told Mies of a report by Heinrich de Fries for Frankfurt's lord mayor, when Mies was considered for the position of building assessor, which ultimately went to Ernst May.
94. Werner Hegemann, "Schräges oder flaches Dach," *Wasmuths Monatshefte für Baukunst* 11, no. 3 (1927): 120.
95. Van der Rohe, *Donna è mobile*, 16.
96. Marx and Weber, "From Ludwig Mies to Mies van der Rohe," 24–39.
97. Fritz Neumeyer, "Beim Wort genommen: Originalton Mies," in *Originalton: Ludwig Mies van der Rohe; Die Lohan Tapes of 1969* (Berlin: Dom, 2021), 9–31.
98. Ada van der Rohe to Ms. Ewald at Salem Boarding School, May 7, 1930; and Ludwig Mies van der Rohe to Director, Salem Boarding School, March 4, 1932, both Generallandesarchiv Karlsruhe, Salem—13, Nr. 355.

Chapter Two. Conventional Houses and Visionary Projects

1. This has been convincingly argued by Andreas Marx and Paul Weber, "Konventioneller Kontext der Moderne. Mies van der Rohes Haus Kempner 1921–1923. Ausgangspunkt einer Neubewertung des Hochhauses Friedrichstrasse," in *Berlin in Geschichte und Gegenwart. Jahrbuch des Landesarchivs Berlin*, ed. Jürgen Wetzel (Berlin: Mann, 2003): 63–107.
2. Published without a title in *Frühlicht* 1, no. 4 (1922): 122–24; English translation quoted in Fritz Neumeyer, *The Artless Word: Mies van der Rohe on the Building Art* (Cambridge, Mass.: MIT Press, 1991), 240. Max Berg, "Die formale Auffassung des Hochhausgedankens. Charakteristische Entwürfe des Berliner Wettbewerbs," *Bauwelt* 13, no. 21 (May 25, 1922): 359–63, 434–35, quote at 363.
3. Si, "Die Hauptversammlung des Bundes Deutscher Architekten," *Zentralblatt der Bauverwaltung*, June 30, 1920, 336.
4. Berg, "Die formale Auffassung."
5. Berg, "Die formale Auffassung." For information about the Friedrichstrasse competition, see Florian Zimmermann, *Der Schrei nach dem Turmhaus* (Berlin: Argon, 1988); Dietrich Neumann, *Die Wolkenkratzer Kommen! Deutsche Hochhäuser der Zwanziger Jahre* (Braunschweig: Vieweg, 1995), 61–112.
6. Code words of all entries were listed in the magazine *Baugilde*: "Wettbewerbe in Berlin. Hochhaus Bahnhof Friedrichstrasse," *Baugilde* 2 (January 18, 1922), repr. in Zimmermann, *Der Schrei nach dem Turmhaus*, 300.
7. Ulrich Conrads and Horst Eifler, "Mies im Gespräch II" (recorded by RIAS Berlin, October 1964), published as a phonograph record as *Mies in Berlin* (Bauwelt Berlin, 1966), quote at 9:16 min., https://www.bauwelt.de/rubriken/videos/Mies-im-Gespraech-II-2123186.html.
8. Julius Posener, "Vorlesungen zur Geschichte der neuen Architektur II," *Arch+* 53 (September 1980): 75.
9. John Zukowsky, *Mies Reconsidered* (Chicago: Art Institute of Chicago, 1986), 37.
10. Franz Schulze, *Mies van der Rohe: A Critical Biography* (Chicago: University of Chicago Press, 1985), 103.
11. Marx and Weber, "Konventioneller Kontext der Moderne," 63–107.
12. Walter Koeppen, *Bauordnung für die Stadt Berlin vom 3. November 1925*, 2nd rev. ed. (Berlin: Ernst, 1927), 29, 35.
13. Quoted in Neumeyer, *Artless Word*, 250.
14. Hermann Seeger, *Bürohäuser der privaten Wirtschaft* (Leipzig: Gebhardts, 1933), 14.
15. The most exhaustive analysis of the different renderings can be found in Pablo Gallego Picard, *Traslaciones Poéticas: Un recorrido por la Friedrichstrasse de Mies van der Rohe en 1921. Arquitectura, fotografía y cine, la percepción en la arquitectura* (PhD diss., Departamento de Proyectos Arquitectónicos, Escuela Técnica Superior de Arquitectura Universidad Politécnica de Madrid, 2014).
16. It is less likely that the label was attached in Germany already, as the competition date of 1921 was widely known there. "Friedrichstrasse" would have probably been written as "Friedrichstraße," with the unique letter only found on German typewriters. Theoretically, Ludwig Glaeser might have attached the label on arrival (based on the wrong information in the 1947 catalogue), but he probably would have written the label in English for the benefit of the museum staff (and he was the one who rectified the date in a publication right after Mies's death).
17. Philip Johnson, *Mies van der Rohe* (New York: Museum of Modern Art, 1947), 24–25; Peter Blake, *The Master Builders: Le Corbusier, Mies van der Rohe, Frank Lloyd Wright* (New York: W. W. Norton, 1960), 180–84; Arthur Drexler, *Mies van der Rohe* (New York: George Braziller, 1960), 31, 115; A. James Speyer, *Mies van der Rohe* (Chicago: Art Institute of Chicago, 1968), 16. Naturally, many reviews adopted the wrong date. Christopher Andreae, "Mies van der Rohe: A Lengthy Career: What Might Have Been," *Christian Science Monitor*, May 8, 1968, 10; Ada Louise Huxtable, "The Miesian

Lesson," *New York Times*, April 28, 1968, D34. Mies repeated the claim as late as 1964 when he was interviewed in Berlin: Conrads and Eifler, "Mies im Gespräch II," quote at 8:26 min.

18. Ludwig Glaeser, *Ludwig Mies van der Rohe: Drawings in the Collection of the Museum of Modern Art* (New York: Museum of Modern Art, 1969), n.p.

19. Published without a title in *Frühlicht*, 1, no. 4 (1922): 122–24. English translation quoted in Neumeyer, *Artless Word*, 240.

20. Schulze, *Critical Biography*, 103, 107. Mies later explicitly rejected that assumption; see Conrads and Eifler, "Mies im Gespräch II."

21. Carl Gotfrid [Carl Gottfried], "Hochhäuser," *Qualität* 3, no. 5 (1922): 63–66.

22. Gallego Picard, *Traslaciones Poéticas* 11, Wolf Tegethoff, "From Obscurity to Maturity: Mies van der Rohe's Breakthrough to Modernism," in *Mies van der Rohe: Critical Essays*, ed. Franz Schulze (New York: Museum of Modern Art, 1989), 28–94, quote at 43; Michele Caja, email to author, June 21, 2023.

23. Bruno Möhring, "Über die Vorzüge der Turmhäuser und die Voraussetzungen, unter denen sie in Berlin gebaut werden können," *Stadtbaukunst Ater und Neuer Zeit* (1920): 375.

24. Spyros Papapetros, "Malicious Houses: Animation, Animism, Animosity in German Architecture and Film—From Mies to Murnau," *Grey Room* 20 (2005): 6–37. Herzog produced models for several modern architects, such as the Luckhardt Brothers' entry for the Friedrichstrasse competition in 1922, the model of Otto Bartning's Sternkirche in 1924, and the model for Mies's entry for the German section at the Brussels World's Fair in 1934.

25. Mart Stam, "Die Neuen Materialien" *ABC-Beiträge zum Bauen* 3/4 (1925): 4.

26. Bruno Taut, *Die neue Baukunst in Europa und Amerika* (1927; repr., Stuttgart: J. Hoffmann, 1979), 111.

27. H. Marcus, "Die Tragfähigkeit und die Wirtschaftlichkeit trägerloser Pilzdecken," *Deutsche Bauzeitung*, supplement Mitteilungen über Zement, Beton- und Eisenbetonbau 16, no. 23 (December 6, 1919): 149–52, no. 24 (December 20, 1919), 155–59, quote at 149. Swiss engineer Robert Maillart claimed authorship in 1926, citing his experiments of 1908 and 1910. Until then only the American experiments were known. R. Maillart, "Zur Entwicklung der unterzugslosen Decke in der Schweiz und in Amerika," *Schweizerische Bauzeitung* 87 (1926): 263–65, 19–21.

28. O. Freud, "Die trägerlose Pilzdecke, eine neuartige Eisenbetondecke für Industriebauten," *Industriebau* 17 (1926): 166–270; Julius Vischer and Ludwig Hilberseimer, *Beton als Gestalter* (Stuttgart: Julius Hoffmann, 1928), 49–50.

29. Reyner Banham, *Theory and Design in the First Machine Age* (London: Architectural Press, 1960), 295.

30. In *Frühlicht* 1, no. 4 (1922), quoted in Schulze, *Critical Biography*, 100.

31. See contemporary critics Karl Scheffler, "Ein Weg zum Stil," *Berliner Architekturwelt* 5 (1903): 291–95; Heinrich Pudor, "Gerüst-Architektur," *Bauwelt* 1, no. 36 (1910): 15.

32. Gotfrid, "Hochhäuser," 63–66. Gottfried wrote under the *nom de plume* Carl Gotfrid. The magazine *Qualität* was published by Carl Ernst Hinkefuss, the business partner of Wilhelm Deffke, who occasionally worked in Mies's office from 1920 to 1924.

33. Gotfrid, "Hochhäuser," 63–66.

34. In 1923, the Verein Berliner Künstler occupied nineteen rooms, the Bund Deutscher Architekten four rooms, and the Novembergruppe six rooms.

35. At 68 1/4 by 48 inches (173.4 by 121.9 centimeters), Mies's presentation drawing was considerably larger than Poelzig's (executed by his draftsman, Erich Zimmermann, at 43 3/8 by 30 3/8 inches, or 110.1 by 77.2 centimeters).

36. Adolf Behne, "Der Wettbewerb der Turmhaus-Gesellschaft," *Wasmuths Monatshefte für Baukunst* 7 (1922–23): 59.

37. Rainer Stommer, "Die Germanisierung des Wolkenkratzers," *Kritische Berichte* 10 (1982): 36–53; Neumann, *Die Wolkenkratzer Kommen!*.

38. Knud Lonberg-Holm, "Moderne Tysk Bygningskunst: Arbejder af arkitekt Mies van der Rohe, Berlin," *Bygmesteren Dansk Arkitektforenings Tidskrift* (August 15, 1923): 203–5. I would like to thank Adrian Täckman for this reference.

39. Walter Curt Behrendt, "Skyscrapers in Germany," *Journal of the American Institute of Architects* 11, no. 9 (September 1923): 365–70.

40. George C. Nimmons, "Skyscrapers in America," *Journal of the American Institute of Architects* 11, no. 9 (September 1923): 370–72.

41. William Stanley Parker, "Skyscrapers Anywhere," *Journal of the American Institute of Architects* 11, no. 9 (September 1923): 372.

42. Nimmons, "Skyscrapers in America," 370.

43. Gerhard Severain to Mies van der Rohe, March 28, 1923, Museum of Modern Art (hereafter MoMA), MvdR; Dietrich Neumann, "Haus Ryder in Wiesbaden und die Zusammenarbeit von Gerhard Severain und Ludwig Mies van der Rohe," *Architectura* 2 (2006): 199–219.

44. Marx and Weber, "Konventioneller Kontext der Moderne," 65–107.

45. Mies's invoice to Karl Vogt (April 30, 1923), for the execution of a stove, fireplace, table, bench, and two cabinets, MoMA, MvdR, General Correspondence 1920s, Folder 2; Mies van der Rohe to factory owner Albrecht in Friedrichroda, February 14, 1923, Library of Congress (hereafter LoC), MvdR, General Correspondence 1920s, Folder 5.

46. Little is known about Ada Ryder. She was registered as "Privatiere" in the Wiesbaden address book, which suggests that she had her own assets.

Information provided by Gerhard Klaiber, Stadtarchiv Wiesbaden, August 17, 2005.

47. The historicist multifamily apartment block at Taunusstrasse 75 by the architect Wilhelm Müller still exists. Sigrid Russ, *Denkmaltopographie Kulturdenkmäler in Hessen, Wiesbaden II. Die Villengebiete* (Braunschweig: Landesamt für Denkmalpflege Hessen, 1988), 414, 415.

48. On the east side, the neoclassical house No. 18 was built in 1861; on the west side, No. 22 was designed in 1897 by master builder Karl Schulze. See Russ, *Denkmaltopographie Kulturdenkmäler*, 310, 312, 313; Ryder House (No. 20) is not listed in the monument topography.

49. Gerhard Severain to Mies van der Rohe, March 7, 1923, MoMA, MvdR

50. Mies van der Rohe to Gerhard Severain, March 23, 1923, MoMA, MvdR.

51. Gerhard Severain to Mies van der Rohe, March 28, 1923, April 12, 1923, MoMA, MvdR.

52. Building application at the civil engineering office in Wiesbaden. Information from Sever Severain, Wiesbaden.

53. Postcard, Gerhard Severain to Mies van der Rohe, June 18, 1923, MoMA, MvdR.

54. Correspondence between Gerhard Severain and Mies van der Rohe, June 18 and 29, 1923; July 5, 7, 17, 18, and 23, 1923. Payment voucher for 50,000 Marks from Severain to Mies van der Rohe, July 14, 1923. Handwritten note by Severain: "L. L. Up to now paid 3,000,000 marks." MoMA, MvdR, Folder House Ryder.

55. Gotfrid, "Hochhäuser," 63–66.

56. Correspondence between Gerhard Severain and Mies van der Rohe, December 3, 1923; December 7, 1923; January 27, 1924; March 6, 1924, all MoMA, MvdR, Folder House Ryder.

57. The latter two have not been identified. *Grosse Berliner Kunstausstellung im Landesausstellungsgebäude am Lehrter Bahnhof* (Berlin: Grosse Berliner Kunstausstellung, 1923), 34.

58. Among them Robert van t' Hoff, Jan Wils, Gerrit Rietveld, J. A. Pauw, J. M. van Hardeveld, Raemaker en Karel Meyer, J. J. P. Oud, Theo van Doesburg, and Frans Smulders. *Grosse Berliner Kunstausstellung,* 37.

59. The exhibition was held from October 15 to November 15, 1923.

60. Franz Schulze and Edward Windhorst, *Mies van der Rohe: A Critical Biography*, new and rev. ed. (Chicago: University of Chicago, 2014), 78. See the photo of Mies's Curvilinear Glass Skyscraper on the wall of van Doesburg's studio and the exhibition list for the Paris exhibition in Dolf Broekhuizen, *Maison d'Artiste. De Stijl Icon* (Rotterdam: nai010, 2006), 47, 95.

61. *Grosse Berliner Kunstausstellung,* 34.

62. Ludwig Mies van der Rohe, "Bürohaus," *G*, no. 1 (July 1923): 3. Here Mies was echoing Hans Richter and Werner Graeff's editorial in *G*: "The fundamental demand of elemental form-creation is economy. Pure relation of power and material. That requires elemental means, total control of means. Elemental order, regularity." English translation quoted from Detlef Mertins and Michael Jennings, eds., *G—An Avant-Garde Journal of Art, Architecture, Design and Film, 1923–1926* (Los Angeles: Getty Research Institute, 2010), 101.

63. Dietrich Neumann, "Three Early Projects by Mies van der Rohe," *Perspecta* 27 (1992): 76–97. Ludwig Glaeser was the first to suggest the layout of the columnar structure and the floor plan with the central courtyard. See Ludwig Glaeser, *Mies van der Rohe: Drawings in the Collection of the Museum of Modern Art* (New York: Museum of Modern Art, 1969). See also Tegethoff, "From Obscurity to Maturity," 28–94.

64. Mies van der Rohe, "Bürohaus." The German text speaks more evocatively of "*Teigwaren*" (doughy matters) and "*Panzertürme*" (tank turretts)—the latter surely a sideswipe at Erich Mendelsohn's Einstein Tower.

65. Neumann, "Three Early Projects," 76–97.

66. Mies famously explained the vertical I-beam mullions on the outside of his Lake Shore Drive Apartments as structural devices stiffening the corner plates, but then conceded that the "real reason" was that it simply had "not looked right" without them. "Mies van der Rohe," *Architectural Forum*, November 1952, 99.

67. J. J. P. Oud, "Über die zukünftige Baukunst und ihre architektonischen Möglichkeiten," in *Holländische Architektur*, Bauhaus Bücher 10 (Munich: Albert Langen, 1926), 8–21, quote at 18.

68. Ludwig Hilberseimer, "Konstruktion und Form," *G*, no. 3 (1924): 24–25. Translation by Steven Lindberg in Mertins and Jennings, *G*, 128.

69. Ludwig Glaeser, interview transcript with Werner Graeff, September 17, 1972, Canadian Centre for Architecture, Montreal; Dietrich Neumann, "Mies's Concrete Office Building and Its Common Acquaintances," *AA Files* (Spring 2017): 70–84.

70. Neumann, "Mies's Concrete Office Building," quote at 77. In a curriculum vitae written in 1945, Deffke mentioned the years 1922–24; in another version, a year later, he claims the years to be 1917–24.

71. Mies van der Rohe to Wilhelm Adolf Farenholtz, December 9, 1925, LoC, MvdR, Personal Correspondence F.

72. Similar vertical lines can be seen in the two colored chalk drawings for the Concrete Country House, also made in the period immediately before the 1923 *Grosse Berliner Kunstausstellung*. Both are of a similar width to the drawing of the Concrete Office Building—90 inches (228.6 centimeters) wide, in comparison with 113 3/4 inches (288.9 centimeters).

73. Philipp F. Reemtsma was interested in modern architecture and later com- missioned Frankfurt architect Martin Elsässer to design his home in Hamburg—the largest modern house in Germany.

74. Before moving operations to Hamburg, Reemtsma briefly considered a move to Berlin—perhaps an inspiration for Deffke (and Mies) to rework the Erfurt project for the capital.

75. Neumann, "Mies's Concrete Office Building," 70–84.

76. "Neuartige Bürohausbauten: Bürohaus mit Fensterwänden (Entwurf des Architekten Ludwig Mies van der Rohe)," Deutsche Allgemeine Zeitung, August 5, 1923, morning edition, Kraft und Stoff supp., 1.

77. See Deutsche Allgemeine Zeitung to Mies van der Rohe, July 18, 1923; August 1, 1923; August 8, 1923, all MoMA, MvdR, Folder 3, MvdR Manuscripts.

78. For Mies's text about the office building submitted too late to the Deutsche Allgemeine Zeitung, see Ludwig Mies van der Rohe, "Office Building," in Neumeyer, Artless Word, 241–42.

79. Schulze, Critical Biography, 110.

80. Tegethoff, "From Obscurity to Maturity," 55.

81. Johnson, Mies van der Rohe (New York: Museum of Modern Art 1947), 30.

82. Schulze, Critical Biography, 116.

83. Ludwig Mies van der Rohe, "Bauen," G, no. 2 (September 1923): 1. Mies surely thought of Thilo Schoder's house for textile merchant Franz Stross in Liberec, Czechoslovakia (1923–25), and van de Velde's Werkbund Theater at the 1914 Cologne exhibition.

84. Mies van der Rohe, "Bauen," 1.

85. For a more detailed analysis, see Neumann, "Three Early Projects," 76–97.

86. Bruno Taut, "Der Regenbogen: Aufruf zum Farbigen Bauen," Frühlicht 1 (1921), repr. in Bruno Taut, Frühlicht 1920–1922. Eine Folge für die Verwirklichung des neuen Baugedankens, Bauwelt Fundamente 8 (Basel: Birkhäuser, 1963), 97–98. The second rendering of the Concrete Country House in red had previously been attributed to the Eliat House project of 1925. The ribbon window on the left, the placement of the chimney, and the overall configuration suggests an earlier version of the Concrete Country House. The drawing style is similar to that of Wilhelm Deffke, who had stopped working for Mies in 1924.

87. Emil von Mecenseffy, Handbuch fir Eisenbetonbau, vol. 10, Die künstleri- sche Gestaltung der Eisenbetonbauten (1911; repr., Berlin: Wilhelm Ernst, 1922), 135.

88. Walter Gropius to Mies van der Rohe, June 7, 1923; Mies van der Rohe to Gropius, June 14, 1923, all LoC, MvdR, Private Correspondence, Folder G.

89. Mies van der Rohe to Walter Gropius, June 5, 1923, LoC, MvdR.

90. Another indication that there were two drawings of the Concrete Office Building is a listing of "two large views, one section, one model from Weimar" of it for a show organized by Mies for the Jena Kunstverein. Kunstverein Gera to Mies van der Rohe, November 24, 1924, LoC, MvdR. See Andreas Marx and Paul Weber, "Zur Neudatierung von Mies van der Rohes Landhaus in Eisenbeton," Architectura 2 (2008): 127–66.

91. Walter Gropius to Mies van der Rohe, June 7, 1923, LoC, MvdR.

92. Mies van der Rohe to Walter Gropius, June 14, 1923, LoC, MvdR.

93. Walter Gropius, "Développement de l'Esprit architectural moderne en Allemagne," L'Esprit nouveau 27 (1924): 40–45.

94. Walter Gropius to Mies van der Rohe, September 18, 1923, LoC, MvdR.

95. Mies van der Rohe to Werner Jakstein, September 13, 1923, LoC, MvdR, Private Correspondence, Folder G.

96. Mies van der Rohe to H. P. Berlage, December 13, 1923, LoC, MvdR, Personal Correspondence 1923–40. (The original is in the Berlage papers of the Het Nieuwe Instituut, formerly Netherlandish Architecture Institute, in Rotterdam.)

97. Adolf Meyer to Mies van der Rohe, November 22, 1923, LoC, MvdR, Private Correspondence, Folder F; Mies van der Rohe to Walter Gropius, September 29, 1923; Gropius to Mies van der Rohe, October 2, 1923, LoC, MvdR, Private Correspondence, Folder G.

98. Mies van der Rohe to Walter Dexel, October 29, 1924, LoC, MvdR, Private Correspondence, Folder D; Mies van der Rohe to Walter Gropius, October 29, 1924, LoC, MvdR, Private Correspondence, Folder G; Kunstverein Gera to Mies van der Rohe, November 24, 1924, LoC, MvdR, Private Corres- pondence.

99. R. P., "Kunstverein Jena. Eröffnung der Ausstellung über Moderne Architektur," Jenaische Zeitung, November 5, 1924. The lecture at the opening event was delivered by Adolf Meyer (because Mies was ill).

100. Walter Dexel, "Jena," Der Cicerone. Halbmonatsschrift für die Interessen des Kunstforschers und Sammlers 18 (1926): 581–82, quote at 582.

101. Walter Curt Behrendt to Mies van der Rohe, January 30, 1924, LoC, MvdR, Box 1, Private Correspondence, 1923–40, Folder B.

102. The exhibition lasted from May 31 to September 1, 1924. See its catalogue, Grosse Berliner Kunstausstellung im Landesausstellungsgebäude am Lehrter Bahnhof (Berlin: Grosse Berliner Kunstausstellung, 1924).

103. Ludwig Mies van der Rohe, "Lecture" (June 19, 1924), in Neumeyer, Artless Word, 250.

104. Early in 1924, Erich Mendelsohn had been honored with a remarkable spe- cial edition of Wasmuths Monatshefte für Baukunst. Both the style of his sketches and some of his early buildings had an influence on Mies's first modern building. Erich Mendelsohn, "Bauten und Skizzen," Wasmuths Monatshefte für Baukunst 1–2 (1924): 1–66. Grosse Berliner Kunstauss- tellung, 97.

105. Theo van Doesburg, "De Nieuwe Architectuur," Boukundig Weekblad 45, no. 20 (May 17, 1924): 200–204; Dolf Broekhuizen, Maison d'Artiste. De Stijl Icon (Rotterdam: nai010, 2006).

106. Alfred Barr, Cubism and Modern Art (New York: Museum of Modern Art, 1934), 156–57.

107. Quoted in Peter Carter, Mies van der Rohe at Work (New York: Praeger, 1974), 180.

108. L'Architecture vivante (Winter 1925): 2–9.

109. Adolf Behne, "Grosse Berliner Kunstausstellung 1924," Die Weltbühne 28 (July 28, 1924): 60–62.

110. Walter Curt Behrendt, "Die Architektur auf der Berliner Kunstausstellung 1924," Kunst und Künstler 22, no. 11 (1924): 347–52, quote at 351.

111. Hans Soeder, "Architektur auf der Berliner Kunstausstellung 1924," Der Neubau 6 (1924): 153–58, quote at 158.

112. Hans Richter, "Der Neue Baumeister," Qualität 4, nos. 1, 2 (January/ February 1925): 3–9.

113. Martin Gaier and Claudia Mohn, "Haus Mosler, Neubabelsberg. Dokumentation einer Zerstörung. Planungs-, Ausführungs- und Veränder- ungsgeschichte des Hauses," in Mies van der Rohe. Frühe Bauten. Probleme der Erhaltung—Probleme der Bewertung, ed. Johannes Cramer and Dorothée Sack (Petersberg: Imhof, 2004), 71–86; Michael Zajonz and Ralf Dorn, "Haus Mosler, Neubabelsberg. Ein Haus, 'das sehr gut in die ernste, märkische Landschaft passt,'" in Cramer and Sack, Frühe Bauten, 87–102.

114. Zajonz and Dorn, "Haus Mosler, Neubabelsberg," 90.

115. Werner Graeff, "Über die sogenannte 'G-Gruppe,'" werk und zeit, no. 11 (1962); English translation in Art Journal 23, no. 4 (1964): 280–82, repr. in Mertins and Jennings, G., 243–48.

116. Quoted in Maria Gough, "Contains Graphic Material: El Lissitzky and the Topography of G," in Mertins and Jennings, G., 21–51, quote at 44.

117. Graeff, "Über die sogenannte 'G-Gruppe,'" 247.

118. Mertins and Jennings, G., 128.

119. Ludwig Mies van der Rohe, "Industrielles Bauen," G, no. 3 (June 1924): 8–13. See "Der Leichtbau," Vossische Zeitung, April 4, 1924, morning edi- tion, economy and technology supp., 1.

120. Lilly Reich to Mies van der Rohe, June 10, 1925, MoMA, MvdR.

121. Hans Richter, "Der Neue Baumeister," Qualität 4, no. 1 (January/February 1925): 3–9.

122. Fritz Jacob to Mies van der Rohe, March 1, 1925; Hermann John to Mies van der Rohe, February 23, 1925, both MoMA, MvdR, Folder Mosler. In 1931, a new law protected the term "Baumeister" by making it dependent on passing an exam, the Baumeisterprüfung. At that point, Mies had been accepted as an architect and stopped using the term. "Verordnung über die Berechtigung zur Führung der Berufsbezeichnung 'Baumeister' (Baumeisterverordnung). Vom 1. April 1931," Deutsches Reichsgesetzblatt, no. 14 (1931): 131.

Chapter Three. Housing and Urban Modernity

1. Referenced in Walter Dexel to Mies van der Rohe, January 24, 1925, Museum of Modern Art (hereafter MoMA), MvdR, Small Projects Folder #2; Mies and Dexel probably met at the Werkbund, which Mies had been invited to join on March 22, 1924. Otto Bauer, secretary of the Deutscher Werkbund, to Mies van der Rohe, March 22, 1924, Library of Congress (hereafter LoC), MvdR, private correspondence, 1923–1940; R. P., "Kunstverein Jena. Eröffnung der Ausstellung über Moderne Architektur," Jenaische Zeitung, November 5, 1924. The lecture at the opening was delivered by Adolf Meyer (because Mies was ill). Franz Schulze, Mies van der Rohe: A Critical Biography (Chicago: Chicago University Press, 1985), 122; Wolf Tegethoff, Die Villen und Landhausprojekte. Wohnen in einer Neuen Zeit (Krefeld: Kaiswer Wilhelm Museum, 1981), 1:52–53.

2. Walter Dexel to Mies van der Rohe, January 7, 1925, MoMA, MvdR, Small Projects Folder #2.

3. Bernhard Dexel to Annemarie Jaeggi, June 14, 1988, in Annemarie Jaeggi, Adolf Meyer: Der Zweite Mann. Ein Architekt im Schatten von Walter Gropius (Berlin: Argon, 1994), 474n19.

4. Walter and Grete Dexel to Mies van der Rohe, January 7, 19, 22, 24, and 28, 1925; February 12, 1925; and March 3, 1925, both MoMA, MvdR, Small Projects Folder #2.

5. See Tegethoff, Die Villen und Landhausprojekte, 52–54.

6. Dexel knew about the speed with which Gropius and Meyer had designed and executed Auerbach House in Jena, where a mere seven months passed from the commission to the finished building (March—October 1924). Jaeggi, Adolf Meyer, 474.

7. In addition, according to Dexel, modern architecture was still hard to get approved by the authorities. As director of the Bauhaus, Gropius had enjoyed a certain clout, but Mies could not count on a similar concession.

8. Quoted in Tegethoff, Die Villen und Landhausprojekte, 52.

9. Werner Graeff, interview by Ludwig Glaeser, September 17, 1972, Canadian Centre for Architecture, Montreal, 78, 79. The Dexels seem to have forgiven Mies. They published his Wolf House in Guben in their book on contemporary residential architecture a few years later. Grete Dexel and Walter Dexel, *Das Wohnhaus von heute* (Leipzig: Hesse und Becker, 1928), 57.

10. Jaeggi, *Adolf Meyer*, 337.

11. E. Ge., "Architektur Ausstellung: Adolf Meyer (im Prinzessinnenschlösschen)," *Jenaer Volksblatt* 37, no. 61 (March 13, 1926): 1. According to Dexel, the exhibit was a great success, attracting twice as many visitors as any painting show. "Der behördlich verhinderte Wohnungsbau: Ein Gutachten des deutschen Werkbundes," *Jenaer Volksblatt* 36, no. 302 (December 28, 1925): 3; Walter Dexel, "Jena," *Der Cicerone. Halbmonatsschrift für die Interessen des Kunstforschers und Sammlers* 18 (1926): 581–82, quote at 582.

12. Werner Hegemann, *Werner March* (Berlin: Friedrich Ernst Hübsch, 1930), xv; Thomas Schmidt, *Werner March. Architekt des Olympia-Stadions 1894–1976* (Basel: Birkhäuser, 1992), 14, 15. For the most detailed discussion of the Eliat House project, see Tegethoff, *Die Villen und Landhausprojekte,* 55–57.

13. The lost rendering drawing appeared in a laudatory essay about Mies by Paul Westheim, intended to introduce him as director of the upcoming Weissenhof exhibition to a broader public. Westheim explained that Mies designed houses as "dwelling devices," not as "decorative backdrops," and his small output was due to his principled belief in "characterful," upright, straightforward architecture. Paul Westheim, "Mies van der Rohe: Entwicklung eines Architekten," *Das Kunstblatt* 11, no. 2 (February 1927): 55–62, image 59, quotes at 57, 62.

14. Telegram from Hermann John to Mies van der Rohe, February 25, 1925, LoC, MvdR, Private Correspondence 1923–40, Folder M.

15. "Ausstellung der Entwürfe," *Vossische Zeitung,* September 10, 1925, evening edition, 4.

16. "Der Verkehrsturm auf dem Potsdamer Platz in Berlin," *Die Voss,* January 3, 1925, 1.

17. Alfred Wedemeyer, "Der geplante Verkehrsturm in Berlin, Ecke Leipziger- und Friedrichstrasse," *Deutsche Bauzeitung* 59, no. 51 (June 27, 1925): 99–101.

18. "From a Traffic Tower: Growing Discipline of New York Crowds to Upraised Arm—Use Psychology's Laws," *New York Times,* March 12, 1922, 102.

19. Kosina had worked for Erich Mendelsohn in 1921, and the dynamic form of the model revealed traces of that influence.

20. "Der neue Verkehrsturm," *Berliner Tageblatt,* June 3, 1925, supp. 1.

21. "Der neue Verkehrsturm," *Berliner Volkszeitung,* June 4, 1925, morning edition, supp. 1; *Berliner Technische Zeitung,* June 4, 1925, 2.

22. "Der zweite Verkehrsturm," *Berliner Börsenkurier,* June 4, 1925, 4.

23. "Der zweite Verkehrsturm," [*Berliner Börsenkurier*], 4.

24. Brief, Heinrich Kosima and Paul Mahlberg and Mies van der Rohe, June 4, 1925, MoMA, MvdR, Early Projects Folder #8.

25. "Der neue Verkehrsturm," [*Berliner Volkszeitung*], 2.

26. "Der zweite Verkehrsturm," [*Berliner Börsenkurier*], 4.

27. Bodo Rasch, "Wie die Weissenhofsiedlung entstand," in *Die Zwanziger Jahre des Deutschen Werkbunds* (Giessen: Anabas, 1982), 107–9.

28. Otto Bauer, secretary of the Deutscher Werkbund, invited Mies to join on March 22, 1924, LoC, MvdR, Private Correspondence, 1923–1940.

29. The most exhaustive source on Lilly Reich is still Matilda McQuaid, with an essay by Magdalena Droste, *Lilly Reich: Designer and Architect* (New York: Museum of Modern Art, 1996), https://assets.moma.org/documents/moma_catalogue_278_300199443.pdf. See also Esther da Costa Meyer, "Cruel Metonymies: Lilly Reich's Designs for the 1937 World's Fair," *New German Critique,* no. 76 (Winter 1999): 161–89.

30. Richard Lisker to Mies van der Rohe, February 2, 1925; Lisker to Mies van der Rohe, February 28, 1925; Lisker to Mies van der Rohe, July 19, 1925, all LoC MvdR, Private Correspondence, Folder L.

31. Sonja Günther, *Lilly Reich, 1885–1947. Innenarchitektin, Designerin, Austellungsgestalterin* (Stuttgart: Deutsche Verlags Anstalt, 1988), 18.

32. Invoices from A. Theuer, Gebr. Hammer, and Wollferts & Wittmer, March 7, 12, and 31, 1925, LoC, MvdR, Private Correspondence, Folder D; Richard Pommer and Christian F. Otto, *Weissenhof 1927 and the Modern Movement in Architecture* (Chicago: University of Chicago Press, 1991), 20–21.

33. LoC, MvdR, Private Correspondence, 1923–1940, Folder R; Invoice B. Damme to Mies van der Rohe, July 1, 1925, LoC, MvdR, Private Correspondence, Folder D.

34. Adolf Rading to Mies van der Rohe, July 1 and July 14, 1925, LoC, MvdR, Personal Correspondence, Folder R.

35. Dietrich Neumann, "Mies's Concrete Office Building and Its Common Acquaintances," *AA Files* (Spring 2017): 70–84.

36. For detailed information on Haus Wolf, see Dietrich Neumann, ed., *Ludwig Mies van der Rohe, Villa Wolf in Gubin: History and Reconstruction* (Berlin: DOM, 2023). Wolf registered his disappointment that he did not hear from Mies for many weeks after their meeting (Mies had failed to mention his skiing vacation in Switzerland). Hermann John to Mies van der Rohe, February 20, 1925, MoMA, MvdR, Folder House Wolf. Money transfer slips addressed to Mies in Zuoz, February 14, 1925; February 28, 1925; and April 3, 1925, all LoC, MvdR, Private Correspondence, 1923–40, Folder M.

37. The different thicknesses of the two cantilevers illustrates the different loads they carry.

38. The preserved plans allow insights into the creation of the design—for example, there is an earlier version with divided window panes.

39. Lilly Reich to Richard Lisker, February 6, 1927, private collection, quoted in Christiane Lange, *Ludwig Mies van der Rohe und Lilly Reich. Möbel und Räume* (Ostfildern: Hatje Cantz, 2007), 99.

40. For example, Adolf Behne, "Holländische Baukunst der Gegenwart," *Wasmuths Monatshefte für Baukunst* 6, no. 1 (1921/22): 1–32; this essay presented mostly buildings by Berlage and the Amsterdam School. Paul Westheim, "Zu den Bauten von W. Dudok," *Wasmuths Monatshefte für Baukunst* 8, nos. 3/4 (1924): 87–104.

41. Heinrich de Fries, *Moderne Villen und Landhäuser* (Berlin: Wasmuth, 1924), v, vi, vii.

42. *Bouwkundig Weekblad,* September 20, 1924, 366.

43. Annette Ludwig, *Die Architekten Brüder Heinz und Bodo Rasch* (Tübingen: Wasmuth, 2009), 118–20.

44. Quoted in Ludwig, *Die Architekten Brüder Heinz und Bodo Rasch,* 142n64.

45. Anon. (probably Guido Harbers, editor-in-chief), "Die 'neue Linie' im alleinstehenden Einfamilienhaus," *Der Baumeister* 29, no. 11 (November 1931): 422–31.

46. Alfred Gellhorn, "Von der Form," *Soziale Bauwirtschaft* 14 (1925): 188.

47. Donald Drew Egbert, *Social Radicalism and the Arts, Western Europe: A Cultural History from the French Revolution to 1968* (New York: Knopf, 1970), 661f.

48. See Wilhelm Pieck, July 12, 1925, in Simon Behringer, "Das Revolutionsdenkmal von Mies van der Rohe: Sinnbild der Masse," in *Baubilder und Erinnerungsmuster,* ed. Wita Noack and Jan Maruhn (Berlin: Form + Zweck, 2022), 41–67. Much additional new material about the monument is in Wita Noack, Ulf Meyer, and Jörn Köppler, eds., *Mies und die 'Unvollendete Moderne' Das Revolutionsdenkaml von 1926* (Berlin: Form + Zweck, 2023).

49. Christian Fuhrmeister, *Beton, Klinker, Granit. Material Macht Politik* (Berlin: Bauwesen, 2001), 212ff.

50. "Den toten Helden der Revolution. Die Enthüllung ihres Denkmals," *Die Rote Fahne,* June 13, 1926, supp. 1.

51. Provisional plan for the execution of the Werkbund exhibition Stuttgart. Württemberg section of the Werkbund, June 27, 1925, MoMA, MvdR, Weissenhof Folder.

52. Sergius Ruegenberg to Karin Kirsch, June 5, 1984, quoted in Karin Kirsch, *The Weissenhofsiedlung: Experimental Housing Built for the Deutscher Werkbund, Stuttgart, 1927* (New York: Rizzoli, 1989), 34.

53. Quoted in Kirsch, *Weissenhofsiedlung,* 38–39.

54. Daybook of the city expansion department, October 15, 1925, in Kirsch, *Weissenhofsiedlung,* 35.

55. Paul Schmitthenner, "Die Werkbundsiedlung," *Süddeutsche Zeitung,* May 5, 1926, evening edition, quoted in Kirsch, *Weissenhofsiedlung,* 36.

56. Paul Bonatz, "Noch einmal die Werkbundsiedlung," *Schwäbischer Merkur,* May 5, 1926, evening edition, quoted in Kirsch, *Weissenhofsiedlung,* 36.

57. Notes from Stuttgart Werkbund board meeting, May 14, 1926, MoMA, MvdR, quoted in Kirsch, *Weissenhofsiedlung,* 36.

58. Richard Döcker, "Zum Bauproblem der Zeit," *Die Form* 1, no. 4 (January 1926): 61–74.

59. Richard Döcker to Mies van der Rohe, May 18, 1926, MoMA, MvdR.

60. Mies van der Rohe to Richard Döcker, May 27, 1926; MoMA, MvdR, quoted in Kirsch, *Weissenhofsiedlung,* 38–39.

61. City council, July 28–29, 1926, in *Amtsblatt der Stadt Stuttgart,* nos. 91 and 92 (August 10–11, 1926), quoted in Kirsch, *Weissenhofsiedlung,* 40.

62. Richard Döcker to Mies van der Rohe, December 14, 1926, MoMA, MvdR, quoted in Kirsch, *Weissenhofsiedlung,* 47.

63. Curt R. Vincentz, *Bausünden und Baugeld-Vergeudung* (Hanover: Deutsche Bauhütte, 1932), 5–6.

64. Rudolf Pfister, "Stuttgarter Werkbundausstellung 'Die Wohnung,'" *Der Baumeister* 26, no. 2 (February 1928): 33–72, esp. 41.

65. Hermann Muthesius, "Die letzten Worte eines Meisters. Die neue Bauweise," *Berliner Tageblatt,* October 29, 1927, 1, Beiblatt, supp. 1, 1.

66. Muthesius, "Die letzten Worte eines Meisters," supp. 1, 1.

67. Ludwig Mies van der Rohe and Walter Riezler, "Zum Neuen Jahrgang," *Die Form* 2, no. 1 (January 1927): 1, 2, 59.

68. Gert Kähler, ed., *Geschichte des Wohnens, 1918–1945. Reform-Reaktion-Zerstörung* (Stuttgart: Deutsche Verlagsanstalt, 1996), 287.

69. Marie-Elisabeth Lüders, "Baukörper ohne Wohnungen," *Die Form* 2, no. 10 (October 1927): 316–19.

70. Max Osborn, "Die Wohnung der Zukunft," *Vossische Zeitung,* August 26, 1927, morning edition, 1–2, quote at 1.

71. Siegfried Kracauer, "Das neue Bauen. Zur Stuttgarter Werkbund-Ausstellung: Die Wohnung," *Frankfurter Zeitung,* July 31, 1927, quoted in Siegfried Kracauer, *Schriften: Aufsätze: 1927–1931* (Frankfurt: Suhrkamp, 1990), 68–74.

72. Theo van Doesburg, "'The Dwelling,' the Famous Werkbund Exhibition," *Het Bouwbedrijf* 4, no. 24 (November 1927): 556–59. English translation quoted in Theo van Doesburg, *On European Architecture: Complete Essays from Het Boubedrijf, 1924–1931* (Basel: Birkhäuser, 1986), 164–72, quote at 167.

73. Alexander Dorner, "Zur Abstrakten Malerei. Erklärung zum Raum der Abstrakten in der Hannoverschen Gemäldegalerie," *Die Form* 3, no. 4 (April 1928): 110–14.

74. See Christiane Lange, *Ludwig Mies van der Rohe. Architektur für die Seidenindustrie* (Cologne: Nicolaische Verlagsbuchhandlung, 2011), 71ff.

75. The name refers to a 1910 poem by the satirical German writer Christian Morgenstern called "Sitzfleischstuhl" (The Aesthete): "Wenn ich sitze, will ich nicht sitzen / wie mein Sitz-Fleisch möchte / sondern wie mein Sitz-Geist sich / sässe er, den Stuhl sich flöchte." This was brilliantly translated into English by Max Knight: "When I sit, I do not care / just to sit to suit my hindside / I prefer the way my mind-side / would, to sit in, build a chair." Max Knight, *Christian Morgensterns's Galgenlieder* (Berkeley: University of California Press, 1969), 185. Rietveld had instructed anyone building it to glue a copy of Morgenstern's poem under the seat. Rasch pitched his own chair as an organic response to the needs of the sitter against the abstraction of Rietveld.

76. Ludwig Mies van der Rohe, *Chair,* US Patent Office No. 1791453, filed August 4, 1928 (in Germany, August 23, 1927).

77. Quoted in Otakar Máčel, Marijke Küper, and James Burge, "The Chairs of Heinz Rasch," *Journal of Design History* 6, no. 1 (1993): 25–44, quote at 39.

78. Kristina Jaspers, "The Adam's Family Store," *AA Files* 75 (2017): 20–27.

79. Mies van der Rohe to S. Adam, April 2, 1928, MoMA, MvdR, Later German Projects, Folder #1.

80. Fritz Adam to Mies van der Rohe, January 3, 1929, MoMA, MvdR, Later German Projects, Folder #1.

81. "Wolkenkratzer in der Friedrichstrasse," *Vossische Zeitung,* March 14, 1929, morning edition, supp. 1, 1; "Blick auf den Grundstücks-Markt," *Vossische Zeitung,* 130, March 17, 1929, real estate and investment supp., 1.

82. Mies van der Rohe to Fritz Adam, July 2, 1928; Fritz Adam to Mies van der Rohe, January 3, 1929, both MoMA, MvdR, Later German Projects, Folder #1.

83. Mies van der Rohe and S. Adam correspondence, January 10 and 17, 1929, MoMA, MvdR, Later German Projects, Folder #1.

84. Arthur Korn, *Glas im Bau und als Gebrauchsgegenstand* (Berlin: Ernst Pollak, 1929): 18; Justus Bier, "Über Architektur und Schrift," *Der Baumeister* 27 (November 1929): 349–59; Guido Harbers, "Neue Fassadensysteme," *Der Baumeister* 27 (November 1929): 360–65.

85. Curt Gravenkamp, "Mies van der Rohe: Glashaus in Berlin," *Das Kunstblatt* 14 (April 1930): 111–13.

86. John Zukowsky and Ines Dressel, "Appendix II: Mies van der Rohe and the Stuttgart Competition," in *Mies Reconsidered: His Career, Legacy, and Disciples,* ed. John Zukowsky (Chicago: Art Institute of Chicago, 1986), 168–71. See also images of the competition entries at 114–16.

87. Inken Gaukel, "Zeppelinbau," Stadtarchiv Stuttgart, October 29, 2019, https://www.stadtlexikon-stuttgart.de/article/e281d841-f34c-4f23-b08f-cae9d30a5dee/Zeppelinbau.html; Wilhelm Lotz, "Wettbewerb für ein Bürohaus am Hindenburgplatz in Stuttgart," *Die Form* 4, no. 6 (March 15, 1929): 151–53.

88. "Mies van der Rohe: Wettbewerbsentwurf für ein Verwaltungsgebäude in Stuttgart," *Das Kunstblatt* 13 (June 1929): 190–91.

89. The most important sources for the Esters and Lange houses are Tegethoff, *Villas and Country Houses;* Lange, *Ludwig Mies van der Rohe und Lilly Reich;* and Lange, *Architektur für die Seidenindustrie.* The suggested chronology and design evolution for the Esters House have been thoroughly changed by the surprising find in 2019 of an entire set of drawings for the house of July 1928 by archivist Christoph Moss at the Krefeld Stadtarchiv.

90. Quoted in Lange, *Architektur für die Seidenindustrie,* 99.

91. A letter of October 16, 1928, reveals the possibility of the clients entirely abandoning the project. Hermann John to Ernst Walther, Jr., October 16, 1928, MoMA, MvdR, Correspondence Esters and Lange Houses.

92. Walter Cohen, "Haus Lange in Kerfeld," *Museum der Gegenwart* (1930): 160–69.

93. Hermann John to Ernst Walter and Hermann Lange, January 23, 1929, MoMA, MvdR, Correspondence Esters/Lange Houses.

94. Henry Thomas Cadbury-Brown, "Ludwig Mies van der Rohe in Conversation with H. T. Cadbury-Brown," *AA Files,* no. 66 (2013): 68–80.

95. Walter Riezler, "Die Bebauung des Alexanderplatzes," *Die Form* 4, no. 6 (March 15, 1929): 129–32; Martin Wagner, "Das formale Problem einer Weltstadt," *Das Neue Berlin* 2 (1929): 33–41.

96. "Der Neue Alexanderplatz," *Vossische Zeitung,* March 3, 1929, "Zeitbilder" supp., 2.

97. Paul Ferdinand Schmidt, "Der Neue Alexanderplatz," *Vorwärts,* April 5, 1929, supp. 5, 1.

98. Justus Bier, "Wettbewerb für eine Umgestaltung des Alexanderplatzes. 1929," *Der Baumeister* 27, no. 11 (November 1929): 356–58.

99. Ludwig Hilberseimer, "Das Formproblem eines Welstadtplatzes," *Das Neue Berlin* 2 (1929): 39–40.

100. Ludwig Hilberseimer, "Entwicklungstendenzen des Städtebaus," *Die Form* 4, no. 8 (April 15, 1929): 209–10.

101. Johannes Grobler, "Hochhaus am Bahnhof Friedrichstrasse in Berlin," *Deutsche Bauzeitung,* February 1, 1930, supp. 2.

102. "Die Leipziger Frühjahrs-Baumesse 1929. Die Stände," *Deutsches Bauwesen* 5, no. 4 (April 1929): 90.

103. "Die Leipziger Baumesse," *Bauwelt* 20, no. 12 (March 1929): after 292, 1–3, advertisements at 17–18; compare also the (different) illustration in "L'Architecture et L'Aménagement d'Expositions," *La Cité* 8, no. 8 (February 1930): 126.

Chapter Four. Politics and Architecture

1. Dietrich Neumann, with David Caralt, *An Accidental Masterpiece: Mies van der Rohe's Barcelona Pavilion* (Basel: Birkhäuser, 2021). For the German sections, see 98–111.

2. Neumann and Caralt, *Accidental Masterpiece,* 67–69.

3. This project was discovered and published for the first time in Valentín Trillo Martínez, *Mies en Barcelona. Arquitectura, Representación y Memoria* (Seville: UEUS, Editorial Universidad, 2017), 69.

4. Raimond Vayreda, "Els moderns seients metàllics," *D'Ací i d'Allà* 19, no. 151 (July 1930): 226–27; Francisco Marroquín, "El Pabellón de Alemania en la exposición de Barcelona," *ABC,* January 25, 1930, 13–14.

5. Marta Romaní [Anna Murià], "Sillas Siglo XX," *Diario Oficial de la Exposición Internacional de Barcelona 1929* 1, no. 35 (November 2, 1929): 25. See also Josep Mainar, "El mobiliari a l'Exposició (I)," *Mirador* 2, no. 61 (March 27, 1930): 8.

6. See Gabriele Neri, *Caricature Architettoniche* (Macerata: Quodlibet, 2015), 126–29; Andrea Klein and Hermann Haarmann, eds., *"Pleite glotzt euch an. Restlos": Satire in der Publizistik der Weimarer Republik. Ein Handbuch* (Wiesbaden: Verlag für Sozialwissenschaften, 2013), 152.

7. Henning Rogge, "Ein Motor muss aussehen wie ein Geburtstagsgeschenk," in *Industriekultur. Peter Behrens und die AEG 1907–1914,* by Tilmann Buddensieg and Henning Rogge (Berlin: Mann, 1979), 91–126.

8. Mies van der Rohe interview, ca. 1967, from the documentary film *Mies,* directed by Michael Blackwood and Franz Schulze (New York: Michael Blackwood Productions, 1986).

9. See "Cahier Spécial sur l'Architecture et l'Aménagement d'Expositions," *La Cité. Urbanisme, Architecture, Art Public* 8, no. 7 (January 1930): 101–20; "Second Cahier sur l'Architecture et L'Aménagement d'Expositions," *La Cité. Urbanisme, Architecture, Art Public* 8, no. 8 (February 1930): 121–32.

10. About Wilhelm Deffke, the Tesma Cigarette stand, and his collaboration with Mies, see Dietrich Neumann, "Mies's Concrete Office Building and Its Common Acquaintance," *AA Files* 74 (June 2017): 70–84.

11. Walter Riezler, "Die Sonderbauten der Pressa," *Die Form* 3, no. 9 (September 1928): 257–63; Ludwig Mies van der Rohe, "Zum Thema: Ausstellungen," *Die Form* 3, no. 4 (April 1928): 121.

12. Eduard Foertsch, "Die Weltausstellung in Barcelona. Die Spanische Stadt," *Vossische Zeitung,* June 11, 1929, morning edition, 4.

13. Walther Genzmer, "Der Deutsche Reichspavillon auf der Internationalen Ausstellung in Barcelona," *Die Baugilde* 11, no. 20 (October 1929): 1654–55.

14. These recollections were recorded in 1970, more than forty years after the event. Quoted in Eva Maria Amberger, *Sergius Ruegenberg. Architekt zwischen Mies van der Rohe und Hans Scharoun* (Berlin: Berlinische Galerie, 2000), 78–81.

15. Interview from February 13, 1952, in "Six Students Talk with Mies," *Master Builder* (School of Design, North Carolina State College) 2, no. 3 (Spring 1952): 28.

16. "Conversations with Mies," in *The Oral History of Modern Architecture: Interviews with the Greatest Architects of the Twentieth Century,* ed. John Peter (New York: Harry N. Abrams, 1994), repr. in Moisés Puente, ed., *Conversations with Mies van der Rohe* (New York: Princeton Architectural Press, 2008), 59.

17. Interview with Mies, issued as a phonograph record as *Conversations Regarding the Future of Architecture* (Louisville: Reynolds Metals Company, 1956), quoted in Wolf Tegethoff, *Mies van der Rohe: The Villas and Country Houses* (New York: Museum of Modern Art, 1985), 77n41.

18. Anon., "El arquitecto Van der Roch [sic] creador del Pabellón de Alemania," *Diario Oficial de la Exposición Internacional Barcelona 1929,* no. 12 (June 2, 1929): 25.

19. Urtzi Grau, "Three Replications of the German Pavilion," *Quaderns* 263 (Fall 2011): 58–63, quote at 61.

20. Ludwig Mies van der Rohe, "Vom Neuen Bauen," *Deutsche Kunst und Dekoration* 66 (1930): 180.

21. Erich von Kettler to Lilly Reich, September 19, 1929, Museum of Modern Art (hereafter MoMA), MvdR, Barcelona Pavilion, Folder 9.

22. Sergius Ruegenberg, Mies's assistant, claims in his recollections that Mies found the living room in Le Corbusier's house in Stuttgart "the only one worth visiting." Sergius Ruegenberg, "Mies und Zeichnung," undated

manuscript (ca. 1969), n.p., Ruegenberg Papers, Berlinische Galerie (hereafter BG), Berlin.

23. Ruegenberg, "Mies und Zeichnung."
24. "Der Skelettbau ist keine Teigware. Sergius Ruegenberg berichtet von Mies van der Rohes Berliner Zeit," *Bauwelt* 77, no. 11 (March 14, 1986): 346–51, quote at 350. In his notes, Ruegenberg stressed the fact that the columns were nickel-plated, not chrome, which was not yet available. Sergius Ruegenberg, "Worte. Mies van der Rohe zum Barcelona Pavilion," undated manuscript (c. 1969), Ruegenberg Papers, BG. See also Bruno Reichlin, "Conjectures à Propos des Colonnes Réfléchissantes de Mies van der Rohe," in *La Colonne Nouvelle Histoire de La Construction,* ed. Robert Gargiani (Lausanne: Presses Polytechniques et Universitaires Romandes, 2008), 454–66.
25. Erich von Kettler to Lilly Reich, September 10, 1929, October 29, 1929, both MoMA, MvdR, Barcelona Pavilion, Folder 9.
26. Eduard Förtsch, "Deutschland in Barcelona," *Tempo,* June 6, 1929.
27. Ulrich Conrads and Horst Eifler, "Mies im Gespräch I" (recorded by RIAS Berlin, October 1964), published as a phonograph record as *Mies in Berlin* (Bauwelt Berlin, 1966), https://www.bauwelt.de/rubriken/videos/Mies-im-Gespraech-II-2123186.html, quote at 9:34 min. Sarah Booth Conroy, "Brief Splendor of Mies van der Rohe's Enduring Pavilion: Mies Van der Rohe," *Washington Post,* October 14, 1979, C1, 2.
28. Guido Harbers, *Das freistehende Einfamilienhaus von 10000–30000 und über 30000 Mark* (Munich: Callwey, 1932). See, for example, houses by Karl Schneider for 16,000 Mark and Sigurd Lewerenz for 14,000 Mark on pages 90 and 118.
29. For a detailed prehistory of the German participation, see Neumann and Caralt, *Accidental Masterpiece,* 30–41. "Generalkommissar von Schnitzler will zurücktreten," *Vossische Zeitung,* March 2, 1929, evening edition, 2.
30. "We understand that the credit will be paid back by you out of the future proceeds of the sale of the pavilion in Barcelona's Park de Montjuïc (currently still under construction), of which you are the sole owner." Reichskreditanstalt to Georg von Schnitzler, April 23, 1929, Bundesarchiv Lichterfelde (hereafter BArchL), Ausstellung Barcelona, AA, Abteilung II, R 9.01, 40029, 142–43. Von Schnitzler fought for two years after the exhibition for additional compensation but ended up paying a substantial amount of the costs.
31. Lilly von Schnitzler, "Weltausstellung Barcelona," *Der Querschnitt* 9, no. 8 (August 1929): 582–84.
32. "La sección alemana en la Exposición Internacional de Barcelona 1929," *Diario Oficial de la Exposición Internacional Barcelona 1929,* no. 10 (May 25, 1929): 18. A German version of the same text exists in the papers of Georg von Schnitzler: "Bericht über meinen Besuch der Internationalen Weltausstellung Barcelona 1929," anon., typescript, Sanofi Hoechst Company Archive, Frankfurt-Friedrichsdorf (Hoechst Archive), ZWA 209, Weltausstellung Barcelona 1929, 13.
33. William J. R. Curtis, *Modern Architecture since 1900* (London: Phaidon, 1996), 270–73, quote at 271.
34. L. S. M. (Lilly von Schnitzler), "Weltausstellung Barcelona," *Europäische Revue* 5, no. 4 (July 1929): 286–88, quote at 287; Guido Müller, "Von Hugo von Hofmannsthal's Traum des Reiches zum Europa unter nationalsozialistischer Herrschaft: Die 'Europäische Revue' 1925–1936/44," in *Konservative Zeitschriften zwischen Kaiserreich und Diktatur,* ed. Hans-Christof Kraus (Berlin: Duncker und Humbolt, 2003), 155–86; L. S. M., "Weltausstellung Barcelona," 288.
35. Köstner & Gottschalk to Mies van der Rohe, September 26, 1929, MoMA, MvdR, Barcelona Pavilion Folder, Reuter gift.
36. "La Semana Alemana," *La Vanguardia,* October 20, 1929, 11; "Inauguració Oficial de la Setmana al Pavelló Alemany," *La Publicitat,* October 20, 1929, 5.
37. Note from Georg von Schnitzler, June 23, 1929, BArchL, Ausstellung Barcelona, Auswärtiges Amt, Abt. II, R 9.01, 40029, 169.
38. Heinrich Simon to Georg von Schnitzler, July 8, 1929, Hoechst Archive, ZWA 209, Weltausstellung Barcelona 1929–1930.
39. Internal memorandum, Foreign Ministry, June 25, 1929, BArchL, Ausstellung Barcelona, Auswärtiges Amt, Abteilung II, R 9.01, 40029, 179.
40. Unfortunately, there is no trace of any choreography by Rudolf Laban for the Barcelona Pavilion in the archives of the Laban Institute in London.
41. Georg von Schnitzler to Ernst Matray, October 10, 1929, Hoechst Archive, ZWA 209, Weltausstellung Barcelona 1929–1930; Georg von Schnitzler to Mies van der Rohe, October 10, 1929; Mies van der Rohe to Georg von Schnitzler, October 16, 1929, both MoMA, MvdR, Barcelona Pavilion Reuter gift.
42. "El Presidente del Club Germania, de Barcelona, señor Rüggeberg . . . ," *Diario Oficial de la Exposición Internacional Barcelona 1929,* no. 35 (November 2, 1929): 3.
43. I would like to thank my friend and collaborator David Caralt, a professor at the School of Architecture at the Universidad San Sebastián in Concepción, Chile, for this information, description, and quote. "El 'Conde Zeppelin' en Barcelona," *La Vanguardia,* October 24, 1929, 6; "El majestuoso vuelo del 'Conde Zeppelin,'" *La Vanguardia,* December 28, 1991, 10.

44. Wilhelm Hack found the pavilion "without a doubt very original, entertaining, perhaps even practical in the southern climate, but it does not seem German. Only the two gigantic German flags: the black-white-red one with its eagle, and the black-red-golden one, let us assume that we are looking at something German. . . . The tiresome affair about the German flag apparently also gave some headaches to the Spanish exhibition organizers. In the ocean of flags, you'll find in the end even three German flags: the pure black-white-red one as well as the two official ones. Again and again it happens that visitors at the exhibition debate which one is really the German flag." Wilhelm Hack, "Die Wunder der Ausstellung," *Deutsche Tageszeitung* (Berlin), June 11, 1929. E. Tatarin-Tarnheyden, "Grundlegende Betrachtungen zur Flaggenfrage," *Archiv des öffentlichen Rechts* 52, no. 3 (1927): 313–36.
45. For additional details on the political aspects of the pavilion, see Neumann and Caralt, *Accidental Masterpiece,* 144–51.
46. Peter Blake, *The Master Builders* (New York: Alfred A. Knopf, 1960), 208–12.
47. Alfredo Baeschlin, "Barcelona und seine Weltausstellung," *Deutsche Bauzeitung,* no. 57 (1929): 497–504; *Deutsche Bauzeitung,* no. 77 (1929), 657–62; Heinrich Simon, "Weltausstellung 1929. Deutsche Abteilung I," *Frankfurter Zeitung,* no. 410 (June 5, 1929): 1; Eduard Foertsch, "Die Weltausstellung in Barcelona," *Vossische Zeitung,* no. 270 (June 11, 1929): 4; Justus Bier, "Mies van der Rohes Reichspavilon in Barcelona," *Die Form* 16, no. 4 (August 15, 1929): 423–30.
48. Claudia Beckmann, "The Statue *Morgen* in the Barcelona Pavilion," in *Barcelona Pavilion and Sculpture,* ed. Ursel Berger and Thomas Pavel (Berlin: Jovis, 2006), 34–51.
49. Wolf Tegethoff, *Die Villen und Landhausprojekte von Mies van der Rohe* (Krefeld: Kaiser-Wilhelm-Museum, 1981), 80; Detlef Mertins, "Architectures of Becoming: Mies van der Rohe and the Avant-Garde," in *Mies in Berlin,* ed. Terence Riley and Barry Bergdoll (New York: Museum of Modern Art, 2001), 107–33.
50. Hans Bernoulli, "Der Pavillon des Deutschen Reiches an der internationalen Ausstellung Barcelona 1929," *Das Werk* 16, no. 11 (1929): 350–51; Helen Appleton Read, "Germany at the Barcelona World's Fair," *Arts* (October 1929): 112–13; Paul Bonatz, "Ein Baumeister spricht über die Bauplastik," *Wasmuth's Monatshefte für Baukunst und Städtebau* 16, no. 8 (1932): 378.
51. Walter Riezler, "Das neue Raumgefühl in bildender Kunst und Musik," presented at *Vierter Kongress für Ästhetik und allgemeine Kunstwissenschaft,* Hamburg, October 7–9, 1930, published in *Zeitschrift für Ästhetik und allgemeine Kunstwissenschaft,* no. 1 (1931): 179–216, quote at 202.
52. Reyner Banham, "On Trial 6. Mies van der Rohe: Almost Nothing Is Too Much," *Architectural Review* 132 (1962): 125.
53. Vincent Scully, *Modern Architecture: The Architecture of Democracy* (New York: George Braziller, 1961), 27.
54. Peter Blake, "Afterword: Conversation at 23 Beekman Place: Interview with Paul Rudolph" (1986), in *Paul Rudolph: The Late Work,* ed. Roberto de Alba (New York: Princeton Architectural Press, 2003), 203–17, quote at 216.
55. Philip Johnson, *Mies van der Rohe* (New York: Museum of Modern Art 1947), 58, 60; Blake, "Afterword," 217. See George Dodds, "Body in Pieces: Desiring the Barcelona Pavilion," *Res* 39 (2001): 173; Scully, *Modern Architecture,* 27.
56. Guido Harbers, "Deutscher Reichspavillon in Barcelona auf der Internationalen Ausstellung 1929," *Der Baumeister* 27, no. 11 (November 1929): 421–27; Bier, "Mies van der Rohes Reichspavilion," 423–30; Francisco Marroquín, "Hacia una nueva arquitectura. El Pabellón de Alemania en la Exposicion de Barcelona," *ABC,* January 26, 1930, 13–14; Nicolau M. Rubió i Tudurí, "Le Pavillon de l'Allemagne à l'Exposition de Barcelone par Mies van der Rohe," *Cahiers d'Art,* nos. 8/9 (1929): 408–11.
57. Gustav Edmund Pazaurek, "Ist der Werkbund auf dem richtigen Wege?," *Münchner Neueste Nachrichten* 83, no. 308 (November 12, 1930): 1; Eduard Foertsch, "Die Weltausstellung in Barcelona," *Vossische Zeitung,* no. 270 (June 11, 1929): 4; Bonaventura Bassegoda, "En la Exposición: Más Pabellones Extranjeros," *La Vanguardia,* October 31, 1929, 5. Alfredo Baeschlin, a Swiss architect, painter, and poet living in Spain, similarly feared that a visitor would stand "perplexed" in front of it, wondering "if he is looking at a building that is still being assembled." Alfredo Baeschlin, "Barcelona und seine Weltausstellung," *Deutsche Bauzeitung* 63, no. 57 (1929): 497–504; no. 77, 657–62.
58. Leberecht Migge to Elisabeth Elsaesser, November 20, 1929; Elisabeth Elsaesser to Leberecht Migge, n.d., both Martin Elsaesser Stiftung, Frankfurt. I am grateful to the late Thomas Elsaesser, Amsterdam, for sharing these two letters with me.
59. Hack, "Die Wunder der Ausstellung"; Bier, "Mies van der Rohes Reichspavilion," 423; Ernst Runge, "Die Baukunst am Scheidewege?," *Deutsches Bauwesen* 6, no. 4 (April 1930): 80–81.
60. Ludwig Mies van der Rohe, "Stuhl," Patentschrift no. 486722, Deutsches Reich, published November 7, 1929. On the Barcelona Chair, see Wolf Tegethoff, "Der Pavillonsessel. Die Ausstattung des Deutschen Pavillons in Barcelona 1929 und ihre Bedeutung," in *Mies and Modern Living: Interiors, Furniture, Photography,* ed. Helmut Reuter and Birgit Schulte (Ostfildern: Hatje Cantz, 2008), 144–73; Christiane Lange, "Barcelona Sessel," in

Ludwig Mies van der Rohe und Lilly Reich: Möbel und Räume (Berlin: Hatje Cantz, 2007), 174–76.

61. Sergius Ruegenberg to Tecta, June 4, 1988, TECTA Archive; Eva-Maria Amberger, *Sergius Ruegenberg: Architeckt zwischen Mies van der Rohe und Hans Scharoun* (Berlin: Berlinische Galerie, 2000), 82–83; Willi Kaiser, "Es war Mies, nicht Lilly," *Der Spiegel* 19, no. 1 (May 1977), n.p., https://www.spiegel.de/spiegel/print/index-1977-19.html.

62. Ludwig Glaeser, *Ludwig Mies van der Rohe: Furniture and Furniture Drawings from the Design Collection and the Mies van der Rohe Archive, the Museum of Modern Art, New York* (New York: Museum of Modern Art, 1977), 10–11.

63. Ludwig Mies van der Rohe, Berlin, "Sitzmöbel mit federndem Gestell," Österreichisches Patentamt, Patentschrift no. 128771, submitted November 18, 1930, published June 25, 1932.

64. See a detailed account of the genesis of the Electric Utilities Pavilion in Neumann and Caralt, *Accidental Masterpiece*, 106–11. Reconstruction drawings in Laura Lizondo-Sevilla, "Mies's Opaque Cube: The Electric Utilities Pavilion at the 1929 Barcelona International Exposition," *Journal of the Society of Architectural Historians* 76, no. 2 (June 2017): 197–217. See also Matthias Horstmann, "Der elektrische Barcelona-Pavillon. Bild-architekturen 1929—Berliner Riesenfotos in Barcelona," *Die Vierte Wand* 7 (May 2017): 80–85.

65. Interview with Wilhelm Niemann, ca. 1979, Werkbund Archiv Berlin, 17–18. Matthias Horstmann kindly provided this reference. Matthias Horstmann, email to the author, January 7, 2017.

66. S. de Llinás, "Apuntes para mi archivo (XIX). Pabellón de Suministros Eléctricos de Alemania," *La Vanguardia,* September 1, 1929, 6.

67. Eliseo Sanz Balza, *Notas de un Visitante* (Barcelona: Imp. Olympia-Pascual Yuste, 1930), 140.

68. Walther Genzmer, "Der Deutsche Reichspavillon auf der Internationalen Ausstellung in Barcelona," *Die Baugilde* 11, no. 20 (October 1929): 1654–55.

69. The company was founded in Switzerland in 1872; since 1897, it also had a large representation in Singen, Germany. See its advertisement in the special Swiss issue of the *Diario Oficial de la Exposición Internacional Barcelona 1929* 1, no. 30 (October 1, 1929): 4.

70. Eduard Foertsch, "Die Weltausstellung in Barcelona," *Vossische Zeitung,* June 11, 1929, 4.

71. "Less Is More," in Rem Koolhaas and Bruce Mau, *S.M.L.XL.* (New York: Monacelli, 1995), 48–61; Alison Smithson, "Barcelona," *La Vanguardia,* November 15, 1985, 44; Peter Smithson, "All the Travertine" (1986), in *Changing the Art of Inhabitation,* by Alison and Peter Smithson (London: Artemis, 1994), 39.

Chapter Five. Success and Changing Tides

1. A detailed history of this project is at Dietrich Neumann, "Mies van der Rohe's Neue Wache Memorial Project," in *Mies van der Rohe: The Architecture of the City: Theory and Architecture,* ed. Michele Caja and Martina Elena Landsberger (Padua: Il Poligrafo, 2022), 65–78.

2. Frida Schottmüller, "Ein Denkmal für die Kriegsgefallenen," *Der Kunst-wanderer: Zeitschrift für alte und neue Kunst* 6, no. 7 (1924/25): 80.

3. King Friedrich Wilhelm III, who had commissioned it, had not lived in the large palace down the street, but diagonally across at the Kronzprinz-enpalais, in direct proximity.

4. Wiesbaden building inspector Eberhard Phillip Wolff found the architecture "not appropriate" for its purpose, as it suggested a "museum, library or archive. . . . The function of a building should determine its form, and one should never—as has happened here—unnecessarily squeeze a building into an architecture invented by the Greeks for an entirely different purpose." Eberhard Phillip Wolff, "Berlin," *Göttingsche Gelehrte Anzeigen* 6, no. 7 (January 11, 1827): 49–64; *Göttingsche Gelehrte Anzeigen* 8 (January 13, 1827): 65–79, quote at 58.

5. Sean A. Former, "War Commemoration and the Republic in Crisis: Weimar Germany and the Neue Wache," *Central European History* 35, no. 4 (2002): 524.

6. Walter Curt Behrendt, "Eine Gedächtnisstätte für die Gefallenen des Welt-kriegs. Zum Umbau der Neuen Wache in Berlin," *Zentralblatt der Bauver-waltung* 50, no. 29 (July 23, 1930): 513–18.

7. Poelzig complained in a letter to the authorities: Paul F. Schmidt, "Für die Opfer des Weltkrieges: Umgestaltung der Neuen Wache?," *Vorwärts,* July 23, 1930.

8. Behrendt, "Eine Gedächtnisstätte," 517–18.

9. Behrendt, "Eine Gedächtnisstätte," 516. Other critics would agree. Max Osborn, "Neue Wache als Ehrenmal. Die Ausstellung der Entwürfe," *Vossische Zeitung,* July 22, 1930, 3. See also the letter to the editor defending Mies's approach. Hans Kurzse, ". . .über das Ehrenmal," *Voss-ische Zeitung,* August 3, 1930, literature supp., 4.

10. Behrendt, "Eine Gedächtnisstätte," 516.

11. "Ehrenmal für Gefallene," *Die Rote Fahne* 13, no. 170 (July 24, 1930): 4.

12. Adolf Behne, "Das Preussische Kriegermal," *Sozialistische Monatshefte* 36, no. 9 (September 26, 1930): 891–93.

13. Dr. Kurt Karl Eberlein, "Das Berliner Ehrenmal," *Münchner Neueste Nach-richten,* August 1, 1930, 5.

14. Dr. Paul F. Schmidt, "Für die Opfer des Weltkrieges. Umgestaltung der Neuen Wache?," *Vorwärts,* July 23, 1930, 3.

15. Paul Westheim, "Zeitlupe," *Das Kunstblatt,* September 14, 1930, 282–83.

16. Siegfried Kracauer, "Tessenow baut das Berliner Ehrenmal," *Frankfurter Zeitung,* July 23, 1930.

17. Fritz Neugass, "Die Weltausstellung in Barcelona," *Kunst und Künstler. Illustrierte Monatsschrift für bildende Kunst und Kunstgewerbe* 28 (1930): 121–22.

18. Eva-Maria Amberger, *Sergius Ruegenberg. Architeckt zwischen Mies van der Rohe und Hans Scharoun* (Berlin: Berlinische Galerie, 2000), 44–45, 86–87.

19. See Georg von Schnitzler to Mies van der Rohe, October 10, 1929; and Mies to von Schnitzler, October 16, 1929, both Museum of Modern Art (hereafter MoMA), MvdR, Barcelona Pavilion, Folder 2010 addition from Eduard Ludwig estate.

20. Thomas Pavel, "Ground Floor House: Ludwig Mies van der Rohe, Georg Kolbe," in *Barcelona Pavilion: Mies van der Rohe and Kolbe: Architecture and Sculpture,* ed. Thomas Pavel and Ursel Berger (Berlin: Jovis, 2006), 112–17.

21. Quoted in Wilhelm Lotz, "Die Halle II auf der Bauausstellung," *Die Form* 6, no. 7 (July 1931): 241–49, quote at 241.

22. Adolf Behne, "Abteilung 'Die Wohnung unserer Zeit,'" *Zentralblatt der Bauverwaltung* 51, nos. 49/50 (1931): 733–35. Behne had previously been supportive of Mies and included his Concrete Office Building in his 1926 publication *Der moderne Zweckbau.*

23. G. Wolf in *Zeitschrift für Wohnungswesen,* quoted in Friedrich Tamms, "Die Deutsche Bauaustellung 1931 im Spiegel der Presse," *Die Baugilde* 13, no. 18 (1931): 1442.

24. Ferdinand Eckhardt, "Epilog zur Bauausstellung," *Die Weltbuehne* 27, no. 2 (1931): 194–96, quote at 194.

25. Karel Teige, *The Minimum Dwelling,* translated and with an introduction by Eric Dluhosch (1932; repr., Cambridge, Mass.: MIT Press, 2002), 197. This was originally published in Prague by Václav Petr.

26. Wilhelm Lotz, "Die Halle II auf der Bauausstellung," *Die Form* 6, no. 7 (July 1931): 241–49, quote at 248.

27. Wilhelm Lotz, "Kritik der Bauausstellung," *Die Form* 6, no. 6 (June 1931): 212, quote at 218; Wilhelm Lotz, "Möbel und Wohnraum," *Die Form* 6, no. 6 (June 1931): 41–59, quotes at 43, 44.

28. Philip Johnson, "In Berlin: Comment on Building Exposition," *New York Times,* August 9, 1931, 97.

29. Helen Appleton Read, "A New Architecture," *Vogue,* October 1, 1931, 58–59, 98.

30. Justus Bier, "Kann man im Haus Tugendhat wohnen?," *Die Form* 6, no. 10 (October 1931): 392–93.

31. Mildred Adams, "In Their Lights the Cities Are Revealed," *New York Times Magazine,* December 11, 1932, 1.

32. Theo van Doesburg, "Architectuurvernieuwingen in het buitenland," *Het Bouwbedijf* 3, no. 15 (November 26. 1926): 477–79. The English translation is Theo van Doesburg,"'Free from Germany': The Czech Struggle," in *On European Architecture: Complete Essays from Het Bouwbedrijf 1924–1931* (Basel: Birkhäuser, 1986), 124–27.

33. Grete Tugendhat, "Zum Bau des Hauses Tugendhat," in *Ludwig Mies van der Rohe: Das Haus Tugendhat,* ed. Daniela Hammer-Tugendhat and Wolf Tegethoff (Vienna: Springer, 1998), 5–9.

34. Max Eisler. "Architekt Ernst Wiesner, Brünn," *Moderne Bauformen. Monatshefte für Architektur und Raumkunst* 27, no. 6 (1928): 209–23, Münz House at 221.

35. Achim Wendschuh, *Brüder Luckhardt und Alfons Anker. Berliner Archi-tekten der Moderne* (Berlin: Akademie der Künste, 1990), 150.

36. See Erich Mendelsohn, *Neues Haus—Neue Welt* (Berlin: Gebrüder Mann, 1932).

37. Walter Riezler, "Das Haus Tugendhat in Brünn," *Die Form* 6, no. 9 (September 1931): 321–32. Here Riezler echoed his elegiac praise of the Barcelona Pavilion at an art historian's conference in Hamburg the year before. Walter Riezler, "Das neue Raumgefühl in bildender Kunst und Musik," presented at the Vierter Kongress für Ästhetik und allgemeine Kunstwissenschaft, Hamburg, October 7–10, 1930, published in *Beilageheft zur Zeitschrift für Ästhetik und allgemeine Kunstwissenschaft* 25 (1931): 179–216.

38. Riezler, "Das Haus Tugendhat in Brünn," 321–32.

39. Riezler, "Das Haus Tugendhat in Brünn," 328.

40. Bier, "Kann man im Haus Tugendhat wohnen?," 392–93.

41. Roger Ginsburger and Walter Riezler, "Zweckhaftigkeit und geistige Haltung," *Die Form* 6, no. 11 (November 1931): 437–38.

42. Guido Harbers, *Das freistehende Einfamilienhaus von 10,000–30,000 und über 30,000 Mark* (Munich: Callwey, 1932). See, for example, houses by Karl Schneider for 16,000 Mark and Sigurd Lewerenz for 14,000 Mark on pages 90 and 118.

43. Czech architectural historian Jan Sapák estimated the cost of the house as 5 million Czech Kronen, the price of about thirty smaller family homes. Lenka Kudelková and Otakar Mačel, "Die Villa Tugendhat," *Mies van der Rohe. Möbel und Bauten in Stuttgart, Barcelona, Brno* (Weil am Rhein: Ausstellungskatalog Vitra/Skira, 1999), 180–210, esp. 189.

44. Walter Riezler, "Kommentar zum Artikel von Justus Bier," *Die Form* 6, no. 10 (October 1931): 393–94.

45. Ludwig Hilberseimer, "Nachwort zur Diskussion um das Haus Tugendhat," *Die Form* 6, no. 11 (November 1931): 431–39.

46. Anon. (possibly Guido Harbers, editor-in-chief), "Die 'neue Linie' im alleinstehenden Einfamilienhaus," *Der Baumeister* 29, no. 11 (November 1931): 422–31, quotes at 422, 428.

47. Quoted in "Stavba architekta Mies van der Rohe," *Žijeme Brně* 1 (1931): 275, quoted in Vendula Hnídková, "Die An- und Abwesenheit der Villa Tugendhat," in *Mies van der Rohe im Diskurs,* ed. Kerstin Plüm (Bielefeld: Transkript, 2013), 159–70, quote at 166–67.

48. Jaromír Krejcar, "Hygiena bytu," *Žijeme Brně* 2 (1932/33): 132–33, in Kudelková and Mačel, "Die Villa Tugendhat," 180–210.

49. Teige, *Minimum Dwelling,* 7.

50. Fritz Tugendhat and Grete Tugendhat, "Die Bewohner des Hauses Tugendhat äussern sich. Zuschrift an die Redaktion," *Die Form* 6, no. 11 (November 1931): 437–38.

51. The best account of life in the house is that of Daniela Hammer-Tugendhat. See Hammer-Tugendhat and Tegethoff, *Das Haus Tugendhat,* 11–28.

52. The Löw-Beers were wealthier than the Tugendhats, and the parents insisted on assigning ownership to their daughter alone. The family had lived for generations in Brno and owned the Aaron & Jacob Löw-Beer and Sons textile factory.

53. Dietrich Neumann, "Haus Ryder in Wiesbaden und die Zusammenarbeit von Gerhard Severain und Ludwig Mies van der Rohe," *Architectura* 2 (2006): 199–219.

54. See the account of the evolution of the plans: Wolf Tegethoff, "The Tugendhat 'Villa': A Modern Residence in Turbulent Times," in *Ludwig Mies van der Rohe: The Tugendhat House,* ed. Daniela Hammer-Tugendhat and Wolf Tegethoff (Vienna: Springer, 2000), 43–97, esp. 60ff.

55. Ludwig Glaeser and Philip Johnson, "Epilogue: Thirty Years Later," in *Mies van der Rohe,* 3rd ed., by Philip Johnson (New York: Museum of Modern Art, 1977), 205–11, quote at 207.

56. Walter Benjamin, "Erfahrung und Armut," *Die Welt im Wort* 1, no. 10 (1933): 2–3, quoted in Michael W. Jennings, ed., *Walter Benjamin: Selected Writings,* vol. 2, *1927–1934* (Cambridge, Mass.: Harvard University Press, 1999), 731–35, quotes at 734–35.

57. Franz Schulze, *Mies van der Rohe: A Critical Biography* (Chicago: University of Chicago Press, 1985), 178.

58. Christiane Lange, *Ludwig Mies van der Rohe und Lilly Reich. Möbel und Räume* (Ostfildern: Hatje Cantz 2007), 78–87, 148–85. No photographs have survived.

59. The two apartments that Johnson inhabited in short sequence in the early 1930s in New York are often conflated in the literature. The floor plan by Mies and Reich at MoMA is for the earlier apartment at Fifty-Second Street.

60. About Philip Johnson's apartments, see David A. Hanks, "Laboratories for Modernism: The Johnson and Barr Apartments," in *Partners in Design,* ed. David A. Hanks (New York: Monacelli, 2016), 66–96.

61. Martha Delano, "Making Space for Modern Living," *House & Garden,* May 1934, 50–51, 88. As his diploma project at Harvard, Johnson designed his own house at Ash Street in Cambridge in 1943; according to Johnson, it was greatly inspired by Mies's Barcelona Pavilion.

62. Delano, "Making Space for Modern Living," 50–51, 88.

63. Correspondence between Mies van der Rohe and Philip Johnson, November 3 and 23, 1934; and December 5, 1934, all MoMA, MvdR, 1934–42, Folder I.

64. Hannes Meyer, "Mein Hinauswurf aus dem Bauhaus. Offener Brief an Herrn Oberbürgermeister Hesse, Dessau," in *Das Tagebuch,* repr. in *Hannes Meyer und das Bauhaus. Im Streit der Deutungen,* ed. Thomas Flierl and Philipp Oswalt (Leipzig: Spector, 2019), 129–38.

65. Magdalena Droste, "Mies van der Rohe als Bauhausdirektor 1930–33: Der lange Schatten von Hannes Meyer und US-amerikanischen Strategien," in *Mies und die 'Unvollendete Moderne' Das Revolutionsdenkmal von 1926,* ed. Wita Noack, Ulf Meyer, and Jörn Köppler (Berlin: Form + Zweck, 2023), 73–92.

66. "Prozess um das Dessauer Bauhaus," *Friesisches Tageblatt,* October 22, 1935, 2.

67. "Zum Wechsel in der Leitung des Bauhauses," *Deutsche Allgemeine Zeitung,* September 12, 1930, 2.

68. "Die Kandidaten für den Posten des Frankfurter Stadtbaurats," *Berliner Börsen Zeitung,* September 23, 1930, morning edition, 8.

69. "Schon wieder Wechsel in der Leitung des Dessauer Bauhauses?," *Badischer Beobachter,* September 26, 1930, 5.

70. "Vom Bauhaus," *Das Neue Frankfurt* 12 (December 1930): 268.

71. Droste, "Mies van der Rohe als Bauhausdirektor."

72. Philip Johnson, *Built to Live In* (New York: Museum of Modern Art, 1931), n.p., https://www.moma.org/documents/moma_catalogue_2044_300153621.pdf.

73. Philip Johnson, ed., *Modern Architecture* (New York: Museum of Modern Art, 1932), 117; Terence Riley, *The International Style: Exhibition 15 and the Museum of Modern Art* (New York: Rizzoli, 1992), 74–78.

74. Magdalena Droste, "Die Architekturdebatte in der Zeitschrift *bauhaus* der Kostufra," in *Linke Waffe Kunst. Die Kommunistische Studentenfraktion am Bauhaus,* Bauwelt Fundamente 175, ed. Wolfgang Thöner, Florian Strob, and Andreas Schätzke (Basel: Birkhäuser 2022), 100–113.

75. "Das Bauhaus auf dem Wege zum Faschismus," *Arbeiter Illustrierte Zeitung* 1 (January 1931): 18, 19.

76. Droste, "Die Architekturdebatte," 108–9; Magdalena Droste, "The Red Bauhaus and CIAM: Contexts of Ludwig Hilberseimer's Teaching in the Early 1930s," in *Architect of Letters: Reading Hilberseimer,* Bauwelt Fundamente 174, ed. Florian Strob (Basel: Birkhäuser 2022), 29–43.

77. Klaus Jürgen Winkler, *Baulehre und Entwerfen am Bauhaus 1919–1933* (Weimar: Universitätsverlag, 2003), 134–38.

78. Edward Glaeser, "Interview with William Turk Priestley," MoMA, Glaeser Papers, cited in Cammie McAtee, "Alien #5044325: Mies' First Trip to America," in *Mies in America,* ed. Phyllis Lambert (New York: Harry N. Abrams, 2001), 143.

79. Christiane Lange, *Ludwig Mies van der Rohe: Architektur für die Seidenindustrie* (Berlin: Nicolai, 2011), 134–45. In 2013, Lange, great-granddaughter of textile magnate Hermann Lange, had a 1:1 model of the golf club design built near its intended location outside of Krefeld by the Gent architecture firm Robbrecht en Daem. It was seen by thirteen thousand visitors during the summer and fall of 2013. The 1:1 model was deliberately assembled with a much-reduced vocabulary. Plywood stood in for walls and floor plates, windows were framed but not glazed, and the shiny stainless steel columns and cantilevered ceiling plates impressively read as a convincing spatial sequence. See Christiane Lange, ed., *Mies 1:1 Ludwig Mies van der Rohe. The Golfclub Project* (Cologne: Buchhandlung Walther König, 2014).

80. I would like to thank Marc Dubois, Gent, for sharing this photo and his research on Belgian architect Gaston Eysselinck.

81. Eric Mumford, "CIAM and Its Outcomes," *Urban Planning* 4, no. 3 (2019): 291–98.

82. Fred Forbát, *Erinnerungen eines Architekten aus vier Ländern,* vol. 5, Bauhäusler (Berlin: Dokumente aus dem Bauhaus-Archiv Berlin, 2019), S. 111. The CIAM conference in Brussels began on November 27, 1930.

83. Martin Gropius, "Berliner Trinkhalle für Selters- und Sodawasser," *Architektonisches Skizzenbuch* 51, no. 3 (1861): 15.

84. Helmut Erfurth and Elisabeth Tharandt, *Ludwig Mies van der Rohe. Die Trinkhalle, sein einziger Bau in Dessau* (Dessau: Anhaltische Verlagsgesellschaft, 1995).

85. Wita Noack, *Konzentrat der Moderne: Das Landhaus Lemke von Ludwig Mies van der Rohe. Wohnhaus, Baudenkmal und Kunsthaus* (Berlin: Deutscher Kunstverlag, 2008).

86. Gerhard Franke, "Das Bauhaus und die faschistische Kulturreaktion," *Wissenschaftliche Zeitschrift/Hochschule für Architektur und Bauwesen Weimar* 29 (1983): 5–6, 479–82; "Dessauer Kulturschande: Das Bauhaus wird geschlossen," *Volksblatt für Anhalt,* August 23, 1932.

87. "30 Architekten im Wettbewerb," *Vossische Zeitung,* February 11, 1933, morning edition, supp. 1, 1. Otto Haesler and Hans Poelzig were also in the modern camp; German Bestelmeyer, Wilhelm Kreis, and Heinrich Tessenow were the conservative representatives; and there was a group of outspoken Nazis, such as Kurt Frick and Pinno & Grund. The jury had Mies's teacher Peter Behrens, as well as Paul Bonatz and Fritz Schumacher, as members.

88. Rosenberg's infamous opus, usually credited with helping the rise of Nazism and anti-Semitism in the 1920s, was called *Der Mythus des zwanzigsten Jahrhunderts* (The Myth of the Twentieth Century). Mies kept a copy in his library.

89. Ludwig Mies van der Rohe, "Gedächtnisprotokoll Unterredung mit Alfred Rosenberg, 12 April 1933" (copy of Wingler from Mies van der Rohe's private archive) in Peter Hahn, ed., *Bauhaus Berlin* (Weingarten: Kunstverlag, 1985), 130; and a second part in Adalbert Behr, "Ludwig Mies van der Rohe und das Jahr 1933," *Wissenschaftliche Zeitschrift/Hochschule für Architektur und Bauwesen Weimar* 33, nos. 4–6 (1987): 277–81, quote at 281.

90. "Bauhaus und Kampfbund. Ein Brief der Bauhausschüler," *Deutsche Allgemeine Zeitung Berlin,* April 15, 1933, repr. in Peter Hahn, ed., *Bauhaus Berlin* (Weingarten: Kunstverlag, 1985), 131.

91. See Hahn, *Bauhaus Berlin,* 142–44; and in response, and with much more detail, Behr, "Ludwig Mies van der Rohe und das Jahr 1933," 277–81.

92. Mies van der Rohe to Max von Schillings, May 18, 1933, in Hildegard Brenner, *Ende einer bürgerlichen Kunst-Institution. Die politische Formierung der Preussischen Akademie der Künste ab 1933* (Stuttgart: Deutsche Verlags-Anstalt, 1972), 130. See also Elaine S. Hochman, *Architects of Fortune* (New York: Widenfels and Nicholson, 1989), 127–40.

93. Brenner, *Ende einer bürgerlichen Kunst-Institution,* 124.

94. "Berlin: Reichsbankbau," *Die Form* 8, no. 7 (July 1933): 223.

95. Philip Nitze, "Grundsätzliches zum Reichsbank-Wettbewerb"; Heinrich Wolff, "Der Wettbewerb der Reichsbank"; and "Der Wettbewerb der Reichsbank," *Deutsche Bauzeitung* 67, no. 32 (August 9, 1933): 605–6, 607–14, 627–34.

96. Behr, "Ludwig Mies von der Rohe und das Jahr 1933," 277–81.

Chapter Six. On the Fence

1. About Frank Trudel, see Magdalena Droste and Boris Friedewald, eds., *Our Bauhaus: Memories of Bauhaus People* (Munich: Prestel, 2019), 319–27; Fritz Neumeyer, *Ausgebootet. Mies van der Rohe und das Bauhaus 1933— Outside the Bauhaus—Mies van der Rohe and Berlin in 1933* (Berlin: Mies van der Rohe Haus, Form + Zweck, 2020), 239–45.

2. Quoted in Droste and Friedewald, *Our Bauhaus,* 326.

3. Neumeyer, *Ausgebootet,* 239–45.

4. Romano Guardini, *Briefe vom Comer See* (Mainz: Matthias-Grunewald, 1927), 82, quoted in Neumeyer, *Ausgebootet,* 243.

5. Quoted in Kerstin Decker, "Die Diagonale von Dessau: Zum Beginn des Jubiläumsjahrs: Hundert Jahre nach der Gründung bewegen das Bauhaus noch immer politische Konflikte," *Tagesspiegel* (Berlin), January 4, 2019, https://www.tagesspiegel.de/kultur/100-jahre-bauhaus-die-diagonale -von-dessau/23825690.html.

6. Ludwig Mies van der Rohe, "Was wäre Beton, was Stahl ohne Spiegelglas?" (1933), in *Mies van der Rohe. Das kunstlose Wort,* by Fritz Neumeyer (Berlin: DOM, 2016), 378. Translation from Fritz Neumeyer, *The Artless Word: Mies van der Rohe on the Building Art* (Cambridge, Mass.: MIT Press, 1991), 314. Mies's term "raumstürzend" (aptly translated as "space-toppling" by Mark Jarzombek), might have been inspired by Fritz Wichert's description of Max Beckmann's city portraits as having the spatial feel of a "dive bomber." Fritz Wichert, "Max Beckmann und einiges zur Lage der Kunst," *Die Form* 3, no. 12 (1928): 337–47, quote at 343.

7. Correspondence between Mies and the office of Mannheim's lord mayor, March 14, 17, and 22, 1934, all Library of Congress (hereafter LoC), MvdR, Personal Correspondence 1923–40, Folder O.

8. Michael Tymkiw, *Nazi Exhibition Design and Modernism* (Minneapolis: University of Minnesota Press, 2018), 21–31.

9. Ivan Bocchio, "Mountain House. Entwürfe einer alpinen Architektur für Südtirol," in *Mies van der Rohe. Zwischen Südtirol und New York* (Bolzano: Raetia, 2018), 48–93.

10. Dr. Matthies of the general commissioner's office for the Brussels World's Fair to Mies van der Rohe, June 11, 1934, Museum of Modern Art (hereafter MoMA), MvdR, Brussels Folder #1.

11. Several letters in the archive document the distribution of blueprints and photographs: MoMA, MvdR, Brussels Folder #2.

12. "World's Fair Brussels 1935. Deutsches Restaurant" (typescript), MoMA, MvdR, Brussels Folder #2.

13. Mies van der Rohe to Reichskommissar for the international World's Fair Brussels 1935, July 23, 1934; Mies van der Rohe to Oswald Herzog, June 25, 1934, both MoMA, MvdR, Brussels Folder #3.

14. Dr. Bährens, *Guidelines Regarding the German Participation at the Brussels World's Fair* (Berlin, May 14, 1934), 1, 2, MoMA, MvdR, Brussels Folder #1.

15. "Entwurf" (typescript), 1, MoMA, MvdR, Brussels Folder #1.

16. Mies van der Rohe, "Zu dem Vorentwurf für ein Ausstellungsgebäude für die Weltausstellung in Brüssel 1935" (typescript), 2, MoMA, MvdR, Brussels Folder #3.

17. Mies van der Rohe, "Zu dem Vorentwurf," 2.

18. Typescript draft of explanatory text for the Brussels Pavilion competition, 1934, MoMA, MvdR, Brussels Folder #5. See Richard Pommer, "Mies van der Rohe and the Political Ideology of the Modern Movement in Architecture," in *Mies van der Rohe: Critical Essays,* ed. Franz Schulze (New York: Museum of Modern Art, 1989), 96–145, image at 131.

19. Josep Quetglas, "Du Pavillon de Mies au Pavillon de la Fondation Mies," *Criticat,* no. 5 (March 2010): 84–91, https://issuu.com/criticat/docs /criticat05/93.

20. Wolf Tegethoff, "Mies van der Rohe's Competition Entry for the German Pavilion at the Brussels World Fair 1935," in *Dutch Connections: Essays on International Relationships in Architectural History in Honour of Herman van Bergeijk,* ed. Sjoerd van Faassen, Carola Hein, and Phoebus Panigyrakis (Delft: TU, 2020), 337–50.

21. Hermann Phleps, "Die Wichtigkeit des Details in der Architektur," in *Deutsche Bauhütte* 37 (1933): 150ff., 159, 187, 211, 244, 268, 297, 379, quote at 244. I would like to thank Dr. Hans-Georg Lippert, Dresden, for this reference. See also Hans-Georg Lippert, "Baugeschichtslehre in der Weimarer Republik (Die conservative Richtung)," in *Almanach 1993/1997* (Darmstadt: Technische Hochschule, Fachbereich Architektur, 1998), 210–13.

22. Laura Lizondo-Sevilla, José Santatecla Fayos, and Nuria Salvador Luján, "Mies in Brussels 1934: Synthesis of an Unbuilt Exhibition Architecture," *VLC Arqitectura* 3, no. 1 (April 2016): 29–53; Paul Sigel, *Exponiert. Deutsche Pavillons auf Weltausstellungen* (Berlin: Bauwesen, 2000), 127– 32; Pommer, "Mies van der Rohe and the Political Ideology of the Modern Movement in Architecture," 96.

23. See Elaine S. Hochman, *Architects of Fortune: Mies van der Rohe and the Third Reich* (New York: Weidenfeld and Nicolson, 1989), 228.

24. Mies van der Rohe to Eduard Ludwig, July 24, 1934, MoMA, MvdR, Brussels Folder #3.

25. Erich von Kettler to Mies van der Rohe, October 15, 1934; Wirtschaftsgruppe Chemische Industrie to Mies van der Rohe, November 6, 1934; Mia Seeger to Mies van der Rohe, November 9, 1934; and Mies van der Rohe to Seeger, November 23, 1924, all MoMA, MvdR, Brussels Folder #4. Mies signs several letters in this correspondence with "Heil Hitler!"

26. Dr. Haupt to Mies van der Rohe, August 13, 1934, LoC, MvdR, Private Correspondence 1923–40, Folder R.

27. "Aufruf der Kulturschaffenden," *Völkischer Beobachter,* August 18, 1934, in Hahn, *Bauhaus Berlin,* 148. Emil Fahrenkamp, who considered himself apolitical, received important commissions in the Third Reich, and the fourth architect was the little-known Walter March, the brother of Werner March, the architect of the 1936 Olympic Stadium.

28. Alfred Durus (also known as Alfréd Keményi), "Kunstpolitik des deutschen Faschismus," *Internationale Literatur* (November 1, 1934): 162–64, quote at 164.

29. "Deutschlands Geistesgarde wählt Hitler," *Deutsche Freiheit,* August 19, 1934, 3. See also "Briefkasten," *Deutsche Freiheit,* October 4, 1934, 8.

30. Alfred Rosenberg to Joseph Goebbels, August 30, 1934, and October 20, 1934, in Ernst Piper, *Nationalsozialistische Kunstpolitik* (Frankfurt: Suhrkamp, 1987), 113–18; "Kunstbolschewisten für Hitler," *Pariser Tageblatt,* October 1, 1934, 2.

31. Sebastian Neurauter, *Das Bauhaus und die Verwertungsrechte* (Tübingen: Mohr Siebeck, 2013), 465–70.

32. Quoted in Neurauter, *Das Bauhaus und die Verwertungsrechte,* 470.

33. "Ein Schmachdokument deutscher Künstler," *Aufbau: An American Weekly Published in New York* 12, no. 8 (February, 22 1946): 4.

34. Karl Nierendorf, "Gefälschte Unterschriften," *Aufbau: An American Weekly Published in New York* 12, no. 9 (March 1, 1946): 19. Mies was the most immediate beneficiary of this letter, since Heckel and Barlach had already died. Megan M. Fontanella, "Unity in Diversity: Karl Nierendorf and America, 1937–47," *American Art* 24, no. 3 (Fall 2010): 114–25.

35. Diether Schmidt, *In letzter Stunde. Künstlerschriften II* (Berlin: Verlag der Kunst, 1963); Sibyl Moholy-Nagy, "Letter," *Journal of the Society of Architectural Historians* 24, no. 3 (October 1965): 255–56; Elaine Hochman, *Architects of Fortune: Mies van der Rohe and the Third Reich* (New York: Weidenfeld and Nicholson, 1989), 47.

36. Werner Graeff, interview by Ludwig Glaeser, Mühlheim, September 17, 1972, Canadian Centre for Architecture, Montreal. While Severain's name is not mentioned, he is identifiable as "brother of childhood friend from Aachen, who had a paint store in Stuttgart."

37. I published images of the house for the first time in 2006, suggesting Mies's influence on Gerhard Severain, before having found the reference with Werner Graeff's recollection. Dietrich Neumann, "Haus Ryder in Wiesbaden und die Zusammenarbeit von Gerhard Severain und Ludwig Mies van der Rohe," *Architectura* 2 (2006): 199–219.

38. Norbert Hanenberg and Daniel Lohmann, "Fabrikbauten für die Vereinigten Seidenwebereien AG," in *Mies im Westen,* ed. Norbert Hanenberg, Daniel Lohmann, Ursula Kleefisch-Jobst, and Peter Köddermann (Aachen: Geymüller, 2022), 138–47.

39. The address was Luisenstrasse 19 in Berlin Nikolassee (today Kaiserstuhlstrasse 19). Nachlass Herbert Hirche, Folder Mies: Atelier am Karlsbad, Verschiedene Projekte, Museum der Dinge/Werkbundarchiv, Berlin. Carsten Krohn found the corresponding building documents in the Landesarchiv Berlin: Carsten Krohn, "Haus Bucren—Ein unbekannter Bau von Mies van der Rohe in Berlin," *Architectura* 44, no. 2 (2014): 101–6. The addition was executed in 1936.

40. Mies van der Rohe to the Royal Institute of British Architects, October 6, 1934, LoC, Mies Private Correspondence 1923–1940 R; Anon., "Trend of Modern Architecture," *Times* (London), December 1, 1934, 10.

41. P. W., "Deutsche Siedlungsausstellung München 1934," *Das Werk. Architektur und Kunst* 21, no. 11 (1934): 340–47.

42. Guido Harbers, ed., *Deutsche Siedlungausstellung München 1934 Juni bis Oktober* (Munich: Deukula, Grassinger, 1934); "Deutsche Siedlungsausstellung in München," *Deutsche Bauzeitung* 25 (June 20, 1934): 457–58.

43. Anke Blümm, "Der Architekt als 'Wahrer und Mehrer der deutschen Baukultur'? Der Bund deutscher Architekten, die Reichskulturkammer und das Scheitern des Architektengeetzes vom 28. September 1934," in *Unplanbar—Weltbaumeister und Ingenieur: Der Architekt als "Rivale des Schöpfers,"* ed. Hans-Georg Lippert, Anke Köthe, and Andreas Schwarting (Dresden: Thelem, 2012), 144–69; Anke Blümm, *Entartete Baukunst? Zum Umgang mit dem Neuen Bauen 1933–1945* (Berlin: Brill, 2013).

44. "Anordnung des Präsidenten der Reichskammer der bildenden Künste betr. den Schutz des Berufes und die Berufsausübung der Architekten v. 28.9.1934," *Baugilde* 19 (1934): 677.

45. Representative of the chemical industry to Mies van der Rohe, December 7, 1934, MoMA, MvdR, Brussels Folder #4.

46. Judith Bartel, Dirk Dorsemagen, and Barbara Perlich, "Das ehemalige Revolutionsdenkmal auf dem Friedhof Friedrichsfelde," in *Mies van der Rohe. Frühe Bauten. Probleme der Erhaltung—Probleme der Bewertung,* ed. Johannes Cramer and Dorothée Sack (Petersberg: Imhof, 2004), 147.

47. Mies van der Rohe, "Haus H. in Magdeburg," *Die Schildgenossen* 14, no. 6 (1935): 514–15; original manuscript dating from August 7, 1935, LoC, MvdR, quoted in Neumeyer, *Artless Word,* 314–15. One drawing and a model photograph were published in "Mies van der Rohe," *De 8 en Opbouw* (March 21, 1936): 15.

48. Romano Guardini, "Der Heiland," *Die Schildgenossen* 14 (1935): 97–116.

49. Lilly Reich to J. J. P. Oud, February 12, 1936, MoMA, MvdR.

50. Ludwig Glaeser cited in Franz Schulze, *Mies van der Rohe: A Critical Biography* (Chicago: University of Chicago Press, 1985), 195.

51. Otakar Máčel has examined in detail the evolution of Mies's patents for the cantilever chair and, in particular, the legal battles necessary to protect it. See Otakar Máčel, *Der Freischwinger. Vom Avantgardeentwurf zur Ware* (Delft: TU Delft, 1992); Otakar Máčel, "Avant-Garde Design and the Law: Litigation over the Cantilever Chair," *Journal of Design History* 3, nos. 2/3 (1990): 125–43.

52. Eric Mumford, "Alvar Aaltos Urban Planning and CIAM Urbanism," in *Alvar Aalto—Second Nature,* ed. Mateo Kries and Jochen Eisenbrand (Weil am Rhein: Vitra Design Museum, 2014), 279–309, esp. 283.

53. Ludwig Mies van der Rohe, "Sitzmöbel," Patentschrift, Eidgenössisches Amt für Geistiges Eigentum, Nr. 151626, submitted November 19, 1930, registered December 31, 1931, published March 16, 1932. Priority: Germany 1929. Ludwig Mies van der Rohe, "Sitzmöbel mit federndem Gestell," Patentschrift Reichspatentamt Nr. 558774, published August 25, 1932.

54. Adolf G. Schneck, *Der Stuhl* (Stuttgart: Julius Hoffmann, 1928), 6.

55. Joseph Mathieu, "Système de pied de sieges et tables permettant l'empilage sous un volume restraint," Brevet d'Invention 510344, June 8, 1920.

56. Schneck, *Der Stuhl,* 59.

57. Schneck, *Der Stuhl,* 6.

58. Alvar Aalto, *Stapelbarer Stahlrohrstuhl* ("Stackable steel tube chair"), Patentschrift 611274, submitted July 26, 1932, published March 7, 1935.

59. Other designers followed suit, in particular prominent Finnish furniture designer Carl-Johan Boman, who patented a similar stackable metal tube chair shortly afterward. Carl-Johan Boman, *Stapelbarer Stuhl,* Patent No. 149818, submitted December 11, 1934.

60. Alvar Aalto, *Improvements Relating to Furniture and the Like,* Patent Specification Great Britain 431563, patented from November 8, 1933, onward, published July 8, 1935; Alvar Aalto, *Improvement Relating to a Process of Bending Wood and to Articles Made Thereby,* Patent Specification Great Britain 423686, patented from November 8, 1933, onward, published February 6, 1935.

61. Ludwig Glaeser, *Ludwig Mies van der Rohe: Furniture and Furniture Drawings from the Design Collection and the Mies van der Rohe Archive at the Museum of Modern Art, New York* (New York: Museum of Modern Art, 1977), 16. See also "Rationelles Mobiliar," "Möbel aus gebogenem Sperrholz," *Das Werk* 21, no. 10 (1934): 300–304.

62. Mies van der Rohe to Gottfried Bueren, July 3, 1935, LoC, MvdR, General Office File, Patents, Folder Patentanmeldung Sitz- oder Liegemöbel aus federndem Blech 1935–8.

63. Jochen Eisenbrand, "The Organic Line: Aalto's Furniture and the International Market," in Kries and Eisenbrand, *Alvar Aalto—Second Nature,* 147–76.

64. Eisenbrand, "Organic Line," 147–76.

65. June Provines, "Front Views and Profiles," *Chicago Daily Tribune,* May 22, 1939, 13.

66. Lilly Reich, *Tragholm eines Gestelles aus federndem Werkstoff für Sitz und Liegemöbel* Patentschrift 734091, Reichspatentamt, August 15, 1935, published March 11, 1943, 22–24.

67. See Glaeser, *Furniture and Furniture Drawings,* 16.

68. Ludwig Mies van der Rohe in Berlin, "Sitz, insbesondere für Kraftfahrzeuge," Patentschrift no. 652791 (patented in the German Reich from October 24, 1935, published October 21, 1937).

69. Gottfried Bueren to Mies van der Rohe, October 3, 1936, LoC, MvdR, General Office File, Patents, Folder Patentanmeldung Sitz-oder Liegemöbel aus federndem Blech 1935–8.

70. Stainless steel had only recently become commercially available to architects and designers. Krupp had registered its Nirosta brand in 1912, but the first major architectural application seems to have been the entrance canopy at the Savoy Hotel in London in 1929.

71. Winfried Nerdinger, *Walter Gropius* (Berlin: Gebrüder Mann, 1985), 304.

72. Ludwig Mies van der Rohe, "Expressways as an Artistic Problem," *Die Autobahn,* no. 10 (1932): 1; Neumeyer, *Artless Word,* 313.

73. The designs of Welzenbacher and Schweizer in August Sarnitz, *Lois Welzenbacher: Architekt 1889–1955* (Salzburg: Residenz, 1989), 117–223; Immo Boyken, *Otto Ernst Schweizer: 1890–1965. Bauten und Projekte* (Stuttgart: Axel Menges, 1996), 169. March's gas station is in Paul Bonatz and Bruno Wehner, *Reichsautobahn-Tankanlagen* (Berlin: Volk und Reich, 1942). The crate list of Mies's office files mentions "Wettbewerb Tankstellen 1934": LoC, MvdR, Folder 47.1.

74. Sergius Ruegenberg, "Ein Fünfzigjähriger," *Bauwelt* 14 (April 1936): 346.

75. Vivian Endicott Barnett, "The Architect as Art Collector," in *Mies in America,* ed. Phyllis Lambert (New York: Harry N. Abrams, 2001), 91–131.

76. Mies van der Rohe to Sergius Ruegenberg [day and month illegible] 1941, Bauhaus-Archiv, Berlin (filed under Gropius Ruegenberg correspondence); Wichert, *Max Beckmann,* 342, 343 ("the spatial character of Beckmann's art. . . space and its development is the key, is really everything"). Mies and Wichert knew each other since 1924. See entry in Wichert's diary on September 5, 1924: MARCHIVUM, Mannheim, NL Wichert, Zug. 22/1980 No. 558.

77. John A. Holabird, letter to Mies van der Rohe, March 20, 1936; Mies, telegram to Holabird, April 20, 1936; Mies, letter to Holabird, May 4, 1936; Holabird, letter to Mies, May 11, 1936; Willard E. Hotchkiss, letter to Mies, May 12, 1936; Mies, letter to Hotchkiss, n.d.; Hotchkiss, letter to Mies, July 2, 1936, all LoC, MvdR.

78. Dominic Ricciotti, "The 1939 Building of the Museum of Modern Art: The Goodwin-Stone Collaboration," *American Art Journal* 17, no. 3 (Summer 1985): 50–76.

79. Hicks Stone, *Edward Durell Stone: A Son's Untold Story of a Legendary Architect* (New York: Rizzoli, 2011), 22, 25; Edward Durell Stone, *The Evolution of an Architect* (New York: Horizon, 1962), 24. It is possible that this memory is a later conjecture, as his travel dates do not quite add up. Stone, *Edward Durell Stone,* 31.

80. The 10,000-square-foot (929-square-meter) Mandel House was widely published. "Residence of Richard Mandel, Mount Kisco, N.Y.," *Architectural Forum,* March 1934, 185–86; "House of Richard H. Mandel," *Architectural Forum,* August 1935, 78–88; "The House That Works: I," *Fortune,* October 1935, 59–65, 94, 96, 98, 100.

81. Franz Schulze and Edward Windhorst, *Mies van der Rohe: A Critical Biography,* new and rev. ed. (Chicago: University of Chicago, 2014), 178, 179.

82. Mies van der Rohe to Joseph Hudnut, September 15, 1936, MoMA, MvdR.

83. For more details, see Dietrich Neumann, "'. . . Wallpaper with Arctic Landscapes . . .': Mies van der Rohe's Designs for Wall Decoration and Printing Technique 1937–1950," in *Mies and Modern Living: Interiors, Furniture, Photography,* ed. Helmut Reuter and Katrina Schulte (Ostfildern: Hatje Cantz, 2008), 265–77.

84. "Method for Printing Wallpaper," Patent no. 158059 in the German Reich, Reichspatentamt (Imperial Patent Office), Austrian branch office, submitted March 12, 1937, published March 11, 1940.

85. "The photographic production of larger screens or larger screened negatives," Patent specification no. 737591 in the German Reich, Reichspatentamt, submitted January 26, 1938, published June 7, 1943.

86. Sebastian Neurauter, *Das Bauhaus und die Verwertungsrechte* (Tübingen: Mohr Siebeck, 2013), 455–58.

87. Mies van der Rohe to Rasch, October 22, 1936, LoC, MvdR, Personal Correspondence 1923–40.

88. Walter Peterhans, *Was, wann, wie vergrössern,* Der Fotorat 3 (Halle: William Knapp, 1936); Walter Peterhans, *Das Entwickeln entscheidet,* Der Fotorat 15 (Halle: William Knapp, 1939); Walter Peterhans, *Richtig Kopieren,* Der Fotorat 34 (Halle: William Knapp, 1942).

89. Christian Spies, "Raster: Eine Infrastruktur des Sehens," in *Designpatente der Moderne 1840–1970,* ed. Robin Rehm and Christoph Wagner (Berlin: Gebrüder Mann, 2019), 398–403.

90. "Verfahren zum Bedrucken von Tapetenbahnen," Patent no. 158059B, German Reichspatentamt, Austrian branch, issued March 11, 1940. US 2282337A: "Apparatus for the Production of Dot-Composed or Screened Negatives," approved May 12, 1942 (also patented in Switzerland, France, and the Netherlands).

91. Ludwig Mies van der Rohe and Walter Peterhans, "Apparatus for the Production of Dot-Composed Negatives," U.S. Patent Office, Patent no. 2532585, registered on June 26, 1946, issued on December 5, 1950.

92. Kurt H. Feist was a German immigrant ("Henry K. Feist" after arriving in the United States in 1939). Feist to Mies van der Rohe, December 13, 1939, LoC, MvdR, Box 46, Patent nos. 242.480 and 252.654; Feist, Henry K., Patents General 1938–47.

93. While Mies took sole responsibility for this idea, and Lilly Reich was not named as coauthor, an agreement dated October 10, 1941, granted her half of all potential revenue. Studio of Lilly Reich to Mies van der Rohe, April 12, 1947, LoC, MvdR. The patent was registered under Mies's name in Austria, France, Belgium, Sweden, England, and Holland, but not in the United States.

94. Protocol of the meeting of May 16, 1939, attended by W. Tiefel, Lilly Reich, and Hauswald concerning the patent application R 98 839 VII/Sa, LoC, MvdR.

95. Gottfried Bueren to Mies van der Rohe, October 10, 1939, LoC, MvdR.

96. Walter Rendell Storey, "How the Camera Gives Us Murals," *New York Times,* January 18, 1931, 85.

97. Julien Levy, "The Photo Mural," in *Murals by American Painters and Photographers,* ed. Lincoln Kirstein (New York: Museum of Modern Art, 1932), 11f. Thanks to Professor Douglas Nickel for this reference.

98. See Edward Alden Jewell, "Photography and Walls," *New York Times*, May 22, 1932, X7.

99. Sandy Isenstadt was the first to point this out. Sandy Isenstadt, *The Modern American House: Spaciousness and Middle-Class Identity* (Cambridge: Cambridge University Press, 2006), 230–34.

100. Drix Duryea, "Notes on Murals by Photographers," *Architectural Record*, July 1936, 57–61. Duryea's process—based on the projection of a single negative—was similar to Mies and Peterhans's approach.

101. John Marsman, "Vanishing Walls," *Arts and Decoration* (April 1937): 8.

102. Mies van der Rohe to Clemens Holzmeister, March 10, 1937, in Clemens Holzmeister, *Architekt in der Zeitenwende* (Salzburg: Bergland-Buch, 1976), 101. I would like to thank Dr. Christoph Hölz, Innsbruck, for this reference.

103. Hanenberg et al., *Mies im Westen*, 186–91.

104. Lilly von Schnitzler, interview by Ludwig Glaeser, September 6, 1974, transcript, 11, Ludwig Glaeser Papers, Box 3, Item 5, Canadian Centre for Architecture, Montreal. Lilly might have mixed up Speer with Troost, who had died in January 1934.

Chapter Seven. Difficult Beginnings

1. Cammie McAtee, "Alien #5044325: Mies' First Trip to America," in *Mies in America*, ed. Phyllis Lambert (New York: Harry N. Abrams, 2001), 132–91.

2. Helen Resor to Alfred Barr, July 12, 1937, Museum of Modern Art (hereafter MoMA), MvdR, Resor Papers.

3. Hildegard Brenner, *Ende einer bürgerlichen Kunst-Institution. Die politische Formierung der Preussischen Akademie der Künste ab 1933* (Stuttgart: Deutsche Verlags-Anstalt, 1972), 144–48, 163. Bruno Paul, Mies's erstwhile teacher and employer, who was also dismissed, felt misunderstood and listed his Nazi and anti-Semitic credentials in a lengthy letter, as did the painters Max Pechstein and Emil Nolde—to no avail.

4. Elaine Hochman, *Architects of Fortune: Mies van der Rohe and the Third Reich* (New York: Weidenfeld and Nicholson, 1989), 280–89.

5. Danilo Udovicki-Selb, "Le Corbusier and the Paris Exhibition of 1937: The Temps Nouveaux Pavilion," *Journal of the Society of Architectural Historians* 56, no. 1 (March 1997): 42–63.

6. McAtee, "Alien #5044325," 155.

7. Betty J. Blum, "Interview with William Turk Priestley," *Chicago Architects Oral History Project*, Ernest R. Graham Study Center for Architectural Drawings (Chicago: Art Institute of Chicago, 1995), 7; Betty J. Blum, "Interview with Bertrand Goldberg," *Chicago Architects Oral History Project*, Ernest R. Graham Study Center for Architectural Drawings (Chicago: Art Institute of Chicago, 1992), 96–99.

8. "Roll 6027 Passenger Lists of Vessels Arriving at New York, New York, 1820–1897," Microfilm Publication M237, 675 rolls. NAI: 6256867, Records of the U.S. Customs Service, Record Group 36; National Archives at Washington, D.C.; "Passenger and Crew Lists of Vessels Arriving at New York, New York, 1897–1957," Ancestry.com.

9. John Peter, *The Oral History of Modern Architecture: Interviews with the Greatest Architects of the Twentieth Century* (New York: Abrams, 1964), 156–73. Howard Dearstyne and Mies signed the card on November 7, 1937. Eduard Ludwig to Mies van der Rohe, MoMA, MvdR, Ludwig correspondence.

10. Passenger List, the SS *Manhattan*, which left Hamburg on November 17, 1937, and arrived in New York on November 25, 1937, Microfilm Serial, National Archives, T715, 1897–1957, line 6, p. 12 (available through Ancestry.com); Christmas telegram at MoMA, MvdR.

11. Vivian Endicott Barnett, "The Architect as Art Collector," in Lambert, *Mies in America*, 91–131.

12. Barnett, "Architect as Art Collector," 99.

13. Julie V. Iovine, "In Its Own Time," *Chicago Tribune*, July 26, 1997, 1.

14. "Domestic Interiors," *Architectural Forum*, October 1937, 239–368, Tugendhat House at 241.

15. Henry Robert Harrison, "Richard J. Neutra: A Center of Architectural Stimulation," *Pencil Points* (July 1937): 407–38.

16. Norman Bel Geddes Database, "Job 133, J. Walter Thompson Assembly Room, 1928–1947," Harry Ransom Center, https://norman.hrc.utexas.edu /nbgpublic/details.cfm?id=120; Katherine Feo Kelly and Helen Baer, "A Visionary's Archive: The Norman Bel Geddes Papers at the Harry Ransom Center," *Journal of Design History* 25, no. 3 (2012): 319–28.

17. Dietrich Neumann, *The Structure of Light: Richard Kelly and the Illumination of Modern Architecture* (New Haven: Yale University Press, 2010), 118.

18. "The Architect and House: No. 6: Don Hatch of New York," *Pencil Points* (October 1941): 617–32, Pittsburgh House of Glass at 626–29.

19. *A New House by Frank Lloyd Wright on Bear Run, Pennsylvania* (New York: Museum of Modern Art, 1938).

20. Daniel Naegele, "Waiting for the Site to Show Up: Henry Luce Makes Frank Lloyd Wright America's Greatest Architect," *Journal of the International Association for the Study of Traditional Environments* 254 (Fall 2014): 89–97.

21. *Time*, January 17, 1938, cover; "Frank Lloyd Wright," *Fortune*, January 1938, 138; "Frank Lloyd Wright," *Architectural Forum*, January 1938, 1–102.

22. Quoted in "Frank Lloyd Wright," 100.

23. Advertisement for *Architectural Forum*'s Frank Lloyd Wright issue on the inside cover of *Life*, January 17, 1938.

24. "Frank Lloyd Wright," 76, 79–82.

25. In New York it could be seen at the Embassy Newsreel Theater.

26. "America Imports Genius," *New York Times*, September 12, 1937, E8.

27. Walter Gropius, "Education Towards Creative Design," *American Architect and Architecture* 81 (May 1937): 26–30.

28. Charles W. Killam, "School Training for Architecture: Some Pertinent Thoughts on Education," *Pencil Points* (July 1937): 441–47. This essay was the summary of a talk he had given in May 1937 at the Association of Collegiate Schools of Architecture, gathered in Boston on the occasion of the annual AIA convention. Jill E. Pearlman, *Inventing American Modernism* (Charlottesville: University of Virginia Press, 2007), 76.

29. Killam, "School Training for Architecture," quotes at 441, 443, 444. American modernist architect, editor, and preservationist Lawrence Kocher, who had thought much about reforming architectural education, was so impressed with Killam's article that he adopted his approach when developing a new architecture curriculum for the Carnegie Institute in Pittsburgh in 1939. Lawrence Kocher, "New Type of Study Faces Architects," *New York Times*, May 7, 1939, G2.

30. Mies van der Rohe to Mr. Heald, University Club, 1 West Fifty-Fourth Street, New York, December 10, 1937 [translation], Library of Congress (hereafter LoC), MvdR; Kevin Harrington, "Order, Space, Propotion—Mies's Curriculum at IIT," in *Mies van der Rohe: Architect as Educator*, ed. Rolf Achilles, Kevin Harrington, and Charlotte Myhrum (Chicago: Illinois Institute of Technology, 1986), 49–68 (Rodgers and Priestley's diagram on 57).

31. McAtee, "Alien #5044325," 172.

32. McAtee, "Alien #5044325," 176.

33. Ludwig Mies van der Rohe, "Resor House project, Jackson Hole, Wyoming (Exterior Perspective. Fireplace. Perspectives, plans, section) c. 1937–38," MoMA, MvdR. The German "Wandbilder"—literally, "wall images"—was translated as "murals." The text in German: "Wanddekorationen? Leuchtende Wandbilder? Raumbeleuchtung durch Projektion von Wandbilder? Bildliche Raumdekorationen? Hell und gedämpft."

34. McAtee, "Alien #5044325," 176.

35. Mies van der Rohe to Peter Carter in response to Alfred Barr's comparison of the Brick Country House and Theo van Doesburg's *Rhythm of a Russian Dance*: Peter Carter, *Mies van der Rohe at Work* (New York: Praeger, 1974), 180; Alfred Barr, *Cubism and Modern Art* (New York: Museum of Modern Art, 1934), 156–57; Peter Carter, *Mies van der Rohe at Work* (New York: Praeger, 1974), 180.

36. Neil Levine, "The Significance of Facts: Mies's Collages up Close and Personal," *Assemblage* 37 (December 1998): 70–101.

37. Walter Gropius to Mies van der Rohe, June 29, 1938, Bauhaus-Archive Berlin.

38. Mies van der Rohe to Walter Gropius, August 2, 1938, Bauhaus-Archive Berlin.

39. Walter Gropius to Mies van der Rohe, September 13, 1938, Bauhaus-Archive Berlin.

40. Correspondence between Mies van der Rohe and Walter Gropius, September 26, 1983, Bauhaus-Archive Berlin.

41. Quoted in "Overseaers," *Architectural Forum*, November 1937, 10, 12.

42. Barry Bergdoll, "Memento Mori or Eternal Modernism? The Bauhaus at MoMA, 1938," *Docomomo* 61 (2019): 9–17.

43. Walter Gropius to Mies van der Rohe, January 19, 1939, Bauhaus-Archive Berlin.

44. See also Fritz Neumeyer, "Giedion und Mies van der Rohe. Ein Paradox in der Historiographie der Moderne," *Architektur Aktuell*, no. 183 (September 1995): 56–63; Sigfried Giedion, *Space, Time and Architecture* (Cambridge, Mass.: Harvard University Press, 1941), 321–22. See also Dietrich Neumann, "Space Time and the Bauhaus," in *Bauhaus Effects in Art, Architecture and Design*, ed. Kathleen James Chakraborty, and Sabine T. Kriebel (London: Routledge 2022), 116–33.

45. He stayed in room 1514 for six dollars a day. Lee Gray, "Addendum: Mies van der Rohe and Walter Gropius in the FBI Files," in *Mies van der Rohe: Critical Essays*, ed. Franz Schulze (New York: Museum of Modern Art, 1989), 146.

46. Gottfried van Bueren to Mies van der Rohe, October 21 and November 6, 1936, MoMA, MvdR, quoted in Franz Schulze and Edward Windhorst, *Mies van der Rohe: A Critical Biography*, new and rev. ed. (Chicago: University of Chicago, 2014), 182, 442.

47. Ines Dresel, "Interview with Werner Buch," *Chicago Architects Oral History Project*, Ernest R. Graham Study Center for Architectural Drawings (Chicago: Art Institute of Chicago, 1990), 2, 12.

48. Dresel, "Interview with Werner Buch," 3, 19.

49. Architect Charles "Skip" Booher Genther recalled spending afternoons with Mies and Hilberseimer at the Berghoff, to "drink beer and talk" in the 1950s, when working on several high-rise housing projects together. Betty J. Blum, "Interview with Charles Booher Genther," *Chicago Architects Oral History Project*, Ernest R. Graham Study Center for Architectural Drawings (Chicago: Art Institute of Chicago, 1995), 7.

50. The blueprints were still in Mies's office when he retired. The building is operated today as the Glessner House Museum.

51. "Mies van der Rohe and Glessner House," The Story of a House: Official Blog of Glessner House, September 10, 2013, http://glessnerhouse.blogspot.com/2013/09/mies-van-der-rohe-and-glessner-house.html.

52. "New Bauhaus School Closes; Director Sues: Asks Back Pay; Accused of 'Hitlerizing,'" Chicago Daily Tribune, October 16, 1938, 18.

53. László Moholy-Nagy, "The New Bauhaus, American School of Design, Chicago," Design 40, no. 8 (March 1, 1939): 19.

54. "An Apparel Store. Benson & Rixon Store. Chicago, Illinois. Alfred S. Alschuler, Architect," Architectural Record, February 1938, 128–29.

55. "Holabird and Root: Masters of Design," Pencil Points (February 1938): 65–98.

56. Dresel, "Interview with Werner Buch," 2. About Bartsch, see also Blum, "Interview with William Turk Priestley," 12.

57. Jan Thomas Köhler, Jan Maruhn, and Nina Senger, eds., Berliner Lebenswelten der zwanziger Jahre—Bilder einer untergegangenen Kultur, photographs by Marta Huth (Frankfurt: Gatza bei Eichborn, 1996), 82.

58. Walter Gropius, "Architecture at Harvard University," Architectural Record, May 1937, 8–11; "Overseaers," Architectural Forum, November 1937, 10, 12.

59. Eleanor Jewett, "Reflections on Modern Architecture Exhibit: Work of Foreigners Held to Be Outstanding," Chicago Daily Tribune, June 19, 1932, G4.

60. "Views and Profiles," Chicago Daily Tribune, September 13, 1938, 15.

61. Eleanor Jewett, "City Maintains a Full Quota of Art Exhibitions," Chicago Daily Tribune, December 11, 1938, F5.

62. Eleanor Jewett, "Art Institute Show Lives Up to Yule Spirit," Chicago Daily Tribune, December 25, 1938, C5.

63. "Exiled German's Art to Be Shown," Buffalo Evening News, September 11, 1939, I17. It closed on October 29, 1939. Walter Curt Behrendt, "Mies van der Rohe," Magazine of Art (September 1939): 591. "Exiled German's Art to be Shown," 17; "Museum Directors and Art Collectors Meet at Princeton: Sherley Morgan and Rufus Morey Hosts to Visiting Archeologists, Architects," New York Herald Tribune, November 5, 1939, D13.

64. Eleanor Jewett, "Armour Institute of Technology . . . ," Chicago Daily Tribune, October 2, 1938, F4.

65. India Moffett, "Mrs. Armour Gives $50,000 to Institute's Architecture School," Chicago Daily Tribune, October 19, 1938, 17.

66. For the most extensive discussion of the evolution of IIT's plan, see Lambert, Mies in America, 222–330.

67. Reich traveled arrived on the passenger ship Hamburg in New York on July 21, 1939. John Barney Rodgers had applied for her two-month visa. The immigration officer noted that she had exactly four dollars at her disposal.

68. Pauline Saliga, "Interview with George Danforth," Chicago Architects Oral History Project, Ernest R. Graham Study Center for Architectural Drawings (Chicago: Art Institute of Chicago, 1993), 35; Blum, "Interview with William Turk Priestley," 7, 8.

69. Schulze and Windhorst, Critical Biography, 201–3.

70. Lilly Reich to Mies van der Rohe, March 23, 1940, LoC, MvdR papers, Box 47.

71. Lilly Reich to Mies van der Rohe, June 12, 1940; April 15, 1940; May 17, 1940, all LoC, MvdR, Box 47.

72. Lilly Reich to Mies van der Rohe, October 8 and 24, 1939, both LoC, MvdR, Box 47.

73. Lilly Reich to Mies van der Rohe, January 13, 1940; February 11 and 18, 1940, all LoC, MvdR, Box 47, Folder 2 (Patents, Lorenz & Reich, 1937–1940). Reich to Mies van der Rohe, January 13, 1940; February 18, 1940; March 23, 1940, May 3/7, 1940, all LoC, MvdR, Box 47.

74. She reminded Mies to send her chocolates and mentioned how "insecure" Ada was in her presence. (Lilly Reich to Mies van der Rohe, October 8, 1939; April 7, 1940, all LoC, MvdR, Box 47.) In loco parentis she corresponded extensively with his daughter Waltraud, who suffered from pneumonia, and persuaded her not to abandon her studies at the university in Munich. Lilly Reich to Waltraud Mies, October 16, 1939, LoC, MvdR, Box 47.

75. Lilly Reich to Mies van der Rohe, December 12, 1939; March 18, 1940; April 7, 1940, all LoC, MvdR, Box 47.

76. Lilly Reich to Mies van der Rohe, October 8, 1939, LoC, MvdR, Box 47, Folder 2 (Patents, Lorenz & Reich, 1937–1940). No letters from Reich to Mies are recorded after 1940. Eduard Ludwig mentioned in her in a letter to Mies in 1946 that she was tirelessly at work but "deserved a better fate." Eduard Ludwig to Mies van der Rohe, November 25, 1946, LoC, MvdR, folder General Office File, Eduard Ludwig 1945–61.

77. Katharine Kuh, "Mies van der Rohe; Modern Classicist," Saturday Review of Literature 48 (January 23, 1965): 22–23, 61, quote at 61.

78. Lambert, Mies in America, 271, quoted in Kevin Harrington, "Interview with George Danforth," Canadian Centre for Architecture, Monreal, tape 4, side 2.

79. Henry Townly Heald, "Whole New Campus Built to House Illinois Technology: Functional Type of Architecture Adopted to Meet Needs of Institute," New York Times, November 9, 1941, D7.

80. "Illinois Tech—Leader in Redevelopment of Blighted Areas," in Technology Center Today and Tomorrow: Illinois Institute of Technology (Chicago: Illinois Institute of Technology, 1947), 46.

81. Marcia Winn, "Her One and Only Dad," Chicago Daily Tribune, January 28, 1942, 17.

82. "Tech Turns on Heat in Drive for Fieldhouse: Bonfire, Snake Dance Open $1,000,000 Campaign," Chicago Daily Tribune, December 6, 1941, 24.

83. Philip Johnson, Mies van der Rohe (New York: Museum of Modern Art, 1947), 156. The date of 1945 given elsewhere seems less likely: Franz Schulze, ed., An Illustrated Catalogue of the Mies van der Rohe Drawings in the Museum of Modern Art, part 2, 1938–1967, The American Work (New York: Garland, 1992), 166.

84. Peter Blake, "A Conversation with Mies," in Four Great Makers of Modern Architecture: Gropius, Le Corbusier, Mies van der Rohe, Wright: A Verbatim Record of a Symposium Held at the School of Architecture from March to May 1961 (New York: Da Capo, 1963), 93–104.

85. "Plant for Lady Esther, Ltd., Clearing, Illinois," Architectural Forum, August 1938, 96–101.

86. George Nelson, Industrial Architecture of Albert Kahn (New York: Architectural Book, 1939).

87. Myron Goldsmith in conversation with William H. Jordy: William H. Jordy, American Buildings and Their Architects, vol. 5, The Impact of European Modernism in the Mid-Twentieth Century (New York: Oxford University Press, 1972), 223.

88. Hendrik Petrus Berlage, Grundlagen und Entwicklung der Architektur: Vier Vorträge gehalten im Kunstgewerbemuseum zu Zürich (Berlin: Justus Bard, 1908); Le Corbusier, Vers une Architecture (Paris: G. Crès, 1924), 61–64.

89. "Metals and Minerals Research Building, Illinois Institute of Technology," Architectural Forum, November 1943, 88–90.

90. Philip Hampson, "Science Makes Speaking Easy at Dedication," Chicago Daily Tribune, January 12, 1943, 21.

91. Al Chase, "Illinois Tech Will Bid for Stevens Hotel," Chicago Daily Tribune, September 4, 1943, 19; Al Chase, "Top Stevens Bid by Illinois Tech: Offer Totals 5 1/2 Millions, with 30 Year Mortgage," Chicago Daily Tribune, September 5, 1943, 1; Al Chase, "3 Million Dollar Expansion Plan at Illinois Tech," Chicago Daily Tribune, September 24, 1943, 22.

92. Telegram from Howard Myers (editor of Architectural Forum) to Mies van der Rohe, February 3, 1943, LoC, MvdR.

93. Architectural Forum, May 1943, 25, 26.

94. "New Buildings for 194X," Architectural Forum, May 1943, 71.

95. "New Buildings for 194X," 69–152, 189–90, Mies's museum at 84–85.

96. Phyllis Lambert, "Project for a Museum for a Small City" (1943), in Mies in America, 426–29.

97. Ludwig Mies van der Rohe, "Museum," Architectural Forum, May 1943, 84; Levine, "Significance of Facts," 70–101, quote at 83. Mies might have seen Guernica at the Paris World's Fair of 1937, or in Chicago, where it was exhibited in 1939–40 at the Arts Club and the Art Institute on its U.S. tour, before returning to the Museum of Modern Art.

98. Mies van der Rohe, "Museum," 84.

99. Katharine Kuh, My Love Affair with Modern Art (New York: Arcade, 2006), 75, 76.

100. Close-Up of Tintoretto (June 29–October 29, 1944); Explaining Abstract Art (July 1, 1947–January 21, 1948); and From Nature to Art (November 8, 1944–February 4, 1945).

Chapter Eight. Formation of a New Language

1. Franz Schulze and Edward Windhorst, Mies van der Rohe: A Critical Biography, new and rev. ed. (Chicago: University of Chicago, 2014), 248, quoted from Edith Farnsworth's handwritten memoir in the Edith Farnsworth Papers (boxes 1 and 2) at the Newberry Library, Chicago, https://ia903004.us.archive.org/24/items/mms_farnsworth/mms_farnsworth.pdf, 615.

2. Edward Duckett, quoted in William S. Shell, interview with Edward A. Duckett and Joseph Y. Fujikawa, in Impressions of Mies: An Interview on Mies van der Rohe: His Early Chicago Years 1938–1958 (n.p., 1988), 18, quoted in Schulze and Windhorst, Critical Biography, 451.

3. Schulze and Windhorst, Critical Biography, 252.

4. See the review of the arrival of the screened-in porch: "The Vanishing Porch in Perspective," Humanities Commons, https://curtainedwallstimeline.hcommons.org/static-timeline-with-large-images/.

5. Mies van der Rohe during court proceedings, quoted in Alex Beam, Broken Glass: Mies van der Rohe, Edith Farnsworth, and the Fight over a Modernist Masterpiece (New York: Random House, 2020), 150.

6. "This Is the First House Built by Ludwig Mies van der Rohe," Architectural Forum, October 1951, 156–61, quote at 159.

7. "This Is the First House Built," 159.

8. "This Is the First House Built," 159.

9. Philip Johnson to Mies van der Rohe, June 4, 1951, Museum of Modern Art (hereafter MoMA), MvdR, quoted in Beam, Broken Glass, 147.

10. Schulze and Windhorst, Critical Biography, 252; Beam, Broken Glass, 135.

11. Mary Roche, "New Canaan Holds Modern House Day," New York Times, May 14, 1949, 10; "Glass House: It Consists of Just One Big Room Completely Surrounded by Scenery," Life, September 26, 1949, 94–96;

Mary Roche, "Living in a Glass House," *New York Times,* August 14, 1949, SM34; Richard Kelly, "Focus on Light: New Techniques Inspire Exciting Use in Décor," *Flair* 1, no. 15 (1950): 66–69.

12. Edith Farnsworth's furniture selection was reassembled at the house on the occasion of its renaming as "Edith Farnsworth House." See Nora Wendl, *Edith Farnsworth House* (Chicago: National Trust for Historic Preservation, 2021), https://issuu.com/edithfarnsworthhouse/docs/edithbook_nov.

13. Betty J. Blum, "Interview with Myron Goldsmith," *Chicago Architects Oral History Project,* Ernest R. Graham Center for Architectural Drawings (Chicago: Art Institute of Chicago, 1990/2001), 67, https://artic.contentdm.oclc.org/digital/collection/caohp/id/4086/.

14. Leigh Atkinson, "Architect Finds Beauty Lies in 'Skin and Bones': Proud of Simplicity in Gold Coast Building," *Chicago Daily Tribune,* June 21, 1951, S6.

15. "This Is the First House Built," 157, 160.

16. Arthur Drexler, "Post-War Architecture," in *Built in USA: Post-War Architecture,* ed. Henry-Russell Hitchcock and Arthur Drexler (New York: Museum of Modern Art, 1953), 20–37, quote at 20, 21.

17. "The American Idea in Houses: A Glass Shell That 'floats' in the Air," *House & Garden,* February 1952, 44–49, 96; Elizabeth Gordon, "The Threat to the Next America," *House Beautiful,* April 1953, 126–30, 250–51, quote at 129.

18. Joseph A. Barry, "Report on the Battle between Good and Bad Modern Houses," *House Beautiful,* May 1953, 172–73, 266–72.

19. Myron Goldsmith to Diagrid Stuctures Ltd., December 17, 1952, MoMA, MvdR, Business Correspondence folder 2, project 5016, Professional Papers; Myron Goldsmith, interview by Kevin Harrington, Canadian Centre for Architecture, Montreal, tape 9: side 1; both quoted in Phyllis Lambert, "Space and Structure," in *Mies in America,* ed. Phyllis Lambert (New York: Harry N. Abrams, 2001), 333–521, quotes at 461, 519nn224, 227.

20. "Mies van der Rohe," *Architectural Forum,* November 1952, 93–111, quote at 110.

21. Luciana Fornari Colombo, "Mies van der Rohe's Core House, a Theoretical Project on the Essential Dwelling," *Vitruvius,* https://vitruvius.com.br/index.php/revistas/read/arquitextos/11.130/3782/en.

22. Anne Douglas, "Dinner in Yesterday's Bedroom: It's Possible in This Flexible Plan," *Chicago Daily Tribune,* August, 24, 1952.

23. "Mies van der Rohe" [*Architectural Forum*], 108.

24. "Mies van der Rohe," [*Architectural Forum*], 108.

25. Gene Summers to Joseph Fujikawa, May 31, 1955, McCormick House Museum Archive, in "Greenwald House Planning," 150 South Cottage Hill, https://www.150southcottagehillave.net/2019/03/23/greenwald-house-planning/.

26. Gilbert Herbert, *The Dream of the Factory-Made House: Walter Gropius and Konrad Wachsmann* (Cambridge, Mass.: MIT Press, 1984).

27. Eliot F. Noyes, *Organic Design in Home Furnishings* (New York: Museum of Modern Art, 1941), 10–17.

28. Mary Roche, "Furniture Design Subject of Context: Nelson Rockefeller Announces $50000 Competition for Modern Home Wares," *New York Times,* October 24, 1947, 26.

29. Philip Johnson, *Mies van der Rohe* (New York: Museum of Modern Art, 1947), 172–73.

30. Mass-producing a plastic chair would involve complicated tooling design, as the plastic would have to be shaped with metal molds in a hydraulic press.

31. Edgar Kaufmann, Jr., ed. *Prize Designs for Modern Furniture from the International Competition for Low-Cost Furniture Design* (New York: Museum of Modern Art, 1950), 19.

32. A. James Speyer, "Mies van der Rohe," *Art News* 46 (September 1947): 20–23, 42–43, quote at 42; A. James Speyer, *Mies van der Rohe* (Chicago: Art Institute of Chicago, 1968), 115.

33. Kaufmann, *Prize Designs,* 44.

34. Werner Blaser, "Furniture by Mies van der Rohe," in *Mies van der Rohe's German Pavilion in Barcelona, 1929–1986,* ed. Rosa Maria Subirana i Torrent (Barcelona: Ajuntament de Barcelona, 1987), 88–89.

35. Peter Behrens, *Kunst und Technik* (1910), quoted in Fritz Neumeyer, ed., *Quellentexte zur Architekturtheorie* (Munich: Prestel, 2002), 358.

36. Ludwig Mies van der Rohe, "Expressways as an Artistic Problem," *Die Autobahn,* no. 10 (1932): 1.

37. Myron Goldsmith, interview by Kevin Harrington, in Lambert, *Mies in America,* 333–521, quotes at 430, 516nn170.

38. "U. Unveils Plans for Frat House of Unusual Type," *Indianapolis Star,* February 10, 1952, sec. 2, 3.

39. Ted Loos, "The Case of the Missing Mies van der Rohe: After Nearly 70 Years, a Forgotten, Unbuilt Design by the Pioneering Architect Ludwig Mies van der Rohe Comes to Life on Indiana University's Bloomington Campus," *Wall Street Journal,* September 22, 2021, https://www.wsj.com/articles/missing-mies-van-der-rohe-11632313895.

40. Quoted in "Break Ground for Apartment Building Today," *Chicago Daily Tribune,* November 9, 1947.

41. Ulrich Middeldorf, foreword in *An Exhibition of Architecture by Mies van der Rohe, May 16–June 7, 1947* (Chicago: Renaissance Society at the University of Chicago, 1947), n.p.

42. *Theo van Doesburg: Paintings, Drawings, Photographs and Architectural Drawings,* October 13–November 8, 1947, Renaissance Society of Chicago, http://archive.renaissancesociety.org/site/Exhibitions/Intro.Theo-van-Doesburg-Paintings-Drawings-Photographs-and-Architectural-Drawings.263.html.

43. Wies van Moorsel, *Nelly van Doesburg 1899–1975* (Nijmegen: SUN, 2000), 188, 197–98. I thank Herman van Bergeijk for this reference. Dietrich Neumann, "Mies und die Niederlande," in *Mies im Westen: Projekte und Spuren im Rheinland,* ed. Norbert Hanenberg, Daniel Lohmann, Ursula Kleefisch-Jobst, and Peter Köddermann (Aachen: Geymüller, 2022), 70–85.

44. Johnson, *Mies van der Rohe,* 165.

45. The show opened on September 16, 1947, and ran until November 23. Museum of Modern Art, "Museum of Modern Art Presents Retrospective Exhibition of the Architecture of Mies van der Rohe," press release, September 17, 1947, https://assets.moma.org/documents/moma_press-release_325576.pdf?_ga=2.246315394.783610340.1654796427-979520300.1626897436.

46. Exhibition records, Mies Exhibition 1947, MoMA, MvdR; Neil Levine, "The Significance of Facts: Mies's Collages up Close and Personal," *Assemblage* 37 (December 1998): 70–101; Lambert, *Mies in America,* 424–25.

47. Johnson, *Mies van der Rohe,* 164.

48. Lambert, *Mies in America,* 424–25, 436–37.

49. Mies's student Daniel Brenner produced a half-size photographic print of Mies's collage (29 1/4 inches, or 74.3 centimeters, wide) and added his own materials on top (now at the Art Institute of Chicago). It preserves the image of the Maillol figure in the foreground.

50. Levine, "Significance of Facts," 84–87. The photograph had been published in George Nelson, *Industrial Architecture of Albert Kahn, Inc.* (New York: Architectural Book, 1939), 38. (Mies owned a copy of this book, which is now in the Mies van der Rohe Collection, Special Collections, University of Illinois at Chicago.)

51. Konrad Wachsmann, "Mies van der Rohe," *Arts and Architecture* 69, no. 3 (March 1952): 16–31.

52. Johnson, *Mies van der Rohe,* 137, 138.

53. Barry Bergdoll, "Walk-In Collage: Mies van der Rohe's Design of His 1947 Exhibition at MoMA," in *Mies van der Rohe Montage Collage,* ed. Andreas Beitlin, Wolf Eiermann, and Brigitte Franzen (London: Koenig, 2017), 172–87, reference at 184.

54. Edward Alden Jewell, "A Van der Rohe Survey," *New York Times,* September 28, 1947, X7.

55. Charles Eames, "Mies van der Rohe," *Arts and Architecture* 12 (1947): 24–27, quote at 27.

56. Robert Woods Kennedy, review of *Mies van der Rohe,* by Philip C. Johnson, *Art Bulletin* 30, no. 2 (June 1948): 156–57.

57. F. G., "An Architect's Search for Best Use of Space: Mies van der Rohe's Exhibition Shows How His Flowing, Open Plans Have Been Modified to Reality of Industrial Building," *New York Herald Tribune,* September 14, 1947, D1.

58. Joseph Rykwert, review of *Mies van der Rohe,* by Philip C. Johnson, *Burlington Magazine* 91, no. 558 (September 1949): 268–69.

59. Rykwert, review of *Mies van der Rohe,* 269. Sibyl Moholy-Nagy agreed in 1964 at a symposium at Columbia University when she said about the IIT scheme: "I think it is ghastly. It is one of the most brutal, symmetrical, and lumpish plans I can imagine." Sibyl Moholy-Nagy, "Letter," *Journal of the Society of Architectural Historians* 24, no. 3 (October 1965): 255–56, quote at 256.

60. Otto Wagner, quoted in Harry Francis Mallgrave and Christina Contandriopoulos, *Architectural Theory,* vol. 2, *An Anthology from 1871 to 2005* (London: Blackwell, 2008), 94. For "Kunstform" and "Kernform," see Karl Bötticher, *Die Tektonik der Hellenen,* 2nd ed. (Berlin: Ernst und Korn, 1874), 1:25.

61. Peter Blake, "The Difficult Art of Simplicity," *Architectural Forum,* May 1958, 126–31.

62. Ludwig Mies van der Rohe, "A Chapel—Illinois Institute of Technology," *Arts and Architecture* 1 (1953): 18–19.

63. Dietrich Neumann, "Promontory to Lake Shore Drive: The Evolution of Space in Mies van der Rohe's High-Rise Apartments," in *Modern Wohnen: Möbeldesign und Wohnkultur der Moderne,* ed. Rudolf Fischer and Wolf Tegethoff (Berlin: Mann, 2015), 1–22.

64. "Illinois Tech Completes 2 Dormitories," *Chicago Daily Tribune,* September 19, 1948, WB. Nathaniel Owens joined IIT's board of trustees in 1950, and many more commissions for SOM at IIT followed. "Illinois Tech Widens Field, Triples Assets in 10 Years," *Chicago Daily Tribune,* October 10, 1950, B7.

65. "The Financing of Promontory," *Architectural Forum,* January 1950, 77, 124.

66. These apartment hotels were aimed at the upper-middle class with amenities such as maid service and a restaurant. Susan O'Connor Davis, *Chicago's Historic Hyde Park* (Chicago: University of Chicago Press, 2013), 255–71.

67. Each pier is one and half feet (0.5 meter) wide, and all eight bays have the same length of 16 and a half feet (five meters), with an interior width of 15 feet (4.6 meters), accommodating rows of exactly twenty-and-a-half facing

bricks in front of the concrete blocks. Betty J. Blum, "Interview with Charles Booher Genther" and "Interview with Joseph Fujikawa," *Chicago Architects Oral History Project,* Ernest R. Graham Study Center for Architectural Drawings (Chicago: Art Institute of Chicago, 1995), 17–28 (Genther), 11–21 (Fujikawa).

68. Samuel Zi, *Manhattan Projects: The Rise and Fall of Urban Renewal in Cold War New York* (Oxford: Oxford University Press, 2010), 114–36.

69. "Glass and Brick in a Concrete Frame," *Architectural Forum,* January 1950, 68–74, quote at 71. Important new scholarship on the Promontory and Lake Shore Drive apartments includes work by David Dunster and Sarah Stevens: David Dunster, "Selling Mies," in *Chicago Architecture: Histories, Revisions, Alternatives,* ed. Charles Waldheim and Katerina Rüedi (Chicago: University of Chicago Press, 2005), 93–103; and Sarah K. Stevens, *Developing Expertise: The Architecture of Real Estate, 1908–1065* (PhD diss., Princeton University, 2012). "Glass and Brick in a Concrete Frame," 71.

70. Ludwig Mies van der Rohe, "Was wäre Beton, was Stahl ohne Spiegelglas?" (1933), in *Mies van der Rohe: Das kunstlose Wort,* by Fritz Neumeyer (Berlin: DOM, 2016), 378. Translation from Fritz Neumeyer, *The Artless Word: Mies van der Rohe on the Building Art* (Cambridge, Mass.: MIT Press, 1991), 314.

71. Blum, "Interview with Joseph Fujikawa," 18.

72. Quoted in "Architect," *Pittsburgh Courier,* December 3, 1949, 9.

73. Frank J. Kornacker, "The Frame and Floor Structure—Design Principle," *Design for Environment: Floor-Ceilings and Service Systems in Multi-Story Buildings,* ed. Charles R. Koehler (Washington D.C.: Building Research Institute, 1955), 79–85, quote at 82.

74. "Glass and Brick in a Concrete Frame," 70.

75. The zoning code also suggested a 30-foot (9.1-meter) distance from the property line, but the construction company received a zoning exemption. See "Builders of Big Apartment Ask Zoning Change," *Chicago Daily Tribune,* July 13, 1947, S2. The building only occupied 18.5 percent of the entire lot measuring 300 by 135 feet (91.4 by 41 meters), and the remaining space was used for parking and a playground. See Al Chase, "Big Apartment Building Will Cost 1.8 Million: Work on South Side Unit to Begin in July," *Chicago Daily Tribune,* May 4, 1947, n.p.

76. The main elevator opens onto the lobby, and the service elevator onto the emergency staircase.

77. William C. Hedrich recalled the process of rephotographing models in 1992: Betty J. Blum, "Interview with William C. Hedrich," *Chicago Architects Oral History Project,* Ernest R. Graham Study Center for Architectural Drawings (Chicago: Art Institute of Chicago, 1994, rev. 2006), http://digital-libraries.saic.edu/cdm/compoundobject/collection/caohp/id/5993/rec/1.

78. Levine, "Significance of Facts," 70–101.

79. Advertisement for Angeles Mesa in the *Los Angeles Times,* May 18, 19, 1919, in Sandy Isenstadt, *The Modern American House: Spaciousness and Middle-Class Identity* (Cambridge: Cambridge University Press, 2006), 169.

80. Isenstadt, *Modern American House,* 168.

81. "Break Ground for Apartment Building Today," *Chicago Daily Tribune,* November 9, 1947, n.p.

82. The chair was at first (1946–47) made for Herman Miller by a company in California (Evans Molded Plywood of Venice Beach), then from 1947 onward at the company headquarters in Zeeland, Michigan. Four Eames DCM chairs were ordered by Mies's office directly from Herman Miller and paid for by Herbert Greenwald. See Felix C. Bonnet (office manager of Mies) to Herman Miller, January 25, 1950, and Greenwald to Herman Miller, February 25, 1950, MoMA, MvdR, Promontory Apartments Folder 1.

83. I would like to thank senior librarian Charles E. Flynn at Brown University for his help with identifying several pieces of furniture in the photos of the Promontory and Lake Shore Drive apartments.

84. Blum, "Interview with William C. Hedrich," 128.

85. Blum, "Interview with William C. Hedrich," 123.

86. Johnson, *Mies van der Rohe,* 162.

87. Folder Algonquin Apartments (sales brochure), Algonquin Apartment Buildings Scheme #1 and #2, MoMA, MvdR; see Arthur Drexler and Franz Schulze, eds., *The Mies van der Rohe Archive,* pt. 2, vol. 14, *1938–1967* (New York: Museum of Modern Art, 1992), 23.

88. Blum, "Interview with Charles Booher Genther," 24.

89. Blum, "Interview with Joseph Fujikawa," 17–18; Stevens, *Developing Expertise,* 155–58.

90. Blum, "Interview with Charles Booher Genther," 26.

91. Al Chase, "South Side Rental Project. 2 Apartment Projects to Be Started Soon," *Chicago Daily Tribune,* January 7, 1950, A7. Greenwald had worked with the Federal Housing Association (FHA), which had just begun to offer billions of dollars in cheap mortgages and insurance (Housing Act of 1949). Its policy prohibited insuring buildings above $500,000.

92. "Glass and Brick in a Concrete Frame," 69–74.

93. Even Elizabeth Wood, the social reformer and CHA director from 1937 to 1954, who had clear misgivings about their suitability for families with children, eventually approved them. Dominic A. Pacyga, *Chicago: A Biography* (Chicago: University of Chicago Press, 2009), 331–34.

94. "Chicago: Open Corridor Design and Unfinished Construction Minimize Costs and Rents," *Architectural Forum,* January 1950, 84.

95. Devereux Bowly, *The Poorhouse: Subsidized Housing in Chicago,* 2nd ed. (Carbondale: Southern Illinois University Press, 2012), 63; D. Bradford Hunt, *Blueprint for Disaster: The Unraveling of Chicago Public Housing* (Chicago: University of Chicago Press, 2009), 124. See also Julian Whittlesey, "New Dimensions in Housing Design: An Appraisal of Chicago's Multistory Public Housing Projects," *Progressive Architecture* 4 (April 1951): 57–68.

96. Here, the infill was red brick; the width of the bays varied in order to accommodate different room sizes; and the apartments were accessed from galleries in the back—a solution that Mies and Genther had also toyed with.

97. Bowly, *Poorhouse,* 65, 66.

98. Lawrence J. Vale, *Purging the Poorest: Public Housing and the Design Politics of Twice Cleared Communities* (Cambridge, Mass.: MIT Press, 2013), 224.

99. "Public Housing, Anticipating New Law, Looks at New York's High-Density Planning Innovations," *Architectural Forum,* June 1949, 87. See also Richard Plunz, *A History of Housing in New York City* (New York: Columbia University Press, 1990), 255–67. SOM's seven fourteen- and fifteen-story Sedgwick houses in the Bronx of 1950–52 were the first of many more to come.

100. Cabrini-Green was demolished in 2009, Ogden Courts in 2007, and Prairie Avenue Courts in 2000; the Harold Ickes Homes were closed and partially demolished in 2007.

101. Quoted in William Mullen, "The Road to Hell: For Cabrini-Green, It Was Paved with Good Intentions," *Chicago Tribune,* March 31, 1985.

102. "Equitable Builds a Leader," *Architectural Forum,* September 1948, 97–106, quote at 105.

103. Al Chase, "Plan Chicago's First Big Co-Op Office Building: Rush-Huron Project to Cost $1,300,000," *Chicago Daily Tribune,* September 12, 1948, A3.

104. Thomas J. Hamilton, "Work Completed on UN Buildings," *New York Times,* October 10, 1952, 1.

105. "Lever Brothers Plans Unusual Office Building: Structure at Park and 53rd to Have Glass-Steel Face, Seemingly No First Floor," *New York Herald Tribune,* April 30, 1950, 46.

106. "Modern Architecture Display Leads Herron Art Exhibits," *Indianapolis News,* February 4, 1933, 18.

107. Roger Budrow, "Glass-Walled Building Will Be First Here," *Indianapolis News,* May 23, 1950, 1, 13; Roger Budrow, "Van der Rohe a Revolutionary Architect Despite His 64 Years," *Indianapolis News,* May 24, 1950, 35.

108. Budrow, "Glass-Walled Building," 1.

109. Budrow, "Glass-Walled Building," 13.

110. Gerald Dreyer, "'All-Glass' Apartments to Be Built: Luxury Project to Have 12 Stories, 50 Units," *Indianapolis News,* March 28, 1953, 1; "New Apartment Features Glass," *Indianapolis Star,* March 29, 1953, sec. 3, 1; "North Side Apartment gets OK," *Indianapolis Star,* June 9, 1953, 1.

111. Bert Grabow, "Co-op Apartment Project Reports 32 Commitments," *Indianapolis News,* December, 5, 1957, 53.

112. Blum, "Interview with Charles Booher Genther," 29.

113. For Richard Kelly's work for Mies, see Margaret Maile Petty, "Illuminating the Glass Box: The Lighting Designs of Richard Kelly," *Journal of the Society of Architectural Historians* 66, no. 2 (2007): 194–219; Dietrich Neumann, ed., *The Structure of Light: Richard Kelly and the Illumination of Modern Architecture* (New Haven: Yale University Press, 2010).

114. "Mies van der Rohe" [*Architectural Forum*], 99.

115. "Mies van der Rohe," [*Architectural Forum*], 101.

116. "Mies van der Rohe," [*Architectural Forum*], 101.

117. "Chicago to Get 25-Story Twin Apartments with Exterior Walls of Steel and Glass," *New York Times,* April 10, 1949, R1.

118. "The Glass House—Home for Gracious Living: 860–880 Lake Shore Drive," advertising brochure, ca. 1957, private collection.

119. "Glass in a Steel Frame," *Architectural Forum,* January 1950, 75–77.

120. Elizabeth Gordon, "The Threat to the Next America," *House Beautiful,* April 1953, repr. in Alice T. Friedman, *Women and the Making of the Modern House: A Social and Architectural History* (New Haven: Yale University Press, 1998), 141.

121. See Hedrich-Blessing Collection, Chicago History Museum, HB-16110-D, Inventory Number 1991.505.

122. David Dunster, "Selling Mies," in *Chicago Architecture Histories, Revisions, Alternatives,* ed. Charles Waldheim and Katerina Rüedi Ray (Chicago: Chicago University Press, 2005), 82–92.

123. Peter Blake, "The Difficult Art of Simplicity," *Architectural Forum,* May 1958, 126–31, quote at 130.

124. Judith Cass, "All Percussion Concert on Arts Club Program," *Chicago Daily Tribune,* February 28, 1942, 13.

125. Brandon W. Joseph, "John Cage and the Architecture of Silence," *October* 81 (Summer 1997): 80–104.

126. "Illinois Tech Will Dedicate S. R. Crown Hall," *Chicago Daily Tribune,* April 30, 1956, 5.

127. Daniel Bluestone, "Chicago's Mecca Flat Blues," *Journal of the Society of Architectural Historians* 57, no. 4 (1998): 382–403.

128. "An Architecture Building for I.I.T. Mies van der Rohe," *Architectural Record,* August 1956, 133–39, quote at 134.

129. Henry Thomas Cadbury-Brown, "Ludwig Mies van der Rohe in Conversation with H. T. Cadbury-Brown," *AA Files,* no. 66 (2013): 68–80.

130. Carsten Krohn, *Mies van der Rohe: Das Gebaute Werk* (Basel: Birkhäuser, 2014), 130.

131. "An Architecture Building for I.I.T.," 136.

132. Blake, "Difficult Art of Simplicity," 128.

133. Cadbury-Brown, "Ludwig Mies van der Rohe in Conversation," 68–80.

134. Graeme Shankland, "Interview with Ludwig Mies van der Rohe," *The Listener* (October 15, 1959): 60. For a detailed look at some unusual event at Crown Hall, see Jan Frohburg, "Ellington under Glass," *BAc Boletín Académico* (November 4, 2019): 45–68.

135. See, for example, the brief treatment at Schulze and Windhorst, *Critical Biography,* 375. For a contextual overview, see Stephen Fox, "Cullinan Hall: A Window on Modern Houston," *Journal of Architectural Education* 54, no. 3 (February 2001): 158–66.

136. "Mies van der Rohe Designs a Museum for Houston," *Architectural Record,* August 1956, 26.

137. Dorothy Adlow, "Two New Homes for the Arts Fit Responsively into Their Environments: Designers Find Answers in Today's Terms," *Christian Science Monitor,* August 15, 1959, 6.

138. Schulze and Windhorst, *Critical Biography,* 242.

139. Ada Louise Huxtable, "Architects Examine New Directions at Summit Meeing," *New York Times,* May 21, 1961, X11.

140. Hugo Weber, "Vision in Flux—Paintings about Space in Space," *Arts and Architecture* 69, no. 3 (March 1952): 32–33.

Chapter Nine. Universal Formulas

1. Ernest Fuller, "6 Apartment Buildings set on North Side: Skyscrapers Will Cost 25 Millions," *Chicago Daily Tribune,* March 15, 1955, B7.

2. Quoted in David Carlson, "City Builder Greenwald," *Architectural Forum,* May 1958, 118–19, 202, quote at 202.

3. "Eight Chicago Apartment Projects," *Architectural Forum,* November 1955, 140–49, quote at 140.

4. "Eight Chicago Apartment Projects," 140.

5. "Easing Steel," *Architectural Forum,* May 1957, 154–55.

6. Franz Schulze and Edward Windhorst, *Mies van der Rohe: A Critical Biography,* new and rev. ed. (Chicago: University of Chicago, 2014), 294.

7. Phyllis Lambert, *Building Seagram* (New Haven: Yale University Press, 2013), 62ff.

8. "Eight Chicago Apartment Projects," 14.

9. Quoted in Carlson, "City Builder Greenwald," quote at 202.

10. Ludwig Mies van der Rohe, "Speech at the Memorial Service for Herbert S. Greenwald at Anshe Emet Synagogue, Chicago," February 12, 1959, Library of Congress (hereafter LoC), LMvdR, Box 61, File: Greenwald, Herbert S. Memorial Speech.

11. Betty J. Blum, "Interview with Joseph Fujikawa," *Chicago Architects Oral History Project,* Ernest R. Graham Study Center for Architectural Drawings (Chicago: Art Institute of Chicago, 1995), 13.

12. Caroline Constant, "Hilberseimer and Caldwell: Merging Ideologies in the Lafayette Park Landscape," in *Hilberseimer/Mies van der Rohe: Lafayette Park Detroit,* ed. Charles Waldheim (New York: Prestel, 2004), 95–111.

13. *Architectural Forum* (also owned by Luce) followed up in its July issue with three superlative-laden articles on the Seagram Building. "Emergence of a Master Architect," *Life,* March 18, 1957, 60–68.

14. "Emergence of a Master Architect," 60. Mies thanked Scherschel and editor Richard Meryman for the collaboration—and ordered fifty offprints for distribution. Joseph Fujikawa to Sally Dolgenos at *Life,* March 18, 1957; Mies van der Rohe to Richard Meryman, and Mies van der Rohe to Frank Scherschel, March 19, 1957; Mies van der Rohe to Scherschel, March 19, 1957, all LoC, MvdR, Generall Office File L.

15. "Emergence of a Master Architect," 64, 65, 67, 68.

16. "Ludwig Mies van der Rohe," *Architectural Forum,* June 1958, 33.

17. Lambert, *Building Seagram,* 240–47.

18. Lambert, *Building Seagram,* 240–41; "Ludwig Mies van der Rohe," [*Architectural Forum*], 33. Others agreed with Phyllis Lambert's judgment. *Architectural Forum,* a few weeks later, compared the design to an "enormous cigarette lighter": "Seagram Plans a Monument," *Architectural Forum,* August 1954, 52.

19. Charles Luckman, *Twice in a Lifetime: From Soap to Skyscrapers* (New York: W. W. Norton, 1988), 323–25.

20. Lambert, *Building Seagram,* 36.

21. Lambert, *Building Seagram,* 18–21.

22. Lambert, *Building Seagram,* 21.

23. "Seagram's Bronze Tower," *Architectural Forum,* July 1958, 67.

24. Providence lawyer and architectural historian Tim More has convincingly argued that since Seagram failed to explain the reasons for the additional expenditure, the court had no choice but to rule in favor of the city and its higher tax valuation. The predictably lost court case greatly helped with the prestige of the building. Tim More, "An Assessment of the Seagram Building," unpublished manuscript (2003), appendix.

25. For the Bronfmans' lucrative liquor import business during Prohibition (and the resulting need for an improved public image), see Michael R. Marrus's brilliant biography of Samuel Bronfman: Michael R. Marrus, *Mr. Sam: The Life and Times of Samuel Bronfman* (Toronto: Penguin, 1991).

26. Lambert, *Building Seagram,* 199.

27. See also Phyllis Lambert, "Light Changes: Philip Johnson, Richard Kelly, and *Stimmung* at Seagram," in *The Structure of Light: Richard Kelly and the Illumination of Modern Architecture,* ed. Dietrich Neumann (New Haven: Yale University Press, 2010), 80–95.

28. John Manley, one of Johnson's collaborators, interview with the author, August 27, 2012.

29. Arnold Nicholson, "Mr. Kelly's Magic Lights," *Saturday Evening Post,* July 5, 1958, 28–29, 64–65.

30. "Seagram's Custom Look," *Architectural Forum,* July 1958, 72–75, quote at 75.

31. Lewis Mumford, "The Skyline: The Lesson of the Master," *New Yorker,* September 13, 1958, 141–51, quote at 147.

32. William H. Jordy, *American Buildings and Their Architects,* vol. 5, *The Impact of European Modernism in the Mid-Twentieth Century* (New York: Oxford University Press, 1972), 262; William H. Jordy, "Seagram Assessed," *Architectural Review* 124 (December 1958): 374–82, quote at 381.

33. Kiel Moe, *Unless: The Seagram Building Construction Ecology* (New York: Actar, 2020), 176.

34. Gene Summers, transcript of interview with Harrington, June 24, 1996, tape 3, side B, 88, quoted in Lambert, *Buildling Seagram,* 62.

35. Quoted in Lambert, *Buildling Seagram,* 62.

36. "Inland Steel's Showcase," *Architectural Forum,* April 1958, 88–93.

37. Blum, "Interview with Joseph Fujikawa," 16.

38. Thomas W. Ennis, "Find Loss of Revenue Is Balanced by a Rise in Prestige: Building Owners Favoring Plazas," *New York Times,* July 3, 1960, R1.

39. Jerold S. Kayden, *Privately Owned Public Space: The New York City Experience* (New York: Wiley, 2000), 12.

40. Conversation with Mies van der Rohe at the Architecture League in New York organized by Philip Johnson, 4, LoC, MvdR, box 62, file "Interviews with Mies," 4.

41. Mumford, "Skyline," 151.

42. William H. Jordy, "The Laconic Splendor of the Metal Frame," in *American Buildings and Their Architects,* 5:221–77, quote at 273.

43. "Seagram's Bronze Tower," quote at 67.

44. Peter Blake, "The Difficult Art of Simplicity," *Architectural Forum,* May 1958, 126–31, quote at 128.

45. Blake, "Difficult Art of Simplicity," quote at 131.

46. Jane Jacobs, "New Heart for Baltimore," *Architectural Forum,* June 1958, 88–92, quotes at 88, 92.

47. Blum, "Interview with Joseph Fujikawa," 13.

48. Blum, "Interview with Joseph Fujikawa," 13.

49. Peter Palumbo, "Lloyds Bank Building," *Times* (London), February 3, 1969, 9; "Van der Rohe now," *Economist,* October 12, 1968, 52.

50. "Mansion House Square Scheme Is Resurrected," *Financial Times,* January 8, 1982, 24. Peter Palumbo had acquired the necessary lease interests surrounding the site, in order to assure compliance. Mies and Palumbo enjoyed a friendly relationship, Mies became the godfather of Palumbo's daughter Laura Elizabeth: "Christening," *Times* (London), March 28, 1968, 12. See Jack Self, *Mies in London* (London: Real, 2018).

51. Richard Rogers, Norman Foster, and James Stirling, "Mies Van Der Rohe's Mansion House Site Design," *Financial Times,* April 22, 1982, 27.

52. John Summerson, "Palumbo Plan for Mansion House," *Times* (London), March 5, 1982, 13.

53. See a comprehensive overview of the project in *UIA International Architect* 3 (1983): 20–39.

54. "Architecture: Palumbo's Pile," *Economist,* June 30, 1984, 24, 29; Charles Knevitt, "Architects Challenge Prince to Think Modern," *Times* (London), June 1, 1984, 3.

55. Gavin Stamp, "A Monument to the Dead," *Spectator,* May 11, 1984, 10, 12.

56. "Architecture: Palumbo's Pile," 24, 29.

57. John Harris, "Was the Design by Mies Van Der Rohe?," *Financial Times,* April 30, 1982, 19.

58. Quoted in Lord Holford, "Architecture in the City," *Times* (London), March 7, 1975, 15; Lord Holford, "Mies Van Der Rohe," *Times* (London), August 23, 1969, 8.

59. Quoted in Charles Knevitt, "Mies Tower 'Would Rival Bomb Ruin,'" *Times* (London), June 29, 1984, 2.

60. Quoted in Charles Knevitt, "Mies Tower 'Not Worthy of Architect or London,'" *Times* (London), June 28, 1984, 2.

61. "Plumping for Palumbo," *Times* (London), May 6, 1985, 11.

62. "Planning," *Times* (London), May 15, 1985, 4.

63. Charles Knevitt, "Say No to This Mies Museum Piece, Mrs Thatcher," *Times* (London), April 29, 1985, 12; "Ruling on City Block Due," *Financial Times,* May 22, 1985, 8.

64. Colin Amery, "New Palumbo Mansion House Plans Today," *Financial Times,* July 4, 1985, 6.

65. Colin Amery, "This Time, It's Not a Monster," *Financial Times,* June 22, 1987, 22.

66. Quoted in Phyllis Lambert, ed, *Mies in America* (New York: Harry N. Abrams, 2001), 480.

67. "Mies's One-Office Office Building," *Architectural Forum,* February 1959, 94–97.

68. Quoted in "Mies's One-Office Office Building," 95.

69. Schulze and Windhorst, *Critical Biography,* 352–53.

70. "New Way to Raise the Roof," *Architectural Forum,* March 1958, 126–28.

71. In 1967, Gertrude Lempp Kerbis started her own firm, Lempp Kerbis, the first woman-owned and operated architecture firm in Chicago. She became the first female president of AIA Chicago, one of the earliest female members of the Cliff Dwellers Club (where she would later serve as president), and in 2008 she received the Lifetime Achievement Award from the AIA Chicago.

72. "Germany: Mies' Roof in Berlin," *Interbuild/Arena: The Architectural Association Journal* (December 1967): 32–35.

73. Ulrich Conrads and Horst Eifler, "Mies im Gespräch I" (recorded by RIAS Berlin, October 1964), published as a phonograph record as *Mies in Berlin* (Bauwelt Berlin, 1966), quote at 13:44 min., https://www.bauwelt.de /rubriken/videos/Mies-im-Gespraech-II-2123186.html.

74. "Ernst Reuters Rede am 9. September 1948 vor dem Reichstag," Berlin im Überblick, https://www.berlin.de/berlin-im-ueberblick/geschichte /artikel.453082.php.

75. Quoted in "Germany: Mies' Roof in Berlin," 128.

76. The German term "*Gründerzeit*" (literally "founders' time," or, better, "entrepreneurs' years") refers to the economic upswing in Germany in the second half of the nineteenth century, in particular after German unification of 1871, characterized by rampant capitalism, a flood of new buildings, and stylistic promiscuity. About the reception of the Nationalgalerie at its opening, see Dietrich Neumann, "Reaktionen auf die Neue Nationalgalerie," *Bauwelt* 112, no. 9 (April 30, 2021): 32–35.

77. *Manifest der Aktion 507* (Berlin: Selbstverlag, 1968), 87, https://issuu.com /textraum/docs/aktion_507-manifest.

78. Ulrich Conrads, "Mies v. d. Rohe muss in Berlin bauen," *Bauwelt* 52, no. 13 (March 27, 1961): 363.

79. Ulrich Conrads, "Der andere Mies," *Bauwelt* 59, no. 38 (September 16, 1968): 1210.

80. Camilla Blechen, "Im Schatten der Architektur: Die Neue Nationalgalerie Berlin in der Bewährungsprobe," *Frankfurter Allgemeine Zeitung,* no. 272 (November 22, 1968): 14.

81. Jürgen Beckelmann, "Eigentlich unmöglich, doch ideal," *Frankfurter Rundschau,* September 17, 1968.

82. Gottfried Sello, "Ein Neuer Tempel für die Kunst," *Die Zeit,* September 20, 1968, https://www.zeit.de/1968/38/ein-neuer-tempel-fuer-die-kunst /komplettansicht.

83. Repr. in Katrin Voermanek, *Typisch Posener* (Berlin: Jovis, 2019), 99–109, quote at 106–7; as well as Julius Posener, "Absolute Architektur. Kritische Betrachtung der Berliner Nationalgalerie," *Aufsätze und Vorträge 1931– 1980,* Bauwelt Fundamente 54/55 (Braunschweig: Vieweg, 1981), 244–59.

84. *Beton, Stahl und Glas,* directed by Georgia van der Rohe und Sam Ventura (Zweites Deutsches Fernsehen, 1968), 16 mm, 58 min., 33:13–34:33.

85. Peter Blake, "The New National Gallery in Berlin," *Architectural Forum,* October 1968, 34–46, quote at 40.

86. "The New National Gallery in Berlin by Ludwig Mies van der Rohe," *Architectural Record,* November 1968, 115–22, quote at 115.

87. "Mies Monument," *Progressive Architecture* (November 1968): 108–13, quote at 113.

88. Blake, "New National Gallery in Berlin," quote at 46.

89. "The Perspiration Affair, or the New National Gallery between Cold Fronts," *Grey Room* 9 (Autumn 2002): 80–89.

90. Ludwig Glaeser, ed., *Architecture of Museums* (New York: Museum of Modern Art, 1968), 1, 3.

Afterword

1. For more information about the fate of Mies's archive, see Dietrich Neumann, "Cold War Odyssey: The Story of Mies van der Rohe's Archive," in *The Routledge Companion to Archives,* ed. Federica Goffi (London: Routledge, 2022), 263–75.

2. In 1926, Mies had asked Sergius Ruegenberg to discard several drawings of earlier projects. Fritz Neumeyer, *Mies van der Rohe: Das kunstlose Wort* (Berlin: DOM, 2016), 220.

3. "Note Hauswald regarding Reichskammer der bildenden Künste," January 20, 1939, Library of Congress (hereafter LoC), MvdR, Private Correspondence 1923–1940.

4. Lilly Reich to Mies van der Rohe, June 12, 1940, LoC, MvdR, Box 47.

5. Andreas Marx and Paul Weber, "From Ludwig Mies to Mies van der Rohe: The Apartment and Studio Am Karlsbad 24 (1915–39)," in *Mies and Modern Living: Interiors, Furniture, Photography,* ed. Helmut Reuter and Birgit Schulte (Ostfildern: Hatje Cantz, 2008), 25–39, esp. 26.

6. Eduard Ludwig to Mies van der Rohe, January 12, 1948, LoC, MvdR, Folder General Office File/Eduard Ludwig.

7. Eduard Ludwig to Mies van der Rohe, September 4, 1951, LoC, MvdR, Folder General Office File/Eduard Ludwig.

8. Wingler's monumental book on the Bauhaus appeared in 1962 (and was later published in English with MIT Press in 1969): Hans M. Wingler, *Das Bauhaus 1919–1933. Weimar-Dessau-Berlin* (Bramsche: Gebrüder Rasch, 1962).

9. Information from Magdalena Droste, Berlin, December 18, 2019. Eduard Ludwig to Dirk Lohan, Munich, December 22, 1958; Ludwig to Lohan, December 22, 1958, both LoC, MvdR, Folder General Office File/Eduard Ludwig.

10. Kurt Liebknecht to Mies van der Rohe, September 20, 1962, LoC, MvdR, Folder General Office File/L.

11. Eduard Glaeser, email message to author, July 18, 2021.

12. Phyllis Lambert, email message to author, July 20, 2021.

13. Franz Schulze and Edward Windhorst, *Mies van der Rohe: A Critical Biography,* new and rev. ed. (Chicago: University of Chicago, 2014), 387; Christiane Lange, "The Collaboration between Lilly Reich and Ludwig Mies van der Rohe," in *Mies and Modern Living, Interiors, Furniture, Photography,* ed. Helmut Reuter and Birgit Schulte (Ostfildern: Hatje Cantz, 2008), 195–207, reference at 206. One thousand drawings from Lilly Reich's estate are still in need of full scholarly attention, despite the pioneering work of Sonja Günther and Mathilda McQuaid. Paul Galloway, MoMA Archives, email to author, April 20, 2021.

14. Phyllis Lambert, email to author, July 20, 2021.

15. Hans M. Wingler, *The Bauhaus: Weimar, Dessau, Berlin, Chicago* (Cambridge, Mass.: MIT Press, 1969); William Barry Farlong, "The Patient Genius of Mies van der Rohe," *Chicago Tribune,* September 14, 1969, 34; "Mies van der Rohe," *New York Times,* August 19, 1969, 42; Ada Louise Huxtable, "Mies van der Rohe 1886—1969," *New York Times,* August 24, 1969, D24.

16. Wolf Tegethoff, *Mies van der Rohe: The Villas and Country Houses* (New York: Museum of Modern Art, 1985).

17. Franz Schulze, *Mies van der Rohe: A Critical Biography* (Chicago: University of Chicago Press, 1985).

18. Arthur Drexler, George Danforth, and Franz Schulze, eds., *An Illustrated Catalogue of the Mies van der Rohe Drawings in the Museum of Modern Art* (New York: Garland, 1986–92), 20 vols.

19. Elisabeth Michahelles, Hamburg, to Mies, November 21, 1925; Hermann John to Elisabeth Michahelles, November 26, 1925, LoC, MvdR. Mies picked the models "Schwarze Oasenziege Goldlinie" and the "brauner Saffian Blinddruck." Lilly Reich to Mies, December 2, 1925, LoC, MvdR, Private Correspondence 1923–1940, folder R; Invoice B. Damme to Mies van der Rohe, July 1, 1925, LoC, MvdR, Private Correspondence, folder D.

20. Ulrich Conrads and Horst Eifler, "Mies im Gespräch II" (recorded by RIAS Berlin, October 1964), published as a phonograph record as *Mies in Berlin* (Bauwelt Berlin, 1966), quote at 9:16 min., https://www.bauwelt.de /rubriken/videos/Mies-im-Gespraech-II-2123186.html.

21. William H. Jordy, "The Return of Mies van der Rohe," *New Criterion* (May 1, 1986): 45–56, quote at 56.

22. Arthur Drexler, "The Mies van der Rohe Archive," in *The Mies van der Rohe Archive,* vol. 1, ed. Arthur Drexler (New York: Garland, 1986), xi–xvii, quote at xvi.

23. Ada Louise Huxtable, "Architecture: Mies; Lessons from the Master," *New York Times,* February 6, 1966, X24, 25.

24. Arthur Drexler, "Transformations in Modern Architecture," lecture delivered at the Museum of Modern Art, April 10, 1979 on the occasion of the exhibition *Transformations in Modern Architecture,* on view February 21– April 24, 1979, Sound Recordings of Museum-Related Events, 79:29, MoMA Archives, quoted in Felicity D. Scott, "An Army of Soldiers or a Meadow: The Seagram Building and the 'Art of Modern Architecture,'" *Journal of the Society of Architectural Historians* 70, no. 3 (September 2011): 330–53.

25. Ada Louise Huxtable, "The Miesian Lesson," *New York Times,* April 28, 1968, D34.

26. Quoted in Edward Barry, "A Mies van der Rohe Panning," *Chicago Tribune,* May 17, 1968, B19.

27. Sibyl Moholy-Nagy, "Hitler's Revenge," *Art in America* (September– October 1968): 42–43.

28. Robert Venturi, *Complexity and Contradiction in Architecture* (New York: Museum of Modern Art, 1966), 17.

29. Charles Jencks, *Modern Movements in Architecture* (New York: Anchor/ Doubleday, 1973), 95–96.

30. Charles Jencks, *The Language of Post-Modern Architecture* (London: Academy, 1977), 14–17.

31. J. M. Richards, "Mies and Missionary," *Times Literary Supplement,* April 25, 1975, 460.

32. Ada Louise Huxtable, "The Making of a Master," *New York Times,* December 1, 1985, BR1, 32–33.

33. Jordy, "Return of Mies van der Rohe," 46.

34. Jordy, "Return of Mies van der Rohe," 45–56, quotes at 56, 45.
35. Mark Girouard, "The Vision of Mies van der Rohe" *Washington Post,* March 2, 1986, BW8.
36. Paul Richard, "The Flawed Facets of Mies' Crystal View: Mies van der Rohe," *Washington Post,* February 23, 1986, K1.
37. Robert Campbell, "Landmark Exhibition on Mies van der Rohe," *Boston Globe,* February 11, 1986, 44.
38. Campbell, "Landmark Exhibition."
39. Kathryn Smith, *Wright on Exhibit: Frank Lloyd Wright's Architectural Exhibitions* (Princeton: Princeton University Press), 185. Smith considered Wright's nine-hundred-piece exhibition of 1951 "possibly the largest one-man architecture retrospective ever assembled."
40. Ada Louise Huxtable, "How Less Became More: Two Shows of Mies van der Rohe's," *Wall Street Journal,* July 25, 2001, A14.
41. Jean-Louis Cohen, *Ludwig Mies van der Rohe* (Basel: Birkhäuser, 2007); Phyllis Lambert, *Building Seagram* (New Haven: Yale University Press, 2013); Detlef Mertins, *Mies* (New York: Phaidon, 2014). See the review Dietrich Neumann, "The Enduring Legacy of a Modern Master: *Mies* by Detlef Mertins," *Architectural Record,* June 2014, 71, 72. Karsten Crohn, *Mies: The Built Work* (Basel: Birkhäuser, 2014). After the publication of two earlier books on Reich—Sonja Günther, *Lilly Reich, 1885–1947. Innen-architektin, Designerin, Austellungsgestalterin* (Stuttgart: Deutsche Verlags-Anstalt, 1988); and Matilda McQuaid, *Lilly Reich, Designer and Architect* (New York: Museum of Modern Art, 1996)—Christiane Lange, great-granddaughter of one of Mies's clients, convincingly explained Lilly Reich's contributions to their furniture designs in Christiane Lange, "Lilly Reich und ihre Zusammenarbeit with Mies van der Rohe," in *Ludwig Mies van der Rohe und Lilly Reich. Möbel und Räume* (Ostfildern: Hatje Cantz, 2007), 97–110. Recently there have been several attempts at unearthing more of Lilly Reich's work and establishing her legacy outside of Mies's shadow. See Laura Lizondo-Sevilla and Débora Domingo-Calabuig, "Lilly Reich: The Architecture and Critique of an Invisibilized Woman," *Frontiers of Architectural Research* 12, no. 1 (February 2023): 15–27. See two documentaries: *[On Set with] Lilly Reich,* directed by Avelina Prat, Débora Domingo-Calabuig, and Laura Lizondo-Sevilla (Barcelona: Fundació Mies van der Rohe, 2022); and *The Mies van der Rohes,* directed by Sabine Gisiger (Zurich: Dschoint Ventschr Filmproduktion AG, SRF Schweizer Radio und Fernsehen, Filmcoopi Zürich AG, 2023). See also Laura Martínez de Guereñu, *Re-Enactment: Lilly Reich's Work Occupies the Barcelona Pavilion* (2020), https://miesbcn.com/project/re-enactment-lilly-reichs-work-occupies-the-barcelona-pavilion-by-laura-martinez-de-guerenu/.
42. Mae Tinee (Frances Peck Grover), "'Fountainhead,' a Best Seller, Is a Bust as a Film," *Chicago Daily Tribune,* July 26, 1949, 22.
43. Ludwig Mies van der Rohe, "Baukunst und Zeitwille!" *Querschnitt* 4, no. 1 (Spring 1924): 31–32.
44. See, for example, the recent reminder from Jean-Louis Cohen: "Field Notes. Jean-Louis Cohen with Ross Wolfe. Architecture and Revolution," The Brooklyn Rail, November 2020, https://brooklynrail.org/2020/11/field-notes/JEAN-LOUIS-COHEN-with-Ross-Wolfe. Jean-Louis Cohen, one of the kindest and most generous of colleagues, unexpectedly passed away while I was writing this conclusion to my book. He is greatly missed.

Index

Credits

Division Washington, D.C. (figs. 7.3, 7.6); Museum of the City of New York / GRANGER (fig. 7.4); © Archives of the Galerie Nierendorf (fig. 7.5); © Cooper Hewitt Design Museum (figs. 7.7, 7.19); © Time/Life Inc. (fig. 7.9); © Museum of Modern Art, New York, 2023, Artists Rights Society (ARS), New York / VG BildKunst, Bonn (figs. 7.10–7.18, 7.28–7.32, 7.41, 7.42); photo: Hassan Bagheri (fig. 7.20); Private Collection (fig. 7.21, 7.26, 7.40); photo: Historic American Building Survey. Library of Congress (fig. 7.22); © IIT Archive (fig. 7.27); from: Philip Johnson, *Mies van der Rohe* (New York: Museum of Modern Art, 1947), 148 (fig. 7.39); © Art Institute of Chicago (fig. 7.43).

Chapter 8

Museum of Modern Art, © 2023 Artists Rights Society (ARS), New York / VG Bild-Kunst, Bonn (figs. 8.1, 8.2, 8.12, 8.14, 8.15, 8.17–8.19, 8.21–8.25, 8.27, 8.30, 8.43, 8.49); © Canadian Centre for Architecture, Montreal (fig. 8.3); © Hassan Bagheri (figs. 8.4, 8.6, 8.7, 8.37, 8.39, 8.41, 8.59, 8.60, 8.70–8.72, 8.74, 8.75); Library of Congress Prints and Photographs Division Washington, D.C. (figs. 8.5, 8.8); © Chicago History Museum (figs. 8.9–8.11, 8.20, 8.26, 8.28, 8.32–8.34, 8.36, 8.44, 8.45, 8.48, 8.50–8.52, 8.55, 8.57, 8.58, 8.61, 8.63–8.69, 8.73); U.S. Patent Office (fig. 8.13); From: Edgar Kaufmann, Jr., ed. *Prize Design for Modern Furniture Museum of Modern Art, 1950* (New York: MoMA, 1950), 45 (fig. 8.16); © Art Institute of Chicago (fig. 8.29); from: Philip Johnson, *Mies van der Rohe* (New York: MoMA, 1947), 145, 154, 171 (figs. 8.31, 8.35, 8.46); © Getty Images (fig. 8.38); from: *Architectural Forum*, 93, no. 1 (January 1950), 71, 73, 76 (figs. 8.40, 8.42, 8.62); Private Collection (fig. 8.47); © Camilo Vergara (fig. 8.53); © Esto (figs. 8.54, 8.56).

Chapter 9

© Hassan Bagheri (figs. 9.1, 9.3, 9.5–9.7, 9.9, 9.10, 9.12–9.14, 9.17–9.19, 9.24, 9.26, 9.27, 9.29, 9.32, 9.34–9.36, 9.39, 9.51); from: *Architectural Review* (February 1972), 104 (fig. 9.4); photo: Hedrich-Blessing, © Chicago History Museum (figs. 9.2, 9.8, 9.30, 9.33, 9.38, 9.40, 9.43); photo: Camillo Vergara (fig. 9.11); Museum of Modern Art, © 2023 Artists Rights Society (ARS), New York / VG Bild-Kunst, Bonn (figs. 9.15, 9.16, 9.25); © Canadian Centre for Architecture, Montreal (figs. 9.20, 9.21, 9.23); © Library of Congress Prints and Photographs Division, Washington, D.C. (figs. 9.22, 9.41, 9.42, 9.44, 9.45, 9.47); Frank Scherschel / The LIFE Picture Collection / Shutterstock (fig. 9.28); photo: Ezra Stoller, © Esto (fig. 9.31); © RIBA Royal Institute of British Architects (fig. 9.37); © Ullstein Bild / Granger, dpa Picture Alliance (fig. 9.46); photo: Simon Menges (figs. 9.48–9.50).

Afterword

Photo: Dietrich Neumann (figs. 10.1, 10.4); Museum of Modern Art, New York © 2023 Artists Rights Society (ARS), New York / VG Bild-Kunst, Bonn (figs. 10.2, 10.6, 10.7); The Ryerson and Burnham Libraries, Art Institute of Chicago (fig. 10.3); © Bauhaus-Archive, Berlin (fig. 10.5); © Thomas Ruff / VG Bild Kunst, Bonn, Courtesy the artist and David Zwirner (fig. 10.8).

Published with assistance from the Graham Foundation for Advanced Studies in the Fine Arts.

**Graham
Foundation**

yalebooks.com/art

Designed by Office of Luke Bulman

Set in Stempel Garamond and Untitled Sans type

Printed in China by 1010 Printing International Limited

Library of Congress Control Number: 2024936220
ISBN 978-0-300-24623-0

A catalogue record for this book is available from the British Library.

This paper meets the requirements of ANSI/NISO Z39.48-1992 (Permanence of Paper).

10 9 8 7 6 5 4 3 2 1

Front cover illustration: Night view from inside an apartment at 880 North Lake Shore Drive, looking toward the apartment building at 860 North Lake Shore Drive and the cityscape to the south, Chicago, Illinois, circa 1955. HB-13809-Z5, Chicago History Museum, Hedrich-Blessing Collection. Photo: © Chicago Historical Society, published on or before 2014. All rights reserved.

Back cover illustration: Ludwig Mies van der Rohe, Friedrichstrasse Skyscraper project, Berlin, 1922. Perspective view from the north. Charcoal and pencil on tracing paper mounted on board, 68 1/4 × 48 in. (173.5 × 122 cm). Museum of Modern Art, New York. The Mies van der Rohe Archive, gift of the architect. Photo: © Museum of Modern Art, New York, Artists Rights Society (ARS), New York / VG BildKunst, Bonn.

Frontispiece: Hugo Erfurth, Ludwig Mies van der Rohe, 1934. Oil pigment print on illustration board, 11 7/8 × 9 1/4 in. (30 × 23.5 cm). Köln, Museum Ludwig, Sammlung Fotografie, Inv.-Nr. FH 02389. Photo: © Rheinisches Bildarchiv Köln.